THE COLLAPSE OF THE WEIMAR REPUBLIC

THE COLLAPSE OF
THE WEIMAR REPUBLIC

Political Economy and Crisis

Second Edition

David Abraham

Holmes & Meier

New York • *London*

Published in the United States of America 1986 by
Holmes & Meier Publishers, Inc.
30 Irving Place
New York, N.Y. 10003

Great Britain:
Pindar Road, Hoddesdon
Hertfordshire EN11 0HF England

Book design by Marilyn Marcus

First edition published by Princeton University Press © 1981.

Library of Congress Cataloging-in-Publication Data

Abraham, David, 1946–
  The collapse of the Weimar Republic.

  Bibliography: p.
  Includes index.
  1. Industry and state—Germany—History. 2. Agri-
culture and state—Germany—History. 3. Pressure groups—
Germany—History. 4. Social conflict—Germany—History.
5. Germany—Politics and government—1918–1933. I. Title.
HD3616.G35A27 1986   338.0943   86-27033
ISBN 0-8419-1083-9
ISBN 0-8419-1084-7 (pbk.)

Manufactured in the United States of America

For my parents—

WHO AT AUSCHWITZ AND ELSEWHERE SUFFERED
THE WORST CONSEQUENCES OF WHAT I CAN MERELY WRITE ABOUT

Contents

List of Figures

List of Tables

Abbreviations

ADGB	General Federation of Unions (Allgemeiner Deutscher Gewerkschaftsbund)
AVI	Working Association of Iron Processing Industries (Arbeitsgemeinschaft der Eisen verarbeitenden Industrie)
BA	Federal Archive, Koblenz, West Germany (Bundesarchiv)
BdI	Union of Industrialists, pre–WWI (Bund der Industriellen)
BdL	Agrarian League, pre–WWI (Bund der Landwirte)
BVP	Bavarian People's Party (Bayerische Volkspartei)
CNBLP	Christian National Peasant and Rural People's Party (Christliche Nationale Bauern- und Landvolk Partei)
DDP	German Democratic Party (Deutsche Demokratische Partei)
DGB	Federation of German Unions, post–WWII (Deutsche Gewerkschafts Bund)
DIHT	Congress of German Industry and Commerce (Deutsche Industrie- und Handelstag)
DII	German Industry Institute (Deutsche Industrie Institut)
DNVP	German National People's Party (Deutschnationale Volkspartei)
DVP	German People's Party (Deutsche Volkspartei)
GHH	Good Hope Mills, Inc., Oberhausen (Gutehoffnungshütte Aktienverein)
HAGHH	Historical Archives of the GHH
HKB	Historical Commission of Berlin (Historische Kommission zu Berlin)
IRG	International Iron Community (Internationale Rohstahlgemeinschaft)
KPD	Communist Party, Germany (Kommunistische Partei Deutschland)
Langnam	Long Name Association (Langnamverein): Association for Furthering the Joint Economic Interests of the Rhineland and Westphalia
MWT	Central European Economic Congress (Mitteleuropäischer Wirtschaftstag)
NL	Personal Papers (Nachlass)
NSDAP	Nazi Party (Nationalsozialistische Deutsche Arbeiterpartei)
RDI	League of German Industry (Reichsverband der Deutschen Industrie)
RLB	Agrarian League, post–WWI (Reichslandbund)

SPD	Social Democratic Party of Germany (Sozialdemokratische Partei Deutschlands)
USPD	Independent Social Democratic Party of Germany (Unabhängige Sozialdemokratische Partei Deutschlands)
VDESI	Association of German Iron and Steel Industrialists (Verein Deutscher Eisen- und Stahlindustrieller)
WTB	Woytinsky-Tarnow-Baade Plan
Z	Catholic Center Party (Zentrumspartei)
ZAG	Industry-Labor Joint Working Committee (Zentralarbeitsgemeinschaft)
ZDI	Central League of German Industrialists, pre–WWI (Zentralverband deutscher Industrieller)
ZSA	Central State Archive, Division I, Potsdam, East Germany (Zentrales Staatsarchiv, Abt. I), formerly Deutsches Zentral Archiv (DZA)
ZSg	Contemporary History Collection (Zeitgeschichtliche Sammlung)

Preface to the Second Edition

The first edition of *The Collapse of the Weimar Republic: Political Economy and Crisis* sparked a wide-ranging and sometimes acerbic controversy. The various issues that came to be involved have received ample treatment elsewhere,[1] and this is not the place to rehearse them once again. Suffice it to say that while I continue to believe that substantive differences over German history and historical method were at the core of the debate from the outset, I certainly helped precipitate and contribute to it through errors in the original edition. I have thoroughly rechecked all the sources in dispute and a large number of other archival and secondary sources germane to the arguments of the book. This edition incorporates the correction of all errors indicated by my critics and found by myself. Aside from these emendations, the text that follows is nearly identical to that of the first edition.[2]

Needless to say, I regret these errors, but I am gratified that none of the corrections alters the fundamental arguments or theses of my book. This, rather than convenience, explains why I have decided to leave the

---

1. The controversy began in early 1983 with widely circulated xerography by Henry Turner, author of the then-forthcoming *German Big Business and the Rise of Hitler* (New York, 1985). It then mushroomed rather quickly. For the published side, see: the exchange of Communications to the Editor from Turner, T. W. Mason, and myself in the *American Historical Review (AHR)* 88(1983):1142–9; the debate between Gerald Feldman and myself, twice each, in *Central European History* 17(1984):159–290; and the debate between Feldman's student, Ulrich Nocken, and myself in the *Vierteljahrschrift für Sozial- und Wirtschaftsgeschichte (VSWG)* 71(1984):505–27 and 72(1985):329–52 (the latter in English). The controversy finally wound down with an exchange in the American Historical Association's newsletter, *Perspectives* 23, no. 9 (December 1985): 20, 21. By the time of our exchange in *Perspectives*, Turner and I were able to cite well over a dozen newspapers, magazines, and journals that had covered the story. The last of these was probably Turner's interview in the *Campus Report from Accuracy in Academia* 1, no. 2 (January–February 1986): 1, 5. Nearly the entire controversy revolved around the single, albeit important, question of Nazi-business relations. A goodly number of the reviews of *Collapse*, about thirty in total, were excerpted in my debate with Feldman, especially 193–5.

2. The most important corrections to the text appear on pp. 155 at fn. 141, 161 at fn. 160, 285 at fn. 43, 302 at fn. 98, 306 at fn. 113, 310 at fn. 126, and 311 at fn. 129. A larger number of less significant corrections have also been made.

text unchanged. Weimar remains an active area of scholarly inquiry, however, and my own thinking about its political economy has not remained stagnant. In the Introduction to the Second Edition, which follows, I provide an overview of some recent literature in the field and offer an examination of the *Deutsche Führerbriefe*, a newsletter for Weimar industrialists and political figures that provides additional documentation for one of the arguments made in *Collapse*.

In preparing this edition of *Collapse*, I have benefitted from the comments, suggestions, and—at times much needed—encouragement of many friends and colleagues. I am grateful to them all. In addition, Dr. Thomas Trumpp of the Bundesarchiv and Mr. Bodo Herzog of the Historical Archive of the Gutehoffnungshütte offered their kind assistance and encouragement during my revisit to their respective archives. Although somewhat less burdened than a decade ago, Mr. Herzog is, to the relief of every researcher, no less irrepressible. Thanks are also due to Dr. Dieter Schuster of the Deutsche Gewerkschafts Bund archive and staff members of the archive at the Berlin Historical Commission. Not least, I would like to thank Holmes & Meier and my editors, Kevin Davis and Katharine Turok, for their assistance in producing a Second Edition of *Collapse*.

Introduction to the Second Edition

The Collapse of the Weimar Republic begins with three questions: First, how did Germany's divided economic elites attempt to articulate a national agenda around which they could unite? Second, how and from whom was popular support won? Third, how did the institutionalization of social peace first work and then fail? These questions originate in a general concern with the functioning of capitalist democracies, but they are also addressed to a situation specific to Weimar Germany. To answer them, the book explores the factors that, from roughly 1925 to 1930, generated cooperation between the more dynamic, export-oriented, and liberal industrialists on the one hand and the leaders of organized labor on the other. I try to demonstrate how this "Weimar System" worked, whom it benefitted, whom it compromised, and whom it hurt. The explanations, based in economic sector analysis, are, I think, advanced clearly enough. With the depression, the end of American loans, severe dissension over reparations strategy, and the shrinkage in world trade, the balance within the dominant classes shifted in favor of more protectionist, labor-intensive, and nationalist-conservative forces. The compromise that was the "Weimar System" could no longer hold. Neither labor nor capital was prepared to make those concessions that might have saved the Republic. *Collapse*'s critique of business interests is clear enough, but it also contains an implicit critique of German labor, one that I am surprised did not draw more fire from the left.[1]

After 1931 no government could successfully win popular support *and also* offer heavy industry a way out of the now unacceptably costly System. The crisis revealed a contradiction between the demands of democracy and the needs of capitalism. Capital withdrew from the social and political compromise that underlay stability; the result was a

---

1. For this kind of critique, directed in this instance at Borchardt, see Claus-Dieter Krohn, "'Ökonomische Zwangslagen' und das Scheitern der Weimarer Republik," *Geschichte und Gesellschaft* 8 (1982):415–26; Carl-Ludwig Holtfrerich, "Zu hohe Löhne in der Weimarer Republik?" *Geschichte und Gesellschaft* 10 (1984):122–41; Holtfrerich, "Alternativen zu Brünings Wirtschaftspolitik in der Weltwirtschaftskrise," *Historische Zeitschrift* 235 (1982):605–31; and some of the literature cited by them.

fierce stalemate that proved the source of Weimar's collapse and provided a political opening for the mass authoritarian populism of the Nazis. Faced with the necessity of choosing among political alternatives not of their own making, industrialists had to address the Nazi groundswell. As hard as they pressed their "own" *bürgerliche* (bourgeois) parties, industrialists were unable to make them popular with the voters. In fact, as the book argues, the harder their patrons pressed them after 1930, the less popular these parties became. Nor were industrialists successful at launching hothouse conservative mass movements, like the League for the Renewal of the Reich. They had to work with the material available and were less savvy and well-positioned for mass organization than the old agrarian elite had once been. They were unable to make their own history just as they wished.

The book argues that the response of industrialists to the Nazis was various, inconsistent, and contradictory. I try to provide some understanding as to why different groups of industrialists (or fractions of capital, to anticipate the terminology used in the book) responded as they did. Simply put, although it is no simple matter, by mid-1932 most significant industrialists could see "no other way out of the crisis" acceptable to them, and "to protect their social dominance," they "exposed themselves to a potentially uncertain future." By that time, for the dominant industrialists and most agrarians, there was no feasible *and* acceptable alternative to the NSDAP. No other force could claim genuine popular support while also demonstrating a credible commitment to eliminating Weimar's fragmented political democracy and generous social welfare arrangements. Industrialists wanted class peace, an economy free to accumulate and generate profits, and a reascendant Germany. Capitalists worried about interests. They meant to "insert their interests" in a power vacuum and "in light of the Nazis' independently achieved successes." But the Nazis extolled will over interest, and this was vexing. Indeed, as I show, the Nazis were inadequate and disappointing in many respects and threatening and disturbing in others; they were not a movement by industrialists, nor were they what industrialists really wanted. Ultimately, however, they were the only real alternative. Just as industrialists—without much enthusiasm—collectively compromised with the Socialists in 1918 in order to maintain what was theirs and improve their future prospects, so by 1932 they did the same with the less threatening National Socialists.

* * *

It would be an injustice to attempt to summarize here the considerable scholarly work that has appeared over the past five years dealing with the various issues raised in the first edition of *Collapse*. Four such contributions, however, dealing directly with industry and politics,[2] must be addressed here, each for somewhat different reasons.

In a series of essays and lectures, gathered together in *Wachstum, Krisen, Handlungsspielräume der Wirtschaftspolitik* (Göttingen, 1982),[3] Knut Borchardt offers an analysis of the structure and core problems of Weimar's political economy very much like that presented in *Collapse*. It is, of course, gratifying that so distinguished a scholar should have arrived independently at conclusions so much like my own.[4] But, in an important sense, it is also ironic. For although Professor Borchardt is generally understood as advancing a conservative argument, few scholars have made the central point as clearly as he has: in capitalist democracies capital rules, and it is *its* logic that enjoys hegemony.

At the core of the "Borchardt thesis" lies the argument that political alternatives after 1930 were heavily constrained by economic necessity: In particular, Chancellor Brüning could do little to save the Weimar System because organized labor's wage and social policy victories had

2. Other issues addressed in *Collapse,* such as peasant-estate owner relations and conflicts between industry and agriculture, which together make up a goodly portion of the text, are not raised here. The subject of popular and party support *for* the Weimar System (as well as for the Nazi rise) has been investigated in electoral terms by Richard Hamilton, *Who Voted for Hitler?* (Princeton, 1982) and especially by Thomas Childers, *The Nazi Voter* (Chapel Hill, 1983). My own treatment of the bourgeois *(bürgerliche)* political parties and their relationship to agrarian and business interests on the one hand, and *Mittelstand* and especially white-collar voters on the other, is highly consistent with though not identical to that of L. E. Jones, *The Dying Middle: German Liberalism and the Dissolution of the Weimar System, 1918–1933* (Chapel Hill, [1987]).

3. The core, and perhaps most provocative parts, of the argument were first presented as addresses and then published as "Zwangslagen und Handlungsspielräume in der grossen Wirtschaftskrise der frühen dreissiger Jahre," in *Jahrbuch der Bayerischen Akademie der Wissenschaften* 1979, 87–132, and "Wirtschaftliche Ursachen des Scheiterns der Weimarer Republik," in K. D. Erdmann and H. Schulze, eds., *Weimar: Selbstpreisgabe einer Demokratie* (Düsseldorf, 1980), 211–49. They have been restated in "Inflationsgefahren in der Weltwirtschaftskrise?" in W. Engels, A. Gutowski, and H. Wallich, eds., *International Capital Movements, Debt and Monetary System* (Mainz, 1984), 21–42, and further substantiated in "Das Gewicht der Inflationsangst in den wirtschaftspolitischen Entscheidungsprozessen während der Weltwirtschaftskrise," in G. D. Feldman, ed., *Die Nachwirkungen der Inflation auf die deutsche Geschichte, 1924–1933* (Munich, 1985), pp. 233–60. The argument was briefly summarized on a full page in the *Frankfurter Allgemeine Zeitung,* 29 January 1983: 13. See also, "Zum Scheitern eines produktiven Diskurses über das Scheitern der Weimarer Republik," *Geschichte und Gesellschaft* 9(1983):124–37. The latter two make frequent favorable reference to *Collapse.*

4. I did not know of Borchardt's 1979 essay before *Collapse* went to press, and, more understandably, Borchardt did not know of my work until he was asked to review *Collapse* for the *Historische Zeitschrift* 236(1983):483-86.

paralyzed German capitalism. A strong labor movement extracted wage increases in excess of productivity growth, thereby squeezing profits, discouraging investment, and antagonizing capital. The entrepreneurial class could then only welcome the growth of a reserve army of the unemployed in order to weaken the bargaining position of labor and strengthen its own. To argue this is to say, in effect, that the vehement objections of Weimar capitalists to high and "political" wages were rationally founded, whatever the ideological functions of such objections. Weimar, in other words, suffered from an economic crisis that was, in good measure, a profit crisis engendered by a militant reformist labor movement. This circumstance left republican and Socialist politicians with little room for maneuver, facilitated the growth of right radicalism, and eventually encouraged the migration of parts of business into the right-radical camp. According to Borchardt, the system suffered from a structural problem that went well beyond the pressure of reparations and high interest rates. Many of the same arguments are made in *Collapse,* especially in chapter 5.

Borchardt grounds his argument in a larger economic analysis, which portrays the Weimar economy as nonfunctional and untenable *("nicht funktionsfähige")* and existing within a barely functional and tenable political system. I believe one can accept his judgment of Weimar's as a sick economy without inferring antilabor conclusions. Borchardt finds: a net social product per capita during Weimar that lay well below the long-term trend line (the 1913 level was not reattained until 1928); real net investment per capita (despite the wave of "industrial rationalization") about 12 percent less than in the immediate prewar years; personal consumption levels 16 percent higher and public expenditures 34 percent higher in 1928 than in 1913; and an unprecedentedly high share of national income (nearly 67 percent) going to wages.[5] He links low investment levels to high levels of public borrowing and spending, disproportionately costly wages to a successful wage policy by labor and the state, and slowness in productivity growth to these and other factors. Due to the political strength of labor, high unemployment did not succeed in adjusting wages downward in time, and the rate of exploitation remained inadequate. The "relative powers of the combatants" Marx referred to in *Capital* seemed to weigh in favor of labor.

In other words, Borchardt credits the SPD and trade unions with succeeding at much of what they had promised to do. Once they experienced defeat and abandoned efforts at revolutionary transforma-

---

5. My own figure in chapter 5, the effective wage share, is about 61 percent. Borchardt underscores that the 67 percent figure, a "bereinigte" wage share, was about 10 points higher than the average for the period 1950–70.

tion after 1918–19, the SPD and ADGB unions militantly and successfully pursued redistributional struggles. These were often facilitated and even encouraged by political and legal mechanisms, such as binding compulsory arbitration by the state, as well as by elections. By the time of the SPD's successful 1928 election campaign, socialist theorists and representatives of capital alike had come to believe that the weekly wage was a political wage, dependent on the political representation of labor. Incremental social and wage gains lay at the center of labor's strategy—and capital's fears. Indeed, successful social democratic reformism appeared as more of a threat than communist agitation.[6] Borchardt provides some of the same evidence adduced in *Collapse* and agrees that wage and social-welfare policy became the sine qua non of left politics in Weimar. Indeed, to labor's ultimate grief, they were the litmus test applied to all governments—before and after 1932. Labor's approach worked for a while, but once it began to fail, there was no *Spielraum* (margin of maneuver) and no simple escape route: the piper had to be paid. Domestic-oriented and heavy industries, partially on account of their greater labor intensity and tighter markets, were the first to call the question and demand an end to the Weimar System. With little change in labor's posture, and with worsening world trade protectionism, the export and dynamic industries lost their relative preeminence within German capital and moved closer to the position of their more nationalist and conservative colleagues.[7]

Social democratic scholars in particular have criticized Borchardt for insisting on the reality of the "profit squeeze," i.e., for blaming (productive) labor,[8] for suggesting a shortage of investments and profits rather than of demand and jobs. Actually, the thesis of labor-induced profit squeezes is not the intellectual property solely of conservatives and neoliberals or the policy property of business. Historically, there has

6. See, in this regard, von Miquel's poignant testimony to Reusch quoted in chapter 4, below.

7. These latter points are developed more fully in chapters 3 and 5 of *Collapse*, more briefly in Borchardt, *FAZ*, 13. Chapter 3, sections 3–5, below seek to provide some economic grounding for the differential tolerance toward labor's demands shown by the two fractions of industry.

8. The Borchardt theses have now witnessed a great deal of debate. The key entries are cited in footnotes 1 and 3, above; see also Werner Conze, "Zum Scheitern der Weimarer Republik," *VSWG* 70(1983):215–21, and Harold James, "Gab es eine Alternative zur Wirtschaftspolitik Brünings?" *VSWG* 70(1983):523–41. Much of what became Borchardt's argument "for" Brüning was presciently criticized by Gerhard Schulz, "Reparationen und Krisenprobleme nach dem Wahlsieg der NSDAP 1930," *VSWG* 67(1980):200–22. The most substantive interlocutor, Holtfrerich, argues the following, "Zu hohe Löhne," 137–40: Between 1907 and 1925 the number of salaried employees and officials doubled while the number of wage workers remained constant (from 10.3 to 17.3

been a left/right confluence on this question.[9] Analyses that stress the profit squeeze have understandably generated a great deal of discomfort among those German scholars who see such arguments as blaming labor for the severity of the depression, the collapse of Weimar, and worse.[10] From the perspective of the present, they seem also to justify the contemporary chastisement of labor by Christian Democratic, Thatcherite, and Reagan-Republican governments while suggesting the sterility of any collective or demand-centered recovery strategy. Today, as in Weimar, the question can be asked: *Are there not enough jobs for people or not enough profits for investment?* And though investment there must be—capital strike and flight notwithstanding—can one assume that private capitalists do it better than socially oriented public organs? Posed this way, Borchardt's argument appears to be intrinsically antilabor, redolent of the desire of Weimar capitalists to *take advantage of* the economic crisis to weaken labor and its organizations and to undermine democracy.[11]

Perhaps the issue ought to be addressed somewhat differently. *Collapse* observes that the Weimar labor movement's search for economic

---

percent and 54.9 to 49.2 percent of the labor force, respectively), and this accounted for much of the apparent increase in wages. In other words, increases went to *unproductive* labor. Further, increased shares of the national wealth distributed to labor tended to come not from industry but from agriculture, parts of the petite bourgeoisie, and especially rentiers. This also marked a shift in wealth from *investing* strata to *consuming* strata, thereby disproportionately raising consumption but reducing savings and forcing up interest rates. For Holtfrerich, the proper approach to recovery would have begun by encouraging or inducing investment through mechanisms such as employee savings and investment funds. In the end, Holtfrerich's recommendation is remarkably like those being put forward in Sweden during the current crisis and those I have myself adumbrated; see my article "Labor's Way: The Successes and Limits of Socialist Politics in Germany," *International Labor and Working Class History* 28(1985):1–24.

9. See, for example, Eugen Varga's essays collected as *Die Krise des Kapitalismus und ihre politischen Folgen* (Frankfurt, 1969), especially part II; Raford Boddy and James Crotty, "Class Conflict and Macro-Policy: the Political Business Cycle," *Review of Radical Political Economics* 7(1975):1–30; Andrew Glyn and Bob Sutcliffe, "The Critical Condition of British Capital," *New Left Review* 66(1971); and *British Capitalism, Workers and the Profit Squeeze* (London, 1972).

10. Krohn is particularly adamant on the neoliberal message of Borchardt's argument—delivered in a context in which big businessmen themselves were "authoritarian capitalists" and real market capitalism no longer existed. For his part, Krohn (418ff.) stresses overcapacity, the rapidity of capital intensification, and weak demand in the Weimar economy along with protectionist policies abroad. In addition, he emphasizes that a goodly portion of public expenditure subsidized the private sector; Weimar state activity *countered* the economy's weaknesses rather than *aggravating* them.

11. *Collapse* stresses that Weimar capitalists by and large sought to use the crisis precisely to these ends. At the same time, it would be difficult to imagine a reader of the article in the famously conservative and anti-Marxist *FAZ* reaching other than anti-SPD, antilabor conclusions.

rationality, social justice, and political participation was inevitably and decisively constrained by the privileged status systematically accorded the logic of accumulation. It seems that the best that can be accomplished is the worst that can be done: paralyzing capitalism without being able to transform it.[12] The Weimar SPD and ADGB were highly effective but also terribly vulnerable. Having mistakenly assumed that democracy would overcome capitalism *within* the new system of capitalist democracy, they were at a complete loss to deal with the system in distress. Having persuaded most of their members that success was to be measured almost uniquely by wage and social welfare gains, the SPD and ADGB had virtually no idea what to do once capitalism ceased producing surplus they could skim. Rather than inferring from Borchardt's persuasive analysis only the possibility of a "right turn" or retreat by labor, is it possible to posit the possibility of a turn away from economism and a politically oriented turn to the left to escape the crisis? At least one of his respected critics, Holtfrerich, citing arguments in *Collapse,* has cautiously suggested something of this sort by stressing the availability, feasibility, and desirability of job-creation and pump-priming programs.[13]

Yet to stress the availability, feasibility, and desirability of job creation and other anti-deflationary measures is not enough to solve Borchardt's riddle.[14] There was no *economic* way because there was neither *political* will nor an alternative political economy. *Collapse* seeks to explain why, under Brüning, this was so. What may be added here is that, in his efforts to balance and further various capitalist interests while also retaining the tacit support of labor, Brüning could not abandon the imperative of accumulation. At least not unless he, as political entrepreneur, was forced to do so. For that to have happened would have required one of two inducements: either the pressure of a broader

---

12. The three essential discussions of the logic and predicaments of capitalist democracy are Adam Przeworksi, *Capitalism and Social Democracy* (New York, 1985); Claus Offe, *Contradictions of the Welfare State* (London, 1984); and Joshua Cohen and Joel Rogers, *On Democracy* (New York, 1983).

13. Thus Holtfrerich, "Alternativen," 627, citing the discussion in chap. 3, section 6 of *Collapse,* writes, "Abraham has clearly demonstrated that industrial opposition, for example to the work creation measures proposed by the ADGB was directed not so much at the measures themselves as at the organizations of the 'class enemy' and at the political system which had secured workers such broad social and political rights." In "Zu hohe Löhne," 141, he makes reference to efforts aimed at "democratization of the economy." For an extension of the discussion of "economic democracy" begun in *Collapse,* see "Labor's Way," 7–18.

14. Borchardt claims they would not have made much difference anyway; Holtfrerich sharply disagrees. Let us assume, for purposes of the argument and because they seem to have mattered elsewhere, that Holtfrerich is right.

worker-salaried employee-popular constituency such as came into being in the 1960s but which was impossible in Weimar, or a rapprochement between the Socialist and Communist movements. Yet Socialist complicity in and commitment to the System seem to have been too great to permit any undoing of the fatal decisions of 1918–19 that split the Labor movement. And if, somehow, the SPD and the KPD had been able to join forces, the evidence suggests that the leftward pressure thereby exerted would have been directed to toppling Brüning. With that, political warfare would have replaced economic constraints.[15]

The second contribution, Michael Grübler's *Die Spitzenverbände der Wirtschaft und das erste Kabinett Brüning: Vom Ende der Grossen Koalition 1929/30 bis zum Vorabend der Bankenkrise 1931* (Düsseldorf, 1982) provides five hundred densely printed pages covering a year and a half in the relations between leading German business associations and the Brüning government. It is a thorough and impressively researched work. In one of the few English-language reviews, Grübler has been criticized for failing to treat adequately "the economic background to political decisions" and for not providing "an analysis of the causes for divisions" within industry.[16] But such criticism notwithstanding, Grübler offers a trove of chronologically and topically organized materials of significant value to future research and not available elsewhere.[17] He matches an examination of the structure and leaderships of the key interest organizations in the heavy and processing industries, commerce and banking, and agriculture with a close-up study of policy formulation in them. They are thus treated as powerful interest groups—both within and outside the state apparatuses—seeking to resolve the economic and political crises to their own advantage.

15. Not a very enticing prospect at the time, but it is difficult to imagine anything worse than the ultimate outcome.

16. Ulrich Nocken, *AHR* 89(1984):149. Nocken's criticisms of Grübler for inattentiveness to economic influences and a lack of parsimony in his analysis are the exact opposite of his criticisms of *Collapse* and of Bernd Weisbrod's *Schwerindustrie in der Weimarer Republik: Interressenpolitik zwischen Stabilisierung und Krise* (Wuppertal, 1978). Weisbrod examines, with broad grasp and rich detail, the politics and economics of German heavy industry from 1924 to 1928 with a projection into the crisis. Weisbrod's work deserved much more attention in the United States than it received. It is essential to any reasoned debate on Weimar political economy.

17. Many of the documents he draws on appeared almost simultaneously in the immensely helpful two-volume collection edited by Gerhard Schulz, Ilse Maurer, and Udo Wengst, *Politik und Wirtschaft in der Krise: Quellen zur Ära Brüning* (volumes 4/1 and 4/2 of series 3 of the *Quellen zur Geschichte des Parlamentarismus und der politischen Parteien in Deutschland* [Düsseldorf, 1980]). Had these latter two volumes been available at the time, I would have been able to avoid most of the errors in the first edition of *Collapse*.

Grübler contends that in 1930 and 1931 moderate industrialists still sought to reach compromise with the unions. Such agreement might also have stabilized the political system, albeit in a more corporatist and less democratic mode. The evidence in *Collapse* also points to the existence of a strategy or approach of this sort on the part of the dynamic-export fraction of capital, but stresses that preponderant influence was already at this time shifting to the heavy industry-national fraction. In addition, and here I differ with Grübler, I think neither side was prepared to assume the costs of compromise. In fact, neither of the constituencies represented by the leadership of moderate industry or organized labor would even entertain it. Especially with the economy promising to contract further, redistributional struggles heightened. Economics and politics thus conspired to make the situation ripe for radicalization, not conciliation.

The third contribution, a major intervention, begins with that radicalization of capital and moves to its consequences. Reinhard Neebe's *Grossindustrie, Staat und NSDAP 1930–33: Paul Silverberg und der Reichsverband der Deutschen Industrie in der Krise der Weimarer Republik* (Göttingen, 1981) appeared shortly after *Collapse* and is well described by its full title. The fruit of over a decade's research, Neebe's book is avowedly and primarily an organizational history that both picks up the Weimar story later than *Collapse* and, in concentrating on business relations with the Nazis, also takes it further, into 1933. Neebe provides a wealth of empirical material and probes insightfully into sources beyond my own. This is an extremely valuable contribution. At the same time, *Grossindustrie* seems governed by a self-denying ordinance, as far as theorization is concerned, and this leads Neebe to stop short of articulating conclusions to which his own evidence leads him.[18]

In spite of the differences in our approaches, the two books discern many of the same patterns in Weimar's political economy and frequently draw similar inferences about the behavior of people and organizations.[19] They agree on general matters, such as the economic basis for political divergences within industry (for example, as between the heavy-industry, Ruhr-based, "national" Langnamverein and the more export-oriented, Berlin-centered "liberal" Reichsverband). They share

18. I reviewed *Grossindustrie* and elaborated on some of these points in the *AHR* 87(1982):1414–15. Neebe's brief conclusions, 200–03, emphasizing the role of "premodernism," are thus remarkably muted in comparison to the evidence he himself has provided.

19. Many of the similarities between Neebe's findings and my own became apparent in the detailed debate with Feldman.

an assessment of the functional basis and characteristics of the welfare-democratic Weimar System. And they agree on many particulars, such as the role of key individuals (for example, the Reichsverband's liberal chief administrator, Ludwig Kastl, and his isolation from heavy industry) and events, including the controversial Bad Harzburg meetings.[20]

It is worth pursuing the Harzburg question a bit further, both for its intrinsic interest and because of the light it sheds on the complex question of the relations between capitalists and the NSDAP. On 11 October 1931, a united right-wing National Opposition led by Hugenberg of the DNVP, Hitler of the NSDAP, and Seldte of the Stahlhelm, met for the first time publicly and staged a large rally at the Braunschweig spa resort of Bad Harzburg. For Henry Turner, a distinguished historian and critic of my own work, Harzburg marks the first of the three cases at the center of big business's relations with the Nazis prior to the latter's assumption of power; and it provides a paradigmatic example of how questions about these relations are to be posed and understood. Turner undertakes to demonstrate that the meetings produced little direct financial support for the Nazis—a conclusion few historians are likely to dispute. In addition, however, Turner argues that big business was not really involved with Harzburg since "no significant industrialists or other men of big business attended" the meetings; and of the twenty-five or so businessmen who were present, only one was of real importance.[21] The force of such an argument is unclear, however. As Neebe so ably shows in his consideration of the same event, other questions may be asked as well, and other facts adduced. Is financial support the only, or most proper, measure of the significance of such a meeting? Is the personal presence of key industrialists an adequate measure of their interest or sympathy? Neebe thinks not. Nor does he take lightly the presence at these meetings—whose avowed purpose was to unify the popular Right and put an end to Weimar democracy—of the former (and future) president of the Reichsbank, and of the chairman of the association of Ruhr coal owners, an industry at the heart of Germany's economy.

Neebe encourages us to ask more about the *non*-industrialists who attended. They too are highly relevant to industry's attitudes toward the meetings. It turns out that among the *non*-industrialists attending were the following: Max Schlenker, the head managing director of the Langnamverein, the leading organization of Ruhr industrialists; Ludwig

20. For my assessment of the response of several representatives of heavy industry to The Bad Harzburg meetings, see, for example, p. 304 below.
21. Henry Turner, *German Big Business and the Rise of Hitler* (New York, 1985), 168f. See also James Joll in the *New York Review of Books*, 26 Sept. 1985, 5.

Grauert, managing director of the Northwest Employers' Association, the other central association of Ruhr industrialists; Martin Blank, who headed the Berlin office of Paul Reusch, probably the single most powerful Ruhr industrialist; and Erich von Gilsa, who shared that Berlin office and who remained one of Reusch's most trusted confidants and party contact man even after he ceased being the parliamentary delegate from Reusch's district. Neebe also mentions August Heinrichsbauer, by consensus the leading publicist of heavy industry, whose budget was provided by Ruhr firms, including Reusch's, whose efforts were critical to the Harzburg meeting ever taking place, and who from 1930 on was industry's chief liaison to the National Opposition and Nazis. Since such men were present, it is reasonable to conclude, with Neebe, that German heavy industry, through its key organizations, was well represented at what was the first meeting of a united rightist National Opposition dedicated to bringing down the Weimar System.[22]

On this touchstone issue, *Grossindustrie,* after exploring the matter in far greater detail than *Collapse,* arrives at very much the same assessment of industry's divergent response to the Harzburg meetings. Neebe's conclusion merits quotation here:

> The general assault by the National Opposition [Hugenberg, Hitler, Seldte, et al.] against the Brüning government on the occasion of the great "Harzburg Front" demonstration on 11 October 1931 was co-supported at least indirectly by heavy industry. Whereas the Reichsverband eschewed participation . . . the Langnamverein and the Northwest Employers' Association [Ruhr groups] sent their Syndici, Schlenker and Grauert. Along with other leading lobbyists, like Blank, von Gilsa, and Heinrichsbauer, they demonstrated their interest in the creation of a unity from against the existing [Weimar] "System."
>
> The leading representatives of western [Ruhr] industry, such as Reusch, Springorum and Poensgen indeed agreed with the basic line of the "National Opposition" but were not ready to come forward openly.[23]

On another and an important matter, *Grossindustrie* and *Collapse* do not agree, and I now find Neebe persuasive. Relying heavily on the obervations of Paul Silverberg's opponents on the Right and on the Left, I tend, for the most part, to identify that major industrialist with Weimar industry's more advanced economy and more liberal forces.

22. Neebe, *Grossindustrie,* 107.
23. Ibid., footnotes omitted.

Although I describe Silverberg as "a politically complex figure, sometimes a progressive initiator, sometimes a pessimistic bellwether," this may be too generous. Neebe argues forcefully for a calculated and shrewd opportunism on Silverberg's part. In the course of 1932, this was increasingly manifest in his efforts to sever the formally Socialist trade unions from the SPD. That effort basically failed, despite General Kurt von Schleicher's similar strategy during his brief tenure as chancellor. Where I stress Schleicher's maneuver, Neebe emphasizes Silverberg's. In his search for a base of mass support for capitalist hegemony, Silverberg in 1932 courted the Nazis—just as in 1926 he had courted the Socialists! This is, as Neebe notes, an important finding, one to be kept in mind.[24]

Unlike the other recent works discussed here, Henry Turner's *German Big Business and the Rise of Hitler* is readily accessible to the English-reading public. Turner's inquiry is guided by the question of industrial support for Hitler and the Nazi party, which he assesses primarily in financial terms. Indeed, the dust jacket poses the core question, "Did Big Business Finance Hitler?" Turner presents his position in the text as unambiguously as he presents his foil in the book's frontispiece: John Heartfield's 1933 photomontage showing Hitler, with money bag in hand, as a puppet dangling from strings held by the industrialist Fritz Thyssen.[25] And Turner shows the inadequacy of Heartfield's view: Few scholars will challenge the conclusion that the NSDAP was well organized to generate its own funds and was largely self-supporting. It is a conclusion consonant with my own contention that the NSDAP was a "modern," broad-based people's party very different from the bourgeois parties whose erstwhile voters it reaggregated—around a generally vague but, in crucial respects, unambiguously clear agenda.

But Turner expands on this conclusion that the financial role of business in the rise of the NSDAP was slight to take positions that are in fact rather dubious. Turner presents a "business community" virtually devoid of political acumen, one that "viewed Nazism myopically and opportunistically."[26] In their ingenuousness, a few eccentric, albeit major, industrialists offered Hitler their support, while important figures in the business world, like Heinrichsbauer and Schacht (whom Turner diminishes as a "political adventurer") championed the cause of

24. Neebe, 117, 118, is also the source of my correction for the previously misidentified December 1930 report and correspondence discussed in chap. 3, section 5.

25. Heartfield's photomontage has been reproduced often. It appeared initially in the Communist *Arbeiter-Illustrierte Zeitung* of 10 Aug. 1933 and for Turner seems to represent the distilled core of marxist analyses of fascism.

26. Turner, *Big Business*, 349.

the Nazi party and from 1931 on urged its participation in governing. The bulk of the monies that did come from industrial circles to the NSDAP was given to "moderate" figures for purposes of enlightening them on economic matters and as a form of "insurance" in the event of eventual Nazi victory. The real support for the Nazis within business, according to Turner, issued from smaller businessmen resentful of the power of the great firms. Turner holds that, in contrast to certain agrarians and the camarilla around the Reichspresident, nearly all leaders of industry were suspicious and fearful of Nazi radicalism and sought instead to rejuvenate the conservative parties—without granting the NSDAP any significant role in the effort. All told, for Turner, the part and efficacy of big business in the upheavals of German politics from early 1930 to January 1933 have been grossly exaggerated.[27]

Given the real differences between *Big Business* and *Collapse,* the extent to which the two books agree on facts, share key conclusions, and ultimately complement each other may be considered surprising. Like *Collapse, Big Business* finds divisions and camps within German capital, although Turner is reluctant to ground them, as I do, in the domestic and international economy. Nevertheless, we identify many of the same individuals as liberals or progressives. Indeed, when citing anti-Nazi sentiments in the ranks of "big business," Turner most often cites men I identify as central to the ranks of the "dynamic" liberal fraction of industry. There is little disagreement on those figures; we differ over some of the others. Turner demonstrates the determination with which many German businessmen completely rejected Weimar's welfare democracy. He shows how some of them participated in undermining the Republic from the time of the Kapp Putsch (March 1920) through the breakup of the last parliamentary majority government (Spring 1930) to Papen's putsch against the government of Prussia (July 1932). Insisting on their distance from the NSDAP, Turner emphasizes how committed the leaders of heavy industry were to Papen's plans: a "fully authoritarian" state, punitive antilabor social policy, a reversal of the peace treaty, and an end to both political democracy and civil liberties. In actual fact, Papen was more of a *Wegbereiter* (pathbreaker) for the Nazi regime than an alternative to it, as Turner tends to suggest. In the end, it is more than a puzzle how Turner, given his own carefully sifted evidence, can conclude that "Only through gross distortion can

---

27. Indeed, Turner argues, 252, for example, that at crucial moments in 1932 major industrialists vigorously opposed Nazi anti-Semitism, which they considered a benighted prejudice, and warned of the dangers of the Nazi penchant for brutality. Cf. the rather different assessment by H.-A. Winkler, "German Society, Hitler and the Illusion of Restoration, 1930–33" in George Mosse, ed., *International Fascism: New Thoughts and New Approaches* (London and Beverly Hills, 1979), 153–55.

big business be accorded a crucial, or even major role in the downfall of the Republic."[28] It is the argument of *Collapse* that such was indeed the role of business in the dissolution of Weimar.

Even when historians choose and agree on the same facts, they may well construe them differently. Thus, *Big Business* refers to the "oft-told tales" of "the business community's representation at the Bad Harzburg meeting" and "the alleged presence in Bad Harzburg of persons identified with industry."[29] Although not all scholars do, Turner and I agree on the attendance list. Seen from his perspective, that list indicates that business "representation" there was not real, merely "alleged." Schacht was not literally a businessman, only "Reichsbankpräsident, a.D." and associate of businessmen. Few of the working industrialists in attendance were key figures (the chairman of the association of Ruhr coal owners being the major exception). Yet, as noted in the discussion of Neebe above, with the same facts but a different focus, "the business community"/"heavy industry" can be said to have been very much and very well represented at the Harzburg meetings.

More generally, by focusing his questions so heavily on financial support and personal contacts, numerous other distinctly political activities, which might occupy a more central place for other scholars, recede to or beyond the margins for Turner: Paul Reusch's strong counsel to the chairman of the conservative Bavarian People's Party as

28. Turner's summary assessment opens his "Conclusions," 340. The disparity between that conclusion and the facts presented was noted by reviewers; see, for example, H.-A. Winkler's balanced and thoughtful review, "Schuldlos am Dritten Reich?" in *Die Zeit*, 21 Mar. 1986, 17. Given Turner's strict commitment to nominalist positivism, it is disturbing that some reviewers are finding the scholarship in *Big Business* inaccurate and unreliable. Charges of misrepresentation, the suppression of contrary evidence, and manipulation of citations have been levelled in regard to both primary sources and the work of other historians. See, in particular, the examples cited in reviews by F. L. Carsten, *German Historical Institute Bulletin* 22 (1986): 20–23; Klaus Wernecke, "In den Quellen steht zuweilen das Gegenteil," *Frankfurter Rundschau*, 17 May 1986, p. ZB4; Volker Ullrich, "Die Grossunternehmer und der Aufstieg Hitlers," *Suddeutsche Zeitung*, 29 July 1986.

The best recent portrait of the Papen government has been provided by Christoph Graf, *Politische Polizei zwischen Demokratie und Diktatur* (Berlin, 1983). Graf concludes that "National Socialism, in accord with Papen's dependence on Hitler and despite occasional differences between the two, became both legalized and respectable" under Papen (437). Papen's personnel contributed "directly and substantially" to the transfer of power to the Nazis. Cf. Turner, *Big Business*, 276ff. on Papen.

29. Turner, *Big Business*, 350, 168. Turner reserves discussion of the "alleged" presence of these men for his endnotes, where it becomes clear that "alleged" can refer only to the participants' "identification with industry" or "business community representation," and not to the matter of their actual attendance—a distinction not at all clear in the text itself.

early as August 1931 discouraging disagreement between that party and the Nazis; his toleration and acceptance after October 1931 of efforts, strongly opposed by the liberal wing of industry, to purge the chief party of business (the DVP) of those who supported the slightest cooperation with labor and to use financial leverage to merge the rump of that party into the National Opposition spawned at Bad Harzburg; his directives in 1932 to newspapers of which he was part owner to desist from criticism of Hitler, and indeed his insistence on publication of a pro-Hitler article the day before the election; and even the presidential election of Spring 1932, marked by the choice between a conservative—but Socialist-supported—incumbent Hindenburg and Hitler, where Reusch opted for the side of the National Opposition. These are facts of a different sort but facts that nevertheless matter, facts fully in accord with German heavy industry's systematic efforts to undermine the sociopolitical compromises with labor that kept the Weimar Republic from collapsing earlier.

In the concluding pages of *Big Business,* Turner presents the principles that inform the arguments and selection of evidence throughout the book. Those pages of *Big Business* indicate clearly how far removed from each other—both methodologically and conceptually—his work and mine are.[30] Both Turner's work and my own seek to present an accurate picture. Yet, where Turner holds the conscious, deliberate choices and actions of men to be the sole legitimate locus of the historian's inquiry, I take those factors, however important, to be only a part of that inquiry.[31] For Turner, those conscious, deliberate choices constitute a universe of relatively nonproblematic evidence that admits of little if any uncertainty. For Turner, differing views of the evidence, especially those held in the past, were and remain the result of distortion: ignorance, bias, and agendas falsely set. Without such distortions, only a single truth would out. Thus, Turner rejects a variety of marxist interpretations, all for the same reason:

> Whereas valid hypotheses tend to generate consensus, versions of Nazism's rise to power based on the assumption that capitalism accounts for its triumph [sic] have given rise to such a high degree of

30. By contrast, the analytical principles informing *Collapse* are explicitly presented in its opening chapter.

31. As Winkler has noted, "Schuldlos," 17, Turner's examination of the relationship between business(men) and Nazis(m) rests at the level of desires and motivation, *"Motiven,"* without addressing the matter of needs and consequences, *"Wirkungen."* Reviewers of the first edition of *Collapse,* on the other hand, uniformly stressed its focus on needs and consequences. Thus, questions of motive may come up a bit short in my work; they are attended to a bit more by Neebe; and they are addressed singularly by Turner.

arbitrariness and disagreement as to result in utter in-conclusiveness.[32]

Interpretations that display what Turner calls "elasticity" cannot do an acceptable job in demonstrating causality. Like schools of explanation grounded in "divine" or "occult" causality, with which Turner brackets them, they perforce violate "the most basic premises of the professional study of history."[33] There is between us a rather considerable and earnest intellectual divide.[34]

Turner rightly stresses empathy as the first task of the historian if he is to understand the actors and the facts. He faults most historians for failing to participate in the feelings and ideas of businessmen and includes this as part of the ignorance and bias that has distorted the work of others. Historians of all sorts, he argues, have consistently been biased against businessmen:

> That bias should not come as a surprise. Professional historians generally have little or no contact with the world of business. Like so many intellectuals, they tend to view business with a combination of condescension and mistrust. As a consequence, most of what historians have written . . . has been largely uninformed by knowledge about businessmen or their institutions.[35]

Moving beyond knowledge to empathy, many historians believe that interpretive understanding—"*Verstehen*"—is what our enterprise is about. For some of them perhaps, and certainly for Turner, the-oretically based examination of behavior and pattern consistency, the attempt to comprehend particular human associations as social sys-tems—"*Erklären*"—is unscholarly. The latter, of course, is central also to the tradition of historical analysis that includes Marx, and historians

32. Turner, *Big Business*, 353. To describe most of these explanations as "based on the *assumption* that *capitalism accounts* for" Nazism's triumph (my emphasis) is itself biased and inaccurate.

33. Ibid., 358.

34. One that can lead to inappropriate analogies. Thus Turner finds arguments about the economic and social functions of fascism to be "basically similar to that employed by nineteenth-century anti-Semites who insisted that the Jews must have caused the French Revolution since they benefited so greatly from it"—ibid., 354. Quite apart from the *cui bono* questions, there is an odd parallelism implied here between numerous scholars of fascism and nineteenth-century anti-Semites.

35. Ibid., 350f. One wonders about the implications of this position for the study of topics in monarchy, slavery, sainthood, or prostitution. Here, this lack of empathy is most pronounced on the Left. "Since almost all of those who have concerned themselves with the relationship between the business community and Nazism have, to one degree or another, stood left or at least left of center in their political sympathies, a great many have found it difficult to resist the temptation to implicate big business" (351).

inspired by that tradition have contributed importantly to our knowledge of the German past. For some, at least, this identification has colored reception of their work. Turner, for example, perceives a body of work that is part of a still-continuing "crusade against capitalism," preconceived for corroborating doctrine and, from the time of the Third Reich to the present, anchored in "political usefulness . . . to discredit and undermine societies with capitalist economies and to legitimize repressive anti-capitalist regimes."[36] The result of perceptions such as Turner's is the attribution of epistemological and explicit political biases to those who approach historical problems differently.

*   *   *

The Deutsche Führerbriefe and the Industry-NSDAP Convergence, 1932

This second edition of *Collapse* rests on the same evidentiary base as the first, and no new sources have been introduced into the text. But there is one documentary source, pertaining to one of the issues raised in the book, that merits introduction to readers of this volume, and that is the *Deutsche Führerbriefe: Politisch-wirtschaftliche Privatkorrespondenz*. The first edition made one or two references to this newsletter for industrialists. Its association with both the Central European Economic Congress (MWT) and the Ruhr heavy-industry Langnamverein suggested that the *Führerbriefe* was an interesting source for gauging the political sentiment of heavy industry. At that time my access to this publication was limited largely to the articles reprinted in a collection by one of its former staff writers, Alfred Sohn-Rethel.[37] A subsequent reading of the press run for the crisis years, along with consideration of Neebe's treatment of the *Führerbriefe*, persuades me that I had perhaps undervalued its significance as a critical barometer and platform for industrial sentiment on the question of the Nazi party. It deserves more extensive treatment than it has so far received in English.[38]

36. These are the overall themes of *Big Business*'s conclusion, entitled "Myths, Preconceptions and the Misuse of History"; Turner, 356, 358.

37. Alfred Sohn-Rethel, *Ökonomie und Klassenstruktur des deutschen Faschismus* (Frankfurt, 1973), cited in chapter 6, below. Cf. Turner, 299 and note 33, where Sohn-Rethel is accounted for as a "covert Communist provocateur."

38. A complete press run of the *Führerbriefe* is available at the Institut für Zeitgeschichte in Munich, which I thank for supplying me with copies.

Big Business, although it focuses precisely on the question of Nazi-business relations, makes only four brief references to the *Führerbriefe*, the two most important of which (290, 298) are remarkably one-sided and merit comparison with the extensive and bal-

The *Deutsche Führerbriefe* was edited in the capital by Otto Meynen, private secretary to Paul Silverberg, and Franz Reuter, Berlin press agent of the Ruhr industrialists' association and disciple of former and future Reichsbankpresident and Ruhr authority, Hjalmar Schacht. The newsletter appeared twice weekly with a run of about 1,250 copies directed to "the leading circles of finance and industrial capital," including "cabinet members, Reichswehr leaders, leading big agrarians, and the circles around [President] Hindenburg."[39] Leaders of heavy industry were tied to it, including Reusch, who exercised pressure, sometimes unsuccessful, on it.[40] In economic and social policy matters, if not always in political ones, the *Führerbriefe* consistently represented the position of Ruhr heavy industry.

With their contacts to Silverberg and Schacht, the editors were in closest touch with the "political matters of industry" and "mandated to maintain formal and informal ties" to the government and bureaucracy. In its movement from 1928 advocacy of a Grand Coalition with the SPD to its 1932 advocacy of coalition government with the NSDAP, the *Führerbriefe* mirrored the movement of industry itself. In 1928, with the interests of the dynamic-export fraction of industry preponderant, a measure of cooperation with labor (and even the SPD) was the preferred path, despite the objections of representatives of the heavy industry fraction.[41] By mid-1932 the situation and strategy were reversed: the NSDAP had become a preferable mass base. The *Führerbriefe* now shared office space at Schöneberger Ufer 35 with the MWT and Schacht's *"Arbeitsstelle,"* which itself collected money for developing an economic strategy jointly with the Nazis.[42] These three organs were in regular and close contact.[43]

By 1932 German industry generally no longer supported Chancellor Brüning. Support had long since become impatience, particularly

---

anced analysis undertaken by Neebe, especially 154-73 and 265-73. The *Führerbriefe*'s positions were too persistent and consistent to be accounted for by the presence of one Sohn-Rethel among the carefully selected staff members, even if he were the Communist provocateur Turner describes him as having been.

39. Neebe, *Grossindustrie*, 155, 265f., cites a number of sources beyond Sohn-Rethel, including editor Meynen, Werner von Alvensleben, and the research thesis of his own student, Grosskurth.

40. Ibid., 154, 157.

41. See, for example, the objections of Martin Blank and Paul Reusch, 24 Aug. 1928, Blank to Reusch, HA GHH/Martin Blank/400 101 202 4/4b, cited also in Neebe, *Grossindustrie*, 155, 266.

42. See 310–12 below and *AHR* 88(1983):1142–49.

43. On the MWT, see chaps. 4 and 6 below, and Reinhard Frommelt, *Paneuropa oder Mitteleuropa* (Stuttgart, 1977), especially 97ff., which adopts a position on the MWT completely different from Turner's, 466.

within heavy industry but even within the ranks of the more liberal export sector. The social and political consequences of Brüning's dependence on SPD toleration were unacceptable. At the same time, state-guided deflation and the broad distribution of suffering and retrenchment (to include even cartel price policy) inspired no confidence. By May 1932 the *Führerbriefe* referred to Brüning's government as "Marxist, or charitably put, plan–socialistic." In the spring 1932 presidential elections, Reusch, the leading figure in Ruhr heavy industry, in effect supported the National Opposition candidate, Adolf Hitler, and opposed any identification with Brüning's candidate, the incumbent conservative aristocrat and general, Paul von Hindenburg.[44]

The pattern of industrial support for and defection from Brüning is examined in several chapters below, but the key shift of support toward and to the NSDAP is perhaps most clearly registered in the *Führerbriefe*. The elections of 13 March, 10 April, 24 April, and 31 July 1932[45] demonstrated beyond doubt that "in the near future liberalism, including economic liberalism, has no political basis in Germany."[46] And Brüning could no longer hold the fort. Some other political basis for the hegemony of capital, some other power bloc, was now necessary. As *Collapse* repeatedly stresses, from the standpoint of his supporters, Papen succeeded Brüning in June *with the right program but with no popular base* in any social strata. By August, the *Führerbriefe* saw and announced the impossibility of a "Papen solution." At a time when numerous other figures in heavy industry and the agrarian elite were still celebrating Papen's ideological principles, the *Führerbriefe* was worried: "How can a government accomplish the necessary goals . . . when virtually the entire nation is opposed, indeed hostile to it."[47] Industry would only isolate itself from mass political forces.

It would be far better for capital if "unpopular measures" like wage reductions were "coimplemented by a large mass party, which would also be responsible for them."[48] This now meant the NSDAP as it had once meant the SPD. A shift from social democracy to national socialism would provide the basis for a social reconsolidation of cap-

44. Neebe, *Grossindustrie*, 120, 121. At this juncture, the *Führerbriefe* no. 13, 16 Feb. and no. 14, 19 Feb. 1932 proposed Schacht for Reichspresident. Schacht did not allow his vanity to stand in the way for long.

45. The first round of the presidential election took place on 13 March, the second on 10 April. The cataclysmic Prussian Landtag election took place on 24 April: in it the Nazis increased their representation from 6 to 162 seats while the non-Catholic bourgeois parties fell like a rock from about 180 to 42 mandates. The results of the Reichstag election of 31 July appear in chapter 1, tables 1, 2 below.

46. *Führerbriefe* no. 39, 29 April 1932.

47. *Führerbriefe* no. 67, 30 Aug. 1932.

48. Ibid.

italism. This position came to be expressed more and more clearly and more and more explicitly in the following months. While this line of analysis is adumbrated in chapter 6 of *Collapse*,[49] close examination of the *Führerbriefe* provides powerful evidence for industry's movement toward such a solution to the crisis. A two-part September article entitled "The Social Reconsolidation of Capitalism"[50] stated the dilemma of capitalist social domination in a liberal democracy with utmost clarity:

> The problem of consolidating a bourgeois regime in post-war Germany is in general determined by the fact that the leading group—namely the bourgeoisie in command of the economy—has become too narrow to uphold its domination by itself. For this hegemony it needs . . . the linking [*Bindung*] to itself of strata that are not part of it socially but which provide it the indispensable service of anchoring its hegemony in the people, thereby becoming the actual or final support of that hegemony.

As *Collapse* argues, the SPD and ADGB trade unions, through their convergence of interests with the dynamic-export fraction of industry, functioned in this manner from 1924 to 1930. After 1930 the costs of this *"Bindung"*—the legitimating basis for capitalist accumulation—were too high. Simultaneously, mass unemployment, SPD policies, and the economism of trade union leaders led to a growing gulf between the Socialist party and the trade unions. The latter remained wedded to a policy the SPD itself had earlier encouraged: assessing governments almost exclusively on the basis of their delivery of social welfare *(Sozialpolitik)*. This fissure "cut the unions loose" from the SPD and, according to the *Führerbriefe*, left the former available for political linkage to other forces. Chancellor General von Schleicher in December 1932–January 1933 made some efforts to co-opt both the ADGB union leadership and Strasser's "labor" wing of the NSDAP. These efforts, addressed in *Collapse*, had begun as early as July and were regarded favorably by a minority within industry. But the *Führerbriefe*, reflecting the views of the less patient dominant fraction within industry, looked on the SPD/trade union fissure as a desirable prerequisite for the "Integration of National Socialism" into capitalism's social reconsolidation.[51] If National Socialism could assume "a new type of lead-

---

49. See especially 315ff. below, grounded in the analysis of Sohn-Rethel Turner, 290, describes this line of analysis as part of "the Communist line."

50. *Führerbriefe*, no. 72 and no. 73, 16 and 20 Sept. 1932.

51. This was the subtitle of the article of 20 Sept.: see 315ff. below. How substantial the split between the SPD and the trade unions had really become remains an unresolved question.

ership" over the unions "and insert the unions into a compulsion-based [*gebundene*] social arrangement, as social democracy previously inserted them into a liberal one, National Socialism would thereby become the executor of a function essential for any future bourgeois hegemony." Neebe is likely correct that these articles were meant to shore up support for the NSDAP in Ruhr industrial circles, where it may have been softening, as well as to facilitate direct contact with Hitler.[52] They succeeded in both respects.[53]

What industry wanted from the NSDAP at this point was precisely what the *Führerbriefe* had demanded already in May. And that was the same as what Schacht, Reusch, et al. had hoped to accomplish through funding Schacht's bureau *(Arbeitsstelle)* with and for the Nazis:[54] "unmistakable clarity as to their real economic and social program." The economic program articulated in May by Strasser was, at the time, not good enough: according to the *Führerbriefe* of 26 August, it "sacrificed export industry" in the name of a "new mercantilism" and was too "simple minded." The gap would be closed in the next several months; industry's position and that of the NSDAP would begin to converge. I maintain in *Collapse* that the risks involved for business never disappeared completely, before or after 1933. Nevertheless, revisions in the NSDAP economic program, announced already in mid-August, were precisely of the sort industry desired, while the *Führerbriefe* recognized the utility of rhetorical radicalism for attracting workers away from the left.[55] On 17 September 1932 the Economics Division of the NSDAP Leadership was reorganized, with the respectable and industry-friendly Walther Funk replacing the verbal-radical Otto Wagener.[56] Around this same time, Strasser began professing that "we [the NSDAP] recognize private property. We recognize private initiative. . . . We are against the nationalization of industry. We are against the nationalization of commerce. We are against the planned economy in the Soviet sense."[57]

52. Neebe, *Grossindustrie,* 161, 166, 167.

53. Ibid., 269, n. 72. Neebe shows that Reusch—one of those whose support for a Nazi role may have been weakening—was indirectly but clearly involved ("eingeschaltet") in the negotiations and meetings with Hitler undertaken in early November by the two editors, Meynen and Reuter. Turner, 238, 299, considers this trivial, and his discussion of the "non-political" talk between Hitler and Meynen (300) is at odds with Neebe's far more persuasive and detailed account.

54. Schacht's bureau, the *Führerbriefe,* and the Ruhr Langnamverein–influenced MWT ultimately shared their office space, as noted above. They also followed much the same program; *Führerbriefe,* 20 May 1932.

55. See Neebe, *Grossindustrie,* 163f. The efforts of Schacht and Reusch, Heinrichsbauer, Silverberg, and others do seem to have had some effect. *Führerbriefe* of 20 May and 21 June.

56. See, for example, H.-A. Winkler, "Unternehmerverbände," 361–62.

57. Neebe, *Grossindustrie,* 164, citing Strasser's interview with the American jour-

Papen's chancellorship limped along through autumn 1932. His continued and absolute inability to build a base of mass support doomed his "cabinet of barons." For the most part, his key principles were accepted and supported by heavy industry, which welcomed the punishment of labor, the coup against the Socialist government in Prussia, the privileging of capital in legislation and edicts, and the dismantling of democratic institutions. Export industry was distressed by his autarkic protectionism and excessive commitment to organized agriculture's limitless demands. In turn, the agrarian elites stood nearly four-square behind Papen, but the value of their support was diminished by their inability to deliver the votes of the numerically significant peasantry. Having the "right" ideas was not enough; the Nazis were the ones with the mass support. Papen's brief successor, General Schleicher, was aware of this and attempted to build mass support for himself. What worried the leading figures in the dominant fraction of industry, and what led them to reject Schleicher, was the fear of a reparliamentarization of politics, indeed of a revivification of Weimar welfare democracy.[58] Such might well have been the consequence of the general's effort to build support across party lines and on the basis of "neither capitalism nor socialism." Nationalization of key industries was mooted; inflationary public spending under the auspices of Schleicher's Commissioner for Job Creation, Gunther Gereke, appeared in the offing; and a complete break with the Agrarian League and its demands in favor of those of the dairy and livestock-producing peasantry was manifest. The more liberal, dynamic, and export industries were not adverse to much of this program. Thus, Schleicher, as *Collapse* argues, enjoyed the distinct support of leading figures in the Congress of German Industry and Commerce (DIHT), such as Eduard Hamm, and in the liberal wing of the League of German Industry (RDI), such as Ludwig Kastl, Gustav Krupp, and Carl Duisberg. Threatened by extravagant agrarian protectionism and less obsessed with the threat of organized labor, they were also less put off by Schleicher's overtures to the prominent trade union leaders Theodore Leipart and Heinrich Imbusch. Yet this fraction of industry was no longer charting the course for industry as a whole. For the dominant domestic-oriented heavy-industry fraction, Schleicher was a dangerous risk.

---

nalist H. R. Knickerbocker, who concluded that "capitalism has nothing to fear from the National Socialists." On 5 July the *Führerbriefe* praised Hitler for his "highly developed sense of responsibility" and "aversion to radical experiments."

58. See, for example, Reusch to Hamm, 22 Dec. 1932, HA GHH/40023/25b; and Neebe, *Grossindustrie,* 152, 168.

In sum, whereas Papen proposed the proper political prescription, he enjoyed no mass support to help him fill it. Schleicher, on the other hand, sought to mobilize mass support but on behalf of a perilous project. The editors and backers of the *Führerbriefe* were acutely aware of this problem. Through the latter months of 1932 and January 1933 they sought to help overcome it—through encouraging a leading role for the Nazi party, either through the Strasser wing, Hitler, or both. There is good reason to believe that, following their earlier meeting with Hitler, the editors and their industrialist sponsors took an active role in conciliating Papen and Hitler, part of the train of events leading to the critical meeting of those two in Cologne on the afternoon of 4 January 1933 at the home of banker Kurt von Schröder.[59] In any case, Papen took his dinner that same evening nearby, at Silverberg's house. We cannot know what they discussed; it is possible that the day's events, as significant as they were, went unmentioned.[60] We do however know that Schacht wrote Schröder the next day, congratulating him for his "courageous initiative" in helping conciliate "two men . . . through whose cooperation a positive solution can be accomplished perhaps most quickly"; Schacht believed or expected that the Papen-Hitler meeting would become "of historical significance."[61]

However they might variously have felt about it—and their feelings were, as *Collapse* indicates, diverse, ranging from Thyssen's enthusiasm to Schacht's pleasure to Reusch's concern to Kastl's rejection—there were no longer any real alternatives to a leading Nazi role in a new government. The Nazis would not be split, despite the hopes of Reusch,

59. Despite Silverberg's subsequent denials, the recollections provided by the French ambassador André François-Poncet, *Souvenirs d'une Ambassade à Berlin* (Paris, 1946), 65ff., and a number of newspaper accounts cited by Neebe, 171, 273, point in this direction. At the 1947 Nuremberg IG Farben trials, Schröder offered that he had prepared his meeting "in consultation with a number" of industrial leaders. Turner, 315, disagrees, stating that the business "community" "remained unaware of his actions." See also Dirk Stegmann, "Kapitalismus," 45–58 and "Zum Verhältnis," 439; Bracher, *Auflösung,* 690–94, where "something of the otherwise opaque role of economic and financial interests behind Hitler's *Machstreben* becomes visible."

60. Silverberg later denied that the topic was raised, and Turner, 461 n. 11, accepts the denial, of which Neebe is more skeptical.

61. Schacht's letter to Schröder has been reprinted in numerous collections, among them Czichon, *Wer Verhalf,* 79. Turner, 314–16, makes absolutely no mention of Schacht's letter but goes to great pains to argue that Schröder had no contacts with significant industrial figures. At the same time, to demonstrate business opposition to Nazis in the government, Turner in these pages avoids the issue at hand by citing Kastl and Hamm, committed supporters of Schleicher and key members of the liberal fraction! Ultimately, "the left," then and now, is guilty of a "willful, biased interpretation of the Hitler-Papen meeting." (317) Not just "the left," but also those who have settled for less than "the full blown leftist version" are guilty. The scholars and work attacked are too numerous to list here; see the endnotes, 461–63.

Heinrichsbauer, and others (dating back to 1930–31) that Strasser might be available and usable.[62] Beginning with their support of the National Opposition at Harzburg in October 1931, leaders of the national heavy-industry fraction of capital embarked on a road that led most of them quite inevitably to this junction. January 1933 marked the reconciliation and reestablishment of the National Opposition and its constellation of supporters. And here again it was the *Führerbriefe* that expressed most clearly the developments of the last three months before Hitler's appointment as chancellor. Let us close this account by following the *Führerbriefe*'s coverage of the final months, particularly its concern with a possible Nazi electoral decline, Schleicher's policies, the state of the economy, and the possible restoration of parliamentary government and social welfare policies.

The lead story of 8 November stressed that, in the absence of an economic upturn and with a cold winter ahead, popular patience with Papen's narrowly based government could run out.

> Under these circumstances, nothing could be more desirable than broadening the hitherto narrow base of the government, above all through the National Socialists. . . . The electoral setback has for now unleashed much bitterness in the National Socialist camp itself and strengthened radical tendencies. . . . But we have developed much too deep an impression of Hitler's sense for sober and lucid Realpolitik . . . to think that he would permit himself to be derailed into anything reckless.[63]

The fear of a return to parliamentary government was the theme of the lead article of 18 November. It called on president Hindenburg to "place his trust in Hitler," to make him *"zum Manne seines Vertrauens."* "One cannot wish urgently enough at this historical moment that [they] come to an agreement." At this juncture, "as Germany's political crisis . . . reaches the high point of its fever," nothing could be more useful than "a union of the two representatives of the spirit of the German nation, that of tradition [Hindenburg] and that of renewal [Hitler]."[64]

The lead article of 22 November warned that, undesirable elements in the NSDAP notwithstanding, Hitler should be appointed chancellor because "the risk involved here seems to us less than what would be faced if National Socialism continues to be kept out of the government."[65] When the Hindenburg-Hitler negotiations broke down, the

---

62. A number of these issues are addressed in *CEH*, 186–94, 232–36; *VSWG*, 330–35.
63. The article was entitled "Was soll werden?", part I.
64. The article was entitled "Nur keine Zwischenlösung."
65. The article was entitled "In letzter Stunde."

newsletter of 25 November attributed "moral and political right" to Hitler. The Wilhelmstrasse was to blame, not the Nazis.

With Schleicher came the fear of renewed parliamentarism and revived *Sozialpolitik*. Thus, the lead article of 6 December openly worried that General Schleicher might abandon industry's struggle: "there are certain fears due to the sphere of comradeship-socialism from which the chancellor hails, due to his good ties to the unions, due to the appointment of Dr. Gereke [as Commissar for Job Creation], etc." On 9 December the lead article expressed the concern that if the NSDAP was not quickly integrated into the government, "the new chancellor would be increasingly compelled . . . to base himself on parties and groups standing further to the left." The same issue put forward the rather interesting proposition that *Hitler was the next Ebert,* who, like that Social Democratic leader and first president of the Weimar republic, would *restrain the radicalism of his followers in exchange for being put in charge of the state.* The lead story of 16 December voiced great alarm that Schleicher had declared himself "an exponent of neither capitalism nor socialism" and had actually withdrawn Papen's antilabor edicts.

In fact, Schleicher's posture might combine with an improvement in the economic picture, leading to both an end to the NSDAP's chances and a return to parliamentary government. This worried *Führerbriefe* circles: "the noticeable improvement in the economy [would] cut the ground from under radicalism" [!] enabling Schleicher "to take care of the National Socialists one way or another"[66] and opening the way to elections and reparliamentarization. The lead article of 23 December already referred to "Schleicher's half-parliamentary regime"; the final "goal of these policies is of course the return to full parliamentary government"—precisely what the dominant group of industrialists did not want.

All of these matters became more acute with the arrival of the new year. The lead story of 3 January 1933 cited as the pivotal question, "how far it will be possible, to make National Socialism, and with it the entire National Front, into the bearer of government power." In accord with sentiments in the Ruhr, Strasser would play a central role in "the entirety of the National Front taking over state power in Germany for the foreseeable future." However long the "foreseeable future," the transfer of power had to be accomplished somehow and soon. For *if not,* "we will then soon again have the old full parliamentary government, inevitably of a left character." The central goal of capital's leading representatives, the extrusion of the organized Left from politics, the

66. 20 Dec. 1932. The German phrase *"so oder so fertig wird"* has a very ominous ring—as in liquidate.

"liquidation of the past" was at risk. According to the *Führerbriefe* of 10 January, only the NSDAP could prevent such backsliding: "Aside from the National Socialist movement there is no longer any general national movement." If the NSDAP was not successfully integrated into the state, it would only be a matter of months before "the state sinks back into being the booty of the left" for the foreseeable future.

As the month progressed, the *Führerbriefe*'s constituency became more impatient. Thus, by 20 January, after the Papen-Hitler reconciliation, it insisted:

> It must finally be clearly decided how and by whom the German nation . . . is to be ruled. . . . The process of eliminating the central role of parliament peaked under Papen, only to begin to regress again under Schleicher. . . . in fact parliament is increasingly pushing back toward its old status. . . . An aberration in [Schleicher's] political conception is permitting the state to encourage forces that . . . are nothing other than the representation of class politics. Contrary to the supposed power position of heavy industry . . . stands much more the steadily growing power of the unions. . . . he [Schleicher] allies himself with the forces of class struggle.

By the time of its lead article of 27 January, the *Führerbriefe* was encouraging the Nazis to hurry up, for they especially "hold to the position that they have time. They should, however, not take all too much more time, if they want to attain their goal; otherwise it could turn out that, in the end, time is working for Mr. von Schleicher." At the very end, it was, as I have argued, the fear of Schleicher's success that impelled the dominant fraction of industry and the agrarian elite to support or accept the only solution to the crisis still possible. Business fear may have been excessive; we will never know where Schleicher would have taken the country. Nevertheless, the Nazi leadership also recognized that time was running short. On 31 January, the day after Hitler's appointment as chancellor, the *Führerbriefe* opened its issue with a triumphant observation: "Through the appointment of Hitler as Reichschancellor, the government crisis has gratifyingly quickly been solved in the way which we have since the summer steadfastly . . . advocated as the best way."

People make history, but not just as they wish. Here stood the dominant forces in German society: If they were to see the "liquidation of the past," they could do no other.

* * *

Abraham Lincoln, in his famous reflection on the conflicts precipitating the bloodbath of America's Civil War, said that "Both parties deprecated war, but one of them would *make* war rather than let the nation survive, and the other would *accept* war rather than let it perish, and the war came."[67] *Making* war was not necessary to prevent the survival of the Weimar Republic, and those who might have *accepted* war in order to save it were too weak and unable to foresee what lay ahead. Hence, civil war did not come to Germany in 1932 or 1933. Pro-republican forces were too weak, weary, and divided to mount a defense of the "System"; the social welfarist basis of stability had given way to a hopeless and hostile stalemate initiated by heavy industry; the export/reparation economy was suffocated by expensive capital and high tariffs; Weimar constitutionality had, for the most part, disintegrated well before Hitler's appointment as chancellor at the end of January 1933; and that appointment was itself both formally legal and very popular in many sections of society. Instead of civil war, Germany got a mass-based Nazi government—without officially abrogating the Weimar constitution. Nearly everyone in German society underestimated where that government was going, perhaps especially those conservative and elite forces that supported and hoped to tame and use the Nazis. The final page of *Collapse* makes very clear the disappointments and restrictions that Nazi government forced on German capitalism. But just as the interests of the leading part of industry had as their practical consequence a convergence with the NSDAP in 1932, so in the years that followed did those leading interests find the uses of venomous adversity irresistibly sweet.

New York City
April 1986

67. Lincoln's Second Inaugural Address, 4 Mar. 1865.

Preface to the First Edition (1981)

This book originated as a dissertation, and there are a number of people to whom I owe thanks and gratitude for their support in furthering this undertaking at that earlier stage. Foremost, I would like to thank the members of my dissertation committee, who in various ways helped me lay the earlier basis for this work: Peter Novick, without whose moral encouragement and critical insight I would likely not have pursued an investigation in historical political economy, and without whose editorial advice the opacity of my prose would probably not have been held in check; Adam Przeworski, to whom I owe the understanding and appreciation of Marxist social theory which inspired the project and which underlies much of the analysis undertaken here; and Friedrich Katz, whose own understanding of the Weimar era is exceeded only by his modesty. Further, for their comments on and assistance with different parts of the manuscript at various stages, I would like to thank John Coatsworth, Arcadius Kahan, Leonard Krieger, and Hans-Jürgen Puhle. Thanks for their assistance are also due Dieter Gessner, Hans Mommsen, and Bernd Weisbrod; our works are parts of the same discourse, as much where we differ as where we agree. Finally, the critical exchange and sense of communal endeavor provided at Chicago by the political scientists, historians, and sociologists gathered in the Marxist-theory and doctoral seminars opened new and fruitful perspectives and were both timely and animating.

Once at Princeton, I began to benefit from the stimulation and range of challenges provided by my colleagues in the History Department. The spirit of critical inquiry that they help nourish assisted me and is, I hope, evident in my work. No one has been a source of greater encouragement and tougher criticism than Arno Mayer; he has both compelled me to clarify my arguments and encouraged me to stand by them. At a time when radical critique is rather out of fashion, if not quite forgotten, he has faithfully supported me in my project while consistently demanding that I be able to put my case before the dubious and even the hostile. For this and other kindnesses, I register my thanks.

As I embarked on the final stages of this book, I was fortunate enough to receive the challenging criticisms of Gerald Feldman, whose own work on politics and economics in late-imperial and Weimar Germany has done so much to illuminate important issues and further interest in many of the right sorts of questions. Although we shall continue to disagree on a number of important matters, his critique has helped me to sharpen my own interpretation and to appreciate its weaknesses as well as its strengths.

For their generosity in making archival materials available to me, I would like to thank the following: the staff of the Bundesarchiv (Koblenz, FRG), in particular Dr. Thomas Trumpp; Mrs. R. Märsenhausen of the Deutsche Industrie Institut (Cologne, FRG); the entire staff of the Zentrales Staatsarchiv I (Potsdam, GDR)—the former Deutsches Zentral Archiv—which was quite accommodating; and Mr. Bodo Herzog, the beleaguered yet irrepressible holder of the keys to the kingdom at the archives of the Gutehoffnungshütte (Oberhausen, FRG).

Financial assistance was provided at various points in my research and writing by the German Academic Exchange Service (DAAD) and the American Council of Learned Societies (ACLS). A grant from the Princeton Committee on Research in the Humanities and Social Sciences facilitated preparation of the final manuscript.

I should like to acknowledge the conscientious and sympathetic treatment received from my editors at Princeton University Press, Miriam Brokaw and Robert Brown, as well as the assistance of Derek Linton in organizing much of the index.

Finally, I thank my wife, Sandra, without whose sage counsel, help, patience, faith, and comfort at innumerable moments this book would never have been completed.

Introduction to the First Edition

For scholars concerned with the apparent phenomenon of corporatism and our own neocorporatist era, Weimar Germany would appear to have pointed the way to the future for developed Western societies. Indeed, bureaucratic administration rather than parliamentary debate, class collaboration and consensus rather than class conflict and repression, integration rather than fractionalization, inclusion rather than exclusion, and so on were all visible elements in the social, political, and economic mechanisms of Weimar Germany that tended to anticipate those arrangements which have become well anchored and "universally" accepted in the decades since World War II. There is, therefore, certainly both some truth and merit to such a conceptualization.[1]

In a much more consequential and historically significant sense, however, the Weimar era was the last act in the drama of Germany's nineteenth century. From November 1918 through 1923 this was not yet entirely clear. During that period, the democratic and briefly social revolutionary impulses of the several wings of the German labor movement may have been in a position to push German history "forward" a quantum leap. But the political and economic class warfare of those years so chastened the socialist movement that that advance never took place. Instead, most of the forces and many of the actors reemerged from the stage of Imperial Germany to pursue their interests and conflicts once again. The period of the German Revolution—one is even uncomfortable with the term—has been thoroughly explored and will not be investigated here. Rather, this study will explore those conflicts and concerns that surfaced after 1923 to assert anew the continuity of German social and political history. Even so, though facing many of the

---

1. One of the most explicit statements of this position is Charles Maier, *Recasting Bourgeois Europe* (Princeton, 1975). See also Philippe Schmitter, "Still the Century of Corporatism?" *Review of Politics* 36 (1974): 85–131, and Leo Panitch, "The Development of Corporatism in Liberal Democratic Societies," *Comparative Political Studies* 10 (1977): 61–90. The rational kernel contained in the liberal view is obscured by the failure to consider the forms of conflict resulting in corporatist mechanisms that are then hidden behind them.

same issues, Weimar was not the Empire, so the gross result of those conflicts was perforce different. The abandonment of the Weimar Republic by those who had been central underpinnings of the later Empire led to the Republic's collapse and the transfer of power to the Nazis. However novel that outcome, the conflicts which played so great a role in producing it were deeply rooted in the political, ideological, and social structures of Germany before the Great War.

The conflicts within *and* between the industrial and agricultural forces in Germany, as well as those between capital and labor generally, are the subjects of this study. Relations among the dominant social groupings in a society cannot be understood without a parallel examination of the relations between the dominant and the subordinate. Similarly, relations between dominant and subordinate classes cannot be fully deciphered without an evaluation of the unity and coherence of the dominant forces themselves. In examining the structures and trajectories of these various conflicts, and in analyzing how they contributed to the demise of the Republic, one is struck by how much they had in common with the developments of the Empire's last decades. Pressure groups, political parties, and areas of contention all bore a remarkable similarity to their prewar predecessors. The republican political and legal system, the defeat in World War I, the Versailles treaty, and numerous economic changes both domestic and international certainly altered the nature of conflict and its rules, but below the surface much remained the same or was restored. Thus, it is the period from the middle of the war to 1923 that appears anomalous. And not only because of the subsequent reemergence of familiar faces—Stresemann, Hindenburg, Hugenberg, and the industrialists were simply the most obvious—but rather because of the renewed salience of old conflicts, old coalitions, and old desires. The not altogether vain attempts to restore the old *Sammlung* (alliance) of agrarians and heavy industry, Germany's "historical ruling bloc," and the off-again-on-again coalitions of left-liberals, dynamic industrialists, SPD, and Catholic unionists were only two manifestations of the old drama.

The key feature in the drama of late imperial politics had been the alliance of estate owners and heavy industry resting on the popular base of the Mittelstand. Economic protectionism and antisocialism brought and held the two economically dominant classes together. The Mittelstand was generally attracted by these same policies and the corresponding ideology of imperial "social protectionism." Although an examination of the emergence and operation of the Sammlung bloc lies outside the scope of this work, it is important to note the primary costs and benefits of the alliance. Heavy industry gained substantial political support in its struggle against social democracy, the unions, and reform of the state system, while the estate owners obtained tariff protection for their declining sector and support for their political preeminence, especially in Prussia. The relationship between these two fractions of the historical bloc was mediated by the state apparatus for which, despite the lofty state-worship propagated by the estate owners, this became an increasingly mundane preoccupation. The alliance cost the rural elite its political maneuverability; it no longer had anywhere else to go and became increasingly dependent on its ability to "deliver" the peasants and the army. Heavy industry was compelled to accept higher production costs—a situation it tried to mitigate through combinations and organization of the market. The two fractions clashed and were forced to compromise over such issues as the building of the fleet and the *Mittellandkanal*. The former was initially viewed by agriculture as a pet project of hostile, liberal commercial and exporting capital, and the latter threatened to bring cheap foreign grain directly into the densely populated industrial heartland.[2] Although agrarian representatives managed to modify the format of both projects, they had to accept them in exchange for higher tariffs. Organized agriculture accepted its increasing economic marginalization in exchange for certain economic guarantees and continued disproportionate political perquisites and spokesmanship. For heavy industry it was an offensive alliance intended to counterbalance the growing dynamic fraction of industry and to repress organized labor while mobilizing the Mittelstand on its own political behalf. For the estate owners it was a defensive alliance intended to brake the decline in their economic status and traditional standing in the state apparatus.[3] Reconstituting this "historical bloc" preoccupied numerous industrialists and agrarians throughout the twenties.

In the prewar period the agrarians could use their political potential to protect their estates and the political status quo. Without their support the three-tiered Prussian franchise would not have lasted, and the rural and small-town Mittelstand's enmity toward organized labor might have been softened. Their strong and homogeneous base in parliament was available to industry in exchange for economic protection, status prerogatives, and the promise not to be abandoned. Whatever the differences in tax, finance, tariff, and military matters, the

2. On the Mittellandkanal, H.-J. Puhle, *Agrarische Interessenpolitik und preussischer Konservativismus* (Hannover, 1966), pp. 226ff., 240ff.; on the fleet, Eckart Kehr, *Battleship Building and Party Politics* (Chicago, 1975); on both, Walther Herrmann, *Bündnisse und Zerwürfnisse zwischen Landwirtschaft und Industrie* (Dortmund, 1965), pp. 15ff. See also chap. 4, n. 3.

3. Cf. the quotations from Gramsci, p. 10 below and those from Max Weber, pp. 48, 49 below.

"social question" kept the members of the Sammlung bloc together. That was most clearly demonstrated in the 1913 Cartel of the Productive Strata, composed of the Bund der Landwirte, Zentralverband Deutscher Industrieller and the Reichsdeutscher Mittelstandverband. Export industry, dissident feed-dependent peasants, and a minority of the Mittelstand were left either to constitute a permanent progressive minority or to take the step over the brink into coalition with the working class.[4] Emil Rathenau of German General Electric reflected the views of this progressive minority toward the social and trade protectionism which underlay the Sammlung when he argued that German agriculture cannot "attract valuable objects from foreign countries and create riches; only commerce and industry can make Germany great. . . . Compulsory regulations based on fear may preserve the weak in their sphere of activity; the strong can develop their powers only in freedom; weakness does not make for growth. . . . representatives of agriculture have demanded the protectionist principle . . . and the artificial limiting of industry. . . . But it is useless to try to protect industry and commerce from foreign forces with weapons while at home we injure them through laws."[5] While the postwar economy never allowed for Rathenau's degree of glibness, the thrust of his position remained dear to many in the dynamic and export fraction of Weimar industry, and, with the postwar economic recovery, their chance would come.

The end of the monarchy severely weakened the political stock of the estate owners, making it easier for the other fractions of the prewar bloc to attempt to form other viable power blocs. But even before military defeat, social upheavals, and the proclamation of a Republic weakened the rural elite, industry had come to certain agreements with labor (mostly through the unions), which pointed the way to future coalitions without the big landowners.[6] In addition, the war brought together the military bureaucracy and heavy industry where previously the rural elite had mediated that relationship. The inadequate provisioning of the war-weary troops and urban population triggered mutinies and riots and

---

4. On the Cartel of the Productive Strata, Dirk Stegmann, *Die Erben Bismarcks* (Cologne, 1970), pp. 352ff.; from the industrial side, Hartmut Kaelble, *Industrielle Interessenpolitik in der Wilhelminischen Gesellschaft* (Berlin, 1967), pp. 226ff. For an overly generous account of the counter-Sammlung "progressive" coalition, see Beverly Heckart, *From Bassermann to Bebel* (New Haven, 1974). See also chap. 1, sec. 1 below.

5. Cited in Kehr, p. 454.

6. For the exigencies of the wartime labor market, strikes, the Auxiliary Service Law, and finally the Stinnes-Legien agreements between industry and the unions setting up the *Arbeitsgemeinschaften,* see Gerald Feldman, *Army, Industry and Labor in Germany, 1914–1918* (Princeton, 1966), and Maier, pp. 58, 59.

could hardly benefit the rural elite, especially when that elite could also take some credit for the war and continued to call for a "victorious peace." The rural elite emphasized its devotion to the monarchy precisely as other social classes came to question the value of continuing that institution. As other social classes began to demonstrate flexibility on the reform of the Prussian franchise, organized agriculture countered with the call for "corporate-vocational" suffrage. Estate owners and peasants united in opposition to the wartime "coercion economy" while demanding higher prices, none of which sat well with either the urban population or those trying to pacify it.

Perceiving the potential danger of socialist insurrection, Jacob Reichert of the iron and steel industry, and certainly no friend of labor, announced in October 1918 that the state owners and traditional Mittelstand were no longer dependable bulwarks against upheaval. Sufficiently strong allies for industry, he argued, could only be found among the workers and therefore the unions. Toward the end of the war, the SPD came to express the interests of the majority of the nation, albeit in a particular way that led Arthur Rosenberg to describe the events of 1918 as "a middle-class revolution won by Labour fighting against feudalism."[7] Though certainly not banished from the historical stage, the estate owners were removed from the center while the industrialists were left stunned and immobilized.

After edging briefly toward that center stage, the organized working class both pulled back and was pushed away. The "middle-class revolution" established a flawed, formally democratic Republic that underwrote a society in which industrial capitalism was economically dominant. Despite their economic dominance, industrial capitalists failed to attain clear political and ideological superiority. Shifting equilibria and stalemates between the fractions of industry and between industry and the rural elite contributed significantly to the political inadequacy of the dominant social classes. Incapable of presenting themselves clearly as the carriers of the national interest, industrial capitalists, as in the prewar era, could not elicit the voluntary support of the great majority of the population, comprising the working class and the various strata identified still as the Mittelstand. This inadequacy, together with the defeat of the revolutionary socialist impulse, made the subsequent reversion possible and led to the tenuous system of class cooperation, extraparliamentary compromise, and corporatism that have come to be seen as at the heart of the Weimar Republic during

7. *Imperial Germany: The Birth of the German Republic* (Boston, 1964), p. 217. The most insightful analysis of Germany during the war is now Jürgen Kocka, *Klassengesellschaft im Krieg* (Göttingen, 1973).

those years when the Republic worked. Thus, the Weimar system disguised old conflicts while never being fully accepted by the majority of the economic and political leaders of the dominant social classes.

The stability of the middle Weimar years was not grounded in any broad legitimacy, and it therefore proved vulnerable to economic and political strains that might cause any of the various participants to withdraw from the compact. Indeed, with the onset of the Great Depression, the bourgeoisie abandoned the program of compromise and competition with the SPD which had provided the basis for stability from 1925 to early 1930. The SPD's tacit program of integrating and representing the interests of the working class in a democratic, capitalist order was judged too costly by its bourgeois partners.

During the decade from the aftermath of the November revolution to the Great Depression, the SPD was divided into what might be termed social-liberal integrationist and structural-reformist camps.[8] The party largely suppressed or ignored its structural-reformist wing and willingly incurred the loss of those interested in revolution. But the integrationist basis of Weimar politics also depended on the cooperation of some of the many bourgeois parties and the industrial, commercial, and agricultural interests they represented. Substantial and significant sectors of the bourgeois (bürgerliche) parties, backed by large numbers of nonbourgeois voters, participated in this integrationist politics once it became clear—as it had by 1923—that the initial insurrectionary impulse had been defeated. Indeed, after 1924, important industrial groups even sanctioned governing with labor (die Arbeiterschaft); for some this meant the SPD, and they grudgingly abandoned active "counterrevolution" in its several forms[9] in favor of the daily conflicts of liberal-democratic society. By 1926, this was an openly avowed if far from

8. By "social-liberal integrationist" I mean the defense of the daily, material interests of the organized working class within the framework of a democratic republic and capitalist economy. This position did not exclude attempts to improve the competitive position of the working class within the system. The overwhelming majority of the SPD stood in this camp. By "structural reformist" I mean a program designed to improve the structural position of the working class in a democratic polity and to create a democratic economy via legal means. A democratic economy would be a step toward public control and socialism. Supporters of this position fell between Hilferding on the right and Paul Levi on the left.

9. "Counterrevolution" should be understood as encompassing one or more of the following: (a) conservative attempts to restore the prewar social order, (b) a general program of antisocialism or opposition to the working class when organized on a class basis, or (c) sometimes in conjunction with b, a populist or Mittelstandish program of "alternate revolution," possessing a mass base and appearing to oppose the existing social order but not in the name of a class. For a further development of the concept, Arno Mayer, Dynamics of Counterrevolution in Europe, 1870–1956 (New York, 1971).

universally shared policy. Several factors made this stabilization possible. One was the defeat of the working class, completed through the inflation, the suppression of communist uprisings, and the reversal of previous wages and hours concessions after the Ruhr occupation. Another was the apparent waning of right wing, *völkisch* radicalism. Still another was the set of requirements for Germany's reintegration into the world economy and the benefits accruing from it. But even the semblance of stability in 1924–29, disguising some social struggles and transforming others, disappeared with the onset of the economic crisis.

Conflicts among the dominant economic class fractions and between them and the organized working class provided the chief impetus for German politics between 1924 and the end of 1932. Under the specific conditions of the period, these conflicts contributed first to the creation of a tenuous capital-labor compromise and political stability from roughly 1924 through the end of 1929, and then, as conditions changed, these same conflicts contributed to the demise of the Republic. Subsequent chapters of this work analyze these conflicts and their course in detail. Primarily, though not exclusively, the conflicts were generated by divergent and sometimes contradictory material interests: within the agricultural sector, between an elite of grain-growing estate owners and an electorally influential body of dairy and livestock-producing peasants; within the industrial sector, between older, cartellized, and frequently labor-intensive heavy industry oriented toward the domestic market, and a more dynamic, often decentralized and capital-intensive processing industry oriented toward the export market. There were also substantial interest conflicts between agriculture and industry as sectors. On the basis of their production and political desiderata, and in the context of shifting political and ideological coalitions, the dominant class fractions adopted different postures toward organized labor and its demands, toward trade, commercial and fiscal policy, and toward reparations. Ultimately, however, attempts to overcome the consequent contradictions within the framework of the democratic Weimar state failed. The period of social upheaval and counterrevolutionary response from 1918 through 1923 did not alter the economic or social foundations of German society, and, in the specific circumstances of the following decade, the democratic political structures of the Weimar Republic produced no acceptable balance among the interests of the dominant class fractions and between them and the subordinate classes and strata.

The dominant class fractions are not divided here between "good" industrialists and "bad" industrialists or between socially minded entrepreneurs on the one hand and tyrannical *Herren* on the other. Both the earlier record of some who will be described as "dynamic" (e.g., the imperialist and annexationist position before and during the First World War held by Gustav Stresemann and Ludwig Kastl, who appear in Weimar as progressive figures) as well as their post-1933 performances under fascism (e.g., that of the once-progressive IG Farben), should make it clear that moral-political postures or even attitudes toward progress are not at the core of this analysis. What separated the fractions of industry was a divergent set of capitalist interests. That Germany's dominant economic groups could not reconcile their differences within the framework of the Weimar Republic tells us both that capitalists may have interests which vary over a rather broad range and that in given, *particular* historical conditions the democratic republican form of state inhibited the reconciliation of those divergent interests. Attempts to realize particular economic interests may engender or entail specific political strategies—different strategies at different times and under different circumstances. As we shall observe, there are few obvious or enduring political consequences that follow from any given set of economic desiderata—though there are always *some*. In the case of Weimar Germany, as in any other, political outcomes emerged from political struggles, but many of these struggles were themselves grounded in economic relations.

At a certain point in its history, Weimar Germany could no longer tolerate the conflict between the costs of integration in a political system that was based on a mixture of strife and cooperation between social classes, and the necessity of private accumulation and control in a capitalist economy. The offensive of the historical ruling bloc, checked since 1924 by the massive influx of American capital, the vitality of certain sectors of German industry, and the partial cooperation of organized labor, resumed by 1929. The factors precipitating the new offensive were largely political; despite nearly continuous high unemployment and low use-of-capacity rates in German industry, the effects of the Depression had not yet become general when the offensive was undertaken. However, certain key industries, members of the former historical ruling bloc, were already facing or anticipating severe profit squeezes and reductions in production levels. The coal, iron, and steel industries, together with the whole of German agriculture, considered themselves to be "suffering." Their difficulties arose from the social, fiscal, and economic policies of a competitive parliamentary government and tacit cooperation with SPD-led labor, an international trade and tariff strategy attendant to these policies, and an approach to the Versailles treaty that was based on fulfilling its conditions while working for their revision.

The eventual recourse to an alliance with the fascist movement, or what might charitably be described as a surrender to the Nazis by the majority of the representatives of Germany's dominant class fractions, issued from the perceived inadequacy of the republican political system: based on tenuous coalition building among fragmented parties, it could not unite the interests of the dominant classes and could aggregate no base of popular support other than the costly one represented by social democracy. Industrial and agrarian leaders were convinced that post-Depression Germany had to be spared the costliness and unreliability of a democratic political constitution and a profit-devouring social-welfare system. Support of fascism was thus not simply an attempt to survive the Depression; it was a way of using the crisis. Fascism did not arise out of a temporary equilibrium of forces between working class and bourgeoisie, and the extent to which the political system after March 1933 was a "Bonapartist" one reflected in what manner the crises *within* the ruling bloc both had and had not been settled. For the rise and coming to power of the Nazi party corresponded to the sharpening internal tensions among the dominant class fractions. No one class or class fraction could entirely impose its leadership on the other dominant fractions, whether through corporate interest and leadership organizations or parties and the parliamentary democratic state. The transition to fascism took place through, or in the course of, a political crisis that caused the rupture of linkages between the various classes and strata and the political parties which had represented them. Accompanying that political crisis was an ideological crisis which nearly permeated the society. At the same time, the growth of fascism corresponded to an offensive on the part of the industrial bourgeoisie and an economist retreat on the part of the labor movement. The Nazi regime that ultimately emerged from the crisis was certainly more than a dictatorship of monopoly capital, a Bonapartist regime based on an equilibrium of forces and standing above all classes, or a dictatorship of the petite bourgeoisie. Finally, even the fascist state's relative autonomy from the dominant social classes stemmed in part from the inherited and deeply imbedded contradictions *within* and among those classes themselves as well as *between* them and the dominated classes.

Our task, then, is to provide a sectoral analysis of the political economy of Weimar Germany and an examination of the linkage between that political economy and the political stability and crises which marked the years after 1924. That examination must begin with a theoretical consideration of the relationship in capitalist societies between politics and society, between the state and social classes.

THE COLLAPSE OF THE WEIMAR REPUBLIC

Chapter One

THE STATE AND CLASSES: THEORY AND THE WEIMAR CASE

1. State and Economy in Weimar

The functions of the state vary from society to society, but every state, except one on the brink of collapse, performs one function above all others—in a sense comprehending all others as well: it underwrites and maintains the principal social and economic relationships of that society. In a capitalist and industrial society such as Weimar Germany, the state functions as the factor of cohesion for economic, political, and cultural processes and relations. Yet, capitalism's economic relations are relatively independent of its political ones, even in a country with an activist state tradition like Prussia-Germany. Production, in capitalism, in comparison to feudalism, for example, does not rely on political mechanisms in order to be set in motion. Thus, political relations can develop independently of economic relations, and the state in capitalist society may both appear and actually be relatively autonomous.[1] In the parliamentary democratic form of state, formally equal competition increases this autonomy. Within limits determined by the specific status or conjunctures of the economic, ideological, and political realms, state policy output is a product of recognized, rule-bound, institutionalized bargaining where the outcome in any given case cannot be determined beforehand.[2] How state revenue is to be

---

1. Recent debates on "refeudalization" or "repoliticization" are concerned precisely with the question of whether and how economic relations are again dependent on political ones. Both those supporting the theory of "state monopoly capitalism" and those opposing it argue that the state has been drawn directly into the process of economic reproduction. See Claus Offe, *Strukturprobleme des kapitalistischen Staates* (Frankfurt, 1972), and on its historical development, H.-A. Winkler, ed., *Organisierter Kapitalismus* (Göttingen, 1974), esp. the contributions by Winkler, Kocka, and Wehler.

2. On the limits to this autonomy and indeterminacy, Ralph Miliband, *The State in Capitalist Society* (London, 1969), esp. chaps. 2, 6. The Marxist analysis presented here of the relationship in capitalism between the state and the economy has recently penetrated liberal scholarship, leading Marxist axioms to appear as liberal revelations; see, for example, Charles Lindblom, *Politics and Markets* (New York, 1977).

distributed, for example, is such a policy question of indeterminate outcome. Indeed, as we shall observe, this policy question was so fiercely contested in Weimar Germany that conflicts over it resulted in major political and social struggles. This happened because the particular situation in Germany after 1928 converted disputes about the distribution of public revenue into conflicts over the possibility of producing private surplus, and this, as the very essence of capitalist production, could not be called into question. At a minimum, the state in a capitalist society must guarantee that capitalist production can take place and that the social relations of that production are reproduced.

The state is the regulating mechanism for the equilibrium of the entire society. Ultimately, it is through the agency of the state that the dominant social classes are organized, i.e., elevated from the level of their "selfish," individual interests to that of their collective, class interest. Alone, the private and competitive nature of the appropriation of surplus would tend to foster systematic disunity among capitalists, even in an economy where monopolies and cartels were prominent. Similarly, it is through the state that the dominated social classes are disorganized, i.e., kept from the level of their class interests and kept at the level of their interests as individuals, citizens, and members of the nation.[3] The older Marxist expectation that the (increasingly) social nature of production in industrial capitalism would by itself engender or foster working-class unity has not, on the whole, proven correct. To organize the interests of the capitalist class and its allies successfully and to turn these into "national interests," the state and its leaders must stand at a distance from individual capitalists; they must not allow themselves to become the creatures of specific capitalist class members or interests.[4] The crisis of the last years of the Weimar Republic stemmed in large part from the inability of the state to organize the interests of the members of the dominant classes in an autonomous fashion, going beyond partial interests. The Republic was unable to safeguard existing social relations, not because of any revolutionary threat, but rather because of the conflicts and contradictions within the bloc of dominant

3. Nicos Poulantzas, *Political Power and Social Classes* (London, 1973), p. 189. For a different formulation of the same view, Georg Lukács, *History and Class Consciousness* (London, 1971), pp. 65ff. Antonio Gramsci, *Selections from the Prison Notebooks* (New York, 1971), pp. 181, 370, labels the selfish level "economic-corporative" and the organized level "ethical-political." It is only at the latter level that hegemony, active consent, can be established.

4. A position too close to individual capitalists is at minimum considered "corruption." Engels's remark that "Bonapartism is the religion of the bourgeoisie" must be understood to encompass almost all forms of the bourgeois state, not just the strictly Bonapartist.

classes, together with the results of the policy indeterminacy of the preceding years.

It can be argued that since the "Keynesian Revolution" the separation between state and economy has collapsed: civil society and state are joined.[5] The state both reflects and acts upon prevailing social and economic relations. The government bureaucracy is now responsible for the planning, direction, and control of economic undertakings whose costs and technological needs are too much even for large monopolies. The security of private property, of economic growth, and of crisis-free economic performance now require constant intervention by the state. Although this was not yet fully the situation in Weimar Germany, we shall encounter substantial elements of such a development and demands for it.[6] The role of the Prussian/German state in nineteenth-century German industrialization, unprecedented at the time, provided the groundwork for later forms of organized intervention.[7] To the extent that there were government attempts to intervene in and alleviate the economic crisis after 1928, and to the extent that such interventions were expected by the great majority of the population, the economic crisis exacerbated the political crisis. There was increased conflict in the political realm precisely at those points when the state was called upon to do more in the economic realm. Brüning, with his limited, largely negative intervention, had trouble maintaining, and Papen and Schleicher, with their more active intervention, had trouble establishing their political legitimacy through mass loyalty partly because their economic intervention was unsuccessful. The failures of their policies were not primarily due to any inherent lack of wisdom. Indeed, some of the Papen and Schleicher policies were quite promising and were adopted a short time later by the Nazi government.[8] The conflicts of needs, interests, and ideologies among the dominant class fractions were largely responsible for the ineffectiveness of government policy, and only once these were resolved was a coherent state policy possible. So long as the economically dominant classes lacked clear and organizing leadership, their members could not rise above the level of *sauve qui peut*.

5. On this, see Jürgen Habermas, *Legitimation Crisis* (Boston, 1975), as well as the work by Offe and the somewhat overly instrumentalist work by Joachim Hirsch, *Wissenschaftlich-technischer Fortschritt und politisches System* (Frankfurt, 1970).

6. A strong argument for the growth of such tendencies is made by Maier, esp. pp. 545ff.

7. There is a vast literature on the role of the Prussian/German state in industrialization; see n. 27, below.

8. See Michael Wolffsohn, *Industrie und Handwerk im Konflikt mit staatlicher Wirtschaftspolitik?* (Berlin, 1977), chaps. 3–5, and pp. 166–70 below.

That Germany was furthest down the road of "organized capitalism" did not alter the need for leadership within any bloc of dominant classes. The development of the first constitutive elements of this system only increased the saliency of state/economy interaction. H.-J. Puhle enumerates those elements which developed even before World War I:

> the increased taxing prerogatives of the state, the growth of public works and services and insurance, the bureaucratization and organizational tendencies of large industry, especially the new strategic growth industries (electro-technical, chemical, motor and engineering) and the workers' movement . . . further that of political and public-oriented pressure groups which contributed decisively to changing the relationship between government, parliament and public thereby lastingly altering both political landscape and style and binding the sectors of the private economy together with each other and with the agents of the state through their intervention in elections, in the press, in parliament and its committees and through the activities of their representatives in regional government and professional organizations.[9]

An indicator of the advanced role of the state is the percentage of the GNP devoted to public, state expenditures. Thus, in the USA the figures for 1900 and 1929 were 4 percent and 10 percent, respectively; in Germany they were already 16 percent and 30.6 percent. But, the increased interpenetration of state and economy did not "free" state activity from nonpolitical constraints, and it did not relieve the dominant social classes of the need to accomplish an internal ordering crowned by a hegemonic fraction. The patriarchal social commitment of the German bureaucracy augmented the state's autonomy but did not determine the nature and outcome of political practice or the form of society (organized precapitalism, organized capitalism, organized socialism).

Care must be taken in any political analysis to avoid reifying the concepts of autonomy and mass loyalty. While there were moments in late Weimar Germany when the state seemed to be functioning as the instrument of capital as a whole, or even of just one sector of it, there were other times when the state seemed "merely" to be sanctioning and protecting the rules and social relationships of the capitalist order. In these latter instances, the state was probably functioning more independently. Yet it is exceedingly difficult to delineate the social

---

9. Hans-Jürgen Puhle, *Politische Agrarbewegungen in kapitalistischen Industriegesellschaften* (Göttingen, 1975), p. 29.

mechanisms that account for one type of functioning or another. The number of contacts between industrial leaders and members of the government or the bureaucracy, for example, did not vary a great deal. Linkages were both constant and institutionalized; there is no evidence of the state's "holding the rifle butt over the heads" of the capitalist class. Describing this autonomy as "relative" is, therefore, not enough. In the following chapters we shall have to analyze very carefully the individual policy formulations, outputs, and outcomes in order to relate the concept of autonomy to the conflicts among the dominant class fractions. Similarly with the concept of mass loyalty: equal votes need not be of equal significance. The percentage of the German electorate that voted for the Nazi party in the autumn of 1932 (33 percent) was not substantially greater than that which voted SPD in 1928 (30 percent). But, these were voters casting their ballots in a different context, and a qualitatively different mass loyalty emerged to replace the rather tenuous loyalty enjoyed by the Republic.

The autonomy of the state is conditioned by the ways in which the economic realm has come to be dependent on state activity. Broadly conceived, we can locate five areas of such state activity: (1) Guarantee of the organizational and legal principles of the capitalist system: such matters as inviolability of contracts, freedom of labor, etc.[10] (2) Establishment and construction of some material preconditions for production (infrastructure and other external economies such as railroads and telecommunications), which are for the benefit of all economic actors but beyond the reach of any one of them. Although this is an old area of activity, the increased dependence of industrial production on technological advance has enlarged the scope of these activities and further socialized the costs of production.[11] (3) Both occasional and regular participation and intervention in the course of economic activity and growth, to secure growth and avoid and remedy crises (government contracts—especially military—fiscal and monetary policies, tariffs). Growing concentration and inflexibility (cartels, monopolies) render commodity production and exchange increasingly incapable of regulating themselves. (4) Regulation of conflicts between capital and labor so as to avoid constant social crises (mediation and even compulsory arbitration have slowly been accepted by capital). Generally, capital shares an interest in keeping these conflicts within limits so as to

10. See Nicos Poulantzas, "L'Examen marxiste du droit," *Les Temps Modernes,* nos. 219, 220 (1964):274–301.

11. James O'Connor, *The Fiscal Crisis of the State* (New York, 1973), pp. 36, 8. These costs are not just infrastructural but also ongoing and social (social capital and social investments), p. 6.

facilitate the final area of state activity. (5) Maintenance of the legitimacy of, and mass loyalty to, the social system as a whole (distributive and social-welfare measures; foreign successes). Whereas activity in the first two areas is undertaken with the full cooperation of representatives of capital, activity in the last three areas is undertaken against the will of some, perhaps even a majority of the representatives of capital. The growth of the state's role is part of a three-stage historical development: organization of the market (monopolies, self-financing) to relieve the pressure of competition faced by individual capitalists; the institutionalization of technological progress (research and development, investment outlets) to relieve the threat of crises faced by the economy as a whole; and state regulation of the entire system to relieve the pressure of social, political, and economic tensions.[12]

What the state needs to execute these activities limits both the possible range of state action and policy output. The state needs financial resources, a capacity for technological rationality, an already existing legitimacy or mass loyalty, and the loyalty of the owners of the means of production. The Weimar Republic after 1929 was progressively deprived of these, and its ability to act diminished commensurately. The loyalty of the representatives of capital was essential for a number of reasons. As Müller, Brüning, Papen, and Schleicher all discovered, the state can only make offers or set parameters in a process in which the owners of the means of production dispose of what is theirs as they see it. Too much state (or trade-union) pressure can precipitate investment and employers' strikes, and a loss of cooperation or "crisis of confidence," thereby exacerbating a crisis instead of mitigating it. In order to be able to stabilize the economy, the state needs mass support; this is forthcoming only when demonstrable economic successes are at hand, and to obtain these, cooperation with the private sector is essential. The owners of the means of production abandoned the Weimar Republic in its attempts to stabilize the economy partially because of the constraints that had been placed upon it by the results of parliamentary democracy, where all citizens were entitled to press equal claims. The capacity for technological rationality which the state also requires is limited by the fact that the private sector is frequently the source from which both trained personnel and economic data are drawn.[13] The financial needs of the state are met

12. These points are elaborated upon by Offe, pp. 21–25. See also Habermas, *Legitimation Crisis,* part 2, and his earlier statement in *Toward a Rational Society* (Boston, 1970), chaps. 5, 6.

13. The activities and reports of both the parliamentary Enquête Ausschuss study of the entire economy and the semiacademic Friedrich List Gesellschaft accord with this contention.

primarily through tax revenue. Although the state may set tax rates that attempt to reflect the interests of all of society, its receipts from business remain particularly vulnerable; the growth of the "economy as a whole" presents itself as the only way out.[14]

Political and economic developments may dictate an increased and ongoing state role in the economy. The state may undertake economic planning so as to maintain, implement, replace, or compensate for particular economic processes. Curiously, however, the more the state needs to intervene in the economy, the more dependent it becomes on the owners of the means of production. This is true regardless of whether the need for intervention is episodic or organic; the need may even be purely a function of developments within the economy. Thus, in the German case, with the onset of the Depression the Weimar state became increasingly dependent on *die Wirtschaft*. The ideological dominance of the propertied limits the range of possible state policies by successfully characterizing some of them as "utopian."[15] The growing expectation of improvements in the standard of living also renders the state more dependent on the dominant economic powers. This is ironic since it is generally social democratic parties and governments which encourage such expectations.[16] Once such expectations are rooted, they are nearly impossible to reverse democratically, and their costs invariably seem to grow, during both normal and crisis periods. Clearly, such was the case in Weimar Germany. From the time of the last SPD-led government under Hermann Müller on, the state was cast in the role and burdened with the responsibility of economic coordination; it could not possibly succeed, since economic decisions remained the private prerogatives of the industrialists and their leaders, and they refused to cooperate. It was in this context that the results of the predepression conflicts and decisions over the distribution of revenue came to threaten the very ability to produce and accumulate surplus. Despite the institution of consumption and other regressive taxes, it was impossible to transfer the entire burden of state costs completely onto the shoulders of wage earners and other taxpayers. So long as revenue sources remained domestic, the areas of state activity came into conflict with each other and further weakened the state. The

14. The identity between "the economy" and the owners of the means of production is even clearer in the German—*die Wirtschaft* means both. Hilferding's fate as finance minister illustrated these constraints; the issue is discussed in chaps. 5 and 6.

15. Cf. Karl Mannheim, *Ideology and Utopia* (New York, 1936), pp. 203, 146, where this process is described.

16. Eugene Varga made much of this dilemma in analyzing the victory of Italian fascism. His 1927 article appears in Theo Pirker, ed., *Komintern und Faschismus* (Stuttgart, 1966), pp. 131ff.

functions of facilitating private accumulation and guaranteeing mass legitimacy could not be reconciled.[17]

2. State and Society in Weimar

The crisis of the Weimar state was not a social crisis of the sort anticipated by many Communists: a "maturation" of class antagonisms that coincided with the "catastrophic development" of the capitalist economy.[18] The Depression was indeed a catastrophe, and class antagonisms of all sorts were rife, but the impetus for the *state* crisis came from the determination of capitalist groups to use the economic situation to their political advantage. This, in turn, exacerbated political instability and legitimated the abandonment of and opposition to parliamentary government. After 1930, both capital and parts of labor, but especially the former, oriented their struggles toward transforming the internal organization of the state; their class struggle became *political* for the first time in nearly a decade. In the course of their political struggle, the possibility of a new mass base and different form of state for German capitalism became apparent. The divergent interests of the various capitalist groups were organized anew, and the new form of government could function as the new guarantor of cohesion for unchanged social relations.

What were the bases of these various capitalist groups; how, and under whose leadership were they formed into and maintained as the "historical bloc of ruling classes"? It is an axiom of Marxist analysis that the manner in which surplus value is extracted from the direct producer determines the social relations involved in production and ultimately the relationship of the rulers and the ruled.[19] Those involved in production are the carriers of the social relations engendered by the given mode of production. The capitalist mode of production allows for the separation of economic, political, and ideological relations, because surplus is extracted solely within the economic realm, virtually unassisted by political or ideological mechanisms. In capitalism, these car-

17. O'Connor develops this thesis for contemporary America as the "fiscal crisis," but in Germany this was only one aspect of the multiple crisis.

18. This catastrophism was the dominant motif in the Comintern's analysis of western Europe, especially after 1928; once the big Depression came, the revolution would surely follow. This view succeeded in pushing other, more penetrating analyses aside. See Nicos Poulantzas, *Fascisme et Dictature* (Paris, 1970), pp. 43ff. Remnants of this view occasionally still appear in East German work.

19. E.g., Karl Marx, *Capital* (New York, 1967), 3:791; *The German Ideology* (New York, 1960), pp. 7–16.

riers of social relations become classes through their activity—through their practice in the political realm.[20] An objective relationship to the means of production, being a carrier of certain social relations, is insufficient to constitute a class in capitalism.[21] As indicated earlier, the state, when functioning coherently, helps organize the owners of the means of production into a class; this same function is performed for wage labor by political parties and, sometimes, unions.[22] Unless so organized, wage laborers will appear in this dominant political sphere simply as individuals, as citizens seeking to achieve their selfish interests. Conversely, the dominant classes will appear as spokesmen for the interests of the nation as a whole, and the actualization of their needs through the state will generally be consented to and accepted as legitimate.[23] This is one meaning of the term *hegemony*. Thus, to overstate the case somewhat, social *relations* become historical *activity*—to modify Thompson's phrase, "class happenings"—in their political embodiments.[24] But not all conflict between or among classes is class struggle: we should distinguish between "classes in struggle" and literal "class struggle." In the former, place of insertion or location in the production process is external to any confrontation. Thus, the German Mittelstand, in the decade after 1923, was involved in a struggle with other classes in the society, but this was not a class struggle in the sense in which Marxists most often use that term, despite the fact that the Mittelstand's demands were political, economic, and ideological.[25]

No society, including Weimar Germany, is characterized by just one mode of production with its attendant social relations. Although industrial capitalism was by far the dominant mode of production in Weimar

20. This is the view derived from the structuralist reading of Marx; cf. Louis Althusser and Etienne Balibar, *Reading Capital* (London, 1970), pp. 225–53; Louis Althusser, *For Marx* (New York, 1970), pp. 104–28; and, explicitly, Poulantzas, *Political Power,* pp. 74–76.

21. For a differing view, Henri Lefebvre, *The Sociology of Marx* (New York, 1969), pp. 104–12.

22. This view seems to reject entirely the "class in itself"/"class for itself" dichotomy. The former simply does not exist, since without consciousness, i.e., without politics, there is no constitution as a class; there is simply a shared relationship to the means of production.

23. This is perhaps the litmus test for whether or not a dominant social class is hegemonic, capable of eliciting spontaneous loyalty. Cf. John Cammett, *Antonio Gramsci and the Origins of Italian Communism* (Stanford, 1967), p. 204.

24. Or, in a different formulation, the uneven development of the different levels of a social formation leads to the overdetermination of its contradictions and their condensation in one of them. Thus, economic contradictions may appear as political ruptures. Cf. Althusser, *For Marx,* pp. 200–216, 250ff.

25. Ernesto Laclau, *Politics and Ideology in Marxist Theory* (London, 1977), pp. 106, 107.

Germany, other modes also existed: the family-peasant, small-commodity, and even vestigial-feudal modes coexisted with industrial capitalism. The economic, political, and ideological practices of all of these partially amalgamated "subsocieties" constituted the German social formation. A half-century earlier, Marx had remarked on the incompleteness of capitalist development in Germany. Even in the Weimar period, it remained true that Germany suffered, "not only from the development of capitalist production, but also from its incompleteness. Alongside of modern evils, a whole series of inherited evils oppress us, arising from the survival of antiquated modes of production. . . . We suffer not only from the living, but from the dead."[26] These "dead" were to play a crucial role in the resolution of conflicts within the historical bloc of ruling classes.

The East Elbian Junkers continued to occupy vital positions in the military, civil service, and judiciary, and remained an important force not only among rural producers but within the capitalist elite as well. Although total agricultural production contributed under 15 percent to the GNP, and the agricultural portion of the population had slipped to 25 percent by 1925, the agricultural elite continued to enjoy vastly disproportionate influence. Up to 1918, industrial development, despite its rapidity, had taken place within a semifeudal integument, and the Junkers preserved a political and ideological supremacy greater than that of any other landed group in industrial Europe.[27] They continued as a class in charge of much of the state apparatus and as a ruling class in the Empire. Gramsci characterized them as

> the traditional intellectuals of the German industrialists who retained special privileges and a strong consciousness of being an independent social group, based on the fact that they held considerable economic power over the land. . . . The Junkers resemble a priestly-military caste, with a virtual monopoly of directive-organizational functions in political society, but possessing at the same time an economic base of its own and so not exclusively dependent on the liberality of the dominant economic group . . . the Junkers constituted the officer class of a large standing army, which gave them

26. Preface to the first German edition, *Capital,* 1:9.

27. There exists a substantial literature on the subject: e.g., Thorstein Veblen, *Imperial Germany and the Industrial Revolution* (New York, 1939); Hans-Ulrich Wehler, *Bismarck und der deutsche Imperialismus* (Cologne, 1969), and *Krisenherde des Kaiserreichs* (Göttingen, 1970); Helmut Plessner, *Die verspätete Nation* (Stuttgart, 1959); Joseph Clapham, *The Economic Development of France and Germany* (Cambridge, 1936); W. O. Henderson, *The State and the Industrial Revolution in Prussia* (Liverpool, 1958); Helmut Böhme, *Deutschlands Weg zur Grossmacht* (Cologne, 1966).

solid organizational cadres favouring the preservation of an esprit de corps and of their political monopoly.[28]

Of course, in the Weimar period, their political monopoly was broken and, as we shall argue in chapter 4, the big agrarians did become increasingly dependent on the liberality of industrialists and the state. But per se, the dominant economic group, the bourgeoisie, had never directly ruled in Germany. The earlier political and cultural monopoly of the nobility impeded the development of an extensive and independent bourgeois political personnel.[29] This had much to do with the continued parliamentary crises and fragmentation of the liberal parties; in turn, the Catholic Zentrum and SPD were aided in their prewar growth precisely by that fragmentation, a fragmentation which continued throughout the Weimar period. Stresemann's narrow circle constituted perhaps the only successful, representatively bourgeois political group of the entire era. Most industrialists greeted his death with a sigh of relief, anxious as they were to disavow him. Representatives of the agricultural elite, on the other hand, despite being even more unhappy with government policies, continued to fill posts and participate in the state apparatus at all levels down to the very end of the Republic and beyond. Although it had partially merged into the bourgeoisie, the agricultural elite continued as an autonomous class or fraction within the ruling bloc dominated by industry.

Thus, viewed strictly in terms of their percentage contribution to the GNP or portion of the population, representatives of the agricultural sector ought to have been little more than junior allies or supporters of a ruling bloc. However, even after World War I the agricultural elite of estate owners continued to occupy vital positions in both political and civil society; all reaches of the military and civil service, for example, continued to bear their mark. An additional factor was at least equally important in preserving the status of the rural elite as members of the ruling bloc: the agricultural and industrial sectors were not of symmetrical composition; the relationship of the peasant majority to the large landowners was very different from that of the worker majority toward the factory owners. Even when organized, peasants, unlike unionized workers, did not generally adopt an adversary posture to-

28. Gramsci, p. 19.

29. On the extended cultural dominance of the nobility, Ernest K. Bramsted, *Aristocracy and the Middle Classes in Germany* (Chicago, 1964). On the political "monopoly," Maxwell Knight, *The German Executive* (Stanford, 1952). The origins and political consequences of a certain philistinism are analyzed in an essay by Max Weber, "National Character and the Junkers," in Hans Gerth and C. Wright Mills, eds., *From Max Weber* (New York, 1958), pp. 386–95.

ward their putative betters. Peasants simply did not hate the big estate owners the way workers hated the Herren of industry. The resolution of the economic and political conflicts between grain-growing estate owners and the body of dairy- and livestock-producing peasants enabled *Landwirtschaft* to appear as a solid front and buttressed the position of the agricultural elite both vis-à-vis industry and in society generally. In the final two years of the Republic, this solid front began to dissolve; many non-Catholic peasants voted for the Nazis, yet even this did not signify abandonment of the agricultural elite's core interests. Toward the end of the Republic, an attempt to reconcile estate-owner and peasant interests through the "Green Front" occurred, with demands crystallizing around autarky. Not only socialists but also important industrial and commercial groups tried unsuccessfully to exploit rural cleavages and break this agricultural front, which even in the 1920s operated to retard capitalist development.

The dominant element within the unity of dominant classes, what we can call the hegemonic class or fraction, did not remain the same throughout the Weimar years. Viewed politically, largely cartellized and domestic-oriented heavy industry vied for hegemony with generally less cartellized dynamic and export industry. These two fractions of industrial capital entertained similar but far from identical interests. Their relations to their commercial, financial, and agricultural partners also varied, and rivalries between and among these fractions were always present.

Thanks to the cheap debt-retirement, bankruptcies, and lowered real wages resulting from the inflation and Ruhr occupation, most of German industry was able, with the assistance of American capital, to rebuild, modernize, and expand capacity quickly after 1923. An already cartellized industrial sector became even further dominated by grand monopolies and cartels. Both the labor unions and the workers' parties were demoralized by a series of defeats between 1919 and 1923, and the election results of 1924 embodied the new "economy-friendly" state of affairs. What various branches of German industry chose to do, or could do, with their plants was conditioned by a number of factors. Conflicts arose out of the divergent production desiderata, trade, and political needs of the various branches of German industry. The first central cleavage during these years was between export- and domestic-market-oriented industry. The former group, including among others the machine, electro-technical, chemical, and textile industries, was generally interested in low prices for basic industrial goods. (Except for brief interludes like the British coal strike of 1926, Germany's basic, heavy industries were not substantial exporters.) Exporters favored a "pacific" expansion through most-favored-nation trade treaties, which came at the expense of domestic heavy industry and especially agriculture, together with the Stresemann foreign policy of international reconciliation and reintegration. So long as these industries enjoyed international preeminence, wage and social costs incurred through a policy of class cooperation and competition were, for them at least, not crucially significant. A quite different orientation characterized the older Ruhr industries at the heart of the domestic market branch. These wanted high prices and low costs. High costs and overcapacity made pacific expansion difficult and, after 1925, the quotas allotted Germany by the international iron cartel (IRG) proved unsatisfactory. Only an expanded domestic market could absorb this sector's production at high prices. Almost all production and ownership units here were large and cartellized, and the burden of wages constituted a much greater share of total costs. The growing and prosperous export industries accepted high protective tariffs for domestic primary industry, so long as they received refunds from the primary producers equal to the difference between world and domestic prices for those quantities subsequently exported. A series of shaky agreements, the AVI accords, laid the basis for a reassertion of the dominance of the domestic-market-oriented industries, but severe conflicts persisted throughout the Weimar years.

Other cleavages involved capital composition and ideology, factors that also contributed to divergent attitudes toward labor and toward agriculture. Within the League of German Industry (RDI), power was wrested after 1930 by the heavy-industry conservatives from the dynamic-export liberals who had held it since about 1925. The processing and smaller finishing industries then buckled under the menacing of heavy industry's vertical cartels and a political campaign against the system of export rebates. Beginning in the late twenties, mining and steel organizations threatened to withdraw from the RDI and from other organs whose policies they deemed insufficiently conservative or overly attentive to export and parliamentary constraints. Industrial circles began to plan a trade strategy that abandoned the pacific market of northern and western Europe and overseas in favor of the "imperial" market of eastern and southern Europe. The relatively virgin markets of the east were presented simultaneously as an inducement to export circles and as a threat to agriculture to encourage their lining up behind heavy industry. The prospects of renewed profitability were thus ultimately tied to a changed social and political system at home and an imperial policy in central Europe presented as autarky.

Relations between the representatives of industry and agriculture did not follow any smooth pattern during the Weimar years. Although the industrial elite was in a position to set both the tone and the agenda for capitalists during the entire period, its willingness to make sacrifices on behalf of its rural partner varied. Viewed from the perspective of general economic policy, agriculture was increasingly shortchanged between 1924 and 1929. The year 1925 marked the beginning of a trend characterized by trade treaties unfavorable to agriculture, growing agricultural imports, disadvantaged access to capital, widening price scissors, and then, by 1928, the onset of the agricultural depression. Since the home market for heavy industry enjoyed only a brief spurt, agriculture was left, until the end of the stabilization, as the only serious proponent of a semiautarkic "domestic market" strategy. Agriculture did share industry's desire to lower the "costs of production," particularly wages and social-welfare measures. With the growing struggle over this issue inside the last bourgeois/working-class coalition government (1928–30), relations between agrarian and industrial leaders improved. As was the case before World War I, organizations representing heavy industry moved toward the policies advocated by agriculture, while more dynamic and successful export industry groups called upon agriculture to make itself more efficient, cut costs, and help itself. Even socialists were no more critical of German agriculture and its elite than were the spokesmen for the dynamic industries, such as machine building, electronics, and chemicals.

Once the Depression deepened, attempts simply to balance the needs of both agriculture and export industry broke down, and a more unified, coherent strategy became necessary. Because of their relative strength, ministerial support, and even international cartellization, industrialists generally espoused a fairly direct laissez faire view of the state's role. Almost all divergences from that norm were, according to industry, a result of unwarranted and ruinous socialist influence. A weak Landwirtschaft, on the other hand, having traditionally supplied the military and bureaucracy with leading personnel, was much more willing to experiment, on the assumption that it could sabotage or overturn any undesired consequences of state intervention in the economy, while standing to profit from most such intervention. Despite routine denunciations of the "coercive" economy of the war period, the agricultural elite was even tempted by reformist SPD proposals to establish government grain and import monopolies intended to guarantee prices. Such proposals, together with agriculture's seemingly endless calls for "nonproductive" subventions, increased disarray among the historical partners. As the Depression worsened, organized cooperation between agriculture and industry seemed to break down. Only the increased salience of other, more fundamental cleavages prevented a complete rupture between these longtime allies and members of Germany's historical ruling bloc.

The content and course of these intraagricultural, intraindustrial, and agrarian-industrial conflicts will be analyzed in succeeding chapters, both at the economic-corporate level represented, for example, by interest-group organizations and at the level of politics and the state. Each class fraction attempted to make its own economic interests into political interests and to present those as the common interests of the classes and fractions in a bloc.[30] In the Weimar context, each was charged with the primary responsibility for "getting us off the current socialist road and enabling industry to speak in the name of the economy and the nation, not just capitalism."[31] Taken as a whole, however, these capitalist class fractions were the power bloc in Weimar Germany, as they had been in the later years of the Empire.

Originally allied to the prewar power bloc politically, albeit not wholeheartedly, and opposed to it economically, was the Mittelstand.[32] Composed of shopkeepers and commodity producers on the one hand and salaried employees on the other, each constituting just under 20 percent of the population, the alliance proved frustrating for the Mittelstand, more so than it had been during the Empire. Whereas the salaried employees found themselves profiting economically from bourgeois/social-democratic collaboration (1924–29) in the realm of employee rights and *Sozialpolitik* (social legislation and policy) they found the value of their political patronage declining and withdrew their support from the bourgeois parties when the bourgeois parties hardened their positions on Sozialpolitik.[33] Their self-consciously separate status prevented them from moving left, however.[34] The shopkeepers and commodity producers, on the other hand, defected earlier. Not

---

30. Poulantzas, *Political Power*, pp. 239, 283.

31. According to a DDP-oriented liberal, *Berliner Tageblatt* 12 Dec. 1929.

32. H. A. Winkler, *Mittelstand, Demokratie und Nationalsozialismus* (Cologne, 1972). Theodor Geiger, *Die soziale Schichtung des deutschen Volkes* (Stuttgart, 1932), pp. 106–8, distinguished among "old, new and proletaroid" Mittelstand with the first two at about 18 percent of the population and the last, overlapping with the other two, at about 12 percent. Winkler, "From Social Protectionism to National Socialism," *Journal of Modern History* 48 (1976):1–18 stresses the authoritarianism of much of the Mittelstand and the tenuousness of its link to the bourgeois parties. Still useful as an introduction to the composition, attitudes, and fate of the Mittelstand is Herman Lebovics, *Social Conservativism and the Middle Classes in Germany, 1914–1933* (Princeton, 1969), pp. 3–48. On how the Nazi party managed to aggregate the disparate elements of the Mittelstand the works by Winkler remain the best; most recently his "Mittelstandsbewegung oder Volkspartei? Zur sozialen Basis der NSDAP," in Wolfgang Schieder, ed. *Faschismus als soziale Bewegung* (Hamburg, 1976), esp. pp. 103ff.

33. Correspondence between the central leadership and local and occupational representatives of the DDP, DVP, DNVP and other bourgeois parties documents this trend which is discussed in chap. 6.

34. Jürgen Kocka, "Zur Problematik der deutschen Angestellten, 1914–1933," in Hans Mommsen, et al., eds., *Industrielles System und politische Entwicklung in der Weimarer Republik* (Düsseldorf, 1974), pp. 792–811, reaffirms this.

only did they suffer more from the inflation, but for them the costs of bourgeois collaboration with social democracy were not offset by any redeeming benefits. Initially, they had nowhere else to go, but once the movement to the Nazi party began, it became a stampede.[35] Losers in the inflation and unable to penetrate the system of industry-labor collaboration, the Mittelstand could be mobilized politically against it. Further support for the old ruling bloc was provided by the bulk of the peasantry. These supporters obtained little materially in exchange for their support. Certain half-truths propagated by rural, antisocialist ideology shored up their support: an identity of interests shared by all agriculturalists, big and small alike, and a fear of antiproperty, urban Reds. Although peasant support was retained within the range of older bourgeois parties until 1930, it too seemed to disappear overnight (amongst Protestants, at any rate) as soon as an uncompromising advocate presented itself. Once the Republic appeared to announce itself to the peasantry only with the tax collector, it announced itself to the Republic with the "Emperor."[36]

There are two ways of looking at coalition politics, both actual and potential, in the Weimar period. The first is in terms of the social classes or forces represented by various political parties; the second is in terms of the political parties and electoral coalitions themselves. We will examine first the actual and potential class blocs and then the electoral results. Several blocs or coalitions of classes were formed (or were possible) during the Weimar years. These blocs were unstable and shifting. In addition, at different moments, different fractions of a bloc were in a position to set the tone and agenda for a bloc as a whole. Economic and political bonds brought and kept bloc partners together; economic and political conflicts kept various bloc possibilities from forming and tore others asunder. In conceptualizing coalitions or blocs we are faced with a dual task: on the one hand, analysis of class blocs as formed from "the bottom up" and involving group intentions, class situations, tensions, and consciousness at the base; on the other hand,

---

35. Theodor Geiger, "Die Panik im Mittelstand," in *Die Arbeit 7* (1930): 637–54. Numerous voting studies confirmed Geiger's analysis, cf. S. M. Lipset, *Political Man* (Garden City, 1963), pp. 138–52.

36. Rudolf Heberle, *From Democracy to Nazism* (Baton Rouge, 1945), details the entire process for Schleswig-Holstein. Though by no means any longer a "sack of potatoes," Marx's characterization remained partially applicable: They are "incapable of enforcing their class interest in their own name. . . . Their representative must at the same time appear as their master, as an authority . . . power that protects them against the other classes and sends them rain and sunshine from above." Marx, *The 18th Brumaire of Louis Bonaparte* (New York, 1963), p. 124. The "announcement" metaphor appears in the same text.

analysis of more tangible power blocs as formed from "the top down" and consisting of organized political activity and interventions, of parties, alliances, policy formation, leadership organizations, etc. It is primarily in terms of the latter that the coherence and strength of blocs can be evaluated. During the Weimar Republic certain policy issues, decisions, and nondecisions were particularly critical and, as our later analysis will demonstrate, blocs formed and dissolved around issues of social policy *(Sozialpolitik)*, trade policy *(Handelspolitik)*, reparations and foreign policy *(Reparationspolitik* broadly conceived), distribution of the national wealth (and burden), democratization (in both the public and private spheres), and the balance between private accumulation and social legitimation. Thus, government coalitions, cooperation and conflict among corporate interest organizations and unions, patterns of social, trade, and fiscal legislation, the policies of state bureaucracies, the public agenda as enunciated by various ideological apparatuses, and the articulation of the tasks at hand by the spokesmen for classes, unions, and parties all help provide the basis for a partially inductive determination of the class coalitions constituting a bloc.

Schematically, for Weimar Germany we can map several blocs composed or rural and urban, dominant and dominated classes. Through these power blocs, the economic sphere, where individuals appear as the carriers of determinate social relations, shaped the political sphere, in which members of all classes appear as equal citizens with equal claims. It was largely through state activity that intrabloc conflicts were mediated and the interests of a bloc as a whole pursued. Although some of the respective blocs here are labelled with dates, these dates only indicate the ascendance, sometimes tacit or de facto, of one or another coalition, not necessarily a formalized shift. The formal goal of the bourgeoisie remained united bourgeois rule, and the form of state might depend on what type of mass base was available for that rule. In figures 1–5, we posit five such class blocs. In each schema the hegemonic class or fraction, i.e., the dominant element within the unity of classes, is represented in capital letters, and ties represented by solid lines are stronger than those represented by dashed lines. In the bloc formation of figure 1, the estate owners and heavy industry together were hegemonic. Their relationship was mediated on the terrain of the state with the estate owners providing cadres for the semiautonomous military and bureaucratic elite. Export industry, consisting of the more dynamic, new processing industries, was also part of the bloc; it was linked directly to heavy industry. Family peasants too were part of this arrangement, although they profited less from their membership. They were linked to the estate owners. Finally, the petite bourgeoisie was an ally of this bloc, profiting as it did from the bloc's social protectionism

FIGURE 1

Sammlung Bloc, pre-1914 Bourgeois Bloc. The "historical ruling bloc."

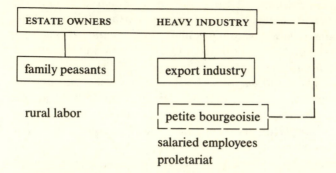

and antisocialism as, for example, the Reichsdeutscher Mittelstandsverband signified. Other groups must be considered as having been in opposition.

In the bloc formation of figure 2, heavy industry was hegemonic. Export industry was allied to heavy industry in this bloc as well, but it demurred from some of the bloc's economic policies. Again, family peasants were linked via the estate owners. The petite bourgeoisie was lost to the bloc because of the effects of the inflation, and other groups were in opposition.

In the bloc formation represented by figure 3, export industry was hegemonic. Linked to it in the bloc were the organized proletariat (including rural labor), insofar as it was represented by the SPD and affiliated unions, and salaried employees. An expansive economy, liberal social legislation, and a shared foreign policy permitted interclass cooperation. Heavy industry, although still within the bloc, had much in the realm of social and economic policy to be dissatisfied with. Estate owners and family peasants were distinct losers in this arrangement, while the petite bourgeoisie became increasingly homeless.

A bloc formation such as in figure 4 would have removed the "pernicious" influence of both the "feudal" estate owners and socialist working class. It failed to emerge because the liberal industrialists could not split the peasants from the estate owners and overestimated the republican potential of the petite bourgeoisie. The progressive aspects of the bloc would have linked salaried employees to export industry, while the conservative ones would have linked the petite bourgeoisie to heavy industry.

The short-lived bloc formation shown in figure 5 was like the "Sammlung Bloc" except for the important fact that it lacked any base of mass support. After over a decade of republican government, it was impossible to stabilize a government that enjoyed no mass support. Further, the agricultural elite was far more dependent on heavy industry than it had been in the prewar bloc. Tables 1 and 2 introduce the political parties, electoral results and party coalitions of the Weimar period.

Broadly speaking, we can say that the parties drew their primary electoral support from the following major groups: KPD—working class and unemployed; SPD—working class, urban and rural, and some middle class; DDP—liberal industry, urban commercial groups, intellectuals, and initially some family peasants; Zentrum—Catholics of all classes, especially workers and peasants; DVP—urban middle class, "white collar" groups, mainline industry, and haute bourgeoisie; Wirtschaftspartei—urban petite bourgeoisie; CNBLP—as per its name; DNVP—various urban middle classes, military and rural elites, and Protestant peasants; NSDAP—urban and rural Mittelstand, especially Protestant, some from all other groups. The key electoral contribution of the NSDAP consisted of uniting on the basis of an authoritarian populism the various Mittelstand groups (petit bourgeois, peasant, "white collar") who were or had become homeless in the course of economic and political changes and whose economic existence provided no basis for unity. By and large, the vote that shifted most between 1920 and 1932 was that of the Mittelstand.[37]

FIGURE 2

Antisocialist Right Bourgeois Bloc, 1922–24. Rolling back the revolution.

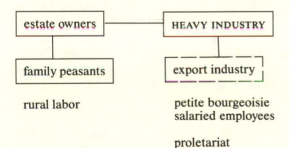

rural labor   petite bourgeoisie
salaried employees

proletariat

37. The importance of the Mittelstand in German society and the ability of the Nazis to organize these economically diverse strata on the basis of a relatively coherent ideological appeal, permit us two generalizations about such crisis situations: (1) the more separated a social sector from the dominant relations of production, the more diffuse are its "objective" interests and consequently less developed its "class instincts"; this has the consequence that the evolution and resolution of the crisis will take place, so far as it is concerned, on the ideological level; (2) the more central the role of this sector in the society as a whole, the more crucial the role of ideologies in the final resolution of the general social crisis. See Laclau, p. 104.

FIGURE 3

Class Compromise Bloc, 1925–30. Republican stability with democratic potential.

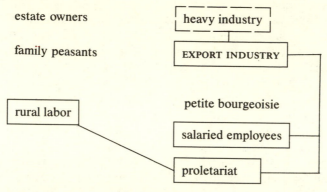

The dotted lines in table 1 indicate the division of the party arena into left, center, and right—according to the policy behavior of the parties, not necessarily according to the intentions of their electoral supporters. The weakness and near disappearance of the "middle" is, of course, the classic story of Weimar Germany. The second classic story is the inability of the left to unite. Consequently, the third classic story is about the instability of cabinets and coalitions. Table 2 examines the vote totals of the three fields and of coalitions other than those actually formed.

Socialist-bourgeois collaboration under socialist leadership (SOCLST/bourg) was rendered impossible once the Zentrum backed away from the SPD and moved to the right. Socialist-bourgeois collaboration under bourgeois leadership (soclst/BOURG) was rendered impossible by the shrinkage of the DDP and DVP and by the latter's move to the right. Before 1924 and the defeat of the working class, the DVP was not prepared to be part of a "republican bourgeois" arrangement; after 1924, this proved the weakest alignment. "Right bourgeois" coalitions were the goal of organized capitalist interests, but the fractiousness of the splinter parties and of the DNVP left them frustrated. Electorally, the most viable possibility remained the socialist/BOURGEOIS, the Grand Coalition. In principle, the SPD remained willing, but once the economic crisis set in, as it did after 1929, the economic costs it exacted proved intolerable. After 1930, no parliamentary government was possible that excluded both SPD and NSDAP; ultimately, both the SPD and parliamentary government itself were rejected.

The political interests of classes are generally represented through parties, and it is through the practice of the parties that struggles among the classes may take place.[38] It was characteristic of the last years of the Weimar state that, except for the workers, classes became detached from their parties, which ceased to be viewed as effective representations of class interests. This break in the link between representatives and represented weakened parliament after 1930 and presaged the movement toward what could be called "parliamentary idiocy." Concomitant with this was the relative increase in the power of the military, the bureaucracy, and private-interest groups.[39] This did not occur against the will of the dominant classes, nor did it indicate a diminution of their power.[40] German industry had, after all, been socially dominant for decades without much of a direct presence on the political scene or direct management of the state apparatus.[41] The Weimar constitution

FIGURE 4

Liberal Bourgeois Bloc. Never formed: the goal of liberal politicians.

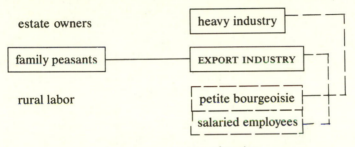

proletariat

38. It is possible to maintain that elections, i.e., party competitions, are a democratic form of class struggle without going so far as to say that it is through parties primarily that class struggle takes place; see Stein Rokkan and S. M. Lipset, *Party Systems and Voter Alignments* (Chicago, 1962).

39. Gramsci, p. 210. For a discussion of parties as vehicles of social and political integration, based on either class or "catchall" perspectives, see Otto Kirchheimer, "The Transformation of the Western European Party Systems," in Joseph LaPalombara and Myron Weiner, eds., *Political Parties and Political Development* (Princeton, 1966), pp. 177–200.

40. The correspondence between Dingeldey, chairman of the DVP, and Paul Reusch, head of the Ruhr industrialists' union, demonstrates this clearly, and these problems will be investigated in chap. 6.

41. On something called a German aversion to a conflict-based constitution of liberty, see Ralf Dahrendorf, *Society and Democracy in Germany* (Garden City, 1967), pp. 137–40, 183–90. On absorption by the state of the practical (in our terms economic-corporative) but not political demands of the German bourgeoisie, see Leonard Krieger, *The German Idea of Freedom* (Boston, 1957), pp. 277, 428, 469ff. Both Krieger and Dahren-

FIGURE 5

Baseless Bloc, 1932. Fascist potential.

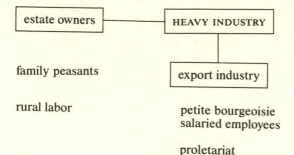

had attempted to establish parliamentary government as the locus for the resolution of social and interest-group conflicts, but so limited and democratic a system would have left too much to be decided by vote counting. The constitution postulated an equilibrium produced by the continuous collision of conflicting interests, almost all of which would have their say.[42]

Additionally, the bourgeois parties from the DDP through the DNVP were singularly unable to unify the interests of the dominant classes. Prominent industrialists constantly bemoaned the fragmentation (*Zersplitterung*) and internal conflicts that rendered the bourgeois parties incapable of merging or acting together to dominate the political scene.[43] And, of course, they were unwilling, once the Depression began, to make the kinds of concessions that had enabled Stresemann to act as if such a dominance had been established. The industrialists themselves, however, provided a recalcitrant base for any unified party formation. They rejected political modification of private interests and were "incapable of accepting co-responsibility . . . for national-political tasks"; they demonstrated irresponsibility, and proved "incapable of building mass support" and providing "moral leadership."[44] Back in 1923, industrialists had demonstrated this same selfishness during the

---

dorf appreciate the importance of the failure of the German bourgeoisie to bring liberty to Germany. Krieger, however, does not make Dahrendorf's mistake of making the "constitution of liberty" a virtual liberal monopoly.

42. Cf. Arthur Rosenberg's comments on Preuss's constitution, *Geschichte der Weimarer Republik* (Cologne, 1961), p. 61.

43. Again, the correspondence between various industrialists and the beleaguered chairmen of the bourgeois parties is full of this concern. The Reusch, Silverberg, and Dingeldey Nachlässe are prime sources; see chap. 6.

44. This was Sigmund Neumann's verdict in 1930 already, *Die Parteien der Weimarer Republik* (Stuttgart, 1965), pp. 24f., 54, 96.

TABLE 1

Percentage of the Vote Obtained by the Parties and Coalitions Formed

	KPD (USPD)	SPD	DDP	Z(+BVP)	DVP	Bourg.[a] Splinter	DNVP	NSDAP	Not Voting
1919[b]	7.7	37.8	18.6	20.0	4.4	1.6	10.3		17.3
1920	20.0	21.7[c]	8.3	18.0	14.0	3.1	14.9		21.6
1924 I	13.3	20.4	5.8	16.7	9.2	8.2	19.4	6.6	23.7
1924 II	9.2	26.0	6.3	17.5	9.9	7.3	20.4[d]	3.0	22.3
1928	10.7	29.8	5.0	15.2	8.6	13.0	14.3	2.6	25.5
1930	13.1	24.6[e]	3.7	14.8	4.6	13.8	7.1	18.3	18.6
1932 I	14.3	21.6	1.1	15.7	1.1	3.0	6.0	37.1	16.5
1932 II	17.0	20.3	.9	15.1	2.0	3.5	8.5	33.0	20.0
1933	12.2	18.4	.8	14.0	1.0	1.5	7.9	44.2	12.1

Sources: Bernhard Vogel, et al., *Wahlen in Deutschland* (Berlin and New York, 1971), pp. 296–97; Heinrich Striefler, *Deutsche Wahlen in Bilder und Zahlen* (Düsseldorf, 1946), pp. 67–68; Max Schwarz, *MdR* (Hannover, 1965), pp. 822–23; S. M. Lipset, *Political Man* (Garden City, 1963), pp. 131–51.

Note: Cabinet composition did not mirror electoral results directly; frequently, there were cabinets of "personalities," e.g., 1922–24, 1930–32. Altogether there were twenty-two governments. The Zentrum was nearly always the fulcrum; after 1924 its right wing tended to dominate. From 1923 to 1930, the DVP enjoyed disproportionate influence. Prosperity and Stresemann's program for reintegrating Germany internationally were essentially responsible for bringing the DVP into the ranks of the "middle parties"; this lasted only as long as they did.

[a] Wirtschaftspartei, CNBLP, Volkskonservativen, and regional splinter parties.

[b] The government of revolutionary delegates declared in November 1918 consisted of 3 SPD and 3 USPD members.

[c] Initial position of SPD yielded to cabinets strongly influenced by DVP.

[d] DNVP was sometimes in but mostly out of the government.

[e] SPD was not in the government, but it depended on SPD toleration.

TABLE 2

Vote Totals of Camps and Potential Coalitions

	Left	Center	Right	SOCLST./ bourg. (SPD+DDP +Z)	soclst./ BOURG. (SPD+DDP +Z+DVP)	Repb. Bourg. (DDP+Z+ DVP)	Right Bourg. (DVP→DNVP)	Actual Coalition (see Table 1)
1919	45.5	38.6	16.3	76.4	80.8	43.0	16.3	76.4
1920	41.7	26.3	32.0	48.0	62.0	40.3	32.0	48/40.3
1924 I	33.7	22.5	43.4	42.9	52.1	31.7+	36.8	55.5
1924 II	35.2	41.0	23.4	49.8	59.7	33.7+	37.6	41.0
1928	40.7	28.8	29.9	50.0	58.6	28.8+	35.9	58.6
1930	37.7	18.5	43.8	43.1	47.7	23.1+	25.5	36.9
1932 I	35.9	16.8	47.2	38.4	39.5	20.9	10.1	...
1932 II	37.3	...	...	36.3	38.3	21.5	14.0	41.5

SOURCES: See Table 1 and K. D. Bracher, *Die Auflösung der Weimarer Republik* (Stuttgart, 1965), p. 645. On the parties generally, Sigmund Neumann, *Die Parteien der Weimarer Republik* (Stuttgart, 1965); Bracher, pp. 64–95; Alfred Milatz, *Wähler und Wahlen in der Weimarer Republik* (Bonn, 1965); E. Matthias and R. Morsey, *Das Ende der Parteien, 1933* (Düsseldorf, 1960), pp. 743–94.

Ruhr occupation and inflation. Their selfishness blocked the national effort even when the government was headed by the bourgeois-conservative shipping magnate Wilhelm Cuno. They had favored militant national resistance only to discipline organized labor and then colluded with the French to ameliorate their economic situations.[45]

The contradictory relations among the fractions of the bourgeoisie disabled its own political parties and augmented both the role of the state as the cohesive factor for any bloc of dominant classes and the bourgeoisie's Bonapartist tendencies. Conflicts over political leadership within the industrial bourgeoisie worsened with the start of the agricultural depression in 1928 and became even more acute with the onset of the industrial depression. These conflicts seemed to immobilize not only the parties but also the state itself; state intervention appeared to be riddled with contradictions. Because of his dependence on both agrarian and SPD toleration, Brüning, for example, was unable to pursue a consistent state policy. Nevertheless, representatives of the dominant classes expected the state to act as the political organizer of their interests. Poulantzas asserts that "the state plays this role because the political parties of the bourgeois fractions are unable to play an autonomous organizational role. . . . [The state's role] emerges as the factor of political unity of the power bloc under the protection of the hegemonic fraction and as organizer of the latter's interests."[46] As the bourgeois parties declined, they took on the role of transmission belts, virtually carrying messages from private interest and pressure groups to the state. In turn, the state moved from a parliamentary to a ministerial to a presidential form, each stage being marked by a narrowing of those circles to which the state was responsive. (In 1930, parliament disposed of ninety-eight laws, while five were enacted by emergency decree. By 1932, five were enacted by parliament, and sixty-six by decree.) The weakening of the bourgeois parties further exposed their already evident class character. Capitalist groups became increasingly concerned with what James O'Connor calls "the private appropriation of state

45. Arthur Rosenberg, *Geschichte*, pp. 178–83; Maier, pp. 364–73, 402.
46. Poulantzas, *Political Power*, p. 299. One may easily quarrel with Poulantzas's contention that the state "plays the role of organizer" of the power bloc, rather than simply providing the terrain. It is by no means self-evident that this was the case in Weimar Germany—either before or during 1932. It is more useful to understand the state as the condensation of existing social relations. We shall also have occasion to question his contention that there is no parcellization, that power is always unitary under the hegemonic fraction. This latter argument leads to a hidden form of "state-monopoly capitalism"—a view that is not borne out by our analysis. See Anson Rabinbach, "Poulantzas and the Problem of Fascism," *New German Critique*, no. 8 (Spring 1976):157–70. Rabinbach's critique of structuralist Marxism is quite trenchant.

power for particularistic ends."[47] Instead of appearing as class-based but popular, the parties became transparent class representatives. Only the Catholic Zentrum and later the Nazis escaped this fate. The consequence of this "demystification" was further loss of support, especially from the Mittelstand. Ultimately, however, the Weimar state was unable, in any of its forms, either to resolve the contradictions within the bloc of dominant classes or the conflicting claims to leadership of it. Before it could do so, the victories won by the working class had to be reversed, and the struggle for hegemony within the dominant bloc had to be resolved, its general interest being distilled from an agglomeration of particular interests; both, of course, "in the interests of the nation."

3. Stability in Weimar: Bloc 3 and Labor's Support

No parliamentary-democratic state can maintain itself without a mass base. Between 1924 and 1930, the German working class, organized primarily in the SPD and trade unions, provided a substantial part of this base. The divisions and conflicts within and among nonworking-class strata were such that governing without working-class participation would have been undesirable even had it been possible. Having accepted the rules of the republican game, it was impossible to deny the strength of the working-class party, which shared adherence to those rules. Indeed, the working class's commitment to those rules was greater than that of any other class. It was after 1923, however, that the policy indeterminacy built into those rules became acceptable to the dominant classes. The defeat of the revolutionary-working-class impulse had been completed by 1923: local Communist uprisings had been suppressed; previous concessions in the realm of wages and hours had been reversed in the context of the Ruhr occupation; the inflation facilitated liquidation of industrial debts; the SPD had rid itself of most of its revolutionaries; völkisch radicalism had subsided; radical tax laws were being rewritten, and their author, Matthias Erzberger, had been killed. And, after 1924, a steady flow of foreign capital facilitated business and industrial rationalization and expansion.[48] Meanwhile, the burial of the socialization committees set up in 1919,[49] the rebuilding of

47. O'Connor, p. 9.
48. The flow of foreign capital was immense. By 1930, a total of 27 billion Marks had been borrowed. The exact figures differ by source; cf. Charles Bettelheim, *L'Economie allemande sous le nazisme* (Paris, 1971), 1:22–24. On the expansion and overexpansion of the industrial structure and plant, Robert Brady, *The Rationalization Movement in German Industry* (Berkeley, 1933). We shall return to both of these issues.
49. See Maier, pp. 138–45, 158–64.

an essentially unreformed military, and the concentration of government power in the ministries—changes sometimes abetted by the SPD—ate away at what the socialists persisted in calling "the achievements of the Revolution." Germany's democrats proved unable to restructure substantially the civil service, judiciary, or the entire ideological structure inherited from the Empire.

It was therefore possible after 1924 for representatives of the dominant classes to accept the necessity of governing with labor, something recognized by leading industrialists as early as 1924, although initially they meant the Catholic workers organized in the Zentrum. By 1926, one such leading industrialist, Paul Silverberg, could tell the annual convention of the League of German Industry (RDI) that government without organized labor (i.e., the SPD) was impossible and undesirable. In a development that furthered this reorientation, Stresemann had been victorious in 1924 over the rightist, pro-DNVP wing of the DVP.[50] Steel magnate Albert Vögler and other dissidents gravitated to the DNVP, while Stresemann found a new source of support in the white-collar-employee wing of his party.[51] Stresemann argued that further counterrevolution would strengthen rather than weaken the Left and would drive the Catholic Zentrum back in that direction.

Industrialists and workers each found the other necessary for social stability; their cooperation was mediated, albeit asymmetrically, by the state.[52] Some elements in industry and agriculture objected from the outset, but their opposition was stilled both by apparent economic prosperity and the political stability engendered by cooperation. Some

50. Paul Silverberg's remarks to the convention of the Reichsverband der Deutschen Industrie (RDI) in Dresden, September 1926. His remarks were not universally accepted; in fact, he came in for considerable criticism, but his general line prevailed, even without the ZAG. Maier, p. 443, discusses the 1924 defection of Vögler and others in the "National Liberal" caucus who wanted to drive the counterrevolution still further. Adam Stegerwald, head of the Catholic unions and later labor minister (1930–32), greeted Silverberg's remarks by announcing gleefully that "Industry is holding its hand out to Labor"; cited in the Pressarchiv of the Reichslandbund/ZSA, series 148/8:21. Organized agriculture was not pleased with the pronouncement of either, and RLB newspapers attacked Silverberg's pronouncement as did the KPD's *Rote Fahne* of 14 Sept. 1926, which spoke of a "Silverberg-Severing alliance," p. 26.

51. Cf., e.g., Larry Jones, "The Crisis of White Collar Interest Politics," in Mommsen, et al., eds., pp. 812–16.

52. The middle Weimar years were not the first time that industry and labor had worked together for their mutual benefit, though now without the ZAG. Gerald Feldman describes a joint triumph of heavy industry and labor during the first years of World War I, *Army, Industry and Labor in Germany, 1914–1918* (Princeton, 1966), pp. 140–248. On the capitalist (Rathenau), unionist (Legien), and statist (Moellendorff) corporatist models and agreements reached during the war, see Friedrich Zunkel, *Industrie und Staatssozialismus* (Düsseldorf, 1974), esp. pp. 172–200.

elements of the working class also objected, but even the bulk of the KPD recognized that a period of "capitalist stabilization" had begun after the thorough defeats of October 1923 and German acceptance of the Dawes Plan in April 1924.[53] Charles Maier employs the somewhat anodyne concept of "corporatist equilibrium" to describe the post-1924 stability, failing to appreciate the role of the state and its apparatus in organizing the dominant classes. He writes, "What permitted stability after 1924 was a shift in the focal point of decision making. Fragmented parliamentary majorities yielded to ministerial bureaucracies . . . where interest-group representatives could more easily work out social burdens and rewards. This displacement permitted a new compromise: a corporatist equilibrium in which private interests assumed the tasks that parliamentary coalitions found difficult."[54] As a statement about the consequences of the fragmentation of the bourgeois parties, this is correct, although there was nothing new in the German bourgeoisie's reliance on state organs. As a statement about some kind of neutral or corporatist state and a social equilibrium, it is false. There was nothing neutral or classless about the Weimar state.

Although the economic recovery and prosperity of the years 1924–29 were both borrowed and uneven, they were experienced as a real turnaround, despite consistently high unemployment. There were good reasons for this optimistic view. In 1923, German industrial production represented 8 percent of world production compared to a prewar share of 16 percent; the volume of industrial production in 1923 was only 55 percent of the 1913 figure. In addition, Germany had lost 75 percent of its iron-ore sources, 31 percent of its blast furnaces, and 23 percent of its other iron and steel facilities in the peace settlement. Yet, by 1927, Germany had reattained its prewar volume of industrial production, and this was increased by 3 percent in the following year, making Germany the world's second industrial power after the United States.[55] In addition, new investment, rationalization, and concentration enabled German industry to attain a level of productivity formerly unique to the United States.[56] Industrial interests could afford to govern with the

53. See the evaluations and lessons of October by Ruth Fischer for the KPD left and August Thalheimer and H. Brandler for the KPD right in *Die Internationale* 6, Ergänzungsheft no. 1 (Jan. 1924); parts reprinted in Helmut Gruber, ed., *International Communism in the Era of Lenin* (Garden City, 1972), pp. 377–83.

54. Maier, p. 353. "Organized capitalism" may be a slightly less opaque concept than corporatism. For a typology of this elusive and too-convenient concept, see Schmitter, pp. 85–131.

55. Ralf Beckenbach, *Der Staat im Faschismus* (West Berlin, 1974), p. 39. The expansion of American power is indicated by the comparable figures for the USA: America's share of world industrial production rose from 36 to 50 percent, and production in 1923 was 141 percent of the 1913 figure.

56. Brady, passim. Using 1924 as a base year, productivity by 1929 had reached an

working class and to accede to some of its demands. Agriculture, on the other hand, never really recovered and was almost immediately the victim of a price-scissors trend. The agricultural sector became compressed both as consumer and producer. Production in 1929, for example, was only 74 percent of the 1913 level, and the agricultural, industrial, and total price indices were skewed accordingly (see table 3). The political consequences of the unevenness of Germany's economic recovery will emerge clearly in the following chapters.

TABLE 3

Critical Economic Indices (1913 = 100)

	Agric. Prices	Indus. Prices	Raw Mate- rials	Cost of Living	Nom- inal Wages	Real Hour Rates	Real Weekly Earn- ings	Indus- trial Produc- tion
1924	128	137	136	131	91	84	70	77
1925	132	157	133	142	123	100	87	92
1926	132	150	130	142	128	105	90	87
1927	138	148	132	148	145	110	97	110
1928	132	159	134	152	164	117	108	113
1929	126	157	132	154	169	123	110	114
1930	107	154	120	148	155	126	105	99
1931	89	142	108	136	137	127	100	82
1932	77	118	88	121	113	122	94	66
1933	84	111	88	118	115	121	98	74

SOURCES: Gerhard Bry, *Wages in Germany, 1871–1945* (Princeton, 1960), pp. 461–67; ZSA/ Büro des Reichspräsidenten 332/104; *Statistisches Jahrbuch für das Deutsche Reich*, 1926–33, passim.
NOTE: Notice the continued high industrial prices and cost of living even when production was down. "Hour rates" tended to be the form of payment for industrial workers, "weekly earnings" for white-collar employees. A reduced work week is also indicated.

For the mass of industrial workers and their political (SPD) and economic organs (ADGB, General Federation of Unions), cooperation offered the possibility of both success and stability. In the course of World War I, the unions had passed from toleration to recognition, and from 1918 to 1924 unions and entrepreneurs had worked together with partially shared and partially divergent goals in the trades and central "joint working committees" (ZAG, Arbeitsgemeinschaften). Once the revolutionary impulse had been defeated, capital and labor formalized their relations through laws and private agreements. A step-by-step system was devised consisting of collective bargaining, mediation, and compulsory arbitration, which institutionalized a certain amount of economic class conflict while simultaneously softening class conflict in general.[57] The unions themselves came to perceive strikes as a means of last resort to be used only when other means failed to yield a compromise. Only secure unions could indulge themselves in such a routinized policy perspective, one based on three important assumptions. First, it was assumed that the unions did indeed enjoy full recognition by the state, the industrialists, and the public as a whole. Second, that through their assumption of "national" tasks and responsibilities, the unions had earned an unassailable, quasi-official or public status. Third, that as institutions they were strong enough to weather even severe economic changes.[58] The extent to which such a policy perspective was durable rather than tenuous was a political question; the answer would depend not primarily on industrial or economic class relations, but rather on political class relations as evidenced in the parties and in the state. After their chastening in 1924, the position of the SPD and the working class as underpinnings of the Weimar state appeared to be permanent, and even all-bourgeois parliamentary governments, such as those that governed from 1924 to 1928, had to respect and make significant concessions to the working class.

The promises of the Weimar Constitution appeared to be bearing fruit. In that constitution, not only were the unions accorded the right to organize *(Koalitionsfreiheit),* but the results of collective bargaining were recognized as well. The state was declared committed to Sozialpolitik, and according to article 165, capital and labor were to enjoy parity in the determination of economic policy. Despite the obvious and severe setbacks organized labor suffered in the four years following promulgation of the Constitution, the ADGB and SPD alike based their efforts on what it, and the democratic republic it signaled, offered. For Rudolf Hilferding, this was the form of state in which the class opposition of workers could be carried furthest without systematic violence; for Hugo Sinzheimer, the privileged position of the unions provided a favorable basis for the further development of society, nation, and state; while for Ernst Fraenkel, the collective rights of

---

index value of 140. See also Elizabeth Schalldach, *Rationalisierungsmassnahmen der Nachinflationszeit im Urteil der freien Gewerkschaften* (Jena, 1930), part II. Whereas industrial production in Germany increased 44 percent between 1924 and 1929, in the United Kingdom the increase was a meager 14 percent, in France only 21 percent. Except for the USSR, only Japan showed a comparable growth rate for these years.

57. The *Gemeinschaften* and the step-by-step approach originated in the agreements reached already in mid-November 1918 between Hugo Stinnes for the industrialists and Carl Legien for the unions (ADGB). Cf. Maier, p. 59.

58. Walter Müller-Jentsch, "Zum Verhältnis von Staat und Gewerkschaften," in Claudio Pozzoli, ed., *Rahmenbedingungen und Schranken staatlichen Handelns* (Frankfurt, 1976), p. 151.

labor represented the positive link between the working class and the Republic. This sense of parity, of labor's co-responsibility for the social, economic, and political common good *(Gemeinwohl)* came to be conceptualized as "pluralist democracy," according to which the democratization of the state could be followed by a democratization of the economy. Thus, it was in 1928, at the height of Weimar's stability, during the period of cooperation between organized labor and the dynamic-export fraction of industry, that the ADGB put forward its program for *Wirtschaftsdemokratie,* for democratizing the economy. Whether or not such a program was feasible within a capitalist democracy or would have taken Germany "beyond" capitalism is moot. The advent of economic adversity, a shift in the balance of power within industry, and the beginning of a general capitalist offensive together led not only to the abandonment of any hopes for economic democracy, but led also to immobility within both the SPD and ADGB and, ultimately, impotence and despair.

During the period of recovery itself, bourgeois/working-class collaboration stabilized the dominance of the former by at once rewarding and depoliticizing the latter. Playing by the rules of the game made the SPD more of an interest-aggregating *Volkspartei*—Sigmund Neumann has suggested that at times, 25 percent of SPD members and 40 percent of SPD voters were other than working class.[59] Strikes were invariably about wages and other distribution questions; gone were vague "political demands" and political strikes. Nevertheless, industrialists paid a price for labor's cooperation in the maintenance of capitalist society. The practice associated with Hilferding's conception of organized capitalism produced certain distinct material gains for the working class, gains generally achieved through the agency of the state, frequently through the Labor Ministry. Among these substantial gains were binding compulsory arbitration of contract disputes, relatively high and industrywide wage rates, unemployment insurance, a broad range of social-welfare measures, and large public expenditures—the whole spectrum of legislation and policy known as *Sozialpolitik*. Although the Communists retained a more violent tenor and archaic vocabulary in both parliament and their unions, actions led by them in this period were not much different.[60] The SPD was simply more forthright in

59. Sigmund Neumann, p. 33; Hans Neisser, "Sozialstatistische Analyse des Wahlergebnisses," *Die Arbeit* 7 (1930):658. However, as we shall observe in chap. 5, pp. 223f., 255ff., the SPD retained a militant reformism and class reductionism—or what has been called a Kautskyian ghetto mentality. The SPD could *not yet* become a real popular alternative or Volkspartei.

60. Cf. Ossip Flechtheim, *Die KPD in der Weimarer Republik* (Frankfurt, 1969), p. 244; see also chap. 5, sec. 3 below.

representing, together with the unions, the day-to-day interests of the working class in a capitalist society. Thus, the major electoral victory of 1928 was in no way interpreted as a mandate for systemic change by either the SPD or the unions. Thus, too, the repression rather than co-optation of rowdy KPD May Day demonstrations; the SPD would not mobilize forces for change. And, finally, in the same line, the toleration of Brüning, the support of Hindenburg, the holding back of the Reichsbanner militia, and the politics of the "lesser evil" up to the final weeks of the Republic.

It was not as if the bourgeois classes and their political representatives were unaware of the costs of this collaboration. In a routine and sometimes successful manner, they opposed the "limitless spending" and "stultification of initiative" that were at the heart of SPD programs. What they could not in general foresee was the exact limit of the economy's ability to absorb popular programs. Hence, their own credibility was damaged, and much of their opposition appeared sporadic and unprincipled, motivated by narrow group interest rather than by concern for the national good. Various conflicts over trade and tariff policy, for example, seemed to underline this selfishness while simultaneously demonstrating how split the dominant classes really were. Important sectors of the Mittelstand came to see themselves as victims of this selfish, weak-kneed policy, and the ranks of the former allies and supporters of the dominant classes were weakened accordingly. The DDP and DVP paid a price in lost support before industry itself concluded that it could no longer afford collaboration.

The major bourgeois electoral victory of December 1924 and the reconsolidation of the left vote under the SPD banner created the conditions for a "popular class state," i.e., a state populated by classes rather than equal citizen-atoms, but nevertheless a state where a bourgeois government seemed to be acting in the interests of all citizens and the nation. Sacrifices of various kinds were demanded of all classes for the good of the nation, but the cooperation of the bourgeois classes and their various interest groups remained tenuous at best. The interests of the dominant classes were not unified, and the links between representatives and represented remained weak. Although the balance within the bourgeois parties (DDP, DVP, DNVP) shifted to the right as did the politics of the Catholic Zentrum, they all remained vulnerable to fissures and splits. Despite the departure of the SPD from the government, the internal coherence of the bourgeois parties was not substantially augmented. Thus, the Zentrum was unable to win the support of its Bavarian sister party for the Zentrum's own conservative presidential candidate, Wilhelm Marx, against the northern Protestant Hindenburg in 1925.[61] The DDP's ranks continued to shrink even during the period of stability. Stresemann was constantly under fire from those within the DVP who perceived too many of their individual interests being sacrificed. The DNVP was torn between abstentionist-rejectionist and compromise-oriented alternatives, as well as between rural and industrial demands. Despite its second-place finish in the 1924 elections, the DNVP participated in the bourgeois government on only two occasions between 1924 and 1928.[62] The bourgeois parties once again suffered from their Imperial maladies.

Indicative of the bourgeoisie's inability to raise itself from the level of economic-corporate interests to the level of political interests was the continuing growth, even before the Depression, of splinter parties, most of which claimed only to represent specific economic groups.[63] The major bourgeois parties never really succeeded in reconciling the various interests of those who comprised their bases. Consequently, the parliamentary and party format for bourgeois/working-class collaboration remained inadequate for serving capitalist interests, while it simultaneously aggravated existing cleavages within the bourgeois parties. This was neither the first nor the last occasion when bourgeois political stability was dependent on more coherent SPD and union support. The latter, in turn, was conditioned primarily by the bourgeoisie's ability to pay the bill.

The state bureaucracy supplemented parliament and the parties as an arena of class collaboration. Many working-class economic victories, both national and in Prussia, were achieved through the agency of the Labor Ministry. Headed most frequently by members of the labor wing of the Zentrum, this ministry tilted toward labor in arbitrating work and contract disputes. Once the Depression began, it came under constant attack from bourgeois forces. The Labor Ministry was also one of the main sources, along with local government, of the costly social welfare and insurance programs (Sozialpolitik), which assumed tremendous symbolic as well as economic importance.[64] The Economics Ministry

61. Georges Castellan, *L'Allemagne de Weimar* (Paris, 1969), pp. 91–95.

62. For a summary of these developments, Larry E. Jones, "The Dying Middle—The Fragmentation of the Bourgeois Parties," *Central European History* 5 (1972):23–54.

63. Among others, the Economic Party of the Middle Class (Wirtschaftspartei), which claimed to represent small business and the victims of the inflation; the Christian National Peasant and Rural People's Party (CNBLP), representing southern and central peasants, and several others of less importance devoted to, among other things, upward revaluation. Cf. Sigmund Neumann, pp. 64–67, and Martin Schumacher, "Hausbesitz, Mittelstand und Wirtschaftspartei," in Mommsen, et al., eds., pp. 823–35.

64. Cf. Ludwig Preller, *Sozialpolitik in der Weimarer Republik* (Stuttgart, 1949), pp. 296–387. We shall discuss Sozialpolitik in substantial detail in chaps. 5 and 6.

served an analogous function in promoting the interests of industry. It, however, reflected the splits in the industrial camp, especially that between export-oriented, small and dynamic industries on the one side and heavy industry oriented toward the domestic market on the other.[65] Major industries and cartels supplied the ministry's leadership and staff, much of which moved back and forth between the ministry and the League of German Industry (RDI).[66] A similar situation existed in the Finance Ministry, although there more democratic commercial and banking interests dominated.[67] In their capacity as ministerial bureaucrats and politicians, these individuals often adopted a certain farsightedness and autonomy which their friends and colleagues back in the interest-group organizations failed to appreciate. Their class origins did not entirely guide their policy formulation.[68] The aristocratic and petit bourgeois members of the bureaucracy did not behave differently because of their different origins.

The relative autonomy enjoyed by the bureaucracy existed as a function of its character as a specific category within the state. Ostensibly, the bureaucracy represented the needs of the entire nation in a neutral fashion. However, conflicts within the bureaucracy reflected arrangements and conflicts on the political scene as a whole, both among the dominant class fractions and between them and the working class. The less obvious the dominance of any particular capitalist fraction, the greater the impact of the bureaucracy and of the executive on the one hand, and of private-interest groups on the other. The political disorganization of the dominant classes, even during the years of stabilization, rendered the bureaucracy a stronger force in mediating interclass conflicts. Beyond this, Weimar Coalition (SPD, DDP, and Z) and socialist governments (as in Prussia) added "republican" personnel to all the previously "antirepublican" organs of state and civil society— schools, police, chambers of commerce, judiciary, church, etc. But they did not restructure these organs; nor, in the absence of real state power, could they have been expected to do so. Since the working class's

---

65. It is instructive that Stresemann's friend and ally, Julius Curtius, experienced difficulties heading this ministry, which paralleled Stresemann's own problems with fractious industrialists.

66. Lothar Albertin, "Faktoren eines Arrangements zwischen industriellem und politischem System," in Mommsen, et al., eds., pp. 658–74. O'Connor's argument that the state sector and the monopoly sector grow together (if not fully in tandem), though essentially correct, is less true for Germany than for the USA with its underdeveloped state.

67. Cf., e.g., Dieter Fricke, ed., *Die Bürgerlichen Parteien in Deutschland* (Berlin-Leipzig, 1968), 1:317–28.

68. Interesting changes in the composition of the political "agents" or "subelite" from 1880 to 1933 are analyzed by Knight, esp. pp. vi, 6, 22, 28, 33, 45.

political practice did not aim at taking state power, the structures of the capitalist state remained intact, despite the conflicts over leadership within the dominant classes.[69]

4. Crisis and the End of Stability

The bourgeois governments of 1924–28, under Stresemann, Marx, and Luther, were able to compromise and maneuver as much as they did only at the expense of the parties which constituted the various coalitions.[70] Cabinets and bureaucracies worked out a host of compromises, but party life showed signs of becoming moribund as the transmission of interest-group pressures became an increasingly central activity.[71] Already, formal and real power began to issue from different sources. As during the late Empire, collaboration did not create consensus, and the centrality of the middle parties masked their decline and the splitting of their constituencies. The political crisis became increasingly acute after 1928, before the economic crisis had really set in. No member of the historically dominant bloc was capable of imposing its direction on the others, either through parliament or other organs of the state. The minimal ideological unity that Stresemann was able to impose dissolved even before his death in October 1929. German capitalism, in brief, could not surmount its own internal contradictions.[72] The political and economic interests of both industry and agriculture were fragmented along several axes, and despite a plethora of organizations and pressure groups, no voice was accepted as guiding. Whereas before 1928 state trade, social, and foreign policies had demonstrated considerable inconsistency and instability, after 1928 incapacitation became a more frequent result of that disunity. As the political crisis deepened and the locus of decision making narrowed from parliament to cabinet to presidential circles, the expression of dominant interests actually became more fragmented. Despite the government's increased emergency powers, it was faced with increased bourgeois disunity.

69. These issues will be dealt with in greater detail in subsequent chapters. On the military during the stable years, see F. L. Carsten, *The Reichswehr and Politics, 1918–1933* (London, 1966), pp. 163–308. Also, Harold Gordon, *The Reichswehr and the German Republic, 1919–1926* (Princeton, 1957).

70. Of the five cabinets in office between June 1924 and June 1928, only two received an actual vote of confidence upon being presented. Two received a weaker "acceptance vote," and the fifth earned a mere "acknowledgment."

71. Michael Stürmer, *Koalition und Opposition in der Weimarer Republik, 1924–1928* (Düsseldorf, 1967), pp. 280–83, demonstrates this point quite effectively without at all sharing the framework guiding the analysis here.

72. Poulantzas, *Fascisme et Dictature*, p. 72.

The SPD electoral victory of 1928 and the Young Plan for reparations revision set off the brewing political crisis, in the course of which fascism reappeared as a mass party and as a possible political alternative. It would be an alternative through which the interests of the dominant classes might be represented less directly but more effectively than they had been. The internal political crisis of the dominant classes and their class offensive were intertwined. In some respects, the situation after 1928 was like that of 1923 when the conservative shipping magnate Cuno had been chancellor: a fragmented bourgeoisie concerned solely with its particularistic interests prevented the state from formulating a "national" policy while simultaneously undertaking an offensive against the working class. The SPD was hardly prepared for such a turn of events: the 1.2 million plus increase in votes it received in 1928 over 1924 was not a reward for steadfast opposition to capitalism and bourgeois rule, for such had not been its policy.[73] And, despite an initially very strong position in the cabinet and parliament in 1928, the SPD program consisted only of the same elements as before: realization of the daily interests of the organized working class within a capitalist system, and continuation of Stresemann's foreign policy. The SPD was, thus, inadequately prepared for the massive lockouts undertaken by employers in Ruhr heavy industry in the fall of 1928. The substantial electoral losses suffered by the bourgeois parties accrued primarily to the benefit of other splinter, rightist and particularist parties. With prosperity largely mortgaged to American capital through the agency of German finance and industry, the prospects of an SPD government mediating the conflicting needs of the dominant fractions were slim.[74]

The political crisis was fueled by the onset of a fiscal crisis worsened by the collapse of the New York stock market and the subsequent shrinkage of loans. The fiscal crisis served as a pretext for the ouster of Hilferding as finance minister and his replacement by the DVP and IG Farben representative, Paul Moldenhauer. Reichsbank president, Hjalmar Schacht, representing another, still more antisocialist constituency, had undermined Hilferding's attempt to restructure government finances in a manner commensurate with the new situation but not entirely at the expense of the working class. Beginning in 1929, unemployment began to rise quickly, an issue that led to the demise of the Grand Coalition, stretching from the SPD to the DVP. With almost three million unemployed by March 1930, the DVP refused to agree to an increase in employers' contributions to the unemployment insurance

73. Arthur Rosenberg, *Geschichte,* p. 140.
74. Cf. Werner Link, "Der amerikanische Einfluss auf die Weimarer Republik—Elemente eines penetrierten Systems," in Mommsen, et al., eds., especially pp. 489–93.

fund, and the coalition collapsed.[75] It was indicative of the SPD's identification with the existing system that it was in no position to ask the working class to accept this setback in the name of a larger struggle.[76] Just prior to his death the previous October, Stresemann had barely convinced his DVP delegation to accept a similar compromise on unemployment benefits and taxation. In the face of substantial opposition to the Young Plan,[77] Stresemann had managed to coerce minimal middle-party unity in its favor. By the time he died, antisocial-collaborationist forces were no longer to be restrained, and the conflicts among the dominant class fractions could no longer be held in check.

The economic crisis first in agriculture, then in domestic, and finally in export industry, together with the state's fiscal crisis, rendered the costs of social collaboration, reparations fulfillment, and a trade policy based on these two, intolerable for the dominant classes. The contradiction between the necessary costs of collaboration and the imperatives of capital accumulation and reproduction could no longer be accepted by the fragmented dominant class fractions. For its part, a series of economic gains unaccompanied by structural changes in the political sphere left the working class all the more vulnerable to a rollback in both spheres. Although the economic and political aspects of the anti-labor offensive emerged almost simultaneously,[78] the political facet was finally of greater significance. The parliamentary system proved weak and indecisive: the fragmentation of interests it encouraged prevented the emergence of a coherent capitalist response to the crisis, while democratic representation assured that the interests of organized labor would continue to be pressed with some success.

Key sectors of industry, including mining, iron and steel, and the whole of agriculture were in the midst of profit crises even before the full brunt of the international Depression was felt. Partially opposed to these sectors, however, was a prosperous export sector consisting

75. Cf. Helga Timm, *Die deutsche Sozialpolitik und der Bruch der Grossen Koalition im März, 1930* (Düsseldorf, 1952). See chap. 5, sec. 3, and chap. 6, sec. 2.

76. See chap. 5 below.

77. In June 1929, the RDI decided not to take an official stand on the Young Plan. Divisions were very sharp, although much of the leadership and most of the membership favored acceptance. In July, the Rhenish-Westphalian industrialists *(Langnamverein)*, under the influence of Ruhr heavy industry, resolved to oppose the Young Plan, as did the "Green Front," the latter purporting to represent all of agriculture.

78. The RDI meetings of September and December 1929 and various gatherings of the Langnamverein inaugurated an economic offensive against Sozialpolitik and the post-1925 compromise with the SPD. The breakdown of the bourgeois/socialist Grand Coalition under the SPD's Herman Müller, and the end of government by parliamentary majority, took place in March 1930 while, as noted, the debate over whether to accept the Young Plan and how to distribute its costs had begun already in the spring of 1929.

mainly of newer industries—ones that had a greater interest in the fulfillment of reparations and less of an interest in the repression of labor. A few of these industries even subscribed to trade-union ideas about the need for increased mass consumption *(Kaufkraft)*. Heavy industry and agriculture were not altogether in agreement either. Whereas industry valued low food costs and high industrial prices, agriculture's preferences were for just the reverse. Whereas both industrial sectors were operating well below capacity and looked favorably upon foreign expansion, pacific or otherwise, agriculture was overproducing and tended toward various autarkic formulas. Once the economic crisis began, it became even more difficult to subsume the diverse economic-corporative interests of the various fractions of the former historical bloc into one political interest. The frequency with which representatives of these fractions found it necessary to remind each other of their common opposition to the organized working class bears witness not only to the depth of hostility toward the SPD and KPD but also to the increased salience and depth of conflicts within that bloc.

The manner in which classes had been organized and inserted into the political struggle up to 1930 led to success first in isolating the economic struggle of the working class from its political struggle and then to the defeat of both facets. No longer able to proceed with the dynamic fraction of industry on the basis of economic recovery and international reintegration, the benefits to labor of "pluralist democracy" proved highly fragile. The economic crisis, which became the Great Depression, eroded labor's wherewithal; unemployment, lower wages, and cutbacks in social insurance programs all undermined trade-union power. After 1930, the representatives of capital first moved away from cooperation with labor and then abandoned previously accepted institutionalized channels for the regulation of conflict in favor of an aggressive strategy of confrontation. Finally, during the terminal crisis of the Republic, the unions and SPD were weakened by their inability to call upon the active energies of their members. Throughout the stable years, both the union and party leaderships had discouraged any real activism among the rank-and-file—partly out of a commitment to the greater efficacy of agreements reached at the top among the leaders of the peak organizations *(Spitzenverbände)* and partly from fear of mass radicalization that might accrue to the benefit of the Communists. Thus, once Weimar's pluralist democracy was shaken, the recognition and incorporation that the unions had enjoyed proved of little service, and may even have rendered defense of the working class more difficult.

But within the Weimar framework the political unity of the dominant classes was not successfully molded out of the diversity of their economic struggles.[79] Further, the political support previously tendered by the Mittelstand in exchange for nonsocialist stability evaporated. By 1930, virtually all sections of the dominant bloc agreed that postcrisis Germany must be spared the costliness and unreliability of an ineffective, democratic political structure and profit-devouring social-welfare system. Beyond that, however, there was little clarity: a presidential dictatorship, a military dictatorship, a restructured but suffrage-based republic with vague corporatist overtones, a government with or one without a mass base—all were conceivable, though each would necessitate a different base of legitimacy and a different internal arrangement of the dominant bloc.[80] Industrialists' impatience with the speed and extent of such a rollback under Brüning's semiconstitutional regime of 1930–32 contrasted with the ambivalence expressed by the leaderships of the bourgeois parties as they lost their constituencies and saw their party structures dissolve.

After 1930, the political front was marked by the growing irrelevance of parliament and its parties. Various attempts to save the disintegrating bourgeois parties by unifying them failed, and the split between representatives and represented was further aggravated. Attempts to govern without an electoral mass base through cabinet and then presidential rule by emergency decree both failed. Tentative attempts in 1932 to weld together a mass base consisting of parts of the Nazi and Zentrum parties proved fruitless. There followed the brief experiments of von Papen's cabinet of barons representing primarily autarkic agriculture and heavy industry, and then General Schleicher's cabinet with its Keynesian overtones and search for a mass base. Treaty restrictions on the Reichswehr together with the overrepresentation of the rural elite throughout the army made a straightforward military dictatorship unlikely. Fed up with their own parties' inability to organize popular support, yet determined not to return to a potentially socialist-domi-

79. Poulantzas, *Political Power*, p. 137, for analysis of the two functions of the political practice of the dominant classes.

80. Even before the Depression, a number of largely reactionary schemes for reorganizing the state structure had been entertained by prominent political and economic figures. Almost all intended to alter federal/state relations and the bicameral legislative structure. Among the more prominent was the League for Renewal of the Reich (Bund zur Erneuerung des Reichs) headed by the former chancellor, Reichsbank president, and DVP politician, Hans Luther. Cf. Fricke, 1:195–200. Otto Kirchheimer captured the social and political context and significance of these developments in his short 1929 and 1930 essays, "Das Problem der Verfassung," "Verfassungswirklichkeit und politische Zukunft," "Artikel 48 und die Wandlungen des Verfassungssystem," and "Die Verfassungsreform" reprinted in *Von der Weimarer Republik zum Faschismus* (Frankfurt, 1976), pp. 64–76, 91–112.

nated parliamentary system, industrialist and agrarian support for the Nazis grew throughout 1932. In moving toward this position, the interests of heavy industry and agriculture coalesced—in the name of both a domestic-market strategy and national reassertion. The historical bloc was reunified, albeit tenuously, under the leadership of heavy industry, but the political crisis was not thereby resolved. For whatever replaced the Weimar system had to be radical; it could be no mere restoration of imperial authoritarianism. What followed would have to be a complete alternative to the existing system, not just a new bartering formula. Any new arrangement would have to rest on or at least accept popular mobilization, but only if identification between radical, anti-status quo popular objectives and socialist goals could be prevented and the very relevance of class denied.[81]

After 1929 Germany witnessed a continuous narrowing of the locus of decision making and decision makers.[82] First parliament ceased to participate in making crucial decisions; then the parties themselves became nearly irrelevant, and finally even the cabinet ministers were shut out. Within the corporate-interest organizations such as the RDI, the general-membership assemblies yielded decision-making power to their presidia and then to a few executive leaders. By the end of 1932, crucial decisions were being made by a handful of men in leadership circles, and one can indeed speak of cliques. Although elections occurred with increasing frequency after 1930, their primary effect was to destabilize the situation further. They served also to indicate that a new Mittelstand mass had been aggregated, more on the basis of ideological and political unity than economic. Since 1924, most industrialists and most bourgeois politicians had remained somewhat aloof from völkisch, populist radicalism and had come to look upon it with suspicion and disdain. After 1930, however, this new popular mass and the Nazi party it supported became objects of their intense interest. Once they established that both the party and its mass were (or could become) supporters of social order, various governmental possibilities involving the Nazis became feasible. In the eyes of those professional politicians and economic leaders for whom the NSDAP was an exogenous force

81. That this was not so simple a matter was demonstrated by subsequent Nazi purges (Strasser, Röhm) and constant internal ideological vigilance and repression through to the very end of the Third Reich; see Laclau, pp. 119ff.

82. Bracher's work, esp. *Die Auflösung der Weimarer Republik* (Stuttgart, 1955), provides the most detailed account of this process. Nevertheless, as we shall observe in chap. 6, his characterization of this as part of the development of a "power vacuum," however suggestive, is also deceptive. The legal political mechanisms of the Republic were certainly undermined and incapacitated, but power hardly disappeared; it was effectively passed into the hands of leading figures in the state executive and private economy whence it was transferred to the Nazis.

and its supporters potential revolutionaries, the preferred strategy was to split the party and enlist its masses. It was only reluctantly that the leading industrial circles became receptive to the idea that the entire NSDAP had to be called upon to take charge of the state and provide that popular base which had been lacking since 1930. But called upon to do what? To assume state power, to be the class in charge of the state for the maintenance of the economic and political order? Would the Nazis constitute a class, or would they merely act as an agent for the capitalist class or for some capitalists? Or were the Nazis simply the only acceptable common denominator for stabilizing the political system and guaranteeing the social system? The leading representatives of the dominant classes thought the Nazis manageable, despite their demands for total power. Industrialists and agrarians do not seem to have feared that, like the mid-nineteenth-century bourgeoisie described by Marx, they were about to "give up the right to rule for the right to make money." As guarantors of capitalism, as proponents of a strong, imperialist Germany, the Nazis appeared to be the best available possibility.

Thus, the rollback of working-class gains, a solution to the fractional struggle among the dominant class fractions, and some settlement with the supporting classes outside the center of the capitalist mode of production (petite bourgeoisie, peasants, and others among the middle strata) were all on the agenda.[83] No one of these tasks required a fascist or imperialist solution; perhaps even all three in their ensemble did not. But the conjuncture and manner in which these tasks appeared in Germany heightened such a possibility. Eventually, the members of the once-dominant bloc "decided" for fascism, although there may have been other ways out of the economic, political, and social crisis that also would not have violated their fundamental interests.[84]

83. Cf. Poulantzas, *Political Power*, pp. 287–88.

84. Cf. Mihaly Vajda, "On Fascism," *Telos*, no. 12 (summer 1972):21. A very insightful contemporary analysis of the needs of the capitalist class and the various ways through which those might be met was provided by Paul Sering [pseudonym of Richard Löwenthal], "Die Wandlungen des Kapitalismus" and "Historische Voraussetzungen des Nationalsozialismus," originally in *Zeitschrift für Sozialismus* (1935), reprinted with the deceptive title of *Faschismus und Monopolkapitalismus* (Berlin, 1967), pp. 1–22, 63–79.

Chapter Two

CONFLICTS WITHIN THE AGRICULTURAL SECTOR

No industrial society can afford to abandon its agricultural sector, and Weimar Germany was certainly no exception. The extreme food shortages endured during the final years of war and the allied blockade after the armistice served to remind the world's second most urbanized country—a country in which more people lived in cities of over 100,000 than on the land—of the importance of its countryside. The territories ceded as part of the peace treaty were largely rural, thereby making agricultural self-sufficiency all the more difficult. Despite the crucial role of international trade, autarky was a central element in German Imperial and imperialist ideology, and a certain antiurbanism accompanied it.[1] More crucial in securing generous treatment for the countryside than this ideology itself was the political and social importance of the carriers and promoters of the ideology. East Elbian Junkers and other large landowners continued after 1919 to exert substantial influence in the military, judiciary, and executive bureaucracy while avoiding much of the fragmentation that plagued German industrialists. The rural aspect of Weimar politics is as illustrative as any of the continuities in German history. Yet, the increased political importance of the peasantry in an electoral system based on equal universal suffrage altered relations both between peasants and estate owners and between the agricultural sector and the rest of society.[2]

---

1. The role of autarky and antiurbanism in this peculiar German ideology has been studied extensively. The ideology is variously described as neofeudal, feudal-imperialist, antimodern, prefascist, Catonist, antiliberal, reactionary, romanticist, neoromantic, cultural pessimist, nostalgic, etc. For a full discussion of this ideology and the unique breadth it enjoyed in Germany, see Klaus Bergmann, *Agrarromantik und Grossstadtfeindschaft* (Meisenheim/Glan, 1970). More interesting than deciding which label is the most appropriate would be an analysis of the political and ideological perspectives that lead to the respective diagnoses.

2. This is an importance which, because of several theoretical bottlenecks, the left failed to appreciate until it was too late. See Hans G. Lehmann, *Die Agrarfrage in der*

The system of most-favored-nation trade treaties negotiated after 1925 was predicated on an expanding export industry, but the conceptions underlying agricultural policy never underwent the corresponding alterations. Organized agricultural interests were able to assure that *Agrarpolitik* during the entire Weimar Republic remained based essentially on the prewar protectionist premises. Weimar agricultural policy did not function for the primary benefit of the peasantry, either before or after the onset of the agricultural crisis in 1928: it was not aimed at correcting the structural weaknesses and deformity of prewar agriculture by encouraging some kind of adjustment to changed domestic and international market conditions. Protectionism could have functioned to ease the pain of transforming agricultural production, but it did not. Agricultural policy served instead to continue protecting the agrarian elite. Once the estate owners no longer could or would protect (and dominate) the peasantry, they lost its support. Ironically, it was the "liberal" Weimar system that ultimately paid the price, not only of protecting the estate owners—who never accepted the Republic—but also the price of the peasantry's final defection from the estate owners, in the form of massive peasant electoral and organizational support for the Nazis.[3]

The German peasant did not stand in relation to the estate owner as the worker stood to the factory owner. In the rural case, conflicts were managed much more easily; contradictions were submerged or mitigated, and a symbiosis was possible in which most peasants voted for and otherwise supported a rural elite that molded but also represented their interests. Until 1930–32, the peasantry was a chief source of electoral support for conservative forces within the parties of the middle and right.[4] A shared interest in protectionism, economic and social,

Theorie und Praxis der Deutschen Sozialdemokratie (Tübingen, 1970). In practice, the left had long been nonsystematically (and unsuccessfully) reformist, but it was only in 1927 that Fritz Baade at the SPD Kiel convention elicited official support for a new peasant line. We shall discuss SPD policy in greater detail below. KPD policy was neither less opportunist nor less confused; cf. note 92, below.

3. Horst Gies, "The NSDAP and the Agrarian Organizations in the Final Phase of the Weimar Republic," in *Nazism and the Third Reich,* ed. Henry A. Turner (New York, 1972), pp. 45–88.

4. Catholic peasants tended to support the right wing of the Zentrum and the BVP as illustrated by the Hindenburg election in 1925 and Kaas's selection as party chairman in 1932; Joseph Becker, "Die Deutsche Zentrumspartei, 1918–1933," *Aus Politik und Zeitgeschichte* 11 (1968):2–12. In 1919, Protestant peasants in the northwest and south gave over 25 percent of their vote to a "leftish," republican DDP, but this high-water mark was never attained again. Some "new Prussian" peasants could not bring themselves to vote for Junkers (cf. Heberle, pp. 39–42), but by 1921 or 1924 at latest, German peasants were back in the fold.

was the keystone of the integration/dependence mechanism that bound most German peasants to the leadership of the big estate owners and set the agenda and tone for organized Landwirtschaft in the Weimar Republic. Because there was little direct political conflict between peasants and estate owners, the divergences between them, as substantial as they might become, generally remained at the level of interest politics rather than class politics. And, although the distribution of rewards was skewed to their detriment, most peasants found this arrangement preferable to any available alternatives and continued to adhere to it until about 1930.

The agricultural sector of the economy benefited less from post-1924 infusions of American capital than the industrial sector; German industry was reintegrated into the world economy, but agriculture was not. Its international and even domestic competitive position was handicapped: its soil and climate were inferior to those of its neighbors, some of which (Belgium, Holland) were closer to population centers than was the German "hinterland"; the territorial losses of the war exacerbated transport and marketing weaknesses; and the post-1925 most-favored-nation trade treaties came largely at its expense.[5] Rural producers jointly opposed the post-1925 national agenda of the dynamic-export industries and organized labor and attempted to win representatives of heavy industry to their side. Once the inflationary period came to an end, German production was disadvantaged and rural income was lowered by taxes and social-welfare costs vastly above prewar levels, a limited access to credit, considerable technical backwardness, a debt-ridden elite, and growing foreign production surpluses. Per capita peasant income was 44 percent less than the national average, whereas in the prewar period it had been only 20 percent less. Between 1913 and 1928, real peasant income rose only 4.5 percent compared to a national average increase of 45 percent; as 25 percent of the population, agricultural producers received only 8 percent of the national income. The politics of social collaboration extracted a considerable price from the countryside while rewarding it with little: "For agriculture the period of prosperity . . . was much more a period of depression between the prewar period and the Third Reich."[6] But what was this countryside, and how did it behave politically?

5. For a full discussion of the conditions under which agriculture produced, see Max Sering, *Die Deutsche Landwirtschaft unter volks- und weltwirtschaftlichen Gesichtspunkten* (Berlin, 1932).

6. Georges Castellan, "Zur sozialen Bilanz der Prosperität, 1924–29," in Mommsen, et al., eds., pp. 104–7. In 1925, 30 percent of the active population and 23 percent of the total population were in agriculture. See also table 3.

1. The Modes of Agricultural Production

The conflicts between estate owners and peasants in the Weimar Republic were partially grounded in their modes of production. Both extensive estate agriculture and intensive peasant farming (usually of units of twenty hectares or less) were part of an overall system of capitalist production. But they were modes that evolved differently from the earlier transformation of feudalism, and they produced surplus in different ways. To what extent economic and political conflicts issue from the existence of differences between the modes of production in a given social formation is uncertain. Modes of production do not contradict or support each other; the classes generated by the respective modes, the carriers of the relations of the modes, may or may not. Nations *can* exist half-slave and half-free. German peasants and estate owners were at odds during the last years of the Weimar Republic; at times the conflicts between them were quite severe. Nevertheless, the estate owners were sufficiently dominant in the political, ideological, and economic life of the countryside and of the state that they were able to avoid being cast in the role of the peasantry's antagonist. Consequently, conflicts with the peasantry were resolved primarily to the elite's advantage, and the peasantry was for the most part retained as an ally. But the peasant/estate-owner symbiosis was an unstable state, and there were pressures pushing the relationship in the direction of parasitism.

Tables 4–6 illuminate the shape and composition of German agriculture, and as they indicate, estates in 1925 comprised about 1 percent of all farm units over two hectares and about 35 percent of total acreage;[7] neither the concentration nor the breakup of holdings appeared any longer to be a trend. Estates characterized the grain-growing regions of the north and east; small-holding dairy and livestock production was most predominant in the south and northwest.[8] De-

---

7. *Statistisches Jahrbuch des Deutschen Reichs* (1934), p. 60. Mode of production, size, and location must all be considered in the definition. Of the approximately 5.2 million farms, over 3 million were of less than 2 hectares (1 ha. = 2.5 acres); under 20,000 were larger than 100 hectares. This meant that 1.1 percent of the landholdings encompassed 38 percent of the land, and the bottom 80 percent of them covered only 40 percent of the land, W. F. Bruck, *Social and Economic History of Germany from William II to Hitler* (Cardiff, 1938), pp. 258, 264. Also, Robert Lorenz, *The Essential Features of Germany's Agricultural Policy* (New York, 1941), p. 131. As table 4 makes clear, there were by 1925 fewer than 10,000 estate owners in all of Germany, but, as less than ½ of 1 percent of the landowners, they owned over 22 percent of the cultivated land (exclusive of garden plots under ½ hectare).

TABLE 4

Units of German Agriculture, 1925

	Units >.5, <2 ha.[a]	Units >2, <5 ha.[b]	Units >5, <20 ha.	Units >20, <100 ha.	Units >100 ha.
# of Units	1,181,210	895,000	956,155	200,000	18,668
Change since 1907	+ . . .	+8,000	+25,370	−28,630	−265
Area under Cultivation (ha.)	1,576,000	2,924,000	12,760,000	9,980,000	7,732,800
# Owners	579,000	710,000	872,000	180,000	9,560
# Adminis- trators	756,000	780,500	920,000	197,000	18,780
Assisting Family	1,400,000	1,750,000	2,450,000	470,000	13,350
Employees	120,000	205,000	620,000	755,000	1,015,500
Employees as % of Labor	4	8	20	56	97

SOURCES: Max Sering, *Die Deutsche Landwirtschaft unter volks- und welt-wirtschaftlichen Gesichtspunkten* (Berlin, 1932), tables 47–49. The most comprehensive description of the size, shape, and texture of German agriculture is F. Beckmann, et al., *Grundlagen und Formen der Deutschen Landwirtschaft* (Berlin, 1933); see also Sering, *Agrarpolitik,* pp. 30, 31, 192.
NOTE: There were 1,880,000 units of less than .5 ha. (1.25 acres). They are omitted since they were rarely the primary source of income.
[a] Owned by people who generally needed to rely on some additional occupation for a livelihood.
[b] Over three-fourths of these owners derived their entire livelihoods from the farm.

population of the countryside through industrialization and emigration had affected the east more severely and served to strengthen estate-owner control there. Between 1806 and 1871, estates absorbed about three million acres of land formerly held by serfs and peasants who could not compete with cheap seasonal and Polish labor. Local manorial government in Prussia *(Gutsbezirke)* was limited in 1872, but remnants remained until 1927, after which all landowning producers enjoyed formal, legal equality. Both Junkers and peasants became integrated into a capitalist system and produced for a sensitive market, domestic and foreign. The privileged position of the Junkers, and their alliance with heavy industry after 1879,[9] rendered them leaders and

8. For detailed breakdowns and maps, Michael Tracy, *Agriculture in Western Europe* (London, 1964), p. 105; and John Holt, *German Agricultural Policy, 1918–1934* (Chapel Hill, 1936), pp. 4–8.
9. This topic has been explored exhaustively. For a recent, comparative analysis of tariff coalitions, see Peter Gourevitch, "International Trade, Domestic Coalitions and Liberty," *Journal of Interdisciplinary History* 8 (1977):281–313.

spokesmen, by virtue of both domination and consent, for almost the whole of agriculture.[10] For most peasants it made real sense to follow the estate-owner lead. In the prewar period, this rural consent was organized into massive support for the Conservative party and for social reaction. During the Weimar Republic, however, the alliance between these two types of producers virtually broke down in the face of structurally determined antagonisms in both the economic and political realms.

Despite occasional feudal remnants, the Junker was a capitalist; he paid wages and invested to show profits. The peasant with his "family-economy" was, however, both laborer and capitalist.[11] The contrast

TABLE 5

Distribution of Agricultural Production by Size of Units, 1925

	Size of Production Unit (in hectares)				
	0–5	5–20	20–50	50–100	Over 100
	Percentage of Sold Products				
Field crops	8	19	25	40	55
Animal products	72	69	62	54	42
Fruit and vegetables	18	10	12	5	4

SOURCE: Sering, p. 929; Lorenz, passim.

TABLE 6

Livestock per 100 Ha. by Size of Unit (Prussia only), 1925

	Size of Production Unit (in hectares)			
	2–5	5–20	20–100	Over 100
	Head of Livestock per 100 Ha.			
Fowl	434	257	148	41
Cattle	91	73	62	34
Dairy cows	61	38	26	14
Pigs	86	60	40	16
Sheep	12	14	20	51

SOURCE: Sering, p. 239.

10. The best analysis of the origins and operation of this arrangement is H.-J. Puhle, *Agrarische Interessenpolitik.* Alexander Gerschenkron, *Bread and Democracy in Germany* (Berkeley, 1943), pp. 21–67, overestimates the role of domination and peasant false consciousness ("irrational predispositions," p. 27) in accepting Junker policies while slighting the extent to which it made both economic and political sense for most peasants to accept Junker protection rather than undertake risky and unrewarding innovations.

11. Here we shall discuss primarily the *operation* of the two modes. A brief but subtle

between the landless and even the poorest landowning peasant was such as to strengthen the bond among all landowners. On estates, employers enjoyed substantial control over the personal and political lives of their employees. Under the Empire, gerrymandering and the three-tiered Prussian ballot partially disenfranchised rural labor; until 1918 agricultural unions and strikes were forbidden; school, church, constabulary, and judiciary were influenced or controlled by the estate owners. Even after 1918 estates could be visited only by guests of the owners, who might observe that even organized rural workers appeared "unskilled . . . apathetic, without social contact . . . and subservient actually and psychologically."[12] The two modes differed in the distribution of the technical culture of husbandry. Among family peasants, requisite technical skills were shared by rich and poor alike, but the estate mode continued to bear some feudal marks: technical culture was largely in the hands of the estate owners, many of whom were, however, incompetent at farming. Finally, intraclass solidarity and political activism differed in the two modes. Small-holding peasants demonstrated considerable solidarity with each other, but their connections to politics outside the countryside were weak, Catholics relying heavily on the Zentrum and almost all on the estate owners.[13] Estate production engendered a highly cohesive, politicized elite well connected to urban and national centers of power and administration, and a rural working class that was often apathetic, sometimes volatile, and organized only with difficulty.[14] Further, in Weimar as during the Empire, estate-owner domination of local government together with membership in the dominant national bloc not only made organization of workers difficult but also tended to prevent the colonization of arable lands by small-holders, as well as rendering dependent those small-

---

discussion of their *genesis* is provided by Max Weber in the essay, "Capitalism and Rural Society in Germany," in Gerth and Mills, esp. pp. 374–84. Whereas a rent system *(Grundherrschaft)* developed in the west, a labor system *(Gutsherrschaft)* developed in the east.

12. Frieda Wunderlich, *Farm Labor in Germany* (Princeton, 1961), p. 19.

13. Much recent literature has attempted to revive "the peasant" as an active, indeed potentially revolutionary, social force, but the conditions under which this can be the case appear rather limited. See Eric Wolf, *Peasant Wars of the Twentieth Century* (New York, 1969), esp. pp. xi–xv, 289–302; Barrington Moore, *Social Origins of Dictatorship and Democracy* (Boston, 1967), pp. 467–79. Scmewhat more cautious is E. J. Hobsbawm, "Peasants and Politics," *Journal of Peasant Studies* 1 (1974):3–22. Marxists have a (deserved) reputation for being unsympathetic to peasants. See chap. 1, n. 36, for the possible basis of this reputation.

14. Wunderlich, *Farm Labor,* pp. 88–90; Jens Flemming, "Grossagrarische Interessen und Landarbeiterbewegung," in Mommsen, et al., eds., pp. 745–62.

holders already resident. Despite an ideological commitment to (re)settling the east with Germans to protect it culturally and militarily, the estate owners consistently hampered the program.[15]

Keeping pace with the income and prestige of urban capitalists did not, however, require estate owners to give up "patriarchal ideology and social pretensions," particularly as these fitted well with the military and bureaucratic professions.[16] Because of the earlier status dominance of the rural elite, urban capitalists, even in the Weimar period, often consummated their rise by buying estates. Together with the movement of some Junkers into industry, there occurred an amalgamation of the two groups, which led to what Max Weber considered "a landed aristocracy corrupted by money making and a capitalist middle class corrupted by aristocratic pretensions."[17] After 1918, the Junkers may have vacated many of their positions in the state, except for a fateful return to center stage during the crisis, but never did they undergo any democratic conversion. They may have been born only once, but they were more than twice saved—first by pseudodemocratization and then by protectionism—from both internal democratization and the effects of social democratization.[18]

Estate agriculture represented one form of capitalist agricultural production—a form of modernization that Lenin dubbed the "Prussian Way," based on large-scale ownership of rent-producing land ("ground rent"). Despite having become capitalists, the estate owners remained an autonomous political and economic force. Small-holding family peasants were also part of a social formation dominated by capitalism, but their mode of production, though market dependent, was not strictly capitalist, and they were connected to the dominant classes

15. For a breakdown on settlement (Siedlung) indicating who profited from it, see *Wirtschaft und Statistik* (1935), p. 156. We shall discuss some of the controversies below.

16. Bramsted, pp. 150–200, 228–55.

17. Reinhard Bendix, *Max Weber* (Garden City, 1960), p. 40. By the Weimar period, none less than Krupp was an established "von" with a brother-in-law, Theo von Wilmowsky, who was a prominent leader of estate-owning interests. Much of Barrington Moore's thesis rests on the danger ("potential for fascist development") of a bourgeois-aristocratic fusion in the absence of a revolutionary impulse, pp. 437ff.

18. Hans Rosenberg, *Probleme der deutschen Sozialgeschichte* (Frankfurt, 1969), details how the Junkers were twice brought back from the abyss. In 1806, the reforms and pseudodemocratization of Stein and then Hardenberg enabled the Junkers to enter a new era. In 1879, the shift from free trade to protectionism sealed the "marriage of rye and iron" and insured that the Junkers would still have a place in a society dominated by industrial capital. On the latter and the ouster of the antiprotectionist liberal Caprivi, see Gerschenkron, pp. 42–67. Even the tariff legislation of 1925 marked a decision not to allow the estates simply to succumb under their own noncompetitiveness.

primarily via the estate owners, who succeeded in speaking for virtually the whole agricultural sector while the peasants remained incapable of enforcing their own interests.

Political activism amongst small-holding peasants tended to be sporadic and marred by a certain lack of intraclass communication; a coherent, disciplined movement simply never emerged, and peasants do not seem to have thought about their situation in class terms. For all their violence, the peasant tax strikes, bombings, and mass marches of 1928 followed in this pattern.[19] Ongoing peasant associations were either organized or penetrated by disciplined political interests (estate owners, the Evangelical and Catholic Churches, the Zentrum, the DDP), and the spontaneous movements of the late twenties, such as the *Landvolkbewegung,* were harnessed by the Nazis. For small-holding peasants, opposition to urban interests was consistently more salient than opposition to the rural upper class. The political activities of the peasantry tended also to be directed primarily at the maintenance of high prices for agricultural commodities and low costs for nonfixed expenses (taxes, interest, fertilizer, etc.). Under most circumstances, conservative and noninnovative attitudes resulted.

As table 4 indicated, of the 2.35 million owners of agricultural properties, generally family heads, over 2.16 million owned units of less than twenty hectares, and these constituted the core of the peasantry. On these peasant farms of less than twenty hectares, a mere 4 to 20 percent of the requisite labor was provided by other than family members, and most of that only at peak harvest periods. Even if one included in the category of family peasants those owning large farms (twenty to one hundred hectares) and employing more substantial amounts of paid labor—their inclusion would be accurate only for parts of the country—this would add the relatively small number of, at most, 180,000 proprietors to the ranks of the peasantry. Thus, the nature of labor inputs was one reason that, contrary to classical Marxist expectations, small-peasant ownership and production remained viable.

One of the striking aspects of the peasant-family mode of production is that, except for short peak periods, two adults were sufficient to run a unit.[20] Most production costs were fixed, and the costs of family labor were not calculable in a capitalist sense. The predominance of fixed

19. Heberle, pp. 48–80. The tax strikes and bombings were never really a movement; Arthur Rosenberg, *Geschichte der Weimarer Republik* (Cologne, 1961), pp. 286–87, does consider the spontaneous rising "a movement," but one directed vaguely against "the system."

20. Folke Dovring, *Land and Labor in Europe, 1900–1950* (The Hague, 1956), pp. 115–18. In this regard, there was very little variation in Europe during the first half of this century.

costs (feeds were an important exception) meant that, generally, production would not fall with a decrease in prices as it would on an estate or in a factory[21]—a fact which exacerbated the rural crisis after 1928. Small and even middle-size peasants would continue to work "harder for less than their employees."[22] By and large, the peasant neither paid wages (see table 4) nor made profits; his goal remained security of support for the family, and his total receipts remained undifferentiable. Cost of production and surplus value were not operative categories. Using the framework developed by the agricultural economist A. V. Chayanov, we can say that the peasant made no distinction between the "family" and the "firm." Indebtedness could become increasingly burdensome, but the family peasant could never declare bankruptcy and begin anew. Not capitalist risk-taking, but adjustable consumption and a "labor-consumer balance between the satisfaction of family needs and the drudgery of labor"[23] motivated peasant family economics. The "desire to maintain a constant level of well-being" underlay many of the peasants' choices. The irksomeness of any extra work would be evaluated against the potential benefits of increased output. The peasant might be more tenacious than the estate owner in making a go of it under any particular set of circumstances, but he might also be more resentful of any disequilibrating force. In conditions where capitalist estates would go bankrupt, peasant families could work harder for longer hours, sell at lower prices, go without a net surplus, and yet manage to go on with their tilling.

Peasant and estate owner were both elements in a social formation dominated by capitalist relations. The need for fertilizer and machinery, the growth of the food industry, and concentration in the marketing of produce affected the peasant's economic relations more than it did his mode of production. As Chayanov observed, "while *in a production sense* concentration in agriculture is scarcely reflected in the formation of new large-scale undertakings, *in an economic sense* capitalism as a general economic system makes great headway in agriculture. . . . [Peasants are subject to] capitalism that . . . in the form of very large-scale production undertakings draws masses of scattered peasant farms into its sphere of influence and, having bound these small-scale commodity producers to the market, . . . subordinates them to its influence."[24] Thus, estate production represented the direct form of the

21. Illuminating on these and other questions is Arthur Stinchcombe, "Agricultural Enterprise and Rural Class Relations," *American Journal of Sociology* 67 (1961): 165–76.
22. Wunderlich, *Farm Labor,* p. 15.
23. A. V. Chayanov, *The Theory of Peasant Economy* (Homewood, Ill., 1966), p. xv.
24. Ibid., p. 257. Italics in the original.

capitalization of agriculture, and the peasant-family economy represented an indirect and for socialists fatefully "anomalous" form.[25] While both estate owner and peasant, but especially the former, were engaged in the primary production of cereals and feeds, and both, but especially the latter, were engaged in the secondary production of livestock from feedstuffs, neither had much control over the third and increasingly profitable area, the marketing of products from farm to retail.[26] This fact lay at the root of "anticapitalist" sentiment in both camps. Estate owners attempted to counter marketing weaknesses primarily through direct influence on government; peasants tried marketing co-ops and political alliances with the estate owners.

When, after 1930, the peasants broke with estate ownership, it was not because the peasantry was in search of new policies or allies. Rather, the protective umbrella of the Junkers had been partially withdrawn and was no longer providing adequate cover. To attain the same ends, the peasants were forced to search elsewhere for leaders and spokesmen. That process, however, was slow and incomplete, and it was based on both structural and circumstantial factors. Without resolution of the economic and political conflicts between grain-growing estate owners and the body of dairy and livestock peasants, Landwirtschaft could not appear as a solid front. Without a solid agricultural front, the rural elite would be weakened in its conflicts with other class fractions.

2. Estate-Owner Domination and the Bases of Rural Unity to 1924

Social and economic protectionism, antisocialism, and the political power of the estate owners linked Germany's peasants to the agrarian elite in a relationship founded on consent and force, spontaneity and manipulation. Junker leadership in production, government, bureaucracy, and the military facilitated and reenforced the integration of the rural sector in Imperial Germany. Protection of inefficient grain production retarded the development of peasant dairy and livestock production, and many German peasants were put at a disadvantage, even in the home market, by the import duties on fodder and feeds

25. The theoretical basis of their discussion, and partially of ours, is Marx's chapter on the "Genesis of Capitalist Ground Rent," *Capital,* (1967 ed.), 3:782–813; see also Lehmann's bibliography.

26. Harold Breimyer, "The Three Economies of Agriculture," *Journal of Farm Economics* 44 (1962):679–80.

(barley, bran, oil cake) that the Junkers had obtained. Maintaining high domestic grain prices shored up the viability of those who were the traditional base of Prussian political power. It was because the peasants accepted the "homogeneity of agriculture" and protection from the urban sector that they innovated only minimally, fell farther behind their Belgian, Dutch, and Scandinavian peasant neighbors in productivity, and accepted a relative (and sometimes even absolute) deterioration of their economic positions in the Wilhelmine period.

The Junker-led Bund der Landwirte (Agrarian League) was formed in 1893 with the dual function of cementing relations with heavy industry in opposition to the policies of Caprivi and bringing all agricultural producers under one umbrella. Throughout the countryside, the Bund became an active force for imperialism, anti-Semitism, and social reaction. It used its network of local organizations, credit institutions, newspapers, and ties to the Conservative party to further these goals and convert public organs (agricultural chambers, co-ops, and labor bureaus) into representatives of its interests.[27] While its leadership argued that "agriculture should not isolate itself by criticizing heavy industry," it nevertheless maintained that a successful "improvement in Germany's international position requires not only developed industry but also a strengthened Landwirtschaft without which the industrial position is not defensible."[28] In its immediate decision to become a political mass organization and to send its representatives to parliament through several parties, the Bund distinguished itself from other less advanced pressure groups, including those of industry. Politics was the key, and even producer co-ops and sales outlets existed not only for narrow cost reductions but for the broader purpose of mass organization. For the peasant, the struggle against urban interests (banks, Jews, socialists) was wed to the policy of protectionism, for allegedly, the German peasant was overly exposed "to the vicissitudes of the world market."[29]

The estate owners were able to portray their interests as national interests and thus everyone's interest, while the interests of the peasants, where divergent, were particularist and narrowly economic. Eckart Kehr makes this point, noting that "among the East Elbian

27. There is considerable literature on the Bund; cf. Puhle, *Interessenpolitik*, especially pp. 165ff., 213ff. Also, Fricke, 1:128–49. For other elements of this simultaneously romantic, reactionary, imperialist development, cf. P. G. J. Pulzer, *The Rise of Political Anti-Semitism in Germany and Austria* (New York, 1964). German conservatives were very quick to discover the favorable potential of mass politics.

28. Bundesarchiv, Koblenz (BA)/Nachlass Roesicke/230, pp. 13, 16.

29. Cited by Tracy, p. 93. Rural schoolbooks taught that the English peasantry was ruined by the repeal of the Corn Laws.

Agrarians the acknowledgement of pure economic interests occurs seldom; they are always simultaneously politicians. They very often emphasize national motives, by which they allow themselves to be led. [They obtain] increased consideration for their class interests by conceding a little to national interests. The pure agrarian tendency appears much more clearly in the case of . . . peasants."[30] Thus, despite changing urban demand, between 1900 and 1915 rye acreage and production increased more significantly than did dairy and livestock production, while the Bund agitated successfully against the suspension of duties on feeds (barley, corn, and oats).[31] Privately, the leadership acknowledged that such a suspension would lower production costs substantially for many peasants, but publicly the proposal was denounced as directed "against the peasantry itself," as a measure that would render animal production "dependent on foreign sources" and on urban middlemen.[32] Better to use more expensive but surplus rye as a feed. Peasant families worked harder as production was deflected to crops for whose production the peasant farm was inferior to the estate.[33]

Why did the peasantry seem to adhere to the Count Kanitz doctrine of 1894 that without a preponderant cereal agriculture all of German agriculture would collapse? Those peasants or groups of peasants slow to adjust production to changing market conditions probably perceived protection of grains as obviating the need to adopt or adapt to new techniques and marketing patterns. Property-conscious peasants were encouraged to fear a supposedly antiproperty working class whose revolutionary threat was unknown, but whose clamoring for cheap food was an established fact. Further, the Bund demanded cheap credit, reduced taxes on agricultural property and inheritance, lower communal taxes, support of the chambers of agriculture, increased duties on livestock, and the cancellation of laws protecting wage labor. The Bund even found ways to mobilize small tenant farmers.[34]

The Bund's influence spread beyond its initial Prussian confines. It sent several hundred of its officials as speakers on the hustings and conducted about ten thousand public meetings a year.[35] In areas for-

30. Kehr, p. 273, note 2.

31. Walther G. Hoffmann, *Das Wachstum der deutschen Wirtschaft* (Berlin-Heidelberg, 1965), pp. 272, 302. Between 1900 and 1913 alone some 540,000 ha. were newly devoted to rye; Sering, p. 264. Between 1880 and 1910 grain production doubled; Tracy, p. 100.

32. BA/Nachlass Roesicke/230, p. 11, letter to von Wagenheim, 23 Sept. 1912.

33. Gerschenkron, *Bread and Democracy*, p. 73.

34. Wunderlich, *Farm Labor*, p. 25.

35. Fricke, 1:138. Other data is provided here on the structure and operation of the Bund.

merly outside Prussia *(muss Preussen)* there had been some earlier resistance to having "Junkers" as spokesmen. In Schleswig-Holstein, for example, it was not until the turn of the century that small and middle peasants reconciled themselves to estate-owner dominance,[36] and the Bund experienced similar difficulties in the Catholic middle Rhine and in Baden. All aspects of the consent-fraud-force continuum came into play. Consent was evidenced when, after the turn of the century, over 50 percent of the Zentrum, representing the Rhenish, Bavarian, and Silesian peasants, began to take a firm stand in favor of increased agricultural tariffs. Force, too, played a role: in addition to well-enforced boycotts against traders, wholesalers, and political unreliables, the Bund sometimes resorted to agrarian terrorism, threatening political opponents with economic sanctions and physical violence.[37]

Other peasant organizations did exist but were unable to mount significant challenges. In 1908, there emerged the *Bauernbund* (Peasants' League) centered among southern small and middle peasants. It declared itself democratic, in the spirit of Stein and Hardenberg, not Junkerdom,[38] and identified with the urban Mittelstand, not the "big" capitalists. Within a decade, the Bund had succeeded in splitting the Peasants' League with the intention of recovering even "the small and smallest" peasant.[39] Although rather numerous, the prewar Catholic Peasant Associations *(christliche Bauernvereine)* could play only a minimal role politically. Organized regionally, there were about thirty with a total membership of 350,000. Primarily, they strengthened the right wing of the Zentrum, which included Catholic estate owners, without thereby being able to exert any influence on the Prussian power centers.[40] The Rhenish and Westphalian Bauernvereine were organized and headed by Catholic members of the titled nobility who went on to become Reichstag deputies for the Zentrum. (One of them, von Schorlemer-Alst, was known as the "king of the peasants.") Initially concerned with organized charity and self-help, their activities expanded to include savings-and-loan associations and technical-aid stations. From the outset they proclaimed that a healthy peasantry would be the strongest support for the existing state and society.[41] Further,

36. Heberle, pp. 29–31.
37. Tracy, p. 96.
38. Günther Franz, *Quellen zur Geschichte des deutschen Bauernstandes* (Darmstadt, 1963), pp. 511–13. They called for cheap money, universal suffrage, disarmament, progressive taxation, free schooling, and federalism. Classical small-producer "populism" or being outside of official, elite "Enlightenment"?
39. BA/Nachlass Roesicke/230, p. 8.
40. This was no less true later, see notes 4 and 80.
41. Walther Herrmann, *Bündnisse und Zerwürfnisse zwischen Landwirtschaft und Industrie* (Dortmund, 1965), pp. 10–12.

they shared the estate owners' reactionary, antidemocratic, antiliberal, and corporatist views; they shared the structural principles of an agrarian ideology.[42]

The peasants had not played a particularly active role in the collapse of the monarchy and the November 1918 revolution, but they initially seemed to welcome these as heralding peace and normalcy. They seemed prepared, too, to tolerate or even support a government led by socialists.[43] The collapse of the monarchy and of the military, together with the workers' upheavals, seemed to have placed estate-owner dominance of the countryside, and the Junker class itself, in danger. Measures designed to make impossible their continued power would have had to be directed against the estate owners' economic and political position.[44] A radical land reform consisting of the socialization or redistribution of estates would have destroyed the economic basis of the rural elite. The creation of a democratic army that would have excluded the old officer corps and replaced it with reliable democrats would have deprived the old elite of a vital power base. The Allies forced a reduction in the army, but the aristocrats remained, and the socialists' utilization of the army to maintain law and order against radical socialists and Communists aided in restoring the legitimacy of that reactionary institution.[45] Ironically, the reduction in the size of the army and even more so of the "bourgeois" navy rendered the military more purely reactionary. The replacement of the upper echelons of the bureaucracy and the dismissal of much of the thoroughly reactionary judiciary would have eliminated another important power base. But the economic basis of the agrarians' strength remained intact, and the cession of the eastern areas came to serve only irredentist purposes. Similarly, the retention of crucial power centers enabled the estate owners to pull their own weight in the counterrevolution and with the leaders of industry. The old moral order of which the Junkers were a central element was neither destroyed nor delegitimized.

The critical food situation and blockade following the ravages of the war made the socialists reluctant to disrupt rural production. Thus, even the radical peasants' soviet (*Bauernrat*) of Bavaria declared in

42. Hans-Jürgen Puhle, *Von der Agrarkrise zum Präfaschismus* (Wiesbaden, 1972), pp. 28–32, 47.

43. Especially in the south, see Arthur Rosenberg, *Geschichte*, pp. 22, 92; *Imperial Germany*, pp. 92–93; and Muth's work on the upheaval in the countryside.

44. This was the cumulative effect of Hitler's physical elimination of a substantial part of the officers corps after July 1944 and especially the later nationalizations in the Soviet occupation zone. Cf. Dahrendorf, pp. 381–96, and David Schoenbaum, *Hitler's Social Revolution* (Garden City, 1966), pp. 193–233.

45. Carsten, *The Reichswehr and Politics*, pp. 3–99.

April 1919 that "socialization must not disrupt production."[46] The wartime supply companies were not converted into cooperatives, and the SPD sought to prevent strikes in fertilizer factories and among agricultural laborers.[47] (The number of unionized agricultural workers rose astoundingly from twenty thousand in November 1918 to one million in 1920; the number then fell precipitously and stabilized at about two hundred thousand.) The Land Settlement (Siedlung) laws of 1919 were not an attack on the latifundia but rather an attempt to create more subsistence possibilities in agriculture, especially for returned veterans. Similarly, the heavy capital and estate taxes imposed by the short-lived Erzberger tax reform of early 1919 represented an attempt to overcome a desperate state-revenue situation rather than any indirect socialization of estates.[48] Total agricultural production in both 1918 and 1919 was less than half the 1913 figure, and the food scarcity militated against any type of land reform during those few months when it might have been politically feasible, had the socialists been interested.

The countryside was pressed hard by the food supply organizations to produce for the cities; controls on marketing and prices (Zwangswirtschaft, literally "compulsion economy") were abandoned only slowly, in good part because of the rampant inflation, some being retained until 1924.[49] As long as the state control of agriculture initiated during the war continued, there was a community of interest between peasants and estate owners in opposition to Zwangswirtschaft. Inducing the peasants to countenance an expropriation of the Junkers under such circumstances would have been all the more difficult.[50] Only the importation of large amounts of grain could have made expropriations possible, but the Russian revolution and the exhaustion of the Allies reduced the amount of grain available. At that, Germany was bankrupt, and the antisocialist allies were not about to do anything to help a so-called Red regime take root.[51] Two other factors militated against

46. Cited in Heinz Haushofer, Die deutsche Landwirtschaft im technischen Zeitalter (Stuttgart, 1963), p. 231. By and large, Haushofer's approach is that the unity of agriculture equaled leadership of estate owners; cf. Hans Rosenberg, pp. 109–16.

47. Indeed, SPD Food Administrator Schmidt in the spring of 1919 blamed radical labor for the food shortage; Holt, p. 19.

48. The accusation that Erzberger had practiced socialization via the Finance Ministry, in any case unjust, certainly did not apply to the estates. The Prussian agriculture minister, Braun, in effect told the estate owners not to worry about socialization, just to produce.

49. Controls on meat were abandoned by the end of 1920; the prohibition on the export of agricultural commodities continued until mid-1924. To "compensate," fertilizer prices were strictly controlled and production placed on a crash program basis.

50. See Gerschenkron, Bread and Democracy, p. 98.

51. See Arno Mayer, Politics and Diplomacy of Peacemaking (New York, 1967).

possible expropriations: low population density in the east, which minimized any land hunger, and the absence of those national antagonisms that facilitated land reforms in the Baltic and Hapsburg successor states. One commentator even goes so far as to say that "only by guaranteeing unimpaired the continued private ownership of land could the Republic enlist the resigned support of the large middle class of peasants."[52]

By 1920 the threat to estate-owner dominance in the countryside posed by the advent of the Republic and urban upheavals had passed. It is telling that while at the end of 1918 the Bund der Landwirte pledged wholehearted support to the social democratic government and recognized the political rights of agricultural workers, by March 1920, the same Bund openly supported the Kapp Putsch. In January 1921, the Bund reorganized itself into the *Reichslandbund* (Agrarian League, RLB), successfully bringing even more peasants under its umbrella.[53] The RLB provided its members with technical, credit, legal, and official help; within four years of its reemergence, its membership reached four and a half million. It was able to take over or at least dominate public institutions such as the chambers of agriculture and reinsert itself into the political and economic life of the small-holding peasantry from whose ranks it drew or withdrew potential leaders.[54] The rapid expansion of the RLB was in part a response to the relatively disadvantaged position of the agricultural sector in the Republic; the RLB promised to get things done for agriculture. Both actively and tacitly the new government also recognized the estate owners as the rightful and capable spokesmen of agriculture. Thus, in October 1922, the *Deutscher Bauernbund* (allied with the DDP and representing the democratic peasants of the south and west) felt compelled to warn Chancellor Wirth, the last of the Catholic left's major figures, that the government was selecting as agricultural representatives "people who are not supporters of the Republic. . . . Official organs are dominated by big estate owners, people who do not support the Republic."[55] Characteristically, the government responded that there was an objective "need for skilled specialists."[56] A similar warning in March 1924 complained that the government was legitimizing the Republic's enemies.[57]

52. Wunderlich, *Farm Labor*, p. 35.

53. On the RLB reorganization and rebirth, Alan Kovan, "The Resurgence of the Landbund and Its Organized Power," Ph.D. dissertation, University of California, Berkeley, 1973. Also, Fricke, 2:526–33, and the new work by Jens Flemming, *Landwirtschaftliche Interessen und Demokratie. Ländliche Gesellschaften, Agrarverbände und Staat 1890–1925* (Bonn-Bad Godesberg, 1978), esp. pp. 250ff.

54. On this co-opting process of "molecular absorption," Gramsci, pp. 58–60.

55. BA/R43I (Landwirtschaftsministerium)/1276, p. 199, 23 Oct. 1922.

56. Ibid., p. 265, 16 Nov. 1922.

3. 1925 to the Crisis: The Absence of Alternatives and Immanence of Conflict

Simultaneously, the estate owners set about demonstrating to the peasants that it was only they who prevented "socialist inspired, discriminatory legislation against the countryside on the part of those who do not consider Landwirtschaft part of the Republic."[58] Rural anti-urbanism and antisocialism were still sufficiently strong in 1925 that even Catholic peasants of the south and west (ostensible members of the Zentrum and BVP) voted in the presidential election for the Junker Hindenburg and against Marx, the candidate of the Weimar coalition (SPD, DDP, Z).[59] The tax legislation of 1926 vindicated the peasantry's strong electoral support of the big agrarians in 1924 and 1925. The radical Erzberger tax laws of 1920 were reversed; property taxes were lightened and to be paid on the basis of income rather than "substance"; sales tax exemptions were granted; inheritance taxes were virtually abolished in the case of takeover by the widow or children.[60]

Similarly, assistance was withdrawn from those consumers' unions that "in the eye of peasants as much as of Junkers forced prices below what a 'free and open' market would bear."[61] Part of the heritage of the pre-1870 multistate system was the continued importance of secondary cities and their conflicts with the countryside. The city was the antagonist of the peasants, many of whose forebears and relatives were driven there by the development of Landwirtschaft. A power-political *(machtpolitische)* unity of the countryside was the only viable response to an urban constellation, which "had abandoned loyalty and faith *(Treue und Glauben)* in social order."[62]

By the end of 1925, both the Prussian and Reich ministries of agriculture had formulated programs based on demands they reported receiving from all sectors of the countryside. The demands were designed to offset the allegedly unfair advantage enjoyed by the urban sector, and in both scope and cost they presaged those programs that emerged later during the crisis. They included: consolidation, reduction, and postponement of debts; regulation and guarantee of grain prices; assistance in the conversion of surplus potatoes into animal feed; a reduction in duty-free frozen meat imports; a cutting back of

57. BA/R43I/1277, pp. 4ff.

58. ZSA/RLB Pressarchiv series 132/vol. 10, p. 2.

59. Alfred Milatz, *Wähler und Wahlen in der Weimarer Republik* (Bonn, 1965), pp. 118–20 and Map 7; Castellan, *L'Allemagne,* pp. 91–95.

60. Cited by Holt, p. 146.

61. Ibid., p. 70.

62. BA/R99F/195, pp. 559, 590. See also the reports sent to Agriculture Minister Hermes by local officials, 1920–22, R43I/2535, pp. 82, 140, 169, Winter 1920.

social welfare programs and taxes; lowered freight rates; and cheap credit.[63] Similar demands were presented directly to Hindenburg, who lent his ear to agricultural groups rather generously.[64] Groups of small and middle peasants from poorer hill regions of the middle Rhine called for similar programs but with additional demands for no more trade treaties, "just prices" to replace the monopoly prices of the cartels, and an end to a situation where "we receive less than the urban unemployed."[65] These demands reveal a willingness to abandon free-market principles and return to principles associated with the prewar tradition as well as with the hated Zwangswirtschaft—but this time to the advantage of the primary producer. Virtually no one, however, shared the agricultural organizations' sense of crisis, and, hence, these proposals were quickly abandoned.

A rather different tendency was ascendant in urban circles after 1925. The domestic market strategy that had dominated since the war (due to the lack of capital, reconstruction needs, and treaty disabilities) was slowly abandoned. In 1925, Germany obtained both access to American capital and trade freedom; the first result was a return to the Bülow tariff rates of 1902. Although these were not low, a series of commercial treaties was soon negotiated under the aegis of Stresemann's Foreign Ministry and with the support of the working-class parties. The result was a precipitous rise in agricultural imports, despite increased domestic production and slightly higher prices. The value of agricultural imports rose to over one-third the gross value of domestic production, and by 1928 the import of dairy and other processed foods nearly tripled (see table 7). Organized Landwirtschaft opposed this new export strategy and the political alliance of industry and organized labor that brought it to pass.

Industry's call for an export offensive and a modus vivendi with labor[66] elicited immediate and diametrically opposed responses from agricultural and working-class representatives. Peace with organized labor and an export offensive were elements of the *same* strategy, one in which the advanced fraction of industry sought to gain the support of

63. For the Prussian version, BA/R43I/2537, 28 Nov. 1925, pp. 470–77; for the Reich version, R43I/2538, pp. 100ff., April 1926.

64. ZSA/RLB Vorstand/113, p. 116.

65. ZSA/RLB Pressarchiv 132/11, p. 9, as reported in the heavy-industry oriented *Kölnische Zeitung*.

66. As indicated above, the first such calls by Silverberg and Kastl of the RDI met with far from universal agreement. But, within a year, their views did become dominant. The lines of cleavage within industry on this issue remained important until the very end of the Republic; they are the subject of chap. 3, and relations between industry and labor are examined in chap. 5.

labor, if need be at the expense of agriculture. Thus, Silverberg's speech at the 1926 RDI convention failed even to refer to agriculture, while leading conservative industrial and agricultural spokesmen referred to an "industrial-socialist alliance" at the expense of heavy industry and agriculture.[67] As chief political spokesman for this alliance, Stresemann said in April 1927 that "autarky is impossible. Our economic problems can only be solved by a reconquest of the German position in the world market. In this task the advanced and processing industries will take the lead."[68]

Responding for the SPD and the unions (ADGB), Fritz Naphtali expressed the organized working class's support for the "full development of industry's potential"—a program that included higher wages, the elimination of tariffs, and a rationalization and toleration of trusts and cartels.[69] The response from agriculture was an angry call for class unity and a reminder of its needs: profitability and accumulation must be assured, and for Landwirtschaft, viability meant protection.[70] For industry to leave agriculture in the lurch while colluding with and finding a mass base in the SPD and unions was adjudged short-sighted, divisive, and dangerous: "on the one hand Industry wants to pursue its

TABLE 7

Agricultural Production, Imports, and Prices (in billions of RM)

	1924	1925	1926	1927	1928	1929	1930
Gross value agric. prod.	12.1	12.6	12.9	14.3	14.6	14.4	13.5
Net value agric. prod.	9.5	9.9	9.7	10.5	11.6	11.1	10.6
Net value ag. imports	2.5	4.1	3.7	4.5	4.4	4.0	3.0
Gross value ag. imports	2.9	4.9	4.5	5.4	5.4	5.1	4.0
Agric. price index (1913 = 100)	128	132	134	138	132	126	107

SOURCE: Adapted from Sering, table 11, and Friedrich List Gesellschaft, *Deutsche Agrarpolitik im Rahmen der inneren und äusseren Wirtschaftspolitik* 6, part 2 (Berlin, 1932):554, 561. Top two rows agricultural year; others calendar year.

67. Reports in ZSA/RLB Pressarchiv 148/8, pp. 17–30; see chap. 1, n. 50.

68. Cited in ZSA/RLB Pressarchiv 132/10, p. 67.

69. *Vorwärts*, 20 October 1926.

70. For example, the *Agrarpolitische Wochenschrift* of 10 September 1927, in ZSA/RLB Pressarchiv 192/22, p. 115.

one-sided politics of profit with the attendant abandonment of Land-wirtschaft, but on the other Industry looks for and expects to find in Landwirtschaft a firm and unselfish partner in the struggle against collectivism. . . . Industry will eventually have to choose one or the other."[71] The alternative preferred by agriculture and most of heavy industry was the domestic market strategy (*Binnenmarktstrategie*) based on protection of agriculture and a more bellicose (*kämpferisch*) attitude toward labor. Thyssen, Vögler, and Reusch—all representatives of conservative, Ruhr heavy industry and leading members of the Langnamverein—together with Graf Kalckreuth of the RLB were pushing their respective parties for a *Bürgerblock* (bourgeois bloc) government and rejection of the still-fresh offer of social peace with labor. If exports must be facilitated for reparations' sake, they argued, then increased work hours and lower wages and social spending were the best way—via a Bürgerblock.[72]

In early 1928, with the export push in full swing, the modus vivendi between industry and labor marked by skirmishes, and the agricultural crisis on the horizon, agriculture's spokesmen increasingly called upon industry to make its choice. For their part, peasants as well as estate owners opposed most of the trade treaties negotiated after 1926, whereas the DVP was the fulcrum for parliamentary negotiations in nearly every case. As one peasant newspaper put it, "We keep getting assurances, then we get screwed."[73] Industry could assume agri-culture's support for its tax and social policies while it paid lip service to, but essentially rejected, plans for massive help for agriculture. Agriculture's ideologists could only counter that,

> in the long run and viewed politically industry cannot survive without agriculture's being healthy. In the name of the producing classes . . . the opening to the unions did not pay. Their demands render profits almost impossible, and they remain essentially red. . . . The de-mands of agriculture, on the contrary, are essential for this state (*eine*

71. This anonymous piece appeared simultaneously in the peasant-oriented *West-fälischer Bauer* and in the conservative voice of Ruhr heavy industry, the *Kölnische Zeitung*, 1 December 1926, in ZSA/RLB Pressarchiv 132/10, p. 10.

72. This according to the *Vorwärts* of 23 Jan. 1927. At the October 1926 Langnam-verein convention, Silverberg received only scant applause, while those like Reusch and Thyssen who spoke of increasing the capacity of the domestic market and forming an alliance of all the "productive strata" ("schaffende Stände") against the socialists re-ceived all the applause; reports in the *Kölnische Zeitung*, 1 Oct. 1926. The interfacing of conflicts within industry with those between industry and agriculture will be discussed in chap. 4.

73. *Rheinische Bauernzeitung*, 2 December 1926, in ZSA/RLB Pressarchiv 132/10, p. 8. For the very revealing party alignments on the various trade treaties, Holt, pp. 218–24.

Staatsnotwendigkeit) and for the economy as a whole. . . . The economic, social and tax policies of recent years are responsible for
agriculture's distress. These have increased costs and made profitability impossible. The Left is our joint enemy; we were its first
victim; industry will be next.[74]

After the war as before, there were essentially three economic-corporate rural organizations, each linked more or less effectively to one of
the national parties. Although they continued to maintain their organizational integrity, they frequently joined for legislative and other political purposes, and their memberships pressed together and called for
mergers precisely as their ties to the respective political parties weakened. The parties were rent by splits, not the least important of which
were caused by the defection of rural constituencies who believed
themselves to be ignored or abandoned. Small farmers in particular
found that their support of the urban bourgeois parties brought them
only limited benefits, even before the crisis. The demands pressed by
these groups served to increase vertical solidarity in the countryside.
Representatives of all three organizations agreed that "only an abiding
solidarity of all farmers—the vine grower of the Mosel, the cattle
breeder of the North and South and the potato and grain producers of
the East—could save those whose fates were in any case tied."[75]

Of the three, the Reichslandbund (RLB) continued to be the largest
and most influential. Its claim of over two million family-head members
was likely inflated, but it was certainly many times larger than any of
the others.[76] Although known as the estate-owner organization par
excellence, its membership consisted overwhelmingly of family peasants and a substantial number of landless laborers (150,000) organized
in the RLB's yellow unions.[77] Before the party splits and the severed
link between representatives and represented, RLB membership was

74. Contributions to a forum in the *Deutsche Tageszeitung*, 3 Mar. 1928, in ZSA/RLB
Pressarchiv 148/8, pp. 151–55. Agricultural spokesmen frequently held the belief that
precisely a reformist SPD rendered capital accumulation and reproduction virtually
impossible. Rather than overthrowing capitalism, the SPD would simply bleed it dry
unless stopped politically; see chap. 4, pp. 205, 206. Such a view partially coincided with
that held by Eugen Varga, a Comintern economist; see *Die Krise des Kapitalismus und
ihre politischen Folgen* (Frankfurt, 1974), pp. 231–61, 337–56.
75. ZSA/RLB Vorstand/50, p. 180.
76. For an assessment of the membership figures, Erwin Topf, *Die Grüne Front*
(Berlin, 1933), pp. 121–23. Topf claims that active membership was only about 500,000.
But, cf. Fricke, 2:521–22, who inclines toward the higher figure; Holt, p. 109, appears to
count family memberships and so arrives at a figure of 5.5 million. Puhle, *Agrarbewegungen*, p. 311, analyzes the figures and concurs.
77. Kovan, p. 184.

virtually obligatory for rural representatives of the conservative- and middle-bourgeois parties. In 1924, of the 102 DNVP members of the Reichstag, 52 belonged to the RLB; the DVP and splinter parties harbored others. Ideologically, the RLB continued to affirm an outlook it described as: Christian-national, corporatist, antiparliamentary, pro-autarky, and Mittelstandish in opposition to Marxism and international finance capital.[78] Over two hundred local and national publications diffused its views. The chambers of agriculture, producer and consumer co-ops, technical-aid stations, and statistics-gathering units were all under its sway. The German Agricultural Council *(Deutsche Land-wirtschaftsrat)* was ostensibly the national coordinating center for the chambers; in fact, it was a virtual affiliate of the RLB performing a quasi-state function.[79] During two particularly critical periods—late 1923 to early 1926 (the institutionalization of stability) and early 1930 to mid-1932 (the heart of the crisis)—the RLB supplied the agriculture minister and much of his bureaucracy.

Although members of the Zentrum and of the DDP headed the Agriculture Ministry between 1926 and 1930, this fact did not accord the peasants of the Catholic Bauernvereine or of the Bauernbund, and its semiautonomous Bavarian section, a commensurate influence in policy formation. Neither organization was able to provide an alter-native to estate-owner domination of agricultural policy. The 580,000 members of the Catholic Associations and 100,000–200,000 members of the Peasant Leagues were small and disunited affiliates of their respec-tive parties. In the case of the Catholics, local leaders tended to favor cooperation with the RLB and overshadowed and disobeyed the na-tional leadership of party-true Andreas Hermes, who was identified with endless compromise, "politics," inconsistency, corruption, and the negotiation of unpopular trade treaties.[80] Whereas the Catholic Zentrum remained the fulcrum of nearly every republican coalition seesaw, its peasant associations hardly followed suit. The leadership of the Bauernvereine in the Rhineland, for example, was fond of referring to the "pig sty of democracy" and "a massive deception" of the people executed by a bungling party system dominated by the socialists in Red

78. The full program is reprinted in Fricke, 2:525; cf. also Puhle, *Präfaschismus.*
79. Topf, pp. 140–46.
80. Thus, the right-wing leadership in the Rhine, in Westphalia, and elsewhere (under von Lüninck and von Loë) often broke discipline and carried the day against the Berlin leadership. On Hermes and corruption, Topf, pp. 93–104. Hermes had the misfortune of being Germany's chief negotiator after 1927 for the Polish trade treaties, which seemed to open the door to cheap foreign foodstuffs. Heide Barmeyer, *Andreas Hermes und die Organisationen der deutschen Landwirtschaft* (Stuttgart, 1971), is altogether too gener-ous in judging Hermes's performance; Topf, p. 112, a bit too harsh.

Berlin.[81] The Bauernvereine continued to oppose the right of agricultural workers to unionize. Even before the crisis, the peasant associations demanded that they be allowed to merge with the RLB and that the party move to the right. Local clergy often spearheaded such actions together with the Catholic nobility. As much as this discordance was bemoaned in the Catholic press,[82] and despite the party's own rightward drift after 1924, the voting masses and patronage possibilities lay essentially elsewhere.

The situation was even worse for the shrinking "left" bourgeois DDP and Hermann Dietrich, the agriculture minister it provided. He had the misfortune to have that portfolio at the outbreak of the crisis (1928–30) and under an SPD chancellor. Torn between the urban-consumer, free-trading core of the party and the rural members of the Bauernbund, who turned to the RLB out of desperation, it was Dietrich who inaugurated a number of new, state-interventionist and protectionist programs, without thereby being able to garner or recoup rural support. His tenure in office marks a central moment in the break between representatives and represented.[83] Already in 1925, a section of the Bauernbund had split from the DDP and affiliated with the less commercial and "socialist friendly" DVP; in the process, the Bauernbund lost one-fourth of its membership to the RLB.[84] In an attempt to consolidate what was left in the countryside, the Bauernbund reorganized and merged with two other small groups in 1927 and became the *Deutsche Bauernschaft*. Under the influence of its strong new Bavarian partner, the organization drifted closer to the RLB rather than providing an alternative to it.[85]

As hopeless as matters in general became for the DDP, its difficulties

---

81. Rhenish Bauernverein leader von Loë, cited in Klaus Müller, "Agrarische Interessenverbände in der Weimarer Republik," *Rheinische Vierteljahrsblätter* 38 (1974):392.

82. E.g., a series on urban-rural problems of the party appeared in *Germania* in August 1928.

83. Dietrich's quandary is well documented in BA/Nachlass Dietrich, esp. folders 342, 240, and 227. We shall return to these in our examination of the break between representatives and represented.

84. Cf. Fricke, 1:73–77, 299–301; Puhle, *Agrarbewegungen,* p. 85.

85. The 1927 merger brought the Bauernbund together with the Bayerische Bauernbund under Anton Fehr and the *Reichsverband der klein und mittel Betriebe* (National League of Small and Middle Owners) under Heinrich Lübke. Fehr's group had provided the main opposition in Bavaria to the yet more right-wing Catholic Bauernvereine under Georg Heim and the BVP; at one time it had been quite radical, but in the new combination it was the most conservative force. As recently as 1924 it had elected ten of its own people to the Reichstag. Lübke's group tried hardest to avoid the RLB and other right-wing forces; for this he was rewarded only after World War II. Details in Holt, p. 110, and Topf, pp. 134–39.

in retaining a peasant constituency were even worse. No party was so identified with urban commercial interests and Jewish-liberal newspapers as the DDP. Even the party's solidly anti-Junker peasant organizer, Tantzen, was trapped between the party's antiruralism and Dietrich's concessions to the grain growers. Differences between these dairy and livestock peasants and the estate owners of the RLB paled in comparison with those between them and groups like the *Deutsche Industrie- und Handelstag* (Congress of German Industry and Commerce, DIHT) whose leaders, like Eduard Hamm, Hermann Levy, and Carl Bosch, were so influential in the DDP. As Dietrich moved further into the "agriculture-friendly" camp, he came under increasingly severe criticism from Hamm and other commercial spokesmen. "The whole economy must be served, and for us that means the *exports of industry*. . . . Agriculture must adjust itself *to the market and to technological development.* . . . Trade must not be endangered." Some new policies did this, making food inordinately expensive and endangering economic ties abroad.[86] Attempting to balance its urban and rural wings was the DDP's dilemma in microcosm: fighting a two-front battle between the socialists on the left and the overwhelming bulk of the middle classes on the right, the DDP's position became increasingly untenable, and by 1930 its share of the vote dropped to under 4 percent. Its peasant support in the Protestant areas of the north and south had disappeared.[87]

The final basis of precrisis unity between estate owners and peasants was that provided by the academic ideologists. There was nothing unique in the nationalism and conservative politics of most Weimar academic economists: like other academics they were state servants and mostly conservative products of the ancien régime; few of them were republicans, fewer yet democrats.[88] What is uncommon about them is the deference they enjoyed as spokesmen for the national good. The dean of the national, agricultural economists was Max Sering, and his comments on the relationship between peasants and estate owners are paradigmatic: "In policy discussion the relations between . . . large and small owners are sometimes considered antithetical. . . . In truth there can be no talk of such a conflict except perhaps for those few who

86. Letter from Hamm to Dietrich, 9 Apr. 1930, BA/Nachlass Dietrich/320, pp. 57, 13.

87. The DDP's case is the prototype for the so-called "disappearance of the bourgeois middle." See Jones, "Dying Middle," pp. 23–54; Werner Stephan, *Aufstieg und Verfall des Linksliberalismus* (Göttingen, 1973); Sigmund Neumann, pp. 48–53; Fricke, 1:322–29. We return to this problem in chap. 6.

88. The circles around Aereboe, Brinckmann, Brandt, Lange, et al., were partial exceptions. Export groups supported these dissidents whose views appeared in DIHT and RDI publications; see chap. 4.

produce in an almost industrial mode[!]." The greatest portion of the land remained dependent on grain production whose elimination would mean economic and political collapse for the nation.[89] To complete the link of millions of peasants to the estate owners, he continues, "without this protection [grain tariffs], not only 19,000 estates but hundreds of thousands of peasant units would surely be abandoned to ruin."[90] The material connection of the peasantry to the dominant classes was not narrowly economic, and it found expression in terms of the nation, property ownership, and the Mittelstand: "Country folk do not simply supply food. They are the nation's energy reserve; all classes are provided by them with the physically and morally healthiest elements produced by breeding *(Zucht)* in tightly knit families in close touch with nature. The agricultural family not only consumes but also produces together; they remain a pillar of even a highly industrial society. Land-tied families constitute three-fifths of the economically independent population and thereby the heart of the Mittelstand."[91] The peasants did indeed support and follow the lead of the estate owners; they had little opportunity or incentive to behave differently. Although peasants bore much of the burden of the trade treaties and social-welfare policies implemented after 1925, they could hardly register their political dissent by supporting either the parties associated with the progressive export and commercial interests or those identified with the working class.[92] Rural unity was to be put to the test: mutual logrolling became less adequate as the estate owners' protectionist umbrella was wielded more selfishly, but to whom else could the peasants turn?

Until the middle of the crisis there was no political development that could separate the peasants from their alliance with the estate owners, an alliance which, though largely negative, nevertheless accorded benefits to both sides. It could hardly be expected that the "normal" politics of Weimar Germany would produce what the "crisis" politics of 1918–23 had not. Grain protection's record was clear: it had slowed, if not reversed, the development of dairy and livestock production and an

89. Sering, pp. 875, 877.
90. Ibid., p. 902.
91. Ibid., p. 874.
92. If political affiliation were strictly a matter of income, the SPD and KPD would have fared much better: in 1925, a good year for agriculture but not yet for industrial wages, over 60 percent of the peasantry lived on gross incomes (i.e., including their partial self-sufficiency in food) less than or equal to "proletarian"; see Geiger, *Schichtung*, pp. 72ff. On the futility of the KPD's emphasis of this, see its peasant expert, Edwin Hoernle, *Die Industrialisierung der deutschen Landwirtschaft* (Berlin, 1928), and *Zum Bündnis zwischen Arbeitern und Bauern, 1928–1951* (Berlin, 1972).

accompanying class of small holders; it had accelerated the depopula-
tion of the east while creating a dependence on miserably paid Polish
seasonal labor; it had limited improvements in the urban diet; and it
subsidized an important, reactionary class of indebted, incompetent
"feudal" capitalists.[93] Young and capable agricultural workers continued to migrate to the cities, even in the face of high urban unemployment. Sozialpolitik seemed to beckon them, and urban employers did
not mind the pressure on the labor force; yet, it was primarily Landwirtschaft itself which suffered the worst consequences.[94] A major
crisis was not really necessary to activate tensions between family
peasants and estate owners; policy conflicts were almost constant,
though they tended to remain at the level of interest rather than class
politics.

Tables 4-6 pointed to the very different types of production and
production requirements to be found in Landwirtschaft. A certain compromise had been reached between two earlier polar possibilities: a
Germany (nearly) self-sufficient in grain agriculture importing vast
amounts of finished dairy and livestock products from its more advanced neighbors, versus one with an intensive peasant-farmer agriculture importing vast amounts of animal feeds and grain from its more
backward neighbors. It was still within the framework of this dichotomy
that policy clashes took place, and it was along this line of cleavage that
export-oriented industrialists and socialists attempted to split the agricultural front. On the one hand, governments intervened on behalf of
estate producers rather than peasants; on the other, it was necessary to
retain the electoral support of the mass of peasants through concessions to them. Thus, the big surplus-producing grain harvest of 1925
resulted in the government's purchase of huge amounts from the estates
at inflated prices.[95] However, the call by peasants for cheap (4 percent)
credits, which they claimed would enable them to modernize and
compete with the Danish and Dutch, fell upon seemingly deaf ears.[96] (A

93. Clapham, pp. 210–14, 229–30. Kehr, p. 281, contends that the agrarians' struggle
was motivated by the desire to drive up the price of estates so as to withstand the social
competition of the wealthy bourgeoisie. On the incompetence of the Junkers as capitalists, Puhle, *Agrarbewegungen,* pp. 44–45, and Dieter Gessner, *Agrarverbände in der
Weimarer Republik* (Düsseldorf, 1976), passim.

94. Von Richthofen's March 1928 consideration of this problem concludes that industry was "too short-sighted" to roll back destructive Sozialpolitik and reduce rural
mobility. ZSA/RLB Verhältnisse zwischen Landwirtschaft und Industrie/246, pp. 13ff.

95. For the politics and details of this action, BA/R43I/2537, pp. 370–414.

96. Whether or not the capital could be mustered for such a program was a political
issue. Sering concurred on the 4 percent figure, p. 912. Interest rates for such loans were
from 1 to 5 percent in the United States, but 10 to 12 percent in Germany (and nearly

successful conversion might have tempered the conflict between peasants and workers.) What the peasants did obtain, at least between 1925 and 1929, was a fixed and minimal tariff on feed barley and corn. The constellation of interests was such that the estate owners (through the DNVP) would have found themselves alone opposing this measure.[97] The persistence of low rye prices after 1929, however, convinced the bourgeois parties, especially the Zentrum, that surplus rye and potatoes could only be disposed of at home through forced use as feeds.

Thus ended what had been a substantial concession by the estate owners to the family peasants; this is made clear in table 8. Even the accommodation on feeds was enjoyed unevenly by family peasants, however. Broken down into three categories, the price indices indicate that those family peasants who produced livestock products but no dairy products (group "b," fairly common in the north) profited considerably less (see table 9). These peasants would become the first to abandon the estate owners in favor of the Nazis. Even during the better years, the latifundian tendency toward indebtedness absorbed a wholly disproportionate share of available credit. Between 1924 and 1929, the indebtedness of the eastern estates rose by nearly one-third, whereas that of small and large farms in the west rose by less than 15 percent.[98] There were three times as many bankruptcies in the eastern provinces of Prussia as in the western, and only 20 percent of units over 50 ha. in the east were able to show a profit.[99]

Beyond any strictly economic concessions, the DNVP had to take seriously its commitment to securing and building a mass conservative base, including a rural Mittelstand.[100] The DNVP party center was, even before 1928, constantly rocked by splits, often in a manner detrimental to the economic interests of the peasants. The "antisystem" wing of the party led by Hugenberg sought to minimize the party's participation in the "republican swindle," but the party's agricultural representatives viewed participation as essential to securing their vital interests. Hence, it was the agricultural wing which most often assumed cabinet portfolios (Kuno v. Westarp, Gerhard v. Kanitz, Martin

---

double that after the bank crisis of mid-1931). The peasants referred specifically to the Dutch and Danish cases, both of which were geographically close to important peasant areas. E.g., BA/R43I/2539, p. 181.

97. Details in Holt, pp. 107–108.

98. Kurt Ritter, *Agrarwirtschaft und Agrarpolitik im Kapitalismus* (Berlin-Leipzig, 1959), 1:261–65. These facts were not lost on the middle- and north-German peasants, even if the consequences were not immediately visible.

99. Sering, p. 57.

100. Cf. the DVP and DNVP party programs on this point, Franz, pp. 522–23.

TABLE 8

Imports (exports) of Feed and Food Grains (in millions of metric tons)

	1924	1925	1926	1927	1928	1929	1930	1931
Wheat	.5	1.5	1.9	2.5	2.2	1.8	1.2	.35
Rye	.5	.2	.0	.7	(.1)	(.4)	(.2)	(.2)
Barley feed	.3	.7	1.7	2.0	1.9	1.7	1.5	.53
Corn	.3	.6	.7	2.1	1.3	.9	.6	.4
Oil cake	.6	.8	1.2	1.9	1.8	1.3	.9	.4

SOURCE: Kurt Ritter, *Agrarwirtschaft und Agrarpolitik im Kapitalismus* (Berlin-Leipzig, 1959), 1:514 and *Vierteljahrshefte zur Konjunkturforschung.*

Schiele; Hans Schlange-Schöningen; Gottfried Treviranus), and it was they who seceded later when Hugenberg consolidated his power and moved toward the Nazis.

In a sense, a long record of influence and dominance in the organs of the state constrained many members of the rural elite to participate in the Republic. Placing interest representation ahead of antirepublican purism, the agrarian organizations developed a governmental con-servatism that was later a principal prop for the Brüning government. Yet here too, the full impact of the Depression, by intensifying social conflict, undermined the prevailing policy of mutual logrolling among organized interests. Small, purely rural parties could not win significant electoral or political influence, and parties that split from the DNVP, like the CNBLP, Landpartei, and later the Volkskonservativen, never obtained more than 5 percent of the vote.[101] The DNVP's loss of two million votes between 1924 and 1928 and again between 1928 and 1930 reflected voter distrust and impatience with this ambivalence. Peasant representatives in the party were in some respects analogous to union representatives in the left parties: they questioned high principles and historical goals in the name of tangible, immediate policy gains. Al-though monarchism, Versailles, the form of the Prussian government, and later the Young Plan were real issues for them, they complained frequently that the party was not concerned with their daily needs and with local problems.[102] Cultural style also separated the easterners from the bulk of peasants: juxtaposed to the austere, class-conscious,

101. On the CNBLP, especially in middle Germany, Topf, p. 119. On the splits in the DNVP, Bracher, pp. 309–22, 337–40; also Jones, "Dying Middle."

102. E.g., Westarp to Hugenberg, in ZSA/DNVP-Reichsleitung, Krisen in der Par-tei/11, p. 75, on local issues, 1926; pp. 38–50 on daily needs and compromising, 1928–30. This was apparent in the DNVP's dealings with Stresemann when it frequently backed itself into a corner where it was ineffective; see Stürmer, pp. 133–38.

bureaucratic, and centralizing Junker prototype was a variegated peasantry, some of it authentically romantic, low in "classness," localistic and federalist.[103] The early defeat of the left in the cities and of union organization in the countryside reduced the possibility of subversion of the village community *(Dorfgemeinschaft)* and way of life.[104] In the name of profitability, state aid, autarky, and lowered production costs, the RLB was able to mobilize peasants while claiming to be a voice of moderation.[105]

Conservative circles in heavy industry continued to support the *Binnenstrategie,* but by 1926 the ascendant groups in industry turned to exports. Thus, the newspaper of the Employers' Association cited the unlikelihood of reestablishing Germany's export dominance and referred to agriculture as the key to an expanded domestic and national market. Similarly, Paul Reusch told the 1927 Langnamverein convention that "increased purchasing power for agriculture would be the best security for industry. The domestic market is the main thing for the future."[106] However, only three months later at the more important

TABLE 9

Agricultural Price Indices by Type of Production (1913 = 100)

	1925	1926	1927	1928	1929	1930	1931	1932
a. Plant	124	127	163	152	128	115	111	106
b. Meat	115	121	113	111	128	114	84	67
c. Other animal products	160	148	149	149	138	120	102	88
b + c	138	129	123	134	134	116	87	74
All agric. (a + b + c)	130	130	136	132	131	116	96	84

SOURCE: Walther G. Hoffmann, *Das Wachstum der deutschen Wirtschaft* (Berlin-Heidelberg, 1965), p. 562.

103. Heberle, pp. 49, 53–54, analyzes the northern, non-Prussian character; Puhle, *Agrarbewegungen,* p. 60, the Catholics of the south and west; p. 83, however, notes how much more they had in common.

104. Flemming, "Grossagrarische Interessen," pp. 747, 752, 759, and Wunderlich, *Farm Labor,* p. 51, both emphasize this.

105. Thus, in April 1926, the RLB organized a demonstration of over fifty-five thousand peasants in Brandenburg against imports. Writing Agriculture Minister Haslinde (Z) afterwards, the RLB claimed to have held back "the enraged mass of peasants" while acknowledging how "gratifying it was that big and small owners marched together." BA/R43I/2538, pp. 170, 173.

106. *Deutsche Arbeitgeber Zeitung* of 21 Mar. 1926 and Reusch at the Langnamverein convention 1 June 1927, cited in ZSA/RLB Pressarchiv 192/22, p. 88.

RDI convention, Carl Duisberg of IG Farben called for a one-third increase in German exports. Under the slogan of "quality production," the ascendant fraction of industry moved toward exports and peace with organized labor. The international iron cartel agreement (IRG) of 1926 further facilitated the export offensive, at least in the short run. This followed by less than a year Silverberg's olive branch to the SPD and constituted a victory for Stresemann and Curtius over the right wing of the bourgeois parties. Some industrial spokesmen even justified increased agricultural imports on the grounds that domestic products were of low quality and high price and ought not to be protected.[107] Those spokesmen, like Kastl of the RDI and Karl Lange of the machine industry, who took seriously lower costs and higher quality in agriculture instead of state aid and protection, were anathema.

The ascendancy of the export fraction of industry further limited the agricultural sector's participation in the national recovery and growing prosperity. Relative adversity was shared by estate owners and peasants and functioned as another factor of unity in Landwirtschaft. In 1927–28, aid to agriculture dropped to under 1 percent of the budget, and the political stock of agriculture's representatives fell commensurately.[108] In the year before the 1928 election, Stresemann sought to move the DVP away from the DNVP and toward cooperation with the SPD, and although his success was rather short-lived, predicated as it was on the assumption that Germany could afford class collaboration, agriculture was the loser. Organized agriculture responded in this immediate pre-crisis period in a fashion that was to become its hallmark during the crisis—unified, vociferous protests, ideological offensives, and pressure applied to the apparatus of state, especially the executive branch. In a move which presaged by a year the organized "Green Front," representatives of the three rural organizations appeared together to present their case to Hindenburg in February 1928. Warning of the proletarianization facing the peasants, the usual litany of complaints and demands was accompanied by dire warnings that it was increasingly difficult for responsible forces to hold back the enraged peasant masses.[109] When an official in the Agriculture Ministry called for rejec-

107. Kastl at the RDI convention, cited in ZSA/RLB Pressarchiv 148/8, pp. 109–12.

108. A figure of .8 percent is calculated by Arno Panzer, *Das Ringen um die deutsche Agrarpolitik* (Kiel, 1970), p. 121. In general, Panzer exaggerates the conflict between industry and agriculture, picturing the latter too much as victim. He is correct, however, that industry played agriculture and labor off against each other. Aid to agriculture hardly disappeared at any time: by *1926* Reich assistance had more than quadrupled and Länder aid more than doubled over prewar levels; *Die Förderung der Landwirtschaft durch öffentliche Mittel* (Berlin, 1930), p. 13 (vol. 13 of Enquête Ausschuss).

109. Report of the meeting in BA/R43I/2539, pp. 95ff. The demands centered around

tion of these exaggerated and threatening demands,[110] he was removed from the case. Further, when the labor and finance ministers called for prosecution of the RLB on the grounds of fomenting massive law-breaking and slurring of Parliament, the president reminded them that it was not the cabinet's task to decide if the RLB had broken the law.[111] How the crisis of Landwirtschaft would have been resolved had it been the only item on the agenda is a moot point, for other crises were soon to develop.

Their inability to obtain credit,[112] concessions made to them on the import of feed grains, protected prices above the world market level, a hostility toward both Sozialpolitik and export industry shared with the estate owners, and the inability to articulate an independent political voice all drove the peasants to join and remain in the camp of autarky, the camp of those who may be described as "located one level below the high point of strength in the [world capitalist] system."[113] After 1926, agriculture was joined in this autarky camp by the coal, iron, and steel industries. Although sometimes not the dominant fraction within industry, they were influential and joined agriculture in a strategy based on internal markets, high tariffs, hostility to labor, further cartelliza-tion, and high domestic prices.[114] In chapter 4 we shall discuss in detail the conflict between this Binnenstrategie and the Exportstrategie after 1927, but the ingredients of the former worked, in the meantime, to resolve conflicts within agriculture. Ideally, Landwirtschaft would be industrialized—without altering its class structure—and become a con-sumer of excess industrial capacity, a supplier of cheaper foodstuffs, thereby justifying lower wages,[115] and a more capable supplier come

---

higher tariffs and prices, and lower social costs, taxes, and credit rates; also strict import quotas/bans and debt relief. Reports from the countryside, e.g., Oldenburg (ibid.; p. 143), did indeed indicate that the peasants were restless and turning violent.

110. Ibid., pp. 251ff. He said they called their program one of patriotic responsibility and all else treason, but "the general picture is not nearly so bad as they claim."

111. Ibid., pp. 310–13.

112. On the endemic shortage of capital for modernization, see the January 1928 report of the Landwirtschaftlicher Hauptverband of the south and west, BA/R43I/2539, pp. 4ff. On the credit shortage in general, Holt, pp. 129–36; Friedrich List Gesellschaft, 1:565–88. See text below, chap. 4, sec. 1, at tables 21–23.

113. Immanuel Wallerstein, "The Rise and Future Demise of the World Capitalist System," *Comparative Studies in Society and History* 16 (1974):402.

114. For details, Dirk Stegmann, "Deutsche Zoll- und Handelspolitik, 1924–1929," in Mommsen, et al., eds., esp. pp. 504–5. Within capitalist circles, they were opposed by Stresemann, the AVI, and other exporters; see chapter 3.

115. Paul Reusch seems to have been aware that, even if cheaper, not all foodstuffs would be affordable. Hence his remarks—in 1926 that workers should eat less meat and more bread, and, in 1928, that they should eat less wheat bread and more of that hearty rye bread! *Berliner Börsen Zeitung*, 19 June 1928.

the next war. Even if credit had been the primary stumbling block[116] there simply was no possibility of investing it in a manner that would have been both productive and consonant with the existing class and political structures of the countryside. As much as bankers like Georg Solmssen, scientists like Aereboe, and industrialists like both Silverberg and Reusch might have advocated the "rationalization" of the countryside, improving the technical capabilities of agriculture was far from a simple matter of investment. A long "passive revolution" like that which characterized the period of German industrialization, the development "of the productive forces of industry under the direction of the traditional ruling classes," was not a fit strategy for agriculture, particularly not in response to a crisis.[117] State aid and protection was the minimum requirement for preserving both a vital fraction of the dominant classes and its popular base. Adaptation had to remain a secondary concern. Political mobilization was the only route possible, and we turn now to an analysis of the forms, activities, and consequences of that mobilization during the multiple crisis after 1929.

4. The Agricultural Crisis, Its Resolution and Contribution to the General Crisis

The fall of grain prices and beginning of the general agricultural crisis in 1928 corresponded in time to the SPD electoral victory of May 1928 and the quickening of conflicts within industry and between industry and the organized working class.[118] The Grand Coalition of SPD through DVP was in trouble from the outset: skirmishes over production costs and Sozialpolitik began immediately, and by autumn nearly three hundred thousand Ruhr ironworkers were locked out by employers who refused to accept binding arbitration by the Labor Ministry.[119] Although we shall not discuss those other conflicts here, agriculture's crisis and the political offensive of its representatives must be viewed in the context of the breakdown of a system of legitimacy based on industrialist/working-class collaboration through the state and the attempt to substitute for it some other mass base. In the course of the

---

116. As claimed, for example, in a long RLB article in the *Deutsche Tageszeitung* of 28 Jan. 1928.

117. Gramsci, pp. 59–60, 106–120.

118. The former conflicts are the subject of chap. 3, the latter of chap. 5.

119. Cf. Ursula Hüllbüsch, "Der Ruhreisenstreit in gewerkschaftlicher Sicht," in Mommsen, et al., eds., pp. 271–89. Further conflicts over distributing the costs of economic stagnation are discussed in Timm, and all these issues are analyzed in chap. 5 below.

agricultural crisis itself, however, the unity of the rural sector under the leadership of the estate owners was placed in jeopardy, and the protective umbrella of the big agrarians became inadequate to retain the direct allegiance of the peasantry. The political struggles to resolve the agricultural crisis contributed substantially to Brüning's fall in May 1932 and the effective end of cabinet and constitutional government in favor of what appeared to be an old-time conservative-authoritarian regime very attuned to the needs of organized agriculture.[120] Further, peasants voted crucially and substantially for the NSDAP, and important figures within the rural elite were essential to Hitler's appointment as chancellor; both were central in the demise of the Republic.

a. Suffering Agriculture and Its Opponents

Rural indebtedness and interest burdens had been rising steadily since the end of the inflation,[121] but data on foreclosures suggest that only with the decline and collapse of world market prices did the situation of Landwirtschaft become critical. The number of foreclosures on farms (over two hectares) grew steadily, if not dramatically, after 1928:[122]

	1927	1928	1929	1930	1931	1932
Foreclosures	2,554	2,292	3,193	4,350	5,061	6,200
Acreage (in ha.)	36,713	48,376	91,153	128,707	152,648	155,000

The declining fortunes of agriculture are best viewed in conjunction with falling world market prices, which are displayed in Table 10.

After 1928, fewer than one-half of the farms in the west and one-third of those in the east were able to cover their interest obligations out of their receipts. The larger the unit, the more frequently such difficulty was experienced. Between 1924 and 1930, farm indebtedness had increased nearly 20 percent for small farms in the west and 35 percent for the eastern estates.[123]

120. An example of this view is provided by Heinrich Muth, "Zum Sturz Brünings," *Geschichte in Wissenschaft und Unterricht* 16 (1965):739–59.

121. See table 22. By 1931 the agricultural debt reached 12 billion RM, 7.3 billion of it short-term!

122. Gerhard Kokotkiewicz, "Der Immobiliarkredit, seine Lage und Aussichten," *Vierteljahrhefte zur Konjunkturforschung*, Sonderheft no. 30 (Berlin, 1932), p. 13. Some areas (e.g., Baden, Thüringen) are omitted, and the figures are, therefore, about 10 percent lower than they ought to be. Emergency decrees limiting and then prohibiting auctions served to hold down the number somewhat after 1930.

123. Friedrich List Gesellschaft, *Agrarpolitik*, 1:399; Puhle, *Agrarbewegungen*, p. 298.

TABLE 10

World Market Prices for Selected Products (in RM per metric ton)
and Cash Returns of Agriculture (in millions of RM)

	1927	1928	1929	1930	1931	1932	% Decline
			Prices				
Wheat[a]	247	227	205	158	92	89	64
Rye	210	222	183	105	77	87	58
Feed (corn/barley)	145	185	152	94	68	63	57
Cattle[b]	855	830	814	804	558	278	68
Hogs	995	889	1,071	876	512	434	56
Butter	3,391	3,530	3,407	2,766	2,205	1,418	58
			Cash Returns				
Veg. production	3.6	3.8	3.6	3.2	3.0	2.6	28
Animal production	5.8	6.5	6.2	5.5	4.4	3.8	35
Total gross	9.4	10.3	9.8	8.7	7.4	6.4	32
Minus expenses	8.0	8.0	7.9	7.0	6.1	5.5	31
Net return	1.4	2.2	1.9	1.7	1.2	.9	36[c]

SOURCES: Based on Hoffmann, pp. 318ff.; *Statistiches Jahrbuch für das Deutsche Reich* (1938), p. 567, agricultural year; *Vierteljahrhefte zur Konjunkturforschung* (1933B), p. 151; Holt, p. 217.

[a] Wheat, rye, and feeds cif. Rotterdam.
[b] Cattle and butter cif. Copenhagen; hogs cif. Polish-German border.
[c] The decline between 1928 and 1932 was a substantially higher 59%.

The combination of effective worldwide overproduction, a sudden curtailment of American capital, and an urban unemployment figure that in early 1929 already exceeded two million (14 percent) served to accelerate the fall in prices. At first, peasants attempted to compensate for declining prices by increasing production, but even once the futility of such measures was recognized and production was cut back, costs remained rigid. Between 1929 and 1932, production decreased by about 26 percent while the value of that production declined by over 60 percent.[124] Tables 3 and 27 indicate that the gap between agricultural prices and the prices of all other goods and services grew constantly between 1927 and 1933. Peasant anger over this continued to be directed primarily at the Sozialpolitik of the organized working class and the trade policies of export industry. In early 1929, RLB representatives asked the agriculture minister rhetorically if it was not preposterous for

124. ZSA/Büro des Reichspräsidenten/333, p. 188. Production dropped from 8.7 to 6.3 million metric tons, and its value sank from 3.8 to 1.5 billion RM. There is considerable variation in the sources.

Landwirtschaft to be paying 850 million Marks in taxes when it was operating at a loss of over 1.5 billion Marks.[125] As state intervention proved to be of only limited success, however, public costs were increasingly viewed as exactions: in 1932, with the price index at less than three-quarters of the prewar level, public costs were still nearly double their prewar level.[126]

Massive peasant protests began in the north in 1928. The feed-dependent cattle raisers of Schleswig-Holstein and Oldenburg were shortchanged in tariff policy (see tables 8 and 9), and neither their party representatives nor the estate owners took up their cause. Besides making credit, tariff, and tax demands, the peasants attacked public officials and installations; one such demonstration may have been attended by one hundred forty thousand peasants.[127] Demonstrations in Oldenburg, in which some thirty thousand peasants participated, presaged many later themes. Under the slogan "From the Welfare State Back to the Work State," a half-dozen peasant and Mittelstand groups issued a list of demands, many of which were later adopted and spread by the Nazis in their agitation: tariff protection like that enjoyed by industry as a step toward barring all food imports, tax relief, cheap credit, reduced state functions and expenses, an end to Prussian dominance, sharp reductions in social-welfare measures, an end to the eight-hour day, protection of small craftsmen, legal action against cartels and monopolies, an end to the pampering of the big cities, a commitment to stop paying reparations, and, finally, a "strong government led by a strong man."[128] For the time being, these demands were taken up by the RLB, but that organization found it increasingly difficult to submerge and adopt peasant grievances.

The RLB had consistently identified the two principal enemies of agriculture as Handelspolitik—the trade and tariff policy pursued by export-industry circles in government, RDI, and DIHT—and Sozialpolitik—the political and economic policy of class competition and cooperation between liberal bourgeois groups and the organized working class. "One-sided commercial and export interests . . . together with the Marxists, are the only ones to benefit from a system" which "they have created for themselves"; one "which harms the

---

125. Cited in BA/R43I/2541, p. 18, 23 Jan. 1929.

126. According to the Agriculture Ministry, the "typical" twelve-hectare unit was scheduled in 1932 to pay 275 RM in taxes, 120 RM in social payments, and 480 RM in interest, for a total of 875 RM; the comparable prewar total was 475 Marks; ZSA/Büro des Reichspräsidenten/332, pp. 197ff.

127. See Franz, p. 531. The figure of 140,000 is from Puhle, *Agrarbewegungen*, p. 318.

128. The demands and events are reproduced in detail in BA/R43I/2539, pp. 58–65, Jan.–Feb. 1928.

German economy, polity, and nation."[129] The Stresemann-SPD coalition that emerged from the 1928 elections was just such a class-collaboration coalition, one that left Landwirtschaft out in the cold.[130] Of the RLB's fifty-four Reichstag deputies, forty-eight were now in opposition. Breaking that coalition was a major priority of organized agriculture. It was a priority shared by estate owners and peasants, but estate owners molded the forms of programmatic opposition, which then yielded results disproportionately beneficial to themselves.

Following the 1928 election, the Mainz Peasant Congress attacked "discriminatory and exceptional legislation against agriculture on the part of the power-holders of November 9 . . . now working together with opportunistic groups in industry."[131] It was these "opportunists" who had kept agricultural tariffs at roughly their prewar level while raising industrial tariffs by 40 percent; it was they who had redirected production in such a way that Germany now absorbed only 65 percent of its own industrial production compared to a prewar figure of 80 percent. Agriculture claimed to be receiving assistance only in those few areas where no export interests were at stake, and this unholy "bourgeois-Marxist alliance" was "the most dangerous opponent of Landwirtschaft and the destroyer of the peasantry."[132] This alliance viewed the interests of agriculture as concessions to be given away in the course of negotiating trade treaties. In February 1929, the RLB issued a booklet entitled *How Can Agriculture Be Made Profitable Again,* and copies were sent to Finance Minister Hilferding (SPD) and Economics Minister Curtius (DVP). The former rejected the pamphlet's proposals out of hand; the latter was initially ambivalent, but after conferring with Hamburg and Bremen importers, he too rejected them.[133] That such would be the reward for tolerating the governments of 1924–28 was something organized agriculture would not accept and would organize against.[134]

The labor-export alliance pressed forward on a trade treaty with Poland: for urban consumers such an agreement held out the prospect of cheaper pork products (especially in Berlin), and for export circles it

129. Cited in Franz, pp. 545–46.
130. Cf. Panzer, pp. 124, 129.
131. ZSA/RLB Pressarchiv 132/10, p. 2. The SPD-export coalition had abandoned "Deutsche Wirtschaftspolitik" in favor of "Weltwirtschaftspolitik."
132. *Westfälische Bauern Zeitung,* 13 Oct. 1930, cited in ZSA/RLB Pressarchiv 132/12, p. 121.
133. This case and the furor it aroused are documented in ZSA/Büro des Reichspräsidenten/329, pp. 161–80.
134. On the one-sidedness of trade treaties and the disappointment and hostility they aroused, Panzer, esp. pp. 47, 52, 111, 129.

promised to open a potentially large market for finished goods, but for the estate owners of the east and the peasant livestock raisers of the north it could only pose a threat to prices. And to nationalists in general it seemed to constitute a tacit acknowledgment of the eastern borders. Agriculture found some support for its position among Ruhr mining interests, who feared an influx of cheap Polish coal, but given the balance of forces within industry, agriculture could expect only very limited support. As for organized labor, its almost dogmatic adherence to a policy of cheap food and minimal tariffs, its opposition in 1929 to a special industrial loan fund for agriculture, and its uncritical support for agricultural "self-help," rendered virtually impossible any rapprochement with organized Landwirtschaft, despite the revised and more conciliatory platforms of various party congresses, Kiel included.

Although rural income had peaked in 1928 (see table 10), food consumption held fairly steady. This was due, on the one hand, to rapidly declining agricultural prices (see table 9) and, on the other hand, to organized labor's ability, at least until 1931, to secure the living standard of its employed members. Table 11 (p. 80) reflects this and indicates the uneven place of food imports in consumption. Rather less ambiguous was the general growth in the volume of food imports compared to 1913. Table 12 (p. 81) indicates the expansion of food imports while demonstrating clearly that the brunt of new imports competed with peasant rather than estate production. In regard to short-term needs, the labor-export coalition was more solicitous of estate owners than of peasants, while failing to convert peasants and peasant production so that they might be in a better position to take advantage of the increased quantity and quality of consumption. The onset of adversity appeared to find the rural sector united within but without substantial allies in either industry or labor.

With the exceptions noted earlier,[135] the agricultural specialists in the scientific-academic community continued after 1928 to support the agrarian ideology of a protected and united rural sector. Like Max Sering, Edgar Salin, and others, Bernard Harms, director of the Friedrich List Gesellschaft, reflected the views of that community when he wrote, "The peasantry is the chief pillar of that vital Mittelstand which is a prerequisite for the continued health of a people and its state." Salin thought only the national market could secure it. The free-trade era was over, and integration into world trade was secondary. And he concluded, "The state must now come to the active assistance of all of Landwirtschaft."[136] By 1931, Sering could find an additional danger

135. See p. 66 above and pp. 194ff., below.
136. Bernard Harms, ed., *Strukturwandlungen der deutschen Volkswirtschaft* (Berlin,

TABLE 11

Total Consumption of Selected Products (in millions of metric tons)
and Percentage Produced Domestically

	1927	1928	1929	1930	1931	1932
	Consumed (in millions of metric tons)					
Bread grains	9.9	9.8	9.7	9.3	9.1	9.0
Potatoes	11.4	11.0	11.6	11.6	12.2	12.3
Meat	3.1	3.3	3.3	3.2	3.3	3.1
Dairy	23.8	25.3	26.1	26.5	26.3	25.5
Fats	1.2	1.2	1.3	1.3	1.3	1.3
Eggs	.4	.5	.5	.5	.5	.5
	Produced Domestically (percentage)					
Bread grains	72	83	91	91	90	99
Potatoes	95	97	98	98	103	101
Meat	90	93	93	96	98	97
Dairy	83	83	82	83	87	90
Fats	40	42	41	42	46	45
Eggs	61	60	63	66	68	68

SOURCE: Horst Denecke, "Die Agrarpolitische Konzeption des deutschen Imperialismus," Ph.D. dissertation, Humboldt University, Berlin, 1972, p. 91.

in agriculture's woes: "the eastern barrier against the Slavs and Bolsheviks" was collapsing, while "tribute payments" led to disastrously high interest rates and "consumed 40 percent of annual new capital."[137] If the rural sector was thus united in its opposition to virtually the entire range of policies promulgated by the export-labor block, it nevertheless continued to experience internal conflicts, many of which were exacerbated by the agricultural depression.

b. *After 1928: Imminent Conflict*

Not all of German agriculture suffered equally from the Depression, and not all of it was left equally helpless to face the collapse of the market. Between 1928 and 1932, farm income plunged 40 percent. But whereas the purchasing power of crops dropped 25 percent, that of other agricultural products dropped 42 percent.[138] Between 1925 and 1928, the exchange value of (peasant) butter to (estate) rye was roughly 1:13.4; between 1929 and 1932, it dropped to 1:11.4—the lowest it had

1929), 1:23–24. Edgar Salin, "Am Wendepunkt der deutschen Wirtschaftspolitik," in Friedrich List Gesellschaft, *Agrarpolitik*, 2:699, 712.

137. Sering's report cited in BA/R431/2549, pp. 246–60. Cf. Topf, p. 234.

138. Tracy, p. 197.

ever been.[139] As tables 8–12 indicate, Landwirtschaft's misery was general but not equal. Even before the end of 1928, special assistance was accorded East Prussia, and excess but high-priced rye was channeled to replace corn and oil cake as a peasant-livestock feed.[140] Thirteen separate acts to help the east were passed between 1928 and mid-1930 when the first general assistance to all of agriculture was voted. Grain and its producers were far sooner and better protected and assisted than any others.

Although they did not attack the estate owners, the disturbances of 1928 in Schleswig-Holstein and Oldenburg took place primarily among feed-short peasants. Peasant spokesmen blamed the Weimar state for high costs and low prices. By 1928, many of these peasants had ceased voting for a DNVP identified with the Junkers and had cast their votes for a variety of splinter and peasant parties.[141] Nevertheless, they did not attribute their problems to the costly preferential treatment accorded the grain growers. Expensive credit, high taxes and social-welfare costs, and agricultural imports bore the burden of their hostility. Yet, it did become increasingly evident that peasants were given short shrift in matters of protection, prices, and government aid. In all three questions, rye-oriented policies reigned, and the few peasant voices that spoke out against them seemed to meet with little resonance.[142] The cost of domestic dairy and livestock production remained relatively high as a result, and labor and export circles consequently called for and obtained continued importation of these products. Agricultural organizations successfully mobilized peasants against this importation

TABLE 12

Import Volume Indices (1913 = 100)

	1927	1928	1929	1930	1931	1932
Grains	103	87	68	48	35	44
Meat	300	216	188	162	91	85
Dairy	141	154	158	152	123	105

SOURCE: Hoffmann, p. 542. See also table 7 above.

139. Lorenz, p. 96.
140. Topf, p. 157, contends that for small peasants, feeds constituted one-third of all costs, for middle and large units, one-sixth.
141. Milatz, pp. 122–23 and map 8. Heberle, pp. 91ff. Denecke interprets the 1928 disturbances as a small- and middle-peasant protest against Junkers and monopolists. I think the "antisystem" themes of those demonstrations cannot be interpreted in that way.
142. For example, the nearly fruitless agitation of the DDP's Tantzen-Heering. BA/ Nachlass Dietrich/240, pp. 27ff, and in the *Berliner Tageblatt* of 21 and 30 Oct. 1930.

and continued the united struggle of all of Landwirtschaft in the name of protection.

This very "protection" was itself immensely inequitable and became increasingly so as the crisis deepened. A comparison of agricultural tariff rates by categories makes this clear. Table 13 divides agricultural tariffs into three groupings: A. food grains competitive with those produced by estates; B. feed grains used by peasants and substitutive for surplus grains produced on estates; C. products competing with those produced by peasants. When estate owners obtained complete protection of their products (group A), they joined and then aggressively led a chorus of calls for protection of peasant products (group C) in opposition to labor and export industry, and successfully muted and redirected peasant opposition to the effective ban on imports of products that would have competed successfully with their own (group B). Price movements would hardly have dictated this kind of protection: in 1931, pig prices were less than three-quarters and cattle prices less than two-thirds their prewar levels, but grain prices averaged over one and a half times theirs. Western and northern peasants were further disadvantaged as livestock production shifted eastward, closer to the supply of available feeds, namely surplus potatoes and rye.[143]

Perhaps unwittingly, the SPD-led Grand Coalition contributed to this rye-centered policy and initial Nazi successes among the peasants. For the sake of ensuring urban consumers a regular and publicly managed supply, the SPD supported a state grain-trade monopoly; for the sake of maintaining their high-cost production and prices, the estate owners were willing to accept controls. The consequence of the last act passed by an SPD government (March 1930) was that the urban consumer was ensured against the peasants but not against the estate owners. Agriculture Minister Dietrich of the DDP and the new grain czar, Fritz Baade of the SPD, thus both failed to conciliate the peasantry, shored up the estate owners, and did nothing to remove the former from the camp of the latter.[144] Neither state purchase of surplus rye nor forced use by peasants of eosinated rye as a feed could stabilize the market or enable the intensive-production peasant to take advantage of cheap foreign feeds. Euphemistically dubbed the "socialization of consumption," this program forced domestic demand for cereals upward—at some expense to consumer food quality and cost and at greater expense to most dairy and livestock producers. All that Baade succeeded in

143. Between 1928 and 1931, the number of pigs raised in the east increased by two million primarily for this reason; BA/R43I/2547, p. 376. Between September 1930 and September 1931, meat prices dropped 25 to 40 percent.

144. On the peculiar SPD-Junker agreement on the grain monopoly and on the program to "socialize consumption," Holt, pp. 113–14, 103; Topf, pp. 208–209, 219.

"socializing" was the losses of the estate owners. Like many in the SPD's ranks, he believed that any state "takeover" of market functions, any "planned economy," was progressive. But the only thing red about Baade's plan was the eosin dye. Helping to restore estate owners and rye, his plan served only to impel peasants back in their direction. Peasant hostility in the most affected regions, though within the old ideological framework, began to accrue to the benefit of the Nazi party.[145] The small and middle peasants saw their narrow profit margins destroyed by the price collapse after 1928 and were unable to obtain the kind of government action that kept the estate owners afloat on the highest domestic cereal prices in Europe.

Table 10 indicates both the sharp drop of cash returns in agriculture after 1928 and the redistribution of those returns to the benefit of the grain producers. The decline in production values, shown in table 7, continued to accelerate: for 1931, the gross- and net-production values were 11.4 and 9.0 billion Marks; for 1932, they were 9.4 and 7.3 billion.[146] But the drop in domestic prices was not as evenly distributed as the drop in world prices shown in table 10. United agriculture's demands for protection did indeed cause domestic prices to be far above world prices across the board, but, again, both suffering and protection were uneven. Table 14 reveals the disparities that operated to the detriment of the peasantry: whereas German rye and wheat prices by 1932 were two and one-half times the world price, pork and butter prices were only about one and one half times the world price. Peasants were also mobilized in a campaign led by eastern estate owners against the allegedly socialistic credit and co-op reforms proposed by the *Preussenkasse*. The very real credit problems faced by peasants were integrated and articulated in such a way as to oppose reforms that would have lessened the influence of estate owners in public and co-op

TABLE 13

Tariffs as Percentage of World Market Price by Type of Product

	Group A		Group B			Group C		
	Wheat	Rye	Corn	Barley	Bran	Pigs	Butter	Eggs
1913	32	38	24	9	0	9	9	3
1931	260	295	255	230	130	35	18	3

SOURCE: Dieter Walz, "Die Agrarpolitik der Regierung Brüning," Ph.D. dissertation, Alexander University, Erlangen-Nuremberg, 1971, p. 93.

145. Heberle, pp. 74–76.
146. Hoffmann, p. 334.

TABLE 14

World and Domestic Price Indices (1925–1928 = 100)

	1929	1930	1931	1932
Rye				
World price	75.0	48.0	38.0	33.0
German price	95.0	72.8	81.3	82.2
Wheat				
World price	89.4	45.6	36.5	31.1
German price	97.0	99.4	86.2	78.5
Pork				
World price	96.8	67.0	34.3	41.0
German price	107.7	84.5	60.0	62.0
Butter				
World price	97.9	68.9	47.2	34.8
German price	96.4	78.0	60.6	60.4

SOURCE: *Wirtschaft und Statistik* (1936), p. 113.

lending.[147] Estate owners formulated protection policies capable of eliciting the consent and support of the mass of family peasants, but those policies were designed to serve estate interests first and foremost.

After 1928, agricultural leaders fostered peasant radicalization so as to be able to demand measures that would allay it. Any government that failed to heed their "moderate" voices would have to contend with unknown dangers. So successful was this strategy that Agriculture Minister Dietrich (DDP), an ostensible representative of the small peasants of the southwest, supported the "socialization of consumption" measures, noting that "the public interest must take precedence over the interests of single groups."[148] Once again Kehr's formula proved correct: the interests represented by the Junkers were the interests of the nation; other rural interests, where divergent, were the interests "of single groups." Realpolitik in agriculture meant meeting the needs of the estate owners, and the same Dietrich who came into office with an SPD chancellor and who promised propeasant policies *(Bauernpolitik)* and increased exports to eastern and southeastern Europe, initiated and presided over policies diametrically opposed to those twin goals.[149]

147. On the Preussenkasse episode of 1928–30: Topf, pp. 91–92, 104; BA/R43I/2426, p. 307; 2540, pp. 329–33; 2547, p. 22; and Panzer, p. 149.

148. Dietrich in March 1930; cited in Holt, p. 117. For examples of fostering radicalism in order to appear moderate, BA/R43I/2542, pp. 102ff., 205ff., and 320. These same pages testify to how Dietrich came around.

149. Tilman Koops, "Zielkonflikte der Agrar- und Wirtschaftspolitik in der Ära Brüning," in Mommsen, et al., eds., p. 857; Topf, pp. 206–7. After the breakup of the Grand Coalition, Dietrich went from agriculture minister to finance minister.

Dietrich could protest afterwards that he had not changed his mind between 1927 and 1931, but that the only way to assist Landwirtschaft was to assist those whose needs were decisive.[150]

Estate-owner interests dominated the formation of state agricultural policy, while family peasants continued to be organized in support of demands that benefited them only within a system which maintained their dependence on those estate interests. Dependence and integration were the two sides of the coin. So far as *policies* were concerned, this symbiotic relationship continued through the crisis; the primary-interest organizations and fronts continued to function. Electorally, however, both the rightist DNVP and leftist DDP—before 1928, the two strongest non-Catholic peasant vote-getters—proved unable, for different reasons, to retain peasant support in the crisis.[151] In the countryside, the DNVP had acted as a conservative Volkspartei, transcending particularist interests and unifying its adherents at the political level. But as the salience of specific economic demands increased, peasants moved toward narrower, interest parties. Thus, the Christian National Peasants' and Rural People's Party (CNBLP) was formed by members of the Agrarian League who thought the DVP and DNVP insufficiently committed to rural interests. Together with the German Peasant's Party (DBP), it proclaimed a peasant form of the agrarian ideology but concerned itself little with other matters. Alternately, the CNBLP might be viewed as an attempt by big landowners to contain nascent peasant rebellion by allowing it some expression.[152] Voting Nazi in 1928 or 1930 enjoyed a similar status. Complementing rather than conflicting with this move toward specific-interest parties was the call, from seemingly all rural quarters, for the unification of agricultural organizations.

Government programs to meet the crisis in agriculture constituted an attempt to save the existing agricultural system, but those programs weakened the unity of the agricultural sector which underlay its strength. At the same time, state intervention in the agricultural sector marked a new plateau of state intervention in the economy in general, an unprecedented level of public assumption of private risks.[153] From

150. The criticisms made of Dietrich puzzled him totally, and his responses were generally quite self-righteous; BA/Nachlass Dietrich, 340/240.

151. On the DDP and the DNVP, chap. 2, sec. 3. Judged by the secessions and expulsions that followed, Hugenberg's victories within the DNVP in 1928 and 1929 severely damaged the party in the countryside. See also chap. 6, sec. 4.

152. On the CNBLP, Fricke, 1:241–44; Sigmund Neumann, pp. 65–67. The alternate explanation is argued by Jones, "Dying Middle," p. 37. For the CNBLP's agrarian ideology in a peasant mode, BA/R43I/2546, pp. 91ff.

153. See Puhle, *Agrarbewegungen*, pp. 12ff., 50; Denecke, pp. 61–63. For precursors in the Kanitz plan, Puhle, *Interessenpolitik*, pp. 230ff., and Gerschenkron, pp. 53–57.

tariffs the state role slowly expanded to include organization of the market, price setting, the limiting of competition, credit control, production quotas, and systematic rescue from bankruptcy; yet these innovations of the later Weimar years applied primarily, if not exclusively, to the agricultural elite of estate owners. Hence, they undermined the political solidarity that Landwirtschaft had for so long enjoyed. The Junkers had never been averse to active and even socialistic state intervention, so long as they derived benefits from it.[154] What began in 1928 as a Help Program produced a new conception of state intervention, one that might save the estate owners but might equally threaten their base of mass peasant support and increase urban opposition. Intervention on behalf of the estate owners short-shrifted the peasantry while fueling the political crisis.

Two programs in particular illustrate how state intervention expanded and for whose benefit it did so. The Eastern Help *(Osthilfe)* and Resettlement *(Siedlung)* programs were expanded by the Grand Coalition and broadened further by the Brüning government between 1930 and 1932. Both had "national" components, and each reflected both aspects of the estate-owner/peasant conflict. The Osthilfe would extend special benefits to the primarily latifundian east in order to keep it a viable part of Germany and protect it from hardier and less demanding Polish peasants.[155] (Never mind that it was the German estate owners who brought in the Polish labor.) The Siedlung program would enable landless and land-short peasants to obtain marginal or defaulted-upon land, primarily in the east. (Never mind that this was during an agricultural depression, that the number of land-short peasants was small and that they lived mostly at the opposite end of the country, in the southwest.) The Osthilfe quickly degenerated into a massive giveaway, and the Siedlung program, in its single biggest year, created only about eight thousand farms.

The primary value of the Osthilfe was stated by one of its reluctant supporters, the industrialist Paul Silverberg, who had hoped to see it used to weed out the most inefficient producers: "long-term political *(staatspolitische)* purposes would be served by the maintenance on their own soil of families who through tradition and character are

154. This was but one of the multiple contradictions of agrarian politics; they are brilliantly illuminated by Kehr, pp. 281–83.

155. More has been written on the Osthilfe than can usefully be read. A biased but nevertheless useful single source is Bruno Buchta, *Die Junker und die Weimarer Republik* (Berlin-Leipzig, 1959). Relating the Osthilfe and Siedlung to party politics, Heinrich Muth, "Agrarpolitik und Parteipolitik im Frühjahr 1932," in *Staat, Wirtschaft und Politik in der Weimarer Republik. Festschrift für Heinrich Brüning,* ed. Ferd Hermens and Theodor Schieder (Berlin, 1967), pp. 317–60.

closely connected to the state."[156] Silverberg acknowledged the wisdom of supporting another dominant social class—even if at the expense of both urban consumers and the peasantry. President Hindenburg's own connections and background undoubtedly served to fatten the program,[157] but virtually the entire nation was captive to the "national" interpretation of the eastern problem. Of the untold billions granted, lent, and spent on the east, no more than one-third was used for investment or rationalization; two-thirds simply went to cover the debts of the indebted, generally as they themselves saw fit.[158] Less than 2 percent of estate owners were refused aid, although Agriculture Ministry analysts rated thirteen thousand of the eighteen thousand estates (71 percent) hopelessly overindebted and not salvageable. Those Prussian officials, socialists, and bankers from the Preussenkasse who objected were successfully frozen out of the decision making.[159] Abuses both major and minor were the norm, and not even the RLB made much of an effort to deny it.[160] Liberal politicians and economists who wanted to help the east but not its inefficient, corrupt, and backward elite found themselves without a (nonsocialist) popular echo.[161] Mostly, these were the same export industrialists who sought, with little success, to split family peasants from the estate owners. Those liberal-democratic successors to Max Weber who entertained bona fide nationalistic positions on the eastern question but who doubted the Junker's ability to bear the German standard missed the point: strengthening the east was one facet of saving the estate owners, not vice versa.

In practice, the Siedlung program also drove a wedge between peasants and estate owners. Himself an eastern estate owner and ex-DNVP representative, the Siedlung commissar, Hans Schlange-Schöningen, was one of those aristocratic reformers willing to yield a little in order to preserve the essentials. He was original to the extent that he was prepared to settle peasants on bankrupted estate lands "in order to renew Germany on the basis of her own soil" and restore the impor-

156. In an article by Silverberg in *Deutsche Kreuz Zeitung,* 30 July 1930.
157. Hindenburg's March 1930 message on the Osthilfe was lavish by any standard, ZSA/RLB Pressarchiv 132/11, p. 185.
158. The one-third to two-thirds ratio is estimated by Gerschenkron, p. 149. See also ZSA/Büro des Reichspräsidenten, Ostprogramm und Agrarmassnahmen/214. Cf. the objections of Prussian Minister President Braun, BA/R43I/2545, p. 212, 23 Dec. 1930.
159. Topf, pp. 258–74. Further details on the entire program are in Dieter Walz, "Die Agrarpolitik der Regierung Brüning," Ph.D. Diss., Erlangen-Nuremberg, 1971, pp. 152–81.
160. The RLB acknowledgment in ZSA/RLB Vorstand/23, pp. 220–30.
161. A characteristic forum for this analysis was the DDP-affiliated *Deutsche Volkswirt:* on the Osthilfe, see especially August Bode, in 3 (23 Nov. 1928):243; Carl Landauer,

tance of agriculture.[162] This was too much for his fellow estate owners, who insisted that settlement meant colonization, not land reform, and that financing settlement was not their problem. They attacked "expropriation" and rejected Schlange's contention that "rural society must show flexibility if it is to survive . . . this is the lesson of Stein and Hardenberg."[163] Schlange's attempt to implement his program (significantly, in cooperation with the labor minister) ultimately led to his and Brüning's dismissal by Hindenburg on the grounds of having engaged in "agrarian Bolshevism."[164] Thus departed the last representative government of the Weimar Republic. Effectively, it was brought down by the entire bundle of social and political conflicts, but its actual fall was precipitated by the rural elite. In fact, the resettlement program was hardly a threat: the estate owners dominated the Land Delivery Associations, whose task it was to procure lands for settlement. They succeeded in having the state buy marginal and wasteland at highly inflated prices and boosted the value of their own real estate. In the proper context, new peasant settlers could provide both cheap labor and political support. In 1929, 4,000; in 1930, 5,800; in 1931, 7,800; and in 1932, 8,450 units of two hectares or more (a rather generous criterion) were resettled. A more generous Siedlung program might well have succeeded in reenforcing estate-owner/peasant bonds and shoring up that base of mass support so vital to the estate owners in their representation and articulation of the interests of the entire rural sector. As with unequal production costs, price collapses, tariff protection, marketing

in 4 (2 May 1930):1040, and again in 5 (23 Jan. 1931):540. Their accusation that funds were being diverted from the peasants to the estate owners did not succeed in bringing peasants to their side.

162. In Germany such stuff passed for reform. The quotation is from Hans Schlange-Schöningen, *Bauer und Boden* (Hamburg, 1933), pp. 56, 76. His overall conception was presented in *Rationalwirtschaft und Nationalwirtschaft* (Berlin, 1927), especially pp. 106ff. See also Denecke, pp. 174–80.

163. Schlange to Hindenburg, ZSA/Büro des Reichspräsidenten, Kabinettsbildungen und Verabschiedungen/47, p. 34. But Hindenburg was no Frederick William and 1930 was not 1806; see note 18.

164. The conflict lasted until Brüning's dismissal in May 1932. Most of the relevant documents are in ZSA/Büro des Reichspräsidenten, Ostprogramm und Agrarmassnahmen/214, pp. 190–283. It was Stegerwald (Z) who insisted that bankrupt estates be split up and settled. Schlange (ibid., pp. 265–68, 27 May) tried unsuccessfully to assure Hindenburg that only the most hopeless and unwanted estates would be resettled; the president was aware, however, that officials in the Agriculture Ministry had judged fully 70 percent of the estates to be beyond saving. Various glosses on these developments are cited by Walz (pp. 182–210), Muth, Koops, and Bracher. The RLB led the attack on the Schlange-Stegerwald proposals, demanding that local associations of owners should decide which properties were available and at what prices. Cf. ZSA/RLB Vorstand/113, pp. 24–31.

and monopoly possibilities, credit availability, subsidies, and giveaways, the Siedlung program generated conflicts between peasants and estate owners. Without altering the essential social, political, and ideological interests that bound them together, the agricultural crisis might drive the two groups in different political directions.

c. Resolving Conflicts within Agriculture

Several solutions to the emerging conflict were possible. One solution would have removed the peasants from the orbit of the estate owners and attached them to a political bloc led by export industry.[165] The resulting liberal-bourgeois coalition would have resembled figure 4 in chapter 1, and would have concentrated on importing cheap feeds and modernizing the peasantry while substantially abandoning the estate owners. A second solution would have been a greater exertion by the estate owners on behalf of the peasantry. With the end of industry-labor collaboration by 1930, such a program would have worked to restore the Sammlung bloc (figure 1) and Binnenmarktstrategie. Estate owners and peasants undertook massive efforts in this direction, ultimately without success. A third solution would have been for each of the two sectors of agriculture to pursue its interests independently, while seeking to ally itself with like-minded urban classes. Such an arrangement would deprive the estate owners of their own mass base in the political process but might lead to a broader penetration and representation of the core interests of all of agriculture within electorally significant urban groups like the Mittelstand.[166] The virtues of such a solution help to explain both partnerships between estate owners and the Nazis and the ambivalence of the former toward the rural success of the latter.[167]

A peasant coalition with the "liberal" dynamic and export industries would, in part, have been a return to the failed prewar Progressive

165. This possibility, like the others, was dependent on the balance of forces within industry: a fluid factor only secondarily dependent on the posture of agriculture. This is discussed in chaps. 3 and 4.

166. Conceivably, in such an arrangement, the estate owners could leave the peasants in the lurch, but only if there existed a form of government where numbers did not count! Peasants could abandon the interests of estate owners only by moving "left"—with export industry or organized labor, and after 1930 these became increasingly nonfeasible partners.

167. A fourth solution, which we shall not discuss here, would have been a worker-peasant coalition advocating autarkic and inflationary policies like those put forward in the Woytinsky-Tarnow-Baade proposals. Wladimir Woytinsky, "Proletariat und Bauerntum," *Die Gesellschaft* 3 (1926):410–40; Fritz Baade, "Richtlinien für ein sozialdemokratisches Agrarprogramm," *Die Gesellschaft* 2 (1924):132–53, and "Die neuen agrarischen Ideen seit 1914," in *Festgabe für Lujo Brentano* (Leipzig, 1925),

(DDP) coalition.[168] Joint opposition to backward estate owners was a necessary but not sufficient condition: the coalition would have to enjoy some support from the urban Mittelstand while facing only minimal pressures from the organized working class.[169] The latter was not inconceivable, since the political benefits to be derived from the weakening of the country's most reactionary and antidemocratic social force *(Junkertum)* would have been quite palpable. Urban consumers were in any case paying inflated food costs because of those big agrarians, so higher food prices would not have been a threat. As we noted earlier, the DDP failed completely in its attempts to form such an alliance. Significant initiatives were, however, taken in this direction by industrial and commercial organizations. Important leaders of industry and agriculture (mostly estate owners) met together on an almost regular basis after 1926. The records of these meetings and commentaries on them by the participants provide an invaluable source for a general analysis of the relations between these two sectors during the later years of the Republic.[170] That analysis is the subject of chapter 4; here we seek to isolate those proposals and initiatives that sought, or tended, to split peasants from estate owners.

In appealing to family peasants, industrialists emphasized the efficiency and potential profitability of intensive dairy-livestock production, which was being retarded by expensive, backward and protectionist estate production. Prosperous Scandinavian and Dutch peasants were the model for what the German peasantry could become; all too clearly a market for their products did exist, as the continuing flow of imports proved. If only the peasantry could be assisted in modernizing its production, and if only it could be brought to see the virtues of a network of trade treaties, then cooperation would be simple and ideological precepts (like self-sufficiency) more malleable. The

---

pp. 227–58. Baade virtually acknowledged the failure of his efforts in "Agrarpolitik und Preussenwahl," *Die Gesellschaft* 9 (1932):289–302. The dominant SPD view remained that articulated by Rudolf Hilferding, "Handelspolitik und Agrarkrise," *Die Gesellschaft* 1 (1924):113–30. See also Lehmann. The SPD never did forge an alliance with the peasantry like that which the Swedish Socialists molded after 1930.

168. On the limitations to the Progressive coalition, Arthur Rosenberg, *Imperial Germany,* pp. 33–67, and Carl Schorske, *German Social Democracy, 1905–1917* (Cambridge, Mass., 1955), esp. pp. 170–80; Kehr, pp. 452–67; cf. Heckart.

169. See Jens Flemming, "Zwischen Industrie und christlich-nationaler Arbeiterschaft," in Dirk Stegmann, et al., eds., *Industrielle Gesellschaft und politisches System* (Bonn-Bad Godesberg, 1978), pp. 259–70.

170. Especially valuable are the Nachlässe of Paul Silverberg, Paul Reusch, and his agent Martin Blank: BA/Nachlass Silverberg/esp. vol. 362, 363; HA GHH/Nachlass Blank 400 101 202 4/vols. 4b–11; HA GHH/Nachlass Reusch 400 101 24/vols. 1–3a, and Reusch's assorted correspondence.

arguments were not new, but the conjuncture was more auspicious. Until sometime in 1929, the concessions that industry had been willing to grant agriculture had fit into the estate-owner model: assistance primarily to the grain growers along with a reduction of taxes, social costs, interest rates, and state interference; all so long as agriculture attempted to modernize and did nothing to endanger industrial exports or the economy as a whole.[171] But precisely as estate-owner demands came to threaten exports and "the economy as a whole," industrialists moved away from the estate-owner model to a peasant model of what was needed to assist Landwirtschaft. This change was accomplished by early 1930.

In January 1930, the RDI told its members that it would oppose all further increases in agricultural tariffs.[172] Concern for exports remained industry's underlying motivation, but the implications for agricultural policy were now different. Priority was now to be accorded to lowering the costs of production and marketing: oil cake, bran, and corn imports would be encouraged for dairy, fowl, and livestock production. Together with a concerted effort to enroll peasants in marketing cooperatives, a general program of co-op assistance and rationalization was in order.[173] Not tariffs and government monopolies were fundamental but, rather, increased production at lower costs. In May 1930, the RDI published its *Contribution to an Agrarian Program;* it was authored by several of the dissident agricultural economists, and was intended to be industry's definitive statement. It advocated "making production suit the market rather than vice versa."[174] Dairy, livestock, fruit, and vegetable production should be encouraged, and that of cereals, potatoes, and legumes restricted. Government aid should flow *only* to those participating in such efforts; it should be withheld from those unwilling or unable to convert, standardize, and cooperate. Substantial estate areas of the east should be removed from production altogether, and those policies which encouraged pig production to move from west to east should be reversed. Productivity levels for herds and flocks could approach Scandinavian levels if peasants were better trained, organized, and supplied with cheaper but richer foreign feeds. In the way of special grants for

171. Thus, the "Six Point Program" of the RDI Executive of June 1929, in *Geschäftliche Mitteilungen für die Mitglieder des RDI,* 11:14, lfd. 247. Grain tariffs were supported (lfd. 249) as were tariffs on feeds (no. 20, lfd. 371). Similarly, Edmund Pietrkowski, "Das Landwirtschaftliche Notprogramm," speech delivered to the Trade Policy Commission of the RDI, 29 May 1929.

172. *Mitteilungen,* 12:2, lfd. 36.

173. Ibid., 12:8, lfd. 194.

174. Karl Brandt, Constantin von Dietze, Friedrich Zorner, *Beiträge zu einem Agrarprogramm* (Berlin, 1930), pp. 11ff.

the east, there was a skimpy 100 million Marks, much of it to be raised by and presided over by industry itself: this an adaptation of Silverberg's plan for a special lending institution, the Bank for Industry Obligations.[175]

Although hardly the stuff of major upheaval, these and similar proposals could have opened new coalition possibilities for the peasantry. Corporate and political carriers were lacking, however; ideologically and organizationally, these proposals could not penetrate the peasantry. Fritz Beckmann took the RDI program on tour, lecturing peasants in several provinces. Although he was pleased with their response, most rural newspapers panned his performance while characterizing the RDI program as "self-righteous" and "nothing but free trade in new dress for agriculture, while industry remains well-protected."[176] Since the Zentrum and BVP went over to grain protection,[177] and Tantzen's wing of the DDP had yielded to Dietrich, only the Deutsche Bauernschaft[178] and smaller front organizations were available as rural vehicles for the new approach. Through the Bauernschaft and another, smaller organization, the RDI published and disseminated two pamphlets, one of facts and figures *(Agrarpolitik in Zahlen)*, one a general attack on the RLB *(The Peasant Struggle Against the RLB).*[179] Both attempted to drive home the RDI's themes, and there was some sign of this agitation's success in convincing family peasants that they were being hurt by estate-owner agropolitics and shortchanged in state policy.[180] But there was little to indicate that the proposed coalition with export industry made significant headway, although some peasant groups like the Schleswig-Holstein Bauernverein adopted basic RDI planks[181] (like

175. With the exception of the Silverberg Bank proposal, the RDI Program bore an uncanny resemblance to the Agriculture Platform of the 1927 SPD Kiel Convention. The Silverberg Bank is discussed in chap. 4.

176. There is no reason to believe that the newspapers were any more objective in their reviews than he was, but they probably were influential locally. See BA/Z Sg Lauterbach 103/1969, 10 May 1930. The most favorable reviews came, of course, from the "democratic" press of Berlin and Frankfurt.

177. See Holt, pp. 123, 117.

178. See note 85. Also, BA/Z Sg Lauterbach 103/1998 indicates which parties and rural organizations thought what of each other.

179. Formally, the Bauernschaft was the publisher of *Agrarpolitik in Zahlen,* while the Wirtschaftsverband bäuerlicher Veredelung edited *Der Bauer in Kampf gegen den RLB* (Bremen, 1930). In fact, the RDI financed the former and the DIHT the latter.

180. Cf. the local reports to the Agriculture Ministry, especially from the west and Bavaria, BA/R43I/2545, pp. 247ff., and 2546, pp. 201–95.

181. Thus, Economics Minister Warmbold wondered in July 1930 why there was no substantial shift in peasant sentiment, ibid., 2546, pp. 3ff. The Schleswig-Holstein Bauernverein wrote Brüning in February 1932 attacking the forced use of surplus rye and potatoes as a feed and the unfair advantage this provided the easterners in dairy and

increasing urban consumption power), and the Bauernschaft as a whole left the Green Front in December 1930 in order to adopt the RDI position.[182] The chief flaw in the RDI program was that industry's attack on inefficient, grain-centered production and its leaders tended to become an attack on all of Landwirtschaft, thereby alienating precisely those peasants whom it was trying to win. Hence, industry's position—more precisely, the position of the dynamic fraction of industry—on feeds and tariffs was not (considered) part of an entirely new strategy and program, but was rather a simple concession for which much was being demanded in return. And, if it were to be simply a matter of concessions, then peasants might be better off bargaining with and through estate owners.

The counterattack was not long in coming. Organized agriculture sought to combat the RDI proposals along a broad front, but of particular interest here was the attempt to reassert the unity of Landwirtschaft by demonstrating to family peasants that there was no other, better way. One strategy of this counterattack was the reconsolidation of the Green Front and a massive offensive within the state on behalf of the protectionist demands of the peasantry. In order to pursue this second solution, the RDI contentions had to be disproven. To this end, a "corrective" pamphlet *(Agrarpolitik mit richtigen Zahlen)* was distributed widely, significantly not by the RLB itself but by the Catholic Peasant Leagues. Its basic thrust was that grain and peasant production could both be sound only if intertwined; they were an organic whole that could only prosper if protected and united. The dissidents were accused of "fighting with weapons stemming from the arsenal of agriculture's enemies."[183] Only a self-sufficient Germany could have a prosperous rural sector. Since urban consumption had not decreased substantially since 1928 and could not increase substantially, protecting what market existed was the only reasonable procedure for Landwirtschaft.[184] These remained the basic premises of the Green Front's ideological and political struggle.

Martin Schiele's replacement of Dietrich as agriculture minister in

---

livestock production. They called for duty-free feeds, noting that it cost them 8 Pf. to produce an egg while the Danes could produce superior eggs for only 3 Pf apiece and the world price hovered around 7 Pf. BA/R43I/2550, pp. 235–38.

182. The Bauernschaft statements are in BA/R43I/2545, pp. 20–29, Nov. 1930; also 2549, p. 368, and 2550, p. 43, 17 Jan. 1932.

183. Karl Wild, *Agrarpolitik mit richtigen Zahlen* (Berlin, 1932), published by the Catholic Vereinigung der deutschen christlichen Bauernvereine, p. 3. Because the Catholic association was less identified with estate owners than the RLB, it was a more effective publisher of this pamphlet than the RLB would have been.

184. Ibid., p. 19.

March 1930 was considered a general victory for agriculture. As a recent RLB president from the moderate, almost republican, wing of that group, his appointment by Brüning, at Hindenburg's and the ministerial bureaucracy's behest, was expected to elicit the support of the rural sector. Schiele was committed only to putting the state's resources at agriculture's disposal, a project fully in accord with the demands of the leaderships of the four principal agricultural pressure groups— united since February 1929 in the RLB-dominated Green Front. Indeed, together with Hermes of the Catholic Peasant Leagues, Brandes of the Landwirtschaftsrat and Fehr of the Bauernschaft, Schiele had founded that umbrella organization designed to reassert the unity of the rural sector.[185] The integration/dependence mechanism with its agrarian-corporatist *(berufsständliche)* ideology was once again at work: once the needs of estate owners were met, united agriculture would seek compatible assistance for the peasants. The only limit to this strategy proved to be the collision of the radicalism it engendered with the basic interests of export industry and organized labor. The constitutional and republican framework was not viable enough to manage that conflict.

The Green Front's offensive began with Hindenburg's "Easter Message" of 1930 and continued for over two years. Emergency and extraparliamentary legislation would lay the basis for rescuing domestic production: along with the Osthilfe and Siedlung, the virtual elimination of food imports through quota allotment *(Kontingentierung),* the abrogation of trade treaties, forced purchase and consumption of domestic surpluses, a moratorium on debt repayment, expanded credit, an end to the eight-hour day and Sozialpolitik, lowered taxes payable partially in kind, welfare payments in kind, a reduction in the profits of "middlemen," a concerted effort to end "tribute payments," and the toppling of the SPD government in Prussia were all part of the Green Front program.[186] Parts of the program were clearly designed in opposition to both partners in the labor-export alliance and the reparations-fulfillment policy of that alliance. Other portions of the program were, however, threats to the operation of market capitalism as a whole, and

185. On the founding of the Grüne Front, Topf, pp. 46–50, 114–15; also Dieter Gessner, "Industrie und Landwirtschaft," in Mommsen, et al., eds., p. 764, and *Agrarverbände.* The "liberal" Bauernschaft left the Green Front in November 1930 and became associated with RDI propaganda. On the question of how wholehearted Hermes may have been, Barmeyer, pp. 96–102; Klaus Müller, pp. 398ff., where it is argued that the impetus came from the rank and file, and Hermes was swept along.

186. Although the precise demands constantly changed, these were the central goals, enumerated emphatically and repeatedly. E.g., Koops, pp. 852–56; BA/R431/2545, pp. 58–62, 22 Nov. 1930; 2546, pp. 47–67, Jan. 1931; 2427, pp. 1–70; 2548, pp. 267–73, Sept. 1931; pp. 260ff., 15 Mar. 1932; BA/Nachlass Silverberg/362, pp. 194ff.

they caused bitter dissension within the cabinet, especially between the Agriculture Ministry, on the one hand, and the Economics and Labor Ministries, on the other.[187] As we have shown, state programs during the first years of the crisis benefited estate owners to the detriment of family peasants. (By 1931, there was, for example, no more "surplus" rye, whereas cattle raisers lost over two billion Marks that year.) Schiele acknowledged this in May 1931 while simultaneously issuing a call for unity. "Those measures taken by the government up to now . . . have benefited the estates. What is needed now is tariff assistance for peasant production." Saxons added that "All agriculture is grievously suffering, without regard to the number of hectares [one owns], or whether one is east or west of the Elbe. . . . The demand of the hour is not the dismantling of grain tariffs, but rather the extension of protection to other products."[188] As the RLB had before it, so now the Green Front was molding and expressing the interests of the peasants, with Schiele and his staff mediating those interests within the state apparatus.

In the months following, local peasant associations flooded Brüning and Schiele with desperate requests for help. Schiele and the Green Front had encouraged a rural radicalization which they then found increasingly difficult to direct. The coalition of interests behind Brüning could not meet all of agriculture's demands, while peasant support of the estate owners became increasingly contingent on having those very demands satisfied. Two typical examples of escalated peasant demands will suffice: In the summer and autumn of 1931, chambers of agriculture, Bauernvereine, local BVP and Zentrum officials, and others wrote to demand assistance: What had been done for grain was correct, commented the Bavarians, but now peasant production, especially dairy, needed help. The devaluation of Sterling had led all of Britain's suppliers to aim for them. Representatives of the Zentrum in Württemberg complained that over half a billion was still being spent on dairy

187. Schiele was regularly opposed by Labor Minister Stegerwald (Z), Finance Minister Moldenhauer (DVP), and Economics Minister Warmbold (DVP). Schiele and Stegerwald, in particular, attacked each other regularly; for example, February 1931, BA/R43I/2546, p. 305. Schiele enjoyed Hindenburg's special trust and frequently reported directly to him; BA/R43I/2543, p. 11. Stegerwald wrote Brüning, 31 Mar. 1931, asking "if Schiele can push through every one of his agitation-based demands against the rest of the Ministers . . . then I would request the Green Front appoint the Labor Minister and make wage and social policy." And this at a time of over 5 million unemployed. BA/R43I/2426, p. 317. Brüning was constantly making peace among his cabinet members, although he, too, finally lost patience with Schiele as it dawned on him that perhaps he was being blackmailed, see BA/R43I/1449, pp. 80ff., 31 Mar. 1931.

188. Statement of 9 May 1932, cited in BA/R43I/2547, pp. 166–67; Saxon peasants, 1 June 1931, p. 363.

imports; butter and cheese tariffs had to be raised immediately; no dairy and livestock products should be imported, and their domestic prices should be guaranteed; finally, no hard currency should be made available for imports.[189] In the 1930 elections, both the DNVP and DVP had lost a large part of their peasant support to splinter parties and the Nazis, and unless the immediate needs of the peasants were satisfied further erosion could be expected. So long as they could find no political interest to transcend their conflicting economic-corporate interests, the members of the Brüning bloc would continue to squabble over what concessions to make to whom. As the weaker partner among the dominant classes, Landwirtschaft stood to emerge on the short end, and the second solution to the conflicts within agriculture was, hence, less likely.[190] Already in February 1931, the RLB warned Brüning that if he did not "free himself from the export and Marxist interests whose prisoner he has become," he would bear responsibility for ruining the nation. Graf Kalckreuth, Schiele's successor as head of the RLB, accused Brüning of being "worse than Caprivi" and of having ignored Hindenburg's wishes while imagining that there was some way Germany could continue to pay reparations.[191] During the following year the missives grew increasingly strident. The radicalism of the Green Front was intended to win back and retain the peasants within the orbit of the rural elite including the DNVP. The RLB needed to demonstrate to the peasants that it shared and cared about their plight and that it could act effectively to ameliorate it. But this project exceeded the ability of the "traditional" organizations: the rural elite could save itself but not its clients, and its radicalism amounted to making promises it could not keep.

The leaders of organized agriculture understood that, in a republican form of government, they could not hope to overcome politically the economic dominance of industry. The rural elite might take advantage of conflicts between industry and labor and of its own peasant support to maximize state activity on its behalf, but the political mechanisms of

189. From the BVP and Bauernvereine, 8 July 1931, in BA/R43I/2427, pp. 49–60; from Württemberg, 7 July 1931, BA/R43I/2548, pp. 40–45, and 4 Dec. 1931, BA/R43I/2549, p. 231.

190. Brüning's compromises had to take export and consumer interests into consideration, and, therefore, always fell short of agriculture's demands. In a February 1931 interview with the Green Front and Schiele, he explained why this had to be so; they responded by citing the indivisibility of their demands; BA/R43I/2546, pp. 338–60.

191. ZSA/RLB Vorstand/146, p. 229. By October, Kalckreuth was accusing Brüning of really wanting to abandon the life-and-death interests of Landwirtschaft; BA/R43I/2427, p. 89. Opposition to Reparations and the Young Plan became increasingly salient to agricultural representatives.

the Republic, unlike those of the Empire, could not provide it with superiority or even equality. In the course of 1931 this understanding came to guide policy as Kalckreuth's tenure in the Green Front and RLB marked a move away from the middle and peasant parties and toward the National Opposition of Hugenberg's purged DNVP and the Nazis.[192] Already in December 1930, Schiele was warned by the RLB that, although *he* was considered a friend of Landwirtschaft, his cooperation with the SPD (Baade?) and DVP (former Finance Minister Moldenhauer) was ruining any chance he had to help agriculture.[193] By January 1932, Schiele, as well as Brüning, was being attacked for failing to carry out Hindenburg's intentions.[194] By May the RLB could write that Schiele too had disappointed Landwirtschaft completely: his approach had been inadequate; "new government modes and methods" would be necessary, and they would come at the expense of existing "tariff, commercial, wage, and social" policies and their supporters. It rejected Schiele's contention that the history of the coalitions of the twenties proved that gains were possible only through governmentalism, not through opposition from outside.[195] Instead, the RLB continued with the policies it had begun the past autumn when it joined the Nazis and the Stahlhelm in running joint lists in local chamber of agriculture elections and assisted Papen and others in efforts to overturn the Brüning government. Finally, in September 1932, the RLB wrote now-Chancellor Papen that the "salvation of the German nation and conversion from a world to a national economy allow for absolutely no more compromises," while "Stände, not parties," would lead "as a weapon in Germany's liberation struggle."[196]

With Papen, this strategy of working to change the system of government *(Systemwechsel)*, while keeping the peasantry within the estate-owner fold, and all the while radicalizing both economic and political demands, almost worked. Ascendant domestic-oriented heavy industry joined agriculture in support of Papen, and, for a moment, it appeared that the Sammlung bloc might be reestablished. The RLB and Green Front paid Papen the highest compliment any Weimar chancellor received from that quarter: he "thought national" and possessed the best

192. See Topf, pp. 131ff.; Puhle, *Agrarbewegungen,* pp. 91–92.

193. ZSA/RLB Schriftwechsel/18, p. 2.

194. ZSA/Büro des Reichspräsidenten, Ostprogramm und Agrarmassnahmen/214, p. 124, Kalckreuth to Hindenburg. Indeed, Hindenburg's support of the two was flagging; see the literature cited in notes 155, 164.

195. ZSA/Büro des Reichspräsidenten, Kabinettsbildungen und Verabschiedungen/47, pp. 10–17; see Stürmer. On the Chambers of Agriculture, ZSA/RLB Vorstand/145, p. 60.

196. ZSA/Büro des Reichspräsidenten, Allgemeine Landfragen/332, pp. 344–45.

intentions; further, the "political tone" of the presidential cabinet was the right one.[197] Not a single member of the Papen government was a deputy in Parliament. Pleased that Germany was now being ruled by a "strong man of strong will" and not by Parliament, the Catholic Bauernverein of Westphalia praised Papen's devotion to Fatherland and Christian Conservatism and his realization that the peasantry "is the ballast of the ship of state."[198] Such praise was warranted. In June 1932, Papen became the first chancellor to attend a Landwirtschaftsrat convention, at which he promised economic autarky, domestic social peace, and national reassertion, all in explicit terms.[199] And in the summer of 1932, Papen accomplished for both peasants and estate owners what Schiele had never been able to do: he unilaterally instituted quotas on imports of dairy and livestock products, banned auctioning of defaulted property nationally (not just in the east), granted a 40 percent land-tax remission, and promised to mandate both a 2 percent reduction of all accrued and present interest charges and a cancellation of the despised turnover (Umsatz) tax. Since almost all conservative and rightist forces had lined up behind Papen, this was all well and good—initially. To show industry its cooperative spirit, the Green Front added to its previous demands the following new ones: immediate further reductions in industrial wages, an end to cash welfare payments, an end to labor arbitration, encouragement of the entrepreneur, and a program for building capital.[200] But the Green Front's hope that the Papen program would win over all of industry for the benefit of all of agriculture was vain; the splits reemerged.[201]

The "second solution" of peasants and estate owners together in a reconstituted Sammlung bloc was not possible over the objections of industry. Even with heavy, domestic-oriented industry ascendant, trade and export requirements could not be jettisoned. Economics Minister Warmbold emphasized this repeatedly. Unilaterally imposed import quotas wold lead to a loss of essential markets, higher costs, and a

197. Von Sybel (Kalckreuth's lieutenant) to von Papen, 21 Oct. 1932, cited in BA/R43I/1275, p. 211.

198. Cited in BA/R43I, Kammern, Behörden und Verbände/1277, pp. 255, 258, 7 and 11 June 1932. One suspects that von Lüninck had a hand in this; see note 80.

199. Ibid., pp. 242–44, 312. Key phrases included "independent of foreign sources for food," "national struggle for liberation," "christian-national and social, not class and internationalist."

200. 17 May 1932, cited in BA/R43I/2550, p. 390.

201. O. Dsenis, "Der Faschismus und die Widersprüche im Lager der deutschen Bourgeoisie," Unter dem Banner des Marxismus 7 (1933):181ff. If one makes allowances for the polemical and tactical qualities of this piece, the analysis still stands up quite well.

slower recovery, the total demise of certain industries, the devastation of whole cities and severely impaired foreign relations. Dozens of industries, chambers of commerce, mayors and industrialists, the RDI, DIHT, and others wrote and telegrammed regularly to express their unwillingness to compromise on this issue.[202] Although Papen persevered and rallied his support, given the absence of a popular urban base for his "New State," it proved inadequate to overcome industrial opposition, and he fell. The election results of 1932 could offer him no succor. General Schleicher replaced him and pursued a program unacceptable to industry for entirely different reasons,[203] but anathema to Landwirtschaft, as we shall see. In the meantime, solution two had blended into solution three.

Not only the Green Front and RLB but peasant associations throughout Germany had thrown their support to the Harzburg Front, the Hitler-Hugenberg opposition. The Green Front dissolved, but whereas the estate owners could return to the DNVP, the peasantry went into isolated, radical opposition, which manifested itself as support for the Nazis.[204] One of the very few staunchly republican peasant representatives, Lübke, remarked that the Green front "made the most demagogic demands in [the peasants'] name while concealing their utter unfeasibility from the peasants . . . thereby discrediting the government in their eyes and making the republic appear hostile to agriculture. The increasingly rapid move to the extreme right and left by the peasants is the consequence of these policies."[205] Oddly, both the RLB and Lübke thus identified the Republic with the social and class forces that dominated it; they simply took opposing stands. The Green Front proved both the limit of what a unified agricultural sector could obtain from the Republic *and* that sector's bridge to the fascist system that would replace the Republic.

Their split with the estate owners impelled some peasants toward the center[206] but a much larger number toward the Nazis. For example, in

202. Warmbold's statements and a selection of communiques in BA/R43I/1275, pp. 301–35, 10, 11, 18 Nov. 1932; also ZSA/Büro des Reichspräsidenten/333, pp. 25–30.
203. On Papen's ouster and his subsequent activities, see the standard, Bracher, pp. 656–93. Bracher's chapters 7–11 remain the best blow-by-blow account of the developments of 1932.
204. On the extent of local and even Catholic support for the Nazis, Klaus Müller, pp. 402–405; Holt, p. 166; Gessner, *Agrarverbände*.
205. Lübke to Brüning, BA/R43I/1301, 5 Aug. 1931. On Lübke, see note 85. Gies, pp. 58ff., overestimates the opposition shown the RLB by other rural groups.
206. Chiefly the same Bauernschaft that had been won over by the RDI proposals of 1930. In February and March 1931, the Bauernschaft and Brüning had toyed with an

the course of the same month, the pig raisers of Lower Saxony, the livestock breeders of Schleswig-Holstein, and the national Fowl Breeders League all complained to the Agriculture Ministry that they and their needs were being sacrificed for the sake of the east, of the estate owners. In 1932, all three of these regions and groups voted heavily for the Nazis.[207] Estate owners and peasants may have separated and pursued their interests via different political routes during the last months of the Republic, but those core interests remained the same, and the two routes converged in support for the Nazis. Nazi electoral success in the countryside was a product of the party's ability to aggregate diverse groups in the manner of a Volkspartei. The party raised no demands regarding agricultural issues which differed from those of any other right-wing party or pressure group; it promised simply to be more effective.[208] Since their own proposals were so similar, the Nazis found it unnecessary to establish counterinstitutions, as was done in the cities and towns, and simply penetrated and captured the existing organizations with remarkable speed and success.[209] This "third solution" had more than one peculiar twist to it: on Christmas eve of 1931, Graf Kalckreuth, speaking as head of the RLB, remarked that "the rapid growth of the National Socialists is very gratifying. . . . Since we are the economic policy *(wirtschaftspolitische)* representatives of agriculture, they want to and should be represented in our leadership."[210] To formalize this, the RLB chose to reserve one of its four presidencies for a Nazi and elected Werner Willikens to the post. In the following year, the RLB turned against Hindenburg himself, and Kalckreuth often arranged Hitler-Hugenberg meetings under the slogan "German Agrarpolitik and German Nationalismus are like siamese twins."[211]

---

alliance, but the Fehr-Lübke group was too weak to be a worthwhile ally. BA/R43I/2546, pp. 121ff. and 2547, p. 23. A similar testing transpired with Schleicher; see note 223, below.

207. The complaints all arrived in December 1931; BA/R43I/2549, pp. 222, 228, 318, respectively. On voting in these areas in 1932, Lipset, pp. 140–48; Heberle, chap. 4; Charles Loomis and J. A. Beegle, "The Spread of German Nazism in Rural Areas," *American Sociological Review* 11 (1946):729; Milatz, maps 4, 6, 8, 12, 14.

208. The party's Agricultural Program is striking for its lack of novelty; see Franz, pp. 535–39; Gerschenkron, pp. 145ff.

209. An account of this is provided by Gies, pp. 61–74; Puhle, *Agrarbewegungen,* p. 322, note 272.

210. The events are recounted in ZSA/RLB Vorstand/145, pp. 1–18.

211. ZSA/RLB Vorstand/146, pp. 200–201, 7 Dec. 1932. Hans Beyer's contention, "Die Agrarkrise," pp. 85ff., that the Green Front was a solid alternative that should have been heeded is, like much of his work, a sheer apologetic.

Hugenberg sought to rally peasants to his Harzburg Alliance with Hitler. Reminding them that "politics, not economics, is fate," he sought to woo them away from the "purely economic and parliamentary Green Front," which could never cease compromising with socialists and Catholics.[212] While still chancellor, Papen himself agreed with Hugenberg that only he together with Hitler could "do a whole job" for Landwirtschaft. As he had previously linked the RLB to Papen, so in the last months Hugenberg linked them both to the Nazis.[213] The readiness of both estate owners and family peasants to support and vote for the Nazis was the final tribute to the ideology of "the unity of Landwirtschaft," which had been so successfully propagated by the estate owners for the preceding half-century.[214] However, since the estate owners could no longer deliver and control the peasant vote, i.e., their previous mass base, they became more dependent on the penetration of their core interests into the National-Socialist Weltanschauung. This proved to be both an initial transeconomic strength of the "third solution" and a long-run weakness after about 1936.[215]

It was not simply class interest that produced such substantial support for the Nazis in the countryside. Obviously, long-run interests do not operate reliably in short-run crisis conjunctures. But, aside from the fact that the Nazi program did elicit massive peasant support well before the 1932 electoral landslides, we must consider the consonance of ways out of a crisis with established and continuing interests. The estate owners had come to be too narrowly self-interested, and that component of hegemony, the representation of generalized interests, which had previously assured them of the support of the peasantry, was called into question. The Nazis entertained a clear advantage, even without offering a particularly different policy: their personnel were not tainted by governmental responsibility, political power, wealth or status. Their talk of autarky, domination of the east, and an end to both class conflict and the vicissitudes of capitalism had not already been discredited. Given their limited political wherewithal, the most econom-

---

212. BA/Nachlass Hugenberg/189, pp. 487, 131, 17 Feb. 1931. Hugenberg's inveterate opposition to the Zentrum and its opportunism rendered nearly impossible any cooperation between his rump DNVP and rightist forces within the Zentrum.

213. BA/Nachlass Hugenberg/38, pp. 166, 159, and vol. 191, p. 157.

214. Puhle, *Präfaschismus;* Gerschenkron, pp. 53–57, 145–53; and Gessner express the view developed here.

215. On this issue, see chap. 4, n. 6 and the literature discussed there. International goals were honored more than ruralist ideology.

ically vulnerable peasants expected the Nazis to solve the crisis of markets, production, and prices as the estate owners, in a particular way, had before them.[216] The patina of revolutionary ideology in the Nazi agricultural program was considerably thinner than in the urban program. Their peasant supporters did not consider the Nazis' program a novel departure; they simply expected more forceful and ruthless, less compromised and self-interested representation and guardianship of their interests.[217] Their toughness and völkisch élan provided the Nazis a drawing card that the estate owners, representatives of a traditional, quietistic authoritarianism, could appreciate but not emulate. The peasantry had been an ally of the imperial ruling bloc, but it was not successfully integrated into any stable Weimar coalition. It had little confidence to lose in the democratic system and an unaltered antagonism toward the organized working class. It was estranged from the leading fractions of industrial capitalism, but it had no vision of a fundamental change of the existing rural order beyond a return to more stable and profitable times.[218] Its interests were now aggregated and politicized by the Nazis.

The corporate representatives of agriculture contributed to the political crisis of the Republic at several crucial points: they consistently opposed the last parliamentary government under Müller and Stresemann; they precipitated the fall of the last "constitutional" government under Brüning, once that government's exertions on organized agriculture's behalf proved to have some limits; and they provided the Nazi Party with crucial electoral support while jockeying within the "inner circles" of the state, and especially the executive, apparatus for Hitler's appointment as chancellor.[219] This latter accelerated as it became clear that the government of General Schleicher was backing away from Papen's previous commitments to the Green Front and was moving toward a Keynesian program of cooperation with the trade

216. Beyer, p. 64; Loomis and Beegle; and Heberle, pp. 64, 100–111, all make much of the peasants' wish to be protected against the uncertainties of the market and class society. See also Gessner, *Agrarverbändtde*, pp. 245ff.

217. Or, what Marx in the *18th Brumaire* identified as "the Emperor."

218. See Arthur Schweitzer, "The Nazification of the Lower Middle Class and Peasants," in *The Third Reich* (London, 1955) esp. p. 594.

219. The last point has been the subject of much discussion. The most fact-filled discussion remains Bracher. See also Gerhard Schulz, *Aufstieg des Nationalsozialismus* (Frankfurt, 1975); Eberhard Czichon, *Wer verhalf Hitler zur Macht?* (Cologne, 1967); Carsten, *Reichswehr and Politics*, pp. 390–97; opposed, Henry A. Turner, "Das Verhältnis des Grossunternehmertums zur NSDAP," in Mommsen, et al., eds., pp. 919ff. At issue here are *not* theories of fascism, rather questions on the order of who talked to whom when and what happened afterwards.

unions and "left" wing of the NSDAP, and perhaps even toward a restoration of party government. Schleicher let it be known that he would reactivate the Siedlung program and pay greater attention to the needs of the peasants of the south and west.[220] He had expected the Green Front to support a presidential-military government and was angered by the failure of that support to materialize.[221] He rejected the Green Front's call for an indefinite moratorium on debt collection and reversed Papen's import quotas. Together with Warmbold and his minister for "Work Creation," Gunther Gereke, he moved back toward export industry and expanded contacts with the trade unions.[222] Simultaneously, he sought alternate rural support, both among estate owners and peasants: in the former area through an appeal to black sheep within the RLB (without success), and in the latter by cultivating and mobilizing the shrinking but friendly Bauernschaft (without much effect).[223] Leaders of the RDI and DIHT supported Schleicher's new turn arguing that "import quotas would make economic recovery impossible; the economy needs quiet and stability."[224]

The Schleicher government, whether viewed as a potential military dictatorship or a potential Bonapartist regime, could not muster the support necessary either to build a coalition or to rule without one. To the right, the General appeared unwilling or unable to remove the threat of a recovery on the part of the left and the unions.[225] Hugenberg accepted this concern in the type of prose that characterized his press empire: "Schleicher is wooing and messing around *(Buhlen)* with the rotten Red masses. . . . His cabinet only appears presidential; in truth

220. For example, in the butter versus margarine question. Cf. Puhle, *Agrarbewegungen*, p. 322, note 273; Beyer, pp. 65–66.

221. BA/Nachlass Schleicher/42, p. 29; Thilo Vogelsang, *Reichswehr, Staat und NSDAP* (Stuttgart, 1962), p. 414.

222. In early January 1933, Schleicher said that the Green Front's demands would "destroy the economy"; BA/R43II/192, pp. 46, 16–19, Schiele to Schleicher, 5 Jan. 1933; also Czichon, pp. 34–47.

223. Schleicher's letter to von Flemming of 12 Jan. 1933 was an attempt to call in some old debts from among the rural elite, BA/R43II/192, p. 2. The Bauernschaft wrote Schleicher on 14 Jan. 1933 agreeing that the situation of the peasants had been worsened by the RLB and calling for an end to latifundist-oriented policy; ibid., p. 66. They further wrote Hindenburg on 27 Jan. 1933 telling him that Schleicher was good for the peasants.

224. ZSA/Büro des Reichspräsidenten/333, p. 34.

225. Presumably, this was the meaning of the constant references by the RLB and others to Communist electoral gains in late 1932 and to allegedly continuous and increasingly successful Communist agitation and organization, not only in the cities but in the countryside as well. See ZSA/Büro des Reichspräsidenten/47, pp. 552–53; BA/R43II/192, p. 38.

he is making himself dependent on parties."[226] Party government would, in all likelihood, portend the reconstitution of a coalition hostile or indifferent to organized Landwirtschaft's demands. With Schleicher himself inadequately devoted to those demands, a showdown between the RLB and the general was unavoidable. Such a meeting took place on 11 January 1933 with the RLB charging that Schleicher's policies marked a return to that export orientation which held no hope for agriculture; only a moratorium on foreclosures and a near-ban on agricultural imports would do. "The impoverishment of Landwirtschaft has with the connivance of the current government reached an extent which even under a purely Marxist government would hardly have been considered conceivable. . . . [We are experiencing] a plundering of agriculture for the benefit of the moneybag interests of internationalist export industry."[227] After this statement, Schleicher broke off all further dealings with the RLB, to which its leadership responded by demanding "the immediate replacement of the government by men finally willing to use a strong hand and follow a National Economic course."[228] Such a move, in the form of the appointment of the Hitler-Papen-Hugenberg government, was to follow in a matter of a few days.

The conflicts, both latent and deflected, historical and conjunctural, between family peasants and estate owners were activated after the onset of the agricultural and political crisis in 1928 and contributed to the demise of the Weimar Republic. A conflict that might have been resolved to the advantage of democratic forces—or at least one that democratic forces had consistently assumed would be resolved to their advantage—took an entirely different course. Separated from their structured dependency on the estate owners, various groups and types of peasants were unable to form alternate coalitions that could have represented their interests within the Republic. Thus, the failure of the moderate agrarians and dynamic industrialists behind Brüning made unlikely any splitting of the agricultural sector, and no effective linkage between the dairy-livestock peasants and the dynamic fraction of industry was established. The short-lived Schleicher government attempted once again to split the peasantry from the estate owners but could not succeed. Deprived of the mass base that had provided their claims popular legitimacy, the estate owners encountered increased resistance

226. BA/Nachlass Hugenberg/37, p. 72, Kleist to Hugenberg, 17 Dec. 1932. On the "social" dangers posed by a Schleicher regime, see below, pp. 163–66, 210–12, 268–70.

227. An account of the meeting is in ZSA/RLB Vorstand/146, p. 229; also, ZSA/Büro des Reichspräsidenten/333, p. 117.

228. The RLB demand was made to an ambivalent Hindenburg, ZSA/Büro des Reichspräsidenten/333, p. 163. He decreed a moratorium on foreclosures a few days later, 17 Jan. 1933.

to their own demands. The opposition of nonagricultural sectors of the population, especially export industry, rendered impossible the policy preconditions for reconsolidating all of Landwirtschaft. The defeat of Papen's autarky program blocked this path while impelling a portion of the peasantry toward the Nazis. Opposing the entire Republic, the Nazi Party was able to build a coalition which included large numbers of both estate owners and peasants and which embodied, or seemed to, the core interests of both. Although its program was not significantly novel, the NSDAP bore none of the accumulated stigmata of the estate owners and appeared willing to "do a whole job" for agriculture. Peasants voted disproportionately for the Nazis, and leading estate owners took part in the elevation of Hitler to the chancellorship. The agricultural sector believed it would thus be saved from abandonment.

Chapter Three

CONFLICTS WITHIN
THE INDUSTRIAL SECTOR

In this chapter we examine the conflicts within the industrial sector and the contribution of those conflicts to the crisis and its resolution. Conflicts existed between branches or fractions of industry and among organized and de facto groups of industrialists. The content of these conflicts was both economic and political, structural and contingent, and any analysis of them must, therefore, be both structural and narrative; it must analyze how different sectors of industry produced, and explain how different industrialists acted. How the industrial sector developed priorities, and how industrialists did and did not organize themselves to affect the outcome of the political crisis after 1928, cannot be fully understood on the basis of developments within industry alone. Examining industry's relationship to agriculture and to the organized working class, particularly after the onset of the Depression, is essential to understanding the changing balance of forces within industry.[1] Nevertheless, the state's inability to organize the interests of the dominant classes and present a consistent economic program was due, in large part, to structural conflicts within the industrial sector itself. Different fractions of industry entertained different coalitional preferences and affinities based on the nature of their own production, capital composition, and international standing. As we have already noted, the dynamic and export branches of industry, in a period of economic recovery and expansion, preferred coalitions with organized labor and salaried employees, whereas the older, heavy and domestic-oriented branches of industry preferred conservative coalitions with the rural sector. Yet, it would be mistaken to infer from the conflicts we are about to discuss a total bifurcation of the industrial sector. Alongside the problem of organizing the interests of the dominant social classes,

---

1. For this reason, the bulk of the discussion of industry's political contribution to the final resolution of the crisis, especially during the critical year 1932, is reserved for chapter 6. The discussion here will stress the structural aspects of the conflict within industry and the events primarily prior to late 1932.

there remained a second problem that never disappeared: incorporating/molding/repressing the interests of the subordinate classes.[2] Accomplishing the latter could easily inflame tensions within the bloc of dominant classes and lead to parliamentary and social coalitions with subordinate classes that would benefit one fraction of industry at the expense of the other. Many industrialists were willing to attempt an incorporation of the organized working class—so long as they could afford it. The increased costliness of working-class demands, economic and political, set limits to the fratricidal potential of Weimar industrialists. Although they could not agree on a program for incorporating the interests of one or more of the subordinate classes, industrialists could agree, especially after 1930 or 1931, on a program for repressing those interests. Even the latter type of program, however, reflected the conflicts within the industrial sector. Some of those conflicts dated back at least to the Empire and remained salient down to the very moment of Hitler's elevation to the chancellorship.

The split within industry had been institutionalized no later than 1895 when, after years of both internecine tension and national economic expansion, the Central League of German Industrialists (ZDI) split into two sometimes hostile organizations. Next to these two, there existed a host of both independent and tributary regional, specialty, and commercial groups. Before the war, these organizations supported a range of social programs and political parties, but with the defeat of German imperialism (which they had nearly all supported) and the attendant social and political upheavals (which they had nearly all opposed), they were constrained to seek greater organizational and political unity. Achieving that unity was rendered more difficult by both the new parliamentary-republican system and a series of structural changes in the economy accelerated by the inflation and Germany's dependence on massive influxes of foreign capital. Continued concentration of industrial holdings and "self-organization," both vertical and horizontal, accompanied an economic recovery which was noteworthy for its sectoral unevenness. Republican stability was facilitated by seeming prosperity and a chastened but still strong organized working class. By 1925 or 1926 much of industry was prepared to reach a modus vivendi with the working class and make its peace with the Republic. At first, this policy was articulated by the dynamic (mostly export) branches of industry and was institutionalized by an all-bourgeois government, but the fullest manifestation of this path was the short-lived Grand Coalition formed after the SPD's electoral victory in 1928.[3]

2. Gramsci, especially pp. 161, 181–82. There is a third problem as well: successfully presenting the interests of the dominant classes as the interests of all of the nation.

3. See chap. 1, secs. 2 and 3; chap. 6, sec. 2.

Even before the onset of the general economic crisis, industrial organizations and their constituents split over support (or toleration) of the Grand Coalition, its various policies and personalities. The lines of cleavage on this issue and the changing balance of forces between the two camps mirrored only imperfectly the internal structures and production desiderata of the several branches of industry. Although the dynamic, capital-intensive, and export industries and their organizations tended, until about 1930 or 1931, to be ascendant over the older, sometimes stagnant, more labor-intensive and domestic-market oriented industries, no unequivocal dominance was established by either. A range of interindustrial agreements, both political and economic, preserved a tenuous equilibrium and prevented a more substantial break between fractions of industry. Chief among these agreements was an export-rebate scheme, which both rewarded and disciplined small producers and many exporters while securing the policy-making role of the older, heavy industries. Nevertheless, had the international economic crisis and the consequent offensive against the previous gains of the working class not "intervened,"[4] the dominant forces within industry might have continued supporting cooperation with the working class and policies like those pursued by the Grand Coalition.

Conflicts within the industrial sector revolved around a number of cleavages that came to assume greater significance after 1925, when Germany regained its trade freedom and foreign capital began to flow. These two factors, together with the international standing of various branches of industry, international production and marketing agreements, the organic composition of capital in various industries, and their respective profitability outlooks, all determined the subjects and locations of conflict within industry. In turn, the ebb and flow of conflicts within industry determined the fortunes and policy-making roles of the various corporate-interest organizations. In addition to conflicts over explicit policy toward the working class and toward the rural sector (both within and outside the framework of the state), other, more internal, issues reflected both the agenda-setting preeminence of the dynamic "liberal" fraction between 1925 and 1930 and the resurgence of the older "national" fraction after 1930. Trade-treaty policy, particularly regarding the touchstone issue of Poland, and approaches to the revision of reparations obligations were especially illustrative issues that generated sharp tensions.

4. Obviously, the crisis and the capitalist offensive were linked, though *either one* might have been possible without the other. Neither was a chance affair; in fact, industry's offensive against organized labor was an element in the evolution of relations between fractions of industry, an element in the *formation* of the capitalist class itself. Here we try to isolate the secular tendencies within industry.

The acceptance of the Young Plan for reparations revision was not only the last significant act for which the Grand Coalition was able to muster a majority, but it was, perhaps, the last significant victory of the "liberal" fraction of industry. Industrialists were crucial in bringing down the Grand Coalition, and they called upon "their" parties and representatives to cease collaborating with labor and to support a strong "economy-friendly" *(wirtschaftsfreundlich)* government instead: the labor-export alliance was finished. From mid-1930 to about mid-1931, both the liberal and national fractions supported Brüning in the expectation that his semiconstitutional, presidial government would be "economy-friendly." But he could build no mass base to support a program which met the needs of both fractions of industry, and he was, therefore, increasingly abandoned by the national fraction. Concomitantly, a series of developments enabled this fraction to reassert itself politically, even though it could not regain its economic leadership. Somewhat ironically, the economically more depressed and paralyzed fraction appeared to enjoy a greater political viability and wherewithal.[5] The liberal fraction's desire to save Brüning's government was inadequate to overcome the national fraction's determination to militate for a regime more wholeheartedly prepared to "restore profitability." From mid-1932 until the end of January 1933, the two fractions more or less checked each other. First, von Papen tried, in conjunction with agriculture, to implement a program attuned one-sidedly to the interests of the national fraction, and then General Schleicher, possibly in conjunction with some segments of labor, toyed with a program attuned one-sidedly to the interests of the liberal fraction. Industrialists from both fractions finally concluded—some gleefully, some hesitantly, and some resignedly—that a National Socialist regime would be that viable alternative which would restore both profitability and political stability while dividing them least.

1. From Prewar Conflict to Post-Inflation Equilibrium

a. *Cartellization and Fractionalization*

Concentration and cartellization had been a tendency in German heavy industry from nearly its very beginnings.[6] The intention of the various

---

5. This paradox dissolves somewhat, but not entirely, when the rural and antilabor components of the capitalist offensive are added back into the equation along with the Mittelstand Rebellion.

6. The active role of the state and the general hostility to "Manchesterian economics" date back to the beginning of industrialization in Prussia. See the literature cited in chap. 1, note 27. On the differential stigmata of early versus late industrialization, Alexander

cartels was to reduce risk, counter or at least dampen both cyclical tendencies and social conflict, and facilitate planning and expansion. This tendency accelerated greatly after the economic crisis of 1873, Germany's turn to protectionism in 1879, and the rapid growth of the Social Democratic and labor movements. The first major cartels were formed among the producers of coke, pig iron, and steel sheeting, but perhaps the most thorough was the Potash Syndicate formed in 1881 and designed to facilitate the monopolistic exploitation of a raw material over which Germany, at the time, enjoyed a virtual monopoly. After the turn of the century, the intervention-ready state even enforced numerous cartels. German industries were not loath to enter international production and marketing cartels, the first of which was the International Rail Makers Association founded in 1883 by the German, British, Belgian, and French manufacturers. Economically more important was the Rhenish-Westphalian Coal Syndicate, which embraced 90 percent of Ruhr coal production. By 1904, iron and steel producers nationwide united in the Steel Work Association.[7] And these production units were large: by 1895, for example, the average coal-mining concern already employed over eight hundred men.[8] By the turn of the century, the new electrical, chemical, and machine industries had joined and surpassed the older industries in "self-organization." Thus, by 1905, Siemens and A.E.G. controlled almost the entire electrical industry. Such self-organization ranged from complete, centralized determination of raw-materials appropriation, production quotas, and marketing allotments to looser groups that "merely" fixed production quotas or distributed market shares or fixed prices. The shape of what was to become the monopoly sector of German industry changed early and quickly. Between 1873 and 1894, for example, the number of mines in the greater Ruhr dropped from 268 to 164, while total production rose from 11.8 to 35.5 million tons and the number of workers grew from 51,400 to 128,000. In that same period, the number of establishments grew by only 13 percent, but the number of employees grew by 56 percent.[9] Very quickly there grew up a whole category of salaried employees *(Angestellten)* whose emergence rapidly and drastically altered the composition and political behavior of both the Mittelstand and the working class. Between 1882 and 1895, the number of plants em-

Gerschenkron, *Economic Backwardness in Historical Perspective* (Cambridge, Mass., 1962), pp. 5–30.

7. On the above, Gustav Stolper, *German Economy, 1870–1940* (New York, 1940), pp. 85–86.

8. Clapham, p. 282. By 1913, net exports had more than doubled.

9. The figures are cited by H.-U. Wehler, "Der Aufstieg des Organisierten Kapitalismus und Interventionsstaates in Deutschland," in *Organisierter Kapitalismus,* ed. Winkler, p. 40.

ploying over 1,000 people doubled from 127 to 255, with 500,000 adults employed in such units. The pattern was similar even in the skilled machine-building trade, of which J. H. Clapham wrote, "In 1882 a few large businesses stood out here and there among a thick undergrowth of small ones. In 1907 the ground was well covered with large businesses and the undergrowth was completely overshadowed, though not killed."[10]

Technological and scientific capabilities and the ability to finance them became more important, especially in the newer capital-intensive branches. The change in the organic composition of capital, with the increased role of fixed capital, was striking from its outset.[11] The role of the major banks and finance institutions grew apace.[12] As the proportion of fixed capital grew, production factors became more rigid and industries less flexible in the face of the business cycle. On the other hand, technological innovation was thereby facilitated, and the institutionalization of research in the laboratories of numerous large industries proved a spur to the entire economy.[13] Thus, next to the organization of the market (through cartels and finance) to relieve the pressure of competition faced by individual capitalists, there began the institutionalization of technological progress (research and development, investment outlets) to countervail the crises faced by the economy as a whole. The role of the state was to grow, slowly and by leaps, as it increasingly attempted to relieve the pressure of social, political, and economic tensions.[14] The growth of a steadily more "organized" capitalism was marked by a number of developments discussed earlier.[15]

Among those developments was the founding of variously organized

10. Clapham, p. 288.

11. Marx in volume 2 of *Capital* and John Stuart Mill in the *Principles of Political Economy* both discussed this change while it was still in its beginnings.

12. One need only recall the rapidity with which steel production changed (Bessemer, Siemens-Martin, and Thomas-Gilchrist processes) to realize how quickly a producer could have his facility turned obsolete if he had inadequate investment funds. On the role of the banks, Rainer Fremdling and Richard Tilly, "German Banks, German Growth and Econometric History," *Journal of Economic History* 36 (1976): 416–24. Banks and science overlapped nicely in the case of Siemens; see Jürgen Kocka, *Unternehmensverwaltung und Angestelltenschaft am Beispiel Siemens 1847–1914* (Stuttgart, 1969). The Siemens enterprise and the Deutsche Bank were intimately related.

13. Carl Duisberg, later the head of IG Farben and the RDI, began as a chemist, and the Siemens house too was renowned for its laboratories. It was between the 1870s and 1900 that theories of "scientific management" were developed. Marx already had some idea of this double effect of fixed capital and science; see his *Grundrisse der Kritik der Politischen Ökonomie* (Berlin, 1943), p. 592.

14. These three stages in the historical development of capitalism, especially the last, remain current; see Offe, *Strukturprobleme*, pp. 21–25.

15. See pp. 3–7 on amorphous organized capitalism.

industrial-interest groups. Between 1872 and 1876, three of the most powerful of these were formed.[16] Their influence over state policy formation was great from the outset; they played a central role in Germany's switch to protectionism in 1879. Their leaders were drawn from the major industries and cartels, and their influence in the political parties and state apparatus altered the political decision-making process permanently.[17] The Wilhelmine state mediated industry's relationship with the rural elite, overseeing numerous compromises and conflicts between the two sectors, the one rising and the one declining. Imperialism was one form of state action undertaken primarily for the benefit of industry; it was a form of both trade-treaty negotiation and Sozialpolitik. (In regard to the latter, it might, together with the social insurance and the antisocialist laws of the eighties, increase mass loyalty. It was a clear instance of incorporation and repression; consent, fraud, and force operating together.) All of these economic and political phenomena may be immanent to the development of capitalism, but in Germany they served to strengthen an authoritarian and partially precapitalist regime that had never been faced with a bourgeois revolution. H.-U. Wehler contends that, in the German case, these various developments led to a reduction in the number of individuals and social groups who exercised power and participated substantially in decision making. In any case, a small group of prominent heads of large industries did become cartel officers, pressure-group leaders, advisors to the ministries, and government officials.[18]

In this economy increasingly dominated by the economic and political presence of organized heavy industry, there remained a very substantial sector composed of small firms engaged mostly in the light industries.[19] Although the sheer number of such firms and the value of

16. In 1872 the Association for the Furtherance of the Joint Economic Interests of the Rhineland and Westphalia (or the Long Name Association—*Langnamverein*—for short); in 1874 the Association of German Iron and Steel Industrialists (VDESI); in 1876 the Central League of German Industrialists (ZDI). In 1895 dissidents from the ZDI formed the League of Industrialists (BdI); it represented primarily the export-oriented light and processing industries, although it was led by representatives of the burgeoning chemical industry. More on this alliance, below. The progressive and free-trading Congress of German Commerce (DHT) was organized in 1861, but, significantly, it did not become the Congress of German Industry and Commerce (DIHT) until 1919.

17. Cf. Kaelble, *Industrielle Interessenpolitik.*

18. Wehler, "Aufstieg," p. 20; Knight.

19. R. T. Averitt, *The Dual Economy* (New York, 1968), presents a schema in which the "central" economy consists of the large producers and the "peripheral" economy of the small firms. This is not the same as O'Connor's distinction (*Fiscal Crisis*, pp. 13–23) between the monopoly and the competitive sectors. Even before the war, substantial penetration between small and large, competitive and monopoly industries had taken place in Germany.

their production is not to be underestimated, either before or after the war, their continued importance was due also to their ability to find allies within the heavy or monopoly sector. The small, craft industries, particularly those of the south and southwest, found new allies in the machine industry and in the giant electrical and chemical industries of Berlin and parts of the Rhineland. This amalgam of some of the oldest craft industries with the most dynamic of the new branches was based on their shared antiprotectionist, export orientation in opposition to much of heavy industry and most of agriculture. Further, the wage demands of labor were secondary for both groups. Many of the light industries employed only a few, very skilled hands—frequently unorganized—whose demands could not be successfully resisted in any event. For the technologically most advanced industries, the importance of variable capital had declined; labor played a lesser role in the creation of what industrialists called "added value."[20] Paralleling this was a distinctly lesser hostility toward social democracy, which even allowed for occasional cooperation, as in the successful antiprotectionist alliance of 1890 and the unsuccessful one of 1902.[21] Many of the small processing, finishing, and consumer-goods industries were hurt by the price-fixing and quota-allotment programs of their heavy-industrial suppliers. Their voices were increasingly stilled and overwhelmed within the Central League of German Industrialists (ZDI) as that organ came to reflect the views of the largest monopolies and cartels.[22]

The dissatisfactions of the oldest small producers and of the most dynamic, newest industries began to coalesce after the official turn to protectionism in 1879. The result was secession, and in 1895 this somewhat odd combination of dissidents formed the Union of Industrialists (BdI). The membership was composed primarily of representatives from the small processing and finishing industries, but much of the leadership emerged from the dynamic and equally export-oriented chemical, electrical, and machine-building industries.[23] The most prom-

20. Even in the prewar period, before the formation of the IG Farben combine, Duisberg became known as the "Welfare Professor" because of his insistence that employers were best off training and paying their employees well and involving them in the operations of the plant. See the testimonial by Hans-Joachim Flechtner, *Carl Duisberg* (Düsseldorf, 1959), pp. 233–43.

21. In the elections of 1890, an SPD-Progressive coalition defeated the Conservative/ National Liberal alliance of agrarians and heavy industry. This victory was reversed in 1902 but made good again in 1912. Cf. Schorske, pp. 225–26; Arthur Rosenberg, *Imperial Germany*, pp. 40ff., 56ff. In some areas, like Baden, the coalition was not just electoral but almost permanent.

22. See Helga Nussbaum, *Unternehmer gegen Monopole* (Berlin, 1966), pp. 36ff.

23. Details on the formation and composition of the BdI and its relationship to the ZDI are in Stegmann, *Die Erben Bismarcks*, pp. 176ff., 236ff., 328ff. Four years earlier, the

inent leader of the BdI was the same Gustav Stresemann who was to play so significant a role in the politics of export-industry/working-class collaboration during the Weimar Republic. The BdI stood for an aggressive and expansive export policy oriented particularly, though not exclusively, to the more developed markets of northern and western Europe and North America. (This was particularly true of the processing and finishing industries, whose high-quality, high-cost products were saleable only in more developed markets.) It rejected the protectionism propounded by conservative agrarian circles, and it considered the ZDI's program for repressing social democracy a fetter on the expansion of the economy. Along with groups like the Hansa Bund, the BdI was involved in a persistent yet primarily defensive struggle to countervail the agrarian/heavy-industry alliance and thereby open the political and economic arenas.[24]

In a sense, this dynamic, free-trading, and export-oriented fraction of industry proved more imperialist than the bulk of conservative agrarians, albeit imperialist with a social component intended to augment the legitimacy of the social order. This became apparent in the turn-of-the-century conflicts over construction of a fleet. Liberals like Max Weber and Friedrich Naumann spoke for this fraction when they hoped to link imperialism to political and social democratization.[25] This pro-

---

chemical industry had led the dissidents in the formation of an Association for Trade Treaties. A more recent and complete work on the BdI is Hans-Peter Ullmann, *Der Bund der Industriellen* (Göttingen, 1976). On the relationship between the two partners in the BdI and for a sympathetic portrayal of their progressive struggle on behalf of modernization and against the political and economic dominance of heavy industry, see Hartmut Pogge von Strandmann, "Widersprüche im Modernisierungsprozess Deutschlands: Der Kampf der verarbeitenden Industrie gegen die Schwerindustrie," in Stegmann, et al., eds., *Industrielle Gesellschaft und politisches System* (Bonn, 1978), pp. 225–40. A changing constellation of forces, the war, and Rathenau's murder marked the defeat of the progressives. We contend here that this defeat was temporary and that the progressives were resurgent in the mid-twenties. Pogge is correct in according a central role to the electrical industry.

24. On the evolution of policy within the BdI and related trade and commercial organizations, see Fricke, ed., 1:117–26. On the Hansa Bund, Siegfried Mielke, *Der Hansa Bund, 1909–1914* (Göttingen, 1976). Mielke's critique of Stegmann's view of the post-Bismarckian Sammlung, pp. 83–90, 166–180, is not entirely convincing. There were differences within heavy industry, but they did not become significant politically.

25. Naumann demanded a democratic basis in domestic affairs and an imperialistic basis in foreign policy. For Weber, Germany's economic development demanded imperialist expansion. The "political education of the nation" could not proceed, according to Weber, because of the nature of the German regime: "half caesaristic, half 'patriarchal,' and in addition recently distorted by a philistine fear of the red spectre!" All this is incisively presented by Kehr, pp. 460, 454. For more on Weber's path to social imperialism, see Gerth and Mills, eds., pp. 32–44. On social imperialism in Germany, Geoff

gram did not, however, become the platform of the whole of German industry because, as usual, the mildest threat from the left drove it to the right.[26] After a brief flirtation in 1905, the ZDI rejected merger with the BdI and in 1913 rejoined the agrarians in the "Cartel of the Productive Strata" (the Sammlung bloc). This, in turn, rendered industry's pursuit of imperialism more difficult.[27] It was compelled to incorporate the demands of a backward rural elite into a program that could not enjoy the support of a working class which was imperfectly integrated at best. The two fractions of industry could only hope to submerge their differences in a maximalist program acceptable to both.

b. *Aftermath of the Revolution and Inflation*

With the defeat of German imperialism and the outbreak of social revolution, the differences between the two fractions of industry suddenly appeared insignificant indeed. Temporarily, at least, the ZDI and BdI were able to overcome their differences; they joined in February 1919 to form the League of German Industry (RDI). In part because of the fear of socialization, the leadership of that new body was intentionally centralized in a sixteen-man presidium dominated by heavy industry. The first chairman of the executive was a Krupp director, Kurt Sorge, who, along with most of his colleagues, made no pretense to republicanism. In order to maximize its political influence, the RDI chose to organize on both a trade and regional basis. Representation was weighted in favor of the largest producers, with one thousand trades organizations subdivided into twenty-seven trades groups. A minority of republicans from the chemical, electrical, and machine industries was virtually shut out of office.[28] Stresemann's defeat clearly indicated that their day had not yet come. From the point of view of industry, internal reconstruction and "reconsolidation" were the order

---

Eley, "Social Imperialism in Germany": Reformist Synthesis or Reactionary Sleight of Hand?", in Joachim Radkau, ed., *Imperialismus im 20. Jahrhundert* (Munich, 1976), pp. 71–86.

26. This is the gist of much of Engels's historical work on Germany after 1848, and, in a different sense, it was the fate of the "idea of freedom" in Germany so long as that idea was carried by the bourgeoisie.

27. On the continuity of the linkage between liberal free trade and imperialism, see in addition to the literature cited above, Joachim Radkau, "Renovation des Imperialismus im Zeichen der 'Rationalisierung,'" in Radkau, ed., pp. 197–264; and Dirk Stegmann, "'Mitteleuropa' 1925–1934: Zum Problem der Kontinuität deutscher Aussenhandelspolitik," in Stegmann, et al., eds., pp. 203–21.

28. On the balance of forces at this early stage, Friedrich Zunkel, "Die Gewichtung der Industriegruppen bei der Etablierung des RDI," in Mommsen, et al., eds., pp. 637–47; also Ullmann, pp. 240ff.

of the day; interclass cooperation and market expansion would have to await a more auspicious time when socialization and socialists were no longer a threat. Although the socialization committees for heavy industry and the anticartel laws of 1919–23 proved to be dead letters almost from the outset,[29] the fear of social revolution and the support of counterrevolution preoccupied the industrial leadership at least through 1923. The course of interindustrial relations was affected by the inflation, the Ruhr struggles, and the terms of the Versailles treaty, as well as by the fear of both social democratic structural changes in the economy and communist insurrection.

But there were several ways to defeat the working class and/or bring it into a constructive relationship to a recaptured state and national economy.[30] (The number of actual supporters of the Kapp Putsch, for example, was quite small.)[31] One of those ways was for industry to lessen its direct presence in the political parties while supporting those whose programs were both acceptable and competitive. Thus, the Siemens group and several textile concerns financed the DDP, hoping it would become a bourgeois concentration that could sap the SPD's strength. Other industrialists and bankers supported the DVP for the same reasons.[32] In 1919 the RDI recognized the unions, their exclusive bargaining rights, the eight-hour day, and the permanence of the Joint Working Committees (Arbeitsgemeinschaften) and factory committees. Although industry was soon to use reparations payments, the Ruhr crisis and the inflation to roll back these concessions, their immediate effect was to neutralize the unions and increase the republican legitimacy of organized industry. In effect, the industrialists had tacitly recognized the Constitution's most social provisions. With the forma-

29. See Gerald Feldman, "Wirtschafts- und sozialpolitische Probleme der Demobilmachung," in Mommsen, et als., eds., pp. 618–36; Stolper, pp. 200–203.

30. We cannot dwell here on either the Social Democratic or Communist failures of 1919–24 or on the successful bourgeois offensive (electoral and institutional) and its limits. Arthur Rosenberg's *Geschichte,* pp. 35–221, remains the best single discussion of the years 1919–23. For a discussion of some of the voluminous German research of the past decade, see the papers of the Second International Colloquium of the Inter-University Centre for European Studies, Charles Bertrand, ed. *Revolutionary Situations in Europe, 1917–1922* (Montreal, 1977). Also, F. L. Carsten, *Revolution in Central Europe* (Berkeley and Los Angeles, 1972).

31. It is illustrative of the splits within industry—and an indication of things to come—that while Albert Vögler, Hugo Stinnes, Emil Kirdorf, and some others in the steel industry indulged Kapp, the chemical industry supported the general strike against the Putsch and chose to pay workers for the strike days. See Gerald Feldman, "Big Business and the Kapp Putsch," *Central European History* 4(1971): 99–130. The former group treated putschists and government with parity.

32. Albertin, "Faktoren," pp. 661–62.

tion of bourgeois cabinets after 1920, industrialists even offered the Republic their expertise through ministerial service. (On the other hand, the so-called Stinnes group continued to call for active opposition to the Republic.) Industry was so successful in recapturing the initiative that in 1923 Robert Bosch and Hermann Cohen even went so far as to suggest that industry fund the revisionist SPD journal *Sozialistische Monatshefte* in order to guide it in the proper direction.[33] The bulk of the RDI, however, opposed organizational intervention in the electoral process, preferring instead to aggregate and form industry's opinions and demands and then present these demands "of the economy" to the different branches of the state.[34] The bourgeois political parties thus enjoyed an autonomy of which they were later to be deprived.

Inflation had begun during the war and continued to worsen afterwards. The inflation contributed to a massive displacement in the national wealth; and this process, like the inflation itself, peaked during the French occupation of the Ruhr in 1923. Ruhr industrialists found that there was a time and a place for patriotism; others would pay the price both for the resistance and its abandonment. First, the inflation could be used to stimulate economic activity while keeping down the real value of reparations payments, and then the stabilization could be used for transferring the costs of both resistance and compliance to other social classes.[35] Together with the massive influx of American capital, which followed upon stabilization of the Mark, the inflation helped to accelerate the concentration of German industry and the rationalization and expansion of its plant. Aside from individual overnight-empire builders and speculators, those who benefited were the owners of the means of production and those who could sell products or shares abroad. Major industries were relieved of their debts, as were most farmers; the urban petite bourgeoisie was relieved of its bonds and savings, and the working class of both its real wages and its eight-hour day. These two classes simply did not profit from the high level of economic activity. By mid-1923, real wages were down almost to half their prewar and 1921 levels despite nearly full employment.[36] Within

33. This proposal was too sophisticated for most industrialists. Paul Reusch, for example, dismissed it brusquely as foolhardy; HA GHH/Nachlass Reusch 400 101 290/43, Bosch to Reusch, 4 Nov. 1923 and reply.

34. In the East German literature the ability to do this successfully is yet another indicator of the existence of "state-monopoly capitalism"; see Fricke, 2:584. For the "incapacitated pluralism" school, this was another step toward "corporatism"; see Maier, chaps. 6 and 8. Later, industry did seek to penetrate and even unite several parties.

35. In 1921 the index of industrial output in Germany was 77 (1913 = 100), whereas in France it was 58, in England 61, in Belgium 55, and even in the United States only 86. The declines in German production in 1923 were a direct result of the occupation, and recovery was very quick. The Allies restored control of Ruhr industry to its owners in

industry, only those with ready access to raw materials could profit from the situation—a boon to vertical concentration and to those who could tap hard-currency sources. Primarily, but not exclusively, the inflation spurred capital expenditure and investment, and German industry as a whole profited rather than lost through the collapse of the currency. It was another round in the political struggle over distribution,[37] uglier because it took place in a period of general misery.

Industry emerged from the inflation period strengthened. Its influence in the state had increased, simultaneously weakening that of the organized working class. Growth of the country's industrial plant had proceeded along lines it dictated. Industrialists could, and did, buy out a great many newspapers and financed several right-wing paramilitary groups while the treasuries of the unions were quickly emptied. Large industry dealt much of the Mittelstand a severe economic setback while rebuilding its own infrastructure and improving its export capabilities with tax funds to which it barely contributed. For years afterward, Mittelstand parties were organized on the basis of the demand for upward revaluation of bonds and savings "expropriated" through the inflation.[38] For much of the Mittelstand, the inflation permanently delegitimized the Republic while arousing hostility toward supposed speculators and representatives of international finance. On the whole then, inflation helped almost all branches of industry. Industry even freed itself somewhat from financial dependence on the banks, whose role was further reduced once the Dawes loans made the United States a primary source of investment capital.

With the stabilization of the currency in late 1923, a number of

---

exchange for their providing the Allies with a portion of their output. The German government would then reimburse the industrialists who could now afford to be generous. On this settlement (the MICUM accords), Maier, pp. 392–96; 414–18; Feldman, *Iron and Steel in the German Inflation, 1916–1923* (Princeton, 1977), pp. 408ff.

36. On the Ruhr conflict and Dawes loans, Maier, pp. 364–73, 402; Arthur Rosenberg, *Geschichte,* pp. 178–83. On wages, Gerhard Bry, *Wages in Germany, 1871–1945* (Princeton, 1960), pp. 214–32. Most of the issues surrounding defeat, inflation, the Ruhr occupation, concentration and counterrevolution are discussed in regard to heavy industry by Feldman, *Iron and Steel.*

37. These are the conclusions reached by Frank Graham, *Exchange, Prices and Production in Hyper-Inflation Germany* (Princeton, 1930), pp. 320–26.

38. Constantino Bresciani-Turroni asserts that "the depreciation of the currency caused in Germany the vastest expropriation of some classes of society that has ever been effected in time of peace," *The Economics of Inflation* (London, 1937), p. 318. Revaluation after 1924 was usually at a rate of about 15 percent of nominal value. Bresciani-Turroni's book discusses in detail all those facets of the inflation which have been merely referred to here. Recent work on the inflationary period by Feldman, Maier, and others has tended to adopt a more agnostic attitude on these issues.

contradictory developments were set in motion. Unemployment at first increased and the eight-hour day virtually disappeared, but the overall demand for consumer goods increased while demand in the production sector declined. Exports declined as imports rose. Within industry, vertical integration gave way to horizontal, as the wild growth of the inflation period needed to be pruned or "rationalized."[39] The process began cautiously but was in full swing by 1926. Simultaneously, the slowdown in coal and iron was reversed, no small thanks to the great British strike of that year.[40] The post-1924 rationalization was characterized by technical progress, new plant and increased stocks, and an infatuation with "Fordism," but even more so by an intensified production that promised both greater productivity and profitability. Public-works expenditures increased significantly, especially on infrastructure and external economies. Both developments depended heavily on American loans, and both showed quick results. Between 1924 and 1927, industrywide productivity increased by about 40 percent. In 1926, the government reported the following percentage of "syndicalization" in sample industries: mining, 98 percent; dyes, 96 percent; electrotechnical, 87 percent; shipping, 81 percent; banking, 74 percent. The two largest trusts of them all, United Steelworks and IG Farben, were formed in 1926 and 1925, respectively.[41] Rationalization, with its emphasis on cartellized ownership and management, fixed capital and science, and industry-state coordination, swept through all the larger industries.

In mining, rationalization led to concentration, mechanization, and overcapacity; together these rendered mining vulnerable to rapid fluctuations. In the iron and steel industries, rationalization above all produced price stability and greater worker-owner conflict. Rationalization and concentration made considerably less headway in the machine industry; despite entry into the field by a few steel producers, production remained basically small scale and undisciplined. In the electrotechnical industry, rationalization facilitated stable growth and augmented Germany's international dominance of the field. In the prosperous chemical industry, rationalization was successful on the inter-

---

39. Ibid., pp. 384–90.

40. During the seven-month strike, the Germans were able to export an extra 225 million RM worth of coal while avoiding the usual import of two million tons of British coal. Further, English iron and steel production dropped eight million tons, and much of it was made up by the Germans; ibid., pp. 409–10.

41. Figures from the state statistical office, cited by Manfred Clemenz, *Gesellschaftliche Ursprünge des Faschismus* (Frankfurt, 1972), p. 197. Some units totally dominated entire industries: United Steelworks, for example, employed 200,000 and produced 35–50 percent of all ferrous and nonferrous metals. IG Farben employed over 100,000 workers.

nal, organizational side, but competition remained substantial and there was little long-range planning. In the nonmonopoly sector (e.g., textiles) and where handicrafts prevailed (optics, instruments and toys, printing), there was much less organizational or technical change. Family ownership remained common, and, despite increased dependence on the electrical and chemical industries, there were few efforts to fashion other than loose organization within this latter sector.[42]

Like concentration and cartellization, rationalization was another means to protect producers from competition and overproduction and to back up, with state power, agreements between private producers. Although all cartel agreements enjoyed legal contract status, perhaps the clearest state underwriting of private accords occurred in the case of the 1926 International Iron Community (IRG) agreements. The private producers of several countries negotiated a production, marketing, and pricing agreement, which the respective governments then underwrote as a virtual treaty.[43] Although the German industrialists later became dissatisfied with the quotas allotted them, they were pleased on three accounts: (1) stability, order, and high prices were bought to west European ferrous production; (2) the state had abdicated to them the determination of "national interests" in a vital area; and (3) German producers were virtually free to charge their customers in the light and processing industries whatever they wanted; there was little recourse to imports. (As we shall see, this last effort created substantial tension between the branches of industry.) The events of the rationalization period provide substantial evidence for any theory of corporatism, neofeudalism, or state-monopoly capitalism. Whichever one chooses, the outstanding characteristic remains the extent of discipline and organization within Germany industry and its interweaving with the state.[44]

42. The best branch-by-branch discussion of rationalization remains that of Robert Brady, *The Rationalization Movement in German Industry.* On coal, pp. 67ff.; iron and steel, pp. 138ff.; machinery, pp. 139–68; electrotechnical, p. 194; chemicals, pp. 235, 250; textiles, pp. 263–71. With greater emphasis on the legal and microeconomic facets, Hermann Levy, *Industrial Germany* (Cambridge, 1935). Elisabeth Schalldach, *Rationalisierungsmassnahmen,* explores the relationship between the technological-organizational and the economic-political. She addresses a number of issues (Fordism, Taylorism, work discipline, industry norms, etc.) which we cannot take up here and observes that the bulk of union leaders and SPD theoreticians, though not all, identified rationalization as a politically neutral but developmentally progressive phenomenon, pp. 94ff., 164ff. The inherent class bias of such technical developments is still being debated.

43. On the details and significance of the IRG agreements, Maier, pp. 540–45.

44. See Brady, pp. 363ff., appendix C. Brady refers to German industry as a "state within the state among the states" and maintains that "there is scarcely an aspect of the

The rationalization movement increased industry's political activism for yet another reason. The recovery the movement facilitated was fragile. Enlarged capacity and the predominance of fixed capital left little flexibility in the event of economic downturn. Given the relative stagnation of the entire western economy during the interwar period,[45] some way had to be found to keep the factories humming. Therefore, industry needed to attend to both economic policy and its political prerequisites. In the steel industry, for example, any utilization-of-capacity rate below 67 percent was bound to be unprofitable. At the height of prosperity (1927–29), the rate barely exceeded 80 percent, and, when it dropped under 40 percent by fall 1931, there was little the industry could do to shrink, besides call for lower wages.[46] Although the margin was not so narrow in other industries, rationalization contributed to the precariousness of industrial prosperity after 1925. There were only three years (1927–30) during which total industrial production exceeded the levels of 1913. The differential nature of that period of prosperity was crucial in determining the political activity and coalitional preferences of the two fractions of industry.

By 1930 the political crisis was full-blown, but its outcome was not determined. The resolution of that crisis was substantially affected by the politics of industry, and those, in turn, were largely conditioned by the economics of the preceding years. In addition to being uneven, Weimar prosperity was neither broad, deep, nor long-lasting. We can briefly characterize the years 1925–30 as follows: 1925 witnessed a reconstruction boom with increased importation of raw materials and agricultural products and increased exportation of finished goods. Capital shortages occasioned by rationalization, trade deficits, and reparations were covered chiefly through foreign loans. The year 1926 saw a

---

normal functions of the state . . . which these economic entities [the cartels] do not possess to some degree, or have not arrogated in some wise to themselves" (p. 368). Whether or not their voice was overwhelming in the councils of state, they had certainly changed the political process.

45. This thesis is convincingly demonstrated by Dietmar Petzina and Werner Abelshauser, "Zum Problem der relativen Stagnation der deutschen Wirtschaft in den zwanziger Jahren," in Mommsen, et al., eds., pp. 57–76. For the entire western economy, Ingvar Svennilson, *Growth and Stagnation in the European Economy* (Geneva, 1954), esp., pp. 41–58 and appendix. The nature of the period was already deciphered, despite the intervening prosperity, by Rolf Wagenführ, "Die Industriewirtschaft: Entwicklungstendenzen der Industrieproduktion 1860 bis 1932," *Vierteljahrshefte zur Konjunkturforschung*, Sonderheft no. 31 (Berlin, 1933), esp. pp. 29–44. We return to a differential analysis of the industrial economy below.

46. Figures cited by Alfred Sohn-Rethel, *Ökonomie und Klassenstruktur des deutschen Faschismus* (Frankfurt, 1973), p. 49. Sohn-Rethel analyzes the dilemma of rationalization from the point of view of the organic composition of capital.

brief though severe recession and then vastly increased exports of coal, iron, and finished products. The industrial plant was expanded further, yet Germany managed a slightly positive balance of payments. In 1927 there was further expansion and prosperity in all sectors. Exports decreased and the trade balance was negative, but both of these were caused by expanded consumption at home. There occurred in 1928 a flattening of overall domestic demand, but improvement continued in the dynamic and export branches. For agriculture, the crisis had already begun. The year 1929 brought an overflow of the market and a collapse of some prices. Domestic demand and imports declined, but exports of finished products continued to rise significantly, leading to a favorable trade balance. An even greater trade surplus was seen in 1930 as exports almost held their own. The dynamic and export sectors now virtually supported the entire economy as agriculture and heavy industry contracted both production and consumption. During these "good years," there was substantial shifting in the balance of forces within industry. In 1925 the two fractions of industry were, politically, roughly in equilibrium. Between 1919 and 1925, the "right" or "national" wing of heavy industrialists successfully accomplished the reversal of the major working-class gains of the revolutionary period and eliminated the SPD from the government.[47] The Republic was made acceptable. After 1925, the dynamic, "liberal" fraction seemed to gain the upper hand. But different groups continued to articulate different political programs grounded in different coalitions and bases of mass support, and it is to that articulation which we now turn.

2. Industrial Politics in the Period of Stability

With the acceptance of the Dawes Plan, the beginning of an economic recovery, and the formation of an all-bourgeois government after the 1924 elections, bourgeois and industrial forces were in a position to create a broader political base for their social dominance. This became evident in Stresemann's attempts to garner the parliamentary support of the SPD, even at the risk of annoying and losing the right wing of his own DVP along with the DNVP.[48] The counterpart of this parliamentary opening to the working class took place within the industrial organizations and reflected the ascent of the dynamic-export fraction. Thus, in January 1925, Carl Duisberg, the "Welfare Professor," late of

47. On this period, Fricke, ed., 2:585–93; see also Bertrand, pp. 159ff.; Maier, chaps. 4, 6; Feldman, *Iron and Steel;* Arthur Rosenberg, *Geschichte*, pp. 178ff.
48. See Stürmer, pp. 280ff.

the Chemical Industries Association and the expanded IG Farben, was elected head of the RDI. Duisberg was chosen over Albert Vögler and Ernst von Borsig—Vögler was a steel industrialist, Stresemann's arch-enemy, who seceded from the right wing of the DVP to join the DNVP in response to the foreign minister's strategy of international reintegration and cooperation with the SPD; von Borsig was the similarly uncompromising chief of the reactionary *Arbeitgeberveband*. Duisberg overcame a somewhat feigned reluctance to be put forward when Silverberg, Abraham Frowein of the textile industry, and Paul Legers of the machine industry warned that Duisberg was the only one of the candidates acceptable to the export and processing industries—who might otherwise secede and form a new BdI.[49] The leaders of Ruhr-based, domestic heavy industry now believed the RDI to be dominated by "Berlin political types," deal-makers of the sort who, during the period of popular upheaval, had exceeded, if not ignored, the wishes of heavy industry in pushing the Stinnes-Legien agreements and the ZAG. Duisberg brought with him, as business chairman, Ludwig Kastl, an active proponent of a fulfillment policy toward reparations and a strategy to reintegrate Germany into the world economy.[50] Kastl's two associates were Hermann Bücher, soon to be an IG Farben and German General Electric (AEG) advisor, and Jacob Herle, a leader of the old BdI; both were known for their moderately progressive social views. The 1925 elections were thus a clear success for the dynamic-export fraction—in distinct contrast to the 1919 contest in which all the presidium candidates of the electrical, chemical, machine, and south German artisanal industries had been defeated.

During Duisberg's tenure, the advisory committee to the *Vositzender* (the *Beirat*), the *Präsidium,* and the *Vorstand* were all expanded—from six to twelve, sixteen to thirty-four, and sixty to one hundred members, respectvely. The previous preponderance of heavy industry was temporarily ended in the course of this expansion. As Weisbrod's research has shown, only five of the twenty figures to belong to Duisberg's Beirat

---

49. Bernd Weisbrod, *Schwerindustrie in der Weimarer Republik* (Wuppertal, 1978), pp. 220ff. In the situation of 1919 such a secessionist threat by the exporters would have carried virtually no weight; see Zunkel, "Gewichtung," pp. 637ff. By 1925 Reusch recognized that "leadership of the RDI might now pass to someone who thinks about [social and commercial matters] differently from us [in Ruhr heavy industry]," Reusch to von Wilmowsky, 23 Dec. 1924, HA GHH/Nachlass Reusch 400 101 290/39. Although Duisberg attempted to allay such anxieties, they were well founded.

50. Before the war, Kastl had been an active social-imperialist propagandizing for German expansion in southwest Africa while supporting progressive reform of the Prussian franchise. For the next seven years Kastl would be a central target of the most uncompromising Ruhr figures.

between 1925 and 1930 were assoicated with mining or iron and steel production, and on a regional basis, the industrialists of Saxony, a very different lot, were accorded greater representation than the Rhenish-Westphalian Langnamverein.[51] The economic policy committee of the Präsidium and Vorstand was chaired by Bücher and his assistant Clemens Lammers of the paper industry (and a Zentrum delegate to the Reichstag). Of its twenty members, three each belonged to the machine-building and small-iron- and steelwares industries, and two each to the electrical and chemical industries—all dynamic-export branches; two each belonged to the paper-and-printing, textile, and construction and shipbuilding industries—a mixed group, but leaning more toward the dynamic-export fraction; and only two each clearly belonging to the mining and basic ferrous metals industries. On the thirty-four-member presidium, between 1925 and 1929 heavy industry was generally represented by only eight (sometimes ten) voices; of the hundred or so delegates to the Vorstand, it sent only twenty-one. Domestic-oriented heavy industry fared just as poorly in all the other RDI committees and bodies.[52] The Duisberg regime inaugurated a period in which the chief body formulating industrial politics was oriented primarily toward the interests and strategies of the dynamic and export branches,[53] and the representatives of heavy industry, now in a distinct policy-making minority, were forced to retreat to their own captive organizations, such as the Langnamverein and VDESI. From these and other outposts, the leaders of western heavy industry attacked the tax, finance, social, labor, trade, and other policies of both the bourgeois and Grand Coalition governments of the years 1925–30. On occasion they were joined in their efforts by the RDI as a whole, but frequently, too, they ignored the central organization and were ignored by it. During these years they set

51. Weisbrod, pp. 223, 217; see also RDI to presidium members, 14 Mar. 1925, HA GHH/Nachlass Reusch 400 101 220/0. One of those five was Silverberg, a politically complex figure, sometimes a progressive initiator, sometimes a pessimistic bellwether. The lignite mining in which his interests were centered was closely associated with the expanding electrical industries and the public utilities.

52. For the representatives' names and affiliations, Weisbrod, pp. 223–24, who holds that heavy industry maintained itself on the *Beirat*.

53. Weisbrod, p. 226 prefers to characterize Duisberg as a mediator within the dichotomy of the old, big heavy industries/small finishing *(verarbeitenden)* industries; he does not here consider that the big, new and dynamic industries, especially chemicals and electronics, joined with or took under wing these smaller finishing industries, and that what resulted was something new. Clearly, they all shared certain capitalist interests, which Weisbrod documents, but this was not the point; the issue was how they might further those interests, and here, as he shows, heavy industry had ample reason to be dissatisfied.

neither the tone nor the agenda for industrial politics; as often and nastily as they may have bristled, they did not lead.

Instead, a revised and more cooperative industrial orientation emerged in the realm of state social policy (Sozialpolitik) and trade policy (Handelspolitik), and accompanying that new orientation was a different posture toward labor and its place in the state. The reestablishment of Germany's economic potential and international stature required a national consensus, which would be based on reintegration of a chastened but still strong SPD.[54] The antisocialist bloc gave way to a class-compromise bloc,[55] a fragile compact for a period of limited growth and progress. It was possible for ascendant members of the dominant economic classes, in this case the dynamic-export fraction, to abandon the interests of other economically dominant fractions, wholly or in part, in favor of more thoroughgoing collaboration with parts of the organized working class.

This collaboration with the working class was feasible because the essential interests of industry seemed no longer to be threatened. A series of compromise equilibria, albeit unstable ones, was now possible. The counterrevolution of 1919–23 had guaranteed for industry that it would continue, in Gramsci's words, to exercise "the decisive function" in "the decisive nucleus of economic activity"; with such a guarantee, a popular class-state was possible.[56] Once the revolutionary and insurrectionary impulse of the working class had been defeated, some of its interests could be incorporated and molded by the ascendant dynamic fraction of industry. Thus, in mid-1925, Herman Bücher called for "labor and social peace." He suggested binding, compulsory arbitration of wage disputes and even recommended a Socialist, former Labor Minister Rudolf Wissell, as chief arbitrator.[57] He also told businessmen to stop cheating on their corporate and personal taxes because their own good was now linked to the public good. In his presidential address, Duisberg professed his personal loyalty to the Weimar Consti-

54. Thus, Duisberg and his associates fully agreed with Stresemann, who justified Locarno to the DVP Central Committee in November 1925 by arguing that "economic power is the only respect in which we are still a Grossmacht, and it is only through it that we can conduct foreign policy." Wielding and developing economic power in such a way as to obtain concessions from France, Poland, and others required domestic social peace and unity, and it was now both safe and worthwhile to pursue such a strategy in tacit cooperation with the SPD. As members of the DVP, Paul Silverberg, Gustav Krupp, and Hans von Raumer (of the electrical industry) supported this position.

55. See figures 2 and 3, for an outline of these blocs and the corresponding electoral results and party coalitions.

56. Gramsci, p. 161.

57. Fricke, ed., 2:594.

tution and, rather hesitantly, even to democracy. He called for a conscious abandonment of prewar industrial attitudes toward the unions and even acknowledged the justice and frequent practicality of the eight-hour day.[58] The interests he expressed were certainly those of capitalist industrialists, but the emphases and programmatic implications were just as certainly different from those favored by heavy industry. In his turn at the podium, von Borsig of Arbeitgeberverbände took direct issue with Bücher and raged against compulsory arbitration. In the conference-closing presentation, however, Kastl not only avoided reference to von Borsig's remarks but proceeded to antagonize heavy industry further by arguing that domestic consumers ought to be freed from the high prices for basic industrial (and agricultural) goods that kept down both their consumption and real income levels.[59]

This more cooperative approach was possible because it issued from a position of strength. The ad hoc institutions of the revolutionary period, which might have, and for brief moments actually had, operated as institutions of counterhegemony or dual power in the hands of the working class (the Joint Working Committees, the Workers' Councils, the Reichs Economic Council) had either been dismantled, penetrated, or recaptured by industry. Foreign policy, national policy, and social policy could now be formed into a coherent whole. Just as acceptance of the Dawes Plan was intended to link Germany's foreign creditors to the fate of its economy, so social policy and the acknowledgment of labor's due were intended to insert the working class through the right wing of the SPD into a national endeavor with a reconsolidated capitalism. In both areas it was a question of costs: costs that at least the dynamic fraction was willing, and could afford, to pay. Both of these tasks were facilitated by the reorientation of RDI policy following the elections of 1924, which had produced heavy losses on the left and large gains on the right.[60] This two-pronged strategy of the dynamic fraction did, however, widen the cleavages within industry. Acceptance of the Dawes Plan precipitated a minor secession from the RDI; as we have suggested, the new policy of social peace and class cooperation and competition precipitated a struggle within it—because of both the economic costs and political implications involved. In this struggle the representatives of heavy industry were unable, before 1929 or 1930, to rally the collective forces of industry on behalf of their stated goals. As

58. DII, Cologne/RDI-Vorbereitungen und Tagungen/23–25 June 1925, Cologne, pp. 10, 11.

59. Ibid., pp. 26, 30. Kastl further indicated support for the Luther-Stresemann-Marx government.

60. Returns and coalitions, tables 1 and 2.

early as 1926, Reusch and Max Schlenker put together a program intended as an alternative to the policies pursued by the RDI and the government, but virtually none of its planks were adopted. Most of them had been or would have been adopted before 1925, and most in fact were again in 1930, but in the situation pertaining between 1925 and the onset of the crisis they could not expect to obtain the assent of the RDI.[61] Almost all of what heavy industry now opposed became either law or policy in the course of the next four years; none of what Schlenker and Reusch here proposed was adopted, either by the new RDI regime or by the governments of 1925 to early 1930.

The election results of 1924 and the establishment of an all-bourgeois government had made "Entrepreneurs and State" and "Industry and Parliament" central discussion topics at the 1925 RDI meetings. The direct, parliamentary influence of industry expanded; numerous industrialists belonged to the victorious parties, and some even became members of Parliament[62] and the executive. The RDI meetings of 1926 sought to come to grips with the opening to the SPD, and therefore they highlighted the splits within industry. The political class struggle of the previous half-dozen years and the outcome of that struggle contributed to a change in the structure and programs of both industry and working class. In the case of the SPD, this manifested itself in a political and theoretical shift from "social politics" to "production politics," in the neutral-state implications of the theory of organized capitalism, and in

61. Among the planks of their program were the following: revision of the Constitution to limit the "luxurious" spending of Parliament and local government, abolition of compulsory arbitration of labor disputes, an end to anticartel legislation, an end to state pressure for price reductions, the abandonment of unemployment insurance (then being proposed), prohibition of foreign "dumping" and severe restrictions on the negotiation of most-favored-nation trade agreements, a state executive strong enough to curb "party-politics," generous use of article 48, and strenuous action to prevent any left cabinet or Grand Coalition. Schlenker to Reusch, 24 Dec. 1925; HA GHH/Nachlass Reusch 400 101 221/6b. The evidence would not seem to suggest that heavy industry had established for itself a veto power within the RDI.

62. This relationship has been most closely explored for the DVP; see Lothar Döhn, *Politik und Interesse: Die Interessenstruktur der DVP* (Meisenheim/Glan, 1970), esp. pp. 91–131 and charts, pp. 401–21. The DVP is, perhaps, the best locus for the discussion of the links between representatives and represented, and we shall return to that issue in chapter 6. For some examples of the links between industry and other bürgerliche parties from the DDP through the Zentrum to the DNVP, see Fricke, ed., 2:597ff. After the 1924 elections, some sixty-five delegates (about 15 percent of the total) occupied 269 seats on the boards of directors and interlocking directorates of industry and commerce. Shortly after taking office, Duisberg argued that industry ought to use, and act through, Parliament rather than simply rejecting it as many of his colleagues in heavy industry were wont to do. He especially valued close relations with parliamentary committees, including their socialist members, and established a standing committee of RDI members of Parliament; see Döhn, p. 423.

an ever-hardening attitude toward the KPD.[63] In the case of industry, Paul Silverberg's keynote speech at the RDI meetings in Dresden of September 1926 set out the new lines of demarcation as articulated by the dynamic figures: social peace and compromise with labor through acceptance of the Republic, and an export offensive through trade treaties that would be negotiated largely at the expense of agriculture and "backward" sections of German industry.

Silverberg announced that industry now had an absolutely affirmative attitude toward the state and that no government was possible without labor. Germany could not only not be governed against social democracy; it could not be governed without social democracy. And, now that the SPD had abandoned the "politics of force, the politics of the street," and had responsibly accepted "the politics of facts rather than of doctrine," that party was needed and ought to be welcomed into government. A "social partnership" was the order of the day for the sake of the nation.[64] Like Duisberg, Silverberg offered a trade-off: industry would accept popular government and the formally democratic Republic in exchange for abandonment of anticapitalist pretensions on the part of the SPD and unions. This, neither more nor less, was the meaning of Silverberg's speech.[65] Of course, Silverberg called on the workers to abandon socialist illusions first, but in fact the SPD was prepared to do that; for the most part it already had. Further, Silverberg expected, naively or otherwise, that cooperating with labor would further tame and integrate it; national leadership would thus be more likely to remain with Germany's entrepreneurs (das Unternehmertum).[66] Such a tacit agreement would mark a labor-industry modus

63. On the theoretical side, see Winkler, ed., *Organisierter Kapitalismus*, pp. 9–18; on the political side, see Arthur Rosenberg, *Geschichte*.

64. Silverberg's speech "The German Industrial Entrepreneur in the Post War Period" is reprinted by Franz Mariaux, ed., *Reden und Schriften von Paul Silverberg* (Cologne, 1952), pp. 49–69. Silverberg entertained the interesting (and insightful) theory that the SPD and ADGB had *always* been responsible except for the few months immediately before and after November 1918, when they picked up an irregular membership and were dizzied. Bücher went on to point to the United States as a place where "social partnership" and "human relations" guided the relations between labor and industry and politics itself. Numerous trade unionists shared some of these conceptions of the United States, see Schalldach, pp. 52ff.

65. This was clear both to Kastl, who saw the text a month before it was presented, as well as to those who were angered by it; BA/Nachlass Silverberg/235, pp. 20–28. At the preconvention meeting of the RDI's economic policy committee, Silverberg's line was approved and endorsed by the chemical, electrical, textile, machine-building, and finished-goods industries, as well as by bank representatives. On the ability of the SPD to abandon socialist illusions while still stifling capitalism, see Laclau, pp. 136ff.

66. Weisbrod argues (pp. 246, 249, 269) that Silverberg's concessions were only tactical, whereas his conditions were substantial, and that, by not explicitly distancing

vivendi and initiate what Duisberg and others within industry's dynamic fraction expected to be a political and economic upwards-development. Ignoring the objections of the Employers' League, top leaders of the RDI had begun weekly secret meetings with members of the ADGB leadership, and although their early sessions dealt with somewhat less contentious issues like tariffs and currency revaluation, the more difficult ones were also to appear on the agenda.[67] Kastl later expanded on Silverberg's theme: what Germany needed, he argued, was an export offensive predicated on "quality production and expanded trade and consumption." This was later the theme of the 1927 RDI convention at which delegates accepted sweeping social and labor legislation and increased public and state expenditures.

Silverberg's speech immediately elicited heated and emphatic responses from labor, both socialist and Christian, all the political parties, agriculture, and heavy industry.[68] Whereas the dynamic fraction, in lieu of other, unavailable popular bases, sought to incoporate the economic demands of labor while enlisting its mass political support (the so-called Silverberg-Severing-Stresemann alliance), the heavy-industry fraction found no solace in a program that threatened both its profitability and pivotal political position. The stage was set for conflicts between the two fractions which would last for the duration of the Republic. Representatives of heavy industry opposed Stresemann in the Reichstag and the Silverberg line in the RDI; in the former arena, they worked for a unification of all the bourgeois parties right of the DDP, and in the latter they pleaded the case, along with agriculture, for a domestic-market and antisocialist strategy. They wanted coalition to the right, not the left, and were not particularly prepared to compromise.[69] Unlike the leaders of the new, capital-intensive industries of the

---

himself from avowed enemies of the Republic like Hugenberg, his words cannot be taken as valid for industry. Instead, they become, like Duisberg's "personal" only, whereas the position articulated by the other wing (Vögler, Reichert) expresses the true or real attitude of industry toward the Weimar state. This is a strained attribution of nearly all power to the villains and none to the others. Representatives of heavy industry were certainly a cohesive and strong-willed force, one which sometimes claimed a veto right in industry generally; one might even contend that they "won" in 1932—though our analysis in chapter 6 will demonstrate that the situation was more complicated than that even then—but certainly in the period 1925–30 their constant vocal objections indicated that they were not getting their way.

67. See Michael Schneider, *Unternehmer und Demokratie* (Bonn-Bad Godesberg, 1975), pp. 69–72.

68. For the immediate responses and their significance, see chap. 1, note 50, and chap. 2, notes 71–73. Press reactions collected in BA/Nachlass Silverberg/706.

69. Dirk Stegmann, "Die Silverberg-Kontroverse 1926," in *Sozialgeschichte Heute—Festschrift für Hans Rosenberg,* ed. H.-U. Wehler (Göttingen, 1974), pp. 594–610, consid-

second industrial revolution or the representatives of the export-oriented skilled-crafts industries, the men of domestic heavy industry (like those of agriculture) were neither inclined nor in a position to compromise with labor. The industrialists from Baden, Middle Germany, and Saxony—indeed, the majority of the RDI Präsidium—might be able to afford and support Silverberg and Stresemann, but not so the captains of the Ruhr.[70]

Reusch, who was angered at not being informed of Silverberg's speech ahead of time, as well as by its content, decided to reply at the first available opportunity, namely the Langnamverein meetings beginning on 1 October.[71] He wanted to be joined by a Rhenish-Westphalian industrialist from outside the mining or steel industries, but he was unable to line up anyone from outside those branches.[72] Instead, he shared the podium with the rather predictable Thyssen, who could manage no better than to insist that "the soul of the workers . . . is neither socialist nor clerical but rather German."[73] On a more programmatic level, Reusch rejected outright the implications of Silverberg's speech, and he informed the assembled Langnamverein convention that only a market *and* coalition strategy based on "the productive strata," especially agriculture, and on the internal market, could make Germany prosperous again and provide industry with tolerable economic policies.[74] If Duisberg wanted his "viable and strong government," it should be one composed of parties representing those "productive strata" rather than unreliable workers' representatives.

---

ers the Silverberg initiative to have been little more than a flash in the pan, almost unintended and supported "only" by the chemical, machine-building, textile, and optical industries and perhaps the big banks (p. 604). The western coal, iron, and steel industries led the majority who opposed it in a "successful" counteroffensive, which continued through the lockout of 300,000 ironworkers in the Ruhr in 1928 down to January 1933. But Stegmann views too many curved lines as straight ones, particularly considering how powerful his "only" industries really were. For a further discussion of both the Silverberg and Reusch approaches toward entrepreneur/union/state relations in this period, see Schneider, *Unternehmer,* pp. 50–60.

70. Weisbrod, p. 268, chides Hilferding for arguing that the balance had swung over to the dynamic, capital-intensive, and export-oriented industries. His criticism is excessive, however: Hilferding was wrong in that he thought their victory was clear and final rather than partial, temporary, and contingent. In fact it did not become final in West Germany until the 1960s.

71. See Reusch to RDI, 26 Sept. 1926, HA GHH/Nachlass Reusch 400 101 220/3. He received encouragement to do so from Reichert, the man of steel and the VDESI's contact with the DNVP, BA/R13I-VDESI/101, p. 111, 16 Sept. 1926, as well as from the Langnamverein's Schlenker, HA GHH/Nachlass Reusch 400 101 221/6b 4 and 7 Sept. 1926.

72. Weisbrod, p. 260.

73. Cited in BA/Z Sg 126/1 Oct. 1926.

74. Cited in ibid.; see note 68.

Thus, whereas the RDI strategy implied the Grand Coalition (figure 3), the heavy-industry strategy implied some variant of the bourgeois Sammlung Coalition (figure 1). Neither fraction could achieve what it wanted *on its own terms:* for a Sammlung bloc, there was insufficient unity; and when the Grand Coalition finally arrived in 1928, it came as a result of the SPD's electoral victory.

Throughout its duration from autumn 1928 to spring 1930, the Grand Coalition was the subject of conflicts between the fractions of industry. Before the Depression led all of industry to reconsider the costs and benefits of coalition with the SPD, industrial opinion had varied within a broad range. At one extreme were commercial and exporting groups like the DIHT who welcomed the trade and social policies of the new coalition and who were willing to pay added social costs in exchange for a counterweight to the protectionist demands of agriculture and monopoly price policies of heavy industry. At the other extreme were groups, especially in Ruhr heavy industry, like the VDESI and Langnamverein, with opposed interests who allowed the Grand Coalition no quarter.[75] So long as the labor-industry compromise remained viable, and so long as Germany's export picture remained bright, the balance of forces within the RDI would continue to favor the dynamic sector. The forces themselves had not changed much over the previous three decades; even some of the chief spokesmen remained the same.[76]

Eduard Hamm, chairman of the DIHT, considered 1928 a boom year and an appropriate time both to increase exports and make concessions to the labor unions. Industry and commerce should, he maintained, "never indulge in simple nay-saying" toward labor. Germany's reintegration into the world economy was the only way out of her dilemma, and even domestic cartels ought to give way before that priority.[77] This

75. Reusch expressed his position consistently from 1925 on: parliamentary majorities were not the way to determine correct policies, parties that had to compete for mass favor would perforce relegate to the background the needs of the economy and the state, and taxes and social spending should certainly not be set by those who do not pay them; Weisbrod, pp. 240ff. Someone, according to Reusch, either a reliable finance minister or the Reichspresident, should be empowered via article 48 to veto parliamentary spending and end assaults on the economy; 28 Dec. 1925, HA GHH/Nachlass Reusch 400 101/220/2a.

76. On this correlation, Ingolf Liesebach, *Der Wandel der politischen Führungsschicht der deutschen Industrie* (Hannover, 1957), pp. 70ff. On the persistence of the split and the spokesmen, Dirk Stegmann, "Hugenberg contra Stresemann: Die Politik der Industrieverbände am Ende des Kaiserreichs," *Vierteljahrshefte für Zeitgeschichte* 24 (1976): 329–78; Pogge von Strandmann, passim.

77. These points appear in BA/R11-DIHT/4449, 4701, 2612, 3942, and 1776, on 4 Oct. 1927, 26 June, 3 Oct., and 24 April, respectively. The DIHT stayed with the Grand Coalition at all times. See Dieter Schäfer, *Der DIHT als politisches Forum der Weimarer*

was tantamount to full support of the Grand Coalition's program. Labor and this fraction of industry agreed that exports equalled jobs[78] and that industrialists had to check those in their own ranks who impeded cooperation. Thus, to counter the veto right within the RDI that the Langnamverein had attempted to claim for itself, moves were undertaken through 1929 nearly to double the size of the RDI executive, thereby increasing the role of the smaller, export- and coalition-oriented producers, many from Saxony and the south.[79]

It was at least partially to counter this tendency within the RDI and the hostility of the DIHT and Hansa Bund that the twelve top leaders of Rhenish-Westphalian industry formed the "Ruhrlade" at the end of 1927.[80] Economics Minister Curtius (DVP) personified the export-labor trade-off supported by those other groups, and he was a special object of heavy industry's ire. It was against him and Stresemann that heavy industry propagated the term *Illusionspolitik* and supported agriculture's demands for high tariffs and a return to the domestic market. While the RDI meetings of June 1929 declared that "a high level of exports is an economic and political necessity," spokesmen for the Langnamverein responded that limiting imports, lowering taxes, reducing Sozialpolitik, and terminating reparations would make a far better national program.[81] Just as the benefits derived from reparations and exports were supposedly illusory, so Curtius's cooperation with the unions in favor of the eight-hour day was perceived as "Illusionspolitik."

Finally, the case of the Ruhr lockouts of autumn 1928 underscored both heavy industry's hostility toward the Grand Coalition and the split within the ranks of industry. About 250,000 Ruhr metalworkers were

---

Republik (Hamburg, 1966), p. 58. The DIHT and like-minded organizations are neglected by Weisbrod.

78. Hamm informed Silverberg that every 1,800-RM worth of exports meant one job, BA/Nachlass Silverberg/646, p. 96.

79. On the Langnamverein's presumption of a veto right, Weisbrod, passim. On the push to "democratize" the RDI, BA/Nachlass Silverberg/274, p. 11. As indicated above, the plan to expand the Vorstand from 60 to 105 members called for the new seats to be allotted to the smaller and newer industries.

80. The Ruhrlade was heavy industry's private cabinet. To facilitate decisiveness, membership was never to exceed twelve. HA GHH/Nachlass Reusch 400 101 24/11. See H. A. Turner, "The Ruhrlade: Secret Cabinet of Heavy Industry," *Central European History* 3 (1970): 195–228.

81. The RDI statement and Langnamverein response are in ZSA/RLB Pressarchiv 132/11, pp. 121, 123. The Langnamverein position reflected the resolution of its meeting of 4 Nov. 1928 at which Reusch attacked Curtius directly. See also the *Deutsche Bergwerkszeitung* of 22 June 1928 and the *Ruhr und Rhein Wirtschaftszeitung* of 20 June 1929. On Curtius's relationship with the unions, see Döhn, p. 183, Weisbrod, pp. 320, 433.

locked out by their employers upon expiration of their contract in mid-October in what amounted to a provocation by heavy industry through the Northwest Employers Organization.[82] Under attack were both the prerogative of the labor minister, now a Socialist, to undertake binding compulsory arbitration and the entire labor-industry modus vivendi, come to fruition in the Grand Coalition.[83] But the lockout did not evoke from the RDI and other central organizations the kind of support industrialists had taken for granted would be forthcoming. Paul Reusch remarked bitterly that "we here in the west are extremely shocked and outraged that the RDI and Berliners are not supporting us in this struggle, one which we have undertaken in the interests of the maintenance of the German and free economy."[84] Not all of industry was yet prepared for the euphemistic "healthy economy in a strong state," which had already become the goal of heavy industry. To understand the political and ideological divergences between the two fractions of industry more clearly, both in regard to the Grand Coalition and the various governments that succeeded it, we must look more closely at the world of production in the industrial economy as a whole and within its fractions or branches. This will then provide a context for examining further the economic conflicts within industry and the political activity of its fractions.

3. Industrial Production

The pessimism and lack of confidence with which the heavy industry fraction greeted the social, trade, commercial, fiscal, and reparations policies of the governments of 1925–30 contrasted sharply with the

82. On the Employers' League *(Arbeitgeberverbände)*, Fricke, ed., 2:751–61. The Ruhr lockouts are discussed in greater detail in chapter 5.

83. Hüllbüsch, "Ruhreisenstreit," pp. 271–89, argues rather convincingly that both the SPD and ADGB failed to appreciate the political significance of the lockouts and compounded that mistake by failing to utilize public sympathy for the workers to launch a counteroffensive. She overlooks the weakness of the "victorious" SPD. Cf. Castellan, *Weimar*, p. 76; Poulantzas, *Fascisme*, p. 187; below, chap. 5, sec. 2; and the sources cited by Schneider, *Unternehmer*, pp. 76–84.

84. Reusch to Schlenker, 19 Nov. 1928; HA GHH/Nachlass Reusch 400 101 221/9a. Even Weisbrod, who generally argues that heavy industry consistently got its way, acknowledges that heavy industry was "politically isolated" at this time, pp. 495, 458. The RDI leadership, including the "spineless" Kastl, opposed the lockout and "refuse[d] to stand on our side"; see Kastl to Reusch, 8 Nov., and Reusch to Kastl, 19 Nov. 1928, HA GHH/Nachlass Reusch 400 101 220/6a. Lange of the machine builders also kept his distance from the steel industrialists.

attitude of the dynamic fraction. As we have noted, it was generally the case that bloc 3 was most acceptable to the modern and profitable industries together with those where fixed rather than variable capital seemed to contribute most to profits. A look at the performance and structure of production in several key industries will facilitate the analysis. Within the framework of the general stagnation of the period,[85] the expansive, dynamic industries were affiliated politicially with the "liberal" bloc, whereas the stagnant industries belonged to the "national" bloc. The striking variation in production levels, highlighted in table 15, found its parallel in the political attitudes of the corresponding industrialists. Table 16 indicates the relative economic importance of the major industries insofar as that was reflected in the size of the work force and the net value of production.[86] These five branches of industry accounted for over half of the total net income from all non-agricultural production. Like the production indices, the employment figures demonstrate substantial unevenness in the extent and duration of industrial recovery and expansion. Juxtaposed, these two tables make clear that the stagnant industries (mining and ferrous metals especially) retained a crucial economic presence despite their relative decline before the dynamic branches. Together, tables 16 and 17 demonstrate the movement and burden of wages in several key industries. The burden of wages in any particular industry is not, however, simply a function of their level and the number of employees, and, as the tables indicate, particularly those industries in the capital-intensive branches where production and work force were expanding, like chemicals and electronics, could generally afford greater wage increases. Further, industries like textiles and clothing characterized by low wages and a large (largely female) work force were increasingly less typical of the German economy. German industrialists were fully aware of the differential impact of labor costs on their production and profits.

The RDI's analysis of taxation, receipts, and wages in 1927 discussed these differences in detail. It was generally argued that there were no profits in production; even in this very good year, 56 percent of "value added" went to wages, 15 percent to salaries, 7 percent to social insurance, 10 percent to taxes, and only 10 percent "to the company

---

85. Wagenführ, pp. 35, 62–64. See note 45, above.

86. In 1927–28 the ten largest "industrial" branches and their percentage contribution to the total value of industrial production were the following: food, 14.7%; textile and clothing, 13.4% (7.6 + 5.8); construction and others, 11.4%; metal and metalwares, 10.3% (a faulty category, however, since half of it consisted of finished wares mostly not in the hands of the same industries); mining, 10%; machinery and vehicles, 8.5%; paper, printing, and cellulose, 5.8%; electrotechnical, 4.2%; raw chemicals, 4%; stone and earth, 4%. Wagenführ, p. 57.

TABLE 15

Production Indices for Sample Major Industries (1913 = 100)

	Stagnant			Borderline	Expansive		
	Coal	All Mining	Raw Metals	Textile, Leather & Clothing[c]	Lignite[a]	Metal Fin- ishing[b]	Chemical
1925	70	79	70	89	160	131	133
1926	76	82	62	75	160	104	123
1927	81	88	86	109	173	143	155
1928	79	88	79	93	190	164	161
1929	86	98	86	85	200	170	186
1930	75	84	63	76	167	157	172
1931	62	70	45	70	153	120	148
1932	55	63	32	73	141	84	139

SOURCE: Hoffmann, pp. 342–43, 392–93.

[a] Lignite was used primarily for electric power production. It was a new and booming field closely linked to those whom it supplied. The most prominent lignite industrialist was our oft-quoted Paul Silverberg. Briquettes not separated from total.

[b] Includes all those industries consuming raw iron or steel and producing finished products or machinery.

[c] Simple average of Hoffmann's two categories.

itself."[87] Of all the industries, mining had the highest proportion of costs devoted to wages, salaries, and social insurance while having a mere 4 percent profit rate. The rate of profit in the iron- and steel-producing industry was less than 2.8 percent. On the other hand, the textile industry enjoyed a 10 percent rate of profit owing largely to low wages, and the electrotechnical branch enjoyed a 7 percent rate, thanks largely to the minor role played by wage costs.[88] Examined on an industry-by-industry basis, the varying place of labor costs becomes dramatic.

Table 18 (p. 138) compares the shares of the component "labor" for several industries in regard to both sales or the "value of Marketed goods" (Umsatz) and the "value added" (Wertschöpfung).[89] The higher raw material and fixed costs, the lower the component or share of labor in total costs and vice versa. The labor component in the value of marketed goods reveals the share of labor in determining the price of marketed goods (costs). The labor component in the value added re-

87. Besteuerung, Ertrag und Arbeitslohn im Jahre 1927, Veröffentlichung des RDI, no. 47 (Berlin, 1929), p. 15.

88. Ibid., pp. 31–33.

89. "Value added" equals "value of marketed goods" minus "costs of materials." Value added is, by convention, defined as labor costs plus profits.

TABLE 16

Employment in Major Industries (in thousands);
and Net Value of Production (1928)

	All Mining	Raw Metal Production	Textile & Clothing[a]	Metal Finishing	Chemical
1925	750	550	2,000	2,350	380
1926	700	413	2,650	1,860	340
1927	715	490	2,150	2,220	375
1928	690	510	2,145	2,300	390
1929	690	487	1,990	2,192	410
1930	620	430	1,790	1,935	360
1931	500	320	1,465	1,560	320
1932	420	262	1,200	1,228	280
Net value of production, 1928 (in billions RM)	4.2	4.5	6	6.4	2.5

SOURCES: Hoffmann, pp. 195, 198. Bry, p. 27, has substantially higher employment figures for some branches, substantially lower ones for others. Earlier ratios have been used to decompose composites. Mining and chemicals rounded.
[a] Employment in the textile and clothing category varies widely in different sources.

veals the share of labor in transforming raw materials into marketed products (profits). In other words, labor, according to table 18, accounts for b percent of the costs in an industry while creating d percent of the profits. The "exploitation ratio" indicates how much an industrialist in a given industry might have "received in return" for his wage inputs. In mining, for example, the share constituted by labor costs was an extremely high 50 percent, while labor contributed only a slightly above average 83 percent to profits. In chemicals, on the other hand, labor costs were an extremely low 15 percent, so that labor's 68 percent contribution to profits made workers in this branch much more "worth their money." By and large, the less "worth its money" the labor force in a given industry, the more opposed were its entrepreneurs to organized labor and the Grand Coalition.[90] There were few anomalies, generally explicable.[91]

90. This leads to the "irony" that it was precisely in the most progressive industries (electrotechnical, chemical) that the work force was most exploited in the technical, economic sense.
91. Thus, the hostility of steel industrialists toward organized labor was grounded in the low profit rate. Also, the unionization of the industry had bred disproportionate animosities, which were reenforced in the twenties by a strong Communist presence. Further, as table 15 indicated, the industry was relatively stagnant after 1925, and it was not very competitive internationally. Conversely, the liberal politics of the metal-finishing

The "bottom line" for entrepreneurs is, of course, profits; the results for 1927 are displayed in table 19 (p. 139), which verifies that the dynamic industries generally enjoyed higher rates of profit and far better net-to-gross-earnings ratios.[92]

Another variable that we have contended helps account for the political and coalitional preferences of different groups of industrialists was export orientation. Although substantial involvement in exports would

TABLE 17

Hourly Income (in Pf.); Annual Earnings (in RM) and Their Index Value (1913 = 100) in Selected Major Industries

	1925	1926	1927	1928	1929	1930	1931	1932
Coal mining								
Hourly[a]	73	78	87	88	89	91	83	74
Yearly[b]	1,838	2,025	2,142	2,265	2,406	2,252	2,028	1,689
Index[c]	121	132	139	148	157	155	137	115
Metal production								
Hourly	...	...	...	...	...	...	...	...
Yearly	2,135	2,197	2,439	2,556	2,565	2,574	2,332	1,951
Index	...	...	...	...	...	...	...	...
Textile and clothing[d]								
Hourly	...	...	88	92	96	97	93	81
Yearly	1,280	1,345	1,440	1,525	1,600	1,656	1,525	1,329
Index	150	156	168	177	187	194	178	154
Metal goods								
Hourly	71	77	80	88	94	95	90	78
Yearly	1,915	1,873	2,126	2,289	2,452	2,519	2,381	2,065
Index	135	132	150	162	173	178	168	146
Chemicals								
Hourly	80	86	92	100	106	108	104	87
Yearly	1,921	2,167	2,241	2,428	2,586	2,540	2,496	2,187
Index	147	164	169	185	197	198	190	165

SOURCES: Hoffmann, pp. 461, 470–71; Bry, pp. 393, 418–21, 473.
[a] 1925–27 hard coal workers only, 1928–32 all coal miners.
[b] All workers.
[c] Based on earnings of all workers and employees in mining.
[d] Figures here are composite; see Hoffmann, p. 470, cols. 5, 7; Bry, p. 473, cols. 7, 8.

and machine industries were undoubtedly furthered by their expansiveness during this period and their extremely strong position in the world market (see table 20). Between 1925 and 1930, they alone provided over 27 percent of all exports.

92. Fairly complete figures demonstrating how much more profitable the dynamic industries were than the other sectors have been compiled by Maxine Sweezy in "German Corporate Profits, 1926–1938," *Quarterly Journal of Economics* 54 (1940):390–392.

TABLE 18

Labor's Share of Total Costs and Labor's Contribution
to Profits (in percent), Key Industries, 1927

		All Mining	Iron & Steel	Tex- tiles[b]	Metal Fin- ishing/ Machines	Electro- technical	Chemi- cals
Costs[a] (in %)							
a.	Fixed costs	35	64	65	56	56	74
b.	Labor costs (workers only)	43	20	18	28	21	9
c.	Labor costs (all employees)	50	26	22	36	31	15
Contribution to Profits							
d.	Labor (workers only)	73	63	55	68	52	41
e.	Labor (all employees)	83	82	68	86	77	68
f.	Capital	8.7	9.6	21	7.1	13.9	19.9
"Exploitation" Ratio							
b:d (or c:e)		1:1.7	1:3.2	1:3	1:2.4	1:2.5	1:4.5

SOURCE: Reichsverband der Deutschen Industrie, *Besteuerung, Ertrag und Arbeitslohn im Jahre 1927* (Berlin, 1929), adapted from tables 13–14, pp. 38, 41.
[a] Taxes, depreciation, and debt retirement are omitted.
[b] Textiles only; the clothing industry is excluded.

not in itself dispose an industry toward political cooperation with the organized working class—the desire to remain competitive could have the opposite effect—the Stresemann policy of reintegrating Germany internationally was dependent on SPD support. In addition, in the case of many export products, their advanced technical "state of the art" quality compensated for any higher prices. Table 20 lists the absolute and index figures for the value and volume of exports and indicates their share of the world trade. The data indicate that the international iron and coal cartels were especially successful in keeping prices up even once volume plummeted. A particularly stark example is provided by comparing the 1930 price and volume indices for coal and chemicals. Further justification is provided for the view that the twenties was a period of general economic stagnation in the west, although Germany's dynamic industries constituted partial exceptions, as their export volumes and world market shares testify. Such industries were the backbone of the liberal fraction of German industry, and the importance of these export branches clearly grew: in 1925, 2.7 million German workers produced 9.3 billion RM worth of goods for export; by 1929, 4.1 million workers produced 13.5 billion RM worth of goods (over one-third of total production) for export—a degree of recovery and even expansion unmatched by the domestic sector.[93] For the period 1926–30, Germany's trade balance was more favorable than the rest of Europe's. Once the Depression began, the export branches not only remained more viable than the domestic branches but gained internationally as well: Germany went from the world's number three exporter in 1929 to number one in 1931, outstripping both Britain and the United States.[94]

Heavy industry lacked the political strength that export industry derived from its superior economic position and cooperation with the SPD in matters of trade, fiscal, reparations, and even social policies. Not only did working-class gains limit heavy industry's profitability, but Stresemann's acceptance of armaments' restrictions was a further "limiting of heavy industry's field of activity."[95] The support of the rural sector, itself even more economically depressed, could not tip the balance in heavy industry's favor.[96] Of all the branches of heavy industry, mining probably suffered the earliest downturn; its fortunes had already peaked in 1926 (see tables 15 and 20). In that year the mines had obtained some 88 percent of the foreign loans made in Rhineland-

TABLE 19

Earnings (in millions of RM) and Profit Rate, 1927

	All Mining	Iron & Raw Metal	Textiles	All Metal Finishing	Electro-technical	Chemicals
Taxable earnings	151	14	132	52	32	31
Net earnings	65	5	75	16	17	17
Profit rate (%)	4.3	2.8	10	4.6	6.2	5.3

SOURCE: *Besteuerung,* table 10, p. 35.

93. The textile, finished-metals, machine, and chemical industries together accounted for about 70 percent of all Germany's exports in the period 1925–32; Hoffmann, p. 154.

94. Thus, the value of finished goods exported quarterly did drop from 2.5 billion in mid-1929 to 2 billion in late 1931. For Britain, however, the drop was from 3 billion to 1.5 billion, and for the United States from 2.7 billion to 1.3 billion. See *Geschäftliche Mitteilungen,* 13:28 (19 Dec. 1931). In the meantime, production for the domestic market dropped 50 percent between 1929 and 1932.

95. NW Iron and Steel, annual report, 1928; HA GHH/Nachlass Reusch 400 101 221/3.

96. The Langnamverein convention of 4 Apr. 1930 supported the rural demand for a Binnenmarktsstrategie, but Reusch was not sanguine about its prospects, ibid.

TABLE 20

Exports of Several Key Industries: Values (in millions of RM), Export Prices
(1913 = 100), Volume (1913 = 100), 1925–1932, and "World" Share
(in percent), 1928

	1925	1926	1927	1928	1929	1930	1931	1932
Coal								
Value	311	895	660	523	590	561	466	275
Price index	140	148	155	137	138	143	123	91
Volume index	39	105	74	66	75	68	66	53
World share 1928 = 10%								
Raw + semi-iron and steel								
Value	457	670	589	650	781	622	531	285
Price index	127	118	127	125	129	130	123	112
Volume index	51	81	66	74	86	68	61	36
World share 1928 = 22%								
Textiles[a]								
Value	1,150	1,167	1,274	1,338	1,399	1,249	1,055	526
Price index	195	183	195	196	189	190	163	133
Volume index	57	62	70	72	79	73	71	42
World share 1928 = 13%								
Metal goods[b]								
Value	2,261	2,445	2,670	3,146	3,769	3,645	2,943	1,835
Price index	138	135	135	140	143	139	131	124
Volume index	76	84	92	104	122	122	104	68
World share 1928 = 30%								
Chemicals[c]								
Value	953	1,137	1,277	1,396	1,460	1,257	1,036	730
Price index	133	138	141	138	129	126	115	104
Volume index	69	80	87	97	109	96	87	67
World share 1928 = 43%								

SOURCES: Hoffmann, pp. 522, 604–7, 534; Svennilson, p. 187. "World" share here means
the eight most industrialized countries of Europe plus the United States. Given the
products being considered, this definition introduces only minor discrepancies.
[a] Includes clothing but not yarn. The export price index for clothing was some seventy or
more points higher than that of cloth and fabric. In the twenties, Germany became a large
importer of clothing. Price index, Hoffmann, p. 607, cols. 11, 12.
[b] Includes machines and vehicles.   [c] Finished goods only.

Westphalia; by 1928 the mine owners received only 22 percent of a
slightly larger gross, and perhaps with good reason. Because of cheap,
primarily Polish, competition, the Ruhr mine owners claimed to be
losing nearly 1.5 RM per ton.[97] In this regard, too, mine owners felt a

97. They blamed this on high wages and overcapacity due to a shrunken domestic
market. They claimed that the English work day was longer than and social costs only
half Germany's. Real wages in England had actually declined 14 percent since 1913 but

distinct kinship with organized Landwirtschaft. These two were bearing the brunt of higher costs, and it was they, according to Arthur Mohrus of the Dresdner Bank, "who are paying off the Dawes Plan"; heavy industry was "slowly but surely going the way of agriculture" toward near bankruptcy.[98]

Because the mining and steel industries belonged to several international cartels, tariffs and quotas were not as salient to them as they were to agriculture. This difference limited the identity of interests between those two fractions, as the ascendance of export industry had limited the identity of interests between the two industrial fractions themselves. Heavy industry's emphasis instead was on the losses it incurred through high wages, Sozialpolitik and taxes—policies emerging from the export-labor coalition.[99] Since no diadic coalition could prove entirely satisfactory to industry, efforts to unify the two fractions of industry were never abandoned. Heavy industry, in particular, was anxious to counteract its declining economic position by establishing mechanisms to bind the two fractions of industry together, preferably in such a way as to reassert its own leadership. Such mechanisms were at once economic and political, private and public. They reflected the conflicts within industry and were attempts to overcome them.

4. Interindustrial Conflicts and Mechanisms: AVI, Tariffs, and Reparations

Some of the tensions between the two fractions of industry can be illuminated by examining three specific areas of conflict and the mechanisms that were established or proposed to manage them. The first set of conflicts arose simply because some industries, the processing branches, were customers of others, the primary producers. The former wanted to buy at low cost, and the latter to sell at high profit. Much of this conflict could be and was settled privately, but recourse to the state was available and used. The second arena was national trade policy:

---

had risen in Germany by almost that amount; *Die Wirtschaftliche Lage des Ruhrbergbaues* (1929), pp. 25–29.

98. Cited in BA/Nachlass Silverberg/362, p. 163, 17 Jan. 1929 and Hugenberg 151/ p. 187, where the same line is argued only more vitriolically. Both suffered from a debt estimated at over 50 percent of capital value. The Langnamverein meetings of 5 May 1928 reiterated the same themes.

99. Already in April 1927, Reusch called for a reversal of these policies in a memorandum to Chancellor Marx; HA GHH/Nachlass Reusch 400 101 293/13.

how and to whose advantage would trade treaties be negotiated and with what compensatory considerations, economic and political? International trade agreements automatically involved the state and reflected, however imperfectly, the balance of class forces. The third arena was the issue of reparations, specifically the Young Plan. There was a clear split between those who believed fulfillment to be the best policy for the German nation and economy and those who preferred a showdown and reckoning. Businessmen represented Germany in international reparations negotiations; the two bankers and two industrialists who led the delegation split down the middle. The outcome of these various conflicts was a dislocation of economic, from political, dominance within industry. One consequence of this dislocation was a quicker end to the labor-export coalition and the foreclosure of certain political options after 1930. The inability of either fraction of industry to emerge as clearly dominant lessened industry's political effectiveness and constrained it to accept a political solution in whose making it had little say.[100]

The first interindustrial conflict we examine was the mechanism used to regulate relations between the buyers of ferrous metals and their producers. This mechanism was an export rebate scheme known as the Iron Processing Industries Agreement (AVI). The thrust of the agreement was that in exchange for not challenging politically the fixed and high price of domestic iron and steel, the producers of these raw goods would refund to the processing and finishing industries the difference between the domestic and world prices for that portion of the iron and steel which the latter industries subsequently exported. While they worked, the AVI Agreements bound the generally smaller, more numerous, less cohesive, and export-oriented finishing industries to the cartels of heavy industry, not just economically but politically as well. Though costly to the primary producers—especially once the Depression began and the world price became otherwise meaningless—these agreements were crucial in preventing a break between the two fractions. Heavy industry obtained complete control over the domestic market, including pricing,[101] while the finishing industries improved their international positions. Freed of pressure from the "left," heavy industry was better able to deal with organized agriculture on its

100. The caveat here was industry's "lowest common denominator," i.e., it had little to say in the making of a solution *besides* that any solution would have to restore profitability to capital *and* eliminate the political influence of the organized working class.

101. In 1928, for example, the domestic iron price was 50 to 70 percent higher than the export price.

"right," and all three fractions could, after 1929, oppose the demands of labor.[102]

The first AVI Accord was reached in 1925, and its consequences were felt immediately. Most representatives of the finishing industries in the DDP, Zentrum, and DVP momentarily deserted their usual partners in Handelspolitik, the SPD, and voted for higher tariffs and against a Saar agreement with France.[103] Suddenly, the finishing industries could accept heavy industry's cartels. They ceased opposing the IRG and, after further assurances, even opposed government surveillance of cartel price policies. High domestic prices were now acceptable because they subsidized exports. Once again a republican government was unsuccessful in interpreting the interests of the bourgeoisie as a whole against its parts,[104] as industrialists preferred to institutionalize their internecine conflicts within their own organizations. So long as the economy was expansive the AVI mechanism continued to work. Thus, a substantial number of processing industries altered their initial positions and supported the Ruhr steel producers' lockout of October 1928. With their significant influence in the liberal and democratic press, they did considerable harm to the unions' efforts.[105]

With the onset of the Depression, both partners turned to an attack on Sozialpolitik rather than to a reconsideration of their own price structures. At least initially, the AVI exporters had little cause to complain. The lower world market prices fell, the higher rose their rebates; and, since the domestic market contracted while their exports actually grew, they became increasingly dependent on their rebates. Hence, many were even willing to join heavy industry's opposition to Brüning's 1931 call for price cuts, even if, unlike heavy industry, they were not prepared to oppose Brüning altogether. The AVI agreements were important to heavy industry because of the declining value and increased costs of alliance with organized agriculture. Of course, the rub was that to retain AVI support, heavy industry had to pay even larger amounts. This, together with the temptation to expand into the profitable finish-

102. See Stegmann, "Zoll- und Handelspolitik," p. 509.

103. Ulrich Nocken, "Inter-Industrial Conflicts and Alliances as Exemplified by the AVI Agreement," in Mommsen, et al., eds., p. 697; cf. Maier, pp. 519, 535.

104. In January 1928, the steel makers and the AVI industries reached an agreement on higher prices for raw iron and steel, together with more generous rebates. A month later the AVI organizations abandoned Economics Minister Curtius (DVP) in his call for policing cartels and possible use of the anticartel laws. BA/R131-VDESI/215, pp. 2–3, 114–70.

105. Nocken, p. 699. The machine-builders association, for example, reversed itself, supported the lockout, and planted prolockout articles in the otherwise anti-heavy-industry *Berliner Tageblatt, Vossische Zeitung,* and *Frankfurter Zeitung.*

ing trades, led to the steel producers' demands for revision of the accords.[106] Between 1925 and 1930, heavy industry had bought a rightward drift (or prevented a leftward one) in the politics of many finishing industries; now a different form of payment was in order.

In 1928 and 1929 the strength of the processing industries within the RDI was enhanced not only by their economic vitality but also by their support of the Grand Coalition and cooperation with the SPD. Because of this greater freedom of political movement, the steel industrialists were forced to be more accommodating. Faced with an RDI resolution critical of the steel industry, Oscar Funcke, describing the multifaceted character of the smaller producers, responded that egos perhaps played too large a role in his industry, but he and his colleagues fully recognized the responsibility to further the exports of the processing industries through the AVI agreements.[107] Paul Silverberg reiterated the complementarity of the two fractions of industry and stressed the "absolute need for both groups to work together to save what [is] left of and attempt to restore the lost position of the entrepreneur." Nevertheless, he chided the processing industries for demonstrating a certain *konjunkturpolitischen Opportunismus* in their dickering with the political left and right.[108] The breaking of the Grand Coalition in March 1930 and the subsequent offensive against the SPD made the attainment of capitalist unity crucial. But the matter was not so simple.

With each in pursuit of individual, entrepreneurial, and corporate interests, conflict between the steel and processing industries grew as the economic situation deteriorated in 1930. Representatives of the two groups met in October under the auspices of the RDI to try to find a compromise. The transcript of that meeting reveals clearly the balance of forces between and political drift of each of the fractions:

> *Director Klemme [steel industry, GHH]*: "Our cartels are in no way to blame; high iron prices are strictly a consequence of a rigid wage

106. The smallest producers in the finishing industries were most vulnerable to this infringement. United in the Esti-Bund, they complained that the AVI associations and the government were doing an inadequate job of protecting them. Many were early supporters of the Nazis, who they believed would halt the takeover of their fields by the big producers and instead establish some kind of artisanal or petit bourgeois justice. See Nocken, pp. 701–2; Winkler, *Mittlestand*. Poulantzas describes this notion of "justice" rather aptly as the petit bourgeois's wanting everybody to be just like himself; *Fascisme*, pp. 262–63.

107. Funcke, BA/R13I-VDESI/221, pp. 215, 221. The RDI complaint against the steel producers was lodged on 24 May 1929. On the conflict between Vögler and Stresemann, see Maier, p. 443, and Stürmer, passim.

108. On the need for unity, BA/Nachlass Silverberg/27, p. 17, 4 Dec. 1930; on oppor-

structure. . . . We must now compel a lowering of wages and follow with lowering prices."

Karl Lange [*machine-building industry and AVI negotiator*]: "As opposed to that of the iron producers, the situation of the processing industries is catastrophic. . . . We view the matter of wages exactly as you do, but our wages are rigid too. But with us sales prices are determined by competition here and abroad. We are delivered up to the free play of forces. We have absolutely no monopolistic cartels. . . . You can maintain constant domestic prices. [We cannot] yet for iron we must pay 68 percent above the world price. . . . You must reduce iron industry prices. . . . [You] say you have losses. Let us not get into that, nor into GHH's dividend increase. . . . To top it all off, you charge your own processing subsidiaries less than you charge us. . . . We will be loyal [for now], but we have to make our position clear on these matters."

Ludwig Kastl [*RDI, mediating*]: "Wage levels need not be maintained until the end of the contract period. But they must be changed through negotiation with the other [labor] side."

Reichert: "Wages are the decisive thing. . . . a general wage reduction affecting coal, ore, railways [etc.] would really make a difference."

Kastl: "Wages and prices must both drop immediately." Given reparations, Germany could not afford to lose any share of the world market. If producers were to convince the public that wages were too high and rigid, they would have to demonstrate that cartel prices were not.

Ernst Poensgen [*steel industry*]: "We must demonstrate the unity of all employers." The government had to saw off the branch on which it was sitting.

Kastl: "The government wants to reduce prices. A great deal of courage is required for that . . . we should not frustrate it."

Paul Peddinghaus [*small-wares spokesman*]: "If I return home without a commitment to lower prices, my colleagues will stone me. . . . The big concerns provision their own subsidiaries at lower prices than they charge us . . . have used favorable deals with local governments for [utilities] . . . and then underbid our firms."

Lange: "We ought to check, if a price reduction may not now be possible. We too will emphasize wage reductions. . . . But . . . one has first to dispel the argument that cartel prices are responsible

---

tunism, p. 36. Kastl estimated that "90 percent of the RDI's work relates primarily to small and middle industry"; ibid., 702, p. 38, 4 Nov. 1930; cf. Weisbrod.

for the current crisis. [Even if losses are entailed] that would show the workers that wages alone are the cause of the crisis."[109]

By mid-1931 the iron and steel producers had lost all interest in the export market that was more crucial than ever to the processing industries. The iron producers could simply no longer afford to pay the export rebates. In 1925, 70 percent of German iron and steel was consumed domestically and 30 percent ultimately exported; in 1928, the ratio was 50:50; by late 1931, it had reached 25:75. By that latter date, numerous steel producers were operating at 25 percent of capacity with the domestic market absorbing only 22 percent of what it had absorbed as recently as 1929. Given the choice between abandoning their cartel pricing and continuing the full AVI rebates, they were highly ambivalent.[110] Heavy industry sought a way out of the 1925 agreements. Its representatives suggested procedures that would have rendered most of the smaller consumers ineligible for refunds. Other proposals would have reduced rebates to the amount of the tariff or some fraction of that amount; still others would have provided the AVI industries a fixed quota of cheap iron to divide as they themselves saw fit.[111] Reichsbank President Luther and the Chancellory were called upon to limit the export industries' access to foreign currency, thereby forestalling their circumvention of the reduced rebate rates. The AVI controversy became a major subject of recriminations in the press, in Parliament, and within the RDI.[112]

In March 1932, the RDI was again called upon to mediate or arbitrate. For the RDI, the issue became a test of the political balance of forces within it. Under the impact of the struggle against organized labor and the SPD, the RDI had swung to the right in mid-1930 and then again in mid-1931. The selection of the "steel man" Krupp to replace the retiring "chemicals man" Duisberg in September 1931 illustrated the renewed organizational dominance of heavy industry. That May, Reusch had indicated to Krupp that the RDI was ready for this change;

109. BA/R13I-VDESI/437, pp. 269, 277–89, 6 Oct. 1930. In the following months a publicity war flared between the two groups.

110. Statements by various spokesmen, ibid., pp. 4–20. Most, of course, wanted to do neither, though the maintenance of cartel prerogatives was a matter of sanctity.

111. At the end of 1931 the German iron price was 107 RM per ton and the world price 62 RM per ton. The prescribed rebate was thus 45 RM per ton, compared to which the tariff was a mere 16 RM per ton. By March 1932 the world price had fallen all the way to 50 RM per ton. The various proposals, objections, and documentation are in BA/R13I-VDESI/438.

112. On foreign-currency limitations, see Reichert's letter to Luther on behalf of the VDESI, 12 Feb. 1932. Cf. HA GHH/Nachlass Reusch 400 101 290/30b. On this episode in the AVI controversy, see Weisbrod, pp. 376–92, where again it is made to appear that the iron and steel producers got their way even though sentiment in all three of these arenas ran strongly against them.

no purge would be necessary.[113] Instead, heavy industry would attempt to integrate the demands of the exporters into an overall program that the former would oversee. Renewed leadership by the heavy, domestic-market-oriented fraction of industry could only facilitate the move toward a new Sammlung bloc.

Trade policy was another area of interindustrial conflict where developments and outcomes both reflected and affected relations between the fractions of industry. It was also an area in which a multitude of organizations sought the intervention of political parties and the executive branch on their individual behalves.[114] During the period of export-labor cooperation from 1925 to 1930, Foreign Minister Stresemann and Economics Minister Curtius pursued a trade-expanding policy of most-favored-nation treaties, which proved damaging to organized agriculture and divisive for industry. While the dynamic fraction profited from these policies, heavy industry gambled instead on the expansion of the internal market together with participation in international cartels. After 1925 it became increasingly apparent that this was not a good wager.[115]

The prototype for fractional conflict over trade policy was the protracted discord over a treaty with Poland. After 1925, the mining and steel industries, especially those of Upper Silesia, joined organized agriculture in opposing a trade treaty with "low-cost Poland." Together, heavy industry and the RLB (and later the Green Front) frustrated the efforts of Stresemann, Curtius, and the export industries to conclude a broad-ranging agreement.[116] Export industrialists attempted to portray trade with Poland as involving essentially the exchange of Polish raw materials for German finished goods. Karl Lange contended that agri-

113. Reusch told Krupp that Kastl and the Berlin liberals and exporters made concessions and "we can work together again. I would be highly grateful if you succeeded Duisberg as chairman. You can be sure you would have the support of the entire West." 5 May 1931; HA GHH/Nachlass Reusch 400 101 290/27. The changes in the RDI are discussed in greater detail below. Certain statutory changes in mid-1930 increased the representation of the Ruhr district within the RDI, reversing the earlier "democratization" and emboldening the representatives of mining interests.

114. See, for example, Carl Böhret, *Aktionen gegen die 'kalte Sozialisierung,' 1926–1930* (Berlin, 1966), pp. 103–16.

115. Much of this is summarized in Stegmann, "Zoll und Handelspolitik," esp. pp. 507–11. In June 1925, the Employers' League anticipated a more profitable and substantially more productive rural sector which might yield lower costs and substantially expand the internal market for German industry. This hardly happened. See BA/R13I-VDESI/358, pp. 288–89.

116. On the similarity of the opponents' arguments, BA/R13I-VDESI/217, pp. 81–92. On the eagerness of the DIHT for such an agreement, despite the evident deleterious effects on German agriculture and mining, BA/R11-DIHT/124, pp. 5523, 4532. On the "pure export" position of the commercial interests attached to the DDP, BA/Nachlass Dietrich/227, pp. 241–45. Heavy industry and the agrarians were strong enough to keep

cultural goods constituted only 13 percent of all imports from Poland and that East Prussia's economic problems were not to be blamed on Poland. The nation must not, he argued in 1928, accept the foolish arguments which the estate owners provided the Langnamverein and which they now both used against Stresemann.[117] Heavy industry's interest in opposing the treaty was increased by the prospect of gaining greater support from agriculture in the fight against the Grand Coalition and its wage, tax, and social policies. Heavy industry's opposition was not severe enough to prevent a treaty supported by the entire labor-export coalition, but the lines of a future autarky coalition did begin to emerge in the course of the debate.

Paul Reusch wrote an "industry-friendly" member of the Agrarian League executive that "Neither I personally nor any of the enterprises I lead has the slightest interest in a trade treaty with Poland. However, [some] eastern and middle-German industries need this agreement badly. . . . Yet agriculture and especially the RLB hotheads reject completely even the most minor concessions." Schlenker held this no way to improve cooperation and join ranks "in our current struggle [the lockouts]" as well as against the entire direction of the government.[118] Reusch's contact man in Berlin, Martin Blank, was informed by the agrarians that heavy industry, if it expected "the shoulder-to-shoulder support of agriculture in social, fiscal, reparations, and political questions," would have to reverse the "slap-in-the-face attitude" toward agriculture which it had let representatives of the dynamic and export industries manifest in the Poland question.[119] Reusch and others were not yet in a position to do that, although they did step up their efforts. Thus, at the very time the RDI was formulating its *Contribution to an Agrarian Program*—a program that met with near-total denunciation by organized Landwirtschaft—some Ruhr steel industrialists raised the slogan "protection of national production."[120] While a majority RDI

---

labor and the exporters from getting all that they desired in a Polish treaty, but not strong enough to prevent what was still a very substantial agreement.

117. Lange's analysis of the composition of Polish trade and his attack on the estate owners are in BA/Nachlass Silverberg/362, pp. 77–83; the criticism of the Langnamverein and defense of Stresemann, pp. 117, 152, Oct. and Nov. 1928.

118. Reusch to Thilo von Wilmowsky (Krupp's brother-in-law and a prominent agrarian "moderate"), 18 Nov. 1928, HA GHH/Nachlass Reusch 400 101 290/39. Panzer's argument, pp. 135–44, that agriculture was entirely on its own, is nonsense. Schlenker to Reusch, 16 Nov. 1928; see n. 120.

119. Von Wilmowsky to Kastl, 17 Nov. 1928, and Blank to Reusch, 21 Nov. 1928; HA GHH/ Martin Blank-Berlinstelle der GHH 400 101 202 4/4b. See Panzer; Gessner, *Agrarverbände*, pp. 128–36.

120. The slogan was raised and its intent made clear by Max Schlenker of the North-west Steel group; HA GHH/Nachlass Reusch 400 101 24/1, 16 Nov. 1928.

report detailed state assistance to agriculture, which it described as thankless and incompetent, and advocated more trade with Poland, heavy industry came to agriculture's defense in the name of the "national economy."[121]

The series of trade treaties negotiated after 1925 resulted largely from the cooperation of the dynamic fraction of industry with labor. The collapse of the Grand Coalition came as a result of domestic factors, primarily the rising costs of that cooperation; but with the Coalition's fall and the slowdown of international trade, the two protectionist fractions, agriculture and heavy industry, reasserted themselves. They began to stage a political comeback even as their economic situations deteriorated. Trade treaties did, at least, help keep heavy industry producing. But in a situation where high labor costs, taxes and social-welfare payments, and ballooning rebate requirements combined to take the profit out of production, heavy industry lost interest in maintaining the volume of production[122] and, hence, in the trade treaties that kept the export branches not only busy but profitable as well. The export drive, which began with great fervor in 1925 and made Germany one of the most adamant supporters of free trade at the World Economics Conference in Geneva in 1927, split the two fractions of industry and, by 1930, became for one of them little more than an onerous burden.

Exports allowed individual capitalists to make substantial profits and extend German influence,[123] but the *national* necessity to export emerged from the assumption of reparations obligations under the Dawes Plan in 1925 as modified by the Young Plan in 1929. The policy of continuing to fulfill reparations was itself the subject of bitter conflicts within industry, and the victory of the fulfillment advocates over the catastrophe advocates, in October 1929 and again in March 1930, however narrow and unenthusiastic, was the last significant victory of the Grand Coalition.[124] Coming as it did at the end of the boom period,

---

121. The Lange-Kastl memorandum of February 1931 was entitled "Post War Help for Agriculture." Reusch wondered if the exporters were "demanding the total destruction of the grain producers." HA GHH/Nachlass Reusch 400 101 24/3a. Such talk clearly undercut the dynamic fraction's program for agriculture; see chap. 4.

122. Thus, both the United Steelworks and the GHH "enjoyed" continuous production and sales volume increases from 1926 through 1929 and into early 1930. Taxes, wages, social payments, and rebate requirements rose faster and farther, however, so that their net profits peaked in 1927, began their decline in 1928, and turned into losses by 1930.

123. This was particularly true for eastern Europe and the Soviet Union, for whom Germany was the number one trading partner. See Sohn-Rethel, pp. 78–99.

124. Cf. Timm, pp. 140–47, 166–67; Bracher, pp. 290–91; chap. 1, note 77.

the majority of industry's representatives were convinced that they needed the Young Plan. A portion of this majority believed that acceptance of the plan would assist in limiting labor's demands and restoring fiscal responsibility. For the large minority at the center of the "national opposition," the Young Plan signified national humiliation, long-term capital impoverishment, and a cementing of the export-labor coalition's strategy of social peace and international reintegration—all on unsatisfactory terms.

Germany's business representatives to the negotiations were split. The banker Carl Melchior of the Hamburg house of Warburg and the industrialists' agent Ludwig Kastl supported acceptance of the plan they had helped negotiate; the banker Hjalmar Schacht and the industrialist Albert Vögler rejected their own work and left the negotiating team.[125] The RDI unofficially supported Kastl, Melchior, and acceptance of the plan. The Langnamverein explicitly supported Vögler, Schacht and its rejection. For the exporters and still more prosperous industries, the Young Plan, although it technically might require a half-century of reparations, promised not only immediate restoration of German sovereignty over important territories and public enterprises but also a continued and even enlarged flow of foreign credits along with a commercialization of reparations and war debts. These final points particularly appealed to Melchior, a prominent figure within the DIHT, and to the representatives of the dynamic and export industries in the RDI echelons. Because they promised little if any benefit to stagnant, domestic-oriented heavy industry, its representatives saw nothing in the Young Plan to recommend itself, not even the planned

125. The four chief delegates to the negotiating sessions led by Owen Young were proposed by the two cabinet members and most directly responsible for reparations matters—Foreign Minister Stresemann and Finance Minister Hilferding, both central figures in the cooperation between the dynamic fraction of industry and labor. Both ministers agreed that as Reichsbankpräsident and someone respected in international finance, Schacht was the obvious choice for the meetings scheduled to begin in Paris in February 1929. Their real first choice, for the reasons indicated below, was Melchior; for these same reasons his appointment was opposed by Vögler, who argued that in "his and his colleagues' opinion," Melchior overestimated Germany's ability to pay and that "commercialization was unacceptable" to them. Silverberg successfully proposed a compromise of sorts to Stresemann: upgrading Vögler's status so as to preempt the criticism that would inevitably come from the rightist "national opposition" once the negotiations were concluded. Vögler spoiled that plan with a dramatic resignation well-orchestrated with some of his Ruhr colleagues. At the behest of the RDI leadership and with the full backing of the electrical and chemical industries especially, Kastl assumed Vögler's functions and helped bring the negotiations to a successful close. See Jörg-Otto Spiller, "Reformismus nach Rechts: Zur Politik des RDI am Beispiel der Reparationspolitik," in Mommsen, et al., eds., pp. 593–95.

restoration of Germany's full control over her finances. For the time being, however, the balance of forces within industry still favored the dynamic fraction and its cooperation with the Grand Coalition government and the Young Plan's opponents had to admit defeat.[126]

Many in heavy industry were prepared to allow the RDI to incur the blame for any consequences of the plan and, hence, did not militate strongly against it or act in support of the Hilter-Hugenberg referendum against the plan and its proponents.[127] The RDI at its October 1929 convention described the Young Plan as exceeding Germany's ability to pay but necessary politically; for heavy industry, the political necessities the plan dictated were of a different order—ending cooperation with organized labor and the SPD. Those supporting acceptance saw it as a necessary evil to be accepted quickly and quietly; and indeed, the RDI convention's discussion was notable for its brevity.[128] In contrast, the Langnamverein meeting was orchestrated to maximize the vehemence of the plan's opponents and to disassociate them from any responsibility for its success.[129]

In addition to manifesting support for the Vögler hard-line, the Ruhr industrialists used the occasion to call for the "immediate reversal of the already impossible burden placed on us by outrageously high wages and taxes." "Especially endangered," said Reusch, "are agriculture,

---

126. Weisbrod, pp. 290ff., admits that this was the case but contends that heavy industry's unsuccessful opposition nevertheless spoiled the victory.

127. See the reports cited in the press, ZSA/RLB Pressarchiv 148/9, pp. 39–43. Some on the extreme right of heavy industry (Thyssen, Kirdorf, et al.) did support the Hitler-Hugenberg referendum; Spiller, pp. 597–98. In opposition to those who wanted "the catastrophe now," Kastl maintained that the next generation of Germans would not be paying reparations even if reparations were formally supposed to continue for forty years. Robert Bosch and Hermann Bücher of the electrical industry and RDI even joined the SPD-led public campaign against the referendum.

128. This was the Kastl-Duisberg-Silverberg position to which Reusch, Reichert, and others took great exception. See HA GHH/Nachlass Reusch 400 101 221/9b, Reusch to Schlenker, 29 June 1929. Reusch rejected Silverberg's suggestion to remain calm and adopt a farsighted perspective. Reusch was also less concerned to mask the division within the RDI on this and other issues. Nevertheless, Duisberg and his associates contrived to hold to a bare minimum the time allotted for discussion of the Young Plan and even managed to keep Thyssen from being scheduled to speak; see Reusch to Kastl, 8 Aug. 1929 and Kastl's response, 13 Aug., HA GHH/Nachlass Reusch 400 101 220/7.

129. HA GHH/Nachlass Reusch 400 101 221/9b, where Reusch's proposed agenda and list of speakers are recorded together with letters of support from the other convention organizers. The list of speakers had to be changed at the last moment when it turned out that some of those expected to oppose the Plan (the economist Stolper, for example) actually supported it and castigated their hosts. For all their supposed Rhenish-Westphalian unity, the Langnamverein program featured no speakers from the AVI processing industries. June 1929.

heavy industry and the raw-material industries."[130] Opposition to the Young Plan became intertwined with the overall critique of policies approved or tolerated by the dynamic fraction. In one and the same paragraph, Reusch could protest that

> Five generations of tribute . . . and the sellout of the German economy are unacceptable. . . . The Young Plan will reduce the German Volk from a nation to a geographical expression. . . . Not counting debts and interest, the demands on the economy have increased [over] 18 billion RM since 1925: 3.5 billion in taxes, 10 billion in wages, 3 billion in salaries, and 1.4 billion in social welfare expenses. . . . Were the social purchasing power [Mehraufwand] theories correct, we should be in the midst of blooming prosperity; we are not! [Precisely those industries which could least afford it had been hardest hit.] The execution of the Young Plan on top of all that is impossible; the enslavement of the German people for the rest of the century is impossible.[131]

Kastl's view was almost diametrically opposed. For him, world economic developments and Germany's ability to export were critical. Responding to the British reparation agent MacFadyan's suggestion that Germany facilitate its debt payments by cutting public expenditures, Kastl wrote that "social-welfare costs are a premium for warding off bolshevism. Were those not paid, then large sections of Social Democracy would wind up in the Communist camp[!]. By preventing this, Germany serves the interests of other European countries as well."[132] Even once allowances are made for the rhetorical components in both statements, the severity of the split between the two fractions remains clear—as does the inadequacy of the mechanisms designed to overcome the division.

5. Political Responses to the Crisis: Bürgerblock, Brüningblock, and "National Opposition"

The abandonment of the Grand Coalition by the bourgeois parties and its subsequent collapse in March 1930 left the dominant social classes without a popular base to support their program for overcoming the

130. Cited in the *Deutsche Bergwerkszeitung*, 9 July 1929.
131. Reusch's keynote speech, cited in BA/Z Sg 126/8 July 1929, BBZ.
132. BA/Nachlass Kastl/9, pp. 87–88, 22 Mar. 1930. Support for the KPD did grow after 1928, but Kastl willfully exaggerated the Communist threat. More important than warding off bolshevism, Sozialpolitik bought the bourgeoisie a mass base and some measure of capitalist stability.

worsening economic situation.[133] Prominent industrialists strove to replace the late coalition with a bourgeois concentration (Bürgerblock), but were unable to marshal either the requisite unity or popular support. Besides their growing electoral weakness, several of the bourgeois parties would not cooperate with each other.[134] Thus, some in the DVP would under no circumstances unite with the DDP, yet others would unite with that party only. The largest bürgerliche party remained the DNVP, but Hugenberg's leadership was unacceptable not only to other politicians but to the industrial proponents of unity as well. Although the unification efforts of the industrialists were multifaceted, they were confused and reflected the salient divisions within industry: Eduard Hamm of the DIHT and August Weber of the textile industry, for example, financed the "Liberal Alliance," which tried to bring about a merger of the DDP and DVP at the same time that Paul Reusch and Fritz Springorum attempted to unite the DNVP (without Hugenberg), the DVP, the Wirtschaftspartei, and other splinter parties while excluding the DDP.[135] And, while all the unity proposals involved the DVP, that party's chief parliamentary and ministerial figure (following Stresemann's death), Curtius, was utterly unacceptable to almost all of heavy industry, which inveighed against him constantly.[136] Heavy industry also found unacceptable the DVP finance minister, Paul Moldenhauer, formerly of IG Farben, because he "ignored the immediate needs of business in the name of some vague long-term goal."[137] Whereas some industrialists viewed the Zentrum as a large and needed pillar of any Bürgerblock, others saw it as too spoils-oriented and a

133. The outlines of that program were drawn in the two RDI memoranda: *Aufstieg oder Niedergang* (Recovery or Collapse), December 1929 (Veröffentlichung des RDI, no. 49) and *Wirtschafts-, Sozial- Steuer- und Finanzpolitik* (Economic, Social, Tax and Fiscal Politics), January 1930 (Veröffentlichung des RDI, no. 50). These documents are written virtually as ultimata and mark a clear break from the politics of cooperation with labor. The specific proposals are discussed in chapter 5.

134. On their electoral problems, see tables 1–2; on problems of unity, Jones, "Dying Middle," pp. 23–54; Bracher, pp. 309ff.

135. These efforts are discussed in HA GHH/Nachless Reusch 400 101 293/9. On the deteriorating relations between representatives and represented, see chap. 6, sec. 4.

136. Curtius was the prototype of the class collaborator. Already in 1928, Schlenker wrote that "Curtius does not have the least ability to represent even the most basic demands of the economy. . . . I have tried emphatically to make clear to the DVP the desperate situation into which Curtius is increasingly dragging the party and *die Wirtschaft*. . . . He must be pushed out." HA GHH/Nachlass Reusch 400 101 221/9a. Schlenker to Reusch, 3 Nov. 1928.

137. The attack on Moldenhauer was particularly sharp in 1930; HA GHH/Nachlass Reusch 400 101 293/4a and 10a. Moldenhauer had succeeded Hilferding at the end of 1929. For example, 8 and 10 Feb. and 10 and 20 Mar. 1930, Moldenhauer to Duisberg, Herle notes on Moldenhauer, 220/8a, 8 Mar. 1930.

major impediment to that goal. Many in the DVP were unprepared to forgive the Zentrum its Prussian Black-Red coalition, but refused, too, to subordinate themselves to the DNVP. While the DVP leadership bore real enmity toward the DDP, Bosch and IG Farben continued to fund it.[138] The various efforts to buy or blackmail the bourgeois parties into combination or coalition continued through 1932, but they all failed. The goals of the forces within industry were too divergent, selfish, and narrowly defined to be amenable to formation into one unified political voice. Despite critical financial support, the heavy-handed involvement of industrialists did nothing to enhance the electoral appeal of the bourgeois parties.

In the absence of any substantial bourgeois unity, both fractions of industry were initially constrained to accept an SPD-tolerated Brüning government as the successor to the Grand Coalition. Initially, too, Brüning's program promised a restoration of profitability through lower wages, reduced state expenditures, a further revision of reparations, and general austerity combined with an expansive trade policy—all in the context of a strong government semiindependent of Parliament. Such a catch-all program was bound to follow a zigzag course, but one that could not meet the needs of both fractions of industry so long as the program did not seek to eliminate all SPD and labor influence. Short of such a commitment, the two competing fractions of industry (and the rural sector) would still need to thwart each other.[139] Dissatisfied with the tempo of Brüning's and Labor Minister Stegerwald's belt tightening in the fiscal, labor, and social spheres, spokesmen for heavy industry began looking for alternatives as early as November 1930. Not only did Brüning leave intact the structural basis of labor's economic gains, but he appeared intent on lowering basic industrial prices in order to facilitate an export drive and revision of reparations.[140] As noted above,

138. On DVP hostility toward the Zentrum, BA/Nachlass Dingeldey/73, pp. 6, 44, 47, and /75, pp. 64ff.; on the animus toward the DDP, /89. In chap. 6, sec. 4, we discuss more fully the relationship of the industrialists to the bourgeois parties.

139. In this sense, Poulantzas is correct in asserting that what he labels "middle capital" (small, nonmonopoly-sector industries in the processing and consumer-goods branches) found it useful to continue collaborating with labor until the Nazis were able to neutralize the conflicts within capital generally; Fascisme, pp. 96–101. In different terms, Silverberg understood this, too, as he observed support for Brüning diminishing in the ranks of heavy industry but not among either smaller producers or export interests, between mid-1930 and mid-1931; BA/Nachlass Silverberg/274, pp. 85–108. On the initial widespread industrial support for Brüning, see Wilhelm Treue, "Der deutsche Unternehmer in der Weltwirtschaftskrise," in Conze and Raupach, eds., p. 107.

140. The strategy behind the export offensive was twofold: it would appear as if Germany were doing its best to meet its reparations obligations; yet it would encourge

Germany became the world's number one exporter in 1930–31, and the exporting branches found the uses of general adversity quite sweet.

August Heinrichsbauer, an associate of Reusch's Berlin representative Martin Blank and chief link to the National Opposition, reported in December 1930 that "the time for a so-called bourgeois concentration is past. . . . It is a matter of providing the masses leaders from those already available. . . . The essential goal must be to maintain and build the unity of the National [Hitler-Hugenberg-Seldte] Opposition. . . . The time for 'not only this but also that' [Brüning's half-measures?—DA] must be past." For his part, however, Reusch, replying to a report by Edgar Jung later in the month, preferred an attempt to create a movement whose goal "is not to fit a point of crystallization between the bourgeois right and National Socialism. Much more the movement should have in mind the creation of one national right," which would also tutor the Nazis. He and several colleagues may have noted Goebbels's "readiness to promote the interests of entrepreneurs" and his statement that "wage cuts for the sake of reparations and the current system are unacceptable," but that "he would put himself completely at the disposal of the entrepreneurial class" if it joined in thoroughgoing opposition to the System. Reusch may also have noted Strasser's remark that "industry has exerted itself too much for exports"; "the economy must be switched over from the world to the domestic market. That would mean the reinvigoration of agriculture; I embrace a feasible form of autarky." It would be too much to infer from these documents a switch to a strategy based on the Nazis; Reusch considered the Jung report so controversial that he asked him to destroy all his copies.[141] Nevertheless, they do help to demonstrate that the split between the liberal (pro-Brüning) and national (pro-Hitler-Hugenberg) fractions of industry began almost as soon as the outlines of Brüning's program became clear, and the National Opposition emerged as a real force.

Brüning earned the wrath of heavy industry and the support of the AVI industries by mandating price as well as wage cuts—under the threat of invoking the long-ignored cartel laws. This was a threat to the only advantage heavy industry still enjoyed: guaranteed high prices. By

competing foreign manufacturers to urge their governments to relent on German payments. On the support this program enjoyed with the dynamic fraction, see Dieter Schäfer, p. 63.

141. Heinrichsbauer, possibly via Blank, to Reusch, [9] Dec. 1930; Reusch's comments on a no-longer-preserved report by Jung, [23] Dec. 1930, and his instructions to Jung, 2 Jan. 1931, HA GHH/Nachlass Reusch 400 101 293/11. (The colleagues who noted Jung's observations are left unnamed.) It is not our intention here to detail the process by which industrialists developed their contacts with and affinities for the Nazis.

1931 the United Steelworks was operating at about one-third of capacity, but its prices had dropped only 8 percent since 1929. Other branches of heavy industry were in a similar position: mine operators faced sharply reduced demand and fresh labor militancy, and to these was now added Brüning's demand for price reductions.[142] The constellation of economic developments and political responses sharpened the split over Brüning and further dislocated political from economic leadership in industry.[143] From the viewpoint of heavy industry, Brüning's program was neither effective nor sufficient. Granted that through both legislation and presidential emergency decree, he increased workers' contributions to the unemployment insurance fund while reducing the amount and duration of benefits. Further, a cut in wages was decreed, while the tax on wages was raised and the tax on capital lowered. General government spending was restricted, and, after much debate, civil-service salaries were reduced. But the attempt to reduce cartel prices by force and the failure to eliminate the influence of the SPD and unions limited Brüning's acceptability to the national fraction of industry. Brüning was weakened well before the conflict with Hindenburg and the estate owners that toppled him.[144]

Brüning continued to receive some support: from the representatives of the more viable industries of the dynamic fraction (especially IG Farben and German General Electric [AEG], but also the machine builders, the AVI, and other export groups), from the bank most closely associated with that fraction (the Deutsche Bank and some of its executives, Otto Wolff, C. F. v. Siemens, Werner Kehl), from commercial and small-industry organizations (the DIHT, the Hansa Bund), from those who considered the Zentrum a stable and reliable mass base (including Catholic industrialists such as Otto Wolff and Peter

142. On steel, Clemenz, p. 198. In 1932 the United Steelworks operated at a bare 20 percent of capacity. The cement industry had fallen under 30 percent in 1930 already. For the various price indices, see table 3. Between 1929 and 1931, the industrial price index in Britain fell 50 percent further than it did in Germany. For an overview of production declines in other industries, Wagenführ, pp. 56–57. On the declines in mining, Rudolf Regul, "Der Wettbewerbslage der Steinkohle," *Vierteljahrshefte zur Konjunkturforschung*, Sonderheft no. 34 (1933).

143. On the shifting balance within industry, cf. the *Vierteljahrshefte zur Konjunkturforschung*, esp. 5:3A (Dec. 1930), pp. 55ff., 71ff.

144. See chap. 2, sec. 4c. It is noteworthy that for all which German labor lost under Brüning, its leaders knew that they retained influence and that "the social-policy system constructed after the war . . . including collective-bargaining rights, binding arbitration, factory committee laws, work-hours legislation, and most forms of social insurance," remained in place under Brüning. See *Jahrbuch des ADGB, 1931* (Berlin, 1932), pp. 85–87.

Klöckner), and from all those who looked with favor or comfort on the efficacious presence of IG Farben executives at the head of the Economics Ministry (Hermann Warmbold) and, earlier, Finance Ministry (Paul Moldenhauer), and as financial advisor to the chancellor (Hermann Schmitz).[145] Impatient and shortchanged, representatives of heavy industry mobilized as they had a few months earlier when Duisberg suggested reestablishing the Arbeitsgemeinschaft.[146] Representatives of heavy industry discovered that united they possessed a greater degree of political maneuverability than the dynamic fraction, despite suffering from greater economic paralysis.[147] With the collapse of the export economy at the end of 1931 they were able to demand the political leadership of all of industry. By that time it was becoming increasingly less clear which fraction held the better position to set the tone and agenda for industry as a whole. Who would integrate whose demands into a program overseen by whom? It was partly this absence of a hegemonic fraction that drove German industry to foster or accept a Bonapartist solution to the political crisis and an imperialist solution to the economic crisis.

Heavy industry stepped up its offensive in early 1931. In January, the Mining Association threatened to withdraw from the RDI because it was "taking only half measures" and had not succeeded in convincing the government to cancel wage agreements.[148] Four months later, when Duisberg and Kastl continued to support Brüning, the Mining Associa-

---

145. See Fricke, ed., 2:605–9; Weisbrod, pp. 493, 498; Jones, "Sammlung," p. 283; Richard Sasuly, *IG Farben* (Berlin, 1952), p. 89. The work of Kurt Gossweiler has gone farther than any other in tracing the linkages, significant *and* otherwise, between German banks, industries, and cabinets; see *Grossbanken, Industriemonopole, Staat* (Berlin, 1971), esp. pp. 314–92. Although it deserves criticism, most noncommunist historians prefer either simply to ignore his work or dismiss it out of hand. On state-monopoly capitalism as a conception see Kocka's contribution in Winkler, ed., *Organisierter Kapitalismus*.

146. In early 1930 Duisberg, perhaps inspired by developments in the British mining industry, called for resurrection of the ZAG as he had under the better economic circumstances of 1927. He was now joined in this proposal by leaders of the electrical (von Raumer, Siemens), chemical (C. Bosch), textile (Frowein), and paper and printing (Kraemer) industries. Although one can certainly appreciate the refusal of the unions to walk into a trap of this sort, the representatives of heavy industry perceived Duisberg's proposal not as extremely shrewd but rather as conciliatory toward labor and as a move in precisely the wrong economic and political direction. See Döhn, p. 896; *Jahrbuch des ADGB, 1929* (Berlin, 1930), pp. 229ff., and *Jahrbuch des ADGB, 1930* (Berlin, 1931), pp. 96–100.

147. Sohn-Rethel, p. 69; Weisbrod, pp. 479ff., stresses the importance of their unity.

148. Cf. Blank to Reusch and Reusch to Blank, 27 and 28 Jan. 1931; HA GHH/Martin Blank 400 101 202 4/8.

tion withdrew and began systematic funding of the Nazis and Harzburg Front.[149] At the same time that Silverberg attempted to involve industrialists directly in government posts, Ruhr industrialists informed Brüning that they were "no longer prepared to tolerate government inaction," even if it meant calling Parliament back into session. Brüning felt certain the Ruhr industrialists were out to topple him.[150] Their anxieties over the 107-man Nazi Reichstag delegation had apparently ebbed. In a long letter to Brüning in mid-August, Reusch and other leaders of Ruhr industry complained that the basic problem of high costs, lost receipts, and no capital had not been resolved or even eased.

Reusch charged the chancellor with "lacking the courage to convert his understanding of the situation into deeds and failing to proceed against the existing resistance [the SPD and unions] with the required aggressive single-mindedness. . . . The political parties can no longer save the Fatherland. Only men who go the way of their own awareness can do that."[151] The primary target of their offensive remained organized labor and the Weimar system that permitted it to retain significant political power and influence. But the representatives of heavy industry increasingly distinguished between themselves and the other fraction, between themselves and those who would accept "hunger exports" as a national fate. At its June 1931 meetings, the Langnamverein became more explicit. The meeting resolved that: "Half-way measures are just making things worse . . . the entrepreneur's hands are still tied. Western industry demands a long-range plan for a balanced budget . . . an end to capital-destroying laws and policies and reestablishment of freedom of movement for the private sector." The Ruhr situation was worse than that of the others because of its cost structure and because for years cabinets had yielded to the unions. Because of its warnings, "we were labeled 'the reactionary band in Düsseldorf,' but this reactionary band proved right." To this, Thyssen added: "I remarked last November [1930]" that the RDI applause for Brüning was unwarranted. He had not substituted national supporters for supporters of class struggle, "and the unions," through the Labor Ministry, "still govern from behind the scenes. . . . Many of the middle [Berliners and the

149. HA GHH/Martin Blank 400 101 202 4/8a; *Geschäftliche Mitteilungen,* 13:14 (26 June 1931), p. 105. The AVI groups launched a counterattack against the mining forces; see Stegmann, pp. 417f. and the threatening letter, Reichert to Schlenker, BA/R131-VDESI/602, 4 Dec. 1930.

150. Springorum and Blank to Reusch, 13 May 1931, HA GHH/Martin Blank 400 101 202 4/8b.

151. HA GHH/Nachlass Reusch 400 101 221/5, 3 Nov. 1931.

dynamic fraction] hissed me then, but we of Rhineland-Westphalia are harder types [Basalt] . . . and demand a national awakening."[152]

Stepping up the offensive was possible only if control of the RDI could be wrested from the export liberals. They had been considerably weakened by the end of 1931, in part because of further declines in international trade and the collapse of several major banks that summer.[153] The liberals were prepared for a compromise candidate to replace the retiring Duisberg. Without attacking the aged "Welfare Professor" directly, representatives of the national fraction attacked his policies, primarily by assailing the RDI's chief administrative officer, Kastl. Intimately involved in the export-labor coalition, he was now accused of "cowardice in the struggle with the unions."[154] That spring, heavy industry had settled upon Gustav Krupp as its candidate for the RDI chairmanship,[155] a post he assumed on September 25. His selection, together with certain centralizing organizational changes in the RDI Senate, reflected the new balance between the fractions.[156] In

152. Reusch and Thyssen at the Langnamverein meetings of 3 June 1931; cited in BA/Z Sg 126, *Deutsche Bergwerks Zeitung*, 4 June 1931.

153. The largest German bank collapse being that of the Darmstädter and National. See Karl-Erich Born, *Die deutsche Bankenkrise 1931* (Munich, 1967). Considerable responsibility for the decline in international trade must be borne by the United States, whose Smoot-Hawley tariff of 1930 led to a wave of protectionism in other countries, dealing a serious blow to the free-trade policies of Germany's dynamic and export industries. Together with the end of American loans, a vital link was broken in the international economic chain that had made possible Germany's relative, albeit uneven, prosperity and the labor-export coalition: American loans to Germany, German reparations to France and England, northern and western European imports from Germany. In the course of 1931, free-trade options became increasingly less viable for an even larger number of major producers. Sharp drops in world oil prices in 1931 and the opening of the vast Texas oil fields meant that even IG Farben was not immune; with its enormous investments in coal-conversion plants, Farben could now apprehend importation of cheap American oil. In the absence of a substantial automobile industry, there could be no civilian need for the Farben ersatz. The absence of a German automobile industry was critical for steel producers as well—especially if one considers that by the mid-twenties already 35 percent of American steel production went into cars! The automobile industry was one dynamic industry ("Fordism") that Germany did not yet have.

154. "[Under its leadership] industry has until now been too cowardly to take up the struggle with the unions in all its sharpness. That great ill from which we suffer is largely due to the unions . . . which have in fact governed from behind the scenes." Reusch to Kastl, 6 Sept. 1931, HA GHH/Nachlass Reusch 400 101 202 0/11. See also *Kölnische Zeitung*, 14 Feb. 1931. The attack on Kastl began earlier. See note 149: Reichert faulted Kastl personally for the Young Plan, for indulging labor, and for weakening the RDI. He also saw attacking Kastl as a way of getting at Duisberg's liberal leadership.

155. See above, note 113.

156. The expansion and democratization of the RDI organs initiated and pursued

effect, Krupp's election moved the RDI to the right, but it also bridged the fractions. He was not the candidate of the outspoken philo-fascists; they had supported Vögler. Krupp's was a true vertical empire: based in mining and steel, it nevertheless produced locomotives and even sewing machines. Its primary market was domestic, but it had substantial export interests. Despite its size, it was self-financed and beholden to no banks whatsoever. The family and firm enjoyed excellent ties to agricultural organizations, the Foreign Office, and to the Reichswehr as well.[157] The moderate interpretation of the change of guard was provided by newspapers close to heavy industry, which spoke of Krupp as "a bridge from heavy industry to the processing industries who [would] smooth out conflicts." An agricultural newspaper surmised that "industry is about to split into autarky and export camps. . . . The accession of Krupp has helped the domestic market strategy . . . the processing industries are still hostile to us, but they may be on their way out of positions of power." For the *Vorwärts,* a different judgment was in order: "In place of chemical capital we now have heavy industry taking over. Krupp's leadership means a stronger emphasis on class conflict directed against the working class."[158]

Immediately after the RDI convention, Brüning shuffled his cabinet with a distinct move to the right—Curtius and Wirth were dismissed, but this hardly began to conciliate or mollify the growing industrial opposition.[159] Duisberg, now retired, and Kastl belonged to the shrinking ranks of those who continued to support Brüning until his dismissal at the end of May 1932. The ambivalence of many industrialists toward the Brüning-orchestrated reelection campaign for Hindenburg—still

---

under Duisberg was partially reversed as greater decision-making power was reinvested in the top leadership. There—in the economic policy Beirat and the presidium—the leaders of heavy industry increased their strength.

157. On Krupp versus Vögler, Fricke, ed., 2:608. On the diversity of Krupp interests and connections, Sohn-Rethel, p. 73; on ties to the Reichswehr, Carsten, pp. 135–41. Krupp had supported the 1928 Ruhr lockouts but was among the more conciliatory of the steel captains. The particularly disappointed Vögler-Thyssen group then invited Hitler to speak to several of the most important industrialists after Christmas.

158. The "moderate" interpretation was provided by the *Deutsche Allgemeine Zeitung;* the rural interpretation by the *Westfälishe Bauern Zeitung.* The interpretation in the *Vorwärts* is striking because *it blames class conflict on capital. All* three appeared on 25 Sept. 1931.

159. The emboldened opponents of Brüning and his industrialist supporters demanded that IG Farben's Warmbold be replaced as economics minister by Vögler, who had acquitted himself so well in the events surrounding the Young Plan and who now maintained contacts with the "national opposition." He proposed establishment of a state Economics Council *(Wirtschaftsbeirat)* with virtually dictatorial power over all economic and fiscal matters.

strongly supported by Duisberg and his former staff—was symptomatic of the internal division. A further indication of the near-stalemate was the absence of any new numbers of the RDI *Publications* series between September 1931 and December 1932. But it was a stalemate that worked to the advantage of heavy industry. The national bloc derived support from Brüning's "avoidance of the struggle against the masses" and his failure to abolish compulsory arbitration of contract disputes. Brüning's government did not enjoy a popular base substantial enough to allow him to divide and conquer the industrialists. Martin Blank remarked that the chancellor was not without anti-Right "hysteria" and had "definitively sold himself out to the Left." He suffered from a "big industry complex" and made "threats against western big industry." Kastl of the RDI, on the other hand, remained "satisfied" and supported Brüning.[160]

Around the same time, Blank enrolled Reusch and several other Ruhr industrialists in the Stahlhelm. Reusch himself participated in attempts to purge the DVP of supporters of Brüning and former backers of the Grand Coalition, and he authorized his agents with ties to the right wing of the DVP, such as Erich von Gilsa, to proceed "without reservations" against such compromisers in the party as the Frankfurt liberal Richard Merton.[161] On his own, Reusch ordered the staffs of several newspapers he owned around the country to cease attacking Hitler and the NSDAP.[162] By January 1932, Brüning was being described as one "who for years has been making compacts with Marxism while treating the National Freedom Movement the same as the [Communists]."[163] Sud-

160. Blank to Reusch, HA GHH/Martin Blank 400 101 202 4/9, 14 Oct. 1931.

161. Von Gilsa was one of the leaders of the campaign against the DVP "left." Gilsa's seamy career included a stint for Noske fighting Red uprisings and a decade and a half later one as an SA district commander in Bavaria. For most of the intervening years he was active in the right wing of the DVP, and after 1928 he represented the GHH district in the Reichstag, regularly corresponding with his patron and chief constituent, Reusch. To facilitate his toil and trouble, Gilsa's office doubled as headquarters of the GHH's Berlin representative, Martin Blank. See HA GHH/Nachlass Reusch 400 101 293/4a, Oct. 1929; and /12, Jan. 1932; also Weisbrod, pp. 467–74. On the campaign against Merton, see BA/ Nachlass Dingeldey/75, pp. 30–40, 70ff. and /36, pp. 3ff., e.g., 2 Mar. 1932. Other aspects of this effort, pp. 300–302 below. (Merton, a scion of the Jewish Frankfurt family that headed the nonferrous Metallgesellschaft, persisted as *Vernunftrepublikaner*.) In reponse to an utterly desperate appeal for funds dated 26 Jan. 1932, Reusch informed DVP Chairman Dingeldey that the party would receive no assistance until the bourgeois parties united and all those who supported Brüning were removed, 30 Jan. 1932.

162. Reusch's new posture toward the Nazis resulted in staff purge threats in April at at least one of these, the *Münchener Neuesten Nachrichten;* see Kurt Koszyk, "Paul Reusch und die 'Münchener Neuesten Nachrichten,' " *Vierteljahrshefte für Zeitgeschichte* 20 (1972):75–103.

163. Memorandum written for Reusch, 6 Jan. 1932, HA GHH/Nachlass Reusch 400

denly, the NSDAP was perceived as behaving "responsibly" and as a fit coalition partner for a right-dominated Zentrum. By April 1932, both fractions had abandoned Brüning, as demonstrated by Hermann Warmbold's resignation as economics minister in early May. By the time he and Homesteading Commissar Schlange ran into trouble with the estate owners over "agrarian bolshevism," Brüning had already been abandoned by the last of his supporters in industry.

Von Papen's ascent to the chancellorship reflected the emerging dominance of domestic-market-oriented heavy industry in conjunction with the estate owners. His coup d'état against the "Red" Prussian government in July virtually eliminated the last vestige of SPD power.[164] Nevertheless, his "New State" was without a mass base, and certainly without any base beyond the countryside. There existed no combination of groupings that could provide him with either a parliamentary or electoral majority, and his inability to integrate the Nazis as junior partners assured that this would remain the case. His unambiguous policy toward the unions and the SPD (not to mention the KPD) earned him the support of both organized agriculture and industry, and the "Christian, *ständisch* organic, corporatist, authoritarian, and beyond-conflict" ideology he propagated also stood him in good stead.[165] The initial lineup of support behind Papen could not last, however. Despite the self-proclaimed *Systemwechsel* and the presence in the government of all three dominant social fractions, the interests of all three could not be harmonized. At the behest of organized agriculture, Papen imposed unilateral import quotas. Export industries responded with the dire warning that this would mean a loss of essential markets, higher costs and slower recovery for all, and the total demise of certain industries. Krupp himself warned Papen that one-sided agrarian measures would only compound the economy's ills. It was an issue on which the dynamic-export fraction could not compromise, and its leaders withdrew their support.[166] The question became how to incorporate the antidemocratic and antilabor components of Papen's program into a viable overall economic program *with* a mass base to support it. The crushing defeat of all the bourgeois parties in the

---

101 293/12. Beginning in February, Reusch expressed his preference for the Stahlhelm's Düsterberg in the presidential election; Blank had earlier enrolled Reusch and the others as "honorary members."

164. Details in Bracher, pp. 571–600; see chap. 6, sec. 3 below.

165. H.-A. Winkler, "Unternehmerverbände zwischen Ständeideologie und Nationalsozialismus," *Vierteljahrshefte für Zeitgeschichte* 17 (1969):341–71. See also Dahrendorf, pp. 129–41, 183–87. In the hands of the Nazis, but not of Papen, this ideology could link the elites to parts of the Mittelstand—as it used to do under the Empire.

166. See chap. 2, sec. 4c; chap. 4, sec. 7.

elections of July 1932 forced even the liberals to give up any final hopes of a bourgeois bloc.[167] The Nazi Party was the only force which could provide that mass base while conceivably offering a program acceptable to both fractions of industry. During the last phase of the Papen government, industry was divided over whether to incorporate the "left wing" of the NSDAP into a coalition with the Zentrum or its mainstream into a coalition with the DNVP. The dynamic fraction tended to favor the former solution, heavy industry the latter; only a few (the Keppler Circle) cared to have the Nazis govern on their own. It would take another few months and the Schleicher interlude to "tame" the Nazis and make them the acceptable lowest common denominator for industry.[168]

Through the manipulations of the military and Hindenburg's camarilla, General von Schleicher was appointed chancellor at the beginning of December. The Schleicher government was possible because the NSDAP would not be split and because numerous industrialists, like Hindenburg, were as yet unprepared to yield full power to Hitler.[169] Schleicher's failures were a mirror image of Papen's: if Papen erred on the side of estate owners, domestic and heavy industry, autarky and the failure to seek a mass base, then Schleicher and his minister for "Work Creation," Gunther Gereke, erred grievously on the side of a minority of peasants, inflation, export and processing industry, integration, and too much dickering with the Nazi "left" and the unions.[170] Gereke's public-works program was not unlike that proposed by some in the ADGB (the Woytinsky-Tarnow-Baade program) and was distinctly pro-labor and inflationary. Both fractions of industry were generally opposed to inflationary policies, frequently citing the horrors the very

167. Election statistics in tables 1, 2. All the parties of the bourgeois right together obtained a mere 10.1 percent of the vote; they were the weakest of any potential coalition and weaker than they had ever been. We shall have more to say about the bourgeois parties during this phase in chap. 6.

168. We do not deal here with how individual industrialists or groups of them were won over to the Nazis, nor with the overworked area of financial support provided the Nazis by industrialists, bankers, and barons. We are interested in the structural question of what types of solutions were acceptable to different fractions of industry and why. The two sets of questions are, however, not irreconcilable; see Czichon, pp. 24–56, and Stegmann, "Kapitalismus und Faschismus 1929–1934: Thesen und Materialien," in *Gesellschaft: Beiträge zur Marxschen Theorie*, eds. H. G. Backhaus, et al. (Frankfurt, 1976), 6:14–75, esp. pp. 32–37, 44–53. Cf. Schulz, Turner, chap. 6 below.

169. Details in Bracher, pp. 670–85; Carsten, *Reichswehr and Politics*, pp. 382–90.

170. On Schleicher and Landwirtschaft, see chap. 2, sec. 4c, and chap. 4, sec. 7. On Schleicher's dealings with both the Nazi "left" and the ADGB, see Michael Schneider, *Das Arbeitsbeschaffungsprogramm des ADGB* (Bonn-Bad Godesberg, 1975), pp. 140–57, 198–202; and below, chap. 6, sec. 6. Woytinsky, pp. 470ff.

idea evoked in the hearts of Mittelstand savings-account holders.[171] The policy shift back in favor of export industry came as a rude shock to those in heavy industry who had previously brought about a shift in their own favor. Thus, Jakob Reichert, director of the VDESI, was astonished that he and his colleagues no longer had direct access to either the chancellor or the economics minister; it was indicative that he had to "depend on hearing things" via Hamm of the DIHT and Lange of the Machine Builders "fourteen days later."[172] Steel industrialists even seemed to fear socialization of their bankrupt companies. Once again, the dynamic fraction set the government's economic agenda: officials of the Deutsche Bank and Hans Raumer of the electrical industry, Schmitz of IG Farben, Kastl, Hamm, Bosch, and, to a certain extent, Silverberg. Conflicts between the two fractions were coming to the fore rather than their joint interest.

That component of Schleicher's program intended to capture a mass base was the same which isolated his industrial backers from their own colleagues. The specter of state socialism and a possible reparliamentarization of political life, even if in military dress, finally tipped the scales in Hitler's favor. The reentry of the unions into the corridors of power, in the form of Strasser's Nazi "left" as well as the ADGB, threatened what was the primary political accomplishment of the previous year and a half: their exclusion. Most industrialists rejected Schleicher's Keynesian, public-sector, and consumption-oriented economic proposals and would have opposed him for that reason, together with the estate owners who feared resettlement of their latifundia. Schleicher had for months been negotiating with Strasser, with representatives of the ADGB and white-collar associations, and the prospect of a dirigist social dictatorship supported by anticapitalist masses was too much to bear.[173] The Nazi electoral losses in November and their subsequent financial difficulties rendered more real the possibility of splitting the party. Most industrialists, however, preferred to make use of the chastening of the party and Strasser's suspension to integrate Hitler himself. It was the *political* fear Schleicher's program inspired

171. Reusch sounded this theme frequently and described inflation as a "French trick to save reparations." He also wrote Luther that the currency was the only healthy part of the economy left; "we can never heal the economy" by making the currency sick. Unlike Vögler, he was unimpressed by the results of the British devaluation. HA GHH/Nachlass Reusch 400 101 290/30b, 1 Oct. 1931, 13 July, 19 Oct., and 16 Nov. 1932.

172. Reichert to Kastl, 17 Jan. 1933, BA/R13I-VDESI/54, p. 8. On the privileged position enjoyed by the DIHT, Dieter Schäfer, p. 74; on divisions, Dsenis.

173. On the reality of anticapitalism in the Nazi left, Arthur Rosenberg, *Geschichte*, pp. 294–96, and the detailed study by Reinhard Kühnl, *Die national-sozialistische Linke* (Meisenheim/Glan, 1966).

that was central and that led, finally, to the appointment of the Hitler-Papen-Hugenberg government.[174] Papen's program, this time with a mass base and a more nationalist tone, appeared to be the lowest common denominator for the three dominant social fractions.

The remaining question was how to reconcile the interests of an autarkic rural elite with the interests of noncompetitive and over-expanded heavy industry and both of those with export-oriented finishing industries. A program for cartellizing agricultural production and guaranteeing prices without altering property relations would satisfy the demands of the estate owners.[175] A program of holding down the costs of production while increasing public spending, especially on armaments, would go a way toward satisfying heavy industry. A vigorous program of trade expansion, especially in middle and southeastern Europe—imperialism—could open avenues for export industry without setting it against either the rural elite or heavy industry.[176] Residual notions of laissez faire entrepreneurship would have to give way to state guidance,[177] and years of ideological homage to the Mittelstand would be honored, after some early confusion, mostly in the breach. A republic which could only infrequently muster a majority in its favor, but which was nevertheless divisive and costly, would have to be abandoned. Initially, given an improvement in the international economic situation, "only" the peasantry, the working class, and Germany's neighbors would have to pay.[178]

174. Fricke, ed., 2:610, overestimates the centrality of the economic aspect and, by describing it as "social demagogy," underestimates the political facet. Trotsky's argument that Germany was too poor and capital-short to be able to afford a "New Deal" also misses the mark. The requisite costs were *not economic;* they were *political.* As we have indicated, what Weimar Germany's dominant classes could not afford was a democratic political system into which seemed to be imbedded a profit-devouring social-welfare system. This conjuncture is analyzed in chap. 6

175. The evolution of this solution is discussed in chapter 4; it was a long and difficult path—for industry. The rural elite was always ready to accept a helping hand. Only a proper trade and imperial strategy could allow for this path to be taken; see Sohn-Rethel, pp. 78–119.

176. On the MWT program to do precisely this, see below, chap. 4, sec. 8.

177. It is unclear to what extent laissez faire was more than a slogan. Papen, like Schleicher, was "Keynesian." What varied was how public money was to be spent or credited; the difference was *political* and therefore of critical importance; see Dietmar Petzina, "Hauptprobleme der deutschen Wirtschaftspolitik 1932–33," *Vierteljahrshefte für Zeitgeschichte* 15 (1967):23; Czichon, pp. 36, 39. We return to the question of their Keynesianism below.

178. On the background for central European imperialism-cum-autarky, see Henry Cord Meyer, *Mitteleuropa in German Thought and Action* (The Hague, 1955). On the development and execution of this policy after 1933, Ernst Wagemann, *Der Neue Balkan* (Hamburg, 1939); Wilhelm Röpke, *German Commercial Policy* (London, 1934); Arno

6. A Note on Industry and "Work Creation"

In early 1932, spokesmen for the ADGB unveiled the Woytinsky-Tarnow-Baade "Work Creation" *(Arbeitsbeschaffung)* program. Envisaging a variety of public-spending and countercyclical approaches, the plan was designed to put a million unemployed Germans back to work within a short time. The designers largely emphasized public programs, especially the sort that might increase mass purchasing power *(Kaufkraft)* without requiring any increase in the size of the nation's production plant. To initiate the WTB program, its supporters called for a state commitment of at least 2 billion RM.[179] The RDI, along with every other organization of industrialists, manufacturers, and commercial interests, loudly opposed the union plan on the grounds that it represented "cold socialization" and a planned economy *(Planwirtschaft)* and would induce massive inflation ruining the currency. Although some industrialists gradually distanced themselves from Brüning's brutal deflationary strategy, they continued to oppose any programs resembling that advanced by the unions. Even in May 1932, with six million unemployed, representatives of the Employers League informed Brüning and Stegerwald that they opposed all publicly financed job creation because it would increase the state debt and reduce the amount of capital available to the private economy. All such measures were considered to be as destructive as the unions' call for reduced working hours at constant pay.[180]

Labor Minister Stegerwald did propose some public-works and job-creation projects, more as a social measure than an economic one, partly out of sympathy for the plight of Catholic workers and partly to allay their political radicalization. Still in May 1932, Dietrich, now finance minister but soon to join the Chemical Industries Association,

---

Sölter, *Das Grossraumkartell* (Dresden, 1941). More recently, Dietmar Petzina, *Autarkiepolitik im Dritten Reich* (Stuttgart, 1968), part 1; and Stegmann, "Mitteleuropa," pp. 216ff.

179. On the substance and presentation of the WTB Plan, see Schneider, *Arbeitsbeschaffungsprogramm*, pp. 36ff., 81ff.; Woytinsky, passim; below, chap. 5, sec. 3.

180. Schneider, *Arbeitsbeschaffungsprogramm*, p. 185; Wolffsohn, pp. 162–66. Wolffsohn's contention that industrial organizations were unable to affect Brüning's, Papen's, Schleicher's, or the bureaucracy's plans is certainly exaggerated. To be sure, as in other matters, industry could not get all that it wanted from Brüning (or the others), but the plans alluded to here simply faded away; there was no need to combat them. In his nominalism and literalism, Wolffsohn demonstrates little sense for any form of causality that lies between public declaration, on the one hand, and conspiracy, on the other. At the same time, he indicates, *malgré lui-même,* how little all this really mattered. What he sometimes takes as auguries of major changes (e.g., the August 1932 RDI meeting, pp. 191ff.) turn out to be expressions of the marginality of the issue.

proposed an extremely modest, not to say marginal, public-works scheme. Over the objections of the Reichsbank, he called for 60 million RM for road construction, 50 million for canal modernization, and 25 million for agricultural improvements in the context of the Siedlung program. Within the ministerial bureaucracy, Lautenbach's plan for an expansion of credit also received an airing.[181] In any event, Brüning was dismissed at the end of May before anything could come of these proposals.

As opposed to what they derided as "employment therapy," representatives of heavy industry preferred what they called "capital-building work," and measures of this sort were, as we have seen, at the center of Papen's economic and social policies. Most "Keynesian" countercyclical thinking remained untrusted, unproven, and unwelcome, but even such proposals as did emerge from Papen's bureaucracy were geared primarily toward building capital and were clearly predicated on the weakening and exclusion of the unions. They addressed the plight of "die Wirtschaft," not of the unemployed. Thus, it was only after he issued the brutal antilabor decrees in September that Papen proposed what might be seen as a countercyclical economic package. Having obtained a drastic reduction in the labor and social costs of production, as well as a fully credible commitment to political authoritarianism, industrialists could afford to adopt a number of divergent views toward what were perhaps novel but still economically marginal and, unlike those to come under Schleicher, politically safe programs. The Papen Plan of fall 1932 offered entrepreneurs tax coupon-credits equivalent to about 40 percent of taxes due in the next nine months; one-fifth of the coupons could then be used toward payment of taxes in each of the next five years. In addition, the plan provided for a state bounty to employers of 400 RM for every new worker employed for a year.[182]

As chancellor, Schleicher not only cancelled many of the wage cuts Papen had ordered, but his own countercyclical plans were combined

---

181. Wolffsohn, pp. 64–72; Schneider, *Arbeitsbeschaffungsprogramm*, pp. 176ff. Dietrich's plan bore considerable resemblance to the IG Farben proposals of January 1932. In these, neither political nor economic considerations had been ignored: highways for civilian and military vehicles, some no doubt using IG Farben's ersatz gasoline; Siedlung and rural improvements to weaken the hostile big agrarians.

182. Wilhelm Grotkopp, *Die Grosse Krise* (Düsseldorf, 1954), pp. 110ff.; Wolffsohn, pp. 78–97, passim. It was estimated that the tax credits could have been worth up to 1.5 billion RM; 300 million RM was set aside for the bounty program. Employers were permitted to pay workers hired or rehired under this program at below prevailing contract rates. Wolffsohn again overestimates both the economic importance of the plan and the debate over it; Arbeitsbeschaffung was bound to remain of peripheral importance and concern unless taken up by *politically* unreliable figures.

with discomforting political experimentation. He instructed Gereke to consult with Strasser and with the ADGB; both recommended labor-intensive programs and proffered the government their support in exchange for continued participation in decision making.[183] With the exceptions noted below, most industrialists rejected Gereke's inflationary proposal for the state to spend up to 2.7 billion RM on various forms of economic stimulation, work and job creation, and assistance to the unemployed.[184] At the same time, Hitler and the NSDAP "right" prohibited Strasser from culminating his cooperation with the government with formal participation, and the ADGB was unable to overcome its hesitancies before Schleicher was himself ousted. Schleicher's political gamble on a mass base was more significant than his economic planning, and, although the two were connected, when the former failed, the latter lost its significance.

By the middle of the crisis, virtually all industrialists had come to hold the democratic Weimar political system responsible for their problems. The system permitted organized labor altogether too much success while badly dividing their own ranks and placing an assortment of impediments in the way of industrial recovery and national reassertion. Insofar as what they faced was either a cyclical or unique crisis in capitalism that affected each sector differently, German entrepreneurs chose instead to blame the Weimar social compromise. Naturally, as capitalists they believed in "the free economy," but certainly they were not and never had been Manchesterians. However precociously Keynesian or anti-Keynesian any one of them or group of them, their central demand was political—freedom for the economy, for capital, for profits; not economic freedom in the sense of laissez faire.[185] Generally, the strongest dynamic industries and the weakest manufacturers put

183. Wolffsohn, pp. 100, 267–69; Woytinsky, p. 474; Schneider, *Arbeitsbeschaffungsprogramm*, p. 154; Richard Breitman, "German Social Democracy and General Schleicher," *Central European History* 9 (1976):352–78. Blank summed up the anxieties of heavy industry in a letter to Reusch, HA GHH/Martin Blank 400 101 202 4/10, 12 Oct. 1932.

184. See BA/R43II/540c, 19 Dec. 1932, pp. 5ff. Representatives of the Bankers League expressed their own uneasiness and that of numerous others when they asked Gereke, somewhat rhetorically, whether the government was moving toward a "free economy" or a "planned economy."

185. Claus-Dieter Krohn, "Autoritärer Kapitalismus: Wirtschaftskonzeptionen im Übergang von der Weimarer Republik zum Nationalsozialismus," in Stegmann, et al., eds., pp. 120–21 argues that many industrialists were prepared to accept planning and direction of various sorts, including what they thought they saw in Italy, if it came under acceptable political auspices. Smaller producers among the AVI industries thought they saw in corporatism possible protection against the heavy-industry monopolies who, in turn, stressed political authoritarianism and repression of the workers. See also Winkler, "Unternehmerverbände," Again, what frightened so many industrialists about Schleicher was not his Keynesianism but rather his overtures to the unions.

some trust in the state and a measure of countercyclical intervention, while those in between tended more often to believe in the adequacy of the privately regulated market. Some liberal figures in industry, such as Lange and the leaders of the Hansa Bund, spoke of the need for "a free economy in a strong state," but here the Langnamverein was both less ambiguous and more typical with its 1932 call for "a healthy economy in a strong state." In either version, however, organized labor and political democracy were the culprits, and the kind of state interventionism they had forced on the German economy would be eliminated by an authoritarian state.[186]

Some representatives of IG Farben (among them Schmitz, Wagemann, Carl Bosch, Moellendorff, and Warmbold) and other members of the dynamic fraction of industry (Hamm, Silverberg, and Pietrkowski) favored some countercyclical measures designed primarily to increase credit as well as aggregate and popular demand. These men made no headway under Papen but were subsequently among the figures who supported and worked with Schleicher, even once most industrialists began to worry about the "social general" and his ambitious plans.[187] Nevertheless, Ernst Wagemann's plan to increase the money supply and the state debt by 3 billion RM was consistently rejected by entrepreneurs of all stripes from heavy industry to the DDP liberals at the *Deutsche Volkswirt.*[188] On the other hand, the assorted public works and work-creation proposals championed by several representatives of smaller manufacturers, in the DIHT and elsewhere, once again linked these oldest branches to the spokesmen for IG Farben, but also predictably set them against official opinion in heavy industry and the post-1931 RDI.[189] For the latter, the economy would heal itself if freed, probably better without intervention than with it, and consequently

186. See Gerald Feldman and Ulrich Nocken, "Trade Associations and Economic Power: Interest Group Development in the German Iron and Steel and Machine Building Industries," *Business History Review* 49 (1975): 436ff.; Krohn, p. 122; see also the attack on Moellendorff in *Der Arbeitgeber,* 15 Jan. 1933. See above, chap. 1, sec. 1, on how the oldest manufacturers and newest industries arrived at a shared position.

187. See Wolffsohn, pp. 67ff., 175ff., 189ff., 199, 216ff., 287, 371ff.; Krohn, p. 124; Czichon, pp. 36ff.; Grotkopp, pp. 24, 31; Petzina, "Hauptprobleme," p. 27; BA/Nachlass Silverberg/644, pp. 31, 33, 19 Dec. 1932.

188. Wagemann was attacked, predictably by *Der Arbeitgeber,* the Langnamverein, most bankers, and those associated with heavy industry, but also by the academic economists and by political liberals like Landauer and Stolper.

189. Details in Grotkopp, pp. 139ff.; Wolffsohn, pp. 188ff., 219ff., 300–305; Turner, "Ruhrlade," p. 150. Neither Krupp nor his associates, for example, seemed the least bit interested in such "nonsense." For some of those anticollectivist yet Keynesian "reformers" in the Esti-bund and elsewhere, the Nazis seemed to promise work, fair competition, perhaps artisanal socialism, and a different kind of social market economy; see Nocken, p. 701, Schweitzer, passim, Wolffsohn, pp. 304ff.

they demonstrated virtually no initiative in formulating such programs. Ultimately, work creation in itself was not a problem, and therefore did not demand unity.[190]

What was needed, in the opinion of nearly all industrialists, was simple (and familiar): the restoration of autonomy for the economic elites and an end to the need for democratic legitimation in favor of a strong, authoritarian state free of the burden of reparations. They had organized the economy sufficiently well on their own; just as they did not believe that their cartel mechanisms deepened the economic depression, so they refused to accept that the state might do anything substantial to dampen it—beyond removing the artificial impediments Weimar had created. Ironically, it was during the period of Brüning's merciless economic orthodoxy that industrial opposition to the Republic was most radicalized, and, for the now-dominant fraction of industry, no policy undertaken within the framework of the Republic and its social compromise could achieve the necessary ends.

190. In the last analysis, the chief defect of Wolffsohn's book is that he assumes that Arbeitsbeschaffung must have been a major issue in its own right when in fact it simply was not.

Chapter Four

CONFLICTS BETWEEN AGRICULTURE AND INDUSTRY

1. Dominant and Dependent Sectors

If, as indicated in chapter 2, the capitalist mode of production, based on wage labor, never fully established itself in or dominated the countryside, it nevertheless became the overwhelmingly dominant economic force in German society. Even in the Weimar period, industrial capitalism developed partially at the expense of agricultural producers, and this was a basis for sometimes inchoate, sometimes violent peasant anticapitalism and antiurbanism.[1] The agricultural elite was nevertheless able to mount a political struggle to countervail the tendency for the economy to develop at agriculture's expense. Although ultimately unsuccessful in its struggles within the dominant bloc, the agricultural elite conditioned and affected state policy. Small-owning peasants supported the agrarian elite so long as the latter could articulate some kind of joint or unified agricultural interest. The rural elite was able to influence the industrial leadership and the state for two reasons: the two groups had, in fact, come to share many of the same members, largely because of the earlier power and prestige of the Junkers;[2] and, a politically weak and chastened bourgeoisie had early on sought the landed aristocracy's help in combating the organized working class.[3] The "feudalization" of the upper bourgeoisie had been a major basis of

---

1. For example, Heberle, pp. 49–53, 72–76.
2. Bramsted, pp. 188–250. See also chap. 2, notes 17 and 18.
3. Most clearly in the Sammlungspolitik; for the original statement see Kehr, esp. pp. 223–358; Moore, pp. 436ff.; summarized by Dirk Stegmann, "Wirtschaft und Politik nach Bismarcks Sturz: Zur Genesis der Sammlungspolitik, 1890–1897," in *Deutschland in der Weltpolitik des 19 und 20 Jahrhunderts: Festschrift für Fritz Fischer,* ed. Imanuel Geiss and B. J. Wendt (Düsseldorf, 1973), pp. 161–84. For an international perspective, see Gourevitch. The literature on Sammlungspolitik is now immense and has become a focal point for numerous debates historical, political, and personal. Cf. *Geschichte und Gesellschaft* 1:4 (1975) and 4:1 (1978).

stability in Imperial Germany and was an important factor in the weakness of Weimar democracy. This alliance (Sammlungspolitik) had cost German industry its own liberal impulse[4] and slowed the unfolding of its productive potential.[5]

We shall argue that, during most of the Weimar period, the fraction of industry we have called heavy, domestic-oriented industry favored continuing the political and economic alliance with the agricultural elite, which would, in turn, pass on limited protective benefits to the peasantry. The fraction of industry we have called dynamic, export-oriented industry, feeling less pressure from the organized working class, favored bypassing, if not abandoning, the agricultural elite and directly incorporating and marginalizing a modernized and capable (leistungsfähig) peasantry. The attitudes toward agriculture of industry's various branches thus mirrored the splits that existed within industry itself and the way in which those had been resolved. After 1930, however, the economic and political crisis cut short this bifurcation, and the offensive of the dominant classes against the working class provided the rural elite a *temporary* reprieve.[6] The political necessities of the dominant class fractions in 1931 and 1932 overrode the internal economic conflicts, which had been worsening since the onset of prosperity based on collaboration with the working class and the beginning of the export offensive in 1925.[7]

4. Represented in different ways by Caprivi and Richter; see Gerschenkron, pp. 51–64; Krieger, pp. 393–97, 458–70; Stegmann, "Sammlungspolitik."

5. "The German economy at no time made more progress than in . . . the [Caprivi] period," Bruck, p. 115.

6. "Temporary" in that it was not long before the needs of an expansive industrial sector and imperialist politics once again conflicted with the protectionist, autarkic needs of agriculture. The Central European Economic Congress, a German industrial organization and program (Mitteleuropäischer Wirtschaftstag, MWT) made clear by 1935 that Germany was an industrial giant which could obtain its food cheaply in an eastern European market (or empire); see Sohn-Rethel, pp. 78–119. Puhle, Agrarbewegungen, pp. 98–102, infers much less conflict (if any) between the agricultural and industrial aspects of the imperialist program. Although he makes no reference to Sohn-Rethel, see also B. J. Wendt, "England und der deutsche 'Drang nach Südosten.' Kapitalbeziehungen und Warenverkehr," in Geiss and Wendt, eds., pp. 483–512.

7. It belongs to the chaos and zigzag nature of the German conjuncture after 1931 that the last pre-Nazi government (General Schleicher, December 1932, January 1933) was, in fact, strongly supported by export industry with an eye toward the unions and vehemently opposed by agriculture. It was in order to avoid this return to collaboration with the unions and some unpredictable Keynesianism (represented on the one hand by Schleicher's minister for Work Creation, Gereke, and on the other by the unions' Woytinsky-Tarnow-Baade plan, WTB) that the scales were tipped for Hitler. We shall discuss these developments further in chap. 6.

The concrete conjuncture after 1930 was characterized primarily by the collapse of international trade and the struggle to roll back the previous gains of the organized working class. Together with the earlier collapse of the domestic market, the collapse of world trade and the struggle against labor created political exigencies that aided the agricultural elite in its attempts to countervail the secular tendency toward conflict between industrial capitalism and forms of agricultural production which posed an obstacle to industry's further development. Earlier, we took the position that there was no inherent conflict between modes of production in a social formation: between the family-peasant and rural-capitalist modes. Analogously, it was not fully inevitable that German agriculture, dominated by the estates, would burden industrial production.

It seems clear that German industrial capitalism could prosper with *or* without the continued existence of big landed property. The land-distribution problem could be avoided; given the increasingly subordinate role of agriculture, it made little *economic* difference whether big landed property was sustained, maintained, abandoned, or destroyed. Hence the rural elite's successful emphasis on *political* "national," and "class solidarity" themes. But, backward, inefficient, trade-hampering German estate agriculture did fetter industrial capitalism and did rely on state assistance and intervention to the detriment of the state's autonomy, mass loyalty, and legitimacy.[8] Eckart Kehr cites an example in a footnote which is characteristically both profound and demystifying. Commenting on the agrarian claim that in the protectionist trade treaties of 1905 " 'for the first time the parity of industry and agriculture is explicit,' " he writes, "Translated from agrarian jargon into German, that means that agriculture hopes finally to have brought the development of industry to a standstill."[9]

A second, farcical version of this position was pronounced in April 1928 when the future agricultural minister, Martin Schiele, proclaimed that an "even balance" *(Gleichgewicht)* existed between industry and agriculture and had to be maintained, for Germany was, in his neologism, an *Agrarindustriestaat*. Actually, in the preceding twelve months, industrial production had been worth about 25 billion marks; agricultural production only about 10 billion. The values of industrial wages and salaries (14 billion) and of industrial exports were each

---

8. This was something that the orthodox Marxists understood better than Baade and the revisionists. However, the former failed to join this understanding with their commitment to saving rather than undermining the state.

9. Kehr, p. 346, note 1.

greater. The rural sector could absorb no more than 15 percent of what industry produced.[10] In the Weimar period the political needs of the socially dominant classes as a whole necessitated support of Land-wirtschaft, particularly once heavy, domestic-oriented industry reasserted its leadership in 1931. The actors found themselves allies in a *historically* developed class struggle whose imperatives were at odds with the general *structural* developments of a capitalist social formation.

The capitalist mode of production interacted with the two modes in the countryside in such a way that resources were systematically transferred from the countryside to the cities. Further, land became somewhat anomalous in the capitalist system; it was the only commodity neither freely extensible nor reproducible at will. In agriculture, investment was faced with the constraint of decreasing returns; German bankers, estate owners, and peasants all complained that increased investments did not lower unit costs.[11] As late as the turn of the century, according to Weber, land rents/profits reduced profits and hampered the development of industrial capital.[12] Peasant producers, however, did not profit from this peculiarity of land and may have had to work harder simply to maintain a constant standard of living.[13] A set of conditions was created characterized by low prices for peasant agricultural products (*partially* countervailed by high tariffs and hence paid for by urban consumers) and high prices for those industrial products necessary for agricultural production. This was a constant complaint of both estate owners and peasants,[14] as was the ensuing difficulty in attracting private capital into agriculture.

The divergence in interest rates and constant demands for more credits for the countryside indicate how unattractive rural investment

10. Schiele cited in ZSA/RLB Pressarchiv 131/11, p. 49. A rejoinder with statistics appeared in the *Berlin Börsen Zeitung,* 6 June 1928, ibid., p. 63. A position similar to Schiele's had been voiced by Agriculture Minister Kanitz in March 1925. See BA/ R431/2537, pp. 271ff. On an earlier phase of this ideological conflict, Herman Lebovics, "Agrarians vs. Industrialists," *International Revue of Social History* 21 (1967):31–65. Max Sering also expressed this view of industrial-agricultural equality within the scientific realm when he asserted that "all urban activity obtains its life-blood from the countryside. There can never be more industry than there is an agricultural ability to supply it," Sering, p. 874.

11. On these two aspects of the perversity of land in a capitalist system, N. Mouzelis, "Capitalism and the Development of Agriculture," *Journal of Peasant Studies* 3 (July 1976):484.

12. Weber, "Rural Society," especially pp. 369, 373, 383; also, Kehr, pp. 283–84.

13. This argument is supported by Gerschenkron, pp. 71–80, as well as by the data in Hoffmann and Chayanov.

14. E.g., ZSA/RLB Pressarchiv 132/11, p. 4: "The lack of capital and credit are our [agriculture's] worst problems." See tables 3, 7, 8, and 9 above.

was (see table 21). A very prominent banker of the Weimar period, Georg Solmssen of the Disconto-Gesellschaft and other banks, admitted that private capital tended to shun the country, preferring to meet the direct producer in the arena of circulation, through the market mechanism: Investment monies were scarce, but all knew that agricultural productivity had to be increased. "[That] is your task. . . . We can be helpful commercializing production" and the business aspects of supply.[15] The semiaborted Silverberg plan for industrial aid to agriculture only proved the rule, as we shall see. This left the state, under pressure from the estate owners and agricultural organizations, as the chief provider of capital for the rural sector. In 1924, 40 percent of commercial credit flowed to agriculture; in 1925, the percentage dropped to 25 percent; by 1927, it was 17 percent, and in 1928, 16 percent. And most of that was in the form of undesirable short-term credits. Agriculture fared even less well in access to foreign capital.[16] An economic problem endemic to a declining primary sector was rendered a "national" and political problem, and the rural elite was powerful enough to guarantee that the urban working and middle classes would foot the bill, not only after but also well before the onset of the crisis.[17]

TABLE 21

Representative Annual Interest Rates for Investment, 1925–1932

	1925	1926	1927	1928	1929	1930	1931	1932
Industry								
Long-term	8.5	6.7	6.5	7.0	7.1	7.2	7.4	9.1
Short-term	7.6	4.9	5.5	6.5	6.9	4.4	6.8	5.0
Agriculture								
Long-term	10.7	9.0	8.8	9.4	11.1	11.2	11.3	8.4
Short-term	11.0	9.7	9.8	11.0	13.0	11.8	13.6	15.1

SOURCES: Robert Lorenz, *The Essential Features of Germany's Agricultural Policy* (New York, 1941), p. 75; Gerhard Kokotkiewicz, "Der Immobiliarkredit, seine Lage und Aussichten," *Vierteljahreshefte zur Konjunkturforschrung,* Sonderheft 30 (Berlin, 1932), pp. 21ff.; Sidney Homer, *History of Interest Rates* (New Brunswick, N.J. 1963), pp. 461, 467.

15. Georg Solmmsen, "Deutschlands Nahrungsnot," in his *Beiträge zur Deutschen Politik und Wirtschaft* (Munich, 1934), p. 779. Similar comments from the Dresdner Bank in ZSA/RLB Pressarchiv 132/11, p. 38. On the general lack of commercial credit for the countryside, see the report of Agricultural Minister Dietrich in 1928, ZSA/Büro des Reichspräsidenten/329, p. 135.

16. ZSA/Büro des Reichspräsidenten/329, pp. 135–38, Dietrich's report.

17. The data is quite clear. The parliamentary committee for the study of the economy (Enquête Ausschuss of 1929) published *Die Förderung der Landwirtschaft durch öf-*

TABLE 22

Agricultural Indebtedness and Agricultural Investment
(in millions of RM), 1925–1932

	1925	1926	1927	1928	1929	1930	1931	1932
Agricultural debt	8,023	8,728	9,884	10,831	11,392	11,630	11,765	11,425
Annual interest	425	610	625	785	920	950	950	1,005
Interest as % of sales	5.6	7.5	7.3	8.3	8.9	9.7	10.7	13.8
Agricultural investment	850	310	1,540	1,270	120	1,440	690	430
Agricultural price index (1913 = 100)	132	132	138	132	126	107	89	77

SOURCES: Lorenz, pp. 75, 91; Holt, p. 137; Hoffmann, p. 237. Hoffmann urges caution with these figures.

TABLE 23

Industrial Investment (in millions of RM), 1925–1933

	1925	1926	1927	1928	1929	1930	1931	1932	1933
Amounts	5,020	560	6,480	5,450	1,690	− 1,740	− 5,020	− 3,340	− 340

SOURCE: Hoffmann, p. 247.

Simultaneously, agriculture was compelled, under the advisement of industry and finance, to modernize constantly and increase productivity. The resulting investment was both expensive and "catch up," designed primarily to keep from sinking further into debt. Chronically indebted peasants and Junkers were both forced to invest and improve productivity simply to keep afloat. A look at the rates of agricultural indebtedness and agricultural investment is illuminating in this regard (see table 22). About 7 percent of farm revenue was necessary to service the agricultural debt in 1913. The inflation lowered this to well under 6 percent, from which the figure rose to 7½ percent in 1926 and 14 percent by 1932. Further, investment in agriculture had to take place even when interest rates and indebtedness were at their highest and the

fentliche Mittel as vol. 13 of its report (Berlin, 1930), see especially pp. 5–14. Also, Tilman Koops, "Zielkonflikte der Agrar- und Wirtschaftspolitik in der Ära Brüning," in Mommsen, et al., eds., pp. 853–68, and Dieter Hertz-Eichenrode, Politik und Landwirtschaft in Ostpreussen, 1919–1930 (Cologne, 1969), pp. 181–337; Topf, pp. 256–69.

price indices for agricultural goods at their lowest. This contrasted sharply with the investment pattern in industry, where no such self-mutilation took place. As table 23 indicates, once the economy weakened, investment ended and disinvestment began.

Industrial capitalism thus interacted with agriculture in such a way as to contribute to the nearly continuous expansion of industrial capital and the marginalization of agricultural production.[18] It was not unreasonable, therefore, that the exemption of land and its primary products from the market, from the capitalist system, had been a real if vainly sought goal of organized agriculture since the turn of the century. By the Weimar period, and until the onset of the Depression, most of industry enjoyed the possibility of allying itself either with labor or with agriculture in passing its own trade and foreign-policy bills. Industry could inflame or dampen the divergences within Landwirtschaft without actually splitting it irredeemably.[19] And the rural elite thus did become, in Gramsci's words, "increasingly dependent on the liberality of the dominant economic group." But it did so partially on its own terms and not without making its own contributions toward resolving the political crisis. To use the Weberian image, its views often acted as "switchmen" determining the tracks along which action would be pushed by the dynamic of interests.

Precapitalist groups generally had retained a disproportionately strong voice in determining what kind of ideological and political framework would accompany "organized capitalism." Increased and systematized state intervention in the economy, and the political framework for that intervention, were in no small part the work of groups whose origins and outlooks were precapitalist,[20] even if they themselves had in time become capitalists (like the estate owners) or become part of a capitalist social formation (like the family peasants). The influence of the dependent sector remained mighty.

2. Strategies for Sectoral Interaction after 1925

A key to understanding the relationship between industry and agriculture during the stable years of the Weimar Republic may lie in the reconciliation of two almost diametrically opposed evaluations of how agriculture fared during this period. On the one hand, there is Georges Castellan's contention that "for agriculture the period of prosperity and

18. Again, Georg Solmssen, *Die Lage der Landwirtschaft und ihre Bedeutung für das Bankgewerbe* (Berlin, 1928), pp. 12–18, 44–49.
19. See Holt, pp. 110ff.
20. See Winkler, *Organisierter Kapitalismus*, p. 216.

stability was much more . . . a period of depression between the prewar period and the Third Reich." On the other hand, there is Hans Rosenberg's assertion that despite routine complaints and thanks to state aid, not only was the agrarian "plutocracy" better off than major industrialists and merchants but landowners in general "were materially better off in the first decade of the Weimar Republic than they were in the first quarter century of the empire."[21] What makes these statements compatible is the fact that the marginalization of agricultural production as a whole and the protection of some agricultural producers were not mutually exclusive processes. So long as the rural elite was able to "deliver" the peasants, its own political standing in the Republic would remain substantial regardless of which industrial fraction was pointing the way toward which larger coalition. The *possibility* of political coalition with agriculture remained a real and effective force, even during the period of the labor-export coalition. Agriculture's economic problems were, therefore, only part of the story, and how the rural sector fared economically was only one component of its political situation. Further, the overall stagnation of agriculture did not prevent either occasional prosperity or the enrichment of certain producers; any number of arrangements could allow for that.

By 1925 industry was in a position to begin determining the place of the agricultural sector in both the national economy and any political bloc. Politically, the defeat of organized labor's insurrectionary moment allowed for its subsequent incorporation and functioning as a popular base for the state. The rural population, like much of the Mittelstand, was reduced to being on the outside much of the time. Economically, the restoration of Germany's trade freedom in 1925, in accord with the provisions of the Versailles treaty, allowed for the reintegration of the industrial sector into the world economy and the growth of that sector under the leadership of the dynamic and export fraction. A tacit labor-export alliance chose a path detrimental to the interests of agriculture. Yet, as we have noted, coalitions remained shifting and unstable, and no single fraction ever achieved unquestioned dominance. All social classes or class fractions participated, therefore, in the formation of policies affecting agriculture, but, because we are analyzing relations between industry and agriculture, the primary actors considered here are the two fractions of industry and the rural elite.[22] The fractions of

21. Castellan, "Sozialen Bilanz," p. 107; Hans Rosenberg, *Probleme,* p. 44.

22. The dominant strand of thought in the SPD, represented by Hilferding, supported free trade and industrial expansion, thereby allying itself with export interests and opposing agriculture's demands. The minority view, represented by Baade, was ready for a program of autarky, inflation, and state ("public") regulation of prices. See the literature cited in chap. 2, note 167. The policy of the KPD was almost a caricature of that of the

industry tried economic and political strategies that would variously have resulted in the integration, marginalization, or virtual abandonment of agriculture's interests. Some groups of industrialists and bankers sought to sustain and maintain the existing structure of agricultural production; others attempted to rationalize, thin out, and reorganize that structure, a few were even content to abandon it to its fate.

Between 1925 and the end of 1932, representatives of industry offered five strategies for dealing with the problems of agriculture. The first was a kind of free-trading, sink-or-swim position characteristic of the more dogmatic thinkers in the DDP and the most aggressive representatives of the dynamic, export-oriented industries. Often with the support of organized labor, representatives of this position, like Karl Lange of the machine industry, were foursquare opposed to the estate owners and any attempt to sustain their high-cost production. A corollary of this strategy was the separation of peasant dairy and livestock production from the estate owners' sphere of influence and the "industrialization" of that production through cheap imported feeds and the construction of a dense network of modern production and marketing cooperatives.

Whereas supporters of the first strategy were prepared to align themselves with family peasants and even with the SPD in order to create a more efficient rural sector, the proponents of the second strategy were more concerned to preserve the unity of the propertied classes. Representatives of the older, domestic-market-oriented heavy industries shared with the estate owners a stake in protectionism and were reluctant to injure the interests of even the most inefficient members of that class—especially so long as the attendant costs were borne by others. Thus, the DVP platform called for agricultural independence to be protected by tariffs and the nurture of units of all sizes, while the postwar DNVP platform added that agriculture was still the economy's first estate.[23] These two strategies, the export strategy and the domestic-market strategy, could exist in relatively pure form so long as the economy was in any case expansive or at least stable. In public discussion and in the voluminous debates of the agricultural economists, the choice between the two remained the paradigm for both science and ideology. Although they never entirely ceased being the framework of analysis for vital agricultural and trade issues, after 1929 they in-

---

DDP free traders. The KPD clung to the position that cheap feeds would help destroy the Junkers *and* create a democratic peasantry. See the memorandum of 28 May 1930 to Brüning from the communist Reichsbauernbund, in BA/R43I/2543, pp. 303–305. As for the peasants, we have demonstrated how their interests were formed, integrated, and expressed.

23. Cited in Franz, pp. 522–23. It is noteworthy how many industrialists were also active latifundists; see Herrmann, pp. 20, 22.

creasingly gave way to policy initiatives grounded in three other, less starkly differentiated conceptions.

The third strategy might be described as one of making agriculture fit for competitive capitalism, a kind of modernization without injury to the existing class structure of the countryside. Given the limitations imposed by that rather severe constraint, this proved to be a compromise approach pursued in two variants. In one form it was articulated by nearly all of industry under the leadership of the dynamic-export fraction and was typified by the RDI's 1930 *Contribution to an Agrarian Program*. As we observed in chapter 2, this form of the competition or modernization strategy was perceived by the rural elite as a near ultimatum and, should the estates not shape up, a threat of abandonment. Some exporters did attempt to fashion this strategy into an attack on the estate owners, but at root it was a program to modernize and integrate agriculture.[24] The other variant of this competitive-fitness strategy was developed much more in cooperation with the estate owners and was articulated by the luminaries of heavy industry. Whereas the first variant was associated with the labor-friendly exporters in the RDI leadership (Kastl, Duisberg, August Weber, Wolff, and Raumer, for example), the latter variant was associated with the notables of both the Ruhr and the estate areas (Reichert, Reusch, Krupp, Wilmowsky, and Brandes, for example), and it took its name, the Esplanade Circle, from the venerable hotel where it held its multipurpose meetings. Both variants of this strategy fell far short of their goals: the former because the dynamic fraction of industry was itself displaced from leadership in 1931, and the latter because its commitment proved much more to protection and preservation than to adaptation.

Just as industrial capitalism itself had by and large evolved beyond the competitive era, so the fourth strategy sought to rationalize agricultural production without placing the main emphasis on competitiveness and international standing. This strategy of organized capitalism for the countryside emphasized instead the regulation of both prices and production; it attempted to move "beyond" the fixation with costs, protection, and trade treaties. (Some facets and precursors of this strategy had emerged during the wartime emergency regime, but the rules, stakes, and form of state were now all different.) Its two primary components, the cartellization of agricultural production and the financing of rural credit through a special bank established, funded, and controlled by industry, constituted an advanced capitalist program.

24. The accelerating world depression together with the normal hysteria of the RLB and other rural organizations made the program seem much more subversive than it was. Most damning was the fact that the exporters' variant of this competition strategy was supported by and resembled the program of the SPD; details below.

And it was advanced capitalists who proposed it: Carl Bosch initiated the cartellization scheme, and Paul Silverberg formulated the program of the Industrial Obligations Bank for agriculture. It was, perhaps, too advanced and was opposed by some representatives of industry and the petite bourgeoisie who feared potential state involvement, and by some representatives of agriculture who appreciated the possibility of better integrating agricultural production into the total economy but who rejected the implied marginalization and increased dependence on the industrial leadership.[25]

The fifth strategy proposed to subsume both the shared and divergent interests of industry and agriculture under a program of imperialism. An expansion and redirection of markets eastward, primarily through the Danube Basin, promised to provide for the most commonly shared interest of agriculture and industry[26] and a potentially popular program for redressing Germany's national grievances. By 1932 the first four of these strategies had been laid out and fought out, not simply on the basis of their "objective" economic merits, but rather in the context of shifting intra- and interclass coalitions and conflicts. During the tenure of the Papen and Schleicher regimes in 1932 all four of these strategies were quickly recapitulated while the fifth strategy became increasingly attractive. Thus, between 1925 and the end of 1932, five strategies governed the relations between industry and organized agriculture: export, protection, modernization, organization, and imperialism were all called upon and available.

3. The Economic Interaction of the Two Sectors

The various tables in chapters 2 and 3 illuminated the changing size and shape of agricultural and industrial production in Weimar Germany; data presented here will illustrate how production in the two sectors interacted. As a consumer, the rural sector was stagnant and poor. In 1928, a good year all around, per capita consumption of industrial goods in purely agricultural areas was only 100 RM, compared to 135 RM in largely agricultural, partly industrial areas, 185 RM in partly agricultural, largely industrial areas, and 200 RM in purely industrial

25. Of course, it was supported by those in the SPD, like Baade, who anticipated greater state-public-democratic involvement in planning. For this reason, the SPD supported the government sugar quota, grain and corn import monopolies. In this they were joined by the DNVP, which would do almost anything to push up agricultural and land prices; they were opposed by the DDP, Wirtschaftspartei, and DVP, which feared state encroachment in the market itself. Most of this has been SPD and Common Market policy since the 1950s.

26. Subject to the constraint mentioned in note 6 above.

TABLE 24

Prices (1913 = 100) and Production Values
(in billions of RM), 1926–1932

	1926	1927	1928	1929	1930	1931	1932
Net value agricultural prod.	9.7	10.5	11.2	11.1	10.6	10.1	8.5
Agricultural price index	134	138	132	126	107	89	77
Net cash returns	1.6	1.4	2.2	1.9	1.7	1.2	.9
Net value industrial prod.	21.3	26.3	31.8	28.4	26.7	18.7	17.3
Industrial price index	150	148	159	157	154	142	118

SOURCES: Adapted from Karl Lange, "Deutsche Industrie und deutsche Landwirtschaft, Ihre Produktionsentwicklung 1925–1931," in Friedrich List Gesellschaft, 2:554, 563. Cf., however, Hoffmann, pp. 310, 313, where the production values are all higher.

areas. The consumption of foodstuffs was also lower, even if allowances are made for peasant consumption of nonmarketed goods. For foodstuffs, the corresponding figures for the four types of regions were 25, 61, 77, and 146 RM, respectively.[27] What was true for individual consumption was also true in aggregate terms; German industry had far better customers than the underconsuming rural sector. Together with the investment figures noted earlier, table 24 indicates the relative strength and profitability of the two sectors. Rural stagnation and decline are striking.

Table 25 demonstrates even more clearly the extent of the unequal exchange between the two sectors and the economic marginality of agriculture. In good years as in bad ones, the rural sector was never more than industry's third-best customer. In good years, industry was its own best customer followed by the export market; and, as importantly, during bad times, the export market became industry's best customer, thereby creating an even worse situation for agriculture. Its own exchange patterns, on the other hand, remained nearly unchanged in most respects. The increasingly important role of exports, through both the fat years and the lean ones, contrasted sharply with the stagnant quality of the rural market.

While industrial exports, particularly those of finished goods, grew in importance throughout the period, German agricultural production ex-

27. Paul Münch, *Die innere Marktverflechtung von Landwirtschaft und Industrie* (Giessen, 1934), p. 67.

perienced difficulties holding its own. The extremely significant impact of agricultural imports was noted in chapter 2:[28] until 1930, agricultural imports had a net worth well over one-third the value of domestic production. And, unlike the voluminous importation of raw materials, food imports served no further productive purpose. (Holding down the costs of reproducing labor power was an argument that appealed primarily to those whom organized Landwirtschaft considered its enemies.) Table 26 provides a rough breakdown of the contribution of each of the three sectors to the German balance of trade. In an export-oriented economy like Germany's, agriculture's negative contribution became at best a very undesirable liability.

TABLE 25

Exchange of Agricultural and Industrial Production
(in billions of RM and percent), Three Sample Years

	1924–25 (pre-prosperity)		1927–28 (prosperity)		1930–31 (depression)	
	Net Value	%	Net Value	%	Net Value	%
Of net agricultural production						
To industry	3.6	38	4.29	40	4.14	40
To commerce	1.5	16	1.93	18	1.55	15
To other urban	1.55	17	1.38	13	1.77	17
To agric. sector	2.6	28	3.14	28	2.8	27
To export	.25	2	.14	1	.23	2
Total	9.46	100	10.8	100	10.5	100
Of net industrial production						
To industry	7.9	36	9.7	32	5.4	24
To commerce	3.0	14	3.8	13	2.2	10
To other urban	3.4	15	3.1	11	2.0	9
To agric. sector	3.7	16	4.4	15	4.0	18
To export	4.2	19	8.2	30	8.7	39
Total	22.2	100	29.4	100	22.3	100

SOURCES: Composed on the basis of Lange, pp. 569, 572; BA/R43I/1275, pp. 270–75, and Paul Münch, *Die innere Marktverflechtung von Landwirtschaft und Industrie* (Giessen, 1934), p. 55. See also Paul Bramstedt, "Die Tauschbeziehungen von Landwirtschaft und Industrie—Probleme des Binnenmarkts," in Friedrich List Gesellschaft, 2:413–52. He reluctantly concludes that the dependency of the two sectors runs one way only, i.e., agricultural prosperity is dependent on industrial prosperity, but *not* vice versa.

28. See table 7 and the accompanying discussion.

TABLE 26

Value of Exports and Imports by Category (in billions of RM), 1926–1932, and as Share of Foreign Trade (1929)

	1926	1927	1928	1929	1930	1931	1932
All food & drink							
Exported	.53	.47	.62	.72	.55	.64	.56
Imported	3.70	4.50	4.35	4.00	3.09	2.63	2.48
Balance	−3.17	−4.03	−3.73	−3.28	−2.54	−1.99	−1.92
Raw materials & halfwares							
Exported	2.73	2.61	2.70	2.93	2.46	2.04	...
Imported	4.95	7.19	7.24	7.21	5.50	3.96	...
Balance	−2.22	−4.58	−4.54	−4.28	−3.04	−1.92	...
Finished goods							
Exported	7.15	7.72	8.70	9.83	9.04	8.35	...
Imported	1.36	2.54	2.46	2.27	1.79	1.42	...
Balance	+5.79	+5.18	+6.24	+7.56	+7.25	+6.93	...

	Imports	%	Exports	%
1929 shares				
All food & drink	3.82	29	.72	5
Raw materials & halfwares	7.21	54	2.93	22
Finished goods	2.27	17	9.83	73

SOURCES: Sering, p. 830, Landmann, p. 606 and Dietmar Keese, "Die volkswirtschaftlichen Gesamtgrössen für das Deutsche Reich, 1925–1936," in *Die Staats- und Wirtschaftskrise des Deutschen Reichs 1929–33*, eds. Werner Conze and Hans Raupach (Stuttgart, 1967), p. 75.

One of the most tenacious problems of agricultural production in developed industrial social formations is that of the price scissors. The data in table 27 demonstrate how agricultural prices first failed to keep up with increases in other prices and then proved to be far more downwardly elastic than the others. With no significant exceptions, the gap between agricultural prices and the prices of those goods consumed by peasants and estate owners continued to grow throughout the period. Although organized labor's wage gains were severely slowed by the inflation and buffeted by high unemployment, its gains were not easily rolled back; this was in very marked contrast to agricultural prices after 1929 and did nothing to help reconcile peasants and workers. No other trend aroused as much anger in the countryside as the price scissors, unless it was the tendency of liberal, pro-export economists to acknowledge that the scissors did exist but that the only way to overcome the trend was through rationalization and more efficient production.[29] The underlying complaint of agriculture's representatives, however, was the lack of profitability, and they would have accepted almost any arrangement providing them that.

4. Strategies 1 and 2: Exports versus Protection, 1925–1931

During most of this period the basic framework for the conflicts among the three economically dominant fractions was provided, on the one hand, by the question of how to deal with the SPD, and, on the other, by the choice between a dynamic-export and a heavy-industry/domestic-market strategy. Sozialpolitik and Handelspolitik were the loci for conflicts between and within classes. For most of this period it was the dynamic, export fraction of industry that set the agenda and tone for the dominant classes as a whole. It relied largely on the support of the organized working class to overcome the objections of an often united agriculture and heavy industry. The search for the national good in economic matters therefore took the form of a conflict between expanding the dominant sector come what may and recognizing a parity or equilibrium between the dominant and the older sectors. In agricultural matters this meant choosing assimilation into an international division of labor and modernization, on the one hand, or protection and subsidy, on the other. After 1925 the dynamic-export fraction had the initiative.[30] Its representatives wanted to ease the burden placed on them

TABLE 27

Agriculture in the Price Scissors, 1926–1932, Indices (1913 = 100)

	1926	1927	1928	1929	1930	1931	1932
Agricultural prices	134	138	132	126	107	89	77
Farm machinery	125	125	127	127	127	125	122
Other fixtures	133	133	139	141	140	130	120
Construction	161	173	173	177	168	148	130
Fertilizer	86	83	82	85	83	78	73
Basic consumer goods	162	160	175	172	160	143	127
Real hourly wages	105	110	117	123	126	127	122

SOURCE: *Berichte über Landwirtschaft* 83 (1933), p. 10; Denecke, p. 94. Holt, p. 218, reports higher figures.

29. The RDI economists were representative of this school. In addition to the 1930 *Contribution,* see Hans Zörner and Lothar Russig, "Die Bedeutung der Industriepreise für die Kostengestaltung im landwirtschaftlichen Betriebe," in Friedrich List Gesellschaft, 1:357–78.

30. For agriculture's response to the ascent of the exporters, see chap. 2, sec. 3.

by the agricultural sector: first, by limiting its political and policy prerogatives; and second, by using the rationalization of peasant dairy and livestock production to force the estate owners either to swim or, preferably, sink.

Despite the SPD's support, representatives of industry failed in their 1925 initiative to absorb the Agriculture Ministry into their "own" Economics Ministry; the very attempt, however, indicated the balance of forces.[31] From the outset of its trade offensive in 1925, German industry made it clear that it would accept the high-quality, low-cost agricultural products of its northern and western neighbors in exchange for its own advanced, industrial products. This opened the way for a comprehensive series of most-favored-nation trade agreements negotiated through Stresemann's Foreign Ministry. Stresemann and the export offensive both enjoyed full SPD support: "High agricultural duties damage industry's ability to export, thereby increasing unemployment and lowering the ability of the home market to consume. We have realized this . . . and are pleased that some industrialists, like Bosch and Lange, also do."[32] For his part, Robert Bosch was quite explicit: "Our own territory [eigene Scholle] cannot, should not, and need not feed all of Germany. We need exports and profit greatly from them; tariffs must be limited so as not to hamper them. . . ." He thought Landwirtschaft had no right to expect an 8–10 percent profit rate; the least profitable farms should be abandoned. "Industry needs to retain its best customer, the rural sector [sic], but it needs even more to expand its [export] markets."[33] Trade treaties were negotiated between 1925 and 1928 on the basis of such positions, and the prewar industry-agriculture trade parity was abandoned. The first major treaties were signed in 1925 with Spain, France, Holland, and Belgium; they directly affected rural producers in the north and east of Germany. Later treaties in 1927 with Czechoslovakia, Poland, and the Baltic and Balkan states spread the adverse effects to southern and western Germany as well.[34] Simultaneously, state expenditures for export credits (and social programs) rose rapidly while outlays for the rural sector dropped. Early symptoms of a crisis in agricultural production were labeled a "purification process" by exporters and socialists alike. It was another case of

31. Details of this effort in Panzer, p. 91.

32. *Sozialdemokratische Agrarcorrespondenz*, 25 May 1927; cited in ZSA/RLB Pressarchiv 132/10, p. 96a. Support for the SPD among the peasantry was further weakened by this policy.

33. Robert Bosch in the *Deutsche Allgemeine Zeitung*, 17 Apr. 1927. Kastl could legitimately maintain in April 1926 that the new position was one "shared by industry, commerce, and labor"; Panzer, p. 80.

34. Panzer, pp. 53, 111, 137.

the strong preaching to the weak about the virtues of the free market, competition, and hard work.[35]

Until the SPD electoral victory in 1928, however, these voices were countered by those in heavy industry who were proponents of a domestic-market strategy. Until the Grand Coalition and the Young Plan reversed the trend, heavy industry and agriculture were, in fact, closing the gap that separated them. The *Industrie und Handelszeitung* commented that the "bad times for agriculture began after the inflation with growing debts, competition, tax, and social costs—all while industry was forced to export. We grew apart. But now men like Vögler and Reusch are bringing industry back to its senses." They needed a reconciliation so that together they could battle "the left and all opponents of a national production policy."[36] At the end of 1926, Reusch told his colleagues in iron and steel that their "primary concern must be the development of the domestic market, for industry and agriculture are more dependent on each other now than ever before." For their part, representatives of agriculture were aware of both who their friends and enemies were in the changing industrial lineup—and of their own trump card. Again, Economics Minister Curtius and the exporters were their primary targets, but the overall lie of the land was perceived clearly:

> Curtius is sabotaging the restoration of profitability in the domestic market. . . . The kinds of attacks Bosch and Lange have made on us are as bad as anything produced by the socialists. We do not constantly tell industry what to do, but they do tell us. . . . Their program for cooperation is a program for our capitulation. . . . In order to combat state socialism we need to develop a really unified position. . . . But we must admit that although certain branches of industry—the ones that used to be decisive (iron, steel, and mining)—are closer to us, the predominant mood in industry—including that of very influential circles (like IG Farben)—is very hostile toward us.[37]

Finally, the 1927 annual report of the Northwest Iron group presented a view of agriculture and the market almost diametrically opposed to that held by spokesmen for the dynamic fraction:

35. Thus, August Weber told the RDI in April 1928 that agriculture's problems were a result of the low quality of its production, its inability to compromise or adapt, and its arrogance. What the nation needed was low production costs and food prices. Cited in ibid., p. 133.

36. Cited in ZSA/RLB Pressarchiv 132/10, p. 185, 25 Nov. 1927, *DTZ*, 17 Nov.

37. ZSA/RLB Verhältnisse zwischen Land und Industrie/126, pp. 68–69. A few months later, Reusch told the Langnamverein that "we are not adversely affected by adequate agricultural tariffs—and want them for ourselves too"; ibid., p. 124. Further, "The rural sector is our largest and most secure market." He was well aware, however, that this was not the predominant mood in industry.

We appreciate with compelling clarity how vital it is for industry to maintain and develop agriculture. [The basis of economic activity is the exchange of rural and industrial production.] Agriculture is only now recovering from ten years of government coercion and catching up with our competitive neighbors. The goal is to make Germany's food supply as independent of imports as possible. This goal of food independence [*Nahrungsfreiheit*] is both supportable and fully attainable. . . . Aside from the national-political grounds for such an effort . . . it would assist our trade balance. . . . An increase in the export of our industrial products will not accomplish these goals.[38]

After 1928, the rift between industry and agriculture grew, first because of the Grand Coalition and then because of the slowdown in domestic production combined with expansion in the export sector. Even conservative groups like the Langnamverein became less receptive to agrarian demands. Legislation for the assistance of rural producers, of the type they themselves favored, met increased resistance from the representatives of industry. Until around 1931, the moderate programs of Agriculture Minister Dietrich and the "reasonable" programs of his successor, Schiele, found only minimal industrial approval. So long as the argument was carried on within the framework of the export versus domestic strategy, opposition to agriculture mounted, as was evident, for example, in the East Prussia/Poland tradeoff.[39] Andreas Hermes ventured into the free-traders' den when he cited Adam Smith and admonished the 1928 DIHT convention, telling it, in the name of agriculture, that all industrial and commercial expansion depended on a thriving rural sector. The delegates were much more impressed, however, when representatives of the Dresdner Bank told them that "there is an indisputable standstill in the growth of the domestic market. . . . [whereas] despite all the barriers, German industry is competing successfully on the world market and can more than

---

38. October 1927, cited in *Stahl und Eisen,* 16 and 23 Feb. 1928.

39. For the debate on 1928 Osthilfe legislation, cf. Hertz-Eichenrode, pp. 217ff. The RDI *Mitteilungen* of 7 Mar. 1928, 10:6, lfd. 110, make clear that the export offensive had just begun! Insofar as this legislation was intended to counter the ill effects of the Polish trade treaty, Lange retorted that the East Prussians had no cause to complain; they were in a better competitive position than ever before, and the chief Polish agricultural imports accounted for only .35 percent of German consumption. See BA/Nachlass Silverberg/362, pp. 76–85. On the position of heavy industry, chap. 3, sec. 4 above. Only the "ultras" like Hugenberg opposed the treaty completely; BA/Nachlass Hugenberg/114, pp. 132–38, 263. Others, like Schlenker of Northwest Iron, lay in between. Cf. Puhle, *Agrarbewegungen,* p. 89, and the literature cited there; HA GHH/Martin Blank 400 101 202 4/4b, and Nachlass Reusch 400 101 290/39 for the relevant correspondence between Reusch and Wilmowsky; Gessner, *Agrarverbände,* pp. 128–36.

compensate for the declining domestic conjuncture through its increased sales abroad."[40]

Capital-short German industries and banks were not prepared to make the sacrifices necessary to build the rural market when the foreign market beckoned. The political strength of the SPD and unions might force industrialists to acknowledge the urban market, but the rural market was more easily slighted. Labor and industrial capital concurred that the cost of living needed to be kept down for the sake of competitiveness, and although industry would campaign for reductions in taxes and social costs, it would not endorse tariff increases likely to result in higher wage demands. Thus, Edmund Pietrkowski, a leader of the Chemical Industries Association and also a textile industrialist, insisted in 1929 that agricultural imports would have to be maintained at their existing levels and industrial exports encouraged. "The notion that the domestic market could absorb lost exports is preposterous. The tradeoff . . . would yield 1.5 billions at a cost of 6 billions per year."[41] The maintenance of continental foreign trade and a low cost of living were joined in the effort to expand the dairy trade with Finland rather than restrict it as demanded by agricultural spokesmen in early 1930. The RDI countered that restrictions would not only raise unemployment and the cost of living and lead to the loss of foreign markets, but would also precipitate reprisals and a trade war whose beneficiary could only be England.[42] Because most industries during this phase adopted similar positions in the name of the national interest, those few that dissented appeared to do so out of selfish interests. The farm-equipment manufacturers could at most claim that "the distress of agriculture is our distress," and that agriculture must be protected "like any young industry." The particularistic motives were apparent when a spokesman for that industry asked rhetorically, "Would we not seek to lower labor costs and increase profitability and productivity in an industry which started out with disadvantages like those faced by agriculture? . . . The German producer produces twice per acre what the American does, but he does so with four to eight times the labor costs,

40. Hermes, cited in BA/R11-DIHT/125, pp. 1516–18; Dresdner Bank, cited in ZSA/RLB Pressarchiv 132/11, p. 38, *BBC,* 1 Apr. 1928.

41. "Agrarprogramm und Handelspolitik," MS of speech of 28 Sept. 1929, p. 22. Here and elsewhere, Pietrkowski did acknowledge the importance of doing something for the "reliably antisocialist and healthy peasants" (p. 26). Spokesmen for the more prosperous export industries, like Kraemer of the paper and printing industries and Raumer of the electrotechnical branch, were even more outspoken in their opposition to tariff increases, particularly once agriculture's demands began to impinge not only on *overseas* markets but on *European* trade as well; see HA GHH/Martin Blank 400 101 202 4/6, Blank's report of 26 Feb. 1930.

42. See, e.g., the RDI statement of April 1930, BA/R43I/2543, pp. 63–64.

despite real wages there being at least double the German level." He went on to ask, if this were any other German industry, would it not be protected?[43] Such outspoken support for agriculture was, however, the rare exception both before and after 1930.

Even once the Grand Coalition collapsed and industry resumed its campaign against the SPD and Sozialpolitik, the primacy of the export market and reparations obligations both remained. Initially, the consequence was increased industry-agriculture tension and general industrial opposition to the Schiele-Hindenburg programs for assistance to agriculture, discussed in chapter 2. On the one hand, the Brüning government attempted to mediate the interests of the two fractions of industry while leaning more toward the dynamic fraction—all the while dependent on organized labor's toleration. On the other hand, Brüning was compelled, largely at Hindenburg's behest, at least to appease the escalating demands of agrarian organizations and maintain the mass support of the rural population as a partial alternative to the support of labor. This nexus could have furnished the possibility for coalitions, but instead the various triads acted only to aggravate the internal contradictions of the Brüning government. As long as the agriculture-industry conflict remained within the export/protectionist paradigm, no real reconciliation was possible.[44] Between mid-1930 and 1932, other paradigms did begin to emerge under the impact of a deteriorating economic situation and a changing class balance. Nevertheless, important debates continued within the framework of export versus protection, and we must follow those to their conclusion before turning to the other strategies.

Through 1930 and into 1931, the discord between the two sectors was personified and summarized as the debate between Agriculture Minister Schiele and the RDI leadership. Outraged that Schiele had formulated his program without "consulting" them,[45] the corporate leaders of industry hastened to point out the bankruptcy of his proposals. The specific points emphasized time and again by industry's spokesmen included the following, culled from the membership newsletter:

43. Walther Hillmann, chairman of the League of Rural Equipment Manufacturers, in BA/R13III-LMV/1280, p. 6, 26 May 1930.

44. See especially Koops, who, however, attributes too much of agriculture's strength to Hindenburg personally. The impossibility of both preserving exports and meeting agriculture's demands was captured by Brüning's remark to Labor Minister Stegerwald that "under the condition of avoiding dangers to exports I have promised the Green Front to exert myself on behalf of their demands" and the latter's response that "not only is this beyond justification; it is impossible" and could only result in a lower standard of living for everyone. BA/R431/2426, pp. 246–50, 17 Feb. 1931.

45. See, e.g., the RDI memorandum to Brüning of 22 Oct. 1930, BA/R431/2544, pp. 326–28.

(1) variable tariffs would render commerce chaotic, (2) the use of veterinary regulations against foreign meat would invite retaliation, (3) the abolition of frozen-meat imports would harm the urban diet and fully endanger 380 million RM worth of exports to Argentina, (4) increased prices and unemployment would strengthen the Left, (5) the compulsory use of German goods in production, such as hops, would be not only a threat to foreign trade but a basic violation of the free economy, (6) the Dutch, Swiss, and others would indeed boycott German goods in retaliation for any new agricultural barriers. German exports to the Netherlands in 1929 were worth 1.4 billion. Over 300,000 German workers depended for their jobs on the maintenance of this market alone. Exports to Holland alone exceeded the total value of German butter production by 300 million marks. (7) the government's cost-cutting measures and agriculture's adaptation to postwar consumption patterns would both be made more difficult, and symptoms masked rather than problems addressed.

For all these reasons the RDI opposed Schiele's program in the cabinet, in parliament and to Hindenburg personally. It sought to demonstrate that guarding the interests of industry and thereby also of the workers it employed was no less "national" than the protection of Landwirtschaft.[46] Even the relatively stagnant iron and steel industry took note of the dangers in Schiele's protectionist program. Together, the Scandinavian countries plus Holland absorbed 25 percent of all German exports, including 24 percent of 500 million RM worth of raw ferrous exports. What ferrous exports there were also went to food-exporting lands, and so even the VDESI argued that the principle of most-favored-nation treaties had to be maintained.[47]

Representatives of the dynamic fraction went beyond this, refusing to discuss with agrarian representatives any measures that affected exports or, in Raumer's words, "protected low quality and inefficient production." Eduard Hamm of the DIHT wrote all the cabinet ministers that "in this time of unemployment and national sacrifice the needs of industry, commerce, and consumers must come first." An RDI delegation headed by Duisberg, Kastl, and Silverberg called on Hindenburg himself in December 1930 and warned him that the measures proposed to protect agriculture would make exports virtually impossi-

46. *Mitteilungen* 12:8, lfd. 194; 12:19, lfd. 441; 12:27, lfd. 593; 12:31, lfd. 705. Rather than modernizing, organized agriculture was protecting its most backward elements. See also the memorandum from the DIHT to Brüning, 2 Feb. 1931, in which it was alleged that the butter and fruit tariffs alone would threaten 38–45 percent of German exports and destroy the base for taxes, reparations, and social peace: BA/R431/2546, pp. 115–17.

47. BA/R13I-VDESI/68, p. 19, meeting of 12 Feb. 1931.

ble, increase unemployment substantially, and jeopardize five billion RM worth of exports, all for minimal benefits.[48] Toward the end of 1930, Brüning was besieged by telegrams protesting the implementation by presidential decree of several of Schiele's proposals. The protest lodged by the Munich Chamber of Industry and Commerce was typical: "We must express our growing concern over steadily rising trade barriers. . . . they ruin our ability to produce and trade and lead to shutdowns, unemployment and price increases, hunger, misery and mass unrest. The life chances of industry and commerce," they maintained, were being destroyed in obeisance to grain-growing estate production which was assumed to represent what was good, not only for all of agriculture, in itself dubious, but for the whole nation.[49] By the end of 1930, industry, under the leadership of its dynamic fraction, and agriculture had arrived at fully antagonistic positions; this contradiction within the dominant economic classes was at its most severe. The democratic *Berliner Tageblatt* of 13 December 1930 summarized this development in an article entitled "From Contradiction to Absurdity": "In its attempts to assert its parity, the sick part of the economy is prepared to bleed the rest white, to make the rest sick without healing itself. There is no reason to wonder when other social strata refuse to continue sacrificing at the altar of agrarian destruction of capital."

Had the representatives of agriculture lacked any support outside the rural sector their demands would simply have been denied or ignored. We noted in chapter 1 the weak political impulse of the German industrial capitalist class and its inheritance of an early compromise with and reliance on the rural elite, a reliance that manifested itself, even during the Weimar years, in the peculiar prominence of rural notables in the various state organs, particularly the executive. In chapter 2 we discussed the importance of the peasantry for non- and antisocialist coalitions and the ability of the rural elite to use integration/dependence mechanisms to "deliver" that peasantry. And in chapter 3 we analyzed why one fraction of industry, at least, was prepared to make disproportionate economic sacrifices on agriculture's behalf. Even so, the relative success of agriculture's representatives remains a remarkable phenomenon. In some sense, Germans of nearly all classes believed that agriculture's interests and well-being were more "national" than those of

48. Raumer of the electrotechnical industry to Silverberg, 12 Oct. 1930, BA/Nachlass Silverberg/363, pp. 93–97; Hamm's letter to all the cabinet ministers, 24 Oct., and minutes of the RDI delegation's meeting with Hindenburg, 12 Dec. 1930, in ZSA/Büro des Reichspräsidenten/331, pp. 146 and 180ff., respectively. Hindenburg received them correctly but coolly.

49. Cited in BA/R43I/2545, p. 177. This and other communiques reflected the RDI's attempt to remove family peasants from the orbit of the estate owners.

industry. This was partly because significant rural areas were border areas, some of which were lost after the war. Conservative ideology sought, with some success, to blame these losses on the working class (through the "stab in the back" theory) and liberal industrialists, while portraying the reactionary rulers of the East as the last bulwark against the Slavic and Semitic tide. Although the diffusion and success of this ideology must be left unexamined here, there is little doubt that its saliency for many among the nonagricultural population led them to accept, passively at least, measures designed to benefit the most rooted and national of classes. Only if one appreciates this does the success of agrarian propaganda become comprehensible, particularly success in portraying most of industry as "internationalist" compared to patriotic and "national" agriculture.[50]

It was out of combined economic self-interest, ideological affinity, and a political commitment that the journal *Steel and Iron* could write: "Despite the losses we have had to incur in our trade with several countries, industry, and especially the iron industry, has supported agriculture in its tariff demands. Industry is aware of the responsibility it must share for the viability of its largest domestic customer [sic]. . . ." Further, all members of the free-market economy had to be protected against state encroachment and further weakening of the nation's strength.[51] These same groups accepted the Osthilfe "not just for economic, but rather much more for political reasons" and supported revision of the Polish and Finnish trade treaties, because rural Germany, as the backbone of the nation, was "entitled to parity in the calculation of economic policy for the nation as a whole." Those in heavy industry who preached self-sacrifice on behalf of protecting agriculture were, however, not about to abandon the mechanisms that protected their own high-cost production. As we noted in chapter 3, through the AVI agreements the steel industry's customers in the finishing industries did not import raw ferrous products, despite the fact that the domestic price was substantially higher than the world price plus tariffs and freight.[52] Thanks to this and international cartel agreements like the IRG, the iron and steel industry never faced the price competition from which agriculture suffered. These same heavy industries

50. One example will suffice: the RLB newspapers of 12 April 1930 all carried the accusation that the "RDI is more worried about maintaining the economic health of our enemies [Poland? France?] and of far-off lands [e.g., Argentina] than of our own Landwirtschaft, which has already collapsed." In important respects the accusation was, of course, true, at least since the Silverberg-Stresemann-Severing alliance.

51. *Stahl und Eisen,* no. 12, 4 Apr. 1930, cited in HA GHH/Nachlass Reusch 400 101 221/3. Agriculture was not really industry's largest domestic customer, something the editors of this journal must have known.

52. See chap. 3, sec. 4.

opposed a unilateral reduction in interest rates on outstanding private-sector loans to rural producers. Nor were they prepared to lower their own prices as part of any rural-assistance scheme.

Until it was displayed from the overall leadership of industry in late 1931, the dynamic fraction continued to support Brüning while opposing almost all aspects of his agriculture minister's program. For Schiele's protectionist program it attempted to substitute its own, one that recognized a growing need for exports while integrating a modernized agriculture into a more subservient or marginal role. Because its preferred mass base was organized labor, and because it had chosen to accept reparations and reintegration into the world economy, it could not let the basis of its viability be undermined by the kind of protectionism needed to save the existing structure of rural production and its elite. Pietrkowski summarized both the acceptable and unacceptable when he wrote: "If the goal of agricultural policy is to be the feeding of Germany entirely through its own production, then that goal is an illusion. If the goal is to make agriculture production profitable, then that is a worthwhile goal."[53] We now examine how the two fractions of industry proposed to have rural production attain that worthwhile goal.

5. Strategy 3: Modernization, Conciliation, and Reform

Like other programs proposed by the dynamic fraction of industry, its program for making agricultural production more efficient and profitable, the *Contribution to an Agrarian Program* (1930), bore a striking resemblance to initiatives put forward by the SPD, in this case at its 1927 Kiel congress.[54] "Industrialization of Agriculture" was the phrase used to describe the program to seek out and assist the capable (leistungsfähig) producers while abandoning the hopeless ones. As early as 1925, the German Engineers Association had published a series entitled *Technology in Agriculture*, in which it was argued that "we have no intention of permitting our industrial state to develop back into an agrarian state. Rather, we want to develop that industrial state further in that we intend to industrialize Germany's single largest occupation, agriculture," one which, they thought, remained socially and technically backward.[55] The dynamic fraction of industry, together with

53. *Mitteilungen* 14:5, lfd. 84, 29 Feb. 1932.
54. Cf. note 22 above on the SPD. On the presentation and details of the RDI's 1930 *Contribution to an Agrarian Program*, see chap. 2, sec. 4c; on the Osthilfe and Siedlung, chap. 2, sec. 4b. For the trade unions' hostile response to the Osthilfe measures, *Jahrbuch des ADGB, 1931* (Berlin, 1932), pp. 64–69.
55. Cited in Denecke, p. 43.

most of the larger banks, groped for a program to overcome the substantial rural backwardness and inefficiency inherited from the "Prussian Way" in the development of capitalist relations in agriculture, which now impeded social peace and international trade as well.

In the same month, September 1927, in which Duisberg had called for a one-third increase in exports, Kastl and the RDI convention called for a new emphasis on quality in German industrial production. A simple extension of that underlying theme prompted Kastl to attribute vastly increased food imports to "a certain deficiency in quality and value characteristic of domestic production." He contended that "honest circles in agriculture admit this" and offered industry's cooperation in remedying the situation, as long as all concerned realized it was "a question of quality and costs, not tariffs and protection."[56] The transformation of production better to suit demand, the rationalization and standardization of all production units and products, and the organization of a dense network of production and marketing cooperatives were all suggested reforms intended to lower costs, not raise prices. The goal was a modern, efficient, and more purely capitalistic agriculture in the Scandinavian or Dutch mode. In this precrisis period, voluntary measures, education, technical innovation, and the provision of easier credits—together with no retreat on tariff questions—were thought sufficient measures. Even representatives of heavy industry were attracted by the early form of the modernization strategy; after all, if industrialization were to take place, there would undoubtedly be a market to tap. They seem not to have feared that such a program would endanger the Junker class; in the precrisis period the program did not seem to threaten existing class relations.[57] If modernization and rationalization were what the dynamic fraction of industry demanded of agriculture for its own purposes, the heavy-industry fraction saw no harm in them either. Hence, Northwest Iron could endorse such programs and did so in 1927 in considerable detail:

> Noteworthy successes in improving production and quality capabilities have already been scored . . . the energetic contribution of others to this self-help would enhance it greatly—the government and banks by providing easier credit, technical assistance and . . . con-

56. Cited in ZSA/RLB Pressarchiv 148/8, pp. 109–12.

57. Although numerous social analysts and historians we have cited (Max Weber, Eckart Kehr, Hans Rosenberg, and H.-J. Puhle, for example) have argued that the Junker class per se could not adapt and modernize its production, before 1930 this judgment was not shared by or forced upon any significant portion of the actors. To be sure, individual estate owners may have been considered parasites and stumblebums, but estate ownership and large-scale production were not thought beyond salvation. Whether they were politically desirable was another question.

sumers by showing a greater readiness to satisfy their needs with German products. . . . Cooperation with agriculture and an increase in its buying power remain the best pledge for industry's prosperity. . . . The farm equipment industry could absorb [an additional] 500,000 tons [of iron] per year. . . . Industry has every reason to cooperate [to facilitate] peasant resettlement. . . . [Despite huge surpluses] per capita consumption of milk averages about ⅕ liter daily compared to 1 liter in America. Dairy production is the keystone for about 2½ million small units. . . . through our company depots we promote the consumption of milk by workers. . . . and more importantly in worker families. . . . As our experience in cooperation grows . . . we can hope to succeed in bringing industry and agriculture to a unified position on general economic policy questions.[58]

As the economic crisis in agriculture worsened after 1928, the strategy of modernization and reform began to threaten the rural elite. As agrarian spokesmen pushed harder for tariffs and other protectionist legislation, the dynamic fraction's version of modernization more and more resembled the export strategy so close to its heart. Initially, the RDI's definitive agricultural policy statement was eagerly awaited in rural circles. Basing himself on preliminary discussions and leaks, Andreas Hermes of the Catholic Peasants Leagues was able, in July 1929, to voice his "spirited approval that the RDI is adopting an attitude so essentially positive toward the necessities of Landwirtschaft." His view was echoed by Ernst Brandes of the German Agricultural Council, who proclaimed that "it is extremely worthwhile for us to be in agreement with the basic principles of the RDI's program."[59] That optimism, however, had given way to anxiety by the time the RDI's long-awaited *Contribution* appeared in May 1930. Drawn up while the RDI was still under the influence of the labor-export coalition, it countered Schiele's proposals on nearly every point and, therefore, soon elicited a chorus of outraged denunciations and protectionist counterproposals from the major agricultural organizations led by the estate owners and the RLB.[60] It was symptomatic that Hermann Dietrich of the DDP, formerly agriculture minister in the Grand Coalition, where he professed to represent the family peasants of the southwest, and now economics minister under Brüning, praised the RDI program as the one "best suited to help those capable of utilizing it while furthering the interest

58. Cited in *Stahl und Eisen*, 16 Feb. 1928.

59. Cited in BA/Nachlass Silverberg/362, pp. 307, 309.

60. See chap. 2, sec. 4c. Publication of the RDI's rural program was followed by a series of case studies of agricultural production, all highly critical and inflammatory.

of the total national economy."[61] Industry's platform clearly implied a move away from simple subventions to agriculture, particularly to the supererogatory and inefficient grain-growing estate owners.[62] However, Karl Brandt, one of the authors of the RDI *Contribution,* revealed perhaps too candidly what industry's agricultural theorists really thought: "In its current constitution Landwirtshaft no longer fits into the national economy."

Declaring the "current constitution" of agriculture "nonviable" was tantamount to a direct attack on the estate owners who personified that constitution. It was they who unified and led organized agriculture from their strongholds in the East, and it was they who could provide a substantial portion of the troops for any antisocialist coalition. The program of the dynamic fraction of industry sought to deprive them of their mass base in the peasantry, and its formula for a "constructive Osthilfe" threatened their very economic base at a time when they were in deep trouble. A newsletter funded by IG Farben described the Osthilfe in a manner that contradicted the intentions of Schiele and his rural supporters and even those of the heavy-industry fraction: "The task of the Osthilfe must under no circumstances be the restoration of incompetent or unfit families; rather it is to encourage and assist capable farmers [*Ökonomen*] and managers in the difficult but promising tasks ahead. Certainly the East must be helped, but help only there where it serves a purpose, and only with a simultaneous and deep alteration of the modes and methods of production and market orientation."[63] In the course of 1930 and 1931, representatives of the dynamic fraction of industry (and some peasants and most of labor) became increasingly active in asserting that this was the only viable way. As organized agriculture's attack on the program grew more acerbic and socialist support more evident, heavy industry turned reticent and began to back away from support of reform. Citing the position of the SPD and the left, the *Deutsche Bergwerkszeitung* announced that there was no need to get so excited or worried about the RDI program: it did

61. Dietrich's speech to the 50th DIHT convention, 10 Apr. 1930, cited in ZSA/RLB Pressarchiv 132/12, p. 2. Silverberg followed Dietrich to the podium, where he announced that the "era of tariffs has given way to the era of rationalization."

62. Hermann Warmbold of IG Farben and a future economics minister argued that domestic grain production was too high and productivity too low. He called for reforestation of over one million hectares of grain land in the east alone. What that could have done to the land values of Junker estates! BA/R431/2546, pp. 52–53, 29 Jan. 1931.

63. Brandt cited in ZSA/RLB Pressarchiv 148/9, p. 183. On the prescription for the Osthilfe, *Deutsche Führerbriefe* 3 (25 Mar. 1930): 24. On this curious publication, Sohn-Rethel, pp. 27–28.

not represent the collective judgment of industry, "it is just the work of three professors."[64]

At least one aspect of the RDI program was no academic's brainchild. One of the most eminent of industrialists, Paul Silverberg, broke new ground with his proposal for an industry-sponsored, -financed, and -directed bank to fund rural rationalization and modernization. Modifying the framework originally devised to funnel reparations payments but now rendered superfluous by the Young Plan, Silverberg wanted to convert the Bank for Industrial Obligations into a special, central credit institution for agriculture. Funding would be both private and public, but control would be strictly private with ultimate authority residing in a mixed industry-agriculture board dominated by the former. The idea germinated in 1929, before the depression in industry, and its scope was subsequently trimmed somewhat. In any case, the bank would help agriculture while extending industry's control over the rural sector and obviating any rural-inspired and state-decreed moratorium on debt repayment. In a systematic way, industry would become agriculture's chief creditor. Beginning in 1931, industry would levy itself 200 million RM per year for five years to supply the bank with funds that would then be lent at a rate not to exceed 6 percent (half the going rate) to reform-minded rural producers for modernization purposes only. This self-feeding fund would continue for thirty years, the length of time believed necessary to rationalize, integrate, and modernize production fully.[65] In practice, however, reform and giveaway were about evenly balanced; much money simply went to pay off bad debts on bad investments made by hopeless landowners. It was precisely the issue of who would determine eligibility which came to bespeak the real nature of the program, and the ensuing struggle very much resembled that over Siedlung. In both cases the estate-owning class triumphed: local landowners' boards, which they dominated, decided on eligibility, while the

64. Cited in ZSA/RLB Pressarchiv 132/12, p. 73. As noted in chapter 2, the most ardent support for the RDI program came from the SPD and the DDP. The *Vorwärts* of 16 May 1930 called the program "like what the SPD has stood for for a long time." The democratic *Berliner Tageblatt* and the *Börsen Zeitung* both supported it unreservedly, while the RLB's *Deutsche Tageszeitung* attacked it for being a self-righteous, leftist program that ignored the basic problem of inadequate protection. The *Vorwärts* awaited an "alliance between the social reactionary aspirations of heavy industry and Schiele"— the wait was not very long, 18 Apr.

65. Details of the program in Walz, pp. 156–69, and Holt, p. 140. Farm mechanization, product standardization, better animal breeding and crop selection, market-based selection of crops, and improved storage and marketing processes were among the items high on the list of loan-worthy measures. To cover interest and other costs, the state would contribute up to 35 million RM per year—but without becoming involved in management of the operation. To raise the additional sum, Silverberg suggested an increase in the tobacco and alcohol taxes! Cf. BA/Nachlass Silverberg/566.

"socialist" Prussian government and state bank were shut out of the matter.

Although the Silverberg Bank program emerged from the industrial "middle," it came to win acceptance from heavy industry. The restoration or renovation *(Sanierung)* of agriculture had always been a tenet of the domestic-market strategy, and in this form, too, it was a worthwhile endeavor, despite the hard times that had already befallen heavy industry. Schacht proclaimed that "if this plan works, it will create a solid front capable of breaking the excessive demands of labor" and weakening parliamentary prerogatives. Further, the plan would "terminate the socialistic plans of the Prussian state bank" and enable industry to speak in the name of the national economy, not just of capitalism.[66] The only real opposition to the Silverberg Bank proposal came from those on the capitalist extreme right, like Hugenberg, who demanded full protection and outright subventions, and those on the left in the capitalist spectrum, like Carl Landauer of the DDP, who could only wish the Junkers an early demise. It was in this vein that Landauer contended that once again industrialists had fallen into the agrarian trap, and "among them is Silverberg, who has missed the point of his own program. Too many of agriculture's demands are being acceded to; profitability is not being analyzed, subventions simply handed out." The more the agrarians got, he argued, "the louder their anti-export propaganda becomes."[67] The agrarians had no intention of reforming, and the program was not operating to help the seriously capable peasants. What little Siedlung was taking place was doing so at prices and under conditions which were totally unacceptable.

The Silverberg Bank proposal became separated from the RDI's *Contribution* and enjoyed far broader acceptance. Silverberg's own endorsement of the two lends credence to Landauer's assertions, however. In July 1930, Silverberg had written, "My proposals are intended to assist those units which are still healthy and capable of improving

66. Silverberg addressed himself on this matter to heavy industry in particular; see RDI Veröffentlichung no. 50, *Wirtschaftspolitik,* pp. 31f. Some members of heavy industry found the plan attractive as a possible way of subverting Hilferding's finance proposals. At the same time, part of the RDI leadership, including Duisberg and Kastl, responded rather coolly, both on account of what they perceived as excessive generosity toward organized agriculture and because they were not ready to undermine the Grand Coalition. Silverberg was initially so upset that he threatened to resign from the RDI Presidium. See Duisberg, Kastl, and Herle to Silverberg, 13 Dec. 1929 and Silverberg to Kastl, 16 Dec., BA/Nachlass Silverberg/235, pp. 141ff. The incident might have marked the beginning of a certain shift toward the right by Silverberg. See Schacht's response to the proposal in ZSA/RLB Pressarchiv 148/9, p. 100. This was but another instance of his acute understanding of the relationship between economic and political struggle.

67. *Der Deutsche Volkswirt* 5 (23 Jan. 1931):539–41.

their production. . . . They are to prevent the healthy from becoming sick. Those that are sick and not to be healed readily should be turned over to the surgeons, i.e., where the soil quality is adequate for Siedlung, where not for reforestation."[68] Most of this program was to be emasculated by the time it was implemented. Brüning's subsequent attempt to combine or reach a compromise between the RDI program of reform and modernization and the Schiele program of protection could not succeed. As demonstrated in chapter 2, the Osthilfe and Siedlung programs may have been conceived of by industry, or parts of it, in the context of a modernization/integration strategy, but in practice they assumed a more conservative form, if not exactly that of an outright giveaway. Schlange-Schöningen and ultimately Brüning were fired for their "agrarian bolshevism" when they chose, or were compelled, to take reform too seriously. Once the primary social contradiction of labor versus industry had reemerged, reforming agriculture enjoyed much less priority than protecting the rural elite.

If the RDI's *Contribution* was a program for rural reform, and the Silverberg Bank was one aspect of a program for modernization, there remained a third and simpler component to this third overall strategy. That was conciliation, and it was undertaken primarily by the luminaries of heavy industry and agriculture in the framework of regular meetings begun in 1926 at the luxurious Berlin Hotel Esplanade. Most of the Esplanade Circle's early discussions focused on the "joint goals and tasks" of heavy industry and agriculture, and its early resolutions focused on opposition to organized labor and the leftward drift of industry's dynamic fraction. Thus, the "critical situation of agriculture" was described as "no exceptional phenomenon, but [rather] one caused by the economic, social, and fiscal policies of recent years—which have brought about a tremendous rise in costs . . . while impeding all capital accumulation."[69] To demonstrate its sincerity, the Esplanade Circle donated 40,000 RM for a feasibility study of meat packing in East Prussia while helping to convince the government to spend 4 million for the same purpose. Later, the Circle arranged a 400,000 RM interest-free loan for the RLB as a way to deflect RLB criticism of key industries.[70]

68. *Deutsche Tageszeitung*, 26 July 1930. By 1932 the vectors of the Silverberg Bank had been reversed: instead of industry's using the bank to tell agriculture what to do, Papen succeeded in making the bank's administrators dependent on local landowners' committees; see Denecke, p. 228; ZSA/RLB Vorstand/113, pp. 24–31.

69. Statement of 3 Mar. 1928, cited in BA/Nachlass Silverberg/362, p. 55. The "Shared Tasks and Goals of Agriculture, Commerce and Industry" were the theme of a major Esplanade conference, 2 June 1927. Representatives of heavy industry expressed their willingness to forego exports if the countryside could become a livelier market. Reusch, for example, chastised Robert Bosch for his impatience and lack of faith in agriculture, HA GHH/Nachlass Reusch 400 101 290/43, letter of 27 Jan. 1927.

70. On meat packing, HA GHH/Nachlass Reusch 400 101 290/0, to von Batocki, 12

The Circle receded somewhat during the period dominated by the export-labor alliance, but it worked always to keep the channels of communication open during the "dark days" of the Grand Coalition. In light of the existing reparations, tax, and social policies, the Circle placed special emphasis on debt consolidation and reduction (see table 22). This concern reflected the anxieties of the Circle's bankers: interested in securing their debts, they opposed measures that would either drive down the price of land or result in rural debt moratoria and cancellations. Some rural representatives were sufficiently satisfied with the work of the Circle that they could profess their "basic agreement with its principles in seeking an organic insertion of agrarian policies into total economic policies."[71] Some of the Circle's positions were so conciliatory as to conflict with the official stand of the RDI leadership, while others were deemed so inadequate by the rural delegates that they boycotted numerous sessions.

It was all as if each of the two fractions of industry were *constantly* choosing whether to stand firm on the left flank or the right. Without losing sight of the larger policy issues or the overall political constellation, industry's members of the Circle shifted positions and fears with each set of issues.[72] Consequently, agriculture's representatives were able to modulate their tones while still pursuing a steady course. They watched the balance between the two fractions of industry shift and repeatedly offered their assistance in the struggle to roll back the economic and political gains of the working class. As one facet of the attempt to encourage and assist reform and modernization in German agricultural production, the Esplanade Circle was essentially a failure. The men of the Ruhr who dominated industry's side were halfhearted about the matter; the members of the rural elite sitting opposite them knew well how to utilize inter-industrial tensions to weaken whatever resolve occasionally manifested itself.

Industry's program for agricultural reform really began too late. Both industrial fractions had long had policies, but they did not articulate a program until 1929—well after the onset of the crisis in the countryside. The RDI's *Contribution* bore witness to the dogmatism and limitations

---

Dec. 1927. On the RLB loan, Martin Blank/400 101 202 4/5a. Grants and loans together were to total 1.5 million, but, as Blank observed, "Rather than helping the RLB all at once, we should help them slowly in order to enjoy a more protracted influence," 1 Mar. 1929.

71. Von Miquel to Reusch, 16 Apr. 1930, HA GHH/Nachlass Reusch 400 101 293/10a. At about the same time, however, the more radical *Westfälische Bauern Zeitung* wrote that "the peasants are fed up being promised help in their struggle for a bare existence at every fancy banquet and then, in reality, being delivered only reproach and criticism."

72. The correspondence between Kastl and Reusch is particularly illuminating in this regard; see HA GHH/Nachlass Reusch 400 101 24/3a, and Fessler's interpretation of these rapid shifts for Brüning, BA/R43I/2426, pp. 100–104 mid-Dec. 1930.

of the export liberals. They wanted to modernize and marginalize agricultural production, but they wanted to do so without admitting that, in Germany, only a full and continued coalition with the organized working class could render that possible. They wanted the city to conquer the countryside: they fomented sedition within the rural populace, but they were unwilling to muster the troops necessary to topple the dominant class of estate owners. They came to fear their potential troops more than the enemy itself. The Silverberg Bank plan mirrored the inadequacy and risk-averse pragmatism of the moderates. It sought to integrate the rural sector by making it industry's client. This plan offered the members of the rural elite a deal they could not resist. But, being both politically wiser and more desperate, they knew how to turn the bargain to their own advantage. Finally, the Esplanade Circle reflected the superficial commitment of heavy industry to rural reform and its greater commitment to solidifying the ranks of those opposing the Weimar system. Heavy industry's leaders and spokesmen did not need to be reminded of the rank order of social contradictions. Secure in that knowledge, the rural elite could attempt to call the Sammlung bloc back into existence.

6. After Exports and Reform: Toward a New National Sammlung Bloc

The heavy-industry fraction rejected collaboration with the organized working class almost from the very beginning of industry's parliamentary and policy cooperation with the SPD in 1925. Declining profitability, combined with the continued high costs in wages and social legislation exacted by the SPD and ADGB, prompted the dynamic fraction to withdraw its support from that coalition in 1930. Partly in response to the loss of that mass base, industry, and particularly heavy industry, turned to the rural sector. As a distinct loser during the labor-export coalition, organized agriculture was eager to oblige. In their opposition to the Grand Coalition, agrarian spokesmen, together with the more conservative representatives of heavy industry, juxtaposed to the existing power bloc their own proposals for a "national" bloc. The electoral fragmentation of the middle classes rendered a parliamentary Sammlung bloc impossible, but by proving its own political and economic worth, agriculture could attempt to assemble the dominant economic classes into one anti-Weimar "national" bloc. Using the schema introduced in chapter 1, we can see that in place of Bloc 3, the rural leadership attempted to substitute a modified Bloc 1. Ultimately, the best they could manage was a baseless Bloc 5, but heavy industry and agriculture together did eliminate the possibility of *any* bloc led by the export fraction, either with the working class (Bloc 3) or without it (Bloc 4). *Together,* the two older fractions could compensate politically for their lost economic preeminence while attempting to reconstitute a domestic-market strategy so as to regain that preeminence.

The first step in such a program was already discernible in the Esplanade Circle: heavy industry's opposition to both labor and exports was leading it to return to Landwirtschaft. Industrialists affiliated with the DNVP had always opposed cooperation with organized labor and urged that "nationally linked industry and agriculture pull together." For their part, agricultural leaders within the Zentrum had also rejected cooperation with labor in favor of national and agriculture-friendly industry.[73] Both of these viewpoints were shut out by the Grand Coalition, but in the immediate aftermath of defeat Reusch was able to console the losers that "industry and agriculture will soon again assume a united stand on the great questions of German economic policy." Industry never burned its bridges; indeed, what aid to agriculture was forthcoming between 1928 and 1930 was directed to the estate owners—in substantial contradiction to avowed RDI policy![74] Even during periods of conflict over trade legislation, the fractions worked on problems of joint concern. Agriculture cooperated with heavy industry in its 1928 attempts to "reform" and dismantle the generous unemployment insurance structure, and both undertook an offensive against "production taxes"—two areas where their interests "run entirely parallel."[75] Among the fruits of this effort was rural support for the Ruhr lockouts in October. By 1930 the alliance between heavy industry and agriculture was building steam. Acknowledging the changed economic picture, the *Ruhr und Rhein* journal urged its readers to support higher grain tariffs and the abandonment of most-favored-nation treaties. In the aftermath of the Young Plan the two fractions launched a united offensive; again the Langnamverein led the way: "Since the acceptance of the [Young] Plan agriculture and indus-

73. On the DNVP industrialists as far back as 1926, ZSA/RLB, Verhältnisse zwischen Land und Industrie/126, p. 53. On the rural Zentrum, Klaus Müller, p. 399; Joseph Becker, "Die Deutsche Zentrumspartei," *Aus Politik und Zeitgeschichte* 11 (1968):3–15.

74. Reusch's consolation, Northwest Iron's statement of 23 Feb. 1928, HA GHH/Nachlass Reusch 400 101 221/3. On the Grand Coalition's aid to agriculture, BA/Nachlass Silverberg/362, p. 278, 3 July 1929. See the comments by Dietrich in BA/Nachlass Dietrich/342, 240, and 227.

75. For the coordinated attack on various tax and social policies, see the correspondence between Reusch and Wilmowsky, HA GHH/Nachlass Reusch 400 101 24/1, letters of 26 Jan. and 30 Apr. 1928, and /2 of 27 Mar. 1930. The joint study committee on social policies was headed by the same Georg Solmssen of the Disconto Bank who could otherwise be so niggardly in regard to the countryside.

try have both experienced disappointment that the long-promised easing of their burdens has remained so many pretty words. Instead, new burdens have been placed on their shoulders. . . . so that the economic demands of both have become one. For that very reason, industry appreciates the special demands of agriculture and will never again raise objections to their being taken into account."[76]

Heavy industry's renewed alliance with agriculture implied both a stepped-up attack on organized labor and a split with the RDI leadership, so long as that leadership was dominated by the liberal Duisberg-Kastl group. Ideologically, the attack on labor assumed the form of a defense of the producers against the demands of the consumers. During precisely the same month that the RDI published its rural reform program, heavy industry found a new way to attack the still-rising wage rate: "for political reasons, the urban population has been living above the level the economy can afford, and agriculture has been footing much of the bill." The theme was repeated often with Reusch providing the definitive statement:

> It is unjustified to call tariffs a burden on the consumer. One could argue that only if one assumed the right of the consumer to claim goods at unhealthily low world market prices way below production costs and the duty of the German agricultural producer to sell— without regard to increased wages, taxes, interest and social costs and without any hope of turning a profit or merely breaking even—at prices way below prewar levels. We have for years been putting too much emphasis on the "rights" of consumers while completely ignoring the profitability of both agricultural and industrial producers. It is high time to emphasize strongly the duties of the consumer toward national production.[77]

Cooperation between agriculture and heavy industry was furthered by the end of the Duisberg-Kastl regime at the RDI in September 1931. The new RDI leader's attendance at joint meetings was appreciated, particularly when he called for the "clearing up of a series of accumulated misunderstandings on both sides in such a way that we can appear united in our demands." While Krupp himself continued to oppose agriculture's calls for import quotas, others to his right added this very demand to the united call for entrepreneur-friendly economic, social,

76. Langnamverein report of 20 Mar. 1930, cited in HA GHH/Nachlass Reusch 400 101 221/3. Shortly thereafter, Otto Weissenberger of the Kommerzbank added that "self-help and modernization are not enough; Landwirtschaft needs state help." ZSA/RLB Pressarchiv 132/12, p. 95.

77. The April 1930 statement appeared in the mine owners' *Deutsche Bergwerkszeitung*. Draft of statement to be delivered by Reusch, 23 Feb. 1931 in the HA GHH/Nachlass Reusch 400 101 24/3a.

and foreign policies. Those furthest right like Jakob Reichert of the VDESI were pleased that they could "sense a return to the old tradition which already in Bismarck's time brought together the two most solid and stable [*bodenständige*] economic branches, agriculture and heavy industry."[78]

In order better to persuade industry to make the requisite economic sacrifices on its behalf, organized agriculture augmented its already strident attacks on the organized working class[79] and its parliamentarism. As we noted in chapter 2, agrarian spokesmen had warned industry in 1926 against any opening to the unions, and they now delighted in reminders of the priority of financial and social policies over trade policy. In an interesting reversal, industry was now charged with having been selfish, shortsighted, and oblivious to the national interest during the period of class compromise and collaboration! Von Miquel of the Property Owners' League had warned Reusch of the consequences of an industry-agriculture split. In an analysis which could almost have been written by Eugen Varga, he maintained that

a split between industry and agriculture can only have one consequence: the certain victory of social democracy. Not the victory of bolshevism, which could precipitate a rapid reaction, but rather the victory of a specifically German, philistine welfare democracy which would only meet its end after having taxed private capital completely away and having spent it all on social welfare. . . . The shared responsibility of industry and agriculture for the preservation of the capitalist economic and moral order far outweighs whatever differences exist between the two. . . . We must build a tightly knit front against the assault of collectivism.[80]

Agriculture's representatives realized that despite the economic manhandling they had undergone and their own limited options, the overall conjuncture could allow them to become a worthwhile, if not

---

78. HA GHH/Nachlass Reusch 400 101 24/3a, 24 Dec. 1932.

79. In a sense, organized agriculture was deprived of political mobility; it was captive to its opposition to labor, and industry could always assume rural backing on social and tax questions. Except for rare, feeble attempts to break the labor-export coalition, it made no overtures to labor. Someone, however, told RLB propagandists of Marx's Second Appendix to the *Poverty of Philosophy,* where he describes the Anti Corn Law League as an attempt to "swindle the working class" and lower wages. Citing this was about all German agricultural spokesmen could do.

80. Von Miquel to Reusch, HA GHH/Nachlass Reusch 400 101 24/2 and 293/9. To demonstrate that they were serious, the agricultural chambers consistently called for the rollback of unemployment insurance coverage and lower taxes on capital. The ultras like Hugenberg made a point of reminding industry that it was to blame for accepting tribute payments and a socialist economic policy; BA/Nachlass Hugenberg/130, p. 122, 4 June 1931.

hegemonic, bloc partner once again. The continuing economic strength and political opposition of the dynamic-export fraction of industry was yet to be overcome, but agriculture could be certain of a friendlier hearing in 1931 and 1932 than at any time since 1925.

As the industrial depression spread to encompass the processing and export industries, including the AVI branches, agriculture's old argument about the potential of the domestic market began to make more sense. (Neither agriculture nor heavy industry had in mind the inflationary, mass-consumption [Kaufkraft] arguments of the Woytinsky-Tarnow-Baade group in the ADGB or the Schleicher-Gereke proposals; what they proposed instead was deflation, assistance to those owning the means of production and rearmament in the "traditional" mode.) Hindenburg had been sympathetic to this position all along, and as the Reichspresident's influence grew in 1931 and 1932, he and the military provided the national bloc additional support,[81] which they generally reciprocated. In opposition to the RDI's rural-reform program, agrarian representatives argued that Schiele's program would expand the domestic market by 50 percent. Reusch concurred in seeing the export market as saturated, whereas precisely its underdevelopment "points to the great market possibilities" of Landwirtschaft, then and in the future. Fritz Springorum went even further, contending that "agriculture is of decisive importance for the recovery of our economy . . . and the adage is true: when the peasant has money, everyone can be satisfied."[82] And if one accepted the Green Front position that the domestic market could compensate for lost exports, that agriculture could prosper if provided the protection necessary to develop its potential, then the circle was closed and the logic of the imperial Sammlung bloc's protectionism restored. In the new context, however, a certain autarky was unavoidable, since, according to a DVP analyst, "increasing exports would require imperialism, which Germany in its current powerlessness is just not up to."[83] By early 1932, the national bloc could claim, as Schiele did, that "everything points in the direction of the domestic market: six million unemployed, the collapse of exports" and of the banks, the lack of foreign exchange, and sharpened international tensions.[84] Industrial combinations, especially the AVI, were

81. Sample statements by Hindenburg in ZSA/RLB Vorstand/113 and throughout BA/R43I. He agreed with the Green Front that agriculture's potential had been ignored.

82. *Stahl und Eisen* reprint of Northwest report, 16 Feb. 1928; Springorum in the *Deutsche Bergwerkszeitung* of 5 Apr. 1930, cited in BA/Z Sg 126/Kiel Institut. (Springorum was a member of the Ruhrlade and Generaldirektor at Hoesch.)

83. BA/Nachlass Dingeldey/35, p. 78. See Stegmann, "Mitteleuropa," pp. 215ff.

84. Schiele's vital speech of 21 Apr. 1932, transcript in BA/R43I/2550, p. 311. 1931 was the first year in which there was no net migration to the cities from the countryside.

challenged to restructure their prices so as to benefit rather than hamper the domestic market and hamper rather than benefit Germany's competitors and enemies. All this might have worked if only German agriculture, particularly the estate owners, had not been quite so hopeless. But even in the eyes of its political supporters in heavy industry, estate production had proven itself to be a bottomless pit. Further, there was another drawback to agrarian resurgence: somewhere between 1930 and 1932, the rural elite of estate owners had lost the ability to "deliver" the peasantry. The rural integration/dependence mechanism had broken down, and without the ability to carry the peasants along in their wake, the rural elite could not hope to speak in the name of the nation.[85]

7. 1932: Ontogeny Recapitulates Phylogeny

Because of the stalemate between the "liberal bloc" and the "national bloc" and between the export and domestic orientations, 1932 witnessed a recapitulation of the strategies and conflicts of the previous half decade. During the first third of the year, Brüning continued his fruitless attempt to reconcile the two opposing perspectives; in the middle third Papen tried to implement the radical protectionist program based on import quotas; in the abbreviated final third, Schleicher sought to resurrect the liberal bloc's program under exclusion of the rural elite. In each case the "unity of state policy" was noteworthy for its absence:[86] the economics minister and agriculture minister, for example, did constant open battle. There was, however, one distinct difference between the form of this conflict in 1932 and its previous form. Increasingly, political struggle had been replaced by the open conflict of interest groups, and by 1932 there was little pretense to the former. The links between representatives and represented had been so weakened that the bourgeois parties, when they bothered to speak at all, did so as mouthpieces for the corporate economic interests that dominated them. Both the world-market camp and the autarky camp entertained antiparliamentary and generally antirepublican political positions. Indeed, the capitalist classes had been organizing politically around variants of such a position vis-à-vis the organized working class and Sozialpolitik. In regard to a trade or economic policy, however, division was far from overcome. Out of this there did develop a strategy

---

85. On the breakdown of the integration/dependence mechanism, chap. 2, secs. 4b, c.

86. Assuming such a unity is one of the flaws in Poulantzas' analysis, see chap. 1, note 46.

to organize and control agricultural production; one that could prove acceptable to both fractions of industry as well as to the rural elite.

Before examining the fourth strategy, organization and cartellization, and the fifth strategy, subsumption through imperialism, we need to examine how the export and protection strategies were recapitulated in 1932. Each of the two was juxtaposed to the practice of the other, i.e., the export strategy was put forward in opposition to the Papen-Braun practice of extreme protectionism and assistance to the estate owners, while the protectionist strategy was articulated in opposition to Schleicher's program of facilitating exports at the expense of the estate owners. (At issue also were old questions about the mass base of support.)[87] Papen's autarky program was so one-sided and unacceptable that the fragmented dynamic branches united in opposition to it. Kastl argued that Papen's measures would wipe out most of Germany's foreign trade overnight. "Autarky for Germany means impoverishment," and an impoverished populace could not buy agriculture's goods. "By helping to restore international trade [we can] assist agriculture," not by quotas and bans.[88] So long as the export sector continued to absorb more than twice the industrial production absorbed by the rural sector, it could rely on some support for its position from heavy industry. Speaking for the entire RDI, Krupp and associates told the Green Front that "autarky would destroy all the accomplishments of the past century. . . . We must discuss and plan our policies together before going to the public. . . . Import quotas would imply the abandonment of every one of our treaties. . . . Under no circumstances can industry do without the most-favored-nation system; this system was the basis for the immense growth of German industry. . . . A general quota system will bring down the protest and wrath of the whole world."[89] Hundreds of regional manufacturers' associations and chambers of commerce telegraphed their opposition to import quotas to both Papen and Hindenburg. Needless to say, the dynamic, export, and AVI industries were most incensed and vociferous in their opposition. Yet even so outspoken a representative of heavy industry and the domestic-market orientation as Reusch found that he could not mince his words in rejecting the Papen program: "Our friendship for agriculture cannot go so far that we just sit by as the government gives in to its boundless

87. As noted elsewhere, this was not simply a conflict over trade policy; each of the trade policies carried with it and implied a particular social policy and mass base/coalition.

88. Statement of 5 July 1932, BA/Nachlass Kastl/5.

89. Krupp and von Simson, 6 July 1932, BA/Nachlass Silverberg/363, pp. 178, 184–85. Speaking for the Green Front, Brandes responded that "you propagandize against us in public all the time" and "we cannot compromise on the question of import quotas, especially for dairy."

demands, thereby severely damaging our export industries. Precisely because we here in the Ruhr have always stood and worked for an understanding with agriculture, a strong word from us now is bound to have a positive effect on agriculture and make an impression on the government."[90] It was, in part, its unmediated reflection of industry's positions that totally vitiated the DVP's popular appeal. True to its acquired status, the DVP's 1932 pronouncements on agriculture were indistinguishable from those of major industrial spokesmen.[91] Although both wanted to support Papen for his antilabor and antiparliamentary stands, they could not do so because of his agricultural program. To the public much of this must have appeared a zigzag course.

Autarky was for a long time a tainted term. To Western scholars it implied preparation for war, or at least a bellicose attempt to shut the nation off from normal international commerce and intercourse. Autarky or, in more genteel terms, self-sufficiency is, however, the normal response of states whose economies lie one level below the summit of strength in the world capitalist system.[92] Today, one is even inclined to view sympathetically such a policy on the part of "new states." In numerous respects, Weimar Germany, because of its capital-dependence and penetration by the United States, was such a one-level-below state, despite its immense industrial plant. In light of both subsequent events and the political, moral, and economic bankruptcy of the estate-owning class Schiele represented, it is difficult to muster any sympathy for his defense of autarky. If, however, Schiele had been a progressive (or better), how would one judge his statement that "we call for a point of view beyond that of simple business covering only immediate interests." *Staatswille,* "not the old recipes of liberalism, can beat the crisis."[93] Clearly, the interests of Germany's dominant economic

90. Reusch to Schlenker, 28 Sept. 1932, HA GHH/Nachlass Reusch 400 101 221/11b. Hamm of the DIHT argued that exports were still the healthiest part of the economy and more important to it than ever and that quotas would be devastating. BA/Nachlass Silverberg/646, p. 95, 5 Oct. 1932.

91. Precious examples are to be found in BA/Nachlass Dingeldey/38, pp. 60–61. The relationship of the DVP to both its constituents and industrial backers is examined in chap. 6; on the DVP in particular, see Döhn; Hans Booms, "Die DVP," in *Das Ende der Parteien, 1933,* ed. Erich Matthias and Rudolf Morsey (Düsseldorf, 1960), pp. 523–39; and Poulantzas, *Fascisme,* pp. 106–107.

92. Wallerstein, p. 402; Link, passim.

93. Speech of 28 Apr. 1932, cited in BA/R431/2550, p. 336. Shortly after this speech, there followed a deal of the type Schiele chastized: to circumvent the import ban, Krupp arranged a barter deal with the Danish Cattle Board—agricultural machinery for beef. Simultaneously, the competition was strengthened and "we import an item our worst suffering producers cannot sell." Details in ZSA/RLB Vorstand/146, pp. 94–96. Similarly, the response of industry and commerce to the September decree lowering by 2 percent the interest rate on all outstanding rural loans was characterized by this same "selfishness."

classes had become so fragmented that none of them could even purport to incorporate and represent the national good. Before that could happen, the interests of the three dominant fractions would have to be harmonized or at least reduced to an acceptable lowest common denominator—a broad minimum to include the most basic needs of each, giving no one undue advantage. The Schiele-Papen autarky program proved unworkable and unacceptable to too much of industry. Since the regime also lacked a mass base, it could do little to defend itself, and it was replaced at the end of November by General Schleicher, who set about searching for both a program and a popular base.[94]

During his brief tenure, Schleicher attempted to reverse *both* the balance within the bloc of dominant classes (economic and trade policy) and between the dominant and subordinate classes (social and political policy). In the former realm he sought to abandon the estate owners and adopt a "left-Keynesian" pump-priming, export-oriented and dynamic program. In the latter arena he searched for a mass base in the unions, Strasser's Nazi left, and, perhaps, even the SPD, while holding out the promise of massive public works, peasant settlement programs, and a possible reparliamentarization of political life. Whether these initiatives were real, as most on the right feared they were, or simply a lure into a "social" military dictatorship is not crucial here.[95] So far as the three dominant fractions were concerned, Schleicher's proposals constituted a *volte face*. Instead of relying on the RLB as Papen had done, Schleicher broke all contact with them.[96] For export interests, the abandonment of Papen's policies meant the retention of 1 billion RM worth of exports, 700 million RM in wages and salaries, and over half a million workplaces. Agriculture would recover through increased urban purchasing power.[97] Schleicher's lifting of the rural debt moratorium and prohibition on auctions threatened many an estate owner and was justified on grounds suggested by the DIHT and

94. See chap. 3, sec. 5; chap. 2, sec. 4c. Again, the most thorough discussion is in Bracher, pp. 617–77.

95. On this much disputed question, see, among others, Czichon; Wolffsohn, esp. pp. 98–106; Stegmann, "Kapitalismus und Faschismus"; Turner; Bracher, pp. 677–85, 694–701; Schneider, *Arbeitsbeschaffungsprogramm,* pp. 140–57; below, chap. 5, sec. 3 and chap. 6, sec. 6.

96. He switched from the Papen-RLB policy centered on the subvention of estate production to a policy centered on public works and the breakup of nonviable estates and their resettlement by peasants. See Denecke, pp. 244–46 and chap. 2, pp. 113–15. This latter, of course, had led to Schlange's being fired for "agrarian bolshevism."

97. The *Deutsche Volkswirt* 7 (20 Jan. 1933):490, estimated that even in 1932 German exports were worth over 6 billion RM generating 4.2 billion RM in wages, over 60 percent of which was spent on food. Hans Wilbrandt argued that "every additional increment of aid of other types costs more and achieves less," p. 467.

Carl Siemens: "Continuation would threaten the basic principles of economic life."[98] Silverberg amplified the charges against the agrarians' program in early January 1933 and went on to hint at acceptable alternatives related to his earlier proposals:

> German industry did everything humanly possible for agriculture. . . . The rural organizations accomplished [nothing but] pure political agitation. . . . It was a major mistake of the Brüning government [to have declared and ordered a reduction in rural interest owed.] This opened the way to the subversion of the sanctity of contract, the very basis of economic life. [Various similar measures] were an attack on civil law, private contracts . . . the very rule of law. . . . and during the last four months, the near ruin of the Bank for Industrial Obligations.

All this while agricultural production and distribution remained planless and not uncorrupt. Production cartels might be a vast improvement.[99] Most of the dynamic fraction of industry supported Schleicher's efforts; heavy industry was wary of the possible reparliamentarization of politics and forthcoming concessions to the working class. Since Schleicher failed, however, to co-opt the left wing of the NSDAP and win the cooperation of the ADGB, these latter fears proved premature.

There was nothing tentative about the threat to the rural elite, and its opposition was immediate and unrestrained. During a crucial visit to Hindenburg, several rural leaders elicited his agreement that "so long as we are concerned with exports, agriculture cannot be saved, and we must return to the quota policy of von Papen. . . . public order cannot [otherwise] be maintained."[100] As indicated earlier, the agrarian onslaught against Schleicher was crucial to his dismissal by Hindenburg and replacement by the Hitler-Papen government. Undoubtedly, the reduction of politics to the struggle among interest groups and, by the end of 1932, to that among mere cliques contributed to the disproportionate influence exercised by the rural elite. The loss of much of their peasant base led the estate owners to ally themselves with those who had won over so many of the peasants. Their link to the peasants

98. Siemens and Hamm contended that "these protective measures for agriculture are destroying the creditors while 90 percent of the agreements are not being lived up to by the agrarian side." ZSA/Büro des Reichspräsidenten/296, pp. 210–12.

99. Comments of 14 Jan. 1933, BA/Nachlass Silverberg/363, pp. 196–99. On the importance of the sanctity of contract for a viable capitalist system, see Poulantzas, "L'Examen marxiste du droit."

100. Kalckreuth, von Sybel, Willikens, et al. to Hindenburg, cited in BA/R43II/192, pp. 34, 38. They also warned against any attempts to split agriculture. The peasants, however, had already split on their own.

nevertheless remained much more efficacious than any link between the industrial fractions and their own former electoral supporters. To the very end, the agrarians remained a party in a sense not applicable to the industrialists and in a manner that constantly enabled them to receive attention beyond their economic due.[101] For the rest, the policy shifts of 1932 were less a demonstration of the autonomy of the state apparatus during moments of crisis than they were an indicator of the fragmentation of the dominant classes.

8. Strategies 4 and 5: Cartellization and Imperialism

The program to cartellize agricultural production was related to the campaign for modernization, but its emphasis lay elsewhere. Not fitness for competition but rather organization was its keystone: organization to transcend questions of tariffs, market competition, and subventions. The tariff approach was too divisive, the subvention approach too costly.[102] By fits and starts, initiatives to cartellize agricultural production sprang from several quarters. From their first peacetime appearance, such schemes seemed to present a way out of the rural dilemma, but most of industry was initially unprepared to grant agriculture what it had created for its own production—a form of advanced organized capitalism that might be called "capitalist socialization," featuring production and marketing quotas, price fixing, and self-policing. For their part, agriculture's representatives had regularly expressed the willingness to accept almost anything that would manifest itself in better margins and higher land values.[103] A nascent or inchoate form of cartellization program was mixed in with the protectionist demands of the Green Front already in early 1929. Besides subventions, credits, and tariffs, they called for stabilized domestic prices, better storage facilities, and a grain advisory board.[104] Although the monopoly industries were later to change their positions, these first rural calls were opposed by almost all industrial groups.

In February 1930, Reusch still believed that a grain monopoly, *with*

101. See Gramsci, pp. 19; 56, note 5; 155–56; 186, note 82. Also, Winkler, *Organisierter Kapitalismus,* p. 216.

102. A Professor Dessauer estimated that in 1930, by no means the worst year, total assistance to agriculture amounted to 4 billion RM or over 35 percent of the total value of agricultural production. Aid to industry and commerce totaled 1.3 billion RM or about 5 percent of their production value. Cited in BA/Z Sg 103/Lauterbach, 1 Feb. 1933.

103. This was but one of the contradictions of the highly principled rural elite; see Kehr, pp. 283–85.

104. Meeting of the Green Front with SPD Chancellor Müller, 21 Mar. 1929, in BA/R43I/2541, p. 340.

state involvement, would be "dangerous for the entire private economy, especially coal and iron, setting undesirable precedents for state intervention"; and that it would be better to make selective tariff concessions.[105] Wilmowsky cautioned sympathetic industrialists that grain producers feared that "only a grain monopoly can prevent a price collapse." "The exporters must understand that their behavior drives agrarian leaders to advocate a monopoly" mooted as "national" by the SPD.[106] The last legislative act of the Grand Coalition was, in fact, to establish such a grain monopoly board in March 1930. The bill passed thanks to the cooperation of the SPD and DNVP. Once again, the SPD was in the forefront of actions to stabilize capitalism, whereas the DDP, Wirtschaftspartei, Zentrum, and part of the DVP were not yet ready for such a program, one both liberal capitalists and the Mittelstand opposed. Subjectively, of course, the SPD and the agrarian DNVP supported the bill for very different reasons: the SPD to establish public control, rationalization procedures, and price stability in a vital area; the DNVP simply to guarantee high prices. As indicated elsewhere, the outcome of this alliance was not what the SPD had anticipated.[107] Soon thereafter, the SPD let itself be forced out the government, and the deparliamentarization of German politics accelerated.

As the agricultural depression deepened and other strategies bogged down in stalemates, industrialists took the initiative in formulating their own versions of agricultural cartellization. In need of advice, however, the RDI invited Fritz Baade to deliver a series of lectures on rationalizing and organizing rural production. Sometimes it takes a socialist to put the best capitalist minds at ease and to work! In July 1929, Baade assured an ambivalent RDI that the "central management [*Bewirtschaftung*] of the grain trade corresponds to actual developments" along the lines of existing monopolies and Konzerne. Only market regulations could stabilize supplies and production—as many industralists knew. "The producers and consumers [DNVP and SPD?] are moderate . . . agreement was possible" and would be preferable, he felt, to the disruptive pattern of fluctuations and intolerable tariffs with which Germany was burdened.[108] Some of the liberal exporters were

105. Wilmowsky to Reusch, HA GHH/Nachlass Reusch 400 101 290/39.

106. Ibid., also to the Esplanade Circle in BA/Nachlass Silverberg/363, p. 6.

107. See Holt, pp. 112–15; chap. 2, sec. 4b; and note 25 above.

108. Baade's address to the RDI executive, 3 July 1929 and 18 July 1929, in BA/Nachlass Silverberg/362, pp. 280, 282, 286. Baade justified this position in his writings, see chap. 2, note 167. This type of position did nothing to advance the cause of worker-peasant conciliation. Rather, it reflected the SPD's commitment to organization and rationalization of the economy—thereby presumably facilitating public control in the long run. Baade's presence before the RDI also suggests the dynamic fraction's willingness to cooperate with socialists when potentially beneficial.

not as advanced in their capitalist thinking as Baade. Hamm and some of the AVI representatives, for example, still took the "free market" seriously, and just as they were unhappy with the treatment they received at the hands of the industrial cartels, they feared the creation of yet another massive one. They were ostensibly anxious over the threat of a socialist "coercion-economy," but what they really feared was an erosion of their economic and political position and a gain in agriculture's.[109] This anxiety did not apply to the largest exporters, some of whom, like IG Farben, were leaders of the dynamic fraction of industry. And it was IG Farben which first promoted a new attitude toward agricultural production. In an article on the "Errors of Liberalistic Land Politics," one of that trust's spokesmen wrote, "Directly or indirectly, the state today exercises a certain economic sovereignty and must intervene in the private economy, even when no socialistic tendencies motivate it. . . . The state has to assume many responsibilities . . . one of them being economic sovereignty over the land economy [Bodenwirtschaft] in order to assure maximally rational production and distribution of its products."[110] The specifics of such a program, however, were yet to be provided. How and under what conditions would state-directed cooperatives shepherd or control both peasant and estate production? Around what principles would distribution of the product take place?

It should not be surprising that a representative of the dynamic fraction proposed a program which might guarantee agriculture a certain prosperity but which would undoubtedly render it more dependent, both as an economic sector and as a political fraction. As they had already done for industry, so now rural cartels would overcome the fragmentation of private property (particularly in its peasant form) and the unbearable competition of the market. Offering peasants and estate owners fixed prices for their products and guaranteeing them some profit ("ground rent") would nullify their objections to being controlled. The state would help set agricultural production levels and support prices, in a way it certainly did not do for industry, because agricultural producers could not be expected to enforce discipline on their own. The mechanism of the cooperatives notwithstanding, the diffuseness of

109. See, for example, the DIHT's position, BA/Nachlass Silverberg/645, pp. 390–92. This is one of the few instances where the dichotomy of monopoly sector/competitive sector makes more sense than the dynamic-export/heavy-domestic distinction. The salaried employees of the DVP "left" also opposed "state socialism for agriculture at the expense of working people, the unemployed and pensioners"; Otto Thiel to Otto Hugo in BA/Nachlass Dingeldey/92, p. 74, 14 Apr. 1932.

110. This piece appeared in the IG Farben publication *Europäische Revue* of January 1932; cited in Sasuly, p. 337, and Denecke, p. 174.

rural production, the sheer number of producers, and the nature of the family-peasant mode of production all militated against the possibility of self-regulation. The specifics of such a program were articulated by Carl Bosch of IG Farben so as to cause minimal disruption of German exports and trade treaties. Other specifics were enunciated by Max Schlenker of the Langnamverein so as to elicit maximum possible support from the estate owners. The conflicts between these two industrial fractions had by no means come to an end in 1932, and their resolve somehow to organize rural production itself had to be mediated, had to assume a form acceptable to both. The forum for this mediation was the Central European Economic Congress (MWT), and the program was one of economic domination, imperialism.[111]

Schlenker signaled a major step when his assistants announced

> we must transcend not only slogans like "autarky versus exports" but also that of "free economy versus planned economy." . . . The market for agricultural products must be thoroughly organized and the experience of industry in this area must be drawn upon and applied rationally and reasonably to agricultural relations. Those cartel-type measures industry has utilized can be effective for limiting agricultural imports . . . without constantly bringing us into conflict with our best foreign trading partners. . . . they should be so constructed that help for agriculture has no disruptive effect on industry or vice versa.[112]

The dynamic fraction's more demanding version of rural cartellization was presented by Carl Bosch in a speech before the Chemical Industries Association. In this version the cartel would be international: imports would be controlled through bi- and multilateral agreements but not really limited. The onus would lie on domestic producers to produce only as much of a given product as could be absorbed by the market at preset prices. Future quota allotments would be set by a new state organ on the basis of past performance, and production and marketing cooperatives would be empowered to recommend exclusion of inefficient producers. Prices and production quotas would be set by

111. The MWT was guided after 1930 by the Langnamverein under Max Schlenker, its executive director, but its own heavy involvement made IG Farben an almost equal partner. Sohn-Rethel, on the MWT, pp. 31–38, on the place of agriculture in the imperialist program, pp. 78–99; and note 6 above. See also Stegmann, "Mitteleuropa," pp. 219, 220, and "Faschismus," pp. 57–64. All the industrial organizations and companies of any standing were represented and served by the MWT. One of the MWT's presidents was Thilo von Wilmowsky, Krupp's brother-in-law, a leader of the moderate agrarians and later a personal opponent of Nazi terrorism and anti-Semitism.

112. *Ruhr und Rhein Wirtschaftszeitung* 13 (23 Sept. 1932):631.

an unspecified central board only some of whose representatives would be agricultural producers. Basic principles of the entire arrangement were "a better adaptation of agricultural production to consumer demand and the facilitation of trade-treaty negotiation."[113] Bosch's avowed goal was a "renaissance of international trade." Such a plan might spell far greater difficulties for the grain-producing estate owners than they had hitherto experienced. Toward the end of 1932, cartellization, in various forms, became increasingly attractive to those industrialists who themselves were involved in such operations and who had learned that organization might succeed where competition failed.[114] The key position was occupied by IG Farben, which was almost unique in being a linchpin of both the dynamic-export fraction and the monopoly sector of industry.[115]

Nevertheless, there remained a very substantial number of smaller export industries which opposed this type of strategy, and it was partly owing to their opposition that these proposals were not yet fully developed by the end of 1932. Hence, too, the recapitulation during 1932 of past struggles within the export/protection paradigm. The smaller export industries were themselves not particularly fond of cartels and would certainly withhold their support from any cartel for agriculture until they could be convinced that their own competitive position would not suffer either on account of higher production costs or foreign retaliation. The fear of increased production costs and reduced competitiveness prompted the usually friendly *Frankfurter Zeitung* to criticize Bosch's proposal. The voice of the AVI industries regretted that the erstwhile policies of rationalization and cost reduction had been abandoned in favor of "monopolistic cartel politics" which would protect the agrarians at the expense of both labor and the Mittelstand in industry and commerce. "That control of the market which has been attained in the industrial sector to the detriment of the economy as a whole now appears in the offing as the recipe for diverting the agrarians from their export-damaging quota demands and aligning them with the monopoly front, which would thereby achieve an extraordinary and dangerous increase in its power."[116] The representatives of the smaller export industries shared Bosch's concern with a "renaissance of international trade" but doubted that they and the agrarians could both be part of

---

113. Reported in the *Berliner Zeitung,* 13 Nov. 1932; Denecke, p. 237.

114. An article in the *Deutsche Führerbriefe* of 25 Nov. 1932 listed several new adherents and called for an end to "dogmatic free market individualism which ends in healthy bankruptcy."

115. This is not to denigrate any of the giants of the chemical or electrotechnical branches, but no one within the dynamic fraction rivaled IG Farben.

116. *Frankfurter Zeitung,* 13 Nov. 1932; further criticism, 15 Nov. 1932.

it.[117] Indeed, no political coalition or economic strategy of the previous decade had successfully encompassed both. There was, however, one strategy capable of subsuming interests as diverse as these, a strategy from the not very distant past.

As long as the dominant social class fractions could only choose either international integration under the leadership of the dynamic-export industries entailing high domestic social costs, or a kind of fortress autarky under the leadership of heavy industry and the estate owners entailing a weak popular base, no coherent bloc or coalition could possibly replace that which had dissolved in 1930. Without the organization of the interests of the dominant social classes, there could be no successful program for incorporating the interests of the subordinate classes, and there could be no clear sense of the national interest. If the interests of the rural sector could be subsumed under a program acceptable to industry without extracting "unacceptably" high costs from urban consumers, then a way out could be found. This was a primary goal of the export and heavy industries united in the MWT. Shifting trade partners away from the northern and western countries in favor of the states of the Danube basin would do much to relieve the import pressures felt by the estate owners (though not those felt by the peasants). It would take place partially at the expense of the most advanced export branches, but some compensation for this loss would be provided by greater domestic consumption and the relatively virgin markets of central and southeastern Europe. This had been a principle underlying the aborted customs union with Austria.[118] In any case, as table 28 demonstrates, this shift was already well under way between 1929 and 1931. German economists and industrialists alike were convinced that British, French, and American policies were such that Germany would have to depend more on its Danube trade.

Although almost all its members agreed on this much, the MWT staff was unable to resolve fully the differences between the dynamic fraction's and heavy-industry fraction's versions of the MWT program. In the view of the former, the MWT stood for a conciliatory approach toward France (a policy shared by both Stresemann and Schleicher), whose captial reserves would then play a substantial role in what Duisberg hoped could be a customs union "from Bordeaux to Sofia"

---

117. Some of them proceeded to support Schleicher, not only because of his opposition to the rural elite but also because he appeared interested in reconstituting a mass base upon whose support they could draw. Never mind that they had previously helped demolish this mass base. Others in this sector were increasingly attracted to the Nazis; see Nocken, p. 702; Petzina, *Autarkiepolitik*, p. 21.

118. See Wendt, pp. 483–512, and Alan Milward, "Der deutsche Handel und Welthandel, 1925–1939," in Mommsen, et al., eds., p. 479.

TABLE 28

Exports to Selected Countries, 1929–1931 (in millions of RM)

	1929	1930	1931	% change 1931–1930
Great Britain	1306	1219	1134	− 7
Danube Basin[a]	1607	1339	1000	−25
Netherlands	1355	1206	955	−21
Scandinavia[b]	1186	1178	957	−19
France	935	1149	834	−27
Belgium/Luxembourg	609	601	464	−23
Soviet Union	354	431	762	+78
Poland	343	250	141	−44
United States	991	685	488	−29
Argentina, Brazil, and Chile	681	508	280	−45

SOURCES: BA/Nachlass Silverberg/363, p. 163. The shift did not go unnoticed by representatives of heavy industry; for example, HA GHH/Martin Blank 400 101 202 4/10, 21 Sept. 1932.
[a] Austria, Czechoslovakia, Yugoslavia, Hungary, Romania, Bulgaria.
[b] Denmark, Norway, Sweden.

(and including the French colonies).[119] A market of such size would not only be more independent of American capital but might even challenge it in selected areas. In the view of heavy industry, the MWT stood opposed to France (a policy more in tune with Schacht and Papen and Foreign Minister von Neurath), and had as one of its chief goals, according to Schlenker, a customs union of Germany, Austria, Czechoslovakia, Romania, and Yugoslavia which, in addition to constituting a substantially enlarged market, would prevent Soviet grain dumping and offer a counterweight to American penetration.[120] Representing something of a middle line, Wilmowsky insisted on improving German trade with the central European countries, not the lands overseas. The proper goal was a Danube federation oriented toward Germany; if the French

119. Duisberg at the Bavarian IHT meetings of 24 Mar. 1931. Stegmann, "Mitteleuropa," p. 216, demonstrates that Duisberg was indeed speaking here for the dynamic fraction: Hamm of the DIHT (in opposition to Reusch); Bücher, Siemens, and Raumer of the electrical industry; Kraemer of the paper and printing industry; Bosch of the chemical industry; Wolfgang Reuter and others from the machine-building industry; Otto Wolff of the Deutsche Bank; and others from this same fraction.

120. Schlenker's reports of 15 and 30 June 1931, BA/R13I-VDESI/130. Before too long, France would find itself out in the cold and Poland isolated. Eventually, fascist Italy might be asked to join; see Gossweiler, pp. 332–40.

alone won dominant influence in the area, Germany would be forced back to agriculture-rich overseas markets.[121]

To manage this transition profitably as well as effectively would require political and conceivably military penetration of the Danube countries. If those markets could be opened to German industrial exports, then the pressure on German grain producers would be lessened considerably, and the rural elite and the dynamic fraction of industry would both be reconciled to a bloc led by heavy industry operating in a vastly expanded "domestic" market.[122] Having groped their way to one such acceptable lowest common denominator, the three dominant fractions still lacked a mass base in the subordinate classes or a form of state capable of implementing an imperialist program against foreign and domestic opposition. The Weimar state and military were too weak to oversee such a policy, but it was the only way to overcome the conflict between export industry and agriculture, and it was implemented after 1933.[123]

121. 6 Apr. 1932, ZSA/RLB Schriftwechsel/14b, pp. 639–56.

122. See Milward, p. 479; Stegmann, "Zoll und Handelspolitik," p. 512, "Faschismus," pp. 57ff.; Duisberg's version, Flechtner, p. 378.

123. Sohn-Rethel, pp. 75–99; Denecke, p. 233. Again, peasants and workers would lose initially, but a restored prosperity would improve the urban market for newly rationalized and competitive German peasant production. In practice, the entire countryside was made subservient by 1938 in Germany's new Grossraumwirtschaft.

Chapter Five

THE REEMERGENCE OF
THE LABOR/CAPITAL CONFLICT

By 1924 the Weimar Republic had attained some stability. The last of labor's insurrectionary impulses, the abortive KPD uprisings, had been soundly defeated, and the paramilitary and quasi-secessionist turbulence on the extreme right, especially in Bavaria, went underground or was quelled. Germany's acceptance of the Dawes Plan prompted a massive influx of foreign capital, especially American. The various settlements associated with the Dawes Plan brought military and civil stability to the Ruhr and the Rhineland. Most of the foreign capital was quickly put to use in the reconstruction, rationalization, and expansion of Germany's industrial plant. Germany soon recovered the right to govern its foreign trade as it saw fit, and a host of most-favored-nation trade treaties were negotiated forthwith. The inflation of 1923 had pauperized substantial sectors of the petite bourgeoisie; it had also freed many industries and virtually the entire countryside from their accumulated debts. The Weimar Coalition (SPD, DDP, Z) had not been equal to the tasks it faced in 1923; it was forced to coopt the DVP into the government, thereby establishing the first Grand Coalition, and it was the DVP chairman, Gustav Stresemann, who as chancellor and foreign minister proved to be the hero of the hour. The election results of 1924, with big losses for the left and substantial gains on the right, merely reflected the string of counterrevolutionary victories since the previous elections in 1920. The year 1924 saw the first all-bourgeois government since the shaky Fehrenbach cabinet of 1920, and the new bourgeois government enjoyed both a substantial majority and apparent stability. Yet if the political representatives of organized labor were indeed considerably chastened, they were certainly not eliminated, and organized labor remained in a good position both to participate in Germany's forthcoming economic prosperity and to take advantage of the various conflicts and policy divergences among the dominant economic classes. In addition, the SPD retained its leading place in Prussia and control over a great many municipal governments.

It was during the period of all-bourgeois governments between 1924 and 1928 that organized labor made its most significant gains in social welfare (Sozialpolitik) and labor legislation. In a real sense, Sozialpolitik and social reform emerged as alternatives to the defeated attempts at socialization and socialism. This somewhat ironic development had two main roots. First, the national product, or economic pie, as a whole was expanding considerably, especially after 1926 as Germany was reintegrated into the world economy. As importantly, the SPD provided the primary support for five different bourgeois cabinets composed of several fractious bourgeois parties, while the largest non-socialist party (the DNVP) virtually abstained from government participation altogether. This enabled the SPD to mediate among the diverse forces within the dominant classes, especially in regard to trade policies and state spending, in exchange for which the SPD managed to build an imposing structure of social and labor legislation. Organized labor clearly benefited from the stabilizing modus vivendi reached with both the dynamic and heavy-industry fractions. In addition, the ascendence of industry's dynamic-export fraction, with its particular production desiderata, lessened the role of wages and Sozialpolitik in industry's view of profitability. This changing attitude, spawned perhaps by changes in the organic composition of capital for the leading branches, was reflected in the statements and reports of the RDI, especially during and after 1926 when quality production, exports, and consumption received greater attention.[1]

The industrial proletariat was not alone in demanding and receiving wage and social-welfare benefits. The increasingly large body of salaried employees (Angestellten), though very different from the working class in life styles and politics, nevertheless supported labor and social-welfare legislation from which it distinctly benefited.[2] Further, these white-collar groups, along with organized labor and the dynamic frac-

1. Thus, in addition to discussing these issues themselves, Duisberg availed himself of the RDI Presidium meeting of September 1927 to express the belief that industry and union leaders could now work together again on economic policy matters. Frowein argued that since industry could now afford wage concessions, the unions might be willing to abandon binding arbitration, a process that diverted rank-and-file interest from the union organizations themselves to the state. Bücher cautioned his colleagues against carping about their profit levels and suggested that the chief task was no longer holding down wages but rather replacing variable costs with fixed capital investments. He told his hard-line colleagues in mining that business was not bad and that the state arbitrator was correct to assert that if they could pay out dividends, then perhaps they could also afford higher wages. Others at the meeting suggested that the unions had become an essential support for the existing, capitalist economic order. DII/RDI Tagungen und Vorbereitungen/1 Sept. 1927; cf. Weisbrod, p. 407, and chap. 3, above.

2. See Kocka, "Problematik," pp. 792–811.

tion of industry, opposed the protectionist and price-inflating demands of agriculture and some of heavy industry. As supporters of several bourgeois parties, particularly the DVP, the Angestelltenschaft pressured those parties into compromising and competing with the SPD on several major issues. Despite their antisocialism, these groups caused the bourgeois parties, both in the national and local arenas, to be more socially minded *(sozial)* and strengthened the moderate and "progressive" wings of the bourgeois parties.[3] In doing so, this white-collar constituency increasingly separated itself from other supporters of the bourgeois parties, the petite bourgeoisie and heavy industry in particular.

If prosperity, quality production, international reintegration, and social peace provided the justification and bases for industry's cooperation with organized labor, the SPD's justification for that cooperation emerged from Hilferding's theory of "organized capitalism." According to that theory—interpretations of which range from state monopoly capitalism to corporatism—capitalism's irrationality could be tamed as planning increased. Certainly cartels in Germany had long sought to master the anarchy of the market (and of production), but now the working class could participate in that planning through the agency of the state. Planning and democratization were linked through the mechanism of what could be a neutral and democratic state. Although the genesis of this theory and its implications are themselves worthy of study (as is his consumptionist theory of pacific and limitless capitalist growth), suffice it here to say that the organized working class did obtain material, economic gains through state mechanisms and especially through the Labor Ministry. State intervention in private contractual matters between capital and labor (literally "work givers" and "work takers") did frequently redound to the benefit of labor, and despite incessant complaints, industrialists accepted state intervention. Chief among the forms of state intervention was binding, compulsory arbitration of labor disputes through the agency of the Labor Ministry (and, upon appeal, the Interior Minister). Between 1924 and 1930 these cabinet portfolios were held almost exclusively by members of either the labor wing of the Zentrum or the SPD. Through state-mediated labor relations organized labor won: relatively high and industrywide wage rates; a broad spectrum of social-welfare measures; huge increases in state expenditures for social purposes, especially on the municipal level and for housing; and, in 1927, the jewel of the system of Sozialpolitik, a generous and comprehensive unemployment-insurance law.[4]

3. See Jones, passim.
4. The stable years of Weimar Germany seemed to produce a situation that has more

As we have demonstrated elsewhere, this labor/dynamic-industry cooperation was not without either its opponents or its limits. Beginning already in 1925, the entire rural sector considered itself shortchanged in trade policy and victimized by labor's tax and social exactions. Efforts by both the SPD and commercial and export groups at least to neutralize dairy- and livestock-producing peasants failed. Domestic-market-oriented heavy industry did not suffer from this arrangement quite as agriculture did, but its objections nevertheless became increasingly strenuous. On the one hand, its boom period was much briefer than that of the dynamic fraction; on the other, it was more constrained by international cartels and, hence, more concerned with the capacity and cost structure of the domestic market. Of particular concern to heavy industry were the ongoing conflicts over the eight-hour day and compulsory arbitration. To further its position, heavy industry, particularly in the Ruhr, engaged in numerous "illegal" lockouts and other measures that subverted the quasi-official modus vivendi. So long as the dynamic fraction of industry continued to set the tone and agenda for industry as a whole, however, the labor-export coalition remained safe, at least in principle.

The SPD electoral victory in 1928 and the onset soon thereafter of the economic crisis, first in agriculture and heavy industry and then generally, pushed against the limits of the compromises and stalemates of the previous several years. For all that has been written and said about the SPD's reformism, one must, nevertheless, emphasize that it was a militant reformism; the party in the twenties had not yet made the full transition from Klassenpartei to Volkspartei. This militant reformism on behalf of organized labor—pursued as much by the party as by the unions—manifested itself in a relatively narrow pressure-group mentality that made the German workers' movement increasingly less appealing to other subordinate classes and strata (including the Mittelstand) as a "popular" political alternative.[5] It was, perhaps, pre-

---

recently been accepted as the norm for advanced capitalist societies; see the Introduction to the First Edition above. Thus according to Habermas: "In the monopolistic sector, by means of a coalition between business associations and unions, the price of . . . labour power is quasi-politically negotiated. . . . The mechanism of competition is replaced by compromises between organizations to which the state has delegated legitimate power. . . . [Through] 'political wages' it has been possible above all in the capital-and-growth-intensive sectors of the economy to mitigate the opposition between capital and wage labour and to bring about a partial class compromise," *Legitimation Crisis*, p. 57.

5. It was for this reason as much as for any other that the SPD was unable to profit politically from the chaotic and potentially revolutionary situation of 1932. On the economism and class reductionism (or purism) of German socialism, see below. The pressure-group mentality was lucidly analyzed and criticized by the reformist theorist Adolf Sturmthal, *The Tragedy of European Labor, 1918–1939* (New York, 1943), p. 37. See also Laclau, pp. 136ff., and Suzanne Miller, "Der Sozialdemokratie in der Spannung

cisely its abandonment of social revolution, without a like abandonment of a purist working-class orientation, which constrained the SPD to sustain its militancy in defending the everyday interests of the organized working class. Under pressure from both the KPD and its own structural-reformist wing, the party, after its 1928 victory, supported the call for "economic democracy."[6] To numerous industrialists and politicians this slogan heralded the opening of a renewed struggle aimed at vast socialization. Others knew better but rejected this new impediment to capital accumulation just as forcefully. Ignoring slogans, several unions took the SPD victory as a sign to increase their wage demands, and SPD labor and finance ministers were compelled to accede. This, in turn, dealt a blow to the labor-industry modus vivendi and strengthened the hand of the heavy industry fraction (supported by agriculture); one result was the great Ruhr lockout of October 1928.

More significant than any labor assertiveness, however, were the onset of the world economic and trade depression, the cut-off of the capital flow from New York, the changing alignments within industry, and the (temporary) reparations settlement. Even before the Grand Coalition collapsed in March 1930 over the issue of increased employers' contributions to the unemployment insurance fund, the industrial associations had begun their offensive against organized labor, the SPD and, ultimately, the Republic itself. Labor's economic gains and the SPD's unwillingness and inability to part with them increasingly col-

---

zwischen Oppositionstradition und Regierungsverantwortung," in Hans Mommsen, ed., *Sozialdemokratie zwischen Klassenbewegung und Volkspartei* (Frankfurt, 1974), pp. 84–105.

6. The SPD adopted Wirtschaftsdemokratie and attempted to convert it into an offensive strategy in 1928. The call for economic democracy first emerged in the ADGB in 1924 as a defensive tactic in the coal fields where the workers were taking a beating: in place of the expected postrevolutionary socialization, the inflation and Ruhr occupation permitted the owners to lower wages, increase work hours, and otherwise reestablish their authority. At the ADGB's 1925 Breslau Congress, Herbert Jäckel articulated Wirtschaftsdemokratie primarily as a way to salvage the daily social and economic functions of the unions, halt the decline in membership, and sustain the faith of the rank and file in a period of vicissitudes. For the next three years, Fritz Naphtali and Fritz Tarnow worked at systematizing the program. In the process, economic democracy took on an offensive cast; first because of the substantial improvement in the economy and socialist electoral gains, and second because Naphtali's analysis compelled him to concede that economic democracy was impossible within the framework of the capitalist order and, therefore, that some struggle toward socialism was a prerequisite. The consequences of this are examined below; see also Rudolf Kuda, "Das Konzept der Wirtschaftsdemokratie," in H. O. Vetter, ed., *Vom Sozialistengesetz zur Mitbestimmung* (Cologne, 1975), pp. 253–74, where all this is unproblematic; and Hans Ulrich, "Die Einschätzung von kapitalistischen Entwicklung und Rolle des Staates durch den ADGB," *Probleme des Klassenkampfs* 6 (1973):1–70, where it, along with Hilferding's concept of organized capitalism, is *only* problematic.

lided with the imperatives of capital accumulation and reproduction. A series of economic gains unaccompanied by significant structural victories in the political sphere left the working class all the more vulnerable to a rollback in both spheres.

Heavy industry's offensive had begun by 1927, but alone its efforts were inadequate, and its attacks on the settlement of the stabilization period failed. The behavior of its representatives underscored the differences that existed between it and other entrepreneurs and may even have contributed to the poor performance of the bourgeois parties in the 1928 elections.[7] Only once the overall conjuncture became more critical and industry's ranks closed could a general capitalist offensive be undertaken successfully. A more general assault by industry on the stabilization period settlement began with the RDI meetings of September and December 1929 and the publication of its new program, "Recovery or Collapse." The shift began from Sozialpolitik to Wirtschaftspolitik, from social-politics to economics-politics, i.e., from politics emphasizing legitimation to politics emphasizing accumulation.[8] This renewed counterrevolution lasted until the demise of the Republic, and its economic and political facets were intertwined. During the next three years, industrialists' impatience with the speed and extent of the rollback contrasted with the ambivalence expressed by the leadership of the bourgeois parties as they lost their salaried employee constituencies. This, in turn, exacerbated the political crisis: the increasingly purist but unappealing bourgeois parties could support no bourgeois government; yet, after 1930 no government could enjoy a majority without including either the SPD or the NSDAP. The industrialist Paul Silverberg's two-pronged 1926 dictum—industry fully accepted the Republic, and no government was possible that excluded the SPD and organized labor—was now fully reversed: industry could no longer accept a republic that divided and weakened its forces, and no government was tolerable that included an SPD seemingly devoted to making capital accumulation and profits impossible. (Certainly industry was neither willing nor able to bear the political and economic costs of overcoming the depression through a union-sponsored program of increased purchasing power and consumption.) It was this basic shift, facilitated by the adoption of the Young Plan and the untimely death of

7. See tables 1 and 2. Certainly the DVP was weakened by the struggle of heavy industry's representatives against Stresemann and his allies, and heavy industry also contributed to the turmoil within the DNVP. These issues are examined further in chap. 6.

8. One should *not* infer, however, that the former arrangement ignored accumulation. What transpired was a shift from export-led accumulation in free markets and in cooperation with labor, to a potentially labor-coercive and imperialistic pattern.

Stresemann[9] (like that of Rathenau and Ebert), which led to the abandonment of the Grand Coalition and the initial support for Brüning's semidictatorial government. The Silverberg-Stresemann-Severing coalition upon which stability had been built was renounced by industry.

Except for its intensity, industry's program changed little from that articulated in the autumn of 1929. Adverse economic conditions led to declines in both union membership and militancy; far more strikes were lost than won, and it was left to the SPD to defend the interests of organized labor at the top, through the political mechanism. The SPD was both conciliatory and hard-nosed on the twin issues of wages and public spending: it accepted both a 10 percent across-the-board wage cut in June 1930 and much of Brüning's fiscal austerity and procapital tax programs; but later the SPD hardened its position as unemployment worsened, Communist strength rose and industry refused to "reciprocate," especially in the area of lowering cartel prices. The party rank and file and the unions had been obstinate in their opposition to the party's swallowing the bitter pill of reduced unemployment insurance coverage in exchange for possible continuation of the Grand Coalition in 1930, but a year and two later it was left to the party center alone to struggle for what could be salvaged of the "achievements of the Revolution." It was, in the face of a divided opposition, perhaps *too* successful in fending off capital's economic onslaught. What that indicated to industrialists, and what others, especially the rural elite, had already appreciated for quite some time, was that the impediments to economic recovery were not to be overcome within a political framework which fostered entrepreneurial fragmentation while permitting the SPD to limit severely the adoption of measures which would lift those impediments.

We have discussed elsewhere the various attempts to overcome the fragmentation of the dominant-class fractions and to transcend or subsume their particular needs through some general capitalist interest. But what was it more specifically that industrialists after 1929 demanded of organized labor, the SPD, and the state? Again, industry's program was elaborated fairly explicitly by the RDI in late 1929. In the precrisis period, the RDI had argued simply that "Sozialpolitik must be limited by the productivity of the economy," but with the crisis this view was highly radicalized. At first, the RDI's program represented an attack on the Grand Coalition; then it became something of a maximum

9. It would be a mistake to attribute the rightward movement within the DVP (let alone industry) to Stresemann's death. Nevertheless, his absence abetted rightist activism within the party: just before his death, he was able to persuade twenty-eight of the DVP's forty-five MPs to vote for Hilferding's tax and finance proposals, but this then quickly changed.

program, which it was hoped Brüning might implement. His inability to do so was, as we have shown, the primary reason he lost industry's support around the middle of 1931. (The impact of the changing balance between the two fractions of industry and the revolt of the agrarians should, however, not be underestimated.) Finally, the Papen government tried its best to implement industry's social program, but it both lacked a mass base of support and ran afoul of the dynamic-export industries. The following summarizes the most salient contentions in industry's analysis:[10]

The policies of recent years had been dominated by an "immense disparity between productivity and profitability on the one hand and public spending on the other." In 1924 Germany began with no investment capital, and the first task ought to have been building it, not attempting to create a welfare state. Too many compromises with socialism led to "politically motivated interference in the economy."

Public costs had skyrocketed: Not counting social insurance, "public spending is more than triple the 1913 level," and taxes were up from 4 to 14 billion annually; social insurance costs had risen from 1.2 to 5.5 billion annually between 1913 and 1929, they claimed.

A 40 percent increase in incomes in five years and luxurious consumption were just not justifiable. "With rising wages, rising taxes, rising interest rates and declining profits, the point is reached where maintaining production itself no longer makes sense. . . . Only responsible economic policies can prevent the collapse of the economy and aid in making Germany free in foreign policy."

"The German economy must be let free. It must be spared experiments and political influences extraneous to the operation of the economy itself." Entrepreneurs and workers "both suffer from poor morale because of mistaken economic, fiscal and social policies." "Economic Democracy" was but a further demoralization of the economy and a step toward socialization and collectivization.

High wages were a part of costs as well as of consumption power. They created only "an apparent consumption power at the expense of the productivity of the economy"; the result was unemployment. A real long-term improvement "in the standard of living of the broad mass" was only possible "through building capital and the restoration of profitability." At present, "production is not worth undertaking." In the boom year of 1928, 30 percent of stock companies and 17 percent of stock capital went without dividends.

10. These points as well as the following nine demands are culled from the RDI's December 1929 manifesto, *Aufstieg oder Niedergang*, RDI Veröffentlichung no. 49, passim, cited hereafter as "Recovery or Collapse."

"Social insurance," put too high a "financial burden on the productive economy. . . . Additionally, the unemployment insurance system is producing a budget deficit which threatens state finances" with bankruptcy. Compulsory arbitration and wage increases threatened "not only capital accumulation" but the very "principle of maintenance of the free, private-enterprise system." Arbitration had led to a reduced "sense of responsibility": workers made all kinds of reckless demands knowing that some were bound to be granted. Compulsory binding arbitration had to be replaced by free "negotiations between free agents."

Besides the abolition of compulsory binding arbitration and other points implicit in its analysis, the following were the RDI's major initial demands: (1) "facilitation of capital accumulation through secured profitability[!]"; (2) a lessening of state intervention in the economy; (3) an end to state borrowing; (4) an end to privileged public competition with the private sector, especially in housing; (5) a cessation of attacks on the cartel system; (6) reductions in the financing and outlays in all areas of Sozialpolitik, especially unemployment insurance; (7) a reduction in national, state, and local government expenditures and a limiting of the taxation and budgetary prerogatives of *Länder* and municipal governments; (8) a reduction of taxes on capital and production and an increase in indirect and consumption taxes, the former through large cuts in property, profit, and various income taxes; and (9) the utilization of economic experts rather than politicians to implement the preceding points.

Again it was Paul Silverberg who in December 1929 summed up the then current status (and form) of the capital/labor contradiction when he argued that "a private, individualist, capitalist economy cannot be successful when the state simultaneously pursues socialistic and collectivistic economic policies, especially in the social, tax, and fiscal realms. It is this contradiction which brought us to our current [sorry] condition."[11] As much as anything else, the political struggles of 1930–32 were directed toward creating the political (pre-)conditions for the resolution of this contradiction to the detriment of its minor "socialistic" aspect. The dominant social classes wanted to make their own history, but they could not make it just as they pleased. They might assume full control over the primary bourgeois parties, and they might support and finance the various forces, both within and outside the

---

11. Silverberg's opening remarks at the December 1929 RDI meetings devoted to the economic, social, tax, and fiscal policy failures of the government; *Wirtschafts- und Sozialpolitik, Steuer- und Finanzpolitik,* ed. Georg Müller (Oerlinghausen) and Paul Silverberg, RDI Veröffentlichung no. 50; notice the coupling of policy pairs.

"national opposition," working to replace the democratic state with an authoritarian one, but they could not be certain of the end to which these efforts would lead. What the dominant social classes did do with all certainty, however, was initiate class conflict from above designed, in Hans Mommsen's words, "systematically to undermine the social-political compromises which underlay the foundation of the Weimar Republic"[12] and which were recodified and developed in the years after 1924. With its links to the army and bureaucracy, heavy industry in particular contributed to the creation of a social climate of class conflict. The pressure of *die Wirtschaft* on the political system substantially weakened the SPD and unions, especially after 1930, and paralyzed the Weimar political system while lending support to those attacking it from the right. Before analyzing this offensive by the dominant classes, we must examine the Sozialpolitik and labor-industry compromises of the period 1924–29 which then became the ground for industry's offensive.

1. Social Compromise: Its Results and Its Limits

The bulk of this work has been concerned with the various conflicts within and between the dominant class fractions and the impediments to unified bourgeois rule engendered and reenforced by those conflicts *and* the Weimar political framework. The strength of the organized working class in the Weimar Republic, in a context characterized by a conjuncture of economic recovery and relative prosperity and bourgeois political fragmentation, led after 1924 to a series of economic and social victories for organized labor. We have already cited a number of the social welfare and labor legislation gains won under the auspices of the labor-export coalition, some even under all-bourgeois party governments. Although the Stinnes-Legien agreements and the Arbeitsgemeinschaften of 1918 were dead letters, Jakob Reichert's panicky remark of that year retained some validity: the traditional middle class and the elite of estate owners were no longer worthwhile or dependable allies; "allies for industry could only be found among the workers; these were the unions."[13] The tacit Silverberg-Stresemann-Severing

12. Hans Mommsen, "Sozialpolitik im Ruhrbergbau," in Mommsen, et al., eds., p. 321.

13. Jakob Reichert of the VDESI (and DNVP) was simply trying to justify his participation in the Arbeitsgemeinschaften. At that time, of course, there were Independent Socialists (USPD) and Spartacists to worry about; in comparison to them the SPD and the unions were forces of order. To that extent, the fears of 1918 were no longer present after 1924. Reichert cited in Maier, p. 59. See also Zunkel, *Industrie und*

alliance continued in force throughout the period of relative prosperity and brought gains to both sides; for the dominant classes these were primarily political, for the working class primarily economic. As the ADGB *Jahrbuch* for 1928 put it, "The basic principles of these [pro-labor] laws of 1924–28 did not issue from the spiritual arsenal of either the Liberals or the Conservatives; they were of the spirit [*Geist vom Geiste*] of the workers' movement, whose political and economic organizations exercise a far-reaching influence on legislation even when the SPD itself is not part of the government."[14] Without analyzing either specific legislation or the debates over enactment, we can examine the underlying principles of labor, fiscal, and social legislation in the period from roughly 1925 to the collapse of the Grand Coalition.[15]

The influx of foreign capital facilitated the rationalization of Germany's industrial plant and contributed to the recovery of much of the economy. But, given the emphasis on infrastructural investment, it also contributed to increased, quasi-structural, levels of normal unemployment. Thus, in the "boom" year 1928, the nominal wage level of employed workers exceeded 155 percent of 1913 levels, but the real wages of the *entire* working class, including the unemployed, were just equal to the prewar level.[16] It was the goal of much Sozialpolitik to redistribute gains within the ranks of the workers and salaried employees themselves, and political devices were employed to mitigate the negative effects of high unemployment on union membership. In considering Sozialpolitik, it is thus important to bear in mind from the outset that social politics took place "at the top," among leaders of labor, industry, and government. Partially as a result of this, internal union organization during the Weimar years concentrated power at the top. Although well organized, the ADGB tended to ignore the plant level, and most of its leaders were pleased that the once-radical and seditious councils *(Räte)* had been integrated and transformed into arms of the unions at the factory level. The unions also failed to keep

---

Staatssozialismus, and Feldman, *Army, Industry and Labor* on various state-, industry-, and labor-sponsored schemes.

14. The assessment of working-class gains under the all-bourgeois governments of 1924–28 appears in *Jahrbuch des ADGB, 1928* (Berlin, 1929), p. 34. The *Jahrbuch* also cited substantial fragmentation within bourgeois circles as well as the desire to appeal to voters. For a general summary, Franz Neumann, *Behemoth: The Structure and Practice of National Socialism, 1933–1944* (New York, 1966), pp. 13ff.; Dietmar Petzina, "Germany and the Great Depression," *Journal of Contemporary History* 4 (1969):59ff.

15. The definitive analysis of Sozialpolitik remains Preller; for these years see pp. 296–387.

16. Preller, p. 507; cf. Bry, pp. 461–67, where the figures are somewhat different. See also the literature cited in chapter 3, note 45. Preller attributes significant importance to this reserve army of the unemployed in the growth of entrepreneurial power.

pace with concentration and rationalization in industry because they never fully converted from trades- to industry-based organization; the plan proposed in 1925 by representatives of the metalworkers to reorganize the ADGB into fifteen large industrial unions stalled. Given their strategic understanding of politics and the state, internal democracy and participation had to appear less important to the union leaders than effective centralization and strong leadership.

State arbitration in the negotiation of industrywide wage rates was one form of Sozialpolitik at the top that partially counteracted the pressure of the reserve unemployed. From 1925 to 1931, compulsory binding arbitration served as the single most important form of wage agreement. It was a form of social compromise embedded in the pluralist democracy of the Weimar Constitution itself,[17] and arbitration received a boost during the heady days of December 1918 when control over wages was vested in the labor minister. Until 1932 the Labor Ministry alone directed arbitration, and occasional attempts by representatives of heavy industry to have the Economics Ministry made coresponsible inevitably failed—in part because the dynamic industries were prepared to continue cooperating within the existing framework.[18] Through 1929, representatives of, among others, the textile, construction, chemical, electrical, and some AVI industries, together with the retail trades affirmed their basic support of state arbitration.[19] All but one or two of the very strongest socialist unions supported arbitration, and the Catholic unions as well as various salaried employee organizations (including the DHV) were fully behind it; on the labor side, only the KPD and its affiliates systematically opposed it.[20] Through the state, arbitration became one part of the format for cooper-

17. Article 165 stipulated that "wage earners and salaried employees are qualified to participate on equal terms with employers in determining wages and work conditions. . . . Organizations on both sides and agreements between them will be recognized." The Constitution promised *both* a free, private economy and a social democracy; see Kirchheimer, *Von Republik zum Faschismus.*

18. Weisbrod, pp. 405–7, acknowledges that heavy industry was unable to get its way, but in doing so he fails to elaborate on those whom he describes as "groups ready to cooperate" with labor and underestimates their influence.

19. See, for example, Hans von Pohl, secretary of the National Retail Trades Association, in the *Textil Zeitung* of 21 Sept. 1928, and "Die Reform des Schlichtungswesens. Die wirtschaftliche Wert der Sozialpolitik," *Schriften der Gesellschaft für Soziale Reform,* no. 83 (1930):120ff. Also, Frieda Wunderlich, "Labor Under German Democracy," *Social Research,* supplement 2 (1940):29, 45.

20. Wunderlich, "Labor," pp. 42–3; Weisbrod, pp. 399, 403. Initially, there had been some skepticism toward arbitration within the ADGB. The *Jahrbuch des ADGB, 1924* (Berlin, 1925), p. 96, still spoke of "the potentially serious danger for labor" posed by arbitration, but each succeeding Jahrbuch, down to 1932, spoke increasingly favorably of the "social function" of Schlichtung while pointing to the consistent hostility of the employers toward it.

ation between labor and the dynamic fraction of industry during the stable years; as in other matters, the state mediated relations that could not occur face-to-face. Although heavy industry campaigned almost constantly against the system as it was organized, it was only after the SPD electoral victory of 1928 and the beginning of economic crisis that industrial opposition became more generalized. Rank-and-file expectations rose with the return of the SPD to the Labor Ministry, and 1928 saw substantial wage increases in a number of large industries, including mining and the metals. These new increases were initially accepted by the dynamic and processing industries, but as the economic situation deteriorated and the balance between the fractions of industry shifted, the entrepreneurial campaign against the socialist Labor Ministry won broader support.[21] Ultimately, as we shall see, the power of the labor minister's delegates to issue Solomonic compromises was undermined; the Emergency Decree of 8 December 1931 lowered all wages governed by collective agreement to their January 1927 levels, and in mid-1932 Papen virtually terminated the labor minister's prerogatives altogether.

Compulsory binding arbitration functioned as a form of compromise and cooperation which grew in scope and importance and increasingly favored organized labor. For 1929, for example, the ADGB reported that 52 percent of all wage agreements were the fruit of compulsory arbitration, and although only 8 percent needed to be declared binding upon appeal, these latter covered 23 percent of all workers. For the same year, the Employers' League reported that 35 percent of "its" workers were covered by agreements concluded in this manner.[22] In fact, according to the Employers' League, from 1925 through 1929, with some annual variation, only about one-quarter of its workers were covered by contracts reached by fully voluntary agreement. Its estimates of the role of compulsion were considerably higher: approximately 30 percent of its workers annually were covered by arbitration awards accepted by both parties, and another 37 percent worked under agreements that had been declared binding.[23] In May 1930 the landmark Oeynhausen arbitration ruling mandated a wage (and price) reduction for nearly 800,000 iron- and steelworkers (and producers) and signaled Brüning's deep commitment to deflationary policies. But until then, arbitration had almost invariably favored the workers, and it was they who turned to it most often. Thus, from 1926 through 1931, over 80 percent of first-instance arbitration requests (before boards) were initi-

---

21. Weisbrod, pp. 379, 403–13.

22. *Gewerkschaftszeitung*, 21 Feb. 1931, p. 118.

23. The rest enjoyed no collective agreement or are unaccounted for; cited in Wunderlich, "Labor," p. 60.

ated by workers compared to about 15 percent by employers. In second-instance arbitration (the larger agreements heard by arbitrators), workers initiated about 60 percent of the requests and employers 20 to 25 percent with the rest undertaken by mutual request or ex officio. Of those arbitration decisions rejected from 1928 through 1931, fully 70 percent were rejected by the employers and 20 to 25 percent by the workers and their representatives.[24] This was understandable if, as Ludwig Grauert claimed on behalf of the Employers' League, arbitration cost entrepreneurs 8 billion RM per year.[25]

Other measures also ate away at the free market in labor.[26] A Work Hours Law in 1927 restored the eight-hour day in most large undertakings by requiring union agreement and mandating a 25 percent wage supplement for hours in excess of eight per day or forty-eight per week. An amendment to a 1924 regulation, obliged installations operating on a twenty-four-hour-a-day basis to switch from a two- to a three-shift system. In 1926 the Labor Courts Law was modified in virtually complete accord with the unions' demands. Health, disability, and social insurance were expanded several times. Putting-out work was regulated and subjected to collective wage negotiation. Occupational health and safety standards were upgraded. Public housing became a substantial undertaking, and tenant protection laws were put on the books. But the jewel of the system was the Employment Facilitation and Unemployment Insurance Law (AVAVG) of 1927, which provided the unions with two new means for helping to manage the labor market.[27] It enhanced the role of the unions in hiring industrial labor through public employment offices, and, more importantly, it relieved the downward pressure of unemployment on wages (and union treasuries) by establishing a system of comprehensive unemployment insurance to which employers, employees, and, indirectly, the state contributed.

Underlying these victories was the ability of the unions to bargain collectively industrywide knowing that compulsory binding arbitration

24. *Reichsarbeitsblatt* (1928):II:12, (1929)II:220, (1930):II:42, 571, (1931)II:368. Between 1926 and 1929 employers had rejected only about 18 percent of arbitrators' decisions.

25. *Magazin der Wirtschaft,* 14 Feb. 1930. Grauert also claimed that between mid-1926 and the end of 1929, the wages of unskilled workers had increased 30 percent and those of skilled workers over 20 percent.

26. Industry's position was that labor market negotiations could be collective (unions and employers' organizations, ultimately cartels) but ought to be free of political interference. On the political nature of state arbitration and for an analysis of its operation and outcomes, see Hans-Hermann Hartwich, *Arbeitsmarkt, Verbände und Staat 1918–1933* (Berlin, 1967), pp. 193–228.

27. On the coalitions and compromises that produced the AVAVG in July 1927, see Stürmer, pp. 210ff.

by the Labor Ministry was available to them. The centrality and increased influence of the labor minister's office prompted Preller to describe it as the "direct and indirect godfather" of all of these developments, if only by virtue of the minister's power to declare arbitration binding.[28] This is entirely consonant with the statement made by Clemens Nörpel, one of the labor-law experts of the ADGB, that the "arbitration function is preeminently political. The results of arbitration depend on labor's political power."[29] Jakob Reichert accused labor's representatives of being even more brazen; he attributed to Hilferding the argument that "it is the ballot which finally determines the amount of wages."[30] The conflicts over social-welfare legislation and arbitration were, like the conflict over wages, part of the struggle over distribution of the social product. How were the burdens and costs of the array of social measures to be divided? Although employer, industrial, and agricultural organizations consistently decried this kind of state intervention in the economy, they were unable to mount a successful political opposition to it—at least until the SPD victory and union "offensive" of 1928 and the onset of economic and fiscal difficulties in 1929. Among the reasons for their temporary weakness was the fact that not only socialist industrial workers derived benefits from Sozialpolitik.

Stresemann used his support of social legislation to consolidate a substantial base among salaried employees; with their backing and that of many dynamic-export industries, he was able to ignore or transcend the clamoring of the industrial wing of the DVP and of most industrialists for the realization of their immediate, selfish interests.[31] Further, the Labor portfolio was, until 1929, in the hands of Heinrich Brauns of the Zentrum, and, in addition to the direct pressure of Catholic unionists and salaried employees, he and his party were

---

28. Preller, p. 509. The mechanics of the Labor Ministry are examined in detail by Hartwich, pp. 231–305.

29. *Gewerkschaftszeitung,* 29 Sept. 1928, p. 613. Apparently Nörpel personally did not want his job to be dependent on labor's political power; he proved to be an organization man capable of switching allegiances. In 1935 he divorced his Jewish wife so that he could go to work for Robert Ley and the Nazis' German Workers' Front (DAF).

30. Reichert in *Der Arbeitgeber,* 1 Jan. 1928, p. 5.

31. On Stresemann and the changing balance of forces within the DVP, see Döhn, and chap. 6, sec. 4 below. On the political and economic position of salaried employees, see the literature cited in chap. 1, notes 32, 34, 35; also Iris Hamel, *Völkischer Verband und nationale Gewerkschaft* (Frankfurt, 1967), on the DHV, and Fritz Croner, "Die Angestelltenbewegung nach der Stabilisierung," *Archiv für Sozialwissenschaft und Sozialpolitik* 60 (1928):103–46, as well as Hans Speier, *Die Angestellten vor dem Nationalsozialismus* (Göttingen, 1977).

guided by a certain affinity for officeholding and a proclivity for social, corporatist, and paternalist solutions to social conflict. The political strength of labor and the economic dominance of capital provided Brauns with a certain autonomy his embattled SPD successor would not enjoy once the ADGB spoke of translating political democracy into economic terms.

Consistent wage gains, various forms of social insurance, a public-housing construction program and rent control, some measure of union control over the labor market, and the available good offices of the Labor Ministry all constituted gains for organized labor and were part of a general social compromise. Public and especially municipal spending increased rapidly, if not always wisely. Even Arthur Rosenberg was prompted to observe that "in the period after 1924 German officials seemed to believe that money was no real obstacle, that as much money was available as one wanted . . . which certainly did not correspond to Germany's true situation. . . . The consequence of these tendencies was that public spending and taxes commensurately reached fantastic heights. [In 1928 with a national income of 50 billion (sic)], total taxation amounted to over 13 billion. . . . [until 1928] this all took place under an all-bourgeois government, including even the DNVP. . . . The entire unhealthy development in German finances after 1924 was the work of capitalists, not workers."[32]

Although the data are incomplete, it seems that a real shift in the distribution of the national income was taking place, as revealed in table 29. During the Weimar years, the share of the national income accruing to labor increased, while that received by capital decreased until as late as 1932. Between 1926 and 1932 industrial capital's annual share dropped 8 percent while labor's rose over 3 percent. (The Nazi regime reversed this trend rather demonstrably.) If, as is likely, worker income peaked in 1929, then the contrast with 1913 and even 1925 is indeed startling. Further, employer allegations that profitability did not benefit from increased production do seem to be verified.

The state's role in arbitrating and sometimes deciding labor conflicts in the long run heightened the importance of control of the government. The politicization of labor relations furthered ADGB activism within the SPD and fostered rank-and-file militancy within the party (but not the unions) between 1928 and 1930. Until the events of 1930 taught them otherwise, many unions seemed to forget the possibility that state

32. *Geschichte*, pp. 164, 166, 169. Some allowance must be made for the rhetorical value of blaming the fiscal crisis on capital. The SPD would have done much worse. Perhaps the KPD could have become a left-wing party of order and austerity, but it certainly did not advertise itself as such.

TABLE 29

Distribution of Income to Entrepreneurs and Employees
(in billions of RM and as percentage of total income)

	Agricultural Entrepreneurs		Non-Agricultural Entrepreneurs[a]		Wages and Salaries		Total National Income	
	Marks	%	Marks	%	Marks	%	Marks	%
1913	6.5	13.0	11.2	22.3	23.3	46.5	50.1	100
1925	5.7	9.5	11.8	19.7	35.0	58.3	60.0	100
1926	5.8	9.2	12.8	20.4	36.1	57.3	63.0	100
1927	5.9	8.3	13.8	19.4	41.7	58.5	71.3	100
1928	5.8	7.7	13.9	18.4	44.6	58.9	75.7	100
1929	5.5	7.2	13.5	17.6	45.8	59.6	76.8	100
1930	5.0	7.3	10.3	15.1	41.2	60.3	68.4	100
1931	4.4	7.7	8.5	14.9	34.6	60.5	57.2	100
1932	3.9	8.6	5.6	12.4	27.4	60.6	45.2	100
1938	6.4	7.8	19.8	24.1	45.7	55.7	82.1	100

SOURCES: The data would require some interpolation for the intervening years, but the tendency remains clear as the inclusion of 1938 underlines by contradiction. Data from Paul Jostock, "The Long-Term Growth of National Income in Germany," in *Review of Income and Wealth V*, ed. Simon Kuznets (London, 1955), p. 109; cf. Bry, p. 122.
[a] Includes handicrafts, trade and commerce, transport, professions, and undistributed corporate profits.

intervention might undermine or even eliminate their gains as easily as it had earlier augmented them.[33] From the vantage point of 1928, the momentum appeared to belong to the unions. The new Unemployment Insurance Law protected 16½ million workers and employees, over 12¼ million of whom were covered by collective wage agreements. A critical weakness within this picture of strength, however, was the fact that only about 40 percent of those covered by collective agreements actually belonged to any union. High levels of structural unemployment and the increased role of state arbitration both took a toll on union membership and activism. It has been argued that workers began to lose interest in their unions as wages were increasingly "fixed by the state";[34] as noted, by the late twenties about one-third of all wage agreements, covering over two-thirds of all workers, were reached by compulsory arbitration. Union membership did rise rather modestly from 1926 through 1930, but the unions never reattained their membership levels of the awful

33. Ursula Hüllbüsch, "Die deutschen Gewerkschaften in der Weltwirtschaftskrise," in Conze and Raupach, eds., p. 130; Hartwich, p. 357. There was a certain violated innocence to the response of union leaders after Oeyenhausen when arbitration decisions began to go against labor; see *Jahrbuch des ADGB, 1931* (Berlin, 1932), pp. 146–47.
34. Wunderlich, "Labor," p. 86.

year 1923, let alone of the peak year 1920.[35] Between 1920 and 1923, about 60 percent of German workers had been organized into unions; the figure fell under 30 percent at the start of 1926 and then climbed gradually and modestly to just under 40 percent in early 1930, after which it fell again. Between 1926 and 1930, then, union power recovered and advanced more substantially than did union membership. Certainly the scope of union-negotiated collective agreements grew, although as table 30 indicates, unemployment here, too, vitiated some of the gains.

Between 1924 and the end of 1929, the average work week was effectively trimmed by nearly two hours.[36] Unskilled workers benefitted more from this reduction than did skilled workers, except, of course, that after 1927 most overtime work was compensated at higher rates. The implicit purpose of reducing hours—creating jobs and reducing unemployment—remained basically unfulfilled, particularly in the stagnant heavy industries, which were far more resistant to any shortening of the work day or work week.[37]

For those employed, both nominal and real wages rose substantially after the depths of 1924. At the start of 1924, average nominal wage rates were almost 10 percent below 1913 levels, and the Employers' League was proven correct in believing that real wage rates could be

TABLE 30

Collective Agreements in Force on January 1, Selected Years

	1920	1924	1929	1931
a. Agreements (in thous.)	11	8.8	8.9	9.1
b. Units Covered (in thous.)	272	813	998	1,068
c. Workers Covered (in thous.)	5,986	13,135	12,276	11,950
Units/Agreement	25	92	112	117
Workers/Agreement	544	1,493	1,379	1,313

SOURCE: Bry, p. 42.

35. Bry, p. 32, provides the following, somewhat low, estimates of union membership for workers only (i.e., excluding salaried employees and other white-collar groups) and excluding yellow, red, syndicalist, and other stray groups: in millions—
    1925—4.90 1927—4.92 1929—5.47 1931—5.18
    1926—4.67 1928—5.47 1930—5.68 1932—4.70
36. The statistics are rather confusing and not always comparable, cf. ibid., p. 48. A union inquiry into actual hours worked concluded that there had been a reduction from 50.4 to 48.6 hours per week between 1924 and February 1930.
37. During the 1926–27 struggles over the length of the work shift and work week, Ruhr industrialists complained that the processing industries, the dynamic industries, and "all of Berlin"–oriented industry had already gone over to the eight-hour day, forty-eight-hour week. See Weisbrod, pp. 321ff.

TABLE 31

Indices of Hourly and Weekly Wages, 1924–1932 (1913 = 100)

	1924	1925	1926	1927	1928	1929	1930	1931	1932
Nominal									
Hourly rates	107	135	146	154	168	177	180	171	144
Hourly earnings	112	146	155	169	190	200	194	180	151
Weekly earnings	91	123	128	143	164	169	155	137	113
Real									
Hourly rates	82	95	102	104	110	115	122	125	120
Hourly earnings	86	103	109	114	125	130	131	132	125
Weekly earnings	70	87	90	97	108	110	105	100	94

SOURCES: Bry, pp. 331, 362; cf. Hoffmann, p. 470.

held to two-thirds of prewar levels: "The wage rate expressed [in real terms] should not exceed two-thirds of prewar levels. The resultant decrease in income should be compensated by additional hours. Prevailing higher rates should be reduced. Arbitration decisions leading to higher rates should be prevented by nonparticipation of employers in the proceedings."[38] With 28 percent of union members unemployed and another 42 percent working short-time, there was not much the unions could expect to do to counter the employers. From 1924 to 1930, however, the cost of living rose rather modestly (about 15 percent) while nominal wages rose substantially (over 60 percent). The general economic upturn, improved industrial productivity, and the stagnation and then decline of agricultural prices all helped make this possible. Hourly real rates rose by 40 percent from 1924 to 1929, reaching a point somewhat more than 20 percent above 1913 levels. Weekly real rates rose almost as much, but owing to the shorter work week and other differences, real weekly rates were less than 10 percent above 1913 levels.[39] Real hourly and weekly earnings rose even further than the corresponding real rates—almost 55 and 60 percent, respectively. Real hourly earnings kept rising until *1931* at which time they were 30 percent above prewar levels. Indeed, nominal hourly wage rates as well as real hourly rates and earnings increased (especially for the unskilled) through 1930—despite economic downturn. Table 31 indicates the pattern of nominal and real wages for the entire period. If the gross annual earnings of fulltime employees in the fifteen largest industries is indexed

38. Cited in Bry, p. 55; see table 3.

39. Bry cautions, however, that these higher rates were themselves "minima set for designated occupations and that, particularly in prosperous years, they were exceeded by rates actually paid and still more by average earnings," p. 75.

(1913 = 100), then annual earnings in 1929 and 1930 exceeded *180*—a level not reattained until the late 1950s at the earliest. It is not surprising, therefore, that as late as 1931, Tarnow could caution his fellow ADGB leaders that "especially seen from abroad, the standard of living of German workers is rather respectable and, beyond that, we have the best Sozialpolitik."[40]

After 1924 the cost of living remained relatively stable. The cost of housing was kept well below the aggregate cost of living, while the cost of clothing and miscellaneous goods and services rose disproportionately. Again with 1913 indexed at 100 the cost of living moved as follows:[41]

1924—131	1927—148	1930—148
1925—142	1928—152	1931—136
1926—142	1929—154	1932—121

Even once the Brüning government began ordering wage reductions by emergency decree after June 1930, and state arbitrators began ruling against labor, the relative level of wages remained high. Because both raw-material and living costs remained relatively stable—in fact, raw materials costs generally declined after 1924—the price-to-wage ratio moved in labor's favor until 1932. Although conservative analysts overestimate the significance of this indicator,[42] it does reveal something about capital's budding hostility as well as about labor's welfare. If the price-to-wage ratio for the boom year of 1928 is set equal to 100, then the index values for the other years are the following:

1925—127	1928—100	1931—79
1926—110	1929—94	1932—81
1927—104	1930—86	(first qtr.)

Table 32 demonstrates quite clearly the economic Achilles' heel of Sozialpolitik—persistently high unemployment and relative stagnation of the active labor force. This was a flaw of which organized labor's

40. On earnings, Bry, p. 473; cf. Keese, pp. 45, 47. Specifically:
      1924—112 1926—148 1928—169 1930—182 1932—145
      1925—142 1927—157 1929—180 1931—168 1933—139
Tarnow's remark in Historische Kommission zu Berlin, HKB/Vorstandssitzungen Protokolle des ADGB/NB 3, 21 Jan. 1931.

41. Bry, pp. 422–24. Hoffmann, pp. 600–601, provides a more specific breakdown of the costs of various goods and services.

42. As does Ferdinand Hermens, "Das Kabinett Brüning und die Depression," in Hermens and Schieder, eds., pp. 296ff.

TABLE 32

Employment and Unemployment, 1925–1932 (in millions and percent)

	1925	1926	1927	1928	1929	1930	1931	1932
Employed								
Industry and mining	12.5	11.2	13.0	13.4	13.0	11.4	9.5	8.0
Trade and transport	5.3	5.4	5.7	5.9	6.1	6.0	5.7	5.3
Total actives[a]	31.0	29.9	32.0	32.5	32.3	30.5	28.1	26.1
Unemployed[b]								
Registered	.7	2.1	1.3	1.4	1.9	3.3	4.6	5.6
% of union membership	6.5	18.4	8.8	8.6	13.3	22.8	34.4	44.2

SOURCES: Data combined from Hoffmann, pp. 205–206, and Bry, pp. 398–400. On stagnation, see the literature cited in chap. 3, note 45. Preller's unemployment figures, p. 394, are somewhat higher.
[a] Includes, in addition to the above categories, agriculture, servants, military, and all others.
[b] These are conservative annual averages; the true figures were likely higher, and wintertime unemployment was substantially higher.

opponents would later take full advantage, particularly once the unions' political guarantors were weakened.

High unemployment challenged the new welfare and insurance measures almost immediately. Thus, in the winter of 1928–29, up to 2.5 million claimed unemployment insurance benefits, thereby severely taxing the fund and necessitating both a direct grant from the already hard-pressed treasury and an increase in contributions to the fund on the part of the employed exceeding the mandated 3 percent of gross wages.[43] In still prosperous mid-1929, nearly 10 percent of ADGB members were unemployed, and 1.5 million Germans were drawing unemployment insurance; over 10 percent of the state budget was being spent on unemployment and social insurance. Already the crisis of the unemployment insurance fund and state spending were exacerbating the fiscal crisis of the state. It was the conflict over remedying these, over determining at whose expense they were to be remedied, that the Grand Coalition and the labor-export alliance collapsed less than a year later. As note 35 and table 32 indicate, increased unemployment meant decreased union membership, and both phenomena weakened the unions as their (defensive) struggle with employers sharpened. In turn, this increased the pressure on the SPD and contributed thereby to the disintegration of the Grand Coalition.[44] That the changing economic

43. Details in Hüllbüsch, "Gewerkschaften," pp. 135–36; Preller, p. 520.
44. We discuss the collapse of the Grand Coalition below. On growing union pressure within the SPD before that, Schneider, *Arbeitsbeschaffungsprogramm*, pp. 47–60.

situation and the entrepreneurial offensive led to a change in the momentum of labor/capital struggles is revealed in table 33, a tabulation of man-days lost due to strikes and lockouts. After 1924, lockouts became an indicator of employer offensives, while strikes (except perhaps in 1927) became an increasingly defensive and reactive labor strategy. By 1931 labor was basically deprived of the wherewithal to strike, and employers, though hardly satisfied, no longer needed to lock out their employees.

Other indicators that help to measure the advance of Sozialpolitik through the second half of the twenties and its slow retreat thereafter show the same double determination by economic conditions and political developments. Thus, employer contributions to health insurance rose 58 percent between 1925 and 1929 and then declined 31 percent by 1932.[45] At first, this would appear to be a direct consequence of changes in (un-)employment, but when these figures are compared with the income share accruing to entrepreneurs (table 29), it emerges that employers yielded increasingly larger portions of their income for this purpose until 1932. State expenditures on social insurance rose by 57 percent between 1925 and 1930 and then declined only 13 percent through 1932; here the issue was more political than employment-based. Similarly, state spending rose a full 25 percent, from 8 billion to 10 billion RM, in three short years from 1925 to 1928. It then declined a mere 2.4 percent in 1930. Only in 1931 did it drop a more substantial 12.5 percent, followed by an additional 11.5 percent in 1932.[46] Another minor example: expanding public education was both a democratic principle of the SPD and labor movement and a tactic to relieve pressure on the labor market. Thus, public spending for education was vastly increased by the republican parties; in 1925 it was already 45 percent above prewar levels, and in 1929 it rested at 208 percent of 1913 levels. Although spending on education was cut by one-third between

TABLE 33

Man-Days Lost, 1924–1932 (in millions)

	1924	1925	1926	1927	1928	1929	1930	1931	1932
To strikes	13.4	4.0	0.8	3.1	8.6	1.6	3.7	1.5	1.1
To lockouts	22.8	5.9	0.4	3.0	11.7	2.7	0.3	0.4	0.0

SOURCE: Bry, p. 327; *Jahrbuch des ADGB, 1931* (Berlin, 1932), pp. 170–74.

45. Hoffmann, p. 684, provides the figures in millions of RM; for 1925–32, they are, respectively: 439, 475, 553, 631, 694, 637, 476, 365.

46. Ibid., pp. 720–21, for the figures.

TABLE 34

Tax and Total Government Revenues, 1925–1932 (in billions of RM)

	1925	1926	1927	1928	1929	1930	1931	1932
Taxes								
Reich and								
Länder	7.37	8.09	9.45	9.90	9.99	9.81	8.51	7.32
Municipal	3.20	3.58	4.09	4.40	4.39	4.33	3.68	2.96
All revenue	12.9	14.7	17.1	18.7	18.9	18.8	16.9	14.1

SOURCE: Hoffmann, p. 801.

1929 and 1932—under substantial pressure from the bourgeois parties—not until the early fifties were the levels of the late twenties reattained.[47]

In general, the political decisions of the Brüning and Papen governments were necessary to accomplish in the sphere of state spending what economic developments themselves had brought to pass in most facets of labor/capital relations. In their efforts to curtail and reduce public spending, these two regimes, of course, pointed to declining tax (and other) receipts caused by the economic crisis and to the imperative of encouraging economic recovery by easing the tax burden[48] on capital and production. We shall examine the Brüning and Papen policies below, with regard to the battle of the budget and the whole range of Sozialpolitik; here table 34 simply lists the state income parameters within which the political struggles took place. Tax and other revenue rose consistently through 1928, increased slightly in 1929, declined a bit in 1930, and then began to drop sharply.

As steadily rising unemployment threatened the private or contractual components of Sozialpolitik after 1929, organized labor called upon the state to plug the financing gap. Thus, in 1931 the unemployment and health insurance funds could be kept solvent only by a transfer of 2.4 billion RM from the general treasury: that amount was equal to 45 percent of the amount paid in by employed workers and their employers and equaled no less than 28 percent of the entire tax revenue of the Reich and Länder governments![49] As larger numbers of the unemployed became fully dependent on those welfare programs financed and operated by municipal governments, about one-third by

47. Ibid., p. 728.
48. See, most recently, Werner Jochmann, "Brüning's Deflationspolitik und der Untergang der Weimarer Republik," in Stegmann, et al., eds., pp. 101ff.
49. Preller, p. 520.

the end of 1931, organized labor sought to expand the prerogatives of local governments, whereas representatives of industry demanded that these fiscally irresponsible units be disciplined and deprived of many of their taxing rights.[50] In general, as the economic crisis deepened, organized labor called for increased state assistance and intervention, while industry consistently demanded the release of the economy from precisely such "political" fetters. For the latter, compulsory arbitration, unemployment insurance, labor, wages and hours legislation, and state spending of most sorts were all impediments to production and Wirtschaftspolitik, to "economics politics"—the only way for the nation and the economy as a whole to recover. Before we analyze in greater detail the conflict between Sozialpolitik and Wirtschaftspolitik during the period of economic and political crisis, we should pause to examine the role played by Sozialpolitik in unifying the otherwise fragmented and fractious interests of the dominant social classes even prior to the onset of the economic crisis.

2. The Politics of Sozialpolitik

The dominant class fractions were divided by their divergent economic, political, and ideological interests. In previous chapters those differences were symbolized by the term *Handelspolitik,* in the broadest sense an abbreviation for the range of differences and conflicts emerging from the competitive nature of capitalism. Other differences—for example, over monarchism and a posture toward the former royal houses, over the degree of religious compulsion to build into the school system, over certain aspects of foreign policy, and some others—were, perhaps, more random with regard to the world of production, if not historically. But if production desiderata and Handelspolitik divided the dominant fractions,[51] Sozialpolitik unified them. It did so especially for representatives of agriculture and heavy industry; the dynamic-export fraction of industry was, as we have seen, more willing to

50. The debate over the prerogatives of municipal governments, often socialist or "popular," is discussed in chapter 6. See also O'Connor for analogies with current "urban crises." A recent analysis of the fiscal problems of New York City compares that situation explicitly with several aspects of the Weimar case: fiscal retrenchment and political demobilization ("contraction") of those who have most recently won some measure of political and economic power, partially with their own connivance but primarily for the sake of restoring economic viability—Martin Shefter, "New York City's Fiscal Crisis," *Public Interest,* no. 48 (Summer 1977):98–127.

51. As shown in chap. 3, this division also affected attitudes toward organized labor, social and reparations questions; see table 35 below.

compromise with organized labor, certainly before 1929 and in some respects afterwards as well.[52] The DVP leadership, for example, recognized in 1925 that "the best possible trade policy would emerge from cooperation with the SPD, but what majority could we then mobilize for tax and fiscal legislation?" Later, it was the tension between SPD and DVP in the area of social legislation which provided the basis for industry's greater willingness to compromise with agriculture.[53]

For those producers to whom Sozialpolitik simply meant increased costs and diminished competitiveness and profitability the issue was clear. The SPD had long been aware, however, that this constraint was not equally salient to all producers. At least as early as 1924, the SPD used its support of free trade and industrial expansion to marshal sympathies within the dynamic-export and nonmonopoly sectors of German industry. In remarks befitting a Cobden or Bright, Hilferding rejected agriculture's demands for high tariffs: "Free trade is an essential part of realistic pacifism since protectionism in the broadest sense [Schutzzollpolitik]" was a weapon of monopoly capital conflict which "can lead to violent international altercations. . . . imperial conquest" and reaction at home. He felt a prosperous processing-finishing industry was the key to German recovery, and that its interests, like labor's, were in low tariffs.[54] The tacit Silverberg-Stresemann-Severing alliance was built on the recognition by each of the parties of these shared interests and of the existence of room for compromise. Each of the primary socioeconomic groups sought allies with which to balance the political or economic weight of its adversaries and competitors.[55]

The conflicts between the industrial fractions and the absence of a clearly and indisputably hegemonic group ultimately weakened bourgeois political coherence and lessened its political power. At the same time, the absence of that coherence provided the organized working class and its demands a certain political entrée they might otherwise not have enjoyed. Unity of the dominant class fractions under the leadership of heavy industry, for example, would probably have ren-

52. We have noted, for example, the RDI's and dynamic industries' cool response to the Langnamverein's and Northwest Iron and Steel's calls for support during the great Ruhr lockouts. The ADGB Jahrbücher constantly distinguished between hostile and compromise-ready groups of industrialists.

53. Schneider's statement for the DVP, 8 June 1925, quoted in Panzer, pp. 39, 91. Gessner, "Industrie und Landwirtschaft," pp. 771–72, argues that first the threat of socialization and then Sozialpolitik kept alive the alliance between the agrarians and heavy industry.

54. Hilferding, p. 129. On the changing SPD position toward agricultural protection, see chap. 2, note 167 and chap. 4, note 22.

55. Stürmer, esp. pp. 120–211. This was also what underlay the weekly meetings begun in early 1926 between RDI and union leaders; see Schneider, Unternehmer, p. 70.

dered impossible the major accomplishments of the mid- and late twenties.[56] At the same time that Paul Silverberg was announcing the dynamic-export fraction's readiness to cooperate with the SPD in autumn 1926, the Langnamverein was attempting to unify the dominant classes, presumably under its own leadership. To Silverberg's legitimation of Sozialpolitik, Reusch counterposed "a healthy Wirtschaftspolitik, which [however] would necessitate that all the productive strata work together more closely."[57] At the next conventions Reusch repeated his basic position; this time with more specific criticism of blossoming Sozialpolitik: "Government measures, especially those of the Labor Ministry, are driving our costs up and making us noncompetitive." Disappointments in exports were, he thought, also "due to fiscal and social-welfare policies" Germany could not afford. "Germany's lack of capital" just did not allow for these luxurious expenses: "receipts in the iron and steel industry are up 7–10 percent over 1913, but wages are up 60–70 percent, and taxes and social levies are up 250–300 percent." "Cigarette consumption has [doubled] . . . and consumption has shifted from simple and hearty rye bread to wheat bread." Germany's industries, argued Reusch, were neither profitable nor competitive. In metals, "our costs are 30–50 percent higher than our competitors', and this pattern would now affect textiles and others as well."[58]

But this period in the history of German industry belonged to the "Welfare Professor" Duisberg and his allies in the RDI and the bourgeois parties; Reusch's day was yet to come. The dire warnings emanating at least since 1925 from Ruhr magnates like Reusch, Vögler, and Thyssen were largely ignored—for the time being. In that year a group of them had complained to the chancellor of "brutal taxation and bloated public services" which, together with short-sighted wage policies encouraged by the prejudiced and political arbitration system, "make profitability impossible. The labor minister must be made to realize that he is responsible to the entire economy, not just the workers. . . . Our economy cannot afford the kind of Sozialpolitik we have." It will "lead to the collapse of the economy, . . . unless we have a quick end to coercive interference in wage policies, a reduction in intolerable social levies and taxation and a corresponding fiscal reform of the

56. Thus, Mommsen, "Sozialpolitik," p. 304, argues that such a unity would probably have prevented acceptance of the unemployment insurance laws, compulsory arbitration, the eight-hour day, and the Young Plan.

57. Reusch at the October 1926 Langnamverein convention, quoted in BA/Z Sg 126/ Kiel Institut.

58. Ibid., Reusch's talks of 2 Oct. 1927 and 15 Nov. 1927; also the analyses in the *Deutsche Bergwerks Zeitung* of 15 Nov. 1927 and speech of 5 May 1928.

national and municipal governments."[59] While there seems to have been little explicit disagreement with this position on the part of other industrialists, the implied programmatic recommendations were largely ignored. Although the Employers' League, RDI, DIHT, and other industrial organs, as well as estate-owner and peasant groups, issued a joint statement in early 1928 decrying various extensions of social-welfare legislation, the dynamic fraction of industry was not yet prepared to support the more militant, pro-lockout position of the Ruhr industrial captains or the protectionist demands of the rural cosigners.[60] Heavy industry and the agrarians, including peasant representatives, reached general agreement, but this was not enough to stop the growth of Sozialpolitik.[61] Hugenberg's warnings that labor's gains (and Reparations) were "slowly but surely driving industry down the road to ruin already traversed by agriculture" were not yet taken seriously; nor, apparently, was his contention that through "levelling" the workers were the only group better off in 1930 than in 1913.[62]

What finally tipped the balance within industry in favor of full-fledged opposition to Sozialpolitik was the decline of international trade, which displaced the dynamic fraction from its leadership position within industry. That was but the final blow, however, and it was preceded by a combined political and economic development of great import: the SPD electoral victory of 1928 and the subsequent small-scale economic and ideological offensive of the trade unions. The first postelection showdown was posed by the Ruhr lockouts of October 1928: an attempt by iron and steel industrialists to prevent a round of accelerated wage demands and simultaneously to attack the state arbitration mechanism. The details of the events and divisiveness they engendered have been discussed elsewhere;[63] here we mean to stress heavy industry's own

59. HA GHH/Nachlass Reusch 400 101 293/13, memorandum to the chancellor, Sept. 1925.

60. Details in BA/R13I-VDESI/217, pp. 126ff.; from the rural side, ZSA/RLB Vorstand/50, pp. 85–90. On the isolation of heavy industry during the lockouts, Weisbrod, pp. 495, 436ff. On the agrarians' attempt to make a splash with the industrialists, see ZSA/RLB Vorstand/144, p. 98.

61. On the near congruence of interests between heavy industry and agriculture on Sozialpolitik, see ZSA/RLB Pressarchiv 132/11, p. 28 and /10, pp. 192, 204. The role of the Esplanade Circle and the Polish trade treaty was discussed in chapter 4. Wilmowsky explained that on the questions of social and unemployment insurance the interests of agriculture and industry were fully parallel; HA GHH/Nachlass Reusch 400 101 24/1, 25 Apr. 1928. Peasants were outraged that jobless workers received more in unemployment insurance than they themselves earned working.

62. BA/Nachlass Hugenberg/151, pp. 185, 226, respectively. See also the Green Front memorandum of 19 Mar. 1929, which called for the restoration of satisfactory capital accumulation in industry.

63. See chap. 3, pp. 132f.; Schneider, Unternehmer, pp. 76–84; Weisbrod, pp. 415–56.

offensive. Reichert had consistently emphasized that the steel industry objected to compulsory arbitration not only for its results, but also "because it deprives [the entrepreneur and worker] of a sense of responsibility."[64] The prospect of an SPD labor minister now determining arbitration outcomes was too much to bear.[65] The Ruhr producers were willing to shut down over 75 percent of Germany's ferrous production as part of a preemptive move against the unions. The steel producers had not fared well even under the bourgeois government of 1927 (with its dynamic-export Economics Minister Julius Curtius of the DVP): the system of the three, eight-hour shifts with wages untrimmed had been forced on them—with the acquiescence of the dynamic fraction of industry—at a time when "we can neither sell our goods nor make a profit." Reichert claimed that this was tantamount to "a general 13.6 percent wage increase" and that the unions could afford "ridiculous and immense demands" since the arbitrator ignored "the facts of reality." "An additional 50,000 workers would have to be hired, and the total cost increase demanded came to no less than 48 percent of current wages . . . it would cost 220–250 million RM [11 percent] of the total value of our production." With the cost of its product increased over 10 percent, he asked how Germany could possibly compete. "With economic operation of the factories impossible, a closing [i.e., lockout] . . . was unavoidable, the decision of the unions, arbitrator and labor minister."[66] An RDI report on the economy in 1927 contended that organized labor was pushing against the limits of what German industry could endure. Without endorsing a strategy of lockouts, the document argued that profit rates had fallen to 4 percent, half their prewar level, and when capital accumulation is virtually impossible, "when labor's share of receipts becomes too great" and when taxes are greater than profits, "capital must simply lose interest in producing."[67]

The Ruhr lockouts lasted over two months, until just before Christmas 1928. They ended, finally, with SPD Interior Minister Severing's revision of the SPD Labor Minister Wissell's arbitrator's decision.[68]

64. Reichert cited in BA/R13I-VDESI/217, p. 6. Background on heavy industry's opposition in /68, pp. 56–60, 20 Feb. 1929.

65. Hartwich, p. 335; Schneider, *Unternehmer*, p. 82.

66. Citations and details in BA/R13I-VDESI/215, pp. 169–76. Reichert laid out the VDESI's position in *Der Arbeitgeber* of 1 Jan. 1928. On heavy industry's defeat on the question of work shifts and hours, Weisbrod, pp. 301–32; see Reusch to Ernst Poensgen, 28 Dec. 1927, HA GHH/Nachlass Reusch 400 101 290/32.

67. *Besteuerung,* RDI Veröffentlichung no. 47, pp. 8ff. On the notion that there is some point at which labor's share of receipts becomes too great for capitalist-democracy to remain stable, see chap. 6, sec. 1 below. The overall situation varied greatly by industry, as shown in chap. 3.

68. The arbitrator was Wilhelm Joetten, perhaps the most respected of all arbitrators

Both sides were left unhappy, while the principle of compulsory arbitration itself did not emerge unscathed. Representatives of heavy industry proclaimed it a fix—labor's political representatives declaring in favor of labor's economic representatives. Rank-and-file union members found quite unsatisfactory a settlement that provided them with only minimal shortening of the work week and average wage increases of barely 4 percent; they had expected considerably more from "their own" newly elected government (they had asked for up to 18 percent and had been awarded 8), particularly as the industry's cartels had already announced price increases. Nevertheless, both sides had their appetites whetted: labor determined that wage and welfare improvements were possible even when the particular industry in question was not doing well, and industry concluded that it was possible to disobey the law of the land and cause real economic dislocation in the name of the general interest. The labor-export coalition was sufficiently intact, however, that the Reichstag, by an overwhelming margin including 30 of 45 DVP delegates, voted substantial public grant funds for the quarter-million locked-out workers. Yet, it was not strong enough to force the iron and steel industrialists to accept the original, procedurally correct, and state-sanctioned decision; the government had to devise an epicyclical appeal procedure, which would incorporate demands for weakening the arbitrator's authority and the procedure itself.[69] Finally, the four-month-old Grand Coalition government of SPD through DVP was itself weakened while tensions increased between the industrial and popular wings of the DVP and DDP.

That the steel industrialists succeeded in politicizing capital's economic struggle on behalf of "die freie Wirtschaft" while undermining the legal-arbitration structure is certain; that the Grand Coalition was

---

and one long familiar with both the industries involved and the situation in the Ruhr basin. His memoranda along with those of the other interested parties are reprinted in Michael Schneider, ed., *Auf dem Weg in der Krise* (Wentorf b. Hamburg, 1974).

69. Weisbrod argues that despite the responses of Parliament, the press, and public opinion and the ambivalence of the other wing of the RDI (pp. 435f., 495), the lockouts were a real success for heavy industry: the Ruhr captains violated the law, weakened the Grand Coalition, struck a blow for the "free economy," ignored the RDI leadership, and cemented their own veto right within that organization (pp. 415–56). See chap. 3, sec. 2 above, and Bracher, pp. 199–228; Preller, pp. 399ff.; Hüllbüsch, "Ruhreisenstreit"; Timm, pp. 97–107. Weisbrod correctly emphasizes the consequent weakening not only of the arbitrator but also of the Labor Minister and the strengthening of the right wing of the DVP in opposition to Stresemann, Curtius, and their pro–Grand Coalition allies within the dynamic-export fraction. He asserts, too (p. 436), that at this stage, the representatives of Ruhr heavy industry wanted to go it alone—a curious argument in view of their own isolation, legal setbacks, and final reliance on Severing virtually to decree a settlement.

given notice of heavy industry's opposition is also clear. On the labor side, skepticism as to what the unions might expect from SPD ministers was nourished. The terms of Severing's revision cost the employers only one-third of Joetten's original settlement and amounted to less than 10 percent of what the unions had initially demanded.[70] The party would soon attempt to compensate for disappointing the unions, who were now even further dependent on the state than before. As a "Macht-probe," the outcome of the Ruhr lockouts was ambiguous albeit ominous for both the forces cooperating in the Grand Coalition and the social compromise embedded in the Constitution. Reusch's threat to resign his leadership of the Langnamverein in protest over his colleagues' inadequate attack on state authority suggests that even within heavy industry different strategies were contemplated.[71] An effort undertaken by the steel industry to defend free enterprise and resist state arbitration was settled, after all, by the arbitration of an SPD minister, yet one who, in the event, acknowledged the economic plight of the industrialists, particularly what seemed at the time to be declining domestic demand uncompensated for by rising indirect (AVI) exports. All sides had had to trade off political and economic demands, and none could claim a decisive victory.

After the lockouts and the start of the economic crisis, it became clearer to the unions that they had been unduly sanguine about industry's readiness to cooperate in the various measures designed to counteract the effects of the labor market. The unions' puzzlement was, therefore, somewhat tempered when, in 1929, most industries announced their unwillingness to raise their contributions to an unemployment insurance fund moving ever deeper into the red.[72] Following the SPD's electoral victory, and only about one year after the unemployment insurance law was passed, union leaders in the ADGB began to articulate an offensive version of the doctrine of economic democracy, a political-economic conception that would enable them to extend and broaden the principles of Sozialpolitik. Perhaps as a correlate to Hilferding's conception of "organized capitalism," Fritz Naphtali, Fritz Tarnow, Hugo Sinzheimer, Erik Nölting, and others, basing themselves in part on the theories of Austro-Marxists like Max Adler, devised a program for *Wirtschaftsdemokratie* or "economic democracy." This

70. See BA/R13I-VDESI/104, p. 220, Grauert's explanation, 20 Feb. 1929.

71. See Reusch to Silverberg, HA GHH/Nachlass Reusch 400 101 290/35, and to Krupp, /27, 10 Dec. 1928; Weisbrod, p. 443.

72. Hüllbüsch, "Gewerkschaften," p. 136. Industrial unwillingness had become apparent before Stresemann's death, that is, before it became clear that the DVP would follow suit and that the Grand Coalition was doomed.

new goal lay nebulously between the tragedy of socialism and the farce of worker participation or co-determination;[73] they both argued that capitalism had to be bent before it could be broken. A crucial weakness of this design for economic democracy was precisely its economism;[74] economism just when the dominant classes were politicizing even the economic aspects of their struggle against organized labor, as heavy industry had in the Ruhr lockouts.

Whatever economic democracy may have meant to its supporters, to industrialists it was folly and mischief, creeping socialism, to be opposed fully and quickly. Thus, Weber and Frowein, more liberal industrialists who even supported the Grand Coalition, felt compelled to insist that "we must counter the plan to reach socialism through democratization of the economy. . . . Political relations have not led to the selection of the best and most capable; economic [democracy] is just as unlikely to. . . . All Sozialpolitik must be limited by the productivity of the economy. . . . higher productivity cannot be achieved through economic democracy. . . . There can be no 'fire and water [mixed] economy' . . . coerceive and communistic undertakings are . . . like sand thrown into a machine."[75] A year earlier, Ludwig Kastl, business chairman of the RDI and also a liberal backer of the Grand Coalition, remarked, "It is grotesque that more than three-fourths of all Germans have social insurance," that the state's social budget had quadrupled since 1913 was a "crime against the economy" worse now that the productive economy was to be turned into something democratic.[76] Other decidedly liberal industrialists, members of the DDP, and representatives of the dynamic-export fraction, men like Robert

73. On responses to the doctrine of Economic Democracy, see H.-A. Winkler, "Unternehmer und Wirtschaftsdemokratie," *Politische Vierteljahresschrift* 11, Sonderheft 2 (1970):308–22. The basic document is Fritz Naphtali, ed., *Wirtschaftsdemokratie: Ihr Wesen, Weg und Ziel* (Berlin, 1928). It is no accident that Woytinsky and Fritz Tarnow, both active in formulating this conception, were three years later the primary architects of the New Deal–like WTB Plan; cf. Wladimir Woytinsky, *Stormy Passage* (New York, 1961), and the plethora of articles cited by Robert Gates, "Von der Sozialpolitik zur Wirtschaftspolitik?" in Mommsen, et al., eds., pp. 217–21. Max Adler's strikingly idealist statement on economic democracy is contained in his *Politische oder soziale Demokratie* (Berlin, 1926), pp. 132–50. See also the literature cited by Kuda.

74. Although its advocates certainly did not abjure politics, in practice Wirtschaftsdemokratie directed worker energies primarily toward economic matters just as the political arena was heating up and about to crack. See Naphtali, p. 23; Kuda, pp. 273–74.

75. August Weber's speech at the RDI meetings of 21 Sept. 1929, reprinted as *Unternehmertum und Kapitalismus,* in RDI Veröffentlichung no. 48 (1929). On the response of industrialists to Wirtschaftsdemokratie, see Schneider, *Unternehmer,* pp. 85–92, 156–62. The fire, water, and sand metaphors were Frowein's as he seconded Weber.

76. Ludwig Kastl's speech "Die Wirtschaftspolitischen Aufgaben des RDI," reprinted in RDI Veröffentlichung no. 42 (1928), pp. 24, 23, 16.

Bosch, Ernst Leitz, and Max Levy, argued that "economic democracy" was pushing the entrepreneur into a corner: "these proposals would take all freedom of movement away from the entrepreneur . . . leading him either to passivity or to reactionary tendencies!"[77] Abraham Frowein of the textile industry summed up the more generous critique in what must have seemed to him a self-explanatory proposition: "Politics corrects, the economy produces; democracy is therefore an ideal in the former but a drag [*Hemmschuh*] in the latter."[78]

The basic point of contradiction had been reached and the basic conflict joined. The unions' desire to translate into economic terms what had been attained in the political realm—democracy—was too much for any fraction of capital to accept, even if the economic situation had been better than it actually was.[79] To complete political with economic democracy would have been a basic violation of the capitalist mode of production and a basic threat to the dominant classes. Fritz Tarnow could contend that capitalism was malleable and bendable, that it could be changed without being completely "turned around" [*umgewendet*] all at once, that "planned direction of the economy in the interests of the general public" was a feasible goal "even before political power is one hundred percent in our hands," but his contentions were mere invitation to the subversion of political democracy, if not full-fledged counterrevolution.[80] At their most ambitious, proponents of economic democracy envisioned concurrent and interdependent advances in the economic and political realms; this was the old partnership between the unions and the party, but the position of an SPD lodged in the Grand Coalition could never be adequate to such an offensive strategy. Beyond that, however, the strategy itself was prisoner of that Second International economism-reformism which underestimated the importance of political struggle.[81] Indeed, the SPD was

77. Their statement of October 1928, cited in BA/Nachlass Dietrich/228, p. 161. Various members of the DDP subsequently began to complain of welfare cheaters, double dippers, and the general abuse of social legislation. They called for a reduction in benefits and the establishment of stricter eligibility categories; see /320, pp. 225–28.

78. BA/Nachlass Frowein/1, p. 10, 17 Feb. 1931. This juxtaposition receives greater attention in chap. 6.

79. Thus Bücher, generally one of the most progressive major industrial spokesmen, warned that "economic democracy" was particularly pernicious precisely because it was not fully utopian but rather potentially practicable; RDI Vorstand meeting, 21 June 1928, DII/RDI Tagungen und Vorbereitungen/1928.

80. See the sampling of statements by Tarnow in Hüllbüsch, "Gewerkschaften," pp. 134–35, and Gates, pp. 217–21.

81. Cf. Poulantzas, *Fascisme*, pp. 34–55, 241–53; chap. 1, secs. 1 and 2, and chap. 6, sec. 1. For an extremely stimulating if pessimistic update on this problem-complex, see Wolfgang Müller and Christel Neusüss, "The Illusion of State Socialism and the Contradiction Between Wage Labor and Capital," *Telos*, no. 25 (Fall 1975):13–90, and the

reduced such that its efficacy was measured by its ability to legislate economic gains, and, worse still, its legitimacy within the working class (including even some of the ADGB leadership) depended on its ability to defend economic gains militantly and successfully! An unsympathetic but perceptive observer like Reusch's assistant Martin Blank was able to summarize this situation quite easily: "not only the unions but the SPD itself stands or falls with the fate of unemployment insurance."[82] And fall it did.

After 1929, as Germany's economic product first stagnated and then shrank, the dominant class fractions sought to unite politically and economically around a program based on dismantling labor's gains. Politically, their program manifested itself in undermining the Grand Coalition based on the alliance of organized labor and the dynamic-export fraction of industry. Economically, the program called for a political and labor-market struggle to improve profitability at the expense of labor and the state programs that had been working to labor's advantage. Industry's incessant demands for "elasticity" instead of "rigidity" in the negotiation of labor contracts was an attack on "political wages" and labor relations, not only those promulgated by state arbitration but also those embodied in public law and state spending.[83] The portion of the social product obtained by labor was to be reduced, while its share of the burdens of a lost war had to increase. Massive unemployment facilitated Wirtschaftspolitik as massive foreign credits had earlier facilitated Sozialpolitik; in both cases political coalitions were affected accordingly. The RDI memorandum of December 1929, "Recovery or Collapse," inaugurated the general offensive of capital, an offensive that heavy industry, for its part, had long sought and had attempted to begin somewhat prematurely with the Ruhr lockouts a year earlier.[84] The collapse of the Grand Coalition in March 1930, ostensibly over the issue of increased employers' contributions to the unemployment insurance fund, was one major step in that offensive. The worsening economic depression and changing political conditions then fired capital's general offensive, and the corporatist patina of a pluralist democracy, of a state above classes and yet representing all classes, simply melted away.[85]

---

responses by Habermas and Offe; cf. Ulrich, pp. 47ff. Clearly, the theoretical issues raised by and for the left in Weimar Germany are nearly all very much with us.

82. Blank to Reusch, 4 July 1929, HA GHH/Nachlass Reusch 400 101 293/9.

83. Details of industry's attack on "political" wages, arbitration, and social insurance in Schneider, Unternehmer, pp. 119–42.

84. For Weisbrod, heavy industry's offensive began even earlier, but his analysis indicates that the returns were initially small and slow in coming.

85. Preller, who like Maier is inclined to take this corporatism very seriously to begin with, emphasizes this last point, p. 514. See Hartwich's critique, pp. 373–84.

3. Implementing Industry's Program

Organized labor and the SPD had been somewhat successful in characterizing the Ruhr lockouts as an affront against the general, national interest,[86] but they could not disarm or split the general capitalist political, ideological, and economic offensive launched in late 1929. The inauguration of class conflict from above and the shift in leadership within industry from the dynamic-export to the heavy-domestic fraction seem to have caught the SPD off guard.[87] The *Vorwärts*, for example, responded quizzically and with undue surprise to the demands voiced in "Recovery or Collapse" and subsequent RDI memoranda: "Industry is using the Young Plan as an excuse against labor." It went on to say that the RDI talked as if it wanted a "feudalism of grand capital" which would come at the expense of the general public and wipe out almost all the social gains of past decades and that indeed the RDI program would yield 7.7 billion RM annually, almost all of it at the expense of the working population. "Silverberg's is a plan for creating a fiscal dictatorship . . . he shows himself [hitherto an outspoken moderate and friend of the Grand Coalition] now to be an enemy not only of the working class and economic democracy, but rather of the democratic state altogether."[88]

In essence, however, the *Vorwärts* was correct. Given a shrinking economic pie, such were the measures leading industrialists believed necessary for easing the burden of Sozialpolitik and restoring profitability. To bring the dynamic-export fraction around to the program articulated in "Recovery or Collapse," George Müller (Oerlinghausen) and Paul Silverberg emphasized the deleterious effect of labor's gains on those yet unconverted:

> The export strategy has not worked well because German Handelspolitik was stabbed in the back by social and tax policies. . . . The kind of coalition politics which allowed that is now impossible. . . . We must lower our costs [not raise them] . . . we must have a reduction in public and social costs—whatever it takes [*um jeden Preis*]. We need production, not consumption . . . a socialist-collectivist tax and finance policy . . . a finance minister [Hilferding] being used as a socialization minister is making success impossible for the private, capitalist economy.[89]

86. See chap. 3, note 83; Weisbrod, pp. 436, 495.
87. See chap. 3, esp. sec. 5.
88. *Vorwärts* of 4, 11, and 13 Dec. 1929, respectively. In the offing was what the KPD described as an "internal Young Plan" designed to shift Germany's various burdens "onto the shoulders" of the country's working people.
89. Cited in ZSA/RLB Pressarchiv 132/11, p. 168.

Reforms had to begin by cutting all public outlays at least 5 percent and all taxes except those on unnecessary consumption (such as alcohol, tobacco) and untaxed government-owned installations.

And the dynamic-export fraction seems to have been convinced. Thus, a leader of that fraction, the "Welfare Professor" himself, Carl Duisberg, came around and announced in January 1930—fully aware of the political implications—that "determining the breadth of the current crisis is the overburdening" of politically supported high taxes, wages, and social-welfare costs. "Capital is being destroyed through the unproductive use of public funds. . . . Only an immediate and radical reversal in state policies" could help. Public funds for private businesses were, somehow, less objectionable.[90]

Representatives of capital repeatedly called for an end to the false popular prosperity based on foreign loans and labor's political pressure, and manifested in inflated wages and state spending at the expense of capital accumulation. Reparations were being paid without tightening the popular belt; the primacy of Sozialpolitik had led to half the national income's being funneled through the state; "political wages"

---

90. *Wirtschafts- und Sozialpolitik*, RDI Veröffentlichung no. 50, pp. 37, 43. The consistent opposition of industrialists and their spokesmen to state intervention in the private economy for the benefit of organized labor was not mirrored by any similar objection to state subvention of failing capitalist enterprises. Besides the persistent efforts of the agrarians to "socialize" agriculture's losses, shipbuilders, railway-equipment manufacturers, and automobile companies, among others, all succeeded in obtaining Reich and local grants, loans, and guarantees in the period after 1925 and especially 1929. Frequently, "national," military and job-protection justifications were offered, but often ailing industries expected assistance as a trade-off for high wages, taxes, and social costs. (Fritz Blaich, "Garantierter Kapitalismus: Subventionspolitik und Wirtschaftsordnung," *Zeitschrift für Unternehmensgeschichte* 22 [1977]:50–70). Jobs were generally not protected for very long.

The case of Borsig Ltd. was particularly ironic. Ernst Borsig was chairman of both that corporation and the Employers' League, VdA. In the latter capacity, he inveighed for years against state intervention in determining wages, prices, work conditions, and other aspects of a free, private economy. Yet in July 1931, he was compelled to request state aid to preserve his firm, though, to be sure, he blamed high social costs and taxes for its difficulties. He further justified state intervention on the basis of the potential importance of his Berlin-based plants for armaments production should munitions factories in the west be eliminated (BA/R43I/2461, pp. 19, 28). Reichswehr Minister General Schleicher supported this contention, and Labor Minister Stegerwald argued that the collapse of Borsig would destroy international faith in the credit-worthiness and contractual reliability of the crucial machine-building industry while resulting in the possible loss of thousands of jobs. In the end, Borsig Ltd. received a grant of 1.5 million RM and large loan guarantees, not a terribly large sum but a victorious violation of principle nevertheless (ibid., pp. 53ff., 97ff.). Borsig apparently did not fear the ultimate socialization of his property. As a display of gratitude and perhaps of resentment on the part of more successful entrepreneurs, the RDI accused the Brüning government and the SPD of moving toward indirect or "cold socialization" measures. See Reusch's position, chap. 6, n. 38 below.

were making much of German industrial production noncompetitive abroad and hindering expansion of its markets; the appearance of national prosperity rendered revision of the Versailles treaty less likely; and, finally, according to the RDI, coercive wage and arbitration measures attempted to pass the cost of wasteful and extravagant public spending from the masses onto the producers and their revenue.[91] Obviously questionable was the capacity of the Weimar democratic republic to restore profitability, alias "a healthy economy." The deparliamentarization of political life, the weakening of the unions, and the internal dynamic of the economic crisis were, together, the primary motors in the dismantling of organized labor's economic gains and the entire edifice of Sozialpolitik. The ultimate goal of capital's offensive—one it did not attain—was control over the state mechanism sufficient to enforce its own economic demands and comprehensive enough to incorporate the divergent interests of its three primary fractions.[92] The political alternatives industrialists came to face were not (directly) of their own making; indeed, subjectively they frequently felt impotent in the face of political developments, but substantively they were able to make good use of the crisis.[93]

State fiscal and social policies up to mid-1930 impeded an alteration of the distribution of the social product to capital's advantage. The attack on state arbitration was grounded in both hostility toward its outcomes and the conviction that it infringed intolerably on the rights of the owners of the means of production. Hence, the watershed Oeynhausen arbitration decision of June 1930, which lowered wages 10 percent, mollified but did not convert the industrialists. Any substantial maintenance of unemployment and social insurance was rejected by industry (and organized agriculture) not only because of a principled desire to balance the state's finances, and not only out of an unwillingness to maintain, let alone increase, their minimal contributions to those funds. Far more, these programs were undermined because they created a floor or base level for wages; they interfered with the "normal" market patterns of wages and labor during a period of massive deflation.[94] The collapse of the Grand Coalition left organized labor

91. *Wirtschafts- und Sozialpolitik,* pp. 12ff. See Weisbrod, pp. 460ff.

92. It might, perhaps, be more accurate to say that direct control of the state mechanism was less of a goal than the certainty that the state mechanism, *in whosever hands,* would *cultivate rather than violate* capitalist interests. This goal was attained, though not in the form most desired.

93. Turner in his analyses has focused chiefly on these subjective feelings of impotence in order to exonerate industrialists of responsibility for the events of late 1932 and early 1933. Döhn and esp. Stegmann, "Faschismus und Kapitalismus," point out Turner's myopia, but their battle continues.

94. Preller, p. 516, emphasizes this point—perhaps too much, although it is corroborated by many of industry's own presentations; cf. BA/R13I-VDESI/230. Within the ranks

without the political force necessary to save these programs. This is not to say that had the Grand Coalition not fallen when and as it did the various social programs would have been salvaged to a substantially greater extent; the SPD might well have presided over their dismantling. Doing so, however, would have been exceedingly difficult for a party whose raison d'être had pretty much been reduced to defending the daily interests of the organized working class, as defined primarily by the labor unions. For that very reason, perhaps, the SPD permitted the Grand Coalition to collapse rather than attempting to make the compromises and concessions which might have enabled it and parliamentary government to continue.[95]

The government of Chancellor Brüning, which succeeded the Grand Coalition, was, however, itself rendered dependent on the SPD's toleration by the election results of September 1930. Consequently, the SPD was able, through Brüning's dependence on it, to participate indirectly in dismantling social programs even while exercising a considerable braking power that both limited the very dismantling and slowly undermined capital's confidence in Brüning's ability to get the job done! Eliminating the SPD from the coalition government was itself central enough to the representatives of capital, however, that a mere four months later Brüning was able to mandate increased contributions to the unemployment insurance fund exceeding those that ostensibly brought down the Grand Coalition. Certainly, other fiscal, social, and political measures under Brüning, as we shall observe, more than compensated for this, but such apparent anomalies underscore the conjunctural primacy of politics. This *half*-responsible posture on the part of the SPD cost it in support lost to the KPD, while the increasingly narrow and antisocial attitudes of the primary bourgeois parties cost them in support lost to the Nazis.[96]

---

of labor there was both a principled and an instrumental commitment to state arbitration. Tarnow tended to stress the inherent virtues of the procedure, whereas Leipart underlined the frequency with which labor won; see, e.g., HKB/Vorstandssitzungen ADGB/NB 3, 24 Feb. 1931.

95. Timm, pp. 178–208; Hüllbüsch, "Gewerkschaften," pp. 138–45; Bracher, pp. 287–303. The ADGB position was that if the price for salvaging labor participation in the government was the sacrifice of Sozialpolitik, then the government was ipso facto not worth saving; Varga's admonitions on the economist trap are germane here. Timm and others have made a major point of the fact that several SPD ministers (but not Labor Minister Wissell) were willing to accept the Zentrum's proposed compromise in order to save the coalition. That they could not carry the day was testimony to the strength of the unions and came as a surprise to the Zentrum, DDP, and DVP.

96. On changing contributions to the unemployment insurance fund, Preller, p. 518. On the SPD's ability to soften the blows under Brüning, see *Jahrbuch des ADGB, 1931* (Berlin, 1932), pp. 85–87, 162–69.

Put baldly, the KPD had been relatively unimportant in German politics between 1924 and 1930. The party had, with Soviet help, wrecked its organization and appeal in the course of its Putsch fiascoes in 1923 and the accompanying repression; by 1924 it could poll only 9.1 percent of the vote. Profiting from the general shift to the left in 1928 (which saw the SPD vote reach 30 percent), the KPD that year obtained 10.7 percent. Of course, neither the SPD nor capitalists spared the Communists venom, and both used fear of the Red specter freely. Nevertheless, the KPD was not a real force during these years in either the labor movement or the larger political arena; its visibility far exceeded its strength. It was only as the Grand Coalition began to founder, and for the reasons elaborated here, that some worker support drifted from the SPD to the KPD. Thus, in the elections of September 1930, the SPD fell to 24.6 percent while the KPD climbed to 13.1 percent. Only with the massive suffering and radicalization of 1932 did the Communists become a real force, polling 17 percent in November 1932 at a time of full political crisis when power might have been available in the streets. During the years of stability, neither the KPD, the Communist splinter unions (abandoned in most industries), nor the Communist caucuses within the ADGB unions made any demands qualitatively different from those of the socialists. A theoretical commitment to the catastrophic collapse of capitalism was more than overshadowed by the party's (and Comintern's) strategic analysis of this as a period of capitalist restabilization. Consequently, Communist demands, goals, and responses to the politics of Sozialpolitik were quite like those of the socialists, and, from the perspective of German capitalists, rather less threatening.

In the years between 1924 and 1928 the Nazi vote fluctuated between 6.5 and 2.5 percent. Suddenly in 1930, the party garnered over 18 percent of the votes. The Nazis appeared as a radical, "antisystem," social but anti-Marxist movement, capable of integrating disparate middle strata, many of which had not benefited from prosperity but were now being hurt by the Depression. At this stage, much of the Nazi vote was also a protest against the fractiousness of the non-Catholic bourgeois parties and the undisguised manner in which those parties frequently represented the interests of rich and powerful industrial and commercial groups (including, somehow, organized labor) who used a weak and corrupt parliamentary form of government as a locus for horsetrading and double-dealing while ignoring the needs of the little man and the nation.[97]

97. On why German capitalists might have seen Communists as less threatening than Socialists, see von Miquel to Reusch, p. 205 above. On the growth of popular support for the Nazis, see Tim Mason, *Sozialpolitik im Dritten Reich* (Opladen, 1977), chap. 2, and

As Brüning attempted through 1931 to cut costs in all areas, he embarked, with the support of labor and the smaller export and finishing industries, on a modest program to have the cartels and monopolies of heavy industry lower their prices. Many industrialists in the export and processing branches supported such an initiative as crucial to economic recovery, but the increasingly dominant fraction of industry rejected the idea that regulation of the market by producers' combinations shared the blame in any way. Only one kind of combination was at fault: "Private enterprise has not failed . . . rather socialistically-inclined political coercion" had created all the burdens along with reparations. Not the cartels, rather wage and social burdens had made costs so high; "the biggest cartel is the wage cartel [the unions]."[98] Next to the wage cartel of the unions there remained the spending cartel of the state which, according to Silverberg in July 1931, "still following socialist ideology, is a badly run organ depending on us but willing to let us perish as it spends on."[99]

To the determined industrialists, Brüning's were only half-measures that whetted the appetite by pointing to, but not accomplishing, all that could be done to reduce wage and social costs. Even Eduard Hamm of the DIHT, one of the more socially progressive spokesmen for commerce and industry and a staunch Brüning supporter, was disappointed with the ability of the parliamentary system to adapt "costs" to Germany's situation. "This Emergency Decree [of 5 June 1931] recognized the importance of capital accumulation" even at the expense of social and wage progress. "Together with the Hoover Moratorium [on reparations payments] this provides us a mere breather." The rigidity of costs remained a political fact because the people "expected to live better after a lost war than before it," and the political system did not allow hard lessons to be learned.[100] Those spokesmen for heavy industry who from the beginning were less patient with Brüning's pace were fully disenchanted by mid-1931. A group of Ruhr industrialists expressed their belief that not much had changed in a letter to the chancellor:

> Just as the creditor countries do not take into consideration our ability to pay, so we entrepreneurs are treated at home. The burden of reparations and the extravagance of public spending continue to fall

Thomas Childers, "Social Bases of the National Socialist Vote," *Journal of Contemporary History* 11 (Dec. 1976):17–42; also tables 1 and 2 above.

98. Speech by Walther Hillmann to the Reichsklub of the DVP, 14 Oct. 1931, cited in BA/R13III-LMV/1280.

99. Silverberg's speech to the RDI presidium, 29 July 1931 in BA/Nachlass Silverberg/32, p. 8.

100. Hamm's comments to the DIHT steering committee cited in BA/Nachlass Silverberg/645, pp. 148, 152, 23 June 1931.

on us. . . . We have no chance to make profits . . . and what we did earn was taxed away. . . . We make the greatest sacrifices and are in turn made scapegoats for the mistakes of others. . . . Self help and private initiative. . . . but [current] economic policies are in certain regards worse than a planned economy: [our] outlays are fixed high by taxes, social costs and coerced wages while the income side is of not the slightest concern. . . . *it is the most urgent task of domestic politics . . . to restore to business profitability, international competitiveness, and especially the possibility of capital accumulation. All other goals must be subordinated to this.* With the economy stand and fall material existence, cultural life, the political organism, and national independence. It is absolutely essential that state administration [at all levels] be reformed . . . and all the collectivist and coercive measures eliminated. . . . The tempo of the turnaround must successfully be accelerated.[101]

These sentiments were then incorporated into a "Joint Statement of German Economic Associations," which demanded of Brüning in October 1931 that he "overcome this distress, not administer it."[102]

Immediately before his dismissal at the end of May 1932, Brüning received a lengthy *aide-mémoire* from Kastl of the RDI, which indicated both industry's unambiguous and largely unsatisfied demands concerning social and fiscal policies as well as its own dilemma in formulating the other components of a program for overcoming Germany's economic troubles. In regard to the former, this no longer seemed to be the same Kastl who, speaking for[103] the dynamic-export fraction two years earlier, had described Sozialpolitik as "an insurance premium against bolshevism."[104] Speaking now for a changed RDI, he demanded free rein for *die Wirtschaft:* no state role in reaching wage agreements, no arbitration whatsoever; rather, "those who want to work should be able to sell their free labor in a free market." Further,

101. Letter of 30 July 1931, HA GHH/Nachlass Reusch 400 101 293/11. "Collectivist measures" included arbitration, high wages, work-hours legislation, social insurance, public housing, etc. Emphasis added.

102. BA/Z Sg 289/Hansa Bund, 30 Sept. 1931 and 8 Oct. 1931. This statement was signed by all the major organizations of industry, commerce, and banking.

103. On some aspects of the relationship between peak association business managers (like Kastl of the RDI, Schlenker of the Langnamverein, and Lange of the association of machine builders) and the leading industrialists themselves, see Feldman and Nocken, passim. As a particular element in the analysis of business behavior, I would contend that the movements of these oft-beholden managers constitute one of the best barometers of shifting sentiments among groups of industrialists themselves. Leading industrialists generally set the parameters and even the policies; the managers frequently developed and articulated them.

104. See chap. 3, p. 152.

tax and tariff revenues should be used to encourage the economy; social welfare and state administrative expenditures must be cut further. National and local government administrations must be made fiscally responsible and their budgets balanced without tax increases. In brief, "capital accumulation must be encouraged and all measures harmful to capital must be avoided in whatever sphere."[105] Two and a half years of industry's pressing these same demands testifies both to their importance in the minds of industrialists and to Brüning's inadequacies—or the inadequacies of the semiparliamentary system itself.

But if industry's program for labor was clear, its program for itself was not. The dominant classes had turned from a program of incorporating the interests of the working class to one of repressing those interests, but they were still divided on how to unify their own interests. Concerning this, Kastl's memorandum revealed a growing hostility toward agriculture's autarkic demands and an awakened interest in imperialist expansion, but there was scant suggestion of a positive program. A real recovery was possible only in an international context, for "if reparations are to be paid, then other countries must accept and encourage our exports." Further, import bans and quotas were symptomatic of the inadequate attention being paid the export industries. Germany had hurt itself with its tariff increases, and Kastl felt compelled to remind the government that trade policies did not exist for the convenience of Landwirtschaft; production could only be strengthened by expanding export markets and competitiveness.[106]

Since the stalemated political situation between 1930 and 1932 failed to permit a total rollback of labor's gains and could not produce capitalist unity on other issues, representatives of both fractions of industry attempted to take advantage of the weakening of the unions to make a separate peace with them. Because the SPD remained more effective in the legislative arena than the unions did in the economic arena, industrialists tried to deal with union representatives directly, bypassing the political mediation of the SPD. If successful, such a strategy would reap the dual fruit of winning concessions in the work place and weakening the SPD's electoral base and morale. This strategy was alluded to already in January 1930 by none other than Duisberg, who, after commenting that "mass-consumption theories may work in rich, self-sufficient America but could not work here," went on to bemoan the critical fact that "unfortunately, workers' organizations are not pure interest representatives but rather are combinations bound to a party."[107] From about this time through the Schleicher interlude, at-

105. Kastl's draft, 14 June 1932, in BA/Nachlass Kastl/5.
106. Ibid.
107. *Wirtschafts- und Sozialpolitik*, p. 43.

tempts to divide the unions from the SPD (and from each other) were a key feature of industry's labor policy. As noted above, the ADGB's militant stand on unemployment insurance in late 1929 and early 1930 contributed substantially to the position adopted by the SPD and the fall of the Grand Coalition. That refusal/inability to compromise was a prime example of both how hemmed in by its economism the SPD had become and how labor's reformist militancy fed the Republic's political antagonists. Sozialpolitik had become not only the litmus test for governments but the very end of politics itself.[108] Whether or not the ADGB came to regret its stand, or should have,[109] it is undeniable that organized labor was weakened by the SPD's exit from the government, particularly as the economic situation deteriorated further rather than improving as had been expected.

As tables 29–31 indicated, the unions remained successful enough in keeping production costs high that negotiating a separate peace with them was, for industry, still a worthwhile endeavor, one that might yield results more tangible than those an SPD-constrained Brüning could produce. This aspect of the class conflict assumed the form of private negotiations aimed at reaching common understandings. Of course, this did not preclude more militant actions, such as those suggested by Reusch, designed to break SPD and union influence on the shop floor and restore the old *Herr im Hause* discipline within the factory.[110] In mid-1930 Fritz Tarnow and Theodor Leipart of the ADGB were approached by Hans von Raumer and Hermann Bücher of the RDI to discuss "joint strategies for alleviating the economic crisis." Raumer and Bücher were as we have observed representatives of the dynamic-export fraction of industry and considered among the most socially progressive of industrialists. The four came close to issuing a joint statement on economic and social policy that might have revived the postwar Arbeitsgemeinschaften, but at the last moment the talks collapsed. Raumer attributed their failure to the "pressure of the steadily deteriorating [economic] situation," but subsequent research has indicated that representatives of heavy industry sabotaged the talks for fear that overly generous compromises were being made by the dynamic-export spokesmen on the wages question. Earlier, Kastl had personally

108. Astonishingly, even in September 1932, Leipart viewed the upcoming election not as a life-and-death campaign for the Republic, but rather as one for "the maintenance of Sozialpolitik." HKB/Vorstandssitzungen ADGB/NB 5, 16 Sept. 1932.

109. Hüllbüsch, "Gewerkschaften," p. 145, argues that it should have and did; for a different formulation of the problem, see chap. 6, sec. 2, below. Also, Martin Vogt, "Die Stellung der Koalitionsparteien zur Finanzpolitik, 1928–1930," in Mommsen, et al., eds., pp. 452–58.

110. See Reusch to Scholz, 17 July 1931, HA GHH/Nachlass Reusch 400 101 293/11; Gilsa to Reusch, 12 Dec. 1931, ibid.: "the *complete* exclusion of the trade-union bureaucracy you desire"—Gilsa believed Reusch's union-busting goal within reach.

assured Hilferding that price reductions would follow wage cuts and that, if only for foreign-policy reasons, most industrialists would go along with the results of joint deliberations. An editor of the *Gewerkschaftszeitung* even went so far as to say that "[if successful] these talks could prove a historical turning point, and we would bear the blame if we failed to heed the opportunity." An agreement with the entrepreneurs would help labor avoid a dictatorship, whether, as Tarnow added, "under Hitler, Hugenberg, or Brüning via Hindenburg."[111]

An associate of Raumer's defended dealing with the unions while bypassing the SPD: "Right now the unions are relatively reasonable, and something can be attained by dealing with them; the social democratic leaders, on the other hand, appear to be incorrigible."[112] In a move sponsored by Brüning and Labor Minister Stegerwald, representatives of the RDI and ADGB met to prepare a joint statement on overcoming the economic crisis for presentation to President Hindenburg and thence to the general public. Although there was some give and take, the talks floundered over whether reductions should come first in costs or in prices. This initiative was also torpedoed by leaders of Ruhr heavy industry who demanded that the ADGB openly renounce binding arbitration and acknowledge that "return to the capitalist system is essential for the salvation of the economy as a whole."[113] The liberal fraction of industry continued to support both Brüning and further negotiations with the unions, but it proved increasingly unable to assume that heavy industry would follow its lead in regard to either.

111. Hans von Raumer, "Unternehmer und Gewerkschaften in der Weimarer Republik," *Deutsche Rundschau* 80 (1954):434; recent evaluations by Hüllbüsch, "Gewerkschaften," p. 146, Döhn, p. 158, Stegmann, "Faschismus," p. 31, Weisbrod, p. 444. Kastl to Hilferding and Umbreit's remarks in HKB/Vorstandssitzungen ADGB/ NB 3, 14 Jan. 1931. For a less sanguine view of these negotiations, along with the official ADGB and RDI statements, see *Jahrbuch des ADGB, 1929* (Berlin, 1930), pp. 229–34, where the split within the ranks of industry is also emphasized.

112. RDI executive committee member Hans Kraemer, 1 Mar. 1931, in HA GHH/ Nachlass Reusch 400 101 24/2.

113. Udo Wengst, "Unternehmerverbände und Gewerkschaften in Deutschland im Jahre 1930," *Vierteljahrshefte für Zeitgeschichte* 25 (1977):103–4. In his attempt to demonstrate the wide-openness and open-mindedness of these discussions, Wengst proves almost the opposite: whatever concessions the industrialists could obtain by mutual agreement, they accept; the rest they would squeeze. By accepting the spirit of compromise, the liberal industrialists convinced some union leaders to make sacrifices while, by refusing even to consider concessions and by withholding cooperation from those ready to compromise, the more militant, national industrialists intensified the pressure. Representatives of heavy industry demanded union renunciation of binding arbitration as one prerequisite for joining the talks even though the Oeynhausen arbitration decision of June 1930 inaugurated a series of rulings favorable to the employers. This turn of events strengthened their cause and their resolve.

While the dynamic fraction continued to see limited compromise with the unions as the best way to depoliticize labor and facilitate joint economic planning, the heavy-industry fraction called for out and out defeat of organized labor first, then negotiation: "The unions are still too strong now [June 1930] . . . for negotiations. . . . first individual battles, like those now imminent, must be fought and blows delivered. . . . Only then will there be a situation in which the workers become disenchanted with their [political and union] leaders."[114] The synthesis of these two approaches was bitter confrontation in all contract, labor-market, and legislative matters, and cooperation in discussing the most general social, agricultural, and trade matters. Under whichever format, however, the deteriorating economic situation would ensure that the bulk of the concessions in matters of wages, prices, public expenditures, and state intervention came from labor. By the end of 1930, for example, industry's representatives no longer felt they had to acknowledge the principle of maintaining social insurance.

At the behest of the Zentrum, the Christian Unions seemed prepared to accept a new Burgfrieden, but the ADGB general assembly rejected the recommendation of its leadership and voted to break off further discussions in January 1931.[115] Following its own politics of the lesser evil, the ADGB leadership had urged a new Burgfrieden because "in the current highly adverse situation the entrepreneurs hold all economic power in their hands . . . the chief weapon of union struggle [the strike] is totally blunted. . . . The fall of Brüning would mean an administrative government [Beamtenkabinett] and finally a dictatorial regime directed against us." In light of general economic and political conditions, Tarnow considered employer agreement to accept and maintain the wage contract a great success. "A Burgfrieden will not hurt us in this situation." He considered it better to make voluntary concessions than have wages lowered by state decree.[116] In rejecting this plea, the assembly delegates demonstrated an economism both more militant and narrower than even that of their leadership. The ADGB leadership had become more political since the debacle surrounding the fall of the Grand Coalition, but it did not convert the rank and file. A representa-

114. Discussion at the joint RDI–Employers' League meetings of 13 June 1930; cited in Wengst, p. 107, and HA GHH/Nachlass Reusch 400 101 293/10b. The quotation is from a Silesian industrialist, Konrad Piatscheck; the moderates warned him that such tactics would only radicalize the workers and strengthen the communists.

115. Wengst, pp. 112–15; and Jahrbuch des ADGB, 1930 (Berlin, 1931), pp. 96–100.

116. Tarnow and Peter Grassmann at the ADGB Congress of 15 Dec. 1930, cited in Wengst, pp. 113–14. Grassmann's prescience about what would follow Brüning did not help in avoiding it. Schneider argues that this led the ADGB leadership to draw away from the SPD, Arbeitsbeschaffungsprogramm, pp. 157–65. This distancing continued throughout 1932. See HKB/Vorstandssitzungen ADGB/NB 5.

tive of the construction workers put the matter revealingly and succinctly: "Acceptance of this arrangement would mean the abandonment of all previous union victories. . . . The unions have much too often subordinated their special trade [*beruflichen*] interests to a general state-political interest. Our responsibility in that regard must end when the interests of our own organizations are at stake."[117] Thus collapsed the attempt to create a systematic, corporatist structure for renegotiation of economic relations between wage labor and capital. It was supported, to varying degrees, by Brüning and Stegerwald, representatives of the dynamic fraction of industry, and much of the ADGB leadership. It was laid to rest by heavy industry and the union rank and file.[118] Several feeble attempts thereafter to revive joint negotiations failed.[119]

Following the SPD's electoral losses in September 1930 (about 5 percent) and their own membership losses, the unions adopted a more generous attitude toward the Brüning government. Despite his government by emergency decree, they considered Brüning as operating "in the spirit of the Constitution," and thereby as "its protector," as working to prevent economic and political collapse, and as the last bulwark against National Socialism.[120] The unions in 1931 outdid the SPD in support of Brüning and perceived correctly, as did heavy industry, that union backing of Brüning operated to take the teeth out of more than one emergency decree; a weakened, tacit form of the labor-export coalition still loomed in the background. Abandoning the now hopeless

117. Cited by Wengst, p. 114. In defense of the assembly delegates, it should be remembered that the fruit of labor's previous participation in the ZAG had been bitter indeed; the resulting distrust weighed heavily on the rank and file and middle-level leadership—along with economism.

118. Recapitulated for Stegerwald and forwarded by the Employers' League, 3 Feb. 1931; cited in BA/Nachlass Silverberg/458. This was another instance of overlapping conflicts between and within classes. Along with the uncertainty after the election of September 1930 and the near-cessation of foreign credit flows, the dynamic fraction's anxiety over the aggressiveness of agriculture and heavy industry made some compromises with organized labor desirable and possible. In September 1931 Brüning blamed heavy industry for rejecting cooperation with the unions; ZSA/RLB Pressarchiv 148/10, p. 44.

119. Thus, one ADGB board member remarked later in 1931 that the export industries, such as chemicals, "are still faring quite well" and "have absolutely no grounds for wage cutting"; HKB/Vorstandssitzungen ADGB/NB 3, 4 Feb. 1931. In January 1932 Leipart wrote Frieda Wunderlich that he had received feelers from Hans Bechly and Abraham Frowein (both identified with the dynamic fraction), but that until he heard from representatives of those now dominant within industry, he could not take any overtures seriously. Leipart closed by adding that "no one can regret more than I do the alienation between the employers and the unions that the former have brought about." DGB/ADGB Vorstandskorrespondenz/18, 13 Jan. 1932.

120. Statements in the *Gewerkschaftszeitung* cited by Hüllbüsch, "Gewerkschaften," p. 149.

question of unemployment insurance and the worthless question of state arbitration, the ADGB in 1931 turned to proposing inflationary and countercyclical work-creation programs, the 40-hour week, and civilian public works in particular. Even before these proposals evolved into the full-blown WTB program, with which Schleicher and Gereke were later to toy, they collided with the basic premises of Brüning's economic program—deflation and a balanced budget.[121] And it was only the rural elite which succeeded, with help from Hindenburg, in altering that aspect of Brüning's course.[122]

Labor's call for active, countercyclical state intervention was basically an atheoretical attempt to create jobs through and in the public sector: Sozialpolitik *as* Wirtschaftspolitik, high wages to increase consumption and thereby production, shorter work hours to create jobs, fiscal manipulation to flatten cyclical changes. That this later emerged, under very different political conditions, as the capitalist wave of the future is probably not something for which the unions ought to be blamed, even if the SPD did reject the WTB Plan as unacceptable in principle, as nonpolitical demagogy. Even for Hilferding, "organized capitalism" had been more a description of the present than a prescription for the future.[123] (A program such as this bore considerable resemblance to what was being said on the Nazi left, and later there were contacts with Gregor Strasser.) Countercyclical state intervention was, in the ADGB's view, "a prerequisite for any real future capability to thwart and counteract the unemployment which our economy [capitalism, the market?] produces. In the future it will have to be the task of the state not only to counteract unemployment with social measures but rather to apply all forces to foster a positive, constructive organization of the economy."[124]

But if the SPD's view of the economic crisis was either orthodox or abstentionist while the ADGB sought to be a certain type of "doctor at the sickbed of capitalism,"[125] neither was in a position to affect the

121. On the emergence of the WTB program, Schneider, *Arbeitsbeschaffungs-programm*, pp. 61–89; on its incompatibility with Brüning's deflationary course, ibid., pp. 167–92; Jochmann, pp. 102–4.

122. In summary, Kopps, pp. 853, 864; Vogt; Bracher, pp. 511ff. The ADGB was simply unable to dissuade Brüning from his deflationary theories. They did not help themselves by conceding a "certain primacy of foreign policy," i.e., reparations revision, since German austerity was essential for revision.

123. See Winkler and Wehler in Winkler, ed., *Organisierter Kapitalismus*, pp. 13, 50–51; Gates, pp. 219, 223.

124. Rudolf Legersdorf and Fritz Tarnow at the ADGB Congress of April 1932, cited in Hüllbüsch, "Gewerkschaften," p. 152.

125. Cf. Gates, p. 220; Schneider, "Vorstellungen," pp. 228–34; Woytinsky, *Stormy Passage,* passim; Sidney Pollard, "The Trade Unions and the Depression," in Mommsen, et al., eds., pp. 246–48.

policies either industry or the Papen government would pursue. Responding to the presentation of the WTB Program, industry spokesmen argued that "not capitalism is at fault for our situation, but rather the decade-long attack against its fundamentals." Reflecting both the new balance of forces within industry and industry's abandonment of Brüning, Gustav Krupp, Duisberg's successor as RDI chairman, joined the attack on the ADGB's proposals, writing that further wage reductions were needed, not inflated wages; elimination of the insurance principle in the event of unemployment was needed, not universalization of that principle. The free play of supply and demand, in which the cartels played a positive function, was to be encouraged, and even the illusion of state works programs was to be avoided.[126] The ADGB Congress of April 1932 was the occasion for a massive industry propaganda attack on the unions, who were held accountable "for the undermining of the free economic system and its internal harmonic from 1918 on to the present day." The SPD and unions were held "responsible for making the development of the private-enterprise system impossible." The industrialists concluded their attack by claiming that, "if production levels are down to turn-of-the-century levels, then public and social expenditures should be too."[127] It was precisely such a policy that the dominant classes expected from Papen's so-called "New State" and "organic rebuilding of the economy" in the second half of 1932.

Whereas Papen, unlike Brüning, was prepared to take adequate and wholehearted economic and political measures against organized labor, his ascension exacerbated the conflicts among the dominant class fractions themselves, particularly those between autarkists and exporters. There was, however, no longer any question of retaining the organized working class as a base of mass support for the dominant classes and the state. To demonstrate the economic side of this, we need to review briefly some of the economic and social measures taken by the Brüning and Papen governments. The fiscal, credit, reparations, unemployment, and world economic crises all presented themselves as one bundle necessitating a unified and coherent approach not easily evolved in the political context of the Republic. From the time of his first emergency decree in June 1930, Brüning's strategy could be summarized as "deflation"; one he pursued in myriad ways. Through Hindenburg, he decreed higher worker contributions to the insurance funds while reducing the amount and duration of benefits; he decreed higher wage, head, bachelor, beer, tobacco, and other consumption taxes, but lower wages and

126. Krupp and Kastl in the *Vossische Zeitung* of 20 Feb. 1932.
127. An RDI article of 13 Apr. 1932, in ZSA/RLB Pressarchiv 148/10, pp. 74–75. This was only a vulgar form of the (still-alive) argument that the proportionate shares of the economic pie are somehow fixed; only the pie as a whole can expand or contract.

taxes on capital; he ordered a shorter work week and lower civil-service salaries, state spending, housing subsidies, and cartel prices; and he pursued an active policy to revise reparations while encouraging German exports.

None of this seemed to work to anyone's lasting satisfaction, while at the same time his authoritarian style of government discredited Parliament, and his brutal deflationary policies deprived much of the population of any hope for improvement within the system.[128] His determination to balance the budget was a particularly hard blow to lower-income groups of all classes. In December 1931 all wages were officially reduced to their levels of January 1927, regardless of existing collective agreements.[129] Prices, however, were not so easily altered by fiat as wages; Brüning's decree of a 10 percent reduction in cartel prices infuriated industrialists without securing full adherence, and industrial prices, like the cost of living, declined only about 10 percent between 1929 and the end of 1931 so that the price-to-wage ratio began rising again in late 1931.[130] The bank crashes of 1931, the end to foreign credits, the decline of exports in response to the spread of the world-trade crisis and agricultural protectionism, and Brüning's continued deflationary strategy led to further cutbacks in production and increased unemployment. By the time Brüning was ousted from office, half of Germany's union members were unemployed. Industrialists accepted production cutbacks and deflation and generally rejected countercyclical and inflationary proposals because of their overriding desire to lower wages and discipline organized labor. In a larger sense, too, they had, with few exceptions, consistently called for a "return to capitalism,"[131] and they expected the classical economic self-healing mechanism to work—especially if the dual burden of Sozialpolitik and reparations could be lifted.[132]

Papen began his labor program by proposing further wage reductions

128. These points are summarized, somewhat tendentiously, by Clemenz, p. 202. At the onset of all this, Stegerwald estimated that a 10–15 percent decline in the standard of living would be unavoidable. Details on the emergency decrees in Preller, pp. 396–97, who also provides a blow-by-blow account of the dismantling of Sozialpolitik, pp. 399–495.

129. See Bry, p. 43.

130. See tables 3 and 27 and chap. 4, sec. 3, above.

131. It is, of course, ironic, if not accidental, that most industrialists, for the half-dozen or so years following the inflation, subscribed to the virtues of free-market capitalism (which certainly did not exist in Germany) but then, after 1930, increasingly turned to authoritarian models that promised to guarantee success. See Krohn, in Stegmann, ed., pp. 113–29, and the discussion of "work creation" in chap. 3, above.

132. Cf. Grotkopp, pp. 24–26. Treue, in Conze and Raupach, eds., pp. 117–21, portrays German industrialists as having been more naive than they could possibly have been.

of from 20 to 50 percent and formulating other policies to facilitate capital circulation and accumulation. In an attempt to mobilize support within the reticent liberal fraction of industry, he described his regime as "the last real opportunity for the private-enterprise system." He set about to abolish what remained of the unemployment and social insurance systems, replacing them with the simple, in-kind dole to be provided by already overburdened municipal governments. Unemployment insurance was reduced to a maximum benefit period of six weeks, and a novel "neediness investigation" was introduced. Numerous burdens were transferred to local governments, which were then punished for their alleged mismanagement: many municipal governments were still SPD-dominated, and so there occurred numerous small-scale Prussia Putsches.[133] The various social insurance funds also lost their rights to administrative autonomy. A presidential decree of September 1932 provided industry with substantial general tax credits and allowed for payment of wages at below contract rates for new employees and "in case of need." Under Brüning, the ability of the SPD and unions to influence policy had slowly been lessened to the advantage of the industrial and employers' organizations; the unions had even been constrained to collaborate in wage reductions and other anti-*sozial* measures. Under Papen, the growing influence of the ministerial bureaucracy was joined to the central leadership of industrial and agrarian organizations so that the influence of the latter became wholly transparent. Wage and contract matters were to be shifted from the Labor to the Economics Ministry and Sozialpolitik reduced to a pure epiphenomenon of free-market considerations.[134]

During his two-month tenure, Schleicher may have been attempting to reverse this two-year-old development. Indeed, we have observed elsewhere that there were definite indications to this effect. Schleicher intervened to cancel wage cuts decreed by the Papen regime; he negotiated with Leipart and others from the ADGB on public-works programs initiated by his minister for work creation, Gunther Gereke; and Schleicher even began to win the grudging support of Severing and others in the SPD itself.[135] For whatever reasons Schleicher may have

133. Bracher, p. 501, emphasizes the linkage between attacking Prussia, narrowing the competences of the Länder generally, and attacking the SPD.

134. Preller, p. 521. The ministerial bureaucracy recommended a complete suspension of unemployment insurance "without bias" as to its eventual status, but representatives of heavy industry insisted that the insurance principle be replaced formally by a welfare-relief principle. (The German for "welfare" or "relief," *Fürsorge,* is even more pejorative than the English.)

135. Leipart's attitude toward the SPD cooled throughout 1932, and in late November he announced rather Delphically that "the unions evaluate every government on the basis of its deeds vis-à-vis the labor movement. . . . A basic hostility toward any and every

sought to return the unions, and perhaps even the SPD, to an active policy-making position, his efforts barely got under way before he was ousted from, and Hitler elevated to, the chancellorship of Germany.

What had begun as a conflict over distributing the costs of reparations and a worsening economic situation became a struggle over the very principles of a democratic Sozialpolitik[136] embodied in the class compromises of 1919 and 1925–29 and embedded in the Weimar Constitution itself. Without control over how those who owned the means of production could dispose of their possessions, the unions were left vulnerable to changes in the overall economic situation, and their success was at least as much conjunctural as structural.[137] The growth of the reserve army of the unemployed could and did partially negate the effects of years of legislation; yet the unions and SPD remained strong enough to ensure that the overall economic crisis would be a profit crisis as well. German workers continued to be the best off in Europe. The economic conflict between labor and capital was politicized by the offensive of the latter, and the SPD could develop no adequate counter-strategy: defense of short-run economic interests and support of the lesser evil deprived the party of any real initiative.

The striking passivity of the non-Communist organizations of the working class toward the end of the Republic resulted from their earlier inability to develop a strategy for achieving labor's social and political demands through reliance on mass activism. The reliance on the state, as in compulsory binding arbitration, and on state-sanctioned bargains among peak organizations proved inadequate. Neither Wirtschaftsdemokratie (during prosperity) nor the WTB Plan (during adversity) could provide a rallying point for popular energies. These plans conceived of social and economic conflicts as being resolved at the top, or from the top down, in the course of capitalist development. Both were *production*-oriented and treated the question of *control* only secondarily. Socialist labor's consistent emphasis on underconsumption analyses of

---

presidial government is of dubious value. Opposition at any price would mean a voluntary surrender of our influence." HKB/Vorstandssitzungen ADGB/NB 5, 29 Nov. 1932. See also, Breitman, pp. 360, 363–70. Leipart's readiness to work with Schleicher and Gereke was made explicit in the *Gewerkschaftszeitung* of 31 Dec. 1932; cf. Grotkopp, pp. 75ff., Schneider, *Arbeitsbeschaffungsprogramm*, pp. 192–202.

136. Preller, p. 525, postulates an inherent contradiction between a democratic Sozialpolitik and a private Wirtschaftspolitik in which the state was the only conceivable mediator, primarily through the agency of binding arbitration. Even Preller seems to suffer from that German penchant for seeing/wanting a class-neutral or class-balanced state. Cf. Hartwich, pp. 373–84.

137. Wirtschaftsdemokratie was intended, at least by some of its supporters, to create structures to insulate organized labor against changes in the economic situation and to constrain the freedom of at least some of the owners of the means of production.

capitalism—inadequate Kaufkraft—left the rank-and-file membership with little to do during an economic crisis. Worse, once the pluralist-democracy, class-compromise model broke down, SPD and ADGB leaders were virtually helpless: during the massive crises of July 1932 (Papen coup, Nazi victories and violence), all they could do was appeal to the workers to vote SPD. Earlier, in March 1931, the ADGB Vorstand had rejected a set of twelve rather progressive economic proposals recommended by Reichsbanner leader Hörsing because, according to the Vorstand, they were "too strongly political and agitational." When Hörsing responded that this was precisely what was needed, Tarnow countered that for the terrain of the unions to be thus preempted by the Reichsbanner "implies that we [the ADGB leaders] have failed in our responsibilities." And yet, though he rejected such an insinuation, less than a week later Tarnow admitted that he saw "no way out of this total misery." Both Brüning and anyone who might replace him were "intolerable"; still, the SPD should not seek power because "the unavoidable tough decisions" would necessarily "lead to mass radicalization," and it was better that Brüning bear the onus.[138] The fear of mass radicalism and of a showdown with the right is transparent.

Subsequently, this class conflict emerged as a key element in a larger political struggle over the form of state itself. It was not by chance that the last parliamentary government collapsed over a central issue of Sozialpolitik, and that the political influence of the dominant classes, if not of the bourgeois political parties, grew steadily thereafter. Grew, that is, within the limits set by their own internal conflicts. Our understanding of the interest conflicts that impeded the formation of a stable consensus among the dominant class fractions and a coherent economic and political program for which they could all stand would be incomplete without an appreciation of the unifying (and sometimes divisive) role played by the organized working class.

138. HKB/Vorstandssitzungen ADGB/NB 3, 9 and 13 Mar., 17 June 1931.

Chapter Six

IN SEARCH OF A VIABLE BLOC

1. Organized Capitalism, Fragmented Bourgeois Politics, and Extrasystemic Solutions

At several points we have noted the three sets of factors facilitating the development of organized capitalism in Germany: the lateness of industrialization and the commensurately increased role of the state even during the abbreviated period of competitive capitalism; the absence of a bourgeois revolution and the continued power of an originally pre-capitalist agrarian elite which "feudalized" the bourgeoisie in the course of a "passive revolution"; and the continued weakness of parliamentary tendencies in both Prussia and the Reich.[1] Through the mediation of a number of "development tendencies," these factors went on to become part of what H.J. Puhle has labeled the "prehistory of fascism." Among those were the privileged access of the estate owners to an "intervention-oriented" executive and an accompanying tendency toward corporate-vocational organization and integration of the Mittelstand—both at the expense of parliamentarism. Beginning in the last quarter of the nineteenth century, the estate owners and heavy industry embarked on a joint course of protectionism which, with the support of the imperial state, facilitated a political alliance and ideological consensus among the owning classes. The rapid growth of the SPD and the workers' movement in general strengthened that Sammlung and added a bitter antisocialism (literally, "hatred of the working class") to the already articulated antiliberalism and anti-Semitism. The resulting Darwinian, imperialist ideology of völkisch nationalism proved to be a successful ingredient in the manipulation of the middle classes and the

---

1. On the stigmata of late industrialization, see the literature cited in chapter 1, note 27, and chap. 1, sec. 1; David Landes, *The Unbound Prometheus* (Cambridge, 1959), pp. 231ff. On the absence of a bourgeois revolution and its implications for the "passive revolution," Gramsci, pp. 59–60, 106–20; Dahrendorf, passim; Moore, pp. 443ff.; and Bendix, p. 40. On the continued weakness of parliamentary tendencies, Krieger, pp. 426–70, and the whole range of Bismarck and post-Bismarck literature by Wehler and Stegmann, as well as that cited by Puhle, *Agrarbewegungen,* pp. 285–86.

denigration of parliamentarism in favor of the "strong state."[2] All this was, of course, a fundament of the prewar Sammlung, and during the Weimar Republic it remained both a latent possibility for and an avowed goal of some representatives of the dominant social classes. Nevertheless, organized capitalism and fascist "prehistory" by themselves did not dictate that no way would be found to organize support for the Republic through a range of political parties.

The class and fraction coalitions described in preceding chapters demonstrated that there was at least one alternative to the Sammlung bloc for organizing mass support. Indeed, that alternative (Bloc 3, see fig. 3) was the basis for relative stability between 1925 and 1930.[3] However, the conflicts within and between the dominant economic classes and the costs exacted by the subordinate classes, primarily the organized working class, rendered that stability tenuous and, after 1930, beyond Germany's means. As we have shown, the unwillingness of organized labor to make far-reaching economic concessions[4] and the determination of both fractions of industry to restore the domestic preconditions for renewed profitability made stability based on the working class increasingly unfeasible. Yet, after the fall of the Grand Coalition, no viable republican political formula or plausible grouping existed to stitch together a coherent economic and national program.

The difficulty in constituting any viable grouping is demonstrated in table 35, which arrays the divergence of sentiment and policy among key social groups and collective actors with regard to a number of crucial political and economic issues. The fragmentation this array reveals was a central factor in the weakness of all Weimer coalitions or blocs, and it affected the potential alliances of both social strata and political parties.[5] The positions ascribed here to the respective actors correspond to no specific date but do reflect our discussion in the preceding chapters. The table also underscores the difficulty of establishing any popular-based alternative to the Grand Coalition within the Weimar framework. A system and set of circumstances that institutionalized the conflict between organized labor and capital as the central axis of politics while at the same time aggravating tensions within the ranks of capital found it exceedingly difficult to aggregate the various broad Mittelstand strata.[6] And the cost of labor's support for

2. Puhle, *Agrarbewegungen,* pp. 103–4.

3. See chap. 1 above, esp. secs. 2–3.

4. This unwillingness characterized the social-liberal as well as the structural-reformist wing of the party. See Sturmthal, pp. 35ff., Laclau, pp. 125ff., and the discussion in chapter 5 above.

5. See chap. 1, sec. 2 above, where the blocs and critical issues are presented.

6. As we shall see below, the failure of the bourgeois and conservative parties, like the subsequent success of the NSDAP, demonstrated that simple antisocialism was no longer enough.

the Weimar capitalist democracy proved excessive. Already in 1929 the RDI stepped up its attack on organized labor's wage exactions, overly generous Sozialpolitik, high levels of public spending, and the attendant fiscal crisis, and by March 1930 the Grand Coalition and the formal labor-export coalition collapsed.

Weimar Germany after 1923 had been a capitalist democracy: after 1930 the SPD's and the ADGB's defense of labor's economic gains undermined the profitability of production and the process of capitalist accumulation; capital "responded" by undermining the democratic political structure on the basis of which those and future gains were possible.[7] No longer were conflicts about short-term distribution questions; the question of production itself was at issue. Whether the possibility of socialist production was or was not "on the agenda" is not central; what is crucial is that capitalists found that their profits were being confiscated—by foreigners through reparations and, more importantly, by organized labor through wage contracts, Sozialpolitik, and certain mechanisms operating through the democratic state. In effect, industrialists argued that minimally necessary profits were unavailable

TABLE 35

The Fragmentation of Group Interests: Array of Stances on Central Issues

Policies	Organized Labor	Dynamic Industry	Heavy Industry	Urban Mittelstand (a)	Urban Mittelstand (b)	Family Peasants	Estate Owners
Sozialpolitik expansion	+	+/−	−	−	+	−	−
Handelspolitik expansion	+	+	+/−	+/−	+	+/−	−
Reparations fulfillment	+	+	+/−	+/−	+/−	−	−
Accumulation fostering	−	+	+	+	+/−	+	+
Democracy expansion	+	+/−	−	−	+	−	−

NOTE: (a) Petit bourgeois strata; (b) salaried-employee strata. We need to know more about the attitudes of the Mittelstand on these and other critical questions. + indicates support, − indicates opposition, +/− indicates either ambivalence or a split within the group.

7. The capitalism/democracy dynamic of capitalist democracies is explored in a powerful essay by Adam Przeworski, "Toward a Theory of Capitalist Democracy," *Political Power and Social Theory* 1 (1980):21–66. The discussion here is illuminated by Przeworski's analysis of profit, wage, and economic crises and their possible political consequences.

for three reasons: the world economic crisis, which decreased the size of the total product or pie; the pressure of reparations payments which, they contended, was borne primarily by capital; and the profit and fiscal crises caused by the policies of the labor-export coalition of 1925–30.[8] As we noted in some detail in chapter 1, popular and electoral support for governments are conditioned by actions of private capitalists; actions which, in a parliamentary-capitalist state, lie beyond the reach of direct political intervention in the arena of private appropriation and investment.[9] Further, as the Hilferding-Wissell dilemma demonstrated in all its sharpness, the state's resources and the ways in which they can be employed depend on revenues derived, regardless of the tax structure, from the *accumulation* process, *not* from the *electoral* process.

The Hilferding-Wissell-Severing dilemma was but a microcosm of the SPD and reformist dilemma: once the economic pie ceases to expand, capitalists and the process of private appropriation will undermine that "philistine welfare democracy which taxes away all private capital" (von Miquel), while its defenders are left without the means to defend their only asset and accomplishment, precisely because there is nothing left to tax away.[10] In a stable capitalist democracy, one could then expect voter desertion, the electoral defeat of the reformist socialist party and a new round of capital accumulation to expand investment and production. But, applied to Weimar Germany with its very strong and mutually antagonistic reformist and communist parties, a fragmented bourgeois political opposition, and no unified or coherent leadership of the dominant economic classes—an internal stalemate—the outcome was a crisis marked by the rupturing of links between representatives and represented and a catastrophic equilibrium that opened the door to extrasystemic solutions.[11]

8. The SPD-led Grand Coalition of 1928–30 was the principal villain in this last area. Przeworski describes precisely the difficulties faced by Finance Minister Hilferding and the SPD: "*any* government in a capitalist society which decreases profits while retaining private property of the means of production runs the risk of undercutting its own fiscal base *and* its ability to tolerate future wage increases." As long as there is private appropriation there must be profits, and these are allocated by capitalists. Ibid., pp. 33–35; see also Varga. Hilferding watched the state coffers empty while his SPD colleagues at the Labor and Interior Ministries, Rudolf Wissell and Carl Severing, acceded to growing wage demands only with great anxieties over the consequences. As a temporary expedient, Hilferding borrowed over $50 million in the United States, and regressive consumption taxes were instituted to balance the budget and allow capitalists to keep paying higher wages.

9. See chap. 1, sec. 1; O'Connor, pp. 5–17, 179–211; Offe, passim.

10. Severing personally felt that the unions had pushed the iron and steel producers too hard, see BA/R13I-VDESI/217, p. 7, 22 Dec. 1928; Schneider, p. 81.

11. See Gramsci, pp. 219–23; Poulantzas, *Fascisme,* p. 106; Przeworski, "Capitalist Democracy," p. 36.

Of course, having the door open and letting Caesar/Bonaparte/Hitler in are two very distinct processes or acts; the collapse of the Republic and the Nazi assumption of power were by no means the same, even though many of the same actors appeared in both dramas.[12] That no stable ruling bloc could be organized under a democratic form of state did not, of itself, indicate that a fascist solution, whatever its nature, would follow.[13] But neither does recognition of the contingent nature of the Nazi victory mean that the problem of organizing support for the various dominant classes of Weimar society could be resolved within the existing framework of democratic politics. The conditions were present for a polarization of political conflict and its removal from the parliamentary theater, as well as for a possible capitalist-fascist alliance: (1) an economic crisis (exacerbated by both the collapse of world trade and reparations payments) in which the national product was insufficient to satisfy both labor's minimal wage demands and the minimally necessary level of profit; (2) a socialist (and a communist) movement, which showed no signs of backing away from costly and successful economic demands; (3) a mass authoritarian populism (especially within the petite bourgeoisie and peasantry), which could be organized and harnessed politically despite the absence of any substantial economic unity; and (4) a politically weak capitalist class frustrated with liberal institutions and prepared to support imperialist and anti-socialist movements in league with preindustrial, statist elites.[14]

The dominant economic classes and fractions did attempt, both before and after 1930, to organize their economic and political interests and ground them in a base of mass support. The Republic, however, proved to be a form of government which divided them, a form of state which highlighted the policy conflicts among the fractions and brought oppositions and competition to the fore. Certainly, it was not simply the nature of private appropriation which led Arthur Rosenberg to write

12. Kirchheimer, *Von Republik zum Faschismus,* pp. 64–76, 91–112; Löwenthal, "Die Wandlungen," pp. 1–22, 63–79; Schulz, passim; Czichon, pp. 24–56; and Stegmann, "Faschismus," esp. pp. 32–37, 44–53.

13. Or, more formally, neither the structure nor the operation of a system is indicated by its genesis. See Maurice Godelier, "Structure and Contradiction in *Capital,*" in *Ideology in Social Science,* ed. Robin Blackburn (New York, 1973), pp. 343, 362; Fritz Stern, ed., *The Path to Dictatorship, 1918–1933* (Garden City, 1966), p. xvii.

14. On the identification of economic crises, Przeworski, "Capitalist Democracy," p. 38; on the tenacity of organized labor's demands, chap. 5 above; Gates; Michael Schneider, "Konjunkturpolitischen Vorstellungen der Gewerkschaften in den letzten Jahren der Weimarer Republik," and Sidney Pollard, "The Trade Unions and the Depression," all in Mommsen, et al., eds., pp. 206–26, 226–37, and 237–48, respectively; on authoritarian populism, Winkler, esp. "Social Protectionism," pp. 1–18, and Geiger, "Panik"; on the capitalists' aversion to liberal institutions, Sigmund Neumann, Winkler, "Unternehmerverbände," and Dahrendorf, to cite but three entries in the field.

that "individual capitalist egoism makes 'national politics' impossible in Germany."[15] The very imperfect attempts to overcome those conflicts, in the countryside, within industry, and between agriculture and industry succeeded, after 1930 or 1931, in creating a united opposition to the organized working class but failed to provide a positive program. (The Nazis exploited this weakness.) What emerged was a stalemate, or a consensus only at the level of the lowest common denominator; there was no hegemonic fraction clearly setting the agenda and tone for the dominant classes as a whole. There was certainly a shift "rightward" after 1930: the formation of the rural Green Front and its activities, the integration of the AVI industries' demands by heavy industry, Stresemann's death and the departure of Curtius and Wirth, the changing balance among the industrial organizations, and the replacement of the RDI's dynamic leadership by one more closely affiliated with heavy industry all testify to this.

One can even equate this shift with a resumption of counterrevolution,[16] social and political, but this does not reveal why the links between representatives and represented broke and an extrasystemic solution became the most feasible. The dominant economic classes aligned with the Nazi party, but that coalition was not their first choice; they entered into it because other solutions, over which they would have had more direct control, did not work. We leave aside the question of how the Nazi party became as strong as it did: those who voted for or joined it did so primarily for reasons other than those which led to its successful assumption of power.[17] One should, however, note the political factors that seemed to accompany the sudden growth of the Nazi party beginning in mid-1929: the constant tension and hostility within the Grand Coalition cabinet, the accelerating attack on Sozialpolitik emanating especially from heavy industry, growing antiparliamentary agitation throughout the right, rightward changes in leadership of the bourgeois parties (DVP, DNVP, and even the Zentrum) and the industrial and agrarian organizations, and the reappearance of the reparations question. But, the question remains how the dominant social

15. *Geschichte,* p. 166.

16. See Mayer, *Counterrevolution.*

17. There is a substantial literature on both who voted for the Nazis and who joined the party. The following attempt to relate these matters to our concerns: Arthur Rosenberg, "Der Faschismus als Massenbewegung," and Otto Bauer, "Der Faschismus," both in *Faschismus und Kapitalismus,* ed. Wolfgang Abendroth (Frankfurt, 1967), esp. pp. 114–68; Moore, pp. 518ff.; Heberle; Lipset, pp. 131–52; Bracher, pp. 106–28, 170–74, 648–55; see also Milatz, and Vogel, et al., *Wahlen in Deutschland* (Berlin and New York, 1971). Despite the vast amount that has been written about Nazi electoral success, the electoral sociology of late Weimar Germany remains somewhat undeveloped. For new beginnings, see Childers, and Mason, pp. 42–98.

classes found themselves in a position where the Nazi party was the best choice they could make, despite the real risks of this alliance.

Could no bourgeois political force organize the political unity of the dominant economic fractions out the diversity and fractiousness of their economic interests? Was no political unity possible and no mass political support available within the Republic, despite the single-mindedness of the dominant classes' antisocialism? Were the maintenance of capitalist economic relations and political democracy so antithetical in *this* conjuncture that abandonment and undermining of the Republic were self-evident necessities for the dominant classes?[18] In a sense it is true that by 1932 few forces outside the SPD were concerned to defend the Republic, and, consequently, not much was needed to topple it. Since they were both demonstrably unable to organize mass support through the bourgeois parties and fearful of a possible socialist reparliamentarization, it is not surprising that industrialists finally turned to the Nazis. Neither was the behavior of the rural elite, military, or executive apparatus surprising. But scenario and cause are not identical:[19] what in the articulation of dominant interests led to the disintegration of the bourgeois parties and the rupture of links between representatives and represented; to the phenomenon of "parliamentary cretinism" and government by emergency decree; to the continuous narrowing of the locus of decision making in both corporate organizations and the state; and to the increasing frequency and futility of the key process in republican government—elections? In the preceding chapters we have analyzed the conflicts within and between the dominant classes and fractions and between capital and labor. Here we continue with an examination of attempts to formulate a political consensus among the dominant classes and to ground that consensus in some party-organized mass constituency.

2. Collapse of the Grand Coalition: End without a Beginning

The labor-export coalition of 1925–30 was contingent on both the preeminence of the dynamic fraction of industry *and* the ability of the

18. This last is the dominant view in East German historiography: cf. Fricke, ed., 2:602–14, and the literature cited there; Wolfgang Ruge and Kurt Gossweiler, eds., *Dokumente zur deutschen Geschichte, 1929–1933* (Berlin, 1975), pp. 11–16. A critique is offered by Iring Fetscher, "Critique of Soviet Marxist Analyses of Fascism," *Marx and Marxism* (New York, 1971), pp. 274–301.

19. Bracher comes close to contending that they are identical, but the richness of his own material forces him further. A more pointed example is Juan Linz, *The Breakdown of Democratic Politics* (Baltimore, 1978).

capitalist economy to afford the wage and social-welfare gains demanded by organized labor. Even during the period of the parliamentary Grand Coalition (June 1928–March 1930), the alliance was tenuous and its two prerequisites were constantly called into question. The Ruhr lockouts of 1928 signaled the objections of heavy industry to both aspects of the arrangement, and in the course of the next three years its view increasingly prevailed. The Grand Coalition collapsed over the twin issues of increased employers' contributions to the unemployment insurance fund and the state budgetary or fiscal crisis. As we have already shown, however, the economy's tolerance of labor's demands was limited even before the onset of the Depression.[20] The SPD's and ADGB's call for "economic democracy" (Wirtschaftsdemokratie) was viewed by industrialists as, at worst, a step on the road to socialism and, at best, a non sequitur: "democracy" was a political concept that could have nothing to do with economics and production. Articulated by the structural-reformist left of the SPD, the call acted as a red flag waved before industry; voiced by the liberal-integrationist unions, the call promised to raise yet another impediment to profitable production and capital accumulation. Few capitalists believed that labor was simply giving up the ghost of socialism free of charge. Theoreticians and leaders within both the SPD and ADGB thought (and hoped) that economic democracy would mark a substantial advance toward the transcendence of capitalism and class society.[21]

For its part, however, the RDI published its manifesto "Recovery or Collapse" and began its outright struggle with labor at the end of 1929. The Grand Coalition could have collapsed immediately after Stresemann's death two months earlier, but labor's support was still needed for ratification of the Young Plan against the opposition of organized agriculture and heavy industry. It was a measure of labor's economist success (and Germany's temporary weakness within the international capitalist order) that the class-collaboration bloc was brought down by a fiscal crisis of the state in conjunction with a political struggle to force employers to increase their contributions to the unemployment insurance fund.[22]

The bourgeois partners in the coalition, including the Zentrum, had

20. On the Ruhr lockouts, pp. 132f., 246–49 above; on the conflict over employers' contributions to the unemployment insurance fund and economic democracy, see Timm, pp. 124–39; on the mounting capitalist offensive, Liesbach, p. 73, Fricke, ed., 2:602–14, Schneider, *Unternehmer*, pp. 85ff., 156ff.

21. See the discussion of Wirtschaftsdemokratie and its implications for working-class politics, pp. 31, 224, 249–51, 269 above. The theoretical bases of such a transcendence are reviewed by Bernhard Blanke, *Kritik der Politischen Wissenschaften* (Frankfurt, 1975), pp. 162–68, as well as by Ulrich, pp. 19–46, and, more optimistically, by Klaus Novy, *Strategien der Sozialisierung* (Frankfurt, 1978), pp. 119–273.

22. The 1924 budget surplus of 880 million RM had turned into a deficit by 1927. In

demanded a general easing of taxes on capital and production and increased taxation of consumption, together with substantial cutbacks in state expenditures. They wanted first to get rid of Hilferding, whose tax-reform plans they considered wholly inadequate, then to reduce unemployment benefits, and finally to split the coalition and constitute a unified bourgeois bloc.[23] Their shared obsession with tax reduction mirrored the increased influence of their industrial and commercial wings and the commensurately lessened influence of their salaried-employee constituents. Several feeble attempts at compromise indicated that industry was no longer interested in pursuing the coalition; the SPD's readiness to raise all taxes in a "just" manner was deemed inadequate. Already in May 1929 the Zentrum had disciplined its worker wing and joined the DVP's call for "self-help" and denunciation of "Father State who provides all." Most of the SPD agreed with Rudolf Breitscheid that "the government's finance situation is not to be improved at the expense of the unemployed." On tax matters the SPD was willing to compromise (and even sacrifice the cabinet portfolio of its chief economic theoretician), but on the unemployment insurance question the majority of the Reichstag delegation and union leaders felt obliged to stand by the workers, not to abandon them to poverty for the sake of a parliamentary coalition.[24]

Indeed, precisely because the SPD had no program for changing the fundamental political and social relations of society on the basis of which it could call for economic sacrifices by the working class, the party had no choice but to defend the workers' short-run economic interests—even at the risk of inviting counterrevolution as Varga had predicted. Hilferding himself regretted the party's and unions' decision to reject Brüning's compromise proposal: "for the sake of thirty pfennings for the unemployed and the unions," he told Gustav Noske, the SPD abetted "the sacrifice of the republic and of democracy"—the only framework within which socialism could be achieved.[25] Indeed, with the fall of the Grand Coalition, government by presidential emergency

1929 there were already over three million unemployed. See Vogt, pp. 439–62; also, Spiller, pp. 593, 599.

23. This post–Young Plan offensive against the organized working class and its political representatives was described as a domestic or "internal Young Plan" by the KPD; see Weisbrod, pp. 457–76, and above, chap. 5, sec. 3. In late 1929, the leaders of heavy industry thought Kastl and the RDI leadership still too solicitous of Hilferding and the SPD. This division between the fractions of industry never fully disappeared.

24. Details and citations in Vogt, pp. 452–58; see also Timm, pp. 149–61, 178–90.

25. Most of the post-1945 SPD has shared this regretful (and too simple) view. Hilferding to Noske, cited in Timm, p. 160; Wissell's contrary view, p. 204. See also chap. 5, note 95, and p. 261, above. One would expect the SPD leaders (and historians) to have been more aware of the determination of most of the DVP and of heavy industry to cut loose from coalition with the SPD, using whatever opportunity presented itself.

decree did replace Parliament, and the SPD was forced to tolerate it, but had not the SPD been deprived of the initiative at a much earlier point? By 1930 the dominant social classes and bourgeois parties were simply seeking an excuse to resume the anti-democratic and anti-welfarist offensive, and one was almost as good as the next![26]

The complaints of the industrialists and the remedies implicit in those complaints indicated the direction policy would take under Brüning. Over a year later, after considerable retrenchment, Jakob Reichert of the VDESI could still write that "it is beyond the capacity of any economy to turn over almost all of its receipts to the treasury and to the victors [reparations] and at the same time to promote the welfare of all citizens." That was how to destroy an economy in which between 1913 and 1929 the national income had risen 55 percent while wages rose 130 percent, taxes over 400 percent, and social welfare costs over 500 percent.[27] Germany had become poor, but its politicians refused to act accordingly; political life had "reached a high point of fruitlessness." In July 1930 Brüning dissolved the troublesome Grand Coalition Parliament and enacted stalled and rejected legislation by presidential decree. He also called for new elections, which resulted in a huge Nazi success and further losses for the bourgeois parties. He could build no mass base to support the gradual implementation of his "compromise" program.[28] To his right, industry pushed for an attack on socialist dominance in Prussia, in general demanding, in Moldenhauer's words, "too much too soon and confusing the long-term goal with tomorrow's."

While the dominant fractions in industry and agriculture were establishing new internal balances and formulating new visions of the national interest,[29] Brüning tried to implement policies consonant with their general interests. But what were those general interests beyond the rollback of working-class gains in labor contracts and state spending; what appeals could elicit or build mass support? Paul Reusch hinted at both the general interest and the popular, national program he and his associates expected of Brüning:

26. Heavy industry and the right wing of the DVP accelerated the attack on the Grand Coalition after adoption of the Young Plan; see von Gilsa to Reusch, 5 Feb. 1930, HA GHH/Martin Blank 400 101 293/4a; Weisbrod, p. 472. The unemployment insurance question was simply one such pretext, and, at this level, Conze's case against the SPD ("Die politischen Entscheidungen in Deutschland 1929–1933," in Conze and Raupach, eds., p. 207) is weak indeed.

27. Reichert in BA/R13I-VDESI/226, p. 35, 4 Nov. 1931, and /232, p. 162. All of industry agreed that whatever relief the Young Plan afforded Germany should benefit private capital accumulation, not social programs and not the exchequer.

28. See tables 1 and 2 for the election results and possible coalitions.

29. On agriculture, chap. 2, sec. 4c; on industry, chap. 3, sec. 5.

The prescription for recovery is the same today as it was five or ten years ago! . . . Sacrifice and work: like old Prussia we either hunger ourselves to the top or remain subservient! . . . We have roughly the same savings as we had in 1895, and the state must return to the modest and simple principles of that time. . . . As a nation we must appreciate the internal and external threats which make this an emergency situation like a war. We must have unity . . . not only for the sake of the economy but also for the struggle against tribute payments and the Versailles [Diktat as a whole]. Our nation will make the needed sacrifices if it is promised reascendance. . . . Yet none of this can be accomplished as long as the political fragmentation of the middle class [Bürgertum] continues. . . . The parties have failed at this so completely that it has become the urgent patriotic duty of economic leaders [die Wirtschaft] to use all their influence to build a strong bloc of all those forces prepared to struggle for and on the basis of the existing economic order.[30]

This statement, and its allusions, pointed to the Sammlung bloc and national reassertion. What the parliamentary parties could not accomplish was now to be undertaken directly by the economic leaders of the nation. The Bürgerblock, which had not been forged by the bourgeois parties, and for which Brüning was acting as a surrogate, remained the political goal of the dominant classes. If such a bloc could be put together, then a quasi-parliamentary republic would remain possible. Otherwise, the choice could only be between some kind of dictatorship and power in the streets; the success or failure of Brüning's strategies would determine which.

3. The Failure of Brüning's Crisis Strategy

Initially, Brüning enjoyed the support of the dominant social classes, but this supported flagged in 1931. His orthodox, deflationary policies, like those of the other Western governments, failed to end the economic depression. Further, he was unable to free himself completely of the economic demands of organized labor, and he could not reconcile the divergent and fragmented interests of the dominant fractions. The brutal deflationary fiscal policies were also intended to demonstrate Germany's inability to pay reparations, and, hence, deflation sharpened international tensions. With the agrarians, Brüning believed that limiting agricultural imports might ruin the adjacent countries and encour-

30. HA GHH/Nachlass Reusch 400 101 221/5, draft speech, 3 June 1931.

age them to oppose the continuation of reparations.[31] With the exporters, Brüning saw the necessity to keep the healthiest branch of the economy going, and he opposed autarkic measures. There simply was no way to accommodate export and rural interests simultaneously, and, as we have indicated, Brüning was ultimately forced to break with the rural elite. As early as January 1931, the agrarians of the Green Front attacked Brüning in a manner that underscored the precariousness of his coalition and the conflicts between two dominant fractions: "Who is to blame for these catastrophic developments? The same circles of commercial and export-industry interests which, harnessed together with the Marxists, previously deprived the German nation of the means of defense. . . . The Brüning government is in hock to them and therefore responsible. It must divorce itself from these Marxist and philo-Marxist forces."[32] Despite its hostility, the rural elite was less victimized by the government's deflationary policies than any other sector: agriculture contributed only 5 to 7 percent to the state's resources, while over 4 billion RM were transferred to it from the rest of the economy.

Although Brüning decreed several wage reductions, the income levels of employed workers remained relatively high; in real terms, some even rose between 1929 and 1931.[33] And though it no longer tilted so clearly toward labor, the state compulsory arbitration mechanism still functioned—all to the great annoyance of heavy industry. Unemployed workers, however, were victimized by deflationary policies, and it was largely at their expense that the budget deficit was kept under control between 1930 and 1932 while unemployment doubled.[34] Reichsbank president Hans Luther impressed on Brüning that doling out welfare was cheaper and more judicious than creating jobs and would not revive the fear and danger of a new inflation. In general, Brüning's policies lacked coherence; so much compromise was necessary that consistency was virtually impossible.

31. This puzzled Agriculture Minister Dietrich, who responded by asking, "What do the United States and England care if Denmark and Holland go bankrupt? England will gladly take our place there as chief trade partner."

32. Green Front statement of 30 Jan. 1931. See also Koops, pp. 859, 862. Less than a month later, Agriculture Minister Schiele praised the Green Front for its "reasonable" and constructive position; BA/R43I/2546, p. 363. Many in heavy industry shared this analysis already, though in a less uncouth form.

33. In 1929 the index value of nominal wages was 169, that of real hourly rates 123; for 1931 the corresponding figures were 137 and 127. See table 3, and Bry, pp. 461–67, for the rise in wages; details, chap. 5, sec. 1.

34. The budget deficit in 1930–31 was 1.53 billion RM; in 1931–32 it was 1.69 billion. Between April 1930 and April 1932, unemployment rose from 2.8 to 5.7 millions, whereas unemployment insurance deficits increased from 443 to only 697 million RM; Koops, p. 866. On creating jobs versus doling out welfare, Koops, pp. 853, 857.

Brüning's residual commitment to constitutionality and his dependence on the SPD's toleration constrained him to provide heavy industry with less than it desired, while his deflationary economic policies prohibited the kind of fiscal, trade, and investment policies that might have stimulated at least the dynamic branches of industry. From the viewpoint of heavy industry, Brüning was from the outset "too slow, indecisive," and too "interested in having parliamentary majorities for his proposals." The results were unacceptable and "[inadequate] half-measures" and inaction on central problems, tantamount, according to Hjalmar Schacht, to "moving full speed into cold bolshevization . . . [and] the death of all private initiative."[35] Paul Reusch indicated more specifically what industry wanted in June 1931: in a speech entitled "Back to 1927," he argued that "the cost of living has declined substantially since 1929 but wages and salaries have not. They must both be returned to 1927 levels; it is socially justified. *In the case of public spending we need more than a return to 1927 levels;* we need a basic renunciation of state socialist economic and finance policies . . . *not only a strong check on expenditures, but a thorough limiting of the state's intervention.*"[36] Of course, 1927 was the year of labor's largest post-1919 gains in Sozialpolitik, and, as Reusch's audience surely knew, 1927 corresponded in most other respects to 1913. Reusch's call for laissez faire was certainly not favored by agriculture, and not even by all industrialists. Some of the advanced, dynamic industries were disappointed that Brüning adopted no countercyclical and trade-inspiring measures;[37] others, in heavy industry, were faring so badly that they simply looked for handouts.[38]

The one type of laissez faire on which they could all agree, however, was that of the *Herr im Hause*—the capitalist as master of work force and factory. In this vein, Georg Solmssen, board member of the Diskonto Bank, used the occasion of a public radio lecture to discuss this most critical aspect of the relationship between politics and economics:

35. The first verdict dates from 24 May 1930; the latter from 25 April 1931; HA GHH/ Martin Blank 400 101 202 4/6 and 8a, respectively. Schacht to Vögler, 21 July 1931, in Nachlass Reusch 400 101 290/33a; he, too, could be uncouth.

36. Reusch's speech of 3 June 1931 in HA GHH/Nachlass Reusch 400 101 221/11b.

37. Aside from facilitating the expansion of the profitable and opportunistic trade with the USSR ("Russengeschäfte," see table 28), the Brüning regime, as we have noted, undertook virtually nothing to create jobs or prime the economy; see Wolffsohn, pp. 75–77. In the first year of his government, exports nevertheless managed to hold their own, but then they also collapsed; see tables 20, 26.

38. Reusch cautioned Ernst Poensgen of the financially troubled United Steelworks against accepting state aid: "It would be a big mistake to ask the state for help . . . instead we should demand healthy economic policies enabling us to manage our businesses freely, independently, and uninfluenced by [state intervention]." HA GHH/ Nachlass Reusch 400 101 290/32, 25 Aug. 1931. This warning presaged the far more famous Friedrich Flick Gelsenkirchen affair.

"The intervention of the state in the determination of costs has been extremely detrimental. Wage rates are no longer the outcome of supply and demand and freely reached agreements between employer and employee; they are determined instead by state arbitration, and this development must lead and has led to steadily rising unemployment. . . . Rationalization has never been able to keep up, and there is no escaping the exponentially bad consequences unless that mechanism is dismantled."[39] Brüning could not do enough for industry to reverse this working-class achievement—state arbitration. Industry's own cartels, however, were another matter; they were sacrosanct because they were private, contractual arrangements. The government's arguments against their price rigidity and, finally, its decree of an across-the-board 10 percent price reduction brought howls of outrage. Brüning responded by telling a meeting of Christian unionists that heavy industry talked only of wage elasticity while rejecting any supervision of cartel pricing. Heavy industry had refused to cooperate with the unions in a program of cost reduction, while "Rhenish-Westphalian industry has for the past thirty years done nothing but cause every Reichschancellor grief."[40] As we shall see below, the Catholic Zentrum itself continued its move rightward and was by no means averse to corporatist and authoritarian schemes[41] (now with papal blessings), but Brüning would not be a simple instrument of industry or of capital.

Under direct pressure from agriculture and heavy industry, and in response to the changes in leadership and balance of power within the RDI, Brüning reshuffled his cabinet in October 1931. Dismissed were Foreign Minister Curtius (DVP) and Interior Minister Wirth (Z)—the two surviving staunchly republican representatives of the bourgeois parties and the last remaining links to the period of labor-export coalition. Neither their own parties not the corporate-interest organizations of the dominant social classes could tolerate their presence any longer. To shore up his declining viability, Brüning offered these and the Finance and Economics portfolios directly to leading industrialists. Albert Vögler, representing the heavy-industry right wing, declined because Brüning could not promise to make the new government sufficiently "dictatorial"; perhaps, too, he preferred to sink rather than save

39. Solmssen's "Der Kampf gegen die Krise," broadcast 10 Dec. 1930, is reprinted in *Beiträge zur Deutschen Politik und Wirtschaft*, p. 335. The post-Ruhr lockout revisions had clearly not gone far enough. Arbitration "created" unemployment.

40. Talk given on 24 Sept. 1931, cited in ZSA/RLB Pressarchiv 148/10, pp. 44, 37.

41. See Arthur Rosenberg, *Geschichte*, pp. 299–300. Rosenberg considers Stegerwald to have been particularly sympathetic to the idea of a dictatorship, along with the post-1928 party leader, Prelate Kaas.

the ship.[42] Paul Silverberg, representing the moderates and with links to both the dynamic and heavy-industry fractions, also refused the offer. He explained the grounds for his refusal to Krupp, the newly installed head of the RDI: Brüning no longer enjoyed the confidence or "even neutrality of western [heavy] industry" which considered him too "cautious, 'political' " to make the changes needed, even if he himself really wanted them, which was also not clear. "Unable to elicit any at all tangible or clear indication of intent," Silverberg told Brüning that "the general opinion was that up to now the government's policies have been decidely hostile to business." "I do not feel myself strong enough to be the only industrialist in the government"; he wanted Schmitz, Vögler and Warmbold to join him and that they "possess a sufficiently strong position in economic, finance, and welfare policies."[43] Silverberg seemed to realize the risks implied in so direct and personal an involvement of prominent industrialists qua industrialists in government: unless Brüning could guarantee them a political basis for their economic dictatorship, they could not appear as spokesmen for the national interest, but only as easily discredited representatives of special, selfish interests. Better to leave political decisions to the politicians, so long as those decisions were based on a correct understanding of national imperatives and could mobilize popular support while yielding at least minimally acceptable policy outcomes.

In light of the dismal 1930 electoral performance of the bourgeois parties,[44] Parliament could not be a suitable theater for the political expression of the will of the dominant classes. Brüning had eased this dilemma by removing policy making from the parliamentary arena, but policy outcomes remained unsatisfactory. The political unity of the dominant classes had still not been molded out of the diversity of their economic interests. At the start of the Brüning regime, Fritz Springorum had hoped for a change in this regard: "We are fragmented" and have no shared consciousness. "We must bring together our broadest circles" to fashion the expression of industry's political and economic needs. Needed was "a unified fashioning of our will"; in lieu of a single

42. BA/Nachlass Dingeldey/36, 13 June 1931; cf. Bracher, pp. 415ff. The president of the Hansa League accused Brüning of "simply administering the national distress rather than overcoming it"—in spite of which his organization expressed the hope that industrial leaders would accept Brüning's offer and work with him: BA/Z Sg 289/Hansa Bund. On the split within industry over support for Brüning, see chap. 3, sec. 5 above.

43. Letter of 12 Oct. 1931 in BA/Nachlass Silverberg/234, pp. 23–25. Brüning ultimately enlisted both Warmbold and Schmitz (of the dynamic fraction's IG Farben, see p. 156f. above), but Vögler's demands in particular were greater than Brüning could promise to meet.

44. See tables 1 and 2.

strong force there was only "horse-trading."[45] But none proved forth-coming. Yet if the Brüning government did not either broaden the base of the dominant classes or unify their interests, it did serve to limit the inputs of other social classes.

Contrary to the contentions of West German pro-Brüning histo-riography, a few political or economic figures expected (or wanted) his government to be the temporary dictatorship that saved the Republic. Except for the SPD and a few souls in the Zentrum, DDP, and DVP, Brüning's nonparliamentary government was a welcome first step in the deparliamentarization of political life.[46] Certainly very few rural pro-ducers, and few industrialists, manufacturers, or members of the petite bourgeoisie saw anything to be gained by a move back to parliamentary rule. Even a considerable number of union leaders came to think that their interests could be attended to by nonparliamentary governments (and hence their later cooperation with Schleicher). Deparliamentariza-tion would not resolve the conflicts within and between the dominant social classes, but it would facilitate their management. Chapters 2 and 3 analyzed how dominant classes and fractions attempted, through their own corporate-economic organs and with the assistance of state appa-ratuses, to resolve or at least transcend these conflicts, in the light of both changed economic and political circumstances and their own production requirements. Under parliamentary rule, the shifts and sta-lemates that resulted would have exacerbated rather than dampened conflicts. One of the leading newspapers close to heavy industry de-scribed the place of the Brüning regime rather trenchantly and crisply: "Brüning's political function can only be described, to borrow a phrase from Bismarck, as the 'precursor' or 'early fruit' [Vorfrucht] of a national dictatorship; i.e., it accustoms the nation to dictatorship and makes it possible for its successors to justify themselves by referring to their predecessors."[47]

45. Speech to the Langnamverein convention of 4 Apr. 1930, cited in ZSA/RLB Pressarchiv 132/11, p. 193.

46. Weisbrod, p. 500, suggests that it was, in fact, only the SPD which hoped Brüning would save the essentials of the Republic. The notion that deparliamentarization would facilitate the management of conflict was a tenet of the League for Renewal of the Reich and had already surfaced before 1928; see Stürmer, pp. 278ff. Brüning was repeatedly credited with removing Parliament from vital decision making—only not fast enough.

47. This interpretation of the function of the Brüning government was contained in the lead article of the Deutsche Allgemeine Zeitung of 4 Oct. 1931. It was much closer to the mark than the position Brüning himself and his historian advocates have argued: he simply ran out of time; he came close to saving the Republic. Had he succeeded, they argue, it would be perfectly logical to claim that a little bit of dictatorship saved the Republic when it was most threatened by extremists taking advantage of the Depression and national indignation. For this view see, for example, Brüning, "Ein Brief," Deutsche Rundschau, 1 July 1947, pp. 1–22; Ferdinand Hermens and Theodor Schieder, eds.,

It was especially in the realm of tax changes and rural aid that Brüning eased the transition to dictatorial "depoliticized" rule. The Osthilfe legislation, for example, was possible only in the absence of parliamentary debate. Quickly, however, this pattern spread to all policy areas: in 1930, parliament enacted ninety-eight laws, whereas five were implemented by emergency decree; in 1931 the legislature passed thirty-four laws, and the President decreed forty-four; by 1932 parliament could agree on only five, while Hindenburg ordered sixty-six into effect.[48] At a joint meeting of the RDI and Green Front in March 1930, Andreas Hermes called for the "removal [of agricultural matters] from the parliamentary scene." Representatives of the RDI responded that "that goes for the entire area of economic and finance policy. . . . The revulsion toward Parliament is general. . . . Their members fleeing them, the unions are desperately seeking to open contacts with industry."[49] This "depoliticization" was accompanied by the increased importance of "trained and neutral specialists," who frequently linked the corporate organizations of industry directly to the ministerial and military bureaucracies. Organizations like the long-somnolent Reichs Economic Council were suddenly touted as founts of wisdom, where employers, producers, workers, and consumers could cooperate as "estates." It was quite in vain that Carl Landauer of the liberal and insignificant DDP warned that, for the commonweal, "It would be a terrible loss to remove decision making from the public light of Parliament and have it placed in the twilight councils of the leading corporate-interest organizations [*Spitzenverbände*]."[50] The neutral and

---

Staat, Wirtschaft und Politik in der Weirmarer Republik (Berlin, 1967). This is the Festschrift for Brüning, and the essays it contains are largely designed to make the case for him. Also, in indirect form, Conze, "Entscheidungen," pp. 211–52, and his "Brüning als Reichskanzler: Eine Zwischenbilanz," *Historische Zeitschrift* 214 (1972):310–34.

48. Brüning's first use of presidential decree powers (article 48) was to implement the previously balked tax laws of 16 July 1930. Article 48, about which much has been written, had been used by Stresemann and President Ebert in 1923 against the communists and Bavarian separatists, but not for ongoing legislative purposes. On Brüning's use of it, see Werner Bratz, "Die agrarisch-industrielle Front 1930–1932," *Schmollers Jahrbuch* 91 (1971):545–69. Brüning admitted the impossibility of implementing rural legislation without article 48; BA/R43I/2426, p. 295, 10 Mar. 1931. Further apologetics for Brüning's use of article 48 in Ulrich Scheuner, "Die Anwendung des Artikel 48," in Hermens and Schieder, eds., esp. pp. 284–86. Basing himself on that destructive legalistic literalism, he manages to argue that abuse of the Weimar Constitution only began with Papen!

49. Meeting notes cited in HA GHH/Martin Blank 400 101 202 4/6. The goal was to get out from "under parliamentary bumbling."

50. On the Reichs Economic Council, Stegmann, "Zoll und Handelspolitik," p. 503; Landauer's warnings in the DDP's *Deutsche Volkswirt* 5 (23 Jan. 1931):541. On this stage generally, Bracher, pp. 377–97.

apolitical experts turned out, of course, to represent the interests of industry, the banks, the army, and the rural elite, and their economic program bore a striking resemblance to that proposed in the RDI's memorandum "Recovery or Collapse." Deparliamentarization clearly aided in shifting the burden of the crisis onto the subordinate classes; when that proved inadequate, Brüning was ousted and replaced by the "fully authoritarian" Papen government, with its "cabinet of experts" expertly representing heavy industry, the rural elite, and the military.[51]

The goals of the dominant social classes and their political representatives were impeded by their very legality, while their own interests were subject to the centrifugal forces of fragmentation and competition. Brüning was forced to limit his attacks on the "achievements of the revolution" by those very achievements: it was not by accident that Sozialpolitik was identified with parliament and the onerous "reign of the ballot." Other structures, similarly identified, also came under attack from "experts" as well as partisans. Whereas conservatives had previously been content to attack SPD domination in Prussia, after 1930 the dormant problem of the Reich/Prussia dualism was rediscovered. Similarly, the taxing and administrative privileges of local government were suddenly found to be "technically deficient and wasteful." During the imperial era, the integrity and prerogatives of both Junker-dominated Prussia and local government were, naturally, sacrosanct, but with the Republic both became major arenas of working-class success. After 1930 there were suddenly a host of reasons for dismantling or eliminating them. Well before Papen's July 1932 coup against the SPD government of Prussia, local taxing prerogatives had been severely curtailed, and the groundwork had been laid for emasculating, if not liquidating, Prussia.[52] The League for Renewal of the Reich was one of the pressure groups devoted to this cause. Together with proposing to alter federal/state relations at Prussia's expense, the Renewal League propounded a new bicameralism with one chamber filled by a mixture of occupational representatives and technocrats. Besides these, there

51. This is, of course, all very abbreviated; see Petzina, "Great Depression," pp. 65, 69; Carsten, *Reichswehr*, pp. 329–63; Bracher, pp. 415–23, 435–42, 511–28.

52. Because the DNVP, the descendants of the Junkers, remembered "their" Prussia, they opposed dismantling it. Their slogan was instead "Free Prussia from Marxism" and the "anti-Prussian dominance of Marxists, democrats, and Jews." The reactionary Bavarians opposed the attack on Prussia for precisely the opposite reason: they were (and remain) fully devoted to the federalist principle and local prerogatives. On the positions of the other parties and their evaluations, as well as on the details of Papen's coup, Bracher, pp. 559–99. In addition to the legislative and ideological aspects of SPD control in Prussia, there was the vital question of the Prussian police force which, after the Reichswehr, constituted the largest repressive agency in the country and yet lay under SPD administrative authority.

were recommendations for a higher voting age and sundry other franchise restrictions. The League was headed by former chancellor, DVP politician, and Reichsbank president Hans Luther; it was a favorite charity and pet project of several industrialists.[53]

Even after German capitalists had generally abandoned active counterrevolution in 1925 in favor of the Dawes Plan, American capital, and domestic stability, a leading steel industrialist could still remark that "Parliament seems unsuited for conscious and responsible consideration of the great issues facing the nation in this time of economic crisis." But the victors seemed intent that Parliament do so. It is not surprising, therefore, that concern with foreign reaction was later to be virtually the only qualm expressed by leading industrialists over the expanded use of presidential decrees for ordinary legislation. Thus, Paul Reusch was concerned to determine how government by Article 48 would affect Germany's credit standing abroad. Lacking the experience of our present-day corporate executives, he was perhaps surprised, but surely pleased, to be reassured that "decisive abroad is not how Germany now puts its financial affairs in order . . . so long as order is established" and maintained.[54] The flow of foreign credits—the mortgage on democracy—did come to a virtual halt in 1931, but not for political reasons.[55] Satisfied of this by November 1930, even the moderate Paul Silverberg urged Brüning to push ahead and "cease catering to the mass psychology of the electorate and the ballot. . . . and pay attention to the psychology of the entrepreneur . . . one of the pillars essential to the rebuilding of the Fatherland."[56] "Objectivity" was what was needed without party agitation. Silverberg and the dynamic fraction of industry thus encouraged a more aggressive policy at home together with a gradualist and conciliatory approach to reparations revision. This was another basis of their support for Brüning and opposition to the autarkists and ultras, like Hugenberg, Schacht, and Thyssen, who called for an immediate end to reparations payments. Because the former still participated viably in world trade, a position on

53. The activities and support of the Renewal League are discussed in Fricke, ed., 1:195–200. The Silverberg and Reusch Nachlässe are replete with favorably inclined memoranda.

54. The prominent 1925 steel industrialist in BA/R13I-VDESI/67, p. 5; Reusch's exchange with his Reichstag delegate, von Gilsa, 17 July 1930, in HA GHH/Nachlass Reusch 400 101 293/4b.

55. On the flow of foreign capital and the bank crisis, first in Austria, then in Germany, see Bettelheim, pp. 22ff., and Born, pp. 56–151. The bank collapses left the Deutsche Bank the only solvent major bank, and on both domestic and reparations questions it was closely connected to IG Farben and the dynamic fraction of industry generally.

56. BA/Nachlass Silverberg/274, pp. 106, 60. See also *Veröffentlichungen des RDI*, no. 55 (Dec. 1930), p. 28.

reparations more militant than Brüning's threatened to provoke economic catastrophe.

Agreement on methods was not enough, however. Although the dominant class fractions supported Brüning's presidential rule and some of the general consequences of that method of governing, they ultimately considered his measures inadequate in the areas of economic and social policy. Just as important, they could fashion no unity among themselves; they could formulate no unified, national program, and Brüning could not do it for them.[57] The state may not be able to unify a power bloc; it may not always be able to unify a bloc's interests, either under the protection of the hegemonic fraction (when there is one) or otherwise. As previous chapters have demonstrated, much impeded the coherent organization of the interests of the dominant classes. Just as these barriers weakened previous governments, they contributed to Brüning's failures and, finally, his fall in April 1932. Beyond that, however, his dictatorial methods were facilitated by a growing alienation between the representatives (the political parties) and the represented (the various fractions). Two years of Brüning's rule succeeded little in camouflaging the crisis of dominant social classes who could no longer organize mass support for themselves through the bourgeois and Mittelstandish parties. Although they did establish nearly complete control over the middle-class parties, that control proved worthless, because those parties were no longer of real electoral significance.[58] With its stable hold on over 15 percent of the electorate, Brüning's Catholic Zentrum (and BVP) assumed greater importance for any attempt to implement programs on behalf of the dominant classes. As long as there remained more than a façade of republican government, however, Brüning would ultimately prove an inadequate executor of capitalist interests. After all, throughout his tenure (and until July 1932) the SPD remained the nation's largest party, while the avowedly middle-class parties lay in shambles.

4. The Break Between Representatives and Represented

The decline of the bürgerliche parties, first into the service of particular interests and then into electoral insignificance, was, perhaps, the key symptom of the political crisis. Throughout the twenties, the non-Catholic bourgeois parties were weakened by their vulnerability to special interests. They reflected the fragmentation of economic and

57. See the discussion of these issues in chapter 3; Poulantzas, *Political Power*, p. 299.
58. See tables 1 and 2.

ideological interests within the dominant classes themselves, and only through Stresemann's leadership and the labor-export coalition was the particularism of those economic and ideological interests transcended for a brief period. When the changed conjuncture (and Stresemann's death) rendered that coalition too costly and no longer viable, the non-Catholic bourgeois parties floundered. What was to be their raison d'être? Whose particular interests would they represent and what agglomeration of voters would they mobilize? Which sectors of the urban electorate[59] would be amenable to new or substitute coalitions with the dominant classes, and what benefits would accrue to the allied and supporting classes?[60] Even after the collapse of the Grand Coalition in March 1930, groups in the dynamic-export fraction of industry and among salaried employees, i.e., groups opposed to the possible hegemony of heavy industry and the rural elite, continued to support Brüning and expected from him a tacit version of coalition with the organized working class, albeit under better terms. It was the possibility of such a continued, tacit coalition that fostered the SPD toleration of Brüning (whom the SPD could have brought down) for over a year and subjected the bourgeois parties to a barrage of conflicting pressures from their financial backers and electoral constituencies.[61] This was one reason that Brüning's government could be both semidictatorial and yet incapacitated. When the dynamic fraction of industry and salaried-employee groups also withdrew their support from Brüning, the rupture of the links between representatives and represented was completed, and the crisis moved into the advanced stage where real and formal power were decisively separate. In Gramsci's words, "conflicts between 'represented and representatives' reverberate out from the terrain of the parties (the party organizations [and] the parliamentary-electoral field . . .) throughout the State organism, reinforcing the relative power of the bureaucracy (civil and military), of high finance . . . and generally of all bodies relatively independent of the fluctuations of public opinion. . . . A 'crisis of authority' is spoken of: this is precisely the crisis of hegemony, or general crisis of the State."[62]

Well into the Weimar crisis, the interests of the dominant classes were represented by several parties, and in some respects by all of

59. Since the agricultural sector was never part of the labor-export coalition (Bloc 3), the end of that coalition produced less dislocation in the rural strategies of the various major and splinter parties, although the same rupture of links and crisis of representation did take place. The rural dynamic was discussed in chap. 2; on the parties and crisis in the countryside, see chap. 2, secs. 3 and 4.

60. See the schema of possible alternate blocs in chap. 1, figures 1–5; on how Bloc 3 provided stability, chap. 1, sec. 3.

61. Cf. Poulantzas, *Fascisme*, pp. 96, 105; chap. 3, secs. 4 and 5, above.

62. Gramsci, p. 210. See chap. 1, sec. 2, above.

them, regardless of the specifics of their platforms or electoral constituencies.[63] Vulnerability to particular interests plagued the bourgeois parties from the start of the Republic.[64] Until its decline in 1928, the DNVP was a successful conservative party based primarily, but not exclusively, in the countryside and on the rural elite in particular, although some of the most conservative industrialists supported it. We have shown in chapter 2 how, as the party came under the control of Hugenberg's extremists, several groups split from it to form narrow governmentalist conservative parties based on peasants and small property owners; it is noteworthy that some of these fared quite well in the elections of 1928 and 1930. Even more than the DNVP, the Zentrum remained, despite its changing politics, something of a Volkspartei—for Catholics. Despite its reputation as the party of commercial and small industrial interests, the DDP drew its support from a variety of liberal, big-city groups as well as from some dissident peasants. The DVP was considered *the* party of heavy industry and high finance, but it received important electoral support from salaried employees and the self-employed. Thus, like the economic and ideological desiderata and preferences of the dominant-class fractions themselves, the bourgeois parties remained fragmented and identified with specific interests—despite their having much in common.[65] It would seem, therefore, that each of the dominant fractions had "its" party, but that none, by itself, could provide an adequate base of electoral support. For historical reasons we have discussed, landowners were far better and more durably organized politically than industrialists, and this provided the rural sector with disproportionate weight in resolving most conflicts. In contrast, industrial interests were spread across several parties with cleavages mirroring economic competition, ideological divergences, historical inheritances, and the egoism of private interests. The industrialists had so many parties it was as if they had no party; this does not, however, seem to have been their intention.[66]

63. Such a statement about dominant classes is bound to be somewhat, but not entirely, tautological; cf. Cammett, p. 204. The electoral constituencies of the various parties are described in Milatz, passim; Stern, ed., pp. 203–5; and in the discussion accompanying tables 1 and 2 above.

64. Arthur Rosenberg, *Geschichte;* Stürmer, passim; Lothar Albertin, *Liberalismus und Demokratie am Anfang der Weimarer Republik* (Düsseldorf, 1972).

65. This description obviously does not do justice to the parties involved. Detailed analyses of their precrisis platforms, supporters, constituencies, and reputations are provided by Sigmund Neumann; Helga Grebing, *Geschichte der Deutschen Parteien* (Wiesbaden, 1962); Ludwig Bergsträsser, *Geschichte der politischen Parteien in Deutschland* (Munich, 1965); and Bracher, pp. 64–95.

66. It is worth quoting Gramsci on this point even though his interpretation is overly voluntaristic:

In the 1928 election, the primary non-Catholic bürgerliche parties (DDP, DVP, DNVP) polled a mere 28 percent of the vote; in 1930 an even lower 17.5 percent. In both cases, four or more bourgeois splinter parties together received over 13 percent of the vote. In the former instance, only SPD and Catholic participation made a majority possible; in the latter, over half a dozen parties were needed to attain a governing coalition, which had received only 37 percent of the vote.[67] Small wonder that overcoming fragmentation was very much a concern of industrialists.[68] Their ideologists and leaders were intent on adding to the representation of interests the representation of a bourgeois world view. But that was underdeveloped in Germany to begin with, and post-1924 developments did nothing to foster such a Weltanschauung. The parties were increasingly unable to draw "living forces" into themselves; more and more strata needed to find new forms of "political, spiritual representation . . . which they found in the 'movements.' "[69] For all their awareness of bourgeois political fragmentation, the industrialists' conception of unity (unlike Stresemann's) was mechanical—balancing interests—and failed to appreciate popular and ideological considerations, with the important exception of nationalism and anti-Marxism. Thus, Max Schlenker noted at the April 1930 Langnamverein meetings: "Economic leaders have so far badly failed and not presented a united front in politics. . . . Unity and decisiveness seem to be present only among the enemies of the entrepreneur. [We] on the other hand, are hopelessly fragmented . . . and lack the political impact which our importance for the future of the nation and the economy would dictate. . . . [we] support too many parties [without] the uniform determination of the Marxist groups. . . . [their] politics

---

[Do] the great industrialists have a permanent political party of their own? [No] the great industrialists utilize all the existing parties turn by turn, but they do not have their own party. . . . Their interest is in a determinate balance of forces, which they obtain precisely by using their resources to reinforce one party or another in turn from the varied political checkerboard. . . . If this is what happens in "normal" times, in extreme cases . . . the party of the great industrialists is that of the landowners, who for their part do have their own permanent party (pp. 155–56).

Gramsci's two examples are Italy and England, but it would seem that German industrialists were too backward politically to have this kind of strategic sense. Their opportunism and susceptibility to Bonapartism reflected their weakness more than it did any interest in a determinate balance of forces. As for turning to the landowners, we have shown how divided industrialists were. Weisbrod, pp. 475, 497–99, makes much the same argument, though in a different fashion.

67. As noted, that coalition was dependent on SPD toleration. Election results and coalition totals in tables 1 and 2.

68. See chap. 3, sec. 5, and chap. 4, sec. 8.

69. Sigmund Neumann, pp. 96, 104. Maier, pp. 545ff., discusses how post-1924 developments took the bourgeois world view out of capitalism.

can only be overcome by [our] politics."[70] Industry helped fund up to seven different parties, but by 1932 they accepted the Papen government, which was formally neither supported by nor dependent on any of them.

At least since 1924 the primary bourgeois integration parties had been breaking up into their constituent social groups. Each formed a party that emphasized limited and particularistic economic interests. Among them was the Wirtschaftspartei, an old-middle-class, urban homeowners party, which sought to regain what the inflation had taken from them and given to big business and organized labor.[71] In chapter 2, we analyzed similar developments in the countryside in 1928 that led to the founding and success of the Christian National Peasant and Rural People's Party (CNBLP), the German Peasants' Party, and the pseudo-tory-democratic Konservative Volkspartei. It is noteworthy that these "special interest" defections afflicted the right as well as the left of the bourgeois parties and that countless attempts to (re-) unify these and the primary parties failed; often they only worsened existing personal antipathies.[72] No reintegration took place until the great successes of the Nazi party overcame bourgeois and middle-class economic divisions under the banner of an authoritarian, antisocialist, popular imperialism. Rather than examining the various attempts to unify the bourgeois parties, we turn instead to look at what weakened them and tore them asunder, what broke the link between representatives and represented, between party and constituency. It is noteworthy, however, that between 1930 and 1933 each successive attempt to unify the bourgeois parties found its center of gravity further and further to the right until authoritarian, antidemocratic preferences, including for Hitler, came to take precedence over any of the preexisting "Mittelparteien," even in the eyes of the politicians themselves.[73]

As noted, its all-Catholic, socially mixed constituency helped guar-

70. Schlenker's talk cited in BA/Z Sg 126/5 April 1930.

71. See chap. 1, sec. 3; Martin Schumacher, "Hausbesitz, Mittelstand und Wirtschaftspartei in der Weimarer Republik," in Mommsen, et al., eds., pp. 832–35; Stürmer; Sigmund Neumann, p. 66; Jones, "Dying Middle," p. 35.

72. Most of these attempts took place during and after 1930; they are richly documented in the DDP and DVP minutes at the BA, Bestände R45III and R45II. A brief summary in Jones, "Dying Middle," pp. 43–46. Reusch and others followed these events very closely, HA GHH/Nachlass Reusch 400 101 293/10. The enmity which emerged around the DDP's attempt to raid the DVP left and, together with several other small groups, form a united bourgeois Staatspartei, was illustrative. Jones provides a richly detailed account of efforts to unify the bourgeois parties in "Sammlung oder Zersplitterung: Die Bestrebungen zur Bildung einer neuen Mittelpartei in der Endphase der Weimarer Republik," Vierteljahrshefte für Zeitgeschichte 25 (1977):265–304.

73. This is especially clear in Jones, "Sammlung oder Zersplitterung," p. 303.

antee the Zentrum an almost fixed 15 percent of the electorate. Yet the party moved rightward, beginning in the countryside with the 1925 presidential election and the pro-Hindenburg defections. From the countryside this drift rightward spread to the cities, especially after 1928.[74] The changes in the party were reflected in the different figures who dominated it during the Republic: from Matthias Erzberger, whom industry considered the most dangerous socializer of them all, to Baron von Papen and Prelate Kaas, via Wirth, Hermes, Brüning, and Stegerwald. This shift could be accomplished relatively smoothly, however, because in Kaas's words, "People do not join our party, they are born into it." Since it was much less vulnerable to fragmentation (and because of its strength in the particularist southern Länder), the Zentrum after 1924 came to play the pivotal role in all governing, and especially bourgeois, coalitions.[75] Beginning in the mid-twenties, there were growing social tensions within the party; these were repressed by the heightened role of clerics, who also led the party to the right. The corporatist, antiliberal, and antisocialist traditions of the Catholic social movement were reemphasized after the 1928 elections in which the Zentrum suffered an 11.4 percent loss of its previous support—most of it to the SPD, and the largest single setback ever.[76] Attempts by the party's labor wing and its newspaper, *Germania,* to slow the Rome-sanctioned move to the right failed. When, just before the collapse of the Grand Coalition, ex-Chancellor and staunch republican Joseph Wirth remarked that "It is the historical mission of the Zentrum to mediate between the DVP and Social Democracy," he was informally censured by the party hierarchy.[77] Thus, the Zentrum was the negative case; a bourgeois party with a mixed constituency it managed to retain despite sharp shifts in policy and political function.

Not so the DNVP. Initially, the DNVP stood for total opposition to the Republic, the "unity of the no." But after the stabilization of the Republic and the defeat of left-wing insurrection by 1924, various constituencies within the DNVP, especially in the countryside, set about defending their daily interests within the republican system. The split between Hugenberg's rejectionists and Kuno von Westarp's compromisers, as well as the divisive question of monarchism, led to heavy

74. On the rightward movement in the countryside and its spread, Müller, pp. 393ff.; Barmeyer, pp. 107–11; and chap. 2, sec. 3 above.

75. See Ruge and Gossweiler, eds., p. 53, for the KPD's rather astute judgment on what made the Zentrum both so flexible and viable. More ponderous is Morsey, in Matthias and Morsey, esp. pp. 283–333.

76. On the party's response to its 1928 losses and the increased prominence of clerics, Becker, pp. 6–9, and Vogt, p. 452.

77. The Wirth episode of February 1930 was related to Reusch by von Gilsa, HA GHH/ Nachlass Reusch 400 101 293/4a. Brüning himself was "horrified"; 11 Feb. 1930.

electoral losses in 1928 and 1930. While a series of rural leaders (West-arp, Schiele, Schlange, Treviranus) argued for participation in order to move governments to the right, Hugenberg's capture of the party chair-manship in 1928 split the party once again and marked a return to the earlier radical opposition to both Weimar and Versailles.[78] Hugenberg ignored the shrinking of the party's constituency and blamed the losses on the collaborators, whom he accused of following "narrow economic and vocational interests" rather than what he perceived as "long-term political" considerations. The schisms led to the founding of the CNBLP, Konservative Volkspartei and populist Christian Socials, while Hugenberg led the DNVP in joining Hitler in the Harzburg (or National) Front in opposition to the Young Plan and to the Republic. The ultras in industry and agriculture who supported Hugenberg's strategy ignored the party's internal breakdown and electoral collapse (1924, 20 percent of the vote; 1928, 14 percent; 1930, 7 percent), and refused those overtures for bourgeois unity which they thought would dilute their stand. Hugenberg utilized his press and film empire to attack the Black-Red (Zentrum-SPD) coalition in Prussia and reject the Brüning strategy of crisis management. By mid-1931 a purged DNVP declared itself for a restored monarchy and a "struggle-alliance" with the NSDAP; together they walked out of parliament.[79] Rejecting calls from the salaried-employee affiliates of the party for a "popular and socially minded conservativism," Hugenberg, assisted by the rural radicals in the RLB and mining interests, pursued an undiluted line of "a bloc not a porridge."[80] The DNVP left the defense of daily interests to those parties which split from it; it concerned itself with "pure political struggle" against the Republic. In this struggle it recruited for the Nazis among former conservatives, especially youth, and aspired to conservatize and civilize some of the plebian and avowedly "socialist" elements among the National Socialists. By 1933 it abandoned the effort to be the tail that wagged the dog and joined the ranks of those who enjoyed the apolitical right to make money.

The DDP was a spent force by 1928, if not already by 1920. That weak liberal bourgeois impulse which survived the events of 1848 and

78. On the splits within the DNVP, Stürmer, pp. 249–54; Bracher, pp. 83–92, 309–30; Sigmund Neumann, pp. 65–70. On the rural compromisers, their programs and dilem-mas, chap. 2, sec. 4b above. Frustrated by Hugenberg's unwillingness to compromise on behalf of their daily interests, significant numbers of former rural DNVP voters went over to the far more uncompromising Nazis.

79. Details in ZSA/DNVP-Reichsleitung/11; Friedrich Hiller von Gaetringen in Mat-thias and Morsey, pp. 543–75.

80. The unfolding of these developments is detailed by Attila Chanady, "The Disin-tegration of the DNVP, 1924–1930," *Journal of Modern History* 39 (1967): 65–90, and Jones, "Dying Middle," pp. 40–42.

1870 was successfully encapsulated in Wilhelmine Germany,[81] but experienced a brief efflorescence between 1918 and 1920 as a result of the collapse of the Empire and the victories of the working class. The culmination of the DDP's efforts was the actual framing of the Weimar Constitution; together with the SPD and a leftish Zentrum, it brought liberal democratic constitutional structures to Germany. Founded, financed, and controlled by representatives of the dynamic fraction of industry, commerce, banking, and small manufacturing, the DDP was staffed by liberal intellectuals and publicists, the Bildungsbürgertum. Its diverse initial constituency consisted of south- and northwestern peasants, various antisocialist, antimonopoly Mittelstand elements, and middle-class Jews; it did not take much to break that grouping apart. The tensions between peasants and urban commercial interests were particularly sharp. The DDP's attempts to defend the interests of feed-short peasants against the estate owners and the Osthilfe went unrewarded.[82] Once the SPD moderated itself, friendly opposition could be replaced by up-front, offensive opposition, and by 1920 most DDP voters had moved to the DVP. Quickly, the DDP was burdened with having subordinated itself to the SPD, and with the pressure from the left removed, that burden proved fatal to the DDP.[83]

The party's gradual and then sharp move to the right after 1929 reflected the changed posture of the dynamic fraction of industry, but it was too late to do any electoral good with the Mittelstand. Thus, a Dr. Goldstein of Flogau warned his DDP colleague, Agriculture Minister Hermann Dietrich, that "We have become an appendage of social democracy, always criticizing its failures but never hindering it with a 'No.' The consequence has been that the middle class and peasants have abandoned us. . . . With the SPD it is impossible to undertake fiscal reform" of which it was incapable, nor make the needed cuts in state sector spending.[84] Because of its pivotal role in any industry-labor coalition or bloc, the DDP during the middle years of the Republic had continued to enjoy governmental and ministerial responsibility despite its lack of real power within any sector of the electorate. DDP industrialists criticized what they considered deficient political coherence: Formally it supported a free, liberal capitalist economy and full par-

81. This is, perhaps, a bit too strongly put; cf. chap. 3, sec. 1a; Krieger, passim.

82. On the DDP's problems in balancing its urban and rural affiliates, chap. 2, pp. 66, 79, 84. Also, BA/R43I/2543, p. 79, 8 Apr. 1930.

83. See Albertin, *Liberalismus und Demokratie,* esp. chap. 1. On the DDP's early rural losses, Heberle, pp. 32ff., 106–20. For an overview, Albertin, "Faktoren," pp. 662ff.; Stephan; Jones, "Dying Middle," pp. 29–32; Hartmut Schustereit, *Linksliberalismus und Sozialdemokratie in der Weimarer Republik* (Düsseldorf, 1975), pp. 185–271; Reinhard Opitz, *Der deutsche Sozialliberalismus, 1917–1933* (Cologne, 1973).

84. Goldstein to Dietrich, 5 Apr. 1930, in BA/Nachlass Dietrich/320, p. 50.

ticipation in the world market. "But the Young Democrats are almost reform socialistic and fully betray any liberal-democratic perspectives. . . . Whatever success we have had among entrepreneurs over the past years have all been fully destroyed by the economic, fiscal, tax, and social policies of our legislative representatives." The party lost all the supporters of free enterprise without winning replacements. It forced some to the right while recruiting for social democracy.[85] The German bourgeoisie may have abandoned the bourgeois revolution at so early a point that there was little potential constituency for the DDP to represent. But the DDP did have a cadre of (mostly Jewish) journalists who provided some of the most astute observations on that very bourgeoisie: "The German bourgeoisie suffers from a pathological lack of responsibility and self-confidence. The stigmata of its degeneration go back to its never having won or even struggled to obtain the status or tradition of a ruling class. It worries about effective slogans while it is incapable of directing or pointing the way beyond anything more than a call for its unmediated material interests. The Bürgertum consumes itself in its individual interests and can act toward no other end."[86] Such a bourgeoisie could generate no party to organize its interests and convert them into a national interest.

The DVP played a more decisive role than any of the other bourgeois parties in the abandonment of the parliamentary and republican form of state. The rupture of links between representatives and represented in the DVP contributed more to the general crisis of the state than did similar breaks in other parties because, both in its personnel and its policy positions, the DVP was the party par excellence of the big industrialists and bankers who dominated the economy.[87] Its leaders attempted to strike a balance between popular appeal and handmaidenship: Stresemann leaned toward the former; his successors, sometimes ambivalently, sometimes wholeheartedly, opted for the lat-

85. Industrialists Robert Bosch, Ernst Leitz, and Max Levy; cited in BA/Nachlass Dietrich/228, pp. 165, 167, 187, 189, 9 Oct. 1928.

86. Berliner Tageblatt, 23 Nov. 1929. On the DDP's reincarnation as the Staatspartei and its final demise, Matthias and Morsey, pp. 31–68. For the argument that the DDP press was actually to the right of the party rather than, as we have suggested, generally to the left, see Modris Eksteins, The Limits of Reason (London, 1975).

87. In 1928, for example, twenty-five of the DVP's forty-five Reichstag deputies either were industrialists or were intimately linked to them. However, during the period of the dynamic fraction's predominance and under Stresemann's pressure, thirty of the forty-five voted for public funds for the locked-out Ruhr workers in 1928, and twenty-eight of the forty-five voted to support Hilferding's finance reforms in late 1929. Cf. Döhn; the Stresemann-Hugo debate of 26 Feb. 1929 over whether industrialists exercised too much control over the party, BA/R45II-DVP/43, pp. 323–33. On Stresemann's strategy for the Grand Coalition, Panzer, pp. 86, 117, 123. The DVP was inevitably seen as the fulcrum for any future Bürgerblock.

ter. Stresemann perceived the long-term interests of German industry as best served through a national, interclass compromise directed toward restoring Germany's place in the world economy. A number of factors we have examined rendered that a viable program, and he cajoled and dragged most of his colleagues along. Operating under changed circumstances, however, his successors, Ernst Scholz and Eduard Dingeldey, determined that labor was to be fought not bought and the parliamentary system undermined not buttressed. With the help of the four-million-strong National Association of Commercial Employees (DHV), Stresemann and his allies had attempted in 1928 and 1929 to reorganize the DVP and change it from "the class party of industry" to a "Volkspartei"; to be sure, one with an antisocialist ideology, yet capable of promoting social- and liberal-welfare programs. With Stresemann's death, the industrialist wing of the party not only swept the DHV insurgents aside,[88] but it even tried to eradicate the influence of Stresemann's junior partner and Grand Coalition enthusiast, Julius Curtius.

Not only did the industrialists pull the DVP out of the Grand Coalition as soon as possible after Stresemann's death, but they apparently believed that DVP leadership in the struggle against socialism was a prerequisite for the formation of a united "Bürgerpartei." Presumably intelligent industrialists contended that the more clearly the DVP stood up for industrial interests, the more popular it would become.[89] It did not particularly concern them that the party would attract more adherents through universalist (though antisocialist) appeals than by eliminating political ambiguity. The Mittelstand could certainly prove to be a reservoir of voters who agreed with the industrialists' opposition to "exaggerated parliamentarism," but the DVP industrialists refused to yield and reach a compromise equilibrium on social-welfare measures that were (almost) as dear to salaried employees as to workers.[90] In opposition to the RDI leadership and the dynamic fraction of industry, the DVP even "recalled" its own minister, Paul Moldenhauer, from the Brüning government, because as finance minister, he demonstrated

---

88. The DHV spokesmen with whom Stresemann worked were Otto Thiel and Frank Glatzel; the former was the chairman of the DVP's Committee on Salaried Employees. On the DHV, Hamel. Thiel's plan for party reform was issued on 5 Feb. 1929, "Volkspartei oder Klassenpartei?" in BA/Nachlass Karl Jarres/41. The entire episode is summarized by Jones, "Dying Middle," pp. 38–40.

89. Reusch to von Gilsa, 25 Mar. 1930: "If the DVP does not take the lead in the struggle against socialism, then the sought-after united Bürgerpartei will never come into existence." HA GHH/Nachlass Reusch 400 101 293/4a. Heavy industry's attacks on DVP participation in the Grand Coalition are summarized here and in ZSA/Büro des Reichspräsidenten/46.

90. Döhn, pp. 888–91. The Nazis never made this mistake.

insufficient alacrity in dismantling social programs and arbitration procedures.[91] As we have shown, the industrialists, by 1932, came to hold the same opinion of the Brüning regime as a whole; even before its fall the DVP split over continued support of Brüning's party-linked government.[92] By mid-1931 the party added to its previous social and economic demands the call for an army-supported presidential dictatorship, the elimination of Prussia's "independence," complete freedom for the employer in contractual, wages, and hours matters, the readoption of black-white-red as the national colors, and freedom for colonial activity.[93] Little in this program could inspire popular as well as industrial enthusiasm. In most respects, heavy industry triumphed more easily within the DVP than within the League of Industry (RDI)!

The ideological battle within the DVP between industrialist backers and salaried-employee representatives was conducted forthrightly. Thus, Hans Bechly of the salaried employees of the DHV wrote to Dingeldey summarizing his position in November 1931.

[Why do not the industrialists realize] that unions are here to stay and are the only form through which the masses can be bound in a positive sense to the state and the economy. . . . The party must put itself before all Germans [or] it is finished as a Volkspartei and will become [as Stresemann warned—DA] an insignificant interest party. . . . Never before have the employers and their spokesmen rode so roughshod [rücksichtlos hinweggesetzt] over the line of the party . . . there seems to be no more room in the DVP for employees. . . . It is intolerable that wages and salaries are repeatedly discussed as if solely they were responsible for our poor economy, with silence on how low they have in fact already sunk.[94]

---

91. Ibid., pp. 896–97. On the RDI's displeasure with the DVP's and heavy industry's haste, von Gilsa to Reusch, 17 June 1930, HA GHH/Nachlass Reusch 400 101 293/4a. Von Gilsa and Reusch complained that the RDI and Kastl in particular continued to support Moldenhauer in the spirit of the Grand Coalition, even once the majority of the DVP delegation had been won over to a more radical line. Heavy industry and the right wing of the DVP considered it inadequate that Moldenhauer had, in his words, "delivered 80 percent of the wishes of die Wirtschaft." Apparently the missing 20 percent were believed necessary to prevent the return of the unacceptable precrisis situation; 8 Mar. 1930, 220/8a. See chap. 3, n. 137, above.

92. See BA/Nachlass Dingeldey/36, pp. 6ff., Feb. 1932, where Richard Merton, Glatzel, Kalle, and the other Brüning supporters within the DVP made their case. For the background to this, Weisbrod, pp. 467–76 and chap. 3, sec. 5 above.

93. Heavy industry's enthusiasm for this program far exceeded that of the party's personnel who sensed its narrowness; see BA/Nachlass Dingeldey/34, pp. 3–5, DVP Kampfziele, 19 Apr. 1931.

94. Bechly to Dingeldey, BA/Nachlass Dingeldey/35, pp. 15, 16, 26–28, 16 Feb. and 12 Nov. 1931.

By the end of 1931, Bechly was prepared to quit the DVP, and many of his followers had begun to vote Nazi. The verdict of one-time DNVP chairman and cofounder of the Konservative Volkspartei, Westarp, was quite similar: "The number of those who will vote for a pure industrial-interest party is obviously minuscule. But that is what the DVP has become; a certain group of industrialists whistles and [Party Chairman] Dingeldey dances." A world view had been replaced by narrow interests. Westarp stated that in Stresemann's day there were struggles between employers and employees, but he tried to be objective and remain socially minded. "But today the party never musters the courage to oppose the employer and industry groups."[95] Industry had become unwilling to incorporate the interests of subordinate classes, unable to organize its own interests except in the most limited manner, and it was in no position to portray its interests as national, rather than selfish interests. Otto Thiel hammered this home to Dingeldey, pointing to the consequence:

> currently salaried employees are very dubious as to the good will of employers . . . [while] no joint committee between them and workers has come to be. . . . When Stresemann was chancellor in 1923 he rejected employer attempts to curtail sharply or eliminate compulsory arbitration. The Employers' League was furious. . . . [but] the Nuremberg party convention embraced my position on social policy. . . . Now our party leaders are seen throughout the land backing social reactionary policies [that alienate our supporters]. . . . while [we] recognize the [social radical] NSDAP as allies [Bundesgenossen]. It is nearly impossible to resist the exit of salaried employees from the . . . reactionary DVP into the camp of the social-radical Nazis.[96]

Logically enough, Bechly and Thiel left the DVP when it formed an electoral alliance with the DNVP in 1932, and they went over to the Nazis precisely because they were "social, not reactionary."

By late 1931, heavy industry had taken complete control of what remained of the DVP. The result was the party's no-confidence vote against Brüning in October and the departure of Ministers Curtius and Wirth. Von Gilsa wrote Reusch of the success of heavy industry's plan: "The vote of the [DVP] majority against the Brüning cabinet can be attributed to this [withholding aid]." Next was to come: "1) Purging the

95. Westarp's observations of 24 Oct. 1931 in BA/Nachlass Dingeldey/38, p. 62, lead column in his *Volkskonservative Stimmen.*

96. Thiel to Dingeldey, 26 Jan. 1931, 17 June 1931, and 30 Oct. 1931, BA/Nachlass Dingeldey/92, pp. 13, 22, 36–39. Thiel added that "nowhere else in the world is Sozialpolitik blamed for causing or continuing the Depression!" 14 Apr. 1932, p. 78.

party of those elements that voted for the Brüning cabinet or abstained. . . . 2) Insertion of the purged DVP into the National Opposition as an autonomous group. . . . 3) Only after the purge [*Reinigung*] . . . would it be right to give the party money, and then only enough to keep it needy."[97]

By early 1932 Dingeldey had to plead for money at the doorsteps of Ruhr industrialists. Their preconditions remained the same: purity in representing the interests of the entrepreneur and the unity of all those prepared to do so. Or, as Reusch told the party leader, "To my great regret, I must refuse to provide financial support" until serious movement toward unity among "all the parties between the Zentrum and the NSDAP is accomplished. . . . all imaginable promises to this end were made but not one kept." In response to Brüning's fall and the upcoming elections, Otto Hugo noted obsequiously that "the gentlemen of industry fully agree that the DVP and DNVP could run together very well; in fact, they could merge."[98] Indeed, throughout 1932 industrialists attempted, with both carrot and stick, to force the bourgeois parties to merge—seeming never to realize how Pyrrhic a victory that would be, for in the course of their efforts they had contributed to destroying the bourgeois parties as viable links between representatives and represented.[99] Since their own economic interests remained divergent, however, they could not settle on policies to be implemented by Papen's fully authoritarian or Schleicher's social-military regime.[100] As we have shown, those governments could organize no mass support in any case; the result was that while cliques quarreled and conspired, the "crisis of authority" grew acute. The door to an extrasystemic solution had opened: who would greet the savior? What were the stages in the

97. Letter of 22 Oct. 1931, HA GHH/Nachlass Reusch 400 101 293/4b. On the fate of the DVP minority that had wished to continue supporting Brüning in opposition to the Harzburg Front, BA/Nachlass Dingeldey/75, pp. 30ff. The Langnamverein and the United Steelworks were in the forefront of this carrot-and-stick purge effort, while Dingeldey identified the "liberal" Brüning supporters as "IG Farben people"; ibid., p. 70 and /36, p. 16, where Dingeldey identifies those pressing him. See also p. 161 above; for Reusch these efforts were but a continuation of the earlier moves to force the DVP out of a "Grand Coalition mentality."

98. Reusch to Dingeldey, 30 Jan. 1932, HA GHH/Nachlass Reusch 400 101 293/12; Hugo's memo, BA/Nachlass Dingeldey/73, p. 40.

99. Curtius was a prime example of what happened to a politician who attempted to interpret industry's long-term interests for it; for Reusch's evaluation of Curtius, see chap. 3, note 136. On the last phases of the attempt to manipulate the parties into unity, BA/Nachlass Schleicher 42/22, 23, and Stegmann, "Faschismus."

100. On the deficiencies and problems of the Papen regime: see pp. 97–100, 162–63, 208–10 above. On the inadequacies and dangers of Schleicher's way, see pp. 100–104, 163–65, and 210–12. Dingeldey referred to "what strikes all of us as the dangerous economic and political experimentation of the Gereke plan," 12 Dec. 1932, BA/Nachlass Dingeldey/34, p. 12.

formation of an alliance between the dominant social classes and the Nazi party?

5. Toward the Extrasystemic Solution

Despite its own internal conflicts, by no later than April 1930 industry as a whole had called for an entrepreneurial offensive, which for many would necessitate a new state leadership and possibly, according to the Langnamverein convention, "a change in the system itself, a possibility from which we should not shrink." Important sectors of heavy industry and agriculture had already determined in 1929 that their miserable economic situation was due much less to cyclical economic developments than to "the System and its operation."[101] They preferred an authoritarian regime and, as we have seen, expected that Brüning would provide that, despite his initial commitment to and dependence on the parties. It was not enough to recognize abstractly the importance of capital accumulation, as Brüning did; it was necessary to organize mass support in its favor, and if that could not be accomplished through parliaments and elections, then other "corporate, vocational and organic" forms merited consideration. In this spirit, Paul Silverberg told the relatively progressive DIHT that "Napoleon was correct: politics determines fate, not economics."[102] For the great majority of industrialists in 1931, this still implied a system-immanent solution grounded in a military-supported, strongly authoritarian regime legitimized by Article 48 of the Weimar Constitution. In a fourteen-page letter to Brüning in August 1931, Ruhr industrialists catalogued their political and economic demands, the final one being that "the tempo of the changeover [*Umstellung*] must be accelerated."[103] Shortly thereafter, however (and just as the leadership change in the RDI was imminent, and the national bloc of NSDAP and DNVP was about to meet at Harzburg), Reusch announced that, despite the rollback of many of the revolution's so-called achievements, "trust in the government is rapidly disappearing . . . its hesitations and delaying tactics are no longer comprehensible."[104] The bank crashes of that summer and

101. The parliamentary republic was referred to by many as "the System"; the desire to get rid of it became broad-based, Döhn, p. 906.

102. Speech to the DIHT gathering, cited in BA/Nachlass Silverberg/645, p. 170, 23 June 1931; his thoughts on "corporate-organic" forms, p. 381; see also Mariaux, ed.

103. The demands were the usual, the sense of urgency more acute; letter of 8 Aug. 1931, HA GHH/Nachlass Reusch 400 101 293/11.

104. Blank to Reusch, 15 Sept. 1931, and Reusch's response, HA GHH/Martin Blank 400 101 202 4/9. On this stage, see Bracher, pp. 407–42, and chapter 3, where I have argued that the dynamic-export fraction generally continued to support Brüning and was not yet fully converted to an extrasystemic solution.

the allied veto of the German-Austrian customs union had added to Brüning's troubles. By October, various industrial agents found their way to the Harzburg meetings, and President Hindenburg, among others, was exploring means for taming and integrating the Nazi Party into the government, for which purposes he and Hitler met. Interest in the mass-base possibilities of a reformed NSDAP grew, and Hitler became an increasingly popular figure on the dinner and lecture circuit, expanding his contacts beyond the old Thyssen-Kirdorf-Vögler crowd.[105]

During the last quarter of 1931, Brüning's stock declined precipitously while that of the Nazis rose. By year's end, an associate of Reusch could describe Brüning as "one who for years has made compacts with Marxism while treating the National Freedom Movement the same as Moscow followers."[106] Brüning's ban of the SA and SS and his agreement to sponsor Hindenburg's reelection campaign in concert with the SPD were, perhaps, the last straw for heavy industry. Brüning stumbled through until May largely because of in-progress negotiations on the suspension and revision of reparations. Finally, "agrarian bolshevism" led Hindenburg to abandon him, and he fell. Papen's ascent represented a victory for heavy industry and agriculture, but it did not solve the problem of a mass base. It was toward this end that contacts with the Nazis were expanded, especially after their succession of election victories, with the hope of "taming" them into providing the mass base for a Papen-type regime.[107] Not a single member of the Papen government was a parliamentary deputy. As Papen's policies increasingly drew the opposition of industry's dynamic-export fraction, this goal took on greater urgency. By mid-1932 the vast majority of industrialists wanted to see Nazi participation in the government—with either the Zentrum or the DNVP—but the possible format remained in dispute. We have examined in detail the conflicts within and between the dominant social classes that rendered impossible a consistent and coherent set of policies capable of satisfying all the fractions. An anti-Marxist, imperialist program was the least common denominator on which they could all agree, and the Nazis seemed capable of providing the mass base for such a program, despite the anxieties and uncertain-

105. Reusch, Springorum, and others in the Ruhr were rather pleased with the results of Bad Harzburg and Hitler's expressed willingness to cooperate; Blank's report of 12 Oct. 1931 in HA GHH/Martin Blank 100 101 202 4/4. On the more general issue: Czichon; Schulz; and Stegmann, "Faschismus"; cf. Turner, "Verhältnis"; Conze, "Die politischen Entscheidungen"; Bracher, p. 410; Schulz, p. 662. (See the Introduction to this edition.)

106. Cited in a report of 6 Jan. 1932, HA GHH/Nachlass Reusch 400 101 293/12.

107. Among the numerous discussions of this process, see Stegmann, "Faschismus," pp. 46ff., and Gossweiler, pp. 384ff., along with the standard, Bracher.

ties their plebeian and populist demagoguery sometimes occasioned. We do not concern ourselves here with the roads traveled by individual industrialists or estate owners, or groups of them, in coming to support the Nazis or, finally, in elevating Hitler to the chancellorship.[108] Rather, we concern ourselves with how industrialists and estate owners, in light of the Nazis' independently achieved successes, attempted to insert their interests into what Bracher has called the "power vacuum" of the last eight or nine months of the Republic.

Heavy industry had scored a symbolic ideological (and bureaucratic) victory already in April 1930 when Brüning reluctantly entertained the appointment as Reichspresschef of Fritz Klein, editor of the heavy-industry-connected *Deutsche Allgemeine Zeitung*. This promised to be a culminating triumph, for through Hugenberg, the RLB, and a few others, the nonparty mass press, especially outside of Berlin, was effectively controlled by heavy industry and the rural elite. Reusch could report that a speech he gave on solutions to the economic crisis was favorably excerpted or reproduced not only by the state radio but by about sixteen hundred urban and rural newspapers as well.[109] Together with some Catholic and sympathetic Lutheran clergymen, the Langnamverein drafted pamphlets and newspaper articles for the "uninformed reader" and later set up a program "to help represent the interests of the economy more effectively among the clergy"[110] "Uninformed readers" were apparently to be found in the army as well; to enlighten them and their kin, five hundred thousand copies of the Langnamverein booklet "Why Unemployment?" were distributed to soldiers and ancillary personnel. For the more informed, the Langnamverein sent Schlenker on a speaking tour: beginning in September 1931, he lectured at military schools and to officer corps on "the objective economic situation" free of "political tendencies."[111]

Although still at a statemate on numerous economic and political policy questions, the two camps within industry, the "national bloc"

108. See Bracher, pp. 592–734 and the literature cited in note 105, above. What follows is of necessity selective; we slight, for example, Hindenburg's camarilla, the similarly pro-Nazi executive bureaucracy, and the somewhat more complicated situation in the military, see Carsten, *Reichswehr,* pp. 309–405, and Vogelsang.

109. Reusch's report to Langnamverein director, Max Schlenker, HA GHH/Nachlass Reusch 400 101 221/9b, 30 July 1929. On Klein, Blank to Reusch, 400 101 202 4/6, 17 Apr. 1930, p. 6. Zechlin chose to stay on, and Klein did not assume the post.

110. On pamphlets for the religious but uneducated, HA GHH/Nachlass Reusch 400 101 221/9a; Schlenker and Reusch, 26 and 30 Mar. 1929; on the churches, Wilmowsky to Reusch, 15 Jan. 1932, 400 101 290/39. As part of these efforts, their associate Sogemeier was co-opted to the Evangelical Church board.

111. Reusch to Schlenker, 5 and 29 Sept. 1931, Schlenker to Reusch, 8 and 16 Sept. 1931; HA GHH/Nachlass Reusch 400 101 221/11b.

and the former "Brüning bloc," both gradually abandoned their attempts to unify the bourgeois parties. As we have demonstrated, the conflicts between the heavy and dynamic fractions of industry never disappeared; neither Papen nor Schleicher was able to transcend or subsume the divergences. Increasingly, however, and especially in the extragovernmental realm, it was heavy industry which set the political agenda for industry as a whole. Heading the agenda during most of 1932 was a project to tame or split the Nazi Party and, after attaching its chastened remainder to one or another of the bourgeois parties, to employ it as a primary support for a nonparliamentary regime that would not impede capital accumulation while securing its legitimacy through a program of rearmament and imperialist expansion.[112]

Those who were initially not of the Weimar system would save those whose dominance the system had threatened. As noted earlier, Reusch had begun to despair of a bourgeois concentration as early as Christmas 1930 and was open to suggestions for off-the-record funding to "creating one national right," out of "the Stahlhelm, Hugenberg, Hitler," and cooperative members of the bourgeois Right.[113] A primary function of unifying the Bürgertum rightward would be to help the "NSDAP move away from its economic utopias." Gilsa thought that if that happened, as it had with the Fascists' "very similar demands, which were then thrown overboard when Mussolini came to power and had to assume responsibility," the NSDAP might also be made capable of governing. At that time he was in a minority; a year later that was no longer so. In October 1931, Carl Siemens, a prominent figure in the dynamic fraction of industry and former DDP supporter, told a New York gathering of industrialists and bankers that Germany's depressed state was the "fault of socialists" and an "exaggerated parliamentarism" and that these were at the root of the success of the "legal and electoral" Hitler movement, which would continue to gain support from many.[114] The NSDAP did indeed continue to win support from industry throughout

112. Bauer, pp. 143–68; see the literature cited in note 105.

113. On Reusch's readiness to fund efforts to "creat[e] one national right," his letters to Jung of 29 Dec. 1930 and 2 Jan. 1931. In the former he writes that the "movement must proceed along the line Berlin-Munich," Berlin being the seat of the bourgeois parties, Munich the seat of the NSDAP—HA GHH/Nachlass Reusch 400 101 293/11. Gilsa repeated the call for "creating one broad national Right" and named who could be included in a letter to Reusch, 31 Jan. 1931. There he urged Reusch and other industrialists to use *all resources at their disposal* to bring this about. Earlier, 30 Oct. 1930, he wrote Reusch of weaning the NSDAP "from its economic utopias" and recalled Mussolini's transformation.—ibid.

114. Carl Siemens's speech at a banquet in New York sponsored by General Electric, 27 Oct. 1931; reprinted in Ruge and Gossweiler, pp. 44–45. For Siemens, anti-Marxism and anti-Bolshevism were *the* key to understanding Nazism's success.

1932. Buoyed by its electoral victories, the party was able to command the increasingly exclusive attention of industrialists, particularly after the Papen regime floundered without a mass base, and Schleicher threatened to embark on dirigist experiments in cooperation with the labor unions.[115] The bourgeois parties that refused to engage seriously with the NSDAP were simply cut off from their primary sources of funding.[116]

The parliamentary Republic weakened organized agriculture and the rural elite much more than it did industry. The labor-based bourgeois revolution of 1918 led to what the agrarians termed a "schematic distribution of spheres of influence" from which it was bound to lose.[117] Despite the privileged access it enjoyed within the executive apparatus, organized agriculture determined early on that it could never be adequately protected by the balance of forces a parliamentary system produced: both Handelspolitik and Sozialpolitik would be stacked against agriculture. Opposition to the parliamentary state and a call for the "strong man" were inherent in the politics of the Green Front from the outset: "We call for a unity front against our suffering and against the state. . . . Agriculture expects the Führer of the German nation . . . to take all the extraparliamentary measures necessary for the salvation of agriculture."[118] Shortchanged by the labor/export-industry alliance, organized agriculture fought the Grand Coalition and appealed to others outside that coalition—the Mittelstand and heavy industry—to join its attack on parliamentarism.[119] "Industry must take advantage of the position of power it still retains to wipe out social democracy. It can only accomplish that if it eliminates parliamentarism. For this purpose it must enter an alliance with agriculture and with German Na-

115. On Schleicher and the unions, HKB/Vorstandssitzungen ADGB/NB 5, Nov. 1932; Breitman, pp. 352–78; Schneider, *Arbeitsbeschaffungsprogramm*, passim; Czichon, passim; Wolffsohn, pp. 98–106.

116. The reactionary BVP was an interesting example: after a year of industry-funded cooperation between the Bavarian party and the Nazis, the BVP sought to pull out because it feared losing its political monopoly in Bavaria. Its industrialist backers responded by cancelling funding for the BVP and threatening to hamper its operations. On the beginnings of that cooperation, HA GHH/Nachlass Reusch 400 101 293/11; on its end 11 June and 14 Aug 1932, HA GHH/Martin Blank 400 101 202 4/10. The BVP had disappointed heavy industry once before when it had allowed some of its delegates in the Reichstag to support assistance to the locked-out ironworkers in the Ruhr.

117. That is, they were cut off from their bastions in the Prussian Parliament, the monarchy, and the military and were left to fend for themselves as one organized interest among several; see Gessner, *Agrarverbände*, and Flemming "Grossagrarische Interessen." On "schematism," ZSA/RLB Pressarchiv 132/11, p. 68.

118. This particularly precious version is from a Green Front and Bavarian Landbund release of February 1929, BA/R43I/2541, pp. 234, 279.

119. For organized agriculture's analysis of the labor-export alliance as a trap, see chap. 2, sec. 3 above.

tionalism."[120] After 1930, "German Nationalism" increasingly came to mean the NSDAP, and the slogan "Agrarpolitik and Nationalism are Siamese twins" achieved considerable currency. We have analyzed in some detail the weakening of the protection-based integration/dependence mechanism that linked peasants to estate owners and the subsequent movement of both family peasants and Junkers, separately and together, into the Nazi camp.[121] In their efforts to bring about a "change of system" (Systemwechsel), peasants and estate owners reenforced each other's radicalization, while the Nazis were able to bridge the differences between them. The appointment of the Papen government seemed to mark the policy and system change for which Landwirtschaft had clamored, and indeed Papen's system and policies earned high marks, but it quickly became apparent that the dynamic fraction of industry and salaried employees would not tolerate the import-quota system which underlay Papen's autarkic Agrarpolitik. Consequently, Graf Kalckreuth, the radical head of the Agrarian League (RLB), refused the Agriculture portfolio and, instead, steered organized agriculture immediately into the Hugenberg-Hitler alliance, which brought the latter to power. Finally, estate owners were prominent in the efforts that culminated in Hindenburg's appointment of Hitler.[122] Had it been the sole dominant class interested in anchoring itself in a Mittelstand-based Nazi mass movement, the rural elite would not have succeeded in its last-minute efforts. Any realization of the Sammlung it had in mind depended on industry.

6. From New Base to New Coalition

As long as Stresemann remained foreign minister and head of the DVP, and so long as the dynamic fraction remained predominant within industry, organized labor, through the Grand Coalition, provided the support base for the social dominance of industry. Much of industry had cause, as we have shown, to be very dissatisfied with this arrange-

120. Statement in the Deutsche Zeitung of 14 Dec. 1929, cited in ZSA/RLB Pressarchiv 132/11, p. 168a.

121. See chap. 2, esp. end of sec. 4c. On the movement of prominent estate owners into the NSDAP, Bratz, p. 547.

122. On the skepticism regarding Papen's durability, ZSA/RLB Vorstand/146, pp. 114ff. On the appreciation of his efforts, ibid., p. 150: "We are grateful that the party-state is gone and has been replaced by an independent, strong, and neutral authoritarianism based on the living forces of German Nationalism." On appointing Hitler, ibid., p. 200: Help had to be given those trying to convince Hindenburg that appointing Hitler was the only way. See also Stegmann, "Faschismus," pp. 85–87.

ment, but tolerated it for a number of reasons, domestic and international. Stresemann's death (3 October 1929) coincided with the changing economic conjuncture and the conclusion of reparations negotiations. Almost immediately the bourgeois parties shifted to opposing the Grand Coalition and commenced looking for other bases of mass support. Within two months, the RDI published its "Recovery or Collapse" memorandum and began its efforts to roll back organized labor's economic gains.

If the bourgeois parties would no longer indulge the economic demands of white-collar groups like the DHV, and were unable to compromise with the protectionist demands of the rural sector and petite bourgeoisie, then what groups could provide a base of support? In October still, Reusch strongly urged the DVP to improve its contacts with the Stahlhelm "lest it lose many supporters around the country if it does not revise the [negative] position it has taken." Reusch recalled that during the 1928 lockouts the Stahlhelm rendered "comradely help which worked well" defending employers against the unions and their organizing work, and it could in the future "down the line and across the Reich struggle against the monopoly unions."[123] Several industrialists were made honorary members of the organization, which may or may not have served its intended purpose. (At the time, the Stahlhelm claimed to have over a million members and was, in any event, the largest of numerous such organizations, certainly larger than the NSDAP.)[124] Industrialists and the Stahlhelm cooperated closely in the Ruhr and Rhineland, and several industrialists continued their support through to the 1932 presidential election, in which they supported the Stahlhelm's candidate. The Nazis distinguished themselves in the 1930 elections, and by the time the assorted antirepublican groups met at Harzburg in October 1931, the Nazis had emerged at the head of the pack. Industrialists split over whether to favor the NSDAP

123. Reusch to Gilsa, 25 Oct. 1929, HA GHH/Nachlass Reusch 400 101 293/4a. The resemblances between the Stahlhelm and groups that had served Mussolini well were not lost on Reusch, who was also interested in the Austrian Heimwehr. On the Stahlhelm's service during the Ruhr lockouts, Blank to Reusch, HA GHH/Martin Blank 400 101 202 4/4b, 17 Dec. 1928, Reusch's affirmations, 19 Dec. 1928. On Reusch's desire to bust the socialist unions, see chap. 5, note 110.

124. On the Stahlhelm, see Bracher, pp. 128–40, and the literature cited there; also, Arthur Rosenberg, *Geschichte*, pp. 246, 294–98. The disillusionment, social dislocations, and ravages of the war and its aftermath produced similar groups throughout central and southern Europe. Gramsci hinted that such groups constituted the "adequate form of organization" for the petite bourgeoisie, a "field army" for those who had never been able to develop their own structures and ideology, for those who now sought a capitalist negation of capitalist contradictions. On all facets of the petit bourgeois ideology, Poulantzas, *Fascisme*, pp. 262ff.

or the nonparty Stahlhelm, but they improved their contacts with both.[125]

By early 1932 at the latest, the leading figures in the now decisive fraction of industry concluded that Nazi participation in or control of the government would provide the best way out of the political crisis while providing auspicious possibilities for a profitable economic recovery. Such a decision was, of course, primarily opportunist but did contribute money and legitimacy to Nazi electoral and popular successes. Conversely, however, electoral successes alone could not guarantee that the Nazis would come to power, and the support and legitimation offered by numerous industrialists, bankers, estate owners, and army officers around Hindenburg proved crucial to such an outcome. An exchange of letters between Schacht and Reusch was characteristic of this legitimation and collaboration. In March, Schacht proposed to Reusch and several others a plan to establish a bureau with and for the NSDAP to draft an economic program. Certain that "the rightward movement in German politics proceeds irresistibly" and that the Nazis were becoming its decisive force, Schacht advocated "working out" economic issues to the satisfaction of both business and the Nazi party. Reusch responded that, after a productive "two-hour talk yesterday with Hitler here in Munich," he could "fully and completely agree with your proposal" and participate financially as well. Several weeks later, Schacht wrote asking for the money for the bureau, whose work had already begun. So far as possible, he wanted "to assure that the policy conceptions emerging from the bureau be in harmony with those views represented from the National Socialist side" by Hitler's two appointees to it.[126]

It was part of the strength of the NSDAP that, until it took power and was compelled to make policy, it propagated a very dexterous and clever mixture of conservative capitalist and populist anticapitalist positions. Compared to its generally pleasing military-diplomatic and racial positions, its economic platform remained ambiguous. One should not, therefore, assume that the industrialists' efforts at "enlightenment" were bound to bear fruit; the point is that they considered

125. Blank to Reusch, 11 Aug. and 4 Sept. 1931, HA GHH/Martin Blank 400 101 202 4/9, where the respective merits and growing popularity of the two are discussed. Blank was particularly enthusiastic about the Stahlhelm.

126. Schacht to Reusch, 18 Mar. 1932; Reusch's response, 20 Mar. 1932; and Schacht's announcement of 6 June 1932; all in HA GHH/Nachlass Reusch 400 101 290/33a. On 21 Sept. 1932 Reusch could write that Nazi "tactlessness" and cooperation with the KPD in recent weeks was disappointing: hitherto he had been "completely sympathetic" toward them; ibid. Schacht's bureau accomplished little but did link its supporters to the Nazi Keppler Circle.

this the necessary and most promising avenue.[127] While the weakened dynamic-export fraction of industry was still supporting Brüning against the onslaught of the agrarians and expending its political energies to combat Papen's autarky plans, efforts by representatives of heavy industry were vital to having the ban on the SS and SA lifted and to effecting a reconciliation among Papen, Prelate Kaas, military leaders, and a more "responsible" NSDAP. Some of industry's worries concerned the potential radicalism of some of the Nazi Party's leaders and their mass following whereas other concerns were prompted by the party's commitment to state intervention and activism in matters of foreign trade, price setting, taxes, and industrial administration.[128] Nevertheless, in March 1932, Fritz Springorum, the treasurer of heavy industry's political fund, notified Krupp, Silverberg, Reusch, and Vögler that in Prussia "a rightist government is possible only with the cooperation of the NSDAP." To obtain a state-responsible NSDAP, as well as to exclude its radicals, "we must extend our active cooperation (also based on financial involvement)" with the party. Strengthening Hugenberg's DNVP was a necessary "detour" [*Umweg*] in "doing everything to engage the NSDAP in practical state responsibility."[129]

The Nazis' demagogic populism remained an issue for industrialists in the second half of 1932. Despite the continued growth of support for them within the ranks of heavy industry, the Nazis still had to win elections. And this sometimes brought out their "anti-capitalist" side— as well as the worries of their industrialist supporters. With a mixture of understanding and annoyance, von Gilsa assessed these factors in a long letter to Reusch of 19 September, written during the crucial Autumn election campaign:

127. Numerous other examples of this in HA GHH/Martin Blank 400 101 202 4/10. See Stegmann, "Faschismus," pp. 32, 46ff., 62, 78. On the Nazi side, Walther Funk was particularly receptive, and Hans Reupke's pamphlets sought to demonstrate the complete compatibility of National Socialism and private property of whatever size. August Heinrichsbauer also worked at harmonizing the economic views of the Nazis and Ruhr heavy industry. One culmination of this effort was Hitler's speech to the Düsseldorf Industry Club of 26 Jan. 1932; see Bracher p. 441, Czichon, p. 27, Krohn, pp. 120–22.

128. This second set of doubts was more pronounced within heavy industry, which had always been more resistant to an expanded state role, than within the dynamic fraction; see Stegmann, *Die Erben Bismarcks*, pp. 458–62. On the wartime and postwar attitudes of the two fractions of industry toward such intervention, see Zunkel, *Staatssozialismus*, passim, and Gossweiler, pp. 57–89, 114–29. The bankruptcies of the Dresdner- and Danatbank and of the United Steelworks seemed capable of putting "cold socialization" back on the agenda. No industrialists at this stage demonstrated any qualms about the antiparliamentary, antiunion, anti-Semitic or antidemocratic facets of the Nazi program; *these* needed no taming.

129. Springorum's circular letter of 22 Mar. 1932 in HA GHH/Nachlass Reusch 400 101 290/36. In fact, neither Krupp nor Silverberg cared particularly for Hitler or the Nazis; see Spiller, pp. 597–98. Von Gilsa to Reusch, 19 Sept. 1932, HA GHH 400 101 293/46.

The National Socialists now consider it their trump also outwardly to appear and behave proletarian in order to affect the masses. Even highly respectable people like Epp [a prominent Bavarian Nazi] and Göring, both of whom I know well, currently place a value on appearing in a manner as much as possible appropriate to proletarian sensibilities. . . . It is a serious matter, that industrial leaders still at this very time stand up for the Nazis instead of saying clearly that they won't take part in the new course. An industrialist, whose name I was not told, said "too much money has already been invested in the Nazis to be able to let them drop financially now." I hold similar thoughts and the hope "that after all things won't be so serious with the Nazis" for a major danger at this time.

It might not be a smooth road, but it was the road taken.

General industrial support for the Nazis grew throughout the summer and reached a crescendo in late autumn. The Langnamverein convention of November 1932, for example, although initially planned to demonstrate support for Papen and his program, instead produced overwhelming support for the appointment of Hitler.[130] There were several reasons for this general swing: after continuous electoral gains, the Nazis suffered their first general electoral setback in November, and they and their supporters feared they might miss that tide in the affairs of men which comes but once.[131] Also, General Schleicher's government was not only building contacts with the Strasser wing of the NSDAP and with some of the dynamic-export industries, IG Farben in particular, but Schleicher talked of nationalizing mining and steel and began dickering with the unions as well. Among the industrialists who supported him, Silverberg, Duisberg, Krupp, and Wolff backed

130. Dr. Scholz, press spokesman for Otto Wolff, wrote Franz Bracht, now commissar for Prussia, that "The Langnamverein convention . . . originally conceived within the framework of the Papen program and intended to support it, revealed [instead] the fact that almost all of industry supports the appointment of Hitler, no matter under what circumstances," report of 26 Nov. 1932, cited by Czichon, p. 73. (Papen had resigned on the 17th and was replaced two weeks later by Schleicher, who had earlier observed that for the Reichswehr to defend Papen would necessitate opposing nine-tenths of the people.)

131. Election statistics in table 1. On 19 Oct. 1932 twenty of Germany's top industrial leaders met at the Klub von Berlin to analyze the elections and discuss postelection strategy. Among those attending were Berkemeyer, Blank (for Reusch), Borsig, Bücher, Frowein, Funke, Herle, Kastl, Krupp, Löwenstein, Piatschek, Pietrkowski, Poensgen, Schlenker, Siemens, Silverberg, Tischbein, and Vögler. (For whatever reasons, Bosch, Duisberg, and Klöckner were missing.) HA GHH/Martin Blank 400 101 202 4/10. The *Deutsche Führerbriefe* from November to January made it clear that the Nazi electoral decline, Schleicher's policies, and the beginnings of economic recovery might combine to restore the status quo ante—parliamentary and Sozialpolitik included! The *Führerbriefe* advocated a Hitler regime. See the discussion in the Introduction to this edition.

Schleicher's attempt to build a base of popular support out of the trade unions—ADGB, Christian and Nazi alike—severed from their party ties. To this end, he held discussions with Leipart, Strasser, and Silverberg, and emphasized his determination to form a viable government without Hitler.[132] Schleicher drew for economic advice on several of those from the dynamic fraction of industry, such as Schmitz, Hamm, Warmbold, and Wolff, who had earlier supported Brüning most consistently, opposed most protectionist measures for heavy industry and agriculture, and even shown some sympathy for the state takeover and nationalization of bankrupt banks and industries. The visions that Schleicher evoked finally tipped the scales for Hitler: visions of some sort of dirigist, social general following reckless, inflationary policies[133] represented, on the one hand, by outsiders like his minister for Work Creation, Gunther Gereke, and the former head of the Statistics Office, Ernst Wagemann, and, on the other, by the "consumption power" proposals of the ADGB.[134] Finally, the chairman of the Catholic Zentrum, Prelate Kaas, told Hindenburg in late November, "There are 12 million Germans in the right opposition [NSDAP] and 13.5 in the left [i.e., 6 for the KPD and 7.3 for the SPD]" with the communists growing stronger daily. He feared the left could unify at any time and that it was going to be a long, bad winter. "The NSDAP must be brought now . . . into a government of national concentration."[135]

It is important to point out that although there were some active Nazi ideologues among the leading figures of industry (few in the dynamic fraction, more in heavy industry; yet more among the rural elite), the important question is not how "fascist" was industry, nor how inti-

132. Thilo Vogelsang, *Reichswehr, Staat und NSDAP* (Stuttgart, 1962), pp. 381, 482ff.; Stegmann, "Faschismus," pp. 53–55, 73; Grotkopp, pp. 75ff.; and above, pp. 163–65; 210–12, 268f.

133. On "consumption power" or Kaufkraft theories, see Schneider, *Unternehmer,* pp. 65ff., 121ff.; Wolffsohn; Woytinsky, *Stormy Passage,* and remarks concluding chap. 5 above. As noted earlier, Schleicher immediately withdrew Papen's September decrees, which had lowered wages and canceled labor contracts. Leipart and Strasser both supported Schleicher's antiagrarian Siedlung proposals (see note 100 above) and a list of nationalizations. On Wagemann and other work-creation policies, see chap. 3, sec. 6 above. Here the *Führerbrief* were most explicit.

134. The literature on Schleicher remains very divided on the issue of his "true intentions." But even if he had been a pure opportunist, perhaps especially if he was, radical economic policies formulated in collaboration with the unions were a distinct possibility; high on the agenda was nationalization of the armaments industries. See Breitman; Gates; Wolffsohn, pp. 98–106; Schneider, *Arbeitsbeschaffungsprogramm,* pp. 195ff.; Woytinsky, *Stormy Passage,* pp. 491–98, for a sampling of opinions.

135. ZSA/Büro des Reichspräsidenten/47, p. 328. Kaas wanted to be certain that the movement went "forwards" rather than "backwards" as it threatened to do under Schleicher. It is worth noting that a number of perceptive observers, German and foreign, thought both civil war and revolution a distinct possibility.

mately involved were its leaders in the backstage events leading to Hitler's appointment.[136] The bourgeoisie saw no other way out of the crisis; it decided "consciously" in favor of the Nazis. The various middle strata, urban and rural, that the Nazis had attracted seemed to be the proper support classes for reestablishing a modified version of the prewar Sammlung under the leadership of heavy industry.[137] These strata, including some salaried employees, were bearing a disproportionate share of the economic costs of the Depression, because the unions and SPD had succeeded, at least to a minimal extent, in protecting their employed industrial workers from the requisite cuts in wages and state-welfare assistance.[138]

Our primary question has been how and why the leading fractions of the dominant social classes came to see the NSDAP as the most reliable or best available basis of support for continuing their own social dominance and for liquidating Weimar democracy. Basically, it seems that the economically disparate collection of urban petite bourgeoisie, peasantry, and some salaried employees which had been shortchanged in all the Weimar coalitions or blocs since 1924 had been reaggregated politically by the Nazi Party, and that the aggregation's demands were such that they could provide for the reconsolidation of German capitalism at a time of economic and political crisis. What the Weimar Coalition of SPD, DDP, and Z had accomplished during and after the traumas of 1918–23 would now be accomplished by or through the Nazis. The SPD had changed the face of imperial German capitalism, perhaps even improved it, but certainly did not destroy it; why should "more" now be expected or feared of the properly nationalistic Nazis? Clearly, the bourgeoisie itself and its parties were by 1932 even less able to bear the weight of the dominant social classes than they had been a decade earlier. To elicit consent, to reach an equilibrium with the subordinate classes, the interests of at least some of them had to be acceded to in some measure.[139] Whereas the interests of the SPD were clearly defined on a class basis—the daily interests of the organized working class—the very lack of an economic or class basis for the NSDAP created the impression that its demands would be less costly to the accumulation process!

---

136. One can, however, appreciate the political place of these arguments in the ideological struggle between West and East Germany as well as in political debate within West Germany. Obviously, Czichon, Stegmann, Turner, and scores of others are engagés.

137. Cf. Blocs 1 and 5 (figures 1, 5), above.

138. See Speier; Geiger, *Schichtung,* pp. 106ff., "Panik," pp. 641ff.; Kocka, "Problematik," p. 806; Arthur Rosenberg, *Geschichte,* p. 314.

139. See Gramsci, pp. 161, 281–82. Force, fraud, *and* consent are all present. Even the most reactionary among German industrialists as well as the military itself realized that a government of pure force, a military dictatorship, was virtually impossible.

The wage and social-welfare policies of 1924 through 1929 integrated employed organized labor[140] (partially at the Mittelstand's expense); conflicts moved from the factories and streets to the chancelleries and ministries, and labor's achievements bound the SPD to the system. This, in turn, had three dire consequences for the SPD and organized labor: first, the SPD's post-1930 policy of always supporting the "lesser evil" was no tactical blunder; it was at the core of a party whose raison d'être depended on saving whatever was salvageable of the parliamentary system.[141] Second, the union leadership was more firmly tied to the state mechanism than to the SPD, and its loyalties could be shifted to whomever or whatever promised to consider its material claims (e.g., Schleicher). Hence, the adhesion of the unions to the SPD would depend primarily on the political fate of the parliamentary republic.[142] Therefore, representatives of the dominant classes might reasonably expect that, once in power, the Nazis, too, would be able to elicit the support of substantial portions of organized labor.

It was the republican political framework which permitted the SPD to make organized labor such an impediment to the accumulation process. In a rather striking article appearing in a newsletter for industrialists but written by a closet-Marxist, the political implications of this are made explicit: "A bourgeois regime which is dependent on a liberal constitution must be much more than just parliamentary; it must use social democracy to support itself, and it must permit social democracy considerable and sufficient accomplishments. A bourgeois regime which wipes out thse accomplishments must sacrifice both social democracy *and* parliamentarism; it must secure a replacement for social democracy and make a transition to a compulsion-based [*gebeundene*] constitution."[143] If the NSDAP could reintegrate the union membership—now separated from the SPD—through some kind of "national corporatism," then social support for both the regime and the dominant classes would be extended considerably beyond the Nazis'

140. But not all of labor. One must remember that unemployment was consistently high in Weimar Germany; see table 32 and accompanying discussions above, and Bry, pp. 398–400. Part of the success of the KPD can be understood on this basis.

141. The "lesser evil" policy and its consequences occupy a central place in nearly every Social Democrat's memoirs whether critical or justificatory. See Hans Mommsen, "Die Sozialdemokratie in der Defensive: Der Immobilismus der SPD. . . ," in Mommsen, ed., pp. 106–33.

142. See Müller-Jentsch, p. 151; Maier, pp. 59ff.; Przeworski, "Capitalist Democracy," pp. 60ff.; Schneider, *Arbeitsbeschaffungsprogramm*, pp. 157–65; and pp. 29–31, 38ff., 127ff., and 269 above.

143. Alfred Sohn-Rethel, "Die Eingliederung des Nationalisozialismus," in *Deutsche Führerbriefe*, Sept. 1932, reprinted in Sohn-Rethel, p. 170. This newsletter was published by the MWT; see chap. 4, sec. 8.

initial Mittelstand base. Further, conflict among the dominant fractions would no longer need to be "mediated" by, or on the terrain of, a socialist-influenced legislature.[144] Here, finally, would be a stable political power capable of meeting both national and economic needs. The permanent state of political crisis caused, in part, by the Weimar Constitution itself could finally be terminated.[145] Those in power could lead without being immobilized by the particularistic demands of a host of parties and interests, and those whose primary interests lay in profitability and production could await real improvements. And most members of the dominant fractions were indeed concerned primarily with improving production and profitability within Germany and expanding markets abroad. This attitude was reflected in a statement made by the liberal DIHT several weeks after Hitler had assumed office and repressive decrees were issued. "Because we are a chamber of commerce we judge the government according to what it does and does not do in the area of *economic policy*." The RDI took much the same position, stressing "internal quiet [*Ruhe*] and social peace [*sozialen Frieden*]." It concluded that "the position of industry toward the new government must depend on its economic policy measures"[146], domestic and foreign.

To paraphrase Arthur Rosenberg, we can say that the "middle-class Republic collapsed because its destiny had been entrusted to the middle classes," and, given a strong organized working class, the Republic divided and weakened those middle classes rather than serving them. Fascism was not simply the outcome of this particular struggle between labor and capital or of any particular kind of equilibrium between the two.[147] It was also, as we have demonstrated, the outcome of the inability of fragmented dominant groups to organize and unify their interests. It was, then, also a product, in Gramsci's words, of the

144. Indeed, Dsenis argued in late 1933 that such conflicts were now settled inside the party rather than in Parliament; Dsenis, p. 187.

145. The Weimar Constitution tried to ensure a situation where every stratum or collectivity could have its own representatives. State policy would emerge from the collision and conflict of the various interests; see Arthur Rosenberg's comment on Preuss's constitution, *Geschichte*, p. 61, and Kirchheimer, *Von Republik zum Faschismus*, passim. The ideal-typical bourgeois pluralist constitution in a land that had no bourgeois revolution!

146. On the willingness to permit the Nazis to engage in some experimental economic programs, Gates, p. 225. The DIHT's concern with the right to make money is from BA/Nachlass Silverberg/646, p. 215, 2 Mar. 1933. On the prospects for expansion eastward and rearmament, see Stegmann, "Zoll- und Handelspolitik," p. 512, Dsenis, p. 182. RDI quoted in the *Berliner Tageblatt* of 8 and 18 Feb. 1933.

147. For the merits and weaknesses of the Thalheimer and Trotsky interpretations of catastrophic equilibrium, see the various numbers of *Das Argument* since 1966 devoted to analyses of fascism.

"interplay of relations between the principal groups (of various kinds, socio-economic and technical-economic) of the fundamental [dominant] classes and the auxiliary forces directed by, or subjected to, their hegemonic influence."[148] Yet, in order to protect their social dominance, industrialists and estate owners exposed themselves to a potentially uncertain future. Of course, they were not without means to defuse Hitler's demagogic promises, but they certainly enjoyed much less influence than they had had among the primary bourgeois parties. "The passage of the troops of many different parties under the banner of a single party" was not without its dangers. The extraordinary political conditions Nazism created and the replacement of bourgeois civility and frock coats with tension and plebian brown inspired some doubts. By and large, those bourgeois politicians who found all this distasteful simply shuffled off stage, but some politicians and prominent economic figures alike must have feared what might be undertaken by this "scum of bourgeois society forming the holy phalanx of order."[149]

In retrospect one can assert that they had good cause. Following Schacht's policies, the Nazis in cooperation with industrialists had by 1936 accomplished most of the tasks necessary to stabilize capitalism—the functional equivalent of the New Deal. Their Mittelstand or artisanal socialism had proven to be a washout virtually from the start; the Nazis were left with "only" their imperialist and racist platforms. They could not choose to increase consumption and return to peaceful capitalism because, without a place in the process of production, there would have been no future for them. Instead, through the mobilization for war, Nazi autonomy increased.[150] Again, the lack of a general class interest beyond their private and fractional interests prevented German capitalists from opposing this. Industrialists were reduced to competing for state orders, but they could tolerate such a situation because organized labor had been eliminated politically.[151] Between 1936 and the initiation of warfare, the fractions of industry were individualized; intracapitalist competition was systematically encouraged. In general, the daily interests of individual entrepreneurs were restricted less than was the case under the New Deal, while at the same time the Nazis were considerably more independent of the social and economic elite than was Roosevelt. The extent of state control over the economy helped deprive German capitalists of their ability to resist Nazi pro-

148. Arthur Rosenberg, *Geschichte,* p. 306; Gramsci, p. 222. See also Richard Löwenthal [Paul Sering], pp. 63–79, esp., p. 78.

149. Gramsci, p. 211; Vajda, p. 18. The similarities between Louis Napoleon's Society of December 10 and the Nazi SA were more than superficial.

150. Mason, chap. 6.

151. Vajda, p. 16.

posals. Many capitalists became so dependent on state contracts that they could not afford to withhold investments in order to express any opposition they might have felt. Rigid control of foreign exchange rendered capital flight very unlikely even if contemplated. Certainly, the dominant social classes and their leaders knew how to make the best of this situation, but, for these very reasons it would appear that the New Deal represented the historical interests of the dominant classes better than did National Socialism.[152] Having, however, chosen "the road to serfdom," German capitalists proceeded to pave it—with gold and blood.

152. According to Angelo Tasca, the fascist state not only replaced the private capitalist as the organizer of production and of the economy, but it also forced its political plans on the private capitalists—while of course preserving and even increasing profits. "Allgemeine Bedingungen der Entstehung und des Aufstieges des Faschismus," in Abendroth, ed., pp. 181–85.

BIBLIOGRAPHY

Archival Sources (Series Designations Only)

Bundesarchiv, Koblenz (BA)

R43I, R43II—Reichskanzlei Akten und Schriftwechsel betreff
 Landwirtschaft und Ernährung
 Kammern, Behörden und Verbände
 Handel und Zölle
R11   Deutscher Industrie und Handelstag (DIHT)
R12I   Vorakten der Reichsgruppe Industrie (RDI)
R13I   Wirtschaftsgruppe Eisenschaffende Industrie (VDESI)
R13III   Verband der Deutschen Landmaschinenindustrie (LMV)
R13XX   Bergbau
R45II   Akten der DVP
R45III   Akten der DDP
R99F   Agrarverbände und Genossenschaften
Nachlässe
 Hermann Dietrich
 Eduard Dingeldey
 Abraham Frowein
 Heinrich Haslinde
 Alfred Hugenberg
 Karl Jarres
 Ludwig Kastl
 Gustav Roesicke
 Hans Schlange-Schöningen
 Kurt von Schleicher
 Paul Silverberg
Zeitgeschichtliche Sammlungen (Z Sg)
 RDI
 Lautenbach
 Bauer
 Kiel Institut
 Chemie
 Hansa Bund

Deutscher Gewerkschafts Bund Archiv, Düsseldorf (DGB)

ADGB Vorstandskorrespondenz
Nachlässe
  Theodor Leipart
  Fritz Tarnow

Deutsches Industrie Institut, Cologne (DII)

Geschäftliche Mitteilungen des RDI und Verschiedenes betreff. Industrie

Zentrales Staatsarchiv, Abt. I, Potsdam (ZSA)

Büro des Reichspräsidenten
  Allgemeine Landfragen
  Kabinettsbildungen und Verabschiedungen
  Kredit Problemen
  Lage der Industrie
  Ostprogramm und Agrarmassnahmen
DNVP-Reichsleitung
  Krisen in der Partei
Reichslandbund (RLB)
  Schriftwechsel
  Sitzungen des Wirtschaftskuratorium
  Verhältnisse zwischen Landwirtschaft und Industrie
  Vorstand
Pressarchiv des Reichslandbundes
  Industrie und Landwirtschaft (132)
  Langnamverein (192)
  RDI und Industrie (148)
Reichsministerium des Innern
  DNVP
Reichswirtschaftsministerium
  Vorläufiger Reichswirtschaftsrat

Historische Kommission zu Berlin, (West) Berlin (HKB)

Vorstandssitzungen Protokolle des ADGB

Historisches Archiv der Gutehoffnungshütte, Oberhausen (HA GHH)

Martin Blank, Berlinstelle der GHH
Nachlass Paul Reusch
  Industrie und Landwirtschaft
  Langnamverein-Schlenker
  Politische und Wirtschaftspolitische Angelegenheiten
  Schriftwechsel

Contemporaneous Newspapers, Journals, and Official Publications

Agrarpolitische Wochenschrift
Die Arbeit
Der Arbeitgeber
Archiv fü Sozialwissenschaft und Sozialpolitik
Berliner Börsen Zeitung
Berliner Tageblatt
Berliner Zeitung
Deutsche Allgemeine Zeitung
Deutsche Arbeitgeber Zeitung
Deutsche Bergwerkszeitung
Deutsche Führerbriefe
Deutsche Kreuz Zeitung
Deutsche Rundschau
Deutsche Tageszeitung
Deutsche Volkswirt
Deutsche Zeitung
Europäische Revue
Frankfurter Zeitung
Germania
Geschäftliche Mitteilungen für die Mitglieder des RDI
Die Gesellschaft
Gewerkschaftszeitung
Industrie und Handels Zeitung
Die Internationale
Jahrbuch des ADGB
Kölnische Zeitung
Magazin der Wirtschaft
Reichsarbeitsblatt
Rheinische Bauernzeitung
Rote Fahne
Ruhr und Rhein Wirtschaftszeitung
Schriften der Gesellschaft für Soziale Reform, no. 83
Sozialdemokratische Agrarkorrespondenz
Stahl und Eisen
Statistisches Jahrbuch des Deutschen Reichs
Statistisches Jahrbuch für das Deutsche Reich
Unter dem Banner des Marxismus
Veröffentlichungen des RDI, nos. 28, 37, 38, 42, 47–50, 52, 55–60
Vierteljahrhefte zur Konjunkturforschung
Vorwärts
Vossische Zeitung
Westfälische Bauern Zeitung
Westfälischer Bauer
Wirtschaft und Statistik

Books, Articles, and Other Published Literature Cited

Abendroth, Wolfgang, ed. *Faschismus und Kapitalismus.* Frankfurt: Europäische Verlagsanstalt, 1967.

Adler, Max. *Politische oder soziale Demokratie.* Berlin: E. Laubsche Verlagsbuchhandlung, 1926.

Agrarpolitik in Zahlen. Bremen: Deutsche Bauernschaft, 1930.

Albertin, Lothar. "Faktoren eines Arrangements zwischen industriellem und politischem System." In *Industrielles System und politische Entwicklung in der Weimarer Republik,* edited by Hans Mommsen, Dietmar Petzina, and Bernd Weisbrod, pp. 658–74. Düsseldorf: Droste Verlag, 1974.

———. *Liberalismus und Demokratie am Anfang der Weimarer Republik: Eine vergleichende Analyse der DDP und der DVP.* Düsseldorf: Droste Verlag, 1972.

Althusser, Louis. *For Marx.* New York: Random House, 1970.

Althusser, Louis; and Balibar, Etienne. *Reading Captial.* London: New Left Books, 1970.

Angress, Werner. "The Political Role of the Peasantry in the Weimar Republic." *Review of Politics* 21 (1959):530–50.

Averitt, R. T. *The Dual Economy.* New York: W. W. Norton, 1968.

Baade, Fritz. "Agrarpolitik und Preussenwahl." *Die Gesellschaft* 9 (1932):289–302.

———. "Die neuen agrarischen Ideen seit 1914." In *Festgabe für Lujo Brentano,* pp. 227–58. Leipzig: Duncker & Humblot, 1925.

———. "Richtlinien für ein sozialdemokratisches Agrarprogramm." *Die Gesellschaft* 2 (1924):122–53.

Backhaus, H. G., ed. *Gesellschaft: Beiträge zur Marxschen Theorie.* Vol. 6. Frankfurt: Suhrkamp Verlag, 1976.

Barmeyer, Heide. *Andreas Hermes und die Organisationen der deutschen Landwirtschaft.* Stuttgart: Fischer, 1971.

Bauer, Otto. "Der Faschismus." In *Faschismus und Kapitalismus,* edited by Wolfgang Abendroth, pp. 143–67. Frankfurt: Europäische Verlagsanstalt, 1967.

Beckenbach, Ralf. *Der Staat im Faschismus.* West Berlin: Verlag für das Studium der Arbeiterbewegung, 1974.

Becker, Joseph. "Die Deutsche Zentrumspartei, 1918–1933." *Aus Politik und Zeitgeschichte* 11 (1968):2–12.

Beckmann, F., et al. *Grundlagen und Formen der Deutschen Landwirtschaft.* Berichte über Landwirtschaft, Sonderheft no. 84. Berlin: Paul Parey, 1933.

Bendix, Reinhard. *Max Weber: An Intellectual Portrait.* Garden City: Doubleday Anchor, 1960.

Bergmann, Klaus. *Agrarromantik und Grossstadtfeindschaft.* Meisenheim/Glan: Verlag Anton Hain, 1970.

Bergsträsser, Ludwig. *Geschichte der politischen Parteien in Deutschland.* Munich: Isar Verlag, 1965.

Bertrand, Charles, ed. *Revolutionary Situations in Europe, 1917–1922*. Montreal: Inter-University Centre for European Studies, 1977.

Bettelheim, Charles. *L'Economie allemande sous le nazisme*. Vol. 1. Paris: François Maspero, 1971.

Beyer, Hans. "Die Agrarkrise und das Ende der Weimarer Republik." *Zeitschrift für Agrargeschichte und Agrarsoziologie* 13 (1965):64–82.

Blackburn, Robin, ed. *Ideology in Social Science*. New York: Random House, 1973.

Blaich, Fritz. "Garantierter Kapitalismus: Subventionspolitik und Wirtschaftsordnung," *Zeitschrift für Unternehmensgeschichte* 22 (1977): 50–70.

Blanke, Bernhard. *Kritik der Politischen Wissenschaft*. Frankfurt: Campus Verlag, 1975.

Böhme, Helmut. *Deutschlands Weg zur Grossmacht: Studien zum Verhältnis von Wirtschaft und Staat, 1848–1861*. Cologne: Kiepenheuer & Witsch, 1966.

Böhret, Carl. *Aktionen gegen die 'kalte Sozialisierung'*. Berlin: Duncker & Humblot, 1966.

Böhret, Carl, ed. *Interdependenzen von Politik und Wirtschaft*. Berlin: Duncker & Humblot, 1967.

Booms, Hans. "Die DVP." In *Das Ende der Parteien, 1933,* edited by Erich Matthias and Rudolf Morsey, pp. 523–39. Düsseldorf: Droste Verlag, 1960.

Born, Karl-Erich. *Die deutsche Bankenkrise 1931*. Munich: R. Piper Verlag, 1967.

Bracher, K. D. *Die Auflösung der Weimarer Republik*. Stuttgart: Ring-Verlag, 1955.

Brady, Robert. *The Rationalization Movement in German Industry*. Berkeley: University of California Press, 1933.

Bramsted, Ernest K. *Aristocracy and the Middle Classes in Germany*. Chicago: University of Chicago Press, 1964.

Bramstedt, Paul. "Die Tauschbeziehungen von Landwirtschaft und Industrie— Probleme des Binnenmarkts." In Friedrich List Gesellschaft, 2:413–52.

Brandt, Karl; von Dietze, Constantin; and Zorner, Friedrich. *Beiträge zu einem Agrarprogramm*. Veröffentlichungen des RDI, 52 Berlin: RDI, 1930.

Bratz, Werner. "Die agrarisch-industrielle Front 1930–1932." *Schmollers Jahrbuch* 91 (1971):545–69.

Breimyer, Harold. "The Three Economies of Agriculture." *Journal of Farm Economics* 44 (1962):676–90.

Breitman, Richard. "German Social Democracy and General Schleicher." *Central European History* 9 (1976):352–78.

Bresciani-Turroni, Constantino. *The Economics of Inflation*. London: Allen & Unwin, 1937.

Bruck, W. F. *Social and Economic History of Germany from William II to Hitler*. Cardiff: Oxford University Press, 1938.

Bry, Gerhard. *Wages in Germany, 1871–1945*. Princeton: Princeton University Press, 1960.

Buchta, Bruno. *Die Junker und die Weimarer Republik*. Berlin-Leipzig: VEB, 1959.

Cammett, John. *Antonio Gramsci and the Origins of Italian Communism.* Stanford: Stanford University Press, 1967.

Carsten, F. L. *The Reichswehr and Politics, 1918–1933.* London: Oxford University Press, 1966.

———. *Revolution in Central Europe.* Berkeley and Los Angeles: University of California Press, 1972.

Castellan, Georges. *L'Allemagne de Weimar.* Paris: Presses Universitaire de France, 1969.

———. "Zur sozialen Bilanz der Prosperität, 1924–29." In *Industrielles System und politische Entwicklung in der Weimarer Republik,* edited by Hans Mommsen, Dietmar Petzina, and Bernd Weisbrod, pp. 104–110. Düsseldorf: Droste Verlag, 1974.

Chanady, Attila. "The Disintegration of the DNVP, 1924–1930." *Journal of Modern History* 39 (1967):65–90.

Chayanov, A. V. *The Theory of Peasant Economy.* Homewood, Ill.: Richard D. Irwin for the American Economic Association, 1966.

Childers, Thomas. "Social Bases of the National Socialist Vote." *Journal of Contemporary History* 11 (1976):17–42.

Clapham, Joseph. *The Economic Development of France and Germany.* Cambridge: Cambridge University Press, 1936.

Clemenz, Manfred. *Gesellschaftliche Ursprunge des Faschismus.* Frankfurt: Suhrkamp Verlag, 1972.

Conze, Werner. "Brüning als Reichskanzler: Eine Zwischenbilanz." *Historische Zeitschrift* 214 (1972):310–34.

———. "Die politischen Entscheidungen in Deutschland 1929–1933." In *Die Staats- und Wirtschaftskrise des Deutschen Reichs, 1929–33,* edited by Werner Conze and Hans Raupach, pp. 176–252. Stuttgart: Ernst Klett Verlag, 1967.

Conze, Werner; and Raupach, Hans, eds. *Die Staats- und Wirtschaftskrise des Deutschen Reichs 1929–33.* Stuttgart: Ernst Klett Verlag, 1967.

Croner, Fritz. "Die Angestelltenbewegung nach der Stabilisierung." *Archiv für Sozialwissenschaft und Sozialpolitik* 60 (1928):103–46.

Czada, Peter. *Die Berliner Elektroindustrie in der Weimarer Zeit.* Berlin: Colloquium Verlag, 1969.

Czichon, Eberhard. *Wer verhalf Hitler zur Macht?* Cologne: Pahl-Rugenstein, 1967.

Dahrendorf, Ralf. *Society and Democracy in Germany.* Garden City: Doubleday Anchor, 1967.

David, Eduard. *Sozialismus und Landwirtschaft.* Leipzig: Quelle & Meyer, 1922.

Denecke, Horst. "Die Agrarpolitische Konzeption des deutschen Imperialismus." Ph.D. dissertation, Humboldt University, Berlin, 1972.

Döhn, Lothar. *Politik und Interesse: Die Interessenstruktur der DVP.* Meisenheim/Glan: Verlag Anton Hain, 1970.

———. "Zur Verschränkung der DVP mit grosswirtschaftlich–industriellen Interessen im Herrschaftssystem der Weimarer Republik." In *Industrielles System und politische Entwicklung in der Weimarer Republik,* edited by

Hans Hommsen, Dietmar Petzina, and Bernd Weisbrod, pp. 884–906. Düsseldorf: Droste Verlag, 1974.

Dovring, Folke. *Land and Labor in Europe, 1900–1950*. The Hague: Mouton, 1956.

Dsenis, O. "Der Faschismus und die Wiedersprüche im Lager der deutschen Bourgeoisie." *Unter dem Banner des Marxismus* 7 (1933):166–90.

Dumont, Rene. *Types of Rural Economy*. London: Methuen, 1957.

Eisfeld, R. *Pluralismus zwischen Liberalismus und Sozialismus*. Stuttgart: Ernst Klett Verlag, 1972.

Eksteins, Modris. *The Limits of Reason: The German Democratic Press and the Collapse of Weimar Democracy*. London: Croon-Helm, 1975.

Eley, Geoff. "Social Imperialism in Germany: Reformist Synthesis or Reactionary Sleight of Hand?" In *Imperialismus im 20 Jahrhundert: Gendenkschrift für G.W.F. Hallgarten*, edited by Joachim Radkau, pp. 171–223. Munich: Verlag C. H. Beck, 1976.

Engels, Friedrich. *The Role of Force in History*. New York: International Publishers, 1968.

Enquête Ausschuss. *Die Förderung der Landwirtschaft durch öffentliche Mittel*. Vol. 13. Berlin: Mittler, 1930.

Feldman, Gerald. *Army, Industry and Labor in Germany, 1914–1918*. Princeton: Princeton University Press, 1966.

————. "Big Business and the Kapp Putsch." *Central European History* 4 (1971):99–130.

————. *Iron and Steel in the German Inflation, 1916–1923*. Princeton: Princeton University Press, 1977.

————. "Wirtschafts- und sozialpolitische Probleme der Demoblimachung." In *Industrielles System und politische Entwicklung in der Weimarer Republik*, edited by Hans Mommsen, Dietmar Petzina, and Bernd Weisbrod, pp. 618–36. Düsseldorf: Droste Verlag, 1974.

Feldman, Gerald; and Nocken, Ulrich. "Trade Associations and Economic Power: Interest Group Development in the German Iron and Steel and Machine Building Industries, 1900–1933." *Business History Review* 49 (1975):413–45.

Festgabe für Lujo Brentano. Leipzig: Duncker & Humblot, 1925.

Fetscher, Iring. "Critique of Soviet Marxist Analyses of Fascism." In *Marx and Marxism*, pp. 274–301. New York: Herder & Herder, 1971.

Flechtheim, Ossip. *Die KPD in der Weimarer Republik*. Frankfurt: Europäische Verlagsanstalt, 1969.

Flechtner, Hans-Joachim. *Carl Duisberg: Vom Chemiker zum Wirtschaftsführer*. Düsseldorf: Econ Verlag, 1959.

Flemming, Jens. "Grossagrarische Interessen und Landarbeiterbewegung." In *Industrielles System und politische Entwicklung in der Weimarer Republik*, edited by Hans Mommsen, Dietmar Petzina, and Bernd Weisbrod, pp. 745–62. Düsseldorf: Droste Verlag, 1974.

————. *Landwirtschaftliche Interessen und Demokratie. Ländliche Gesellschaften, Agrarverbände und Staat, 1890–1925*. Bonn-Bad Godesberg: Verlag Neue Gesellschaft, 1978.

————. "Zwischen Industrie und christlich-nationaler Arbeiterschaft: Alternativen landwirtschaftlicher Bündnispolitik in der Weimarer Republik." In *Industrielle Gesellschaft und politisches System*, edited by Dirk Stegmann, B. J. Wendt, and P. C. Witt, pp. 259–70. Bonn-Bad Godesberg: Verlag Neue Gesellschaft, 1978.

Franz, Günther. *Quellen zur Geschichte des deutschen Bauernstandes.* Darmstadt: Wissenschaftliche Buchgesellschaft, 1963.

Fremdling, Rainer and Tilly, Richard. "German Banks, German Growth and Econometric History." *Journal of Economic History* 36 (1976): 416–24.

Fricke, Dieter, ed. *Die Bürgerlichen Parteien in Deutschland*. Vols. 1 and 2. Berlin-Leipzig: Das Europäische Buch, 1968, 1971.

Friedrich List Gesellschaft. *Deutsche Agrarpolitik im Rahmen der inneren und äusseren Wirtschaftspolitik*. Vols. 1 and 2. Friedrich List Gesellschaft series, Vols. 6 and 7. Berlin: Reimar Hobbing, 1932; Oeynhausen: n.p., 1933.

Gates, Robert. "Von der Sozialpolitik zur Wirtschaftspolitik?" In *Industrielles System und politische Entwicklung in der Weimarer Republik,* edited by Hans Mommsen, Dietmar Petzina, and Bernd Weisbrod, pp. 206–26. Düsseldorf: Droste Verlag, 1974.

Geiger, Theodor. "Die Panik im Mittelstand." *Die Arbeit* 7 (1930):637–54.

————. *Die Soziale Schichtung des deutschen Volkes.* Stuttgart: F. Enke, 1932.

Geiss, Imanuel; and Wendt, B. J. *Deutschland in der Weltpolitik des 19 und 20 Jahrhunderts: Festschrift für Fritz Fischer.* Düsseldorf: Bertelsmann Universitäts Verlag, 1973.

Gerschenkron, Alexander. *Bread and Democracy in Germany.* Berkeley: University of California Press, 1943.

————. *Economic Backwardness in Historical Perspective.* Cambridge: Harvard University Press, 1962.

Gerth, Hans; and Mills, C. Wright, eds. *From Max Weber.* New York: Oxford University Press, 1958.

Geschichte und Geselleschaft. 1:4 (1975) and 4:1 (1978).

Gessner, Dieter. *Agrarverbände in der Weimarer Republik.* Düsseldorf: Droste Verlag, 1976.

————. "Industrie und Landwirtschaft." In *Industrielles System und politische Entwicklung in der Weimarer Republik,* edited by Hans Mommsen, Dietmar Petzina, and Bernd Weisbrod, pp. 762–78. Düsseldorf: Droste Verlag, 1974.

Gies, Horst. "The NSDAP and the Agrarian Organizations in the Final Phase of the Weimar Republic." In *Nazism and the Third Reich,* edited by Henry A. Turner, pp. 45–88. New York: Quadrangle Books, 1972.

Godelier, Maurice. "Structure and Contradiction in *Capital.*" In *Ideology in Social Science,* edited by Robin Blackburn, pp. 334–68. New York: Random House, 1973.

Gordon, Harold. *The Reichswehr and the German Republic, 1919–1926.* Princeton: Princeton University Press, 1957.

Gossweiler, Kurt. *Grossbanken, Industriemonopole, Staat: Ökonomie und Politik des staatsmonopolistischen Kapitalismus in Deutschland 1914–1932.* Berlin: Akademie Verlag, 1971.

Gourevitch, Peter. "International Trade, Domestic Coalitions and Liberty:

Comparative Responses to the Crisis of 1873–1896." *Journal of Interdisciplinary History* 2 (1977):281–313.

Graham, Frank. *Exchange, Prices and Production in Hyper-Inflation Germany*. Princeton: Princeton University Press, 1930.

Gramsci, Antonio. *Selections from the Prison Notebooks*. New York: International Publishers, 1971.

Grebing, Helga. *Geschichte der Deutschen Parteien*. Wiesbaden: Franz Steiner Verlag, 1962.

Grotkopp, Wilhelm. *Die Grosse Krise: Lehren aus der Überwindung der Wirtschaftskrise, 1929–32*. Düsseldorf: Econ Verlag, 1954.

Gruber, Helmut, ed. *International Communism in the Era of Lenin*. Garden City: Doubleday Anchor, 1972.

Habermas, Jürgen. *Legitimation Crisis*. Boston: Beacon Press, 1975.

———. *Toward a Rational Society*. Boston: Beacon Press, 1970.

Hamel, Iris. *Völkischer Verband und nationale Gewerkschaft: Der DHV, 1893–1933*. Frankfurt: Europäische Verlagsanstalt, 1967.

Harms, Bernard, ed. *Strukturwandlungen der deutschen Volkswirtschaft*. Vol. 1. Berlin: Reimar Hobbing, 1929.

Hartwich, Hans-Hermann. *Arbeitsmarkt, Verbände und Staat: Die öffentliche Bindung unternehmerische Funktionen in der Weimarer Republik*. Veröffentlichung der Historischen Kommission zu Berlin. Vol. 23. Berlin: Walter de Gruyter, 1967.

Haushofer, Heinz. *Die deutsche Landwirtschaft im technischen Zeitalter*. Stuttgart: Eugen Ulmer, 1963.

Heberle, Rudolf. *From Democracy to Nazism*. Baton Rouge: Louisiana State University Press, 1945.

Heckart, Beverly. *From Basserman to Bebel: The Grand Bloc's Quest for Reform in the Kaiserreich, 1900–1914*. New Haven: Yale University Press, 1974.

Henderson, W. O. *The State and the Industrial Revolution in Prussia*. Liverpool: Liverpool University Press, 1958.

Henning, Eike. *Thesen zur deutschen Sozial und Wirtschaftsgeschichte 1933–1938*. Frankfurt: Suhrkamp Verlag, 1973.

Hermens, Ferdinand A. "Das Kabinett Brüning und die Depression." In *Staat, Wirtschaft und Politik in der Weimarer Republik: Festschrift für Heinrich Brüning*, edited by Ferdinand A. Hermens and Theodor Schieder, pp. 287–310. Berlin: Duncker & Humblot, 1967.

Hermens, Ferdinand A.; and Schieder, Theodor. *Statt, Wirtschaft und Politik in der Weimarer Republik: Festschrift für Heinrich Brüning*. Berlin: Duncker & Humblot, 1967.

Herrmann, Walther. *Bündnisse und Zerwürfnisse zwischen Landwirtschaft und Industrie*. Dortmund: Gesellschaft für Westfälische Wirtschafts Geschichte, 1965.

Hertz-Eichenrode, Dieter. *Politik und Landwirtschaft in Ostpreussen, 1919–1930*. Cologne: Westdeutscher Verlag, 1969.

Hilferding, Rudolf. "Handelspolitik und Agrarkrise." *Die Gesellschaft* 1 (1924):113–30.

Hirsch, Joachim. *Wissenschaftlich-technischer Fortschritt und politisches System.* Frankfurt: Suhrkamp Verlag, 1970.

Hobsbawm, E. J. "Peasants and Politics." *Journal of Peasant Studies* 1 (1974):3–22.

Hoernle, Edwin. *Die Industrialisierung der deutschen Landwirtschaft.* Berlin: C. Hoym, 1928.

———. *Zum Bündnis zwischen Arbeitern und Bauern, 1928–1951.* Berlin: Akademie Verlag, 1972.

Hoffmann, Walther G. *Das Wachstum der deutschen Wirtschaft.* Berlin-Heidelberg: Springer Verlag, 1965.

Holt, John. *German Agricultural Policy, 1918–1934.* Chapel Hill: University of North Carolina Press, 1936.

Homer, Sidney. *History of Interest Rates.* New Brunswick, N.J.: Rutgers University Press, 1963.

Hüllbüsch, Ursula. "Die deutschen Gewerkschaften in der Weltwirtschaftskrise." In *Die Staats- und Wirtschaftskrise des Deutschen Reichs, 1929–33,* edited by Werner Conze and Hans Raupach, pp. 126–54. Stuttgart: Ernst Klett Verlag, 1967.

———. "Der Ruhreisenstreit in gewerkschaftlicher Sicht." In *Industrielles System und politische Entwicklung in der Weimarer Republik,* edited by Hans Mommsen, Dietmar Petzina, and Bernd Weisbrod, pp. 658–74. Düsseldorf: Droste Verlag, 1974.

The International Council for Philosophy and Humanistic Studies. *The Third Reich.* London: Weidenfeld & Nicolson, 1955.

Jochmann, Werner. "Brünings Deflationspolitik und der Untergang der Weimarer Republik." In *Industrielle Gesellschaft und politisches System,* edited by Dirk Stegmann, pp. 97–112. Bonn-Bad Godesberg: Verlag Neue Gesellschaft, 1978.

Jonas, Erasmus. *Die Volkskonservativen, 1928–1933.* Düsseldorf: Droste Verlag, 1965.

Jones, Larry. "The Crisis of White Collar Interest Politics." In *Industrielles System und politische Entwicklung in der Weimarer Republik,* edited by Hans Mommsen, Dietmar Petzina, and Bernd Weisbrod, pp. 812–16. Düsseldorf: Droste Verlag, 1974.

———. "The Dying Middle—The Fragmentation of the Bourgeois Parties." *Central European History* 5 (1972):23–54.

———. "Sammlung oder Zersplitterung? Die Bestrebungen zur Bildung einer neuen Mittelpartei in der Endphase der Weimarer Republik." *Vierteljahrshefte für Zeitgeschichte* 25 (1977):265–304.

Jostock, Paul. "The Long-Term Growth of National Income in Germany." In *Review of Income and Wealth V,* edited by Simon Kuznets, pp. 98–116. London: Bowes & Bowes, 1955.

Kaelble, Hartmut. *Industrielle Interessenpolitik in der Wilhelminischen Gesellschaft.* Berlin: Duncker & Humblot, 1967.

Keese, Dietmar. "Die volkswirtschaftlichen Gesamtgrössen für das Deutsche Reich, 1925–1936." In *Die Staats- und Wirtschaftskrise des Deutschen*

Reichs, 1929–33, edited by Werner Conze and Hans Raupach, pp. 35–81. Stuttgart: Ernst Klett Verlag, 1967.

Kehr, Eckart. *Battleship Building and Party Politics.* Chicago: University of Chicago Press, 1975.

Kirchheimer, Otto. "The Transformation of the European Party Systems." In *Political Parties and Political Development,* edited by Joseph La Palombara and Myron Weiner, pp. 177–200. Princeton: Princeton University Press, 1966.

————. *Von der Weimarer Republik zum Faschismus: Die Auflösung der demokratischen Rechtsordnung.* Frankfurt: Suhrkamp Verlag, 1976.

Knight, Maxwell. *The German Executive.* Stanford: Stanford University Press, 1952.

Kocka, Jürgen. *Klassengesellschaft im Krieg: Deutsche Sozialgeschichte, 1914–1918.* Göttingen: Vandenhoeck & Ruprecht, 1973.

————. *Unternehmensverwaltung und Angestelltenschaft am Beispiel Siemens 1847–1914.* Stuttgart: Ernst Klett Verlag, 1969.

————. "Zur Problematik der deutschen Angestellten, 1914–1933." In *Industrielles System und politische Entwicklung in der Weimarer Republik,* edited by Hans Mommsen, Dietmar Petzina, and Bernd Weisbrod, pp. 792–811. Düsseldorf: Droste Verlag, 1974.

Kokotkiewicz, Gerhard. "Der Immobiliarkredit, seine Lage und Aussichten." *Vierteljahrhefte zur Konjunkturforschung,* pp. 11–86. Sonderheft no. 30. Berlin: n.p., 1932.

Koops, Tilman. "Zielkonflikte der Agrar- und Wirtschaftspolitik in der Ära Brüning." In *Industrielles System und politische Entwicklung in der Weimarer Republik,* edited by Hans Mommsen, Dietmar Petzina, and Bernd Weisbrod, pp. 852–67. Düsseldorf: Droste Verlag, 1974.

Koszyk, Kurt. "Paul Reusch und die 'Münchener Neuesten Nachrichten.' Zum Problem Industrie und Presse in der Endphase der Weimarer Republik." *Vierteljahrshefte für Zeitgeschichte* 20 (1972):75–103.

Kovan, Alan. "The Resurgence of the Landbund and Its Organized Power." Ph.D. dissertation, University of California, Berkeley, 1973.

Krieger, Leonard. *The German Idea of Freedom.* Boston: Beacon Press, 1957.

Krohn, Claus Dieter. "Autoritärer Kapitalismus: Wirtschaftskonzeptionen im Übergang von der Weimarer Republik zum Nationalsozialismus." In *Industrielle Gesellschaft und politisches System,* edited by Dirk Stegmann, et al., pp. 113–29. Bonn-Bad Godesberg: Verlag Neue Gesellschaft, 1978.

Kuda, Rudolf. "Das Konzept der Wirtschaftsdemokratie." In *Vom Sozialistengesetz zur Mitbestimmung,* edited by H. O. Vetter, pp. 253–74. Cologne: Bund-Verlag, 1975.

Kühnl, Reinhard. *Die nationalsozialistische Linke.* Meisenheim/Glan: Verlag Anton Hain, 1966.

Kuznets, Simon, ed. *Review of Income and Wealth V.* London: Bowes & Bowes, 1955.

Laclau, Ernesto. *Politics and Ideology in Marxist Theory.* London: New Left Books, 1977.

Landes, David. *The Unbound Prometheus.* Cambridge: Harvard University Press, 1959.

Lange, Karl. "Deutsche Industrie und deutsche Landwirtschaft, Ihre Produktionsentwicklung 1925–1931." In Friedrich List Gesellschaft, 2:530–78.

LaPalombara, Joseph; and Weiner, Myron, eds. *Political Parties and Political Development.* Princeton: Princeton University Press, 1966.

Lebovics, Herman. "Agrarians vs. Industrialists." *International Revue of Social History* 21 (1967):31–65.

———. *Social Conservatism and the Middle Classes in Germany, 1914–1933.* Princeton: Princeton University Press, 1969.

Lefebvre, Henri. *The Sociology of Marx.* New York: Random House, 1969.

Lehmann, Hans G. *Die Agrarfrage in der Theorie und Praxis der deutschen Sozialdemokratie.* Tübingen: JCB Mohr (Paul Siebeck), 1970.

Levy, Hermann. *Industrial Germany.* Cambridge: Cambridge University Press, 1935.

Liesebach, Ingolf. *Der Wandel der politischen Führungsschicht der deutschen Industrie.* Hannover: Wiesel Verlag, 1957.

Lindblom, Charles. *Politics and Markets: The World's Political-Economic Systems.* New York: Basic Books, 1977.

Link, Werner, "Der amerikanische Einfluss auf die Weimarer Republik—Elemente eines penetrierten Systems." In *Industrielles System und politische Entwicklung in der Weimarer Republik,* edited by Hans Mommsen, Dietmar Petzina, and Bernd Weisbrod, pp. 489–93. Düsseldorf: Droste Verlag, 1974.

Linz, Juan. *The Breakdown of Democratic Politics.* Baltimore: Johns Hopkins University Press, 1978.

Lipset, S. M. *Political Man.* Garden City: Doubleday Anchor, 1963.

Loomis, Charles; and Beegle, J. A. "The Spread of German Nazism in Rural Areas." *American Sociological Review* 11 (1946):724–34.

Lorenz, Robert. *The Essential Features of Germany's Agricultural Policy.* New York: Columbia University Press, 1941.

Löwenthal, Richard [Paul Sering]. "Historische Voraussetzungen des Nationalsozialismus." In *Zeitschrift für Sozialismus* (1935). Reprinted in *Faschismus und Monopolkapitalismus,* pp. 63–79. Berlin: n.p., 1967.

———. "Die Wandlungen des Kapitalismus." *Zeitschrift für Sozialismus* (1935). Reprinted in *Faschismus und Monopolkapitalismus,* pp. 1–22. Berlin, n.p., 1967.

Lukács, Georg. *History and Class Consciousness.* London: Merlin Press, 1971.

Maier, Charles. *Recasting Bourgeois Europe.* Princeton: Princeton University Press, 1975.

Mannheim, Karl. *Ideology and Utopia.* New York: Harcourt, Brace & World, 1936.

Mariaux, Franz, ed. *Reden und Schriften von Paul Silverberg.* Cologne: Presse der Universität Köln, 1952.

Marx, Karl. *Capital.* Vols. 1–3. New York: International Publishers, 1967.

———. *The 18th Brumaire of Louis Bonaparte.* New York: International Publishers, 1963.

———. *The German Ideology.* New York: International Publishers, 1960.

————. *Grundrisse der Kritik der Politischen Ökonomie*. Berlin: Dietz Verlag, 1953.

Mason, Tim. *Sozialpolitik im Dritten Reich*. Opladen: Westdeutscher Verlag, 1977.

Matthias, Erich; and Morsey, Rudolf. *Das Ende der Parteien, 1933*. Düsseldorf: Droste Verlag, 1960.

Mayer, Arno. *Dynamics of Counterrevolution in Europe, 1870–1956*. New York: Harper & Row, 1971.

————. *Politics and Diplomacy of Peacemaking*. New York: Knopf, 1967.

Meyer, Henry Cord. *Mitteleuropa in German Thought and Action*. The Hague: Martinus Nijhoff, 1955.

Mielke, Siegfried. *Der Hansa Bund, 1909–1914: Der gescheiterte Versuch einer anti-feudalen Sammlungspolitik*. Göttingen: Vandenhoeck & Ruprecht, 1976.

Milatz, Alfred. *Wähler und Wahlen in der Weimarer Republik*. Bonn: Schriftenreihe der Bundeszentrale für politische Bildung, 1966.

Miliband, Ralph. *The State in Capitalist Society*. London: Weidenfeld & Nicolson, 1969.

Mill, John Stuart. *Principles of Political Economy*. Harmondsworth: Penguin, 1970.

Miller, Suzanne. "Die Sozialdemokratie in der Spannung zwischen Oppositionstradition und Regierungsverantwortung in der Anfängen der Weimarer Republik." In *Sozialdemokratie zwischen Klassenbewegung und Volkspartei*, edited by Hans Mommsen, pp. 84–105. Frankfurt: Athenäum Verlag, 1974.

Milward, Alan. "Der deutsche Handel und Welthandel, 1925–1939." In *Industrielles System und politische Entwicklung in der Weimarer Republik*, edited by Hans Mommsen, Dietmar Petzina, and Bernd Weisbrod, pp. 472–85. Düsseldorf: Droste Verlag, 1974.

Mommsen, Hans. "Die Sozialdemokratie in der Defensive: Der Immobilismus der SPD und der Aufstieg des Nationalsozialismus." In *Sozialdemokratie zwischen Klassenbewegung und Volkspartei*, edited by Hans Mommsen, pp. 106–33. Frankfurt: Athenäum Verlag, 1974.

————. "Sozialpolitik im Ruhrbergbau." In *Industrielles System und politische Entwicklung in der Weimarer Republik*, edited by Hans Mommsen, Dietmar Petzina, and Bernd Weisbrod, pp. 303–21. Düsseldorf: Droste Verlag, 1974.

————, ed. *Sozialdemokratie zwischen Klassenbewegung und Volkspartei*. Frankfurt: Athenäum Verlag, 1974.

Mommsen, Hans; Petzina, Dietmar; and Weisbrod, Bernd, eds. *Industrielles System und politische Entwicklung in der Weimarer Republik*. Düsseldorf: Droste Verlag, 1974.

Moore, Barrington. *Social Origins of Dictatorship and Democracy*. Boston: Beacon Press, 1967.

Mouzelis, N. "Capitalism and the Development of Agriculture." *Journal of Peasant Studies* 3 (1976):483–92.

Müller, Klaus. "Agrarische Interessenverbände in der Weimarer Republik." *Rheinische Vierteljahrsblätter* 38 (1974):386–405.

Müller, Wolfgang; and Neusüss, Christel. "The Illusion of State Socialism and the Contradiction between Wage Labor and Capital." *Telos*, no. 25 (Fall 1975):13–90.

Müller-Jentsch, Walter. "Zum Verhältnis von Staat und Gewerkschaften." In *Rahmenbedingungen und Schranken staatlichen Handelns*, edited by Claudio Pozzoli, pp. 150–56. Frankfurt: Suhrkamp Verlag, 1976.

Münch, Paul. *Die innere Marktverflechtung von Landwirtschaft und Industrie.* Giessen: n.p., 1934.

Muth, Heinrich. "Agrarpolitik und Parteipolitik in Frühjahr 1932." In *Staat, Wirtschaft und Politik in der Weimarer Republik: Festschrift für Heinrich Brüning*, edited by Ferdinand A. Hermens and Theodor Schieder, pp. 317–60. Berlin: Duncker & Humblot, 1967.

———. "Zum Sturz Brünings." *Geschichte in Wissenschaft und Unterricht* 16 (1965):739–59.

Naphtali, Fritz. *Wirtschaftsdemokratie: Ihr Wesen, Weg und Ziel.* Berlin: Verlagsgesellschaft des Allgemeinen deutschen Gewerksschaftsbundes, 1928.

Neisser, Hans. "Sozialstatistische Analyse des Wahlergebnisses." *Die Arbeit* 7 (1930):654–59.

Neumann, Franz. *Behemoth: The Structure and Practice of National Socialism, 1933–1944.* New York: Harper & Row, 1966.

Neumann, Sigmund. *Die Parteien der Weimarer Republik.* Stuttgart: Kohlhammer, 1965.

Nocken, Ulrich. "Inter-Industrial Conflicts and Alliances as Exemplified by the AVI Agreement." In *Industrielles System und politische Entwicklung in der Weimarer Republik*, edited by Hans Mommsen, Dietmar Petzina, and Bernd Weisbrod, pp. 693–704. Düsseldorf: Droste Verlag, 1974.

Novy, Klaus. *Strategien der Sozialisierung: Die Diskussion der Wirtschaftsreform in der Weimarer Republik.* Frankfurt: Campus Verlag, 1978. 1978.

Nussbaum, Helga. *Unternehmer gegen Monopole.* Berlin: VEB, 1966.

O'Connor, James. *The Fiscal Crisis of the State.* New York: St. Martin's Press, 1973.

Offe, Claus. *Strukturprobleme des kapitalistischen Staates.* Frankfurt: Suhrkamp Verlag, 1972.

Opitz, Reinhard. *Der deutsche Sozialliberalismus, 1917–1933.* Cologne: Pahl-Rugenstein, 1973.

Panitch, Leo. "The Development of Corporatism in Liberal Democracies." *Comparative Political Studies* 10 (1977):40–61.

Panzer, Arno. *Das Ringen um die deutsche Agrarpolitik.* Kiel: Walter Mühlau, 1970.

Petzina, Dietmar. *Autarkiepolitik im Dritten Reich.* Stuttgart: Deutsche Verlags Anstalt, 1968.

———. "Germany and the Great Depression." *Journal of Contemporary History* 4 (1969): 58–72.

———. "Hauptprobleme der deutschen Wirtschaftspolitik 1932–33." *Vierteljahrshefte für Zeitgeschichte* 15 (1967):18–55.

Petzina, Dietmar; and Abelhauser, Werner. "Zum Problem der relativen Stagnation der deutschen Wirtschaft in den zwanziger Jahren." In *Industrielles System und politische Entwicklung in der Weimarer Republik,* edited by Hans Mommsen, Dietmar Petzina, and Bernd Weisbrod, pp. 57–76. Düsseldorf: Droste Verlag, 1974.

Pietrkowski, Edmund. "Agrarprogramm und Handelspolitik." MS, Berlin, 1929.

Pirker, Theo, ed. *Komintern und Faschismus: Dokumente.* Stuttgart: Deutsche Verlags Anstalt, 1966.

Plessner, Helmut. *Die verspätete Nation.* Stuttgart: Kohlhammer, 1959.

Pogge von Strandmann, Hartmut. "Wiedersprüche im Modernisierungsprozess Deutschlands: Der Kampf der verarbeitenden Industrie gegen die Schwerindustrie." In *Industrielle Gesellschaft und politisches System,* edited by Dirk Stegmann, pp. 225–40. Bonn-Bad Godesberg: Verlag Neue Gesellschaft, 1978.

Pollard, Sidney. "Trade Union Reactions to the Economic Crisis." *Journal of Contemporary History* 4 (1969):101–14.

———. "The Trade Unions and the Depression." In *Industrielles System und politische Entwicklung in der Weimarer Republik,* edited by Hans Mommsen, Dietmar Petzina, and Bernd Weisbrod, pp. 237–48. Düsseldorf: Droste Verlag, 1974.

Poulantzas, Nicos. *Fascisme et Dictature.* Paris: François Maspero, 1970.

———. "L'Examen marxiste du droit." *Les Temps Modernes,* no. 219 and no. 220 (1964):274–301.

———. *Political Power and Social Classes.* London: New Left Books and Sheed & Ward, 1973.

Pozzoli, Claudio, ed. *Rahmenbedingungen und Schranken staatlichen Handelns.* Frankfurt: Suhrkamp Verlag, 1976.

Preller, Ludwig. *Sozialpolitik in der Weimarer Republik.* Stuttgart: Franz Mittelbach Verlag, 1949.

Przeworski, Adam. "The Process of Class Formation." *Politics & Society* 7 (1977):342–401.

———. "Toward a Theory of Capitalist Democracy." *Political Power and Social Theory* 1 (1980): 21–66.

Puhle, Hans-Jürgen. *Agrarische Interessenpolitik und preussischer Konservativismus.* Hannover: Verlag für Literatur und Zeitgeschehen, 1966.

———. *Politische Agrarbewegungen in Kapitalistischen Industriegesellschaften.* Göttingen: Vandenhoeck & Ruprecht, 1975.

———. *Von der Agrarkrise zum Präfaschismus.* Wiesbaden: Franz Steiner, 1972.

Pulzer, P.G.J. *The Rise of Political Anti-Semitism in Germany and Austria.* New York: John Wiley & Sons, 1964.

Rabinbach, Anson. "Poulantzas and the Problem of Fascism." *New German Critique,* no. 8 (1976):157–70.

Radkau, Joachim, ed. *Imperialismus im 20. Jahrhundert: Gedenkschrift für George W. F. Hallgarten.* Munich: Verlag C. H. Beck, 1976.

———. "Renovation des Imperialismus im Zeichen der 'Rationalisierung.'" In *Imperialismus im 20 Jahrhundert: Gedenkschrift für George W. F. Hall-*

garten, edited by Joachim Radkau, pp. 197–246. Munich: Verlag C. H. Beck, 1976.

Raumer, Hans von. "Unternehmer und Gewerkschaften in der Weimarer Republik." *Deutsche Rundschau* 80 (1954):428–40.

"Die Reform des Schlichtungswesens: Die Wirtschaftliche Wert der Sozialpolitik." *Schriften der Gesellschaft für Soziale Reform,* no. 83. Jena: n.p., 1930.

Regul, Rudolf. "Der Wettbewerbslage der Steinkohle." *Vierteljahrshefte zur Konjunkturforschung,* Sonderheft no. 34 (1933).

Reichsverband der Deutschen Industrie. *Aufsteig oder Niedergang.* Veröffentlichung des RDI, 49. Berlin: RDI, 1929.

———. *Besteuerung, Ertrag und Arbeitslohn im Jahre 1927.* Veröffentlichung des RDI, 47. Berlin: RDI, 1929.

———. *Unternehmertum und Kapitalismus.* Veröffentlichung des RDI, 48. Berlin: RDI, 1929.

———. *Wirtschafts- und Sozialpolitik, Steuer- und Finanzpolitik.* Veröffentlichung des RDI, 50. Berlin: RDI, 1930.

Ritter, Kurt. *Agrarwirtschaft und Agrarpolitik im Kapitalismus.* Vol. 1. Berlin-Leipzig: Akademie Verlag, 1959.

Rokkan, Stein; and Lipset, S. M. *Party Systems and Voter Alignments.* Chicago: University of Chicago Press, 1962.

Röpke, Wilhelm. *German Commercial Policy.* London: Longmans & Green, 1934.

Rosenberg, Arthur. "Der Faschismus als Massenbewegung." In *Faschismus und Kapitalismus,* edited by Wolfgang Abendroth, pp. 75–141. Frankfurt: Europäische Verlagsanstalt, 1967.

———. *Geschichte der Weimarer Republik.* Cologne: Pahl-Rugenstein Verlag, 1961.

———. *Imperial Germany: The Birth of the German Republic.* Boston: Beacon Press, 1964.

Rosenberg, Hans. *Probleme der deutschen Sozialgeschichte.* Frankfurt: Suhrkamp Verlag, 1969.

Rüegg, Walter; and Neuloh, Otto. *Zur soziologische Analyse der Geschichte des 19 Jahrhunderts.* Göttingen: Vandenhoeck & Ruprecht, 1971.

Ruge, Wolfgang; and Gossweiler, Kurt, eds. *Dokumente zur deutschen Geschichte, 1929–1933.* Berlin: Deutschen Verlag der Wissenschaften, 1975.

Sanmann, Horst. "Daten und Alternativen der deutschen Wirtschafts- und Finanzpolitik in der Ära Brüning." In *Hamburger Jahrbuch für Wirtschafts- und Finanzpolitik* 10 (1965):111–17.

Sasuly, Richard. *IG Farben.* Berlin: Verlag Volk & Welt, 1952.

Schäfer, Dieter. *Der DIHT als politisches Forum der Weimarer Republik.* Hamburg: Verlag Weltarchiv, 1966.

Schäfer, Gert. *Die Kommunistische Internationale und der Faschismus.* Offenbach: Verlag 2000, 1973.

Schalldach, Elisabeth, *Rationalisierungsmassnahmen der Nachinflationszeit im Urteil der freien Gewerkschaften.* Jena: Verlag Gustav Fischer, 1930.

Scheuner, Ulrich. "Die Anwendung des Artikle 48." In *Staat, Wirtschaft und*

Politik in der Weimarer Republik: Festschrift für Heinrich Brüning, edited by Ferd A. Hermens and Theodor Schieder, pp. 249–86. Berlin: Duncker & Humblot, 1967.

Schieder, Wolfgang, ed. *Faschismus als soziale Bewegung.* Hamburg: Hoffmann & Campe, 1976.

Schlange-Schöningen, Hans. *Bauer und Boden.* Hamburg: Hanseatische Verlagsanstalt, 1933.

————. *Rationalwirtschaft und Nationalwirtschaft.* Berlin: n.p., 1927.

Schmitter, Philippe. "Still the Century of Corporatism?" *Review of Politics* 36 (1974):85–131.

Schneider, Michael. *Das Arbeitsbeschaffungsprogramm des ADGB.* Schriftenreihe des Forschungsinstituts der Friedrich-Ebert-Stiftung. Vol. 120. Bonn-Bad Godesberg: Verlag Neue Gesellschaft, 1975.

————. "Konjunkturpolitischen Vorstellungen der Gewerkschaften in den letzten Jahren der Weimarer Republik." In *Industrielles System und politische Entwicklung in der Weimarer Republik,* edited by Hans Mommsen, Dietmar Petzina, and Bernd Weisbrod, pp. 226–37. Düsseldorf: Droste Verlag, 1974.

————. *Unternehmer und Demokratie.* Schriftenreihe des Forschungsinstituts der Friedrich-Ebert-Stiftung. Vol. 116. Bonn-Bad Godesberg: Verlag Neue Gesellschaft, 1975.

————, ed. *Auf dem Weg in der Krise: Thesen und Materiallen zum Ruhreisenstreit 1928–29.* Wentorf b. Hamburg: Bers & Klöcker, 1974.

Schoenbaum, David. *Hitler's Social Revolution.* Garden City: Doubleday Anchor, 1966.

Schorske, Carl. *German Social Democracy, 1905–17.* Cambridge: Harvard University Press, 1955.

Schulz, Gerhard. *Aufstieg des Nationalsozialismus.* Frankfurt: Propyläen-Verlag, 1975.

Schumacher, Martin. "Hausbesitz, Mittelstand und Wirtschaftspartei in der Weimarer Republik." In *Industrielles System und politische Entwicklung in der Weimarer Republik,* edited by Hans Mommsen, Dietmar Petzina, and Bernd Weisbrod. pp. 823–35. Düsseldorf: Droste Verlag, 1974.

————. *Mittelstandfront und Republik in der Weimarer Republik.* Beiträge zur Geschichte des Parlamentarismus und der politischen Parteien. Vol. 44. Düsseldorf: Droste Verlag, 1972.

Schustereit, Hartmut. *Linksliberalismus und Sozialdemokratie in der Weimarer Republik.* Düsseldorf: Verlag Schwann, 1975.

Schwarz, Max. *MdR.* Hannover: Verlag für Literatur und Zeitgeschehens, 1965.

Schweitzer, Arthur. "The Nazification of the Lower Middle Class and Peasants." In *The Third Reich,* edited by The International Council for Philosophy and Humanistic Studies, pp. 576–95. London: Weidenfeld & Nicolson, 1955.

Sering, Max. *Die Deutsche Landwirtschaft unter volks- und weltwirtschaftlichen Gesichtspunkten.* Berichte über Landwirtschaft, Sonderheft no. 50. Berlin: Paul Parey, 1932.

Shefter, Martin. "New York City's Fiscal Crisis." *Public Interest,* no. 48 (Summer 1977):98–127.

Sohn-Rethel, Alfred. *Ökonomie und Klassenstruktur des deutschen Faschismus.* Frankfurt: Suhrkamp Verlag, 1973.

Solmssen, Georg. *Beiträge zur Deutschen Politik und Wirtschaft.* Munich and Leipzig: Duncker & Humblot, 1934.

————. *Die Lage der Landwirtschaft und ihre Bedeutung für das Bankgewerbe.* Berlin: Paul Parey, 1928.

Sölter, Arno. *Das Grossraumkartell.* Dresden: Meinholds Verlag, 1941.

Speier, Hans. *Die Angestellten vor dem Nationalsozialismus.* Göttingen: Vandenhoeck & Ruprecht, 1977.

Spiller, Jörg-Otto. "Reformismus nach Rechts: Zur Politik des RDI am Beispiel der Reparationspolitik." In *Industrielles System und politische Entwicklung in der Weimarer Republik,* edited by Hans Mommsen, Dietmar Petzina, and Bernd Weisbrod, pp. 593–602. Düsseldorf: Droste Verlag, 1974.

Stegmann, Dirk. "Deutsche Zoll- und Handelspolitik, 1924–1929." In *Industrielles System und politische Entwicklung in der Weimarer Republik,* edited by Hans Mommsen, Dietmar Petzina, and Bernd Weisbrod, pp. 499–513. Düsseldorf: Droste Verlag, 1974.

————. *Die Erben Bismarcks.* Cologne: Kiepenheuer und Witsch, 1970.

————. "Hugenberg contra Stresemann: Die Politik der Industrieverbände am Ende des Kaiserreichs," *Vierteljahrshefte für Zeitgeschichte* 24 (1976):329–78.

————. "Kapitalismus und Faschismus 1929–1934: Thesen und Materialien." In *Gesellschaft: Beiträge zur Marxschen Theorie,* edited by H. G. Backhaus, 6:14–75. Frankfurt: Suhrkamp Verlag, 1976.

————. "'Mitteleuropa' 1925–1934: Zum Problem der Kontinuität deutscher Aussenhandelspolitik." In *Industrielle Gesellschaft und politisches System,* edited by Dirk Stegmann, et al., pp. 203–21. Bonn-Bad Godesberg: Verlag Neue Gesellschaft, 1978.

————. "Die Silverberg-Kontroverse 1926." In *Sozialgeschichte Heute—Festschrift für Hans Rosenberg,* edited by Hans-Ulrich Wehler, pp. 594–610. Göttingen: Vandenhoeck & Ruprecht, 1974.

————. "Wirtschaft und Politik nach Bismarcks Sturz: Zur Genesis der Sammlungspolitik, 1890–1897." In *Deutschland in der Weltpolitik des 19 und 20 Jahrhunderts: Festschrift für Fritz Fischer,* edited by Imanuel Geiss and B. J. Wendt, pp. 161–84. Düsseldorf: Bertelsmann Universitätsverlag, 1973.

Stegmann, Dirk; Wendt, B. J.; and Witt, P. C., eds. *Industrielle Gesellschaft und politisches System: Beiträge zur politischen Sozialgeschichte. Festschrift für Fritz Fischer.* Bonn-Bad Godesberg: Verlag Neue Gesellschaft, 1978.

Stephan, Werner. *Aufstieg und Verfall des Linksliberalismus.* Göttingen: Vandenhoeck & Ruprecht, 1973.

Stern, Fritz, ed. *The Path to Dictatorship, 1918–1933.* Garden City: Doubleday Anchor, 1966.

Stinchcombe, Arthur. "Agricultural Enterprise and Rural Class Relations." *American Journal of Sociology* 67 (1961):165–76.

Stolper, Gustav. *German Economy, 1870–1940*. New York: Reynal & Hitchcock, 1940.

Striefler, Heinrich. *Deutsche Wahlen in Bilder und Zahlen*. Düsseldorf: Wende-Verlag Hagemann, 1946.

Stürmer, Michael. *Koalition und Opposition in der Weimarer Republik, 1924–1928*. Beiträge zur Geschichte des Parlamentarismus und der politischen Parteien. Vol. 36. Düsseldorf: Droste Verlag, 1967.

Sturmthal, Adolf. *The Tragedy of European Labor, 1918–1939*. New York: Columbia University Press, 1943.

Svennilson, Ingvar. *Growth and Stagnation in the European Economy*. Geneva: United Nations Economic Commission for Europe, 1954.

Sweezy, Maxine. "German Corporate Profits, 1926–1938." *Quarterly Journal of Economics* 54 (1940):384–98.

Tasca, Angelo. "Allgemeine Bedingungen der Entstehung und des Aufstieges des Faschismus." In *Faschismus und Kapitalismus*, edited by Wolfgang Abendroth, pp. 169–86. Frankfurt: Europäische Verlagsanstalt, 1967.

Tilly, Richard and Rainer Fremdling. "German Banks, German Growth, and Econometric History." *Journal of Economic History* 36 (1976):416–24.

Timm, Helga. *Die Deutsche Sozialpolitik und der Bruch der Grossen Koalition im März, 1930*. Beiträge zur Geschichte des Parlamentarismus und der politischen Parteien. Vol. 1. Düsseldorf: Droste Verlag, 1952.

Topf, Erwin. *Die Grüne Front*. Berlin: Rowohlt, 1933.

Tracy, Michael. *Agriculture in Western Europe*. London: Jonathan Cape, 1964.

Treue, Wilhelm. "Der deutsche Unternehmer in der Weltwirtschaftskrise." In *Die Staats- und Wirtschaftskrise des Deutschen Reichs 1929–33*, edited by Werner Conze and Hans Raupach, pp. 82–125. Stuttgart: Ernst Klett Verlag, 1967.

Turner, Henry A., Jr. "The Ruhrlade: Secret Cabinet of Heavy Industry." *Central European History* 3 (1970):195–228.

———. "Das Verhältnis des Grossunternehmertums zur NSDAP." In *Industrielles System und politische Entwicklung in der Weimarer Republik*, edited by Hans Mommsen, Dietmar Petzina, and Bernd Weisbrod, pp. 919–31. Düsseldorf: Droste Verlag, 1974.

———, ed. *Nazism and the Third Reich*. New York: Quadrangle Books, 1972.

Ullmann, Hans-Peter. *Der Bund der Industriellen. Organisation, Einfluss und Politik klein- und mittelbetrieblicher im Deutschen Kaiserreich, 1895–1914*. Göttingen: Vandenhoeck & Ruprecht, 1976.

Ulrich, Hans. "Die Einschätzung von kapitalistischen Entwicklung und Rolle des Staats durch den ADGB." *Probleme des Klassenkampfs* 6 (1973):1–70.

Vajda, Mihaly. "On Fascism." *Telos*, no. 12 (Summer 1972):3–26.

Varga, Eugen[e]. *Die Krise des Kapitalismus und ihre politischen Folgen*. Frankfurt: Europäische Verlagsanstalt, 1974.

———. "Uber dem Faschismus." In *Komintern und Faschismus: Dokumente*, edited by Theo Pirker, pp. 131–40. Stuttgart: Deutsche Verlags Anstalt, 1966.

Veblen, Thorstein. *Imperial Germany and the Industrial Revolution*. New York: Viking, 1939.

Vetter, H. O., ed. *Vom Sozialistengesetz zur Mitbestimmung.* Cologne: Bund-Verlag, 1975.

Vogel, Bernhard; Nohlen, Dieter; and Schultze, R. O. *Wahlen in Deutschland.* Berlin and New York: Walter de Gruyter, 1971.

Vogelsang, Thilo. *Reichswehr, Staat und NSDAP.* Stuttgart: Deutsche Verlags Anstalt, 1962.

Vogt, Martin. "Die Stellung der Koalitionspartein zur Finanzpolitik, 1928–1930." In *Industrielles System und politische Entwicklung in der Weimarer Republik,* edited by Hans Mommsen, Dietmar Petzina, and Bernd Weisbrod, pp. 439–62. Düsseldorf: Droste Verlag, 1974.

Wagemann, Ernst. *Der Neue Balkan.* Hamburg: Hanseatische Verlagsanstalt, 1939.

Wagenführ, Rolf. "Die Industriewirtschaft: Entwicklungstendenzen der Industrieproduktion 1860 bis 1932." *Vierteljahrhefte zur Konjunkturforschung,* Sonderheft no. 31 (1933):8–52.

Wallerstein, Immanuel. "The Rise and Future Demise of the World Capitalist System." *Comparative Studies in Society and History* 16 (1974):387–415.

Walz, Dieter. "Die Agrarpolitik der Regierung Brüning." Ph.D. dissertation, Alexander University, Erlangen-Nuremberg, 1971.

Weber, Max. "Capitalism and Rural Society in Germany." In *From Max Weber,* edited by Hans Gerth and C. Wright Mills, pp. 363–85. New York: Oxford University Press, 1958.

———. "National Character and the Junkers." In *From Max Weber,* edited by Hans Gerth and C. Wright Mills, pp. 386–95. New York: Oxford University Press, 1958.

Wehler, Hans-Ulrich. "Der Aufstieg des Organisierten Kapitalismus in Deutschland." In *Organisierter Kapitalismus: Voraussetzungen und Anfänge,* edited by H.-A. Winkler, pp. 29–43. Göttingen: Vandenhoeck & Ruprecht, 1974.

———. *Bismarck und der deutsche Imperialismus.* Cologne: Kiepenheuer & Witsch, 1969.

———. *Krisenherde des Kaiserreichs.* Göttingen: Vandenhoeck & Ruprecht, 1970.

———, ed. *Moderne deutsche Sozialgeschichte.* Cologne: Kiepenheuer & Witsch, 1966.

———, ed. *Sozialgeschichte Heute—Festschrift für Hans Rosenberg.* Göttingen: Vandenhoeck & Ruprecht, 1974.

Weisbrod, Bernd. *Schwerindustrie in der Weimarer Republik: Industrielle Interessenpolitik zwischen Stabilisierung und Krise.* Wuppertal: Hammer Verlag, 1978.

Wendt, B. J. "England und der deutsche 'Drang nach Südosten.' Kapitalbeziehungen und Warenverkehr." In *Deutschland in der Weltpolitik des 19 und 20 Jahrhunderts: Festschrift für Fritz Fischer,* edited by Imanuel Geiss and B. J. Wendt, pp. 483–512. Düsseldorf: Bertelsmann Universitätsverlag, 1973.

Wengst, Udo. "Unternehmerverbände und Gewerkschaften in Deutschland im Jahre 1930." *Vierteljahrshefte für Zeitgeschichte* 25 (1977): 99–119.

Wild, Karl. *Agrarpolitik mit richtigen Zahlen.* Berlin: Vereinigung der deutschen christlichen Bauernvereine, 1932.

Winkler, H.-A. "From Social Protectionism to National Socialism." *Journal of Modern History* 48 (1976):1–18.

————. *Mittelstand, Demokratie und Nationalsozialismus.* Cologne: Kiepenheuer & Witsch, 1972.

————. "Mittelstandsbewegung oder Volkspartei? Zur sozialen Basis der NSDAP." In *Faschismus als soziale Bewegung,* edited by Wolfgang Schieder, pp. 97–118. Hamburg: Hoffman und Campe, 1976.

————. *Pluralismus oder Protektionismus.* Wiesbaden: Franz Steiner Verlag, 1972.

————. "Unternehmerverbände zwischen Ständeideologie und Nationalsozialismus." *Vierteljahrshefte für Zeitgeschichte* 17 (1969):341–71.

————. "Unternehmer und Wirtschaftsdemokratie." *Politische Vierteljahresschrift,* 11 Sonderheft no. 2 (1970):308–22.

————, ed. *Organisierter Kapitalismus: Voraussetzungen und Anfänge.* Göttingen: Vandenhoeck & Ruprecht, 1974.

Die Wirtschaftliche Lage des Ruhrbergbaues. N.p., 1929.

Wirtschaftsverband bäuerlicher Veredelung, ed. *Der Bauer in Kampf gegen den RLB.* Bremen: n.p., 1930.

Wolf, Eric. *Peasant Wars of the Twentieth Century.* New York: Harper & Row, 1969.

Wolffsohn, Michael. *Industrie und Handwerk im Konflikt mit staatlicher Wirtschaftspolitik? Studien zur Politik der Arbeitsbeschaffung, 1930–1934.* Schriften zur Wirtschafts- und Sozialgeschichte. Vol. 30. Berlin: Duncker & Humblot, 1977.

Woytinsky, Wladimir. "Proletariat und Bauerntum." *Die Gesellschaft* 3 (1926):410–40.

————. *Stormy Passage.* New York: Vanguard Press, 1961.

Wright, Erik. *Class, Crisis and the State.* London: New Left Books, 1978.

Wunderlich, Frieda. *Farm Labor in Germany.* Princeton: Princeton University Press, 1961.

————. "Labor under German Democracy." *Social Research,* supplement 2 (1940).

Zörner, Hans; and Russig, Lothar. "Die Bedeutung der Industriepreise für die Kostengestaltung im landwirtschaftlichen Betriebe." In Friedrich List Gesellschaft, 1:357–78.

Zunkel, Friedrich. "Die Gewichtung der Industriegruppen bei der Etablierung des RDI." In *Industrielles System und politische Entwicklung in der Weimarer Republik,* edited by Hans Mommsen, Dietmar Petzina, and Bernd Weisbrod, pp. 637–47. Düsseldorf: Droste Verlag, 1974.

————. *Industrie und Staatssozialismus: Der Kampf um die Wirtschaftsordnung 1914–1918.* Düsseldorf: Droste Verlag, 1974.

INDEX

ADGB (General Federation of Unions), xix, xxi, 29, 61, 128n, 133n, 168, 230, 231n, 232, 235, 239, 240, 257, 266, 268, 270, 313; centralization of leadership in, 230–31; collapse of Grand Coalition and militancy of, 256n, 261, 264n; RDI meetings with, 129, 261–62; Schleicher's search for mass base and, 163–64, 167–68, 211; Wirtschaftsdemokratie program of, 30–31, 224n, 249–52, 269n, 269–70, 278; "Work Creation" program of, *see* WTB. *See also* labor unions.

Adler, Max, 249

AEG (German General Electric), 110, 123, 156

Aereboe, Friedrich, 66n, 74

agrarian-industrial relations, 13–15, 37–38, 44, 46–47, 97–98, 106, 114, 139–41, 142–43, 160, 162, 171–219, 271; ability of estate owners to "deliver" peasants and military in, 39–40, 56, 206–207; Bank for Industrial Obligations and, 92, 180–81, 198–99, 202; cheap food policy and, 38, 79–80; collapse of world market and, 173, 206–207; discriminatory legislation against agriculture and, 77–78; disproportionate power of agriculture in, 171, 192–94, 211–12, 292–93; domestic vs. export marketing strategies and, 13–14, 39, 49n, 60–63, 71–74, 90–92, 103–104, 132, 179, 185–94, 196–97, 199–200, 206–12, 271; Esplanade Circle and conciliation in, 180, 200–202; estate owners vs. peasants as base in, 89–94, 104–105, 172, 179, 192n; industrial capitalism vs. agricultural production in, 171, 173–75, 181; investement and rates of return in, 175–77, 182; offensive against working class and, 172–73, 201–202, 203–205, 243; relative strength and profitability in, 182–85; rift in, after 1928, 14, 188–92; strategies for increased agricultural productivity and, 179–81, 185–202, 212–19; unevenness of economic recovery and, 28–29.

Agrarian League, *see* Bund; RLB

agricultural crisis (1928), 43, 67–68, 74–105; breakdown of peasant/estate-owner alliance and, 43, 74, 80–93, 98–100, 103–105; domestic market prices in, 80–81, 83–84; increased support for Nazis and, 82–83, 95–96, 99–102, 103–105; indebtedness and, 75–76; preferential treatment accorded to estate owners in, 80–89, 94–96, 203; world market prices in, 75–77, 83–84

agricultural sector, 42–105, 245–46, 291n; access to capital in, 69, 73–76, 83–85, 174–77, 180–81; capitalist relations in, 12–13, 47–48, 49–52; capitalist socialization in, 212–15; cartellization in, 165, 180–81, 211–19; consumption in, 173, 181–82, 183; in Imperial Germany, 45–49; imports and import quotas in, 60, 78–80, 82, 97–98, 102–103, 162–63; 183–84, 189, 204–205, 208–209, 209n, 215–16, 282, 308; migration to cities from, 67–68; modes of production in, 45–52, 171, 173, 177; noncompetitiveness of, 44, 49n, 67, 173, 177–81, 191n, 191–92, 194–202, 206–207, 211; participation in Republic seen as essential by, 69–70; price scissors and, 28, 184–85; rationalization and modernization in, 73–74, 179–80, 186, 194–202, 213–15, 216–17; RDI program for, 91–93, 148–49, 180, 187n, 189, 191–92, 193n, 194–98, 199n, 199–202, 206, 208, 213, 213n; retailing of products from, 51–52; rural debt moratorium and, 98–99, 102–103, 210–11; socialization and unionization in, 56–57; state aid to, 72–73, 80–82, 175, 212n; state intervention in, 57–58, 82–83, 85–89, 212–19. *See also* agrarian-industrial relations; estate owners; peasant/estate-owners alliance; peasants

Anti Corn Law League, 205n

anti-Semitism, 53, 271–72, 311n

antisocialism, 271; in agricultural sector, 16–17, 52–53, 59, 197; in industrial sector, 115–16; of Sammlung bloc, 18–19. *See also* labor-capital conflict